A gift from
The
Association of
Fundraising Professionals -
Brandywine Chapter

Fundraising Fundamentals

A Guide to Annual Giving for Professionals and Volunteers

SECOND EDITION

JAMES M. GREENFIELD

John Wiley & Sons, Inc.

*To all those who choose fundraising as their
profession and those who volunteer their time,
talent, and treasure, year after year, to fulfill the
vision and mission of their nonprofit organizations*

ISBN: 0-471-20987-2

Printed in the United States of America.

10 9 8 7 6 5 4 3 2 1

THE AFP/WILEY FUND DEVELOPMENT SERIES

The AFP/Wiley Fund Development Series is intended to provide fund development professionals and volunteers, including board members (and others interested in the not-for-profit sector), with top-quality publications that help advance philanthropy as voluntary action for the public good. Our goal is to provide practical, timely guidance and information on fundraising, charitable giving, and related subjects. AFP and Wiley each bring to this innovative collaboration unique and important resources that result in a whole greater than the sum of its parts.

Association of Fundraising Professionals

AFP is a professional association of fundraising executives that advances philanthropy through its more than 25,000 members in over 159 chapters throughout the United States, Canada, and Mexico. Through its advocacy, research, education, and certification programs, the society fosters development and growth of fundraising professionals, works to advance philanthropy and volunteerism, and promotes high ethical standards in the fundraising profession.

2001–2002 AFP Publishing Advisory Council

Linda A. Chew, CFRE, Chair
Associate Director, Alta Bates Summit Foundation

Nina P. Berkheiser, CFRE
Director of Development, SPCA of Pinellas County

Samuel N. Gough, CFRE
Principal, The AFRAM Group

Guy Mallabone, CFRE
VP, External Relations, Southern Alberta Institute of Technology

Robert Mueller, CFRE
Director of Development, Alliance of Community Hospices & Palliative Care Services

Maria Elena Noriega
Director, Noriega Malo & Associates

R. Michael Patterson, CFRE
Regional Director of Planned Giving, Arthritis Foundation

G. Patrick Williams, MS, ACFRE
Vice Chancellor of Development & Public Affairs, Southern Illinois University—
Edwardsville

John Wiley & Sons

Susan McDermott
Editor (Professional/Trade Division), John Wiley & Sons, Inc.

AFP Staff

Richard B. Chobot, Ph.D.
Vice President, Professional Advancement, AFP

Jan Alfieri
Manager, AFP Resource Center, AFP

Beyond Fund Raising: New Strategies for Nonprofit Innovation and Investment
Kay Sprinkel Grace, CFRE
ISBN 0-471-16232-9
Inspirational yet practical, this book teaches you how to "put away the tin cup" and take fundraising to a new level. An experienced fundraising consultant and volunteer, Grace shows you how to establish a true relationship between philanthropy, development, and fundraising. You will also get forms, checklists, and flow charts to help you understand, visualize, and incorporate this new philosophy into your own nonprofit organization.

Careers in Fundraising
Lilya Wagner, Ed.D., CFRE
ISBN 0-471-40359-8
Careers in Fundraising provides expert guidance on professional opportunities in the field of fundraising, including topics on professional development, on-the-job issues, and the significance of fundraising as a career. This comprehensive resource covers all aspects of the profession, and also addresses the personal mission and commitment necessary for success in the field.

The Complete Guide to Fundraising Management
Stanley Weinstein, ACFRE
ISBN 0-471-24290-X
This book is a practical management how-to tailored specifically to the needs of fundraisers. Moving beyond theory, it addresses the day-to-day problems faced in these organizations, and offers hands-on advice and practical solutions. The book and accompanying disk include sample forms, checklists, and grids to help the reader plan and execute complicated fundraising campaigns.

Critical Issues in Fund Raising
Dwight F. Burlingame, Ph.D., CFRE, editor
ISBN 0-471-17465-3
This book examines the most pressing issues facing fundraising professionals today. Extensive chapters cover donors, innovative fundraising, marketing, financial management, ethics, international philanthropy, and the fundraising professional. Written by a team of highly respected practitioners and educators, this book was developed in conjunction with AFP, the Council for the Advancement and Support of Education, the Association for Research on Nonprofit Organizations and Voluntary Action, and the Indiana University Center on Philanthropy.

Cultivating Diversity in Fund Raising

Janice Gow Pettey

ISBN 0-471-40361-X

Cultivating Diversity in Fundraising offers an overview in cultivating successful fundraising and an enhanced understanding of philanthropic motivation in four selected racial/ethnic populations—African American, Asian American (Chinese, Filipino, Japanese, Korean, and South Asian), Hispanic/Latino (Cuban, Dominican, Salvadoran, Mexican, and Puerto Rican), and Native American. By understanding the rich philanthropic traditions of the individuals they are working with and soliciting funds from, fundraisers will be better equipped to serve their communities and their organizations.

Direct Response Fund Raising: Mastering New Trends for Results

Michael Johnston

ISBN 0-471-38024-5

This guide offers fundraisers, managers, and volunteers an excellent understanding of how to plan and execute successful direct response campaigns. The success of a nonprofit direct response program requires staying on top of recent trends in the field. These trends include appealing more effectively to aging baby boomers as well as tapping into powerful new databases, the Internet, CD-ROMs, diskettes, and videos. The book includes a CD-ROM, with all the full-color, complete examples from the book as well as many more.

Ethical Decision-Making in Fund Raising

Marilyn Fischer, Ph.D.

ISBN 0-471-28943-3

A handbook for ethical reasoning and discussion. In her provocative new book, Dr. Fischer provides conceptual tools with which a nonprofit can thoroughly examine the ethics of how and from whom it seeks donations. With the book's Ethical Decision-Making Model, the author explains how fundraisers can use their basic value commitments to organizational mission, relationships, and integrity as day-to-day touchstones for making balanced, ethical fundraising decisions.

The Fund Raiser's Guide to the Internet

Michael Johnston

ISBN 0-471-25365-0

This book presents the issues, technology, and resources involved in online fundraising and donor relations. A practical "how-to" guide, it presents real-world case studies and successful practices from a top consulting firm, as well as guidance, inspiration, and warnings to nonprofits learning to develop this new fundraising technique. It also covers such important factors as determining your market, online solicitation pieces, security issues, and setting up your Web site.

Fund Raising Cost Effectiveness: A Self-Assessment Workbook
James M. Greenfield, ACFRE, FAHP
ISBN 0-471-10916-9
A comprehensive, step-by-step guide that will help nonprofit professionals ensure that their department and campaigns are as efficient and cost-effective as possible. It combines a thorough explanation of the issues critical to fundraising self-assessment with easy-to-use worksheets and practical advice. The accompanying disk contains all the sample worksheets plus software for downloading a nonprofit's fundraising data from major software products into charts, graphs, and P&L-like spreadsheet templates.

Fund Raising: Evaluating and Managing the Fund Development Process
James M. Greenfield, ACFRE, FAHP
ISBN 0-471-32014-5
Covering initial preparation in 15 areas of fundraising and the ongoing management of the process, this book is designed for fundraising executives of organizations both large and small. Included are numerous examples, case studies, checklists, and a unique evaluation of the audit environment of nonprofit organizations.

International Fundraising for Not-for-Profits: A Country-by-Country Profile
Thomas Harris
ISBN 0-471-24452-X
The only comprehensive book of its kind, it examines and compares the fundraising environments of 18 countries around the world. Each chapter is written by a local expert and details the history and context of fundraising for the country, local and global economic factors, legal and fiscal practices, sources of funding, and what fundraising practices are considered acceptable by the culture and government.

The Legislative Labyrinth: A Map for Not-for-Profits
Walter P. Pidgeon, Jr., Ph.D., CFRE
ISBN 0-471-40069-6
Currently, only a fraction of the nonprofit community takes advantage of the legislative process in representing their members and furthering its missions. Nonprofits are missing a significant way to fulfill their mission of gaining visibility and attracting new members and funding sources. This book answers the questions of nonprofits thinking of starting a lobbying program.

The Nonprofit Handbook: Fund Raising, Third Edition
James M. Greenfield, ACFRE, FAHP
ISBN 0-471-40304-0
The third edition of this invaluable handbook provides a complete overview of the entire development function, from management and strategic planning to hands-on, practical guidance for the various kinds of fundraising. Written by leading fundraising professionals, edited by James M. Greenfield, this invaluable resource brings together more than 40 contributors who are vanguard experts and professionals in the field of fundraising.

Nonprofit Investment Policies: Practical Steps for Growing Charitable Funds
Robert P. Fry, Jr., Esq.
ISBN 0-471-17887-X
Written in plain English by an investment manager who specializes in nonprofit organizations, *Nonprofit Investment Policies* explores the unique characteristics of nonprofit investing. Covered topics include endowment management, planned gift assets, socially responsible investing, and more. This book includes charts and graphs to illustrate complex investment concepts, tables and checklists to guide nonprofit managers in decision making, and case studies of organizations of various sizes to show how to successfully develop and implement investment policies.

The NSFRE Fund-Raising Dictionary
ISBN 0-471-14916-0
Developed by NSFRE experts, this book provides clear and concise definitions for nearly 1,400 key fundraising and related nonprofit terms—from development and accounting to marketing and public relations. It also offers additional resource material, including a suggested bibliography.

Planned Giving Simplified: The Gift, the Giver, and the Gift Planner
Robert F. Sharpe, Sr.
ISBN 0-471-16674-X
This resource, written by a well-known veteran of planned giving, is a down-to-earth introduction to the complex world of planned giving, a sophisticated fundraising strategy that involves big money, complex tax laws, and delicate personal politics. This book shows charities, and in particular the charities' planned givers, how to understand the process—both the administration of planned gifts as well as the spirit of giving.

The Universal Benefits of Volunteering
Walter P. Pidgeon, Jr., Ph.D., CFRE
ISBN 0-471-18505-I
Volunteering is good for nonprofits, individuals, and corporations because it builds strong interpersonal and professionals skills that carry over into all sectors. A concise, hands-on guide to maximizing the use of business professionals in the nonprofit volunteer context, this workbook is a vital resource for all those involved in volunteering efforts. Included is a disk with all the worksheets and model documents needed to establish effective, successful, and ongoing volunteer programs.

Preface

To help finance their annual operating budgets, nonprofit organizations must raise money every year. It is fair to state that *annual giving* is the fundraising method that acts as a fuel source; without it, nonprofit organizations would not be able to provide their programs and services to the public. Annual giving contributions are equally valuable because they are available for capital improvements, equipment, education, research, and a variety of other forms of quality improvement. Only a few organizations are financially independent, although many strive toward that goal. Organizations that have alternative revenue sources, and those that can draw on endowment earnings raised years before, may be less dependent on annual giving revenue for the substance of their operating budgets, but even these well-funded organizations will want to raise money every year to maintain the quality of their programs and to expand the services they provide for public benefit.

This book will concentrate on the methods and techniques of annual giving, one of the three areas of fund development practice. The other two areas—soliciting major gifts in capital campaigns and offering estate planning programs—depend on having a comprehensive annual giving program in place to prepare the volunteers, donors, and prospects they will need to succeed. Most nonprofit organizations use annual giving methods to raise money they will spend immediately and to give donors the satisfaction of knowing that their money was used right away for the good works promised in the solicitation.

Annual giving is not an investment opportunity; there are no stockholders or venture capitalists investing gift dollars in hopes of making a profit in 12 months. Instead, volunteers and donors are investing their time, talent, and treasure by giving these personal resources away. They give them to the vision, mission, purposes, goals, and objectives of each nonprofit organization they serve, because they believe their sacrifice will make a difference in the lives of others.

Nonprofit organizations always seem to be asking for money. Well, that is what an annual giving program is supposed to do. Many programs ask for a single gift each year; some ask more often but offer a variety of options for giving. Others, mostly churches, ask every week. (Churches raise *half* the money given away each year in America.) Asking for money is only one part of what annual giving is all about. A comprehensive annual giving program is endlessly engaged in finding new donors and renewing prior donors, involving them as friends of the organization, and building a relationship that may eventually expand the level of their giving. Annual giving is the best way to initiate and expand this kind of relationship. Fundraising executives are the temporary custodians of the exchange between their organization and the people who invest in it; if the executives' efforts are successful, the number of friends and donors will increase each year, as will their commitment to a mutually beneficial partnership. Annual giving programs possess all these and other benefits:

- Offer an active means for the organization to market its vision, mission, purposes, goals, and objectives to a wide audience
- Promote programs and services (and their benefits) to the public
- Build respect, confidence, and trust through a positive interaction with the community
- Invite active public participation in accomplishing recognizable worthwhile goals that deliver benefits back to the community

This book is an in-depth presentation of the various methods and techniques of annual giving carried out by organizations that raise friends and build lasting relationships. Annual giving is the process that finds the many friends every nonprofit organization needs. Annual giving campaigns solicit gifts and then renew and increase them year after year. Annual giving is *one of the most reliable sources* of revenue available to nonprofit organizations; major gifts and planned giving activities are the *sources of the most money.* The annual giving area requires hard work but it delivers high satisfaction. Managing an annual giving program is a complex and difficult skill because it is both art and science; yet, every fund-raising executive must learn how to succeed at it. Annual giving involves large numbers of people as donors; it also asks people for their time and energy while offering only a thank-you and good feelings in return. Most donors make several gifts each year, usually to six or eight nonprofit organizations plus their church or synagogue. Annual giving is expensive to conduct but it is also profitable. Nonprofit organizations tend to underutilize annual giving because boards of directors and management too often see only its high cost, not its ability to deliver money quickly.

All of these issues and perceptions are dealt with in conjunction with fulfilling the purposes of this book:

1. To explain the nine principal methods used in annual giving and to describe how each of them functions (Chapters 2 through 11);
2. To explain how each method builds on the others to raise money, make friends, and build lasting relationships with donors
3. To explain other ways to raise money every year and demonstrate how they add to (but do not replace) the nine principal methods
4. To describe how to manage a comprehensive annual giving program for maximum success

The sequence of chapters will direct the reader through all the necessary steps, from beginning an annual giving program (by testing lists) to managing a comprehensive enterprise that uses multiple methods every year and is carried out at maximum efficiency and effectiveness. The principles discussed in Chapters 2 through 11 are illustrated with exhibits for their use in everyday practice. Sample letters, gift reports, and other documents show how each of these methods is put into action.

The Campaign to Clean Up America (CCUA) is a fictitious organization invented by Bruce R. Hopkins to illustrate the principles presented in his book, *Starting and Managing a Nonprofit Organization: A Legal Guide*, Third Edition (John Wiley & Sons, 2000). With his permission, I have created a Clean Up Cleveland Chapter of the CCUA and have focused on the decisions, actions, program implementations, and recordkeeping methods of the Cleveland Chapter in relation to the topics covered in each chapter. The CCUA device links this book to the Hopkins classic as a companion book directed toward newer organizations. A short cast of characters has been created for the CCUA's Cleveland Chapter. These are the "people" who will bring these annual giving examples to life. The letters and reports emanating from the Cleveland Chapter add reality to each chapter's topics:

The Campaign to Clean Up America—Clean Up Cleveland Chapter

National Chairman	Michael M. Activist
Cleveland Chapter Board of Directors	
Chair of the Board	I. Harvey Clout
Vice Chair	Mary M. Moneybanks
Treasurer	Sidney M. Secure, CPA

Secretary	Theodosius "Ted" Worthy
Assistant Secretary	Titus Brown, APR
Members–at–Large	Steven Generous
	Iris B. Radiant
	Trafalgar "Telly" Temple

Board Committees
Fund Development	Harold H. Connected
Gala Benefit Evening	Mary M. Moneybanks
	Trafalgar "Telly" Temple
	Iris B. Radiant

Fund-Development Office
Director	Karen I. Anderson
Executive Assistant	Alice B. Nice

A wealth of information is now available on the methods of annual giving described in this book. Chapter notes will identify the major resources where additional details are available. My advice to readers is: Search out and trust these experts; their wisdom is based on years of experience in doing exactly what you might be attempting to do for the first, second, or fifteenth time. Additional resources and recommended readings are listed by topic, in the book's Selected References section. The volume of these materials is a sign that fund development has an evolving body of knowledge—a necessary step toward becoming a recognized profession. My hope is that those who use this book will find it helpful in building a reliable base of faithful friends whose annual gift support will move their nonprofit organizations forward.

The six keys to success in annual giving are easy to memorize:

1. Vision is mission.
2. Leadership is key.
3. Volunteers are golden.
4. Asking is required.
5. Giving is voluntary.
6. Donors must be recognized.

From this book, you will understand their meaning and their importance to successful annual giving efforts.

JAMES M. GREENFIELD
Newport Beach, California
March, 2002

Acknowledgments

Annual giving may be the most challenging area in all of fund-raising because it demands constant creativity, enthusiasm, energy, and immediate results. After 38 years in this profession and 38 annual giving campaigns, I can state with confidence that no two campaigns are alike. Most of what I have learned about annual giving methods and techniques has come from (a) the experience of directing them, (b) evaluation of their performance and application of the lessons learned, and (c) the thoughtful suggestions of many volunteers, donors, and staff colleagues.

Eight nonprofit organizations have been my schoolhouses; thousands of board members, volunteers, and donors have been my teachers. Friends and colleagues in professional associations have been my coaches and mentors, as have several of my office colleagues. We have learned together, through conferences and workshops, articles and books, informal meetings and networking. One of the true pleasures of this profession is the sharing nature of all its members; we benefit our organizations and ourselves by learning from one another. For this reason, I have dedicated this book to all those who practice annual giving every day.

The resource libraries of the Association of Fundraising Professionals (AFP), formerly NSFRE, and the Association for Healthcare Philanthropy (AHP) proved valuable resources for many of the references cited in this book, as well as Jan Alfieri and Reed Stockman in the AFP Resource Center; I am indebted to the staff at both for their consistent helpfulness and rapid response to my many inquiries for service.

A special thank you to my friend, Susan Golden, president of The Golden Group in Cleveland, Ohio. With her unfailing good humor and special knowledge of her hometown, she verified that all names, addresses, and telephone numbers in the Clean Up Cleveland feature were indeed fictitious! For this and all your helpful suggestions, Susan, I thank you.

I remain indebted to the team at John Wiley & Sons for all their support, especially to Susan McDermott, Editor, for her assistance in updating this second edition to my 1994 book, as well as her many helpful suggestions for its improvement. Special thanks are also due to Beth Childs, Copy Editor and Louise Jacob, Associate Managing Editor, whose ability to grasp any new subject gives quality to this effort. Their support of this book from start to finish is appreciated.

J.M.G.

Contents

List of Exhibits

CHAPTER 1

Developing Annual Gift Support by Raising Friends and Building Relationships

For all philanthropic practice, there are two overarching questions:

1. Why do we exist?
2. What's the money for?

These questions deserve great answers; in fact, many great answers will be needed. The purposes of annual giving go beyond merely raising money; that alone is an inadequate and insufficient answer to why we exist. The true objective is to find and build a constituency of friends who are willing to join a cause. During the period of their friendship, they will be encouraged to expand their relationship to active involvement that may last a lifetime. To build such friendships and lifelong relationships between people and causes, charitable organizations must send these encouraging messages every year, communicating them through the medium of annual giving. Effective communication through annual giving programs will require careful thought, extensive preparation, and an efficient and effective delivery system.

A nonprofit organization begins by identifying the values that characterize it and by studying its "vision" of itself—what it has done and is doing now, and, most important to fundraising success, what its plans are for the future. This vision contains the fundamental values incorporated into the mission statement. The mission statement, in turn, explains why the organization was formed, what its continuing goals are, what benefits it intends to provide to others, and why its functions are of value and should continue. Henry Rosso[1] writes that the mission statement "expresses more than justification for existence and more than just a definition of goals and objectives. It defines the value system that will guide program strategies. The mission is the magnet that will attract and hold the interests of trustees, volunteers, staff, and contributors." The mission statement should use clear language to describe the programs and services to be offered and to explain how the vision will be carried out and how the results will be achieved. Charitable organizations use several philanthropic practices—stewardship, volunteerism, a charitable purpose, and public advocacy, among others— to enable them to achieve their vision and fulfill their mission. "People helping people" is both the method and the model; *helping*, which implies action, is something everyone can do. Philanthropy, or what Robert Payton[2] calls "voluntary action for the common good," connotes association with others in the community and is the chief means to carry out the mission.

Once the mission is understood and the programs to fulfill it are in place, an organization must study its charitable purpose, an attribute that denotes altruism and enlightened self-interest. Donors give time or money to a charitable purpose that will help other people because they appreciate the implied mutuality of dependence that people have for one another.

A charitable act is a social exchange that occurs each time a gift is made. The decision to make a gift comes after being asked by someone else, someone who is trusted by the donor. A gift implies a considerable amount of confidence and trust in both the solicitor and the charitable organization's ability (and faithfulness) to "do the right thing" with the money or, at the very least, to do no harm.

Charitable behavior is a personal virtue advocated in every religious tradition; every citizen has the freedom to practice charity. To help another person or a cause can be practiced alone, between two people, or among millions acting together. Over centuries, the concept of charitable action has evolved into the practice of philanthropy today. Philanthropy requires a generosity of spirit that can be practiced anywhere and everywhere, at any time; it can accomplish any "charitable" purpose, and often will be accompanied by public recognition. Philanthropy has flowered in America, partly because of the protection it has enjoyed from the federal government since the ten amendments known as the Bill of Rights were added to the Constitution of the United States. The First Amendment states:

> 1. Congress shall make no laws respecting an establishment of religion, or prohibiting the free exercise thereof; or abridging the freedom of speech, or of the press; or the right of the people peaceably to assemble, and to petition the government for a redress of grievances.

Government has joined in philanthropic practice by legitimizing its reason to exist. Government also advocates that its citizens engage in charitable acts because these acts improve the common good. In most nations, government is responsible for a wide spectrum of public services. By contrast, whole areas of American enterprise, from the arts to education, from social welfare to health care, from religion to civic causes, are often carried out by citizens, acting alone or together. The consensus in America is that government cannot and should not be involved in many of these areas. There is also agreement that some areas of public activity can be better served when government, business, and philanthropy act together. This agreement is one of the most sacred privileges in the people's possession, a personal freedom that encourages them to practice philanthropy. Brian O'Connell[3] has given this perspective on the freedoms of the First Amendment:

> It is important to be reminded of the basic values of American society; the freedom, worth, and dignity of the individual; equal opportunity; justice; and mutual responsibility. Our largest vehicles for preserving and enhancing those basic values are:
>
> Representative government starting with one person/one vote;
> The freedoms of speech and assembly
> The free press
> A system of justice beginning with due process and presumption of innocence
> University public education.

Philanthropic practice, or people acting together through charitable organizations, begins when active participation and financial support are requested from individuals, business, and the government itself. To be able to respond, the charitable organization must embody its vision and mission into a structure and an action plan. First, it must qualify as a charitable organization by being incorporated as a nonprofit, public benefit corporation in 1 of the 50 states. Second, it must be granted tax-exempt status by the federal government by qualifying as a pure public charity. The organization is then granted several privileges in exchange for its agreed-on obligation to perform one or more charitable activities, as described by Bruce Hopkins:[4]

> The federal tax definition of a charitable organization contains at least 15 different ways for a nonprofit entity to be charitable. These characteristics, found in the income tax regulations, IRS rulings, and federal and state court opinions, include: relieving the poor and distressed or the underprivileged; advancing religion, education, or science; lessening the burdens of government; beautifying and maintaining a community; preserving natural beauty; promoting health, social welfare, environmental conservancy, arts, or patriotism; caring for orphans or animals; promoting, advancing, and sponsoring amateur sports; and maintaining public confidence in the legal system.

More than 20 subgroups or types of charitable organizations qualify under Section 501(c) of the Internal Revenue Code (IRC). Charitable organizations that demonstrate "charitable purposes" enjoy tax exemption privileges on income, sales, and property, plus a charitable contribution deduction for donors who make gifts. Organizations that quality as "501(c)(3) organizations" (Section 501(c), subsection (3) of the IRC) are also permitted to engage in tax-exempt bond financing, to claim school tax exemptions, to enjoy reduced postal rates, and to be relieved of federal unemployment taxes and corporate net income taxes, except where they might qualify for unrelated business income tax (UBIT).

This impressive array of privileges is enhanced by the public benefits and "good works" performed by each charitable organization. In all of this activity, it is not organizations that act; it is the people within them and the people who act through them on behalf of others. People exercise a mutual obligation to care for one another through their voluntary association. In so doing, they take upon themselves certain duties and responsibilities as owners of charitable organizations and stewards of the public's trust. Their efforts succeed in building a new community, one that will be held together by their commitment to carry out a charitable purpose. This new community adds to its membership volunteers and staff, friends and donors, clients and their families, and others who share in the responsibility of doing their best to improve the human condition by fulfilling the mission of the charitable organization.

Philanthropy holds a mirror to society's pluralism where the acts of others fulfill the needs of all of its members. Hopkins,[5] describing a truly democratic state, warns that "the power to influence and cause changes cannot be concentrated in one sector of that state or society. There must be a 'pluralization of institutions' in society, a fancy way of saying that the ability to bring about changes and the accumulation of power cannot belong to just one sector—inevitably, the government." Those who become active as members of a charitable organization become directly responsible for its welfare, whether they are board members, management, employees, or clients; all are bonded to the vision and mission and become advocates of the organization's reason to exist. Other memberships are filled by government, business, nonclients (or not-yet clients), volunteers, and donors, who also join and become partners to the mission. John Gardner,[6] founder of Common Cause, has summarized the status of nonprofits in the United States: "In the realm of good works this nation boasts a unique blending of private and governmental effort. There is almost no area of educational, scientific, charitable, or religious activity in which we have not built an effective network of private institutions." With everything in order, and having been sanctioned with legal form by the government, charitable organizations go forth to fulfill their mission to benefit others. The philanthropic process has begun.

THE PHILANTHROPIC PROCESS

The philanthropic process has many parts. We have touched briefly on only the most essential ingredients: the vision and mission; rights of assembly, association, and community; charitable purposes and public benefits; and legal form. Legal form might be complex but it is necessary to all that follows. A charitable organization established by citizens must be constituted correctly as a nonprofit, public benefit corporation. Each such entity is a substantial enterprise and, as the chrysalis becomes the fragile but beautiful butterfly, it will require vigilant attention by all its members to preserve its life and to enhance its beauty. Volunteers who serve on its board of directors assume the stewardship of the public's trust on their collective shoulders; it is their duty to demand that everything be completely legal. To lose the government's endorsement is to cause the association to forfeit its benefits and privileges, cease to provide its public benefits, divide its property, and "wind up" its existence. Worst of all, it will lose public trustworthiness, a failure in its purpose for existence. Without legal form and public trust, no matter how lofty the vision or how humane the mission, they will go unfulfilled. Gardner[7] evaluated the importance of the independent sector in this ringing tribute:

> If it were to disappear from our national life, we would be less distinctly American. The [independent] sector enhances our creativity, enlivens our communities, nurtures individual responsibility, stirs life at the grassroots, and reminds us that we were born free. Its vitality is rooted in good soil—civic pride, compassion, a philanthropic tradition, a strong problem-solving impulse, a sense of individual responsibility and, despite what cynics may say, an irrepressible commitment to the great shared task of improving our life together.

To live up to these ideals, the members of each charitable organization must be active participants in the philanthropic process. They must recruit community residents and business executives to serve as board members, ask others to volunteer their time and talents, and invite the public to share in the organization's financial support. The domain of philanthropy has remarkable diversity, substantial numbers, economic power, and enormous public impact, all of which should be represented in the board, volunteers, and donor membership. Collectively, America's charitable organizations or independent sector are referred to as the third sector, after business and government, out of respect for their accepted value to the nation. When the domain of philanthropy joins in partnership with business and government, philanthropy shines as the uniquely American example of a democratic triumph.

John D. Rockefeller 3rd,[8] long associated with highly visible philanthropic achievements, once commented:

> A healthy third sector keeps government honest, provides alternative ways to solve problems, helps maintain institutions that should *not* be taken over by government, and provides opportunities for the initiative and sense of caring that are the indispensable bedrock of a thriving democracy. . . . There is, however, a common thread that runs through

the third sector; a belief in being of service to one's community and other people, without relying on government and without any expectation of personal profit. At the heart of the third sector is individual initiative and a sense of caring. . . . This means that the oldest form of support, philanthropic giving, is still the most important. It provides the crucial margin that gives third-sector institutions their most precious asset— independence.

The sections that follow will discuss philanthropic practice, the independent sector and the nature of charitable organizations, and the fund development process, all in preparation for study of the comprehensive annual giving program.

PHILANTHROPIC PRACTICE

The vision and mission of a nonprofit organization will answer the first of the two overarching questions: Why do we exist? and What's the money for? The second question is far easier to answer when the vision and mission are known; without them, the message is only about money. In the vision and mission statements, dreams take shape and form, practical applications become visible through actual programs and services delivered, and defined purposes, goals, and objectives measure the results. All of these goals are brought to life through philanthropic practice. Philanthropic practice is volunteerism in action, and, says Payton,[9] "[I]t might be argued that philanthropy is an essential defining characteristic of civilized society." It is expressed by people in several forms, from leadership and governance to public solicitation and giving. Hours of time and energy are given freely by people every year; they also share their personal talents, their assets, and other human and material resources. Why do they do it? A trio of leading analysts has offered these reasons:[10]

> People benefit from serving others. The most important benefits are satisfactions: spiritual, moral, and psychological. We accept the psychological evidence that voluntary service in behalf of others enhances self-esteem and self-worth. The secret seems to lie in the liberation of the self from its own preoccupations by sympathy for and empathy with others. . . . Voluntary acts of compassion and acts of community are always needed, in all societies, and always will be.

None of these valued attributes should be taken for granted; they must be developed with care and attention by charitable organizations.

Leadership is essential to success in any enterprise, including the charitable organization; volunteerism is second only to leadership in its importance to philanthropic practice. Leadership and volunteerism encourage others to make the effort to join in. Everyone is not a leader, and all leaders cannot serve at the same time. Nonprofit organizations are no more alike than are the types of business or the levels of government, and they do not act alike. Despite their high motives and good intentions, some people may not have the knowledge and skill needed to govern others nor the experience required to manage charitable organizations with effectiveness and efficiency. Their place may be as volunteers, and there is much to be done by volunteers, including asking others for their annual gift once a year.

Philanthropic practice includes this asking for gifts. Few gifts are made without a request first being delivered in some way. Solicitation is believed by some people to be a confrontational, one-way conversation. Saying no is seen as a far easier thing to do than asking. For some people, asking for gifts is another form of sales, and, like sales everywhere, it is assertive, even aggressive at times. They are uncomfortable with this assignment. What is most important to the solicitation is that making gifts is a **voluntary act** each and every time. Giving is the result of an invitation; a reply is requested. Asking for money for charitable purposes is not begging. Gift appeals by charitable organizations, says Harold Seymour,[11] "should aim high, provide perspective, arouse a sense of history and continuity, convey a feeling of importance, relevance, and urgency, and have whatever stuff is needed to warm the heart and stir the mind." Philanthropic practice is carried out by sharing valid needs with selected audiences who are invited to lend their support. The act of giving is the servant to philanthropic practice and is carried out whenever money or time is given. Not everyone is willing to ask friends for money; those who prefer not to ask can give their energy and talents to other areas. What is valuable in all of these actions is the volunteerism itself. Every citizen has this opportunity. More should try it; they might like it. For philanthropic practice to succeed, gifts of money are required. Everyone who asks others to give should first make his or her own personal gift each year. Those who are asked should consider the invitation seriously; many do, and they make a contribution. In fact, most of the people who decide to give will make more than one gift to a charitable organization each year. Despite this generosity, raising money is not the end to be achieved; it is only the means to the end. Fundraising follows leadership, volunteerism, and public generosity toward fulfillment of the vision and mission. Of all the acts of philanthropic practice, the privilege and freedom of voluntary giving may be the least understood and the least appreciated.

THE INDEPENDENT SECTOR AND THE NATURE OF CHARITABLE ORGANIZATIONS

After many years of acting alone or in groupings by type of organization or service provided (the arts, colleges, museums, and so on), the great variety of charitable organizations active in America began to come together, drawn by common needs for advocacy, communications, research studies, and threats of governmental regulation. The Tax Reform Act of 1969, which imposed operating regulations and excise taxes on private foundations, might have served as the catalyst for this awakening. The 1975 report of "the Filer Commission"[12] included a specific recommendation "that a permanent national commission on the nonprofit sector be established by Congress." True to the American tradition, private citizens began the organization instead, and Independent Sector was founded in 1980 under the leadership of John Gardner and Brian O'Connell. Within its mission was the responsibility to serve as the collective spokesperson and rallying point for the variety of nonprofit organizations that exist in America. The sheer size and diversity of the independent sector may come as a surprise to many readers. Harvey Dale[13] described these dimensions in 1991:

> It is estimated to comprise more than 1.3 million organizations, of which more than two-thirds are charities or social-welfare entities (which together make up the so-called independent sector). Nearly 10 percent of the U.S. labor force works in that sector. The net value of assets held by charities alone is probably in excess of $300 billion today. Charitable giving in this country has exceeded $100 billion annually for the past few years. Even that large number has accounted for less than 30 percent of the receipts of the independent sector; *total* annual receipts—which also included dues, fees, charges, investment income, and government payments—exceeded $325 billion in 1987 and must be greater now. By any measure, the independent sector in our country is very substantial.

The Internal Revenue Service (IRS) reported that the number of 501(c) tax-exempt organizations registered as of September 1999 was 1,312,647, of which 773,934 were classified as 501(cc)(3) religious and charitable, 59 percent of the total. These figures do not include churches, integrated auxiliaries, subordinate units, and conventions or associations of churches that do not need to apply for recognition of exempt status.[14] The rate of growth in new organizations receiving approval remains at about 6 percent a year. Of the 72,161 applications for exempt status received by IRS in that fiscal year, 58,138 were approved, including 52,773 as 501(c)(3) organizations. Total giving in 1999 was $190.16 billion and in 2000 was $203.45 billion, a 3.2 percent increase over 1999 and the lowest increase in the prior five years (see Exhibit 1-1).

The authority to guide each of these charitable organizations rests with the board of directors. The directors are men and women who act on behalf of their organization's self-interest; they guide their enterprise toward fulfillment of its vision and mission, its reason to exist "Mission is entrusted to the governing board, and governance entails stewardship."[15] The directors accept with equal duty their accountability to the public for the actions of the organization, its employees and staff, its clients, and its financial affairs, and for all of its assets. It is not an overstatement that the ultimate responsibility for the existence and welfare of the organization rests with the board of directors. It is also fair to propose, although each board has its well-defined duties, that board members serve as a collective example to everyone else within the entire independent sector, not just one organization. Given such levels of responsibility, the members of the board of directors are well-advised to study the following standards:[16]

> First, the nonprofit board has and uses a systematic process for assessing the strengths and weaknesses of the composition of the current board. Strengths and weaknesses are usually assessed in terms of demographic characteristics, expertise, and skills, and the result is a board profile.
>
> Second, the board profile is used to identify the personal characteristics and expertise/skills desired in new recruits to the board.
>
> Third, recruitment of potential board members is systematic and rigorous in that potential members are thoroughly informed as to the mission and goals of the organization; its financial condition; and the time, effort, level of contributions, and fundraising activities expected of them. Potential members are interviewed by a board committee (and perhaps

EXHIBIT I-I   NATIONAL ANNUAL GIVING DATA*
TOTAL PHILANTHROPY IN THE
UNITED STATES (IN BILLIONS)

Sources of Contributions	1998	1999	2000*	Percent of Total
Individuals	$148.50	$143.71	$152.07	75%
Bequests	$ 12.63	$ 15.61	$ 16.02	7.70%
Foundations	$ 17.10	$ 19.81	$ 24.50	12%
Corporations	$ 8.97	$ 11.02	$ 10.86	5.30%
TOTALS	$174.52	$190.16	$203.45	100.00%

Uses of Contributions	1998	1999	2000*	Percent of Total
Religion	$ 76.10	$ 81.78	$ 74.45	36.60%
Education	$ 24.61	$ 27.46	$ 28.10	13.80%
Health/hospitals	$ 16.90	$ 17.95	$ 18.90	9.30%
Human services	$ 16.90	$ 17.36	$ 17.90	8.80%
Unallocated/foundations	$ 16.98	$ 15.11	$ 32.20	15.80%
Arts/culture	$ 10.50	$ 11.07	$ 11.60	5.70%
Public/social benefit	$ 10.90	$ 10.94	$ 11.60	5.70%
Environment/wildlife	$ 5.30	$ 5.83	$ 6.10	3.00%
International/foreign	$ 2.10	$ 2.65	$ 2.60	1.30%
TOTALS	$174.50	$190.16	$203.45	100.00%

*Source: The Chronicle of Philanthropy, May 31, 2001, charts on pages 29 and 36.

the full board) as to their motives and interests in volunteering for board service.

Fourth, new board members receive additional, thorough training and orientation beyond that provided during recruitment and selection.

Fifth, board members commit significant time to board duties, not only attending board and committee meetings but also preparing for meetings and undertaking other assignments, perhaps including fundraising activities.

Sixth, board meetings are characterized by a process through which all are encouraged to participate and disagreement is welcomed, while relationships are collegial and consensual. The board works as a team.

Seventh, the board uses processes of assessing the performance of the board as a whole and the performance of individual members. The board has and follows standards of removing members who do not perform.

Eighth, the board's chief tasks are to (a) select, evaluate, and, if necessary, dismiss the chief executive; (b) define and periodically reevaluate the organization's mission and major goals, develop a strategic plan, and approve budgets and policy statements consistent with the plan; and (c) ensure that the organization obtains the resources necessary to meet the plan.

THE ROLE OF FUND DEVELOPMENT

Vision and mission can lift the spirit; leadership and volunteerism provide the example others are to follow. What are others asked to do? How can the public be involved in the mission and in the programs and services that carry out that mission? Great answers will again be required. The fund development department has the major responsibility for financial support but also has many duties other than raising money. Fund development is often where the public's invitation to participate is centered, where communications begin and continue, and where opportunities for a lifetime of involvement can be fulfilled.

Fund development performs a variety of essential services for nonprofit organizations because its methodology demands planning, marketing, promotion, and community relations. Some may choose to believe that these services are the result of fund development activities, but it is important to understand that they must be carried out before fund development can succeed. Fund development is the area with primary responsibility for raising friends and building relationships for nonprofit organizations. These uses for fund development in philanthropic practice have been defined in many ways; one of the best was provided by Seymour:[17] "Development is the planned promotion of understanding, participation, and support." Fund development is how and where the public is invited to join the cause, to give of their time, talent, and treasure, and to become an active part of a solution to meet human needs.

The several methods and techniques of fundraising are the tools used for (not the purpose of) fund development. The grand design for their use can be illustrated as a pyramid that has three levels of fundraising activity: (1) annual giving, (2) major giving, and (3) estate or planned giving (see Exhibit 1-2). Volunteers and donors are invited to begin their relationship by accepting information about the organization. Building the relationship will take time and will involve repeated opportunities for giving. In this way, their interest and personal involvement will increase to a level where

EXHIBIT 1-2   THE PYRAMID OF GIVING

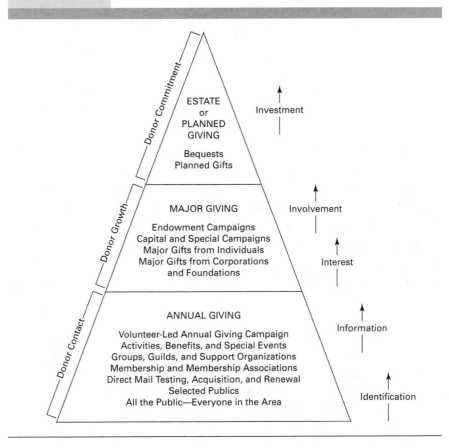

investment decisions will be made. To spearhead the attainment of these levels of continuing relationships, the fund development department will be asked to play several roles:

- Building community
- Responding, not directing
- Being a catalyst to facilitate action
- Finding opportunities for investment in humanity
- Being dynamic because the mission and cause are dynamic
- Seeking a design to accomplish objectives, not merely to give money away

- Viewing solicitations as a "contact sport," not a duty or chore
- Offering a means for donors to fulfill their aspirations
- Using social exchange to achieve higher purposes
- Working always, *always* in the future
- Being more artist than scientist

Fundraising is a " 'responsibility system,' ethical at its base and tied to a larger complex of authority, control, and responsibility. Honesty, openness, and accountability are therefore essential to the integrity and credibility of fundraisers. The professional fundraiser is ethical and virtuous as well; wholehearted, persistent, and impartial."[18] The purpose of fundraising is more than marketing, more than promotion, more than the money raised. Its value is in the results accomplished by the organization's use of the money. Fund development is the process where mission and purposes are matched with the public's desire to help; "people helping people" is carried out through fund development activities. Peter F. Drucker[19] has described its evolution:

> [A] non-profit institution that becomes a prisoner of money-raising is in serious trouble and in a serious identity crisis. The purpose of a strategy for raising money is precisely to enable the non-profit institution to carry out its mission without subordinating that mission to fundraising. This is why non-profit people have now changed the term they use from "fundraising" to "fund development." Fundraising is going around with a begging bowl, asking for money because the *need* is so great. Fund development is creating a constituency which supports the organization because it *deserves* it. It means developing what I call a membership that participates through giving.

The stars of fund development are donors. They are the best friends a nonprofit organization can hope to have; retaining their friendship and expanding their relationship are the primary duties of the fund development program. The value of donors and of what they give enables charitable purposes to be carried out and aids realization of the vision and mission. The objectives may be clear, but donors' motives for giving are complex. They are a mixture of feelings, values, fond wishes, and a sincere desire to make a difference—all of which can be nurtured with praise and public recognition. Donors possess considerable influence within this relationship.

They can be offended and upset by errors and mistakes and, in the next instant, can be consumed with satisfaction about the good they have made happen. Many donors begin giving with a glow of enlightened self-interest. In time, these same donors grow to appreciate that what they can do with their money is less important than what philanthropic practices can do with their money for others. Donors have various motives for making gifts:

- They want to be charitable and to help others.
- They enjoy ego satisfaction.
- They want to gain public recognition.
- The public respects philanthropists.
- Their religious guidelines call for charitable action or promise rewards in the afterlife.
- They want to participate in a worthy cause.
- They want to join with others in a common purpose.
- The organization has a good public image.
- They have confidence in the organization and they trust it to use their money well.
- The organization has good people in leadership positions.
- The organization is fiscally sound and operationally well-managed.
- They were asked to give.

Many more factors are at work in each gift decision. Some donors give on impulse, others because of a genuine interest, and a few according to an integrated giving plan.[20] People possess any number of complex (even competing) motives that occur with each gift decision. The objective of fund development is not to manipulate donor motives but, by understanding them better, to assist donors in fulfilling their aspirations through gift support.

Donor behavior is much more than a single gift decision or one episode of giving, and it may be triggered by internal motivations and external influences (see Exhibit 1-3). Donors achieve personal values from giving—beyond the tax deduction, if they choose to claim it. The spirit of altruism, of "people helping people," is an act of charity at the highest level. Such gifts are made without expectation of anything in return other than the courtesy of a thank-you letter or a receipt. "Philanthropy is misunderstood

EXHIBIT I-3   FRAMEWORK FOR DETERMINING WHY PEOPLE GIVE

Internal Motivations	External Influences
Personal or "I" Factors	*Rewards*
Acceptance of self or self-esteem	Recognition
Achievement	Personal
Cognitive interest	Social
Growth	
Guilt reduction or avoidance	*Stimulations*
Meaning or purpose of life	Human needs
Personal gain or benefit	Personal request
Spirituality	Vision
Immortality	Private initiative
Survival	Efficiency and effectiveness
	Tax deductions
Social or "We" Factors	
Status	*Situations*
Affiliation	Personal involvement
Group endeavor	Planning and decision making
Interdependence	Peer pressure
Altruism	Networks
Family and progeny	Family involvement
Power	Culture
	Tradition
Negative or "They" Factors	Role identity
Frustration	Disposable income
Unknown situations	
Insecurity	
Fear and anxiety	
Complexity	

Reprinted with permission from *Principles of Professional Fundraising* by Joseph R. Mixer (San Francisco: Jossey-Bass Publishers, 1993), 14.

when it is reduced to any one of its elements; therefore, fundraising is not the whole of philanthropy and is about more than money, being inextricably tied to philanthropic values, purposes, and methods."[21]

All donors may not be satisfied with the mere exchange of money; some may want to participate in philanthropic practice. For this type of donor, volunteerism is the answer most of the time. Donors will benefit from actions taken on behalf of others, even if they perform no action and receive no material rewards for their efforts. The fund-development process must acknowledge that donors are deserving of appropriate recognition for their good works.

Donor relations affirms the quality of action taken more than the amount given. Every gift is worthy of justifiable praise and should be acknowledged by the nonprofit organization. Those who are able to give more in a single donation may indeed receive more attention, but their accolades should be the same as those for every other donor whose cumulative giving eventually achieves the same level of support. Nonprofit organizations must be alert to the danger of selling recognition in exchange for the promise of rewards, no matter how much a donor has indicated a desire to receive them. Among the ethics of philanthropic practice are fairness and equality to all who give and to whom appropriate recognition can be offered.

> Ethical fund raising is the prod, the enabler, the activator to gift making. It must also be the conscience to the process. Fund raising is at its best when it strives to match the needs of the not-for-profit organization with the contributor's need and desire to give. The practice of gift seeking is justified when it exalts the contributor, not the gift seeker. It is justified when it is used as a responsible invitation, guiding contributors to make the kind of gift that will meet their own special needs and add greater meaning to their lives.[22]

THE ROLE OF ANNUAL GIVING

Annual giving programs, the front lines of fund development, are where most people become involved with nonprofit organizations, where most of the gift exchange takes place, and where the greatest variety of fundraising methods and techniques is found. Annual giving may be the entire fundraising program of nonprofit organizations that depend on the income from their annual giving appeals to cover their annual operating expenses.

Annual giving combines identifying and recruiting new donors with renewing and upgrading previous donors. Annual giving is also a means to expand the involvement and participation of current donors at all levels through membership associations or induction into donor clubs, guilds, and support organizations. Annual giving offers a great variety of opportunities for donors to become active as volunteers and to exercise leadership, especially in the popular areas of activities, benefits, and special events. Identification and recruitment of new donors and continuation of the commitment of prior donors remain constant through all of these annual giving methods. These techniques offer a rich multitude of opportunities for taking philanthropic practice beyond just asking for money. Friend-raising and relationship-building should be at their peak when all these opportunities are available!

What to Use in Making Annual Gifts

Does every gift qualify as being tax deductible? No; tax deductibility depends on what is given, to whom it is given, and the amounts of other charitable deductions in the same year. What, then, can people use to make a gift each year? People can give cash and currency, pledges, gifts of securities, gifts of personal property, gifts-in-kind, and donated services.

Cash and Currency

Cash, checks, and money orders are the most common forms of giving. Credit-card charges are also available with most nonprofit organizations. Depending on the card used, a small service fee (up to 3 percent) may be assessed. The amount charged is received by the organization right away as a full-value donation. The IRS rules permit a total charitable contribution deduction of up to 50 percent of a donor's adjusted gross income for the year of the gift, with a five-year carryover of any excess deduction value. However, only a donor who files an itemized ("long form") return will be able to claim the deduction. (Nonitemizers lost their deduction for gifts to charity under the 1986 Tax Reform Act. Efforts to reinstate this privilege have yet to succeed, up to and including the tax reform legislation of 2001.)

Pledges

The use of pledges for annual gifts is less common than cash and currency and incurs administrative costs for recordkeeping, billing, and collections. Because of the general nature of annual giving, cash is preferred: the organization will use the money as soon as it is received. Pledges are necessary when solicitation is performed over the telephone or on radio or television, or if payment is arranged via payroll deductions by the employer. (United Way has pioneered this simple but effective payment plan.) Because most annual giving programs are tied to the calendar or tax year, the pledge period normally ends on December 31. Alternatively, it may end on the fiscal year-end date of the organization. Pledges have the potential for some amount of nonpayment, depending on the solicitation method used and the time period allowed. Accounting for pledges, now termed *unconditional promises to give*, has been changed in light of Financial Accounting Standards Board (FASB) recommendations that they be counted as revenue for their full value when received, and then treated as assets.[23] If unpaid, the organization has the obligation to pursue payment, including legal redress—a set of conditions not likely to be viewed as conducive to donors' making formal pledges in the future.

Gifts of Securities

Stocks and bonds are valuable assets, but they have changing market value. Donors may choose to act when stock values are up, or a securities gift decision can be deferred until market conditions are favorable. Most annual gifts involving securities are modest in size (under $5,000 in value) and will occur before the tax year ends. Donors expect the stock to be sold so that the proceeds can be used toward annual giving priorities. If securities are sold by a donor and the proceeds are delivered as a gift to charity, the donor will be assessed a capital gains tax on the sale. Donors should be advised to give the securities to the charity instead of proceeds from their sale. Using this method, capital gains are deductible at full market value, subject to the deduction limit of 30 percent of the donor's adjusted gross income in the year of the gift, with a five-year carryover. The tax law changed in mid-1993 regarding gifts of appreciated property. Qualified gifts were removed from the alternative minimum tax (AMT) calculation—good news for generous donors and their favorite nonprofit organizations. Calculation of the charitable contribution value for gifts of securities requires three steps, in keeping with IRS regulations:

1. Establish the value for gifts of securities by calculating the mean average price of the stock on the date when ownership was transferred to the charity.
2. Verify the calculation (a) with a broker *and* (b) in the next business day's edition of a newspaper that carried the stock exchange listing (*The Wall Street Journal* or *The New York Times*, for example).
3. Confirm the gift value in writing to the donor.

Gifts of Personal Property

This category includes anything other than cash, securities, and real estate, and has two subcategories: intangible personal property and tangible personal property. The method to complete the transfer of a gift of intangible personal property (stocks and bonds, patents, copyrights) is the same as for gifts of securities. Transfer of tangible personal property is more complex and requires extreme care. Examples of tangible personal property include real estate, art works, antiques, collectibles, cars, boats, computers, china, silverware, and similar valuables.

IRS rules regarding deductibility are clear but not widely understood. Nonprofit organizations are advised to observe IRS procedures with exactitude in order to protect their donors. If a donor created the donated item, this donor may deduct only his or her cost of materials. If the donor purchased the item, the donor may claim full appreciated value if the donee organization's use of the item is related to its exempt purpose. If the item is for unrelated use, the donor may claim only the cost of acquiring the item. If the value of any item is $5,000 or more, the claim for deductibility must be authenticated in writing by a certified professional appraiser, at the donor's expense. Further, a copy of the appraisal must be signed by the donor and the nonprofit organization and attached to IRS Form 8283, which accompanies the donor's annual tax return. If the organization sells the item within two years after its receipt, it must report the amount of the sale to the IRS on Form 8282. The IRS will compare the appraisal value with the sale value and may challenge the donor's claim if there is a noticeable difference between these two figures.

Gifts-in-Kind

Some donors are in a position to give goods and services that can be used for charitable purposes in lieu of cash, securities, or personal property. Called gifts-in-kind, these are donations that can be valuable when they are directly usable for the organization's charitable purposes or in direct support of an activity, benefit, or special event. Examples are free or reduced-price printing of invitations, programs, or tickets by a professional printer; decorations and flowers from a florist; food from a caterer or wholesaler; table favors from local merchants; wine and similar items from appropriate sources. Gifts-in-kind can help to reduce the direct costs of staging an event and allow greater net proceeds to the nonprofit organization. As with gifts of personal property, tax deductibility rules are precise and the same validation procedures must be followed each time.

Donated Services

People's time has value and the time and talent they give to nonprofit organizations is no less valuable, but the IRS does not allow any charitable deduction for contributions of personal time and talent for any fundraising volunteer work. Deductions are allowed for unreimbursed expenses connected with a donation of services, mileage, tools, and parking (or the cost of transportation to and from the site where the services were provided). The FASB has allowed contributions of services to be recognized at the fair value of services received (but not recognized as revenue). The qualifications include whether "the services received (a) create or enhance nonfinancial assets or (b) require specialized skills, are provided by individuals possessing those skills, and would typically need to be purchased if not provided by donation."[24]

This book will present the entire panorama of annual giving programs, illustrating how the various methods and techniques are used to invite people to become donors, and how to build an initial gift relationship into long-term active participation by the donor in the life of the organization. The relationship begins with list selection and testing by mail and, through a series of expanding steps, it progresses into a comprehensive annual giving program. The testing determines who should receive the invitations and how to explain the vision and mission. "Roll out" invitations are part of the direct mail program, and a renewal cycle follows quickly afterward. Membership adds *belonging*—being part of a group of other donors—and other forms of association, such as by telephone, donor clubs, guilds, and support organizations, plus applications of Internet technology, offer further enhancement. With structured groups and volunteer leadership in place, the annual giving program gains advantages from inviting the public to join in its activities, benefits, and special events. All of these resources help the organization to build a base of continuing donors that is broad enough to support volunteer-led personal solicitation. Using an "annual campaign" model, the organization can give these most faithful donors the personal attention they require. Along the way, there will be multiple opportunities to experiment with one or more of the "other ways to raise money every year" (see Chapter 12). The scope and magnitude of this entire effort, which can be implemented within a period of three to five years, require professional management and direction by fund development staff from the beginning.

The methods and techniques used in annual giving are not the most efficient forms of fundraising. Each can and should be managed with efficiency and productivity on its own merits, but that is all that can be expected. The methods' greater value is in their collective ability to generate enthusiasm and a broad base of faithful followers. By tracking the results, using the formats shown in Exhibits 1-4, 1-5, and 1-6, progress can be monitored in three areas of activity, respectively: (1) sources of giving, (2) purposes and uses of funds raised, and (3) results of each annual giving method. Monitoring the sources of gifts will disclose where increases and decreases in the number of donors occur as well as their level of support and average gift size. The report on purposes and uses of funds raised reveals the degree to which the public has accepted the priority of needs requests with funds in the areas needed. Each fundraising method used in annual giving will perform differently and each method used should be

EXHIBIT 1-4   GIFT REPORT ON SOURCES OF GIFTS RECEIVED

Sources of Gifts	Number of Gifts	Gift Income	Average Gift Size
Trustees/directors	15	$ 25,500	$ 1,700
Professional staff	21	3,025	144
Employees	65	3,675	57
New donors (acquisition)	285	8,030	28
Prior donors (renewal)	282	18,010	64
Corporations	17	8,500	500
Foundations	12	38,800	3,233
Associations/societies	6	2,850	475
Bequests received	3	31,500	10,500
Unsolicited gifts	42	2,950	70
Other gifts received	12	21,500	1,792
Grand Total	760	$164,340	$ 216

Reprinted with permission from *Fundraising Cost Effectiveness: A Self-Assessment Workbook* by James M. Greenfield (New York: John Wiley & Sons, 1996), 15.

EXHIBIT 1-5   GIFT REPORT ON PURPOSES OR
USES OF GIFTS RECEIVED

Purposes or Uses of Gifts Received	Number of Gifts	Gift Income	Average Gift Size
Unrestricted Funds	225	$ 34,519	$ 153
Temporarily Restricted Funds			
Capital/equipment purposes	295	$ 26,950	$ 91
Programs/services purposes	138	18,500	134
Education/training purposes	14	22,500	1,607
Research/study purposes	15	26,450	1,763
Staff/employee purposes	58	3,016	52
Other restricted purposes	12	905	75
Subtotal	757	$132,840	$ 175
Permanently Restricted Funds			
Unrestricted endowment	2	$ 6,500	$ 3,250
Restricted endowment	1	25,000	25,000
Subtotal	3	$ 31,500	$10,500
Grand Total	760	$164,340	$ 216

Reprinted with permission from *Fundraising Cost Effectiveness: A Self-Assessment Workbook* by James M. Greenfield (New York: John Wiley & Sons, 1996), 16.

reported. A summary report should compare gift income against budget for a cost–benefit ratio (see Exhibit 1-7).

Throughout the book, there will be references to several basic principles. As already stated, the first purpose of annual giving is to raise friends and build relationships for the organization. Money follows people; if enough people join in the cause, if the organization serves the cause well, and if a comprehensive annual giving program is in place, the money will follow. Annual giving programs must also possess flexibility. The roster of priority needs will be constantly changing as the nonprofit organization carries out its programs and services year after year. The unique challenge to annual giving is to be able to plan and execute as much activity as possible within 12 months, and to continue those plans and activities with the same enthusiasm, energy, and success in the next year, and the year after that. After three to five years, the results should begin to be reliable enough to forecast performance from year to year. Some advice, from experience: Go back and review the results of each method used. Review again the

Solicitation Activities	Number of Gifts	Gift Income	Average Gift Size
A. Annual Giving Programs			
Direct mail (acquisition)	285	$ 8,030	$ 28
Direct mail (renewal)	282	18,010	64
Membership dues	0	0	0
Donor clubs	0	0	0
Support groups	0	0	0
Telephone gifts	0	0	0
Benefit events	2	12,850	6,425
Volunteer-led solicitations	65	3,675	57
Unsolicited gifts	42	2,950	70
Other gifts received	16	21,500	1,344
Subtotal	692	$ 67,015	$ 97
B. Major Giving Programs			
Corporations	17	$ 8,500	$ 500
Foundations	12	28,800	2,400
Individuals	36	28,525	792
Special projects	0	0	0
Capital campaigns	0	0	0
Bequests received	3	31,500	10,500
Subtotal	68	$ 97,325	$ 1,431
Grand total	760	$164,340	$ 216

Reprinted with permission from *Fundraising Cost Effectiveness: A Self-Assessment Workbook* by James M. Greenfield (New York: John Wiley & Sons, 1996), 17.

reasons why selected fundraising programs were chosen. Measure how well they are doing today. When guidance is called for, turn to Tom Broce's "nine cardinal principles" of fundraising:[25]

I.   Institutional or organizational objectives must be established first.

II.   Development objectives must be established to meet institutional goals.

III.   The kinds of support needed determine the kinds of fundraising programs.

IV.   The institution must start with natural prospects.

EXHIBIT I-7   GIFT REPORT OF SOLICITATION
ACTIVITIES WITH GIFT INCOME
MEASURED AGAINST APPROVED
BUDGET AND ACTUAL EXPENSES
(BY PROGRAM)

Activities	Gift Income	Approved Budget	Actual Expenses	Cost per $ Raised
A. Annual Giving Programs				
Direct mail (acquisition)	$ 8,030	$10,500	$ 9,855	$1.23
Direct mail (renewal)	18,010	3,750	3,890	0.22
Membership dues	0	0	0	0
Donor clubs	0	0	0	0
Support groups	0	0	0	0
Telephone gifts	0	0	0	0
Benefit events	2,850	1,800	1,350	0.47
Volunteer-led solicitations	3,675	500	485	0.13
Unsolicited gifts	2,950	0	0	0
Other gifts received	21,500	0	0	0
Subtotal	$ 57,015	$16,550	$15,580	$0.27
B. Major Giving Programs				
Corporations	$ 8,500	$20,215	$18,250	$2.15
Foundations	38,800	34,525	33,555	0.86
Individuals	28,525	3,210	3,250	0.11
Special projects	0	0	0	0
Capital campaigns	0	0	0	0
Bequests received	31,500	500	550	0.02
Subtotal	$107,325	$58,450	$55,605	$0.52
Grand total	$164,340	$75,000	$71,185	$0.43

Reprinted with permission from *Fundraising Cost Effectiveness: A Self-Assessment Workbook* by James M. Greenfield (New York: John Wiley & Sons, 1996), 19.

V.   The case for the program must reflect the importance of the institution.

VI.   Involvement is the key to leadership and support.

VII.   Prospect research must be thorough and realistic.

VIII.   Cultivation is the key to successful solicitation.

IX.   Solicitation is successful only if Cardinal Principles I through VIII have been followed.

Within the 365 days in each year, there is just enough time to stop and reflect on what is in operation and how well it is performing. Repetitious activities are slightly at risk of becoming fixed because everyone accepts how well they are working. Measurement and evaluation make people nervous; they are afraid something might be discovered to be wrong, especially when the cost of fundraising is added to the analysis. The opposite result is more likely: improvements might be found and might make even better performances possible (see Exhibit 1-7 for a sample analysis). If assessments are not made, improvements will not be found. Perhaps more important to leaders and volunteers is the fact that studies of current activities may yield ideas that can keep annual giving programs fresh and exciting. Here are five basic rules that annual giving can live by:[26]

1. An annual fund drive is annual. Don't skip a year for any reason.

2. Select the best possible people you can find to serve in the leadership positions of the campaign.

3. Develop your case for support.

4. Involve as many volunteers as possible. The more people who ask for money, the more money you will receive.

5. Work closely with each volunteer and provide every tool needed to get the job done. Be absolutely certain to give recognition when the campaign is over.

Annual giving can bring great satisfaction to all who are involved in its practice. It has pace and excitement and is hardly ever dull. It calls for creativity and experimentation and gets instantaneous results. It involves the best of people working for the best of causes: helping others. It has influence in the community and importance to the organization. The friends it finds and develops into committed donors will remain thankful for the opportunity. The money it raises is put to work immediately, and all can see the results. Nonprofit organizations that have comprehensive annual giving programs working on their behalf can depend on their reliable performance, year after year, and can continue with confidence to pursue the fulfillment of their vision and mission.

CHAPTER 2

Asking for Money: Begin with Testing by Mail

Asking for money goes on all the time, among friends and neighbors, men and women, parents and children, and even among children, their siblings, and their classmates. Everyone does it; some people do it many times a day. Sometimes, it works! For example, a person might approach a prospect and say, "Can you please help me? I need money for food." The prospect will decide instantly and will either reach into a pocket or reply, "No; I'm sorry." If no, the asker moves on to the next prospect and tries again with the same approach. Whether it is called begging, panhandling, mooching, or soliciting, asking for money is much the same every time.

What separates fundraising from begging? Is it the request for money for someone else or something else, such as a nonprofit organization and not for oneself? If the same prospect was approached by a volunteer solicitor, the opening line might be the same as a beggar's: "Can you please help me?" But the volunteer solicitor might then add, "I'm a volunteer with The Campaign to Clean Up America; we need money to help clean up our city streets." The prospect is likely to decide right away, yes or no. If the reply is, "No; I'm sorry," the volunteer moves on to the next prospect and tries again.

How is asking for money for a cause different from asking for money for oneself? The words used are not all that different. Was either asker uncomfortable when asking a stranger for money? Did both feel like beggars? Why is asking for money so difficult for so many people? There are people for whom asking for a charitable cause lifts the request to a higher plane, adding morality, humility, honor, and dignity to both the giving and the receiving. But most askers are afraid to be turned down, do not want to be embarrassed, or are fearful of the confrontation required in asking for money.

The mission of every nonprofit organization is to fulfill a charitable purpose by helping others—providing public benefits, advancing the community, improving the world's condition in some large or small way. Commitment, dedication, hard work, and leadership are all necessary. So is money; money is needed every day to make these good deeds possible. To get the job done, people must be willing to ask their friends for money throughout the year. Prospects surround us; the challenge is to find good askers! Finding good askers requires time and attention. It begins with the first efforts to recruit people who are willing to ask their friends for money, which happens to be one of the more difficult first-time assignments people are likely to encounter. Once they have tried this task and succeeded, watch their enthusiasm grow!

ACQUISITION: THE EVERLASTING SEARCH

Asking people for money can be done in a variety of ways. Each technique is quite different and, as this book will illustrate, several tested and proven fundraising methods can be used with success. There are three basic ways to ask:

1. In writing (impersonal)
2. By voice or video (at a distance)
3. In person (face to face)

In-person solicitation is more effective than telephone contact (voice or video); telephoning is more effective than direct mail letters or e-mail messages. Despite this confirmed performance difference, most nonprofit organizations conduct the majority of their annual giving solicitations by mail. Why? Perhaps because it's easier, hundreds, thousands, even millions can be asked, the organizations do not have to recruit and train volunteers, and no one has to actually "confront" a donor or prospect and ask for a gift.

Several decisions are needed before asking can begin. After deciding who will be recruited, persuading them to help, and training them in how to solicit, the final step is selecting who will be asked. Two rules apply:

1. Concentrate on those who are most likely to respond positively.
2. Consider what else the people being asked might be able to do besides being donors. Might they volunteer for other tasks?

Nonprofit organizations need all the help they can get if they are to succeed in areas other than fundraising. The entire process is one of "friend-raising" and "relationship-building." Making new friends for a nonprofit organization is the most significant contribution that can be achieved. Friendships and relationships built with care over time become enormously beneficial to an organization. Two axioms should be kept in mind throughout this book:

1. Friend-raising precedes fundraising.
2. Money follows people.

The more new and old friends a nonprofit organization has, the more giving can be achieved. Friends bring with them their time, talents, and energy as well as their money. All four are equally valuable to a nonprofit organization. These multiple goals should be highlighted constantly, beginning with the first time a new volunteer is asked to help out. A future relationship with each of these potential new friends is possible. Can they help with community relations and legislative activities? Become active leaders in annual giving, major giving, and estate planning programs? Each of their talents will benefit the nonprofit organization for many years, but it will never know how until it asks.

Not everyone who is asked will be interested in being a volunteer or in giving money. Not everyone will want to become a friend to the organization or to develop a relationship with it. But some will, and these valuable people must be found. Acquiring a few new friends who are able to volunteer *and* give money is well worth the effort, which is why such activity is an everlasting search. Nonprofit organizations must continuously recruit new friends, new volunteers, and new donors. There are never enough new people who are trained, experienced, and ready to replace those who are already active but then move on to new tasks, higher levels of assignment, or new locales. Where to begin? How to begin? Who should be recruited first, prospects or volunteers? Will those asked to participate become donors, too?

In the warmup area just behind the starting gate are the prospect selection criteria: knowing the organization well enough to understand its areas of possible public appeal, and knowing the targeted community well enough to understand its preferences, style of volunteerism, giving potential, current concerns, economic conditions, and general demographics. These criteria will provide insight into whom to approach and how best to communicate with possible volunteers. The first means available for contact with them will be either first-class personal letters or third-class, bulk-rate letters. With either choice, the objectives are to identify and then select those within the community who are considered the best *prospects*. Suspects are less qualified candidates than prospects because they are judged to be much less likely to respond to mailed invitations. These questions should be answerable for each name on the mailing list to qualify them as valid prospects, not just suspects: Why has this person been selected? What will this person be invited to contribute—time, talent, energy, advice, counsel, and/or money? If the letter is an invitation to work in some capacity, will this person's capabilities match the "job description" for the work that needs to be done? Invitations by mail should recruit the best talent available to fill these jobs. If the invitation is just to give money, does the letter provide adequate information about the projects that need money, the uses that the organization has planned for the funds received, the numbers of people who will be served, the quality and value of what they will receive, and the benefits that will be rendered to the community? All these messages can be woven into direct mail letters. But the first (and most challenging) task is to locate exactly the people who should receive the letters. Call them *qualified prospects* and pursue them!

Why is this first task so important? If enough willing people cannot be found, the nonprofit organization will not meet its mission to conduct charitable purposes and to provide public benefits. The mission explains why the organization wants and needs more than their money. True, their first and second gifts will be essential as operating cash; but each new donor will be done a great disservice if offered only a single-minded, mercenary goal. Nonprofit organizations that are successful year after year—and even decade after decade—begin by carefully selecting those who are invited to be their friends. From among the prospects and suspects available to them, these organizations find those people who have the potential to become personally involved and will commit to be supportive in multiple ways for many years. Seven criteria are recommended for this initial selection process. Each is discussed in the sections that follow:

1. Identification
2. Qualification
3. Influences
4. Education and Training
5. Participation
6. Leadership
7. Recognition

Identification

Everyone who is invited will not agree to serve in some capacity, so it is important to be selective right from the start. The people contacted and what they are asked to do are the primary search criteria. Any search for prospects and suspects must begin with people who are available—within reach and interested. If possible, the invitation letter should have data to which they are likely to reply favorably. The people most qualified to be volunteers should be asked to come to work. Those most qualified to give should be asked to consider a contribution at a level well within their financial range. It helps when people recognize the name of a nonprofit organization or know about its charitable purposes when they first receive an invitation, but a proper invitation form matters most of all.

Inviting people to consider helping a good and worthy cause is not offensive. If something that coincides with the interests and concerns of those being invited can be included in the message, they might more readily accept. Some people might not have the time or money right now, or care that much about the cause, or even know enough about it to make an informed decision. Asking will stimulate their thinking. Some people will reply that they are fully subscribed to other organizations at this time. Raising friends is a continuous process, and education begins with the first contact. If the interests of those invited are known to be similar or favorable, they will not resent being asked to help, especially where a recognized problem is presented and they are being asked to be part of the solution. The invitation message should also explain why they were selected and be clear about what they are being asked to do to help.

Selection criteria define who will be invited and measure the probability of their acceptance. The next step is to sort them according to the purposes or tasks they are being asked to do. If you are only asking for money, verify financial ability. If you are asking for voluntary service, verify other volunteer experience and performance matched to the job descriptions. Some people are asked over and over again because they have already proved they are interested and willing to help, and they enjoy charitable work. They have also decided how and where they will give their time and their money to philanthropic activities. From experience, most will have narrowed their choices and will reply only to causes they prefer and have verified to be sound. When their interests match the vision, mission, and needs of the organization, these are the best candidates to ask. The first request may not succeed unless a current, urgent reason that makes sense is offered, such as sympathy for the cause or need, respect for the person asking (a peer or a high-level and respected volunteer), and trust that their energy and talents plus the time they have to serve will be put to good use. If all these criteria are in order, their commitment and their money are sure to follow.

Surveys by Independent Sector estimate that in 1993, 89.2 million Americans (47.7 percent of the adult population) were volunteers for a charitable purpose, who gave an average of 4.2 hours per week, for an estimated total of 19.5 billion hours. More than half these hours were spent in four activity areas: religion (19 percent); informal volunteering (14 percent); education (12 percent); and youth development (9 percent), which translate to an equivalent of 8.8 million full-time employees at an estimated value of $182 billion. Despite these impressive figures, Independent Sector estimates that volunteer hours are in decline, a legitimate concern for all nonprofit organizations. Regarding individual giving and its link to volunteer activity, these surveys also have shown that contributions by household members that volunteer are more generous than household members who do not volunteer by a factor of three and a half times as much money. The average percentage of household income given was 1.7 percent, or $646 in 1993; for contributing households in which respondents also were volunteers, the average percentage was 2.6, or $1,193, and in households in which respondents were not volunteers, the percentage was 1.1, and $425 average gift.[1]

Beyond the time and dollars involved, every nonprofit organization has a variety of job opportunities that need volunteer help. The area or task that needs help can be defined in terms of time, or money, or both. As with any other job description, it is essential to recruit people who are matched to the work to be done. If they enjoy what they do, believe it is helpful, and see it as an assignment they can perform successfully, they will come back and work again. These are the volunteers who are so vital to any organization. Some will move on to higher levels of responsibility. Their financial support, growing alongside their involvement, will become a firm commitment to serve the current and future needs of "their" organization.

People generally do not have a lot of experience with well-defined volunteer work. They may be a bit hesitant or suspicious when asked about taking on a new assignment area, or when recruited to a new cause or organization—and for good reason. There are many unknowns to be mastered yet again. Also, others might have abused their good intentions or failed to utilize their skills or their time well. People are also a bit suspicious of requests for their money that are actually asking for their time and skills as a ruse to try to get more of their money. Again, well-defined selection criteria matched to specific duties that point with clarity to the value of the work to be performed are the important ingredients in successful invitations.

Finding people with a capacity to become volunteers, donors, *and* leaders is hard work but they are exactly the "triple-threat" candidates that are needed. Finding people who have only one attribute can also be worthwhile. With a little time and effort, all three attributes might be realized. People bring their own potential for expanding their interests, enthusiasm, and commitment. They also bring access to a larger circle of family, friends, club members, business associates, and contacts, and may share these resources later. Finding such valuable individuals within the community and asking them to become an active part of an organization is worthy of the best hours of the day. The steps involved are: spend time identifying as many qualified people as possible, designate solid assignments for them, prepare to train them to do the work needed, and formulate a plan to supervise, evaluate, and reward them for all they do. Every nonprofit organization can meet its most urgent needs for today and for its future with just a few triple-threat stars on its team.

Qualification

Assuming that people who have similar interests, prior experience, and some financial ability have been identified, what should they be asked to do? The exact tasks assigned will depend on how what is known about them matches the work that needs to be done. People who are available to nonprofit organizations as volunteers bring with them a variety of usable skills as well as wide experience and infectious enthusiasm. Matching their interests with individual tasks related to the mission, purpose, goals, and objectives of the organization will take time and effort, but the results will be enormous, for each of them and for the future of the organization.

Some people are available only to give money. Their chief qualification will be a track record of a generous habit of giving, usually with some public notice. They are quite likely to reply to invitations because they seek involvement, visibility, and public recognition. They want to make a difference, to become a respected member of the community. Each organization needs to recruit these proven donors, not because they have given to others, but because of their potential to give repeatedly to each organization they choose. Donors who will give often are needed more than people who will give only one gift. The time and effort (not to mention the cost) required to recruit a single gift are reason enough to seek out donors who have a proven potential for repetitive giving.

Identifying qualified current and future leaders for nonprofit organizations is the most difficult task of all. Other nonprofit organizations will not train their leaders and then give them away. The best leaders are developed within each organization. They are a product of extensive knowledge, proven ability, demonstrated commitment, and a history of faithful gift support. Such preparation takes a lot of time and should follow a carefully prepared program that has leadership as its objective. Leadership positions will not be immediately available to everyone, but recruitment of potential leaders should never be off the organization's agenda.

Perhaps the most important criterion when identifying leaders from early lists of potential donors and volunteers is whether their abilities will have the opportunity to flower within an organization, allowing them to rise to its highest levels of leadership. First invitations sent to selected prospects may be received by future leaders. What plans are in place for their training and development?

The list of tasks available for volunteer work should be matched with abilities and talents that can be put to good and efficient use. Some people look for a chance to volunteer in order to do something new and different, or to learn new skills. The only qualifications needed may be prior experience in nonprofit voluntary work, rapport with the cause or mission, time to give, reliability, a willing spirit to work within the structure or system offered, and some financial ability. Strong personalities who prefer (or demand) their own way of doing things are not always a happy match, even if they are quite successful on their own. They know how to get things done, but their domineering style may drive others away—a bad outcome for nonprofit organizations. If they cannot fit into a committee system, they may be productive with a task that is not managed in a group or by a committee, or with a one-on-one manager–volunteer arrangement. This kind of arrangement should be reserved only for people who have a high potential to help.

Influence

Recruiting people of influence will be essential to the future of each nonprofit organization. Some individuals can be selected for invitations because they are known to influence others and can bring their influence to benefit the nonprofit organization's cause. Boards of directors are often composed of individuals chosen because their influential affiliation adds prestige to the cause. Influence can be applied through access to others, which is most important for success in fundraising. Influence is a means to get things done—usually the types of things that managers and staff, and even other volunteers, cannot accomplish on their own. Influential leaders who accept leadership assignments inspire people to follow them. They also attract others like themselves into supportive roles. Bless them all— each and every one!

Education and Training

Each organization must provide fairly complete information to those invited to serve. Assimilating new information takes time. Training can be met only partially with printed materials; people need a translator to interpret details in person. An orientation program can explain operating procedures and provide details on the mission, purposes, goals, and objectives of the organization. When a newcomer accepts an invitation to serve, a planned program of education and training will keep excitement and enthusiasm at a high level. Much more information is required for new board members than for new volunteers or new donors, because of the degree of obligation involved. However, all newcomers need information that will build their confidence, commitment, interests, and involvement and enable them to continue their intended level of support.

The information given at the time of first contact can be limited, but it must be adequate for the invitee to make an informed Yes decision. Once the relationship begins, there is more time to add details, expand knowledge, and lay the foundation for a long-lasting relationship. A plan for continuing education should aim to systematically bring everyone to (1) a level of understanding about the organization and (2) an appreciation of the value of time donated by volunteers to help fulfill the mission and purposes that are being advanced.

Participation

An organization that plans how everyone who volunteers can be a part of the organization is more likely to channel qualified people into positions where they will be most effective. High levels of personal involvement are important to leaders among the volunteers. One of the reasons they choose to become associated with nonprofit organizations is the access it gives them to others who share in their commitment for community service. They join because they enjoy being part of something larger than themselves; they stay if they are given some *active* role to play. Without it, they will soon lose interest and move on to another organization that is better prepared for their active involvement. Other volunteers will be satisfied with a more distant relationship and will rely on communications to maintain their interest and to continue their support.

Every organization that plans and uses its volunteers well will receive added benefits from their commitment. Personal involvement counts highly with volunteers. Those who participate feel more closely attached to the organization and will remain close for many years—some, for the balance of their lifetimes. Out of this pool of talent and commitment come the people who will help the organization realize its future. Some will serve at the highest levels of leadership, others will donate the largest gifts.

Communications such as thank-you letters, newsletters, invitations, informative reports, brochures, and annual reports maintain their interest and provide them with all the information necessary for their success in this relationship.

Leadership

The most effective nonprofit organizations are those blessed with people who can lead others. Volunteer leaders aid in the direction and management of internal and external activities at several levels. Their example of stewardship responsibility is a stimulant for action. Leaders within nonprofit organizations can be carefully prepared for this level of duty through on-the-job experience. They may be assigned several jobs with several organizations over time. They benefit from careful orientation for each new assignment and from some form of performance evaluation. Each nonprofit organization has its own style of management, its "corporate culture" or behavior patterns, its policies and procedures, rules of operation, and internal politics. Leaders want to be successful in their assignment (some will not accept a position until they are assured of that success), but they also want to help the organization realize its current and future plans. They bring their talents and experience and they offer advice, counsel, and hard work. Every idea will not be useful at every moment, but their energy and enthusiasm are invaluable and must be cultivated at all times.

Recognition

This criterion is last on the list, but preparations to thank, recognize, and reward volunteers should be made at the beginning of planning, when job descriptions are written. People who give of their energy and skills want to know that their efforts are helpful. The best way to acknowledge their good work and to encourage them to do more is to thank them properly. There are ways to express this appreciation again and again. Recognition can include reporting their names and accomplishments to others and presenting them with token forms of appreciation (certificates, paperweights, plaques, and other mementos). These tokens of appreciation will be graciously accepted and acknowledged in the spirit of gratitude in which they are given. The object itself is not as important as the sincerity behind it. The presenting should be made with honesty, at the right time, in the right setting, and with the right people present. It represents grateful feelings of true appreciation for what they have done to advance the organization's mission.

These selection criteria will be revisited throughout this book because they are so essential to every part of fundraising. Volunteers are the arms and legs as well as the eyes and ears of nonprofit organizations. They represent the community and its willingness to support the mission and purposes of the organization. These leaders, volunteers, and donors are ambassadors who are willing to speak to others with knowledge and positive praise about the organization. Such dedication sets an example others will want to follow.

FINDING LIKELY FIRST-TIME DONORS

When asked what is the most important investment they will make, small business owners are likely to cite the amount of effort and cost they believe must be put into finding new customers. A multinational corporation, asked the same question, is likely to deliver a crash course on advanced applications of modern marketing and advertising techniques. Both entities invest heavily in finding first-time customers because their business (and their profits) depend on being successful at both finding and retaining customers to buy their products. Are nonprofit organizations any different? The selection criteria and techniques used to acquire first-time donors are much the same as those used by small businesses and multinationals to acquire customers. The limiting difference may be the amount of money available to be spent.

Most nonprofit organizations have to reach out widely to identify likely first-time donors. Some nonprofit organizations, because of their mission, have no natural constituency to begin with. Some are unpopular or unknown. For many organizations, the people who use their services and participate in their programs are their first source of prospective donors. Most nonprofit organizations are small in size, locally based, and comparatively unknown. Fewer than 100,000 out of more than 1 million nonprofit organizations in the United States are large enough to be widely known; these are America's colleges and universities, and its prominent hospitals, national health agencies, and museums, which have achieved a positive image and reputation with the public. Smaller, local, unknown organizations find it difficult to compete with these established organizations because the public begins with comparisons. Another factor is that the better known organizations have already captured much of the time and money available in the community. One of the compelling reasons for founding United Way was to help the smaller, weaker, lesser known organizations to gain the attention, respect, and support of a wider public. Competition is a harsh reality. Thoughtful effort will be required to recruit new volunteers and first-time donors for nonprofit organizations. No one should expect that every organization can become an instant celebrity and use that brief moment of fleeting fame to gain enough public attention to attract all the necessary donors and leaders.

The best way to find and recruit new donors is to use tested and proven techniques:

- Start with people whom those in the organization know.
- Ask these people to expand the list of candidates by selecting among their friends, relatives, neighbors, business colleagues, club members, and social contacts.
- Expand beyond this new circle of friends and contacts, reaching out to *their* friends and contacts.

This ripple-effect of "circles of influence" process is an effective way to begin, but it has limits, takes a lot of time, and loses its selectivity in finding well-qualified prospects fairly soon.

Multinational corporations as well as small businesses learned long ago that using only one method to recruit new customers was inadequate. Several avenues must be explored, and each of these sales promotions must be coordinated to reinforce and be reinforced by the others wherever possible. Today, an advertising campaign to introduce a new product is test-marketed in several communities across the country at the same time. A combination of local newspaper, radio, and television advertising is matched with visible promotions in outlet stores—all reinforced with direct mail distribution of product samples to the homes of selected customer groups. The message is almost impossible to miss! A telephone and mail market research study is conducted in each community prior to the campaign, to establish base-line buyer attitudes toward the new product. A second survey, adding web page surveys and Internet promotions, after the testing campaign, measures changes in public attitude. All these data are added to sales results and all input is used to refine the strategy. Only the methods of communication that work best will be used when the new product is offered to other, equally select audiences of customers in the next test. Testing is the proven first step.

Nonprofit organizations can utilize strategic marketing to establish their public image, the value of their cause, their mission, and their charitable purpose. Modern communications methods are necessary to tell their story widely, to influence public attitudes about the quality of their programs and services, and to persuade people to become active supporters. Most nonprofit organizations do not use for-profit marketing and advertising tactics because they endorse a conservative attitude, or they lack the marketing expertise and money for such a campaign. Competition is more likely to bring change in their approach in the future. A few nonprofit organizations have begun to use multimedia techniques including Internet applications (both active and passive) with the same skill and success shown by for-profit corporations; however, as yet most do not. Until they do, their leadership and management are likely to endorse only the most modest and cost-effective promotions, even when executives on the board are effectively using technology for their own businesses. The results can be predicted to be modest and of low impact. When fundraising communications are the only means used for marketing and promotion, they, too, will yield a poor response.

To compete for public attention and to stimulate the public to act, nonprofit organizations must use the same channels as everyone else. Successful communications result from studying the marketplace and surveying public opinion to target those who need to hear the organization's messages using one or more media options singly or (better) in multimedia combinations for added effectiveness. No channel stands alone, nor do any messages have much impact when using just one channel, although each has a separate area for use.

Communications about annual giving activities is an additional message opportunity for reaching select audiences and helping to promote programs and services. Such communications inform and educate these same target markets and stimulate requests for service as well as for financial support.

People want to know what their time and money are being used for before they decide to give; therefore, it is necessary for all messages to be consistent. Listeners or viewers should sense that the messages point to the same organization, highlight the same goals, and encourage the same responses, regardless of whether its purpose is marketing, communicating, or soliciting. Marketing, communications, and solicitation activities perform most effectively and with greatest efficiency when used in a coordinated and cooperative effort that, like a mathematical formula, will produce desired results for all three (see Exhibit 2-1).

Everyone has to start finding prospects somewhere, even if at modest levels. There are several ways to get started. Who lives nearby? Who is using the services offered, attending the programs, learning what services the organization is providing? Who is the organization trying to serve? How is it getting its message to those it wants to serve, those who are supposed to hear about its programs? These people are natural candidates for

EXHIBIT 2-1	MEASUREMENT OF COORDINATION OF MARKETING, COMMUNICATIONS, AND FUND DEVELOPMENT ACTIVITIES

	SCORE
	Low High
Marketing Objectives	
Establish an image	1 2 3 4 5
Create clients for programs	1 2 3 4 5
Elicit a positive response	1 2 3 4 5
Stimulate the public to act	1 2 3 4 5
Communications Objectives	
Inform and educate	1 2 3 4 5
Tell a story, and repeat it often	1 2 3 4 5
Report results, accomplishments, outcomes	1 2 3 4 5
Build confidence and trust	1 2 3 4 5
Build community consensus	1 2 3 4 5
Fund Development Objectives	
Friend raising and relationship building	1 2 3 4 5
Develop a willingness to volunteer	1 2 3 4 5
Develop a willingness to give	1 2 3 4 5
Develop gifts to meet priority needs	1 2 3 4 5
Provide continuous contact with donors through donor relations activities	1 2 3 4 5 _____
Median Score:	

Source: James M. Greenfield, *Fund Raising: Evaluating and Managing the Fund Development Process,* 2nd ed. (New York: John Wiley & Sons, 1999), p. 60. Used with permission.

a request to support the organization. Why not start by making a list of them? Exhibit 2-2 identifies two groups of likely candidates to become first-time donors. Some choices will have to be made; these available audiences can often be interrelated. A list of natural candidates is likely to include some of the same people. The nonprofit organization should make an effort to coordinate its mailing lists, the messages being sent, their means of delivery, and the type of response(s) being requested. Only then can it begin to measure the results.

Before beginning to reach out and stimulate constituents to become new volunteers and donors, a review of the objectives and advantages of the use of direct mail as the chief means of communication and solicitation will be helpful. Direct mail is the most thoroughly tested and proven method to find prospects and to recruit their first gift and their repeated gifts. Robert Torre and Mary Anne Bendixen[3] believe that mail communications have several other uses that support fundraising:

> Direct mail can and should be used in annual, capital, and planned giving campaigns. Few development professionals now feel that direct mail should be used only to solicit "smaller" gifts from prospects, former donors, and current donors. Direct mail, telemarketing, and personal calls are equally powerful ways to approach our constituencies.

EXHIBIT 2-2	LIKELY CANDIDATES FOR FIRST-TIME DONORS
Suspects	People living nearby
	People who have been served
	People to whom service is directed
	People who work for suppliers
	People who respond to invitations
	People who respond to media messages
	People who respond to similar causes
	People identified by selection criteria
Prospects	All who qualify as suspects
	People who participate in similar causes
	People who currently participate in the organization
	People identified by others who are involved
	People buying tickets to activities
	People of influence
	People with proven leadership skills
	People who were donors in prior years

These researchers have identified 14 objectives and advantages for the use of direct mail:[4]

1. A direct mail program should raise funds cost-effectively.

2. Direct mail can dramatically increase the number of donors to an organization.

3. A direct mail program can broaden an organization's visibility and make it more recognizable.

4. A direct mail program can identify more substantial prospects for capital or planned giving campaigns.

5. A direct mail program can identify new volunteers or workers for the organization.

6. Direct mail will reach the great majority of those you wish to contact in the way that you want to contact them.

7. Direct mail can take advantage of current events because it can be formulated and implemented in a very short time period.

8. A direct mail program gives more control to the development office.

9. A direct mail program provides instant gratification.

10. A direct mail program requires less staff time to implement than a phonathon or in-person calls.

11. A direct mail program gives the organization a full opportunity to tell the complete story.

12. A direct mail program can be individualized/personalized and segmented to a specific audience.

13. A direct mail program should be looked upon as a continuing program in the upgrading of donors.

14. A direct mail program provides an easy "follow-through" advantage in solicitation.

TESTING, TESTING, TESTING

Before any invitation, solicitation, or other form of mass communication is mailed, it is essential to test the package, message (copy), offer, timing, and, most important of all, the mailing lists that will be used. Testing proves what will work best for this organization today, not someone else's a year ago. Substitution of guessing for testing is a highly visible and expensive way to prove that an organization is out of touch with its constituency. Failure to test also can cause unemployment for fundraising executives! In one of my personal experiences, we prepared for our first venture into mass direct mail solicitation for a large, well-respected nonprofit organization by testing 45 separate lists within a six-state area. The results were quite promising in every respect save one; we neglected to pay a bit extra for a merge-purge—a computer technique that searches for similar names and addresses and reduces them to a single mailing label. The chairman of the board (naturally!) received 40 copies of the test package! He was forever convinced that direct mail was not worth the powder to blow it up, no matter how many donors were acquired or how much money was raised. He also concluded that we did not know what we were doing, and professional help was brought in.

Testing requires professional help for every part of the mailing process, beginning with the lists to be used and the size of the test for each list. Costs for rental, lease, or purchase of lists start at $35 per 1,000 names; testing is an added expense. Professional direct mail consultants make their living by *being successful* in mail solicitation. To prevent disaster and ensure success, they all recommend testing prior to mailing ("roll out") to the entire mailing list. Besides, testing works!

There is much wisdom in the advice of professionals like Mal Warwick:[5] "The most important factor to test at the outset is whether or not direct mail acquisition is even feasible for your organization. Direct mail fundraising won't work for every organization—but you've got to try to find out for sure." Direct mail solicitation is a complex method of fundraising. Before any venture into either mass mailings or testing, quickly review the following seven rules, issued by Kay Lautman and Henry Goldstein:[6]

1. All tests should have as their goal a measurable increased percent of return and/or average gift. . . .

2. To be accurate, test only one thing at a time. (This rule excludes lists, which you are *always* testing.)

3. Mail test packages within the same week.

4. Mail test packages at the same postal rate, unless it is postage you are testing.

5. Mail test packages to the same lists and split your list for testing on an *n*th (or random sample) select. . . .

6. Any test conducted using fewer than five lists of 2,500 names each is rarely valid. Ten lists of 5,000 names each is preferable.

7. After test results are in, test the same thing once again.

Exhibit 2-3 provides a list of the basic elements in a mail package, all of which can be tested with several variations. A few elements will have the

EXHIBIT 2-3 **COMPONENTS AND OPTIONS IN THE DIRECT MAIL PACKAGE**

Basic Components	Options
Mailing lists	Prior donors
	Members and volunteers
	Prospects and suspects
	Clients and neighbors
	Rented/leased/purchased lists
Outer envelope	Addressee information
	Complete return address
	"Address Service Requested"
	Indicia/stamp/metered postage
	Special "teaser" message
Appeal letter	Official stationery
	Personalized salutation
	Personal message style
	Persuasive wording
	Request for a gift amount
	Typed/printed/computer-output text
	"P.S." message
Enclosure	Brochure, card, or giveaway
	Photograph and message
	Reprinted news article or ad
Response form	Donor's name, address, phone number
	Gift amount options
	Membership option
	Gift club option
	Information for inquiries (on wills, bequests, special gifts)
Reply envelope	Preprinted and preaddressed
	Space for return address
	Postage (blank/metered/stamped)
	Combination response form/envelope (business reply envelope)

biggest impact on the results; all the rest will have only moderate to low impact. Those high-impact elements are the ones that will demonstrate the mail program's potential for success, according to Warwick:[7]

> In other words, if anything's going to give your mailing program a big lift, it's probably one or the other of the following . . . items:
>
> - LISTS!
> - Higher or lower minimum suggested gift
> - Telephone follow-up
> - Offering a product to those who give
> - Involvement device
> - New package
> - Outer envelope design and copy
> - Sweepstakes offer

But, be very cautious if you elect to acquire donors using a sweepstakes offer or offering a product in exchange for an initial gift. Your response rate may, indeed, be higher. But respondents to sweepstakes or premium offers may lack interest in your cause or organization, and their value over the long haul may be substantially less than that of donors or members acquired without such inducements to greed.

Once the mail program is a success, later tests can experiment with other elements. Subtle changes can help to improve results already achieved. Here are some of the possible options:

- Postage (use of stamps/meter/indicia)
- Endorsement by celebrity/recognized community leader/executive director
- Computer-personalized/"Dear Friend" printed letter
- Envelope design (name and address in a window envelope/on a label/ personally printed)
- One-page/four-page letters
- Front-end/back-end premiums
- Enclosures (brochure/card/photo/nothing)
- Reply envelope (postage paid/envelope needing a stamp)
- Survey form
- Timing (seasonal/year-round)

To be as fair as possible and to realize truly valid results, new elements should be tested only against one another, not against prior experience with other mailings or against disparate elements.

There are accounting rules that must be followed regarding joint costs of information materials included in any mailings, even test mailings. Joint costs arise when the solicitation package includes an information brochure that was not prepared for use in fundraising. Rather, it is a document that accurately informs or promotes the programs and services of the organization. The accounting profession will then permit a portion of the mailing cost to be allocated to the programs and services budget, thus reducing fundraising cost calculations.[8] For full details on allocating joint costs of mailings, organizations should consult their professional auditors.

Analysis of the results of test mailings requires some level of experience and—usually—professional help. A reasonable guide for whether a list has been successful in a test mailing uses three measurements:

1. A minimum of 1 percent response rate (at least 30 responses for each list tested)
2. An average gift size of $20 or more
3. A direct cost of $1.25 to $1.50 per dollar raised

As it gains more experience with testing lists and measuring their success, an organization may adopt more sophisticated methods of evaluation:

- Number of replies received
- Percent of respondents who send money (minimum of 30 responses for any test list)
- Number and percent of mail pieces returned as undeliverable (accuracy of the list)
- Average gift size
- Gross revenue received
- Total direct costs for the mailing
- Net revenue received
- Cost per dollar raised (for each mailing)

Applying these eight quantitative measures to each list's performance will show whether the list is valid for the message sent. These same eight factors can be used to compare the performance of one list against another.

Which list had the highest number of respondents? the highest gross revenue? the lowest cost per dollar raised? Other information that may be beneficial to subsequent fundraising programs can be culled from the lists: demographic data on age of respondents, home value, length of ownership, income level, and similar facts. ZIP codes are a key to geographic areas or zones (ZIP + four digits) with higher response rates. Like a giant puzzle, all these pieces of information fit together to deliver a clear picture that points the way for future testing and better results. The marketing, planning, and public relations staff in the organization also can use all these data for enhancement of public image and awareness, choice of product line, strategic marketing, market penetration, and related activities. These staff members' interpretation of the tests can add unique insight that will help in the preparation of the package, message, contents, and lists for the next mailing.

Use of the three basic measurements mentioned earlier will indicate whether there is sufficient evidence to justify continued testing, whether a full *roll out* (mailing) to the entire list is validated, or what segments of the list have met or exceeded the desired minimums. Direct mail fundraising is a way to find the donors needed for an organization; it reveals more than just how much money might be received or how soon it can be delivered. Direct mail can find those people who will respond again to future requests and those who will contribute their time and talent as part of their response. These select people will help to fund the future needs of the organization and will become its faithful volunteers and leaders. Remember: Friend-raising precedes fundraising, and building lasting relationships is one of the primary goals of every annual giving program.

Because cost usually is *the* controlling factor, successful direct mail packages are simple and direct in design and message, and are mailed with the lowest postage allowed (third-class, presort, bulk rate). Responsiveness is being tested first: What elements will stimulate both the numbers of respondents and their average gift size? Cost–benefit analysis (1) correctly places limits on all the variables that do not affect responsiveness and (2) provides the data that help guide decisions on which lists (or pieces of lists) to use again, what message works best, and what giving levels to suggest. U.S. Postal Service regulations control a few parts of every direct mail package—size, weight, and cost. Money and creativity should be invested in lists, packages, and messages that can be proven to yield the best results.

The primary indicators of how direct mail will continue to succeed in acquiring new friends, new donors, and new dollars are results based on tested responses.

The first test mailing initiates the solicitation program. Replies with money will arrive quickly, so systems for gift processing, donor records, and acknowledgment should all be in place. Each test response form should be coded so that accurate results can be tabulated. Test mailings produce the organization's first group of new friends and new donors. They become the control group and the model; their performance sets the standard all the other mailings will have to meet or exceed.

Testing should be conducted often, at least once every other year. Future testing will reveal how a little variety in the package or message can help improve the results. Lautman and Goldstein[9] advise:

Following are elements that usually can remain the same:

- Length of letter;
- Size and format;
- Colors;
- Postage;
- Premiums or other special offer;
- Size of gift requested;
- Mail date;
- Lists.

Future testing must be focused on one or more of those key elements; they can make a real difference in replies when everything else remains the same.

The decision to "roll out" a major mailing to a full list selected from results analysis can now begin with high confidence. The final variables are beyond the organization's control: rapid political and economic change, natural disasters, fiscal realities, and national crises can work for or against any mailing. Knowledge of the fixed details (lists, message, envelope, contents, postage) that have been proven to work in multiple tests is the best prevention available against unpredictable variables.

There are two remaining variables: (1) timing, which is a matter of judgment that can be enhanced by being observant and by having good counsel, and (2) letter texts, which require a writing skill that hits the bull's eye of people's awareness of and sensitivity to the cause and stimulates them to action.

LETTER TEXTS: WRITE LOVE LETTERS!

Much has been written and said about how to write successful annual appeal direct mail letters. Their mission is simple: to inspire people to action. Who writes these letters? What is the key to their success? Francis Prey provided one great answer: Write love letters! He was suggesting that the direct mail letter writers think about the last love letters they wrote: their preparation time, their careful choice of words, all the emotions the letters contained, even the letters' length (more than one page, no doubt). Much was at stake with each love letter. What were the essential ingredients that inspired a reply of equal enthusiasm? Or, where or why did the message fail? The answer to either of these questions will ensure success with direct mail letters! When given equal time and attention, writing letters for friend-raising purposes is not all that different from writing love letters.

Most appeal letters written for nonprofit organizations are drafted by professional staff in the fund development office. They have written them before; their letters have received lots of replies with money enclosed. Other organizations invite professional letter writers and direct mail consultants to help them. Two of the better books of instruction on how to write direct mail letters are Jerry Huntsinger's *Fund Raising Letters*, a series of study guides,[10] and *Dear Friend*, written by Kay Lautman and Hank Goldstein.[11] As an example of the wisdom shared in these texts, here are Huntsinger's four basic marketing principles for fundraising letters:[12]

Principle 1	The techniques you employ to create your letter and package must be determined by the nature of the audience receiving the package.
Principle 2	Any direct mail package that is not personalized is compromised.
Principle 3	The only certain method of discovering exactly what works best for your audience is to engage in extensive and ongoing testing.
Principle 4	You must learn the basic principles, but you must break the principles to be successful.

The primary purposes of a direct mail appeal letter, especially the first one sent to carefully selected suspects and prospects, are to be read and to be acted on. How can a few simple words perform such magic when the mission or cause of a nonprofit organization cannot be contained in one letter? The intent when writing direct mail appeal letters is *not* to tell the whole story all at once. Instead, another part of the story is told in each letter. The writer adds interesting facts, expands on what people have heard about or read before, tells about the people served, introduces the people who provided this service, educates readers about the cause and its direct relationship to their lives, and even tries to influence the readers' thinking. Can anyone hope to do all this in *just one letter*? No; but the organization intends to write more than once. How many times can it write? As often as it gets enough replies! How long should a letter be—one page, two pages, four, six? Will anyone read a six-page letter today? Lautman and Goldstein have declared:[13] "Of course you would—*if* the information was presented in a lively, interesting manner that aroused your curiosity, convinced you the author knew his or her subject, and taught you something. And that is exactly what a good appeal letter should do—arouse curiosity, stimulate interest, instill conviction, and one more thing: inspire action: *a contribution to your cause!*" All this from a first letter, whether it is on one page or six. Lautman and Goldstein recommend attention to four key ingredients in any direct mail letter text: style, format, credibility, and appearance.[14] They also have compiled this list of 13 basic rules for effective direct mail copy:[15]

1. Don't typeset the letter. Reproduce it from perfectly typewritten copy. (When was the last time you sent a typeset personal letter?)

2. Don't have the copy photographically reduced to cram a long letter into a short format. Remember, most of your donors are likely to be over 40 and may have difficulty reading small type. (We do!)

3. Don't omit the "Dear Friend" salutation, and do try to include a dateline if possible. They are part of the real letter look.

4. Long paragraphs are admittedly hard to read, but don't overreact with a letter composed of a series of short paragraphs identical in length. They are equally difficult to read.

5. Don't overdo the underlining. Call attention to pertinent phrases or paragraphs through indented copy blocks, check marks, bullets, giant quotation marks, color, and photographs. The longer the letter, the more important this is.

6. Pretend you are writing to one person. Indeed, you are.

7. Rework the opening and closing paragraphs until they "sing."

8. Don't wait until the last page to mention money. It's okay to ask on page one.

9. Don't try to be funny. Your cause is serious and so is charitable giving. We've tried humor. It doesn't work.

10. Don't bore the reader with the merits of your organization. Rather, write about the people it serves. Give the people names— real people and real names, if possible.

11. Write with emotion and back it up with facts, not vice versa. People don't give because your organization needs the money. They give because they are touched or angry or saddened and want to do something to help!

12. Use your P.S. wisely because it will be read. Too many postscripts just take up space.

13. Don't use big words or jargon.

My best recommendation about writing letter texts is to get professional help from the fund development staff and from an outside adviser or counsel. This book focuses on annual giving as a program that will work effectively year after year to build relationships with new and old donors and volunteers. In the pyramid of giving shown in Exhibit 1-2, direct mail is one of the elements in the base that supports the entire fund development process. The burden laid on direct mail letters is a large responsibility indeed! The letters are crucial to the many successes that will need to follow; an exceptional beginning is not always a guarantee of continuing effectiveness. Solicitation begins with careful list selection and testing. The final ingredient for success is letters that inspire people to reply. When the addressees have been carefully selected and the lists, message, and package have been tested, everything else rides on the letter text.

Letters arrive in an outer jacket that sometimes has extra enclosures (a response form, a reply envelope, maybe an eye-catching throw-in). What is most important about the letter itself? Personalization! Readers can do some firsthand research here; among the solicitation letters recently received:

Were the letters personally addressed (did your name appear) on the outer envelope *and* at the start of the letter?

Did the letters begin "Dear Friend" even though your name was on the outer envelope?

Have you ever begun a love letter (or any letter to someone you knew well and/or wanted to know better) with "Dear Friend"?

If you received a love letter that began with "Dear Friend," would you characterize it as open, direct, and seeking closer ties, or as a bit stiff, less appealing, or perhaps defining new parameters for the relationship?

Personalization costs extra but it provides the best results.

The advent of computers has enabled the segregation of mailing lists by census data, demographics, ZIP codes, and other factors. Computers and their faithful servants, laser printers, now produce personal letters that appear to have been individually typed to the person whose full name, full address, and salutation (by name) appear in their proper places at the top of the page. With refinements, added bits of personal information—a reference to the city of residence (contained in the address above), or the exact amount of the donor's last gift (from the donors' gift record file)—can be inserted at other places in the text. Computerized, personalized direct mail is the minimum standard today. The Arthritis Foundation has mastered the use of personalization in mass mailings at the lowest possible cost. The Foundation's tidy envelope with windows reveals the complete mailing address. When the packet is opened, the name and address appear at the beginning of a personal message. And, representing the ultimate in one page letters, the entire message is presented in full on one side of a 3″ × 5″ piece of paper! The reverse side describes the Foundation's use of funds raised and offers several available giving levels, which prospects are invited to consider. Should every nonprofit organization be using this same package design? No; every organization is not as well known as the Arthritis Foundation and will not send out more than 100 million pieces of mail a year. Economies of scale are working in the Foundation's favor because of instant name recognition and a modest gift request (a minimum donation of $5).

Literally hundreds of details are associated with direct mail appeal letters. The Direct Marketing Association's annual conferences are attended by hundreds of professional direct mail experts who discuss and debate the merits of every facet of "direct response advertising." There are differences in response rates, gift sizes, and costs required, depending on the choice of such details. All these elements are important for each user to consider because mailings are often in the thousands or even millions of pieces. When reviewing options and possibilities regarding the design of a direct mail package and the all-important letters, some basics should be kept in mind. Huntsinger[16] recommends including these six "vital elements" to create the "look" of a real letter:

1. Date line
2. Name and address
3. Dear somebody
4. Body copy
5. Signature
6. Postscript

To have a letter "look right" and serve its primary purpose of stimulating action, Huntsinger provides seven layout suggestions:[17]

1. Make everything easy to read, use short paragraphs, indent the first line of every paragraph.
2. Use underlining to capture the eye.
3. Avoid all caps. CAPITAL LETTERS ARE DIFFICULT TO READ, AND GIVE THE FEELING THAT YOU ARE SHOUTING. But when you underline your words, the effect is stronger.
4. Keep your lines short, don't discourage the eye with long lines and skimpy white space. Wide margins increase readership.
5. Use dashes instead of commas—at times—to break up the routine look.
6. Be sure and put one eye grabber on each page.
7. Use large typefaces. Only 1% of the population has perfect eyesight.

A nonprofit organization can rely on direct mail appeal letters to stimulate large numbers of new friends who will join in the cause. The appeal letters will cultivate, educate, and inspire these newfound friends and donors to continue their faithful support year after year. The letters serve as invitations to encourage participation in other ways, such as to volunteer or to attend events and activities and bring their friends with them. All this is a heavy burden for any letter to bear, whether one page or six pages long. These fragile messengers will often need some help. They can be part of a larger message linked to other annual giving activities. In the continuing example in this book, the activities of the Clean Up Cleveland Chapter are linked to the vision and mission of the fictional national organization called The Campaign to Clean Up American (CCUA).[18] The CCUA's cause is larger than just one person or one organization. The workings of the Cleveland chapter of this national campaign are a microcosm of the events, decisions, documents, personnel, and problems that form both the challenges and the routines when relationships are built through annual giving campaigns. At the end of each chapter, the topics covered will be illustrated in a focus on the CCUA Clean Up Cleveland Chapter.

FOCUS: CCUA CLEAN UP CLEVELAND CHAPTER

The Campaign to Clean Up America (CCUA) is a newly formed, national nonprofit organization dedicated to improving the environment and public health through wide public participation in helping to clean up America's cities and using all this trash to generate electricity for public use. The national board of directors, headed by Michael M. Activist, a prominent conservationist, is headquartered in New York City. Members of the board of directors were selected by Activist from among his personal friends in the environmental and conservation movement. I. Harvey Clout, Chairman of the Cleveland Cast Iron Works, has been invited to head the CCUA Clean Up Cleveland Chapter.

Clout has recruited a few other volunteers from the greater Cleveland area to serve on the board of directors of the Clean Up Cleveland Chapter. The new organization is housed at Clout's accounting firm, which is headed by Sidney M. Secure, CPA. Clout and the board have begun to recruit a director of development. Clout and Secure will pay salaries and operating costs out of their own pockets until local funds become available.

At the May meeting of the national board of The Campaign to Clean Up America, held in New York, each chapter chairperson was given a notebook with detailed instructions on initiating a combined marketing, public relations, and fundraising program in each of several major American cities. The notebook calls for a test mailing to at least six separate lists in the area. The objective of this first mailing is to begin a combined public awareness and fundraising campaign. A sample first-appeal letter was provided in the notebook, along with other details. Clout returned to Cleveland and recruited two volunteers, Mary M. Moneybanks and Theodosius Worthy, to join the local chapter's board. The board members, plus Titus Brown, president of The Brown Agency, an advertising and public relations counsel to Harvey Clout and the Cleveland Cast Iron Works, have begun to develop six mailing lists to be used for the first test mailing. Each list is to have at least 2,500 separate names following merge-purge or duplicate-elimination processing. The notebook provided a sample letter for test mailing purposes (Letter B). Titus Brown and Harvey Clout believe they should also test a letter written earlier by Clout (Letter A), to see which one receives better response. Both test packages are to be mailed on July 10. The six test lists defined for the Cleveland area will be evenly split for Letter A and Letter B:

List	Definition
1	5,000 Cleveland Heights residents
2	5,000 East Cleveland residents (Chagrin Falls, Gates Mills, Mentor, and Solon)
3	NE Ohio members, National Audubon Society
4	NE Ohio members, Nature Conservancy
5	Subscribers (Browns/Cavaliers/Indians)
6	Subscribers (Cleveland Orchestra/Cleveland Play House)

The texts of Letter A and Letter B are presented in Exhibits 2-4 and 2-5. The test results are in Exhibit 2-6.

Analysis of the results suggests the following findings and directions:

1. Through the letters, 348 new donors were acquired!

2. Funds raised did not cover the cost of mailing, but that result was expected in the test program.

3. The cost of testing is high, but will be reduced by one-half when the full mailing is prepared (unit costs for envelopes, bumper stickers, letter preparation, and data processing will be cut).

4. Average gift size, at $24.50, is inadequate to build upon for larger gifts, as is the cost per dollar raised at $1.74.

5. Clout's Letter A did not appeal very well to any audience except Cleveland Heights residents and Audubon Society members

(more than .01 percent response). The most cost-efficient gifts came from Audubon Society members (at $0.84 to raise $1.00).

6. Letter B clearly outperformed Letter A, suggesting this style of message will get the best results.

7. Poor response to Letter B by affluent communities and sports subscribers suggests testing them again later; all other lists look quite promising and should perform well in a mailing to the full list, scheduled to be received by October 30.

EXHIBIT 2-4 FIRST-TIME ACQUISITION DIRECT MAIL: LETTER A

Letter A

THE CAMPAIGN TO CLEAN UP AMERICA
CLEAN UP CLEVELAND CHAPTER

July 10, 200X

Dear Fed Up with Trash:

I don't know about you, but I'm fed up with all the trash on our city's streets.

Cleveland boasts of its "emerald necklace," its theaters and museums, but we are the butt-end of jokes as the city whose river caught on fire and whose lake died.

Well, we cleaned up the Cuyahoga River and restored Lake Erie, didn't we? Now it's time to clean up our streets. How about it; do you want to help me do it? Great. Here's how we can get it done together.

The Campaign to Clean Up America is at work in every big city right now. But there's more to it than picking up trash. Our goal is to recycle our trash into new, clean energy we can all use. You might say we've found the way to cut our electric bills, right under our feet.

We estimate about 100,000 tons of trash is lying in our streets right now that can be converted into 32,000 megawatts of electricity to meet the needs of 18,000 homes for a year, plus reduce *everyone's* electric bills by *$12 a month* and *$144 a year*.

Here's what you and I can do to help make this happen.

First, stop being a "trasher." Pick up after yourself.

Second, bag all the trash you find around your house, garage, and yard, and put it out with your garbage next week.

(continued)

EXHIBIT 2-4 (CONTINUED)

Third, join with me in our Clean Up Cleveland Chapter. Your gift of $12 is what you will save on electric bills each month from our new energy plant.

Fourth, spread the word. Talk about what we are doing; tell your neighbors and the people you work with. Ask them to get involved and join in cleaning up Cleveland. Put your bumper sticker on your car or truck (it's magnetic). Let everyone see that you support a cleaner Cleveland.

As the saying goes, "Every litter bit helps." Your bit of cleaning up and giving will help out a lot. The money we raise is divided equally between our public awareness and education efforts, and construction of our new energy plant.

The energy conversion plant has been approved by the City Council. Land for the plant has been given to the city by Centurion Energy Corp., who will operate this new plant the same as the one already in operation near Perry, Ohio. Estimated cost is $3.5 million, two-thirds of which will be provided by federal and state matching funds. All we need to do is raise $1,250,000 from the people who live and work in Cleveland.

It's all up to us now. Let me see those bumper stickers and let me hear from you real soon.

Many thanks, friend.

Sincerely,

I. Harvey Clout
Chair of the Board
Cleveland Cast Iron Works

P.S. Last week, my son and I picked up three bags full of paper, cans, and bottles around our plant during lunch time in less than 30 minutes. On Friday, 35 managers will go all over this plant to pick up all the trash they can find in 30 minutes. Their goal is to match our three bags full. We have begun!

EXHIBIT 2-5   FIRST-TIME ACQUISITION DIRECT MAIL: LETTER B

Letter B

THE CAMPAIGN TO CLEAN UP AMERICA
CLEAN UP CLEVELAND CHAPTER

July 10, 200X

Dear Friend for a Trash-Free Cleveland:

Every day when I drive to and from work I see a lot of paper and other trash on our streets, along with cans and bottles, boxes and plastic bags.

We all know the city has cut back on trash collecting and street sweeping because of a tight budget, but it is not keeping up with the trash, not at all. And, our city is not the only city that has this problem.

When I was invited to New York last month to hear about The Campaign to Clean Up America, I wanted to go for two reasons. First, this is a serious plan to do something about all the trash that is polluting our country. Second, they've got a great idea. Build a new energy conversion plant that uses trash to make electricity and cuts our energy bills at the same time!

We estimate there are 100,000 tons of trash lying in our streets and around our buildings right now. With energy conversion in a new plant, this trash can become 32,000 megawatts of electricity to meet the needs of 18,000 homes for one year. And, this plant will *reduce* everyone's electric bills by *$12 a month* and *$144 a year.* This great idea got my attention and I volunteered to chair this program for Cleveland. We all will benefit from this effort. We need your help to do it. Each one of us can participate quite easily. Here's what we would like you to do.

First, stop being a "trasher." Pick up after yourself.

Second, bag all the trash you find around your house, garage, and yard, and put it out with your garbage next week.

Third, join with me in our Clean Up Cleveland Chapter of The Campaign to Clean Up America. Your gift of $12 stays in Cleveland. It also is what you can expect to save on electric bills each month from our new power plant.

Fourth, spread the word. Talk about what we are doing; tell your neighbors and the people you work with. Ask them to get involved and join in cleaning up Cleveland.

(continued)

EXHIBIT 2-5   (CONTINUED)

Put your bumper sticker on your car or truck (it's magnetic). Let everyone see that you support a cleaner Cleveland.

You know the saying, "Every litter bit helps." Each of us can help to make our city a lot cleaner. Your contribution of $12 will help, too.

Contributions will be divided between our public awareness and education programs and the cost of construction of our new energy plant.

As you may know, the new energy conversion plant has been approved by the City Council and the land for the plant has been given to the city by Centurion Energy Corp., who will manage this new plant the same as their plant now in operation near Perry, Ohio. Estimated total cost is $3.5 million. Two-thirds of this cost will be met by federal and state matching funds. What we need to do is raise $1,250,000 in private contributions from the people who live and work in Cleveland.

I hope you can join with me and others who are working for a cleaner Cleveland. Let me hear from you soon.

Sincerely yours,

I. Harvey Clout
Chair of the Board
Cleveland Cast Iron Works

P.S. Last week, my son and I picked up three bags full of paper, cans, and bottles around our plant during lunch time in less than 30 minutes. On Friday, 35 managers will go all over this plant to pick up all the trash they can find in 30 minutes. Their goal is to match our three bags full. We have begun!

EXHIBIT 2-6	TEST RESULTS: ACQUISITION LETTER A AND ACQUISITION LETTER B

| | Number | Replies | | Gift | Average | Cost per Dollar |
List No.	Mailed	Number	Percent	Income	Gift	Raised
Letter A						
1	2,500	26	0.0104%	$ 512	$20.00	$1.98
2	2,500	18	0.0074	216	12.00	4.69
3	2,500	48	0.0192	1,200	25.00	0.84
4	2,500	24	0.0096	600	25.00	1.68
5	2,500	18	0.0072	360	20.00	2.81
6	2,500	22	0.0088	480	22.00	2.11
Total/Avg.	15,000	156	0.0104%	$3,368	$22.00	$1.82
Letter B						
1	2,500	38	0.0152%	$ 895	$24.00	$1.13
2	2,500	12	0.0046	124	12.00	8.17
3	2,500	52	0.0208	1,800	28.00	0.56
4	2,500	44	0.0176	900	20.00	1.13
5	2,500	18	0.0072	480	27.00	2.11
6	2,500	28	0.0112	960	29.00	1.06
Total/Avg.	15,000	192	0.0128%	$5,159	$27.00	$1.19
Grand Total/Avg.	30,000	348	0.1160%	$8,527	$24.50	$1.74

Expenses: Costs for each mailing are identical

Unit (Individual Letter)	Cost per Unit
List (@ $35/1,000 names)	$0.035
Outer envelope	0.080
Reply envelope	0.050
Bumper sticker	0.080
Letter/reply form	0.060
Data processing	0.080
Mail preparation	0.020
Postage	0.090
Total	$0.495
	× 2,500 units per list
	$1,237.50 per list

Total cost ($0.495 × 30,000 mailed) = $14,850

CHAPTER 3

Direct Mail Acquisition: Constituency Building

Before beginning an annual giving program, it's worthwhile to take a moment to think about why asking for annual gifts is so important. What can the asking do? What ought it to do? How can it help a nonprofit organization? The one-word answer is: Money. Asking can raise money quickly. The main reason for conducting annual giving programs is to build a constituency of faithful friends and generous supporters. Annual giving has the following characteristics, which yield a multitude of added benefits:

1. It raises money, usually for operating purposes.
2. It lasts 12 months each year and is designed to be repeated every year after that, with increased results each time.
3. Multiple solicitations can occur within each 12-month period.
4. It communicates with more people than any other means available to a nonprofit organization.
5. It is a reliable source of annual revenue to meet current priorities of need.
6. New donors are found and recruited each year.
7. There is heavy reliance on prior donors to repeat their gifts.
8. There are opportunities for volunteer recruitment, training, and participation, and for leadership development.

9. It complements the marketing and community relations programs because of its high visibility.

10. It is a well-planned, highly coordinated, and well-executed activity.

These characteristics must be used to full advantage, channeled and coordinated for positive effect. From 40 years' experience, I am convinced that *planning* is the most important ingredient for success in any annual giving program.

Planning a successful annual solicitation campaign requires close coordination among management staff, volunteers, and leaders, sometimes facilitated by professional fundraising staff, consultants, and vendors. Together, they define why public support is needed (the case), how the funds will be used (the priority), how much is required (the goal), when the money is needed (the deadline), and how much it will cost to succeed (the budget). These decisions are based on an assessment of the organization's public image (through market research), the prior performance of volunteers (their training), solicitation methods and fundraising staff (the results), and an analysis of productivity (a.k.a. efficiency). In short, a plan for success is based on measurable performance, not on speculation or wishful thinking.

Acquisition is also the base, the necessary foundation for the entire fundraising program of every nonprofit organization. To be successful with the full range of annual giving program options demands serious time and attention to finding and keeping scores of donors. Much more is possible when new donors are being recruited in a steady stream. This type of effort is a commitment to build the future constituency of the organization. In time, maximizing the performance of each annual giving program helps the organization meet its priorities of need. Coordination of these programs year after year requires attention to every detail of annual giving activity prior to, during, and after each solicitation effort. To many individuals, especially fundraising office staff and management staff, the routine of annual giving can be boring; the activities have to be repeated year after year. By developing annual giving to its maximum potential and by preserving enthusiasm for it, a nonprofit organization will be guaranteed that it can recruit all the new friends and funds it needs, market its programs and services, and raise money to fulfill its mission within the targeted 12-month cycle. Reliable financial support is a wonderful asset for any nonprofit organization; annual giving programs that deliver plenty of dollars with reliability are gold mines and should be treasured.

As proof of the value of annual giving, this entire book has been created as a comprehensive guide to that one facet of fundraising/friend-raising/constituency building. Once in place and blended with ongoing marketing and communications activities and with donor relations techniques, annual giving will yield a multitude of benefits. Edith Falk[1] has summarized them as follows:

Establishing an annual program is the first step for any organization dependent on outside support for its operating budget. In addition to generating critical, immediate dollars, the complete annual giving program:

Develops public awareness and understanding of the organization. A successful annual campaign demands effective communication with donors and potential donors. Organizations whose annual giving program includes—at the very least—an end-of-the-year mailing are generally better known in their communities than those that do little or no fundraising.

Stimulates unrestricted support. Unrestricted gifts are essential to an organization because they can be applied where they are needed the most. Many annual programs include opportunities for both restricted and unrestricted giving.

Identifies new prospects for giving and upgrades current donors. Securing broad-based philanthropic support is one of the primary goals of annual giving programs. A growing core of loyal donors—rather than a series of one-time givers—is essential to maintain a stable, creative organization.

Cultivates essential volunteer and donor involvement. Annual giving programs are ideal for the identification and training of new volunteer leaders. They provide an important opportunity for donors to become active in special events and other fundraising and public relations activities.

Identifies future capital and planned gift prospects. Annual giving is the bottom rung of the donor acquisition ladder. A strong annual support program can provide leverage in persuading prospective donors to make major gifts and grants, help attract gifts of property or deferred gifts, and build a strong base for a successful capital campaign.

There are numerous opportunities for variety and creativity in the design of annual giving programs. Most of the successful solicitation methods—those used by thousands of organizations and proven after repeated applications in every city and town in America and most parts of the world—are presented in this book. This text will help anyone to design and get started with a program for success. Improvements can always be made to what each organization is doing now. One benefit that comes from inviting new people to join in the annual fundraising activities is that their new ideas are encouraged and can be tested against what is being done now. Perhaps they can add some sparkle (or just sparks) to a tired program and reignite the enthusiasm of volunteers and donors.

Society changes rapidly. So do individuals and their perceptions about urgent community (and personal) needs. Nonprofit organizations must be flexible and able to respond to the changing needs of their communities. Newcomers bring energy and creativity; they breed excitement and increase the potential to maintain continuous improvements in annual giving activities. New fundraising ideas, however, must be evaluated on their own merits first, and then compared with the known performance of existing programs to assess their short-term and future potential. Can they help to find new donors? Can they inspire prior donors to give again? Can they improve the organization's image? Do they complement the overall fundraising program's design? Before committing volunteers, staff, and resources to any new idea, testing is required to find out what the idea will bring to the total solicitation program. A note of caution: Just because a nifty fundraising idea worked for someone else yesterday does not mean it will work for any other organization, today or any day.

MEETING CHANGING NEEDS

Nonprofit organizations must analyze their solicitations each year in order to resolve how ideas for change or improvement can affect their ability to achieve multiple benefits. These annual evaluations guide the selection of the activities that will stimulate the greatest public response and produce the most cash. As with any investment, organizations must commit sufficient time and financial backing to each annual solicitation method that they believe can help to meet their needs. Each fundraising method must be given the opportunity to grow to its own level of maturity, and to demonstrate the numbers of donors it can acquire and retain and the amounts of reliable annual support these donors can give in the future. It takes usually a minimum of three years for annual giving programs to begin to pay off with a dual return (numbers of participants and amounts of gifts) on the initial investment.

Adherence to those activities that work well becomes a reliable plan, especially if it proves it can enhance the relationship of new donors to the organization. The objective is not just to convince donors to give one time; the idea is to enlist their *commitment* to the mission, purposes, goals, and objectives of the nonprofit organization such that their annual gift becomes reliable. These reliable and faithful friends are destined to become the foundation on which secure financial development for the future will be built. Their first-time gift is the beginning of a relationship that can last a lifetime. The grand design is for an overall fundraising program, one that becomes a constant and reliable source of new volunteers and leaders and, in time, major gift donors, as well as annual contributions. Each individual donor must be encouraged to develop a strong commitment to assist in meeting the current and future needs of the organization. Through a variety of programs, multiple benefits beyond cash can be gained from the broadest amount of participation by the widest segment of local residents. It must be understood from the beginning that another objective of a complete fundraising program of annual giving is to find the people who may become potential clients for programs and services at some future time.

Most annual giving programs succeed because of attention to two separate sets of criteria: (1) overall design ingredients and (2) individual performance yardsticks. Both are used for each fundraising method. Design and results work in combination; they complement one another. Performance measurement of each annual giving method is essential, to assess not only the method's results but also its effect on each of the other programs being offered within the same year.

In evaluating results, comparative analysis between nonprofit organizations—even those using the same fundraising methods—is never quite fair. No two nonprofit organizations are identical in how they provide programs and services, any more than in how they solicit their community residents for money. No two organizations solicit at the same time, in the same way, or to the same donors and prospects. They do not have the same volunteers and leaders or possess the same history. Consequently, their results will always differ.

What is similar and worth studying is how each solicitation method performs when measured against its own results from prior years. This type of comparative analysis leads to an accurate understanding and appreciation of how existing solicitation activities are working, what improvements can be made based on results, and what reliable expectations might be made for higher levels of productivity and profitability. The nine-point performance index in Exhibit 3-1 can be used to evaluate the unique performance of each fundraising method based on its results; using the same index also provides a uniform grid for comparative analysis between methods.

The audiences available to nonprofit organizations for participation in their choice of several annual solicitation techniques throughout any one year are often the same people; consideration must be given to the number of requests made of them, the constant message each receives, the timing of all the requests, and their ability to continue to respond as often as possible.

Among the great variety of solicitation options used in annual giving programs, seven critical elements are required for individual and collective success:[2]

EXHIBIT 3-1   THE NINE-POINT PERFORMANCE INDEX

Basic Data

1. Participants   = Number of donors responding with gifts
2. Income   = Gross contributions
3. Expense   = Fundraising costs

Performance Measurements

4. Percent participation   = Divide participants by total solicitations made
5. Average gift size   = Divide income received by participants
6. Net income   = Subtract expenses from income received
7. Average cost per gift   = Divide expenses by participants
8. Cost of fundraising   = Divide expenses by income received; multiply by 100 for percentage
9. Return   = Divide net income by expenses; multiply by 100 for percentage

---

Source: James M. Greenfield, *Fund-Raising Cost Effectiveness: A Self-Assessment Workbook.* (New York: Wiley, 1996), 31. Used with permission.

1. A well-defined purpose
2. Extensive planning
3. An efficient organization
4. A realistic timetable
5. Meaningful fare
6. Realistic assignments
7. Logical order

Each of these elements should be incorporated into the design of the total annual giving plan prior to beginning each year's program. Their performance should be measured after the campaign, to understand their effect on the overall effort as well as their individual results.

A unique value of each annual giving method is its brevity. Only its ability to produce immediate results (cash) is more valuable. Nearly every annual fundraising activity can be carried out quickly, start to finish. Mailings take a few weeks to prepare, but most replies arrive within two to four weeks of mailing. Benefit events, usually held only once a year, are planned and promoted over three to six months and are over in one evening or one weekend. Membership drives are promoted for a month or two, held within a 30- to 60-day period, and concluded by a well-published deadline. Evaluations can be held immediately after all the results are in, and corrections can be implemented in time to help improve the next mailing or event or drive. The cycle continues endlessly, as does the expectation to do better each time.

THE CASE FOR ANNUAL GIFT SUPPORT: GOALS AND POTENTIAL

The *case* for annual gift support is a written statement that lists the reasons why certain identified funds and projects are needed by the nonprofit organization. The case is a story that explains how the funds raised will be used to achieve beneficial purposes—usually, the conducting of charitable and public benefit programs and services to fulfill the nonprofit organization's mission. The case also must demonstrate measurable outcomes that will be delivered as community benefits. The *case statement* is a summary of essential details arranged to encourage understanding of a need and to spark a positive response. The case statement may be one paragraph or an entire letter, or it may be printed in a brochure or proposal.

Most case statements for annual giving are based on the nonprofit organization's carefully developed, long-range strategic plan. It explains this year's design, reports progress made in the past year, and enlists support to continue making progress. By telling this story in yearly chapters, annual case statements form a record of the organization's progress and describe the most urgent current priorities that must be met in order to continue to move forward. The intended result is to be able to inform the public, several times throughout each year, how the organization is progressing, where it is going, how public support has helped, and how it will be needed again if the organization is to continue to benefit the community it serves.

A case statement will translate the specific areas of need identified each year into uncomplicated stories that can be appreciated as opportunities for public participation. The case simultaneously describes and advocates programs and services that are of value. The story may offer specific details about equipment, construction and personnel costs, operating expenses, and similar items, to explain how these areas of expense will improve the organization's ability to provide existing programs that serve people or causes. Exhibit 3-2 lists the 10 basic elements of a case statement. The causes that need attention are stressed, as are areas that are publicly recognized as unmet needs crying out for action.

The role of the case is to communicate how the funds needed will be spent, what results will be achieved, and how the community will benefit. Projected results have public appeal; performance that fulfills the projections seals the relationship. Achieving promised positive results merits the time and attention of all those invited to join as volunteers and as donors.

After issuance of the case statement, with its definition of public benefits, the financial details are revealed. How much will this program or service cost to provide? Was there a process of investigation to search out various solutions? Is the solution picked as most likely to succeed also the one that is most cost effective? In short, can the financial details withstand public scrutiny? Are they reasonable figures? Operating budgets have dual roles as internal guides for management of every area of activity and as "shopping lists" where the public can see the valid use of donated funds. A high degree of trust is implied in every gift; the organization must spend donors' money carefully and wisely.

EXHIBIT 3-2   ESSENTIAL FEATURES OF A CASE STATEMENT

1. The case must reflect the mission of the nonprofit organization.
2. The case must demonstrate fulfillment of a charitable purpose.
3. The case must reflect the validity, relevance, and public benefits to be gained from the programs and services being offered.
4. The case must enunciate the goals, objectives, and long-range plans of the organization.
5. The case must be measured against the competence of the organization to provide these services.
6. The case must demonstrate the organization's competent leadership and sound financial management.
7. The case should advance arguments in favor of monetary support for its cause with truthfulness and confidence.
8. The case should demonstrate how the gift support received will be used and to whom these benefits that make a difference will be provided.
9. The case should explain the community benefits to be gained by successful completion of this work or a solution to this problem.
10. The case should explain the benefits gained by all who join in to provide support to this effort—volunteers and donors alike.

Once the case statement and financial projections are complete, those responsible for fundraising must match the stated goals and objectives, including the amount of funds needed, against the ability and potential of annual solicitation methods to raise the funds needed to operate such well-defined programs and services. An accurate matchup requires an understanding of how each annual giving solicitation method described in this book actually raises money. There is an equal need to appreciate the importance of designing and directing each solicitation method to achieve its maximum capability for raising some or all of the money needed. There are limits, even in the best circumstances, to how much performance each fundraising method can achieve within one year. Accurate estimates are complicated because performance is so often dependent on such factors as leadership, the number of volunteers involved, the availability of support materials, competent staff support, and similar factors. Many of the methods of annual solicitation can be used only once a year; others offer multiple opportunities within each annual cycle. For example, direct mail letters can be used several times within 12 months, but a major golf tournament or a black-tie ball may be held only once or twice a year. All three methods will require most of the year to plan, prepare, and execute. Each technique's potential for results is composed of a mixture of elements that can point to future success. Results are a function of four key features:

1. Access to qualified prospects
2. The relevance and urgency of the need or cause
3. The ability of volunteers and their leaders to perform well
4. Adequate staff and budget

When a fundraising activity is already in place and ready to be used again, its potential can be measured for the ability to maintain and increase its own prior-year performance. An activity's potential depends on an ability to fit volunteers, donors, and prospects into the area or project that needs funds *this year*. Priority projects will change from year to year, and, despite a past level of popularity, each must be sold all over again, with conviction, to all the volunteers, donors, and prospects. Each method of solicitation must measure its ability to attract and retain volunteers, donors, and prospects when their willingness to participate must be redirected to the changing, and not always popular, needs of the organization. Because every fundraising method has a finite potential in numbers of donors and amount of dollars, realistic goals should be estimated for each solicitation activity and predictions should reflect actual results realized when everyone works together each year. After three or more years of operation, predictions become easier and more reliable. Solid estimates of performance become increasingly valuable to managers as the nonprofit organization attempts to plan the programs and services supported by the cash received in the annual giving campaign. With each method, efforts to improve performance and achieve full capacity in subsequent years will continue.

Each of the several fundraising methods used for annual giving solicitation has different performance levels for effectiveness and efficiency, and each is exposed to a multitude of uncertain facts that affect performance:

1. The nonprofit organization's image and reputation
2. The public's understanding and acceptance of the urgency of the need (the appeal of the case)
3. Perceived public benefits to be achieved

4. Local economic and demographic conditions

5. Public acceptance of the method of solicitation used

6. Time of year when the solicitation occurs

Analysis of these factors helps to estimate how each solicitation method will compete for public attention. Add to this analysis the length of time each solicitation method has been in use, the competence of its volunteers and leaders, continued access to new prospects and donors, and confidence in the fundraising program plan, and the forecast of performance begins to take on confidence and insight. All of these realities will affect results fairly quickly; an economic downturn or a local fundraising scandal can defeat, overnight, the best case story ever written. These elements do not have an identical effect when different nonprofit organizations use them in their annual giving programs. Using the same fundraising methods year after year does not guarantee the same performance, either. Fundraising, like every other human endeavor, does not perform at the same level every time it is in operation. Year after year, each organization must define its own annual giving program plan, evaluate the individual results of each fundraising method it uses, and measure the levels of performance achieved. This process will demonstrate which methods work best and why they will continue to perform well. Those methods to which the public responds best should be selected for continued use, provided they are capable of producing the same level or a continued growth of donors and dollars each year *and* are cost effective in their operation. Growth is an implied objective in all annual giving.

GOAL SETTING FOR ANNUAL GIVING SOLICITATION

Goal setting for each fundraising activity is a challenging exercise; setting goals for a group of solicitation activities to be conducted within the same year is considerably more complex. (See Exhibit 3-3.) Goals are, at best, informed estimates of program behavior based on prior results and proposed improvements. Goals cannot be based only on how much money the nonprofit organization wants or needs. The need for money might be valid, but the ability of any one solicitation method—or any combination of methods—to meet an income goal might be unrealistic this year. Other

EXHIBIT 3-3   THE GOAL-SETTING PROCESS FOR ANNUAL GIVING

1. *The Project*
   - Select a project or program that will have immediate public recognition as being valuable or an unmet need.
   - Identify the number of community residents who can and will benefit from this project or program.
   - Summarize the credentials the organization has for providing this service with quality as well as competence, based on past experience.
   - Evaluate how gifts will expand the numbers served, the quality of service, and the expected benefits to the community.

2. *The Audience*
   - Evaluate how many local people are qualified to receive this service and how they will have access to it.
   - Identify potential numbers of available prospects and donors who would be interested in supporting this effort, including whether they might also need or use this program or service at some time.
   - Evaluate the financial value this program may have to the community; calculate the per-person cost of providing it.

3. *Gift Size*
   - Define gift options linked to the per-person cost (above) to deliver this service.
   - Ask for a number of gifts that is linked to the projected number of people who will receive service from each dollar received.

4. *Goal Setting*
   - Estimate the total dollars required this year to fully fund this program; express the costs in amounts or units of service to be provided.
   - Estimate each annual giving program's potential to produce funds to support this program; set goals.
   - Secure all approvals for the fundraising plans and budget required, based on the estimated net proceeds to be raised.
   - Establish a master solicitation schedule for meeting the goals on schedule.

---

fundraising options and other revenue sources will be necessary. When the money needed is raised by using annual giving solicitations year after year, that success illustrates how each method chosen has been highly coordinated with all of the organization's other annual fundraising activities. Each method can be prepared, according to its own multiyear program plan, for budget support, revenue estimates, and assessments of various benefits from broad public participation. By bringing all these critical factors to light,

goal-setting exercises assist with realistic preparations and selection of reasonable goals. As with any investment program, some level of continuing
commitment is necessary to achieve the full flowering of potential. A single fundraising program or its once a year use as a solicitation activity is
only its beginning; it is not the culmination of that program's capacity nor
the apex of its achievement. Because each method of fundraising does not
perform the same as others, each will return a different yield from its investment from year to year. It is recommended that individual goals be set
for each activity as a sound management practice.

Annual giving achieves the highest levels of success when managed as a
combination of programs that strongly support one another. Careful planning involves thoughtful use of a variety of annual solicitation methods,
awareness of their timing, and knowledge of their relationship to audiences
recently solicited. Factors to be considered include external conditions
(such as the local economy), competition from other nonprofit organizations, leadership and volunteer commitment, and even a bit of luck.
A constant evaluation of the performance of each method in use is necessary for informed decisions on what to offer next, when, and to whom.
Great flexibility is needed to design a plan that can continue to be productive throughout the year and will enhance the potential for repeated use
next year.

As an example, five mail donors gave $500 each in response to a letter
appeal program last year. In the next campaign, these five donors will be
solicited by the volunteer-led personal solicitation committee (whose goal
also will increase by their potential to deliver another $2,500). This strat-
egy ensures that a volunteer will talk with each of these five donors about
continuing their gifts at $500 or perhaps giving more. It works; three give
$500 again and two increase their gift to $1,000. Personal solicitation has
been effective in renewing all five gifts; the organization has received
$3,500, which is $1,000 above the $2,500 given in annual support last year.
However, the direct mail renewal program, which brought in these five
gifts last year, has now been challenged to find new donors or to upgrade
others within the donor pool in order to replace the gift amount of $2,500.
To meet this goal, the direct mail program personnel will have to work
harder, expand the lists and the number of solicitations, and spend more
budget. A likely result may be 25 new donors at $100 each, or 250 new
donors at $10 each, or some combination. If the organization is to receive

added funds each year from each technique of annual solicitation, each program must complement the others and receive adequate support for its own separate objectives.

THESE ARE DONORS, NOT NUMBERS

Annual giving goals must be based on expectations of how each method of solicitation will be used and its relationship to the other methods being used. If the overall annual goal is $250,000, the solicitation plan might well include four mailings, three benefit events, two telephone calling nights, two personal solicitation campaigns, one membership drive, and both renewal and new grant applications to qualified corporations and foundations. To illustrate the flexibility needed, let us assume the largest annual donation is from a local businessman who gave $25,000 in each of the past three years, but who has just been promoted and has moved to another state. The organization is likely to lose this gift; and chances of replacing the businessman with another single donor are slim. However, active solicitation of five other businessmen who are major gift prospects has begun; each has a $25,000 gift potential. Unfortunately, none of the five can give the full amount of $25,000 this year. The back-up plan is to ask all five to consider a gift of $5,000 each. Their prior best gifts were between $1,000 and $2,500 each. Business is poor, and they cannot increase their current level at all this year. It is not reasonable to expect each donor to increase his giving by a factor of five, just because the campaign needs to replace one donor at $25,000.

What other facts are in this year's case statement that, along with its package of priority needs, provide quality motives for giving? For solution of its $25,000 shortfall, the organization is likely to have to turn to other fundraising activities. How flexible are the other annual giving programs? Can they increase their performance by $25,000? The solution will depend on existing donors; no new donor is likely to make such a large first-time gift. One or more of the other fundraising programs might agree to ask 25 of its donors for an extra $1,000 each, or 100 donors for an extra $500 each, or 250 donors for an extra $100 each to achieve this goal. What effect will this extra pressure for performance have on these donors? Will they reduce other gifts to the organization, normally given at other times in the year? How will they respond to next year's appeals? Some caution must be exercised in the "solution" being considered, beginning with a respect for donor preferences of amounts, timing, and purposes of their current gifts. The bottom line reads: Anticipate that every donor (major or not) will stop giving some day. Time and attention must be given *now* to the identification, cultivation, and preparation of replacement donors and prospects who will pick up where others have left off. There is more to annual giving then just asking last year's donors for money again.

Fundraising does not perform "by the numbers," despite good intentions and hard work by volunteers and staff. Without an urgent, compelling reason, people cannot be pushed or pressured into higher levels; they will not give more frequently just because the extra money is needed. They can be asked and asked well, but these extra solicitations may appear greedy and could sour their continued relationship. The decision of how often to ask requires sensitive and considerate evaluation. The value of multiple annual solicitation programs is threefold:

1. Some methods may be able to exceed their goals, making up part or all of the difference when others fall short.

2. Other methods may appeal to the same group of donors; they will not object to being asked to participate in different ways more than once a year.

3. Introduce new solicitation techniques or combine existing and new methods focused on renewing current donors to increase net income.

A well-balanced array of activities is desirable for other reasons, besides greater reliability in meeting dollar goals. Prior donors may not have the ability to increase their gift each year, even when well asked; in fact, solid work may be required just to renew their gifts at the same level year after year. But they may be able to be more generous in future years; their retention is essential.

The potential to increase the amount of money raised from the same constituency is dependent on two factors: (1) the number of loyal and committed donors who are matched with energetic and well-trained volunteers, and (2) a continuous effort to recruit new donors. Whatever each donor will give at any one time in response to any one request will be valuable. If the amount falls short of a desired goal, donors must still be told that their efforts did make a difference and are deeply appreciated. With this approach, they will be more inclined to give again next year. Managing donors' enthusiasm and confidence year after year is as valuable a goal as realizing the targeted dollar amount.

Analyses of prior-year results and of current external conditions are essential to realistic goal setting. What activities and individuals worked well or did not work well? What amount of true costs was required and how were the results produced? (Results can and should be measured on several levels when setting new goals. It is essential to understand, to the degree possible, *exactly* how these results occurred.) How many donors responded? What percentage of those who were solicited replied? What was their average gift size? What was the number of volunteer solicitors who helped, and what was their performance level? There is a lot of good data to study. The budget required to support solicitation activities can be measured against results as a way of understanding efficiency and gathering information for next year's budget requirements. Exhibit 3-4 provides several internal and external evaluation areas or options in an acquisition mailing that can be helpful when results must be measured or when an income amount, if these activities are repeated in the next solicitation sequence, must be predicted.

Realistic goal setting can be performed for each of the annual giving activities in use. Measurement of prior performance should begin with a review of the organization's priority of needs and the public's acceptance of the priority list. Next, the organization should review the timing of solicitations, the training and performance of volunteers, the budget available to support each effort, the competence of staff members who supervise these activities, and much more. Among the external conditions to be considered are: fundraising competition, economic and political conditions, demographic and diverse cultural influences, and media and other communications influences. Society changes rapidly today, and it is immensely complex. Consultants and vendors will enhance a general understanding of external factors. Unforeseen events can also have an immediate effect on the best of plans. Examples are: natural disasters and their immediate fundraising responses, which can claim priority over other needs; major elections, which spawn extensive political fundraising activities; an unexpected change in the organization's leadership; a fundraising scandal widely covered by the media; or the inroads of a nearby, competing organization whose multimillion-dollar capital campaign has been in full swing for several months.

EXHIBIT 3-4   ASSESSMENT CRITERIA FOR
ACQUISITIONS MAILINGS

1. Accuracy and Usefulness of the List
   - Complete mailing addresses
   - Correct name spelling and ZIP code
   - No duplications or "salting" of names
   - Number of incorrect address pieces returned
   - Number of address service requests returned

2. U.S. Postal Service
   - Technical advice on successful preparation
   - Handling time at drop site location
   - Average delivery time (14 days or less for third class, bulk rate letters)
   - "Address Service Requested" service

3. Printing Services
   - Comparative bids for services
   - Art work and package design
   - Established and met deadlines
   - Quality of finished product

4. Test Mailing Procedures
   - Random selection of names to test
   - Quality control on test package
   - Tabulation and analysis of test results

5. Mail House Services
   - List processing and consolidation
   - Duplicate-elimination procedures
   - Package assembly and accuracy in preparation
   - Advance deposit to postal account
   - Correct preparations for U.S. Postal Service acceptance
   - Address correction procedures

6. Mail Solicitation Response (by List)
   - Percentage rate of return
   - Average gift size
   - Average cost per gift
   - Individual list cost-effectiveness
   - Overall cost-effectiveness
   - Overall performance analysis (each mailing)

Sometimes, unforeseen events can provide an opportunity to bring an organization's needs to the attention of the public. Awareness of external events and conditions is important; anything that receives high visibility within the area of service may either help or hurt an organization's solicitation activities. Positive effects might be: easier recruiting of leaders and volunteers, greater public confidence in the organization because of its thoughtful response, and more motivation for people to participate in service efforts that have proven to be successful.

Achieving annual goals can be a success story that gives pride and confidence to volunteers and adds credibility to the entire goal-setting process for next year. Failure to meet goals, on the other hand, can be quite damaging to the entire annual giving program even after those involved are provided with full details to help them understand the failure. If, for example, volunteers were excluded from the goal-setting discussions, they can lose confidence in those who set them along with a sense of their ability to meet these demands in the future. Perhaps goals should be called *targets*, with the inner circle to be aimed at and the bull's eye to be hit whenever possible. Failure will not motivate people to donate their time and their money again.

THE ANNUAL FUND—MASTER SCHEDULE

Each nonprofit organization has exactly the same 12 months in which to schedule its annual solicitation activities. The first step is to review the calendar and keep each fundraising activity unopposed and unduplicated in the time slot that is assigned. A savvy approach to scheduling will permit the best efforts of volunteers and donors to have a clear run to their goal. A master schedule may be possible but it must take into account the plans of all concerned and the value of each fundraising method in case overlap occurs. With such a schedule in place, annual giving solicitations can be taking place all year long. Competing organizations will be actively soliciting at the same time, no matter when a program is in progress, and community and seasonal events may erode interest for brief periods. Being aware of competitors' activities and their structure is helpful but each organization must follow its own best course of action.

Among the positive features of a master schedule are: (1) reinforcement of public attention to and support of the needs of the organization and those whom it serves, (2) the ability to compete effectively with other organizations, and (3) consistency in all of its messages during the year. By setting a schedule (being mindful of other organizations, where direct conflict may be unwise), a claim to certain times of the year is established, and the others must decide how to compete with the strength of the announced activity. The quality of an organization's performance is its strongest asset. It will gain respect from others while it reinforces the confidence of volunteers and donors. Everyone believes too much mail arrives and too many telephone calls are received, all asking for money. Fundraising has become pervasive. To avoid an immediate negative response to an appeal directed toward select donors and prospects, an organization must plan each of its appeals and all of its other communications on a master schedule that best meets its needs, has the competition in mind, and allows each of its activities the best hope of success.

Several factors should be considered when making a master schedule for annual giving solicitations:

1. When was the solicitation conducted last year and the year before?
2. Was the calendar year-end used (for tax motives)?
3. Was there any conflict with known dates of others?
4. Did people reply at the same time as in prior years?
5. How did people reply? Did they give more or less?
6. Did volunteers follow the schedules in fulfilling their asking assignments?
7. Did the organization send out its own communications pieces, and how did these requests affect this effort?
8. Which programs met their goals and why?
9. Which programs fell short of their goals and why?
10. What back-up plans had to be used and why?
11. Did the back-up plans help to meet the goal?
12. How will all these factors affect next year's goals?

There are many pieces to the scheduling puzzle. Two of the most important factors involve determining, from everything available, (1) what is the best time for the organization to ask for money and (2) what amount of time (and budget) will be needed to plan, organize, and conduct each solicitation activity at the performance level that is necessary to achieve the annual giving goal. Both factors lead back to the need for planning.

MAKING AND FOLLOWING PLANS: THE FREQUENCY OF APPEALS

There are traditional calendar periods when most nonprofit organizations actively solicit annual gifts. The months of October through December are considered to be the best because of the favorable combination of traditional holiday spirit and the end of the tax year (an unbeatable combination). The second best period extends from March through June; for many organizations, the fiscal year ends on June 30. That leaves the third best period as January to March (publishers often renew subscriptions at this time). The least productive period is the summer months, when vacations consume most discretionary income. Even with good coordination among ongoing solicitation activities, there will be months, usually October through December, when more than one solicitation activity will be in progress at the same time.

Some programs, such as direct mail and personal solicitation, can complement one another because they can work in sequence (a letter is followed by a phone call or appointment) and they use common lists of donors and prospects. Other solicitations may be in direct conflict: one letter may be asking for an annual gift, another for a special campaign gift, and a third for attendance at an event. What is needed is a plan that prevents confusion and reduces the appearance of uncoordinated and excessive overlapping solicitation. It is acceptable to deliver, with a solicitation, an invitation to a popular benefit event that is six to eight weeks away. Donors usually have to make choices when more than one appeal arrives from the same organization (hopefully not on the same day!), but loyal donors may spread their giving decisions among several options. Those who have to make a choice most of the time will still be choosing one of the organization's activities. They are unlikely to respond with separate gifts to each appeal and may ignore the third one entirely, but the message that important needs exist and that their help is vital has been delivered.

The point of sensitivity must be stressed here. Appeals can be too aggressive, no matter how noble the cause or how desperate the need. Stirring the ire of the public is never wise. At times, management and volunteers stress the need for action over the need for sensitivity. It's a tough call; jobs may be on the line. Writing to current donors about an emergency that has developed (which may include failure to meet a goal) will be more acceptable than writing to nondonors who know little about the organization and its goals. What schedule of contacts and what messages have already been sent to both groups? What is the potential for their conclusion that the appeals are ill-timed and inconsistent, appear to use pressure, and may even border on harassment? It is impossible to predict how each person will respond to repeated solicitation, except to know that more people will become upset as appeals become more aggressive and repetitive. Nonprofit organizations do not have the right to bombard the public with relentless appeals. Free speech rights stop where harassment begins. First and foremost, this is a friend-raising business; second, it is a fundraising business. Each appeal must be financially successful in order for an organization to raise the money it needs; it cannot act with financial irresponsibility and expect to receive public support.

After a few years of supporting an organization, its constituency will become more comfortable with multiple solicitations *if they make sense* and do not border on abusive practices. The donors will have learned that several annual giving solicitation programs coincide and that they will be regularly invited to participate in more than one. When they receive a letter appeal for an annual gift, a second letter about a special campaign, and an invitation to a benefit, they may become more willing to at least consider a response to each request, depending on the extent of their interest in (and enthusiasm for) the organization and its needs. Consistency in the annual case statements can help here. Recipients will be less upset when multiple requests arrive if they have been informed, via the case statements, of the full spectrum of targeted needs. An organization must remain sensitive to the frequency with which appeals are sent to its existing donors, and the master schedule acts as a control sheet for communications to every audience.

At times, other organizations may have to revise their schedules to avoid the risk of directly competing with an organization that has well-established patterns of solicitation. A highly respected annual benefit event sponsored by a leading community organization in a charitable fundraising field is likely to be supported and attended by representatives of other organizations in the same field. For example, during National Heart Month (February), donors to the American Heart Association and hospitals with specialized cardiac facilities can be expected to interchange their responses and their appearances at annual giving activities and benefit events. The focus moves from individual organizations' goals to the overriding goal of emphasizing the successes of cardiac research and treatment and the need to contribute toward their continuation and growth.

The time needed to organize annual solicitation programs varies. The cheerful estimate, "As long as is needed for good results," denies the need for an organization to plan thoroughly, measure the results, and then improve the plan if necessary. Estimates of the time to be invested in each fundraising program may be general, but they must be made. Usually, planning and organizing an annual volunteer-led, volunteer-staffed, personal solicitation program scheduled for, say, the month of October, will require intense effort in the entire 11 months between appeals. An annual benefit can take three to six months to prepare but the effort disbands for six to nine months after the event is held. Direct mail programs, often a fundraising staff activity that requires only limited volunteer participation, can be prepared and executed in 60 days.[2] No single calendar period is magically successful; careful planning and realistic measuring of results will indicate whether the date or time period was well chosen or should be rescheduled in the following year.

PLAN TO BE FLEXIBLE

Murphy's law—"If something can go wrong, it will"—can affect the best of plans and schedules. Flexibility is a virtue in any plan, but Murphy's law seems to apply less often when solid planning is implemented and flexibility is reserved for "just in case" situations. Well-made plans are good protection against the unexpected; for some activities, they may even be able to push performance beyond the goals because they allow volunteers, donors, and prospects to concentrate on the urgency of the nonprofit organization's need for funds. Solicitation activities are sensitive to timing, and schedules must be carefully planned to facilitate success and to avoid inordinate pressure on volunteers and donors. Good planning can prevent annual giving programs from turning into last-minute panics in which everyone abandons carefully designed plans, just to achieve a dollar goal. When returns are lower than anticipated, some people may question their own ability to meet defined goals. Others will question the merits of the plan. It is important for board members, managers, volunteers, and staff to appreciate that the willingness of the public to respond with personal gifts cannot be controlled with an on–off switch. Giving is voluntary. Reliable public support is built slowly and carefully. It is based on confidence and trust in the organization and the proven solicitation methods used, and it works best when following highly coordinated annual solicitation plans.

Emergencies do occur. When they are not caused by lapses in steward-ship and are well communicated, they do not lessen the public's confidence and trust in the organization's judgment. Conditions can change. When the changes are understood, they can become enlightening footnotes to the story already being told in the case statements. If public confidence and trust are lost, however, even the best of plans or the strongest case state-ment cannot help. Broad consensus on annual giving methods and ad-herence to fundraising plans are the best protection against unwise, just-get-the-money pressure. Every "quick buck," "quick fix," or "easy money" idea I ever heard about had the same major flaw: It showed that the organization was not well managed, did not plan well, was unable to anticipate common emergencies, and was willing to sacrifice sound busi-ness practices for the sake of money. Quick fixes can do irreparable harm to public confidence and can lead to less than professional conduct or even to unethical practices that promise easy money. Great damage is done to all charitable organizations when a scandal in one of them becomes a major news story. The entire telemarketing industry has become suspect because of a few widely publicized abusive practices. This same suspicion has also been implanted in the public's mind about potential fraudulent uses of the Internet for charitable giving purposes. When a highly visible negative event occurs, wise nonprofit organizations will review their own activities for any improprieties and then reassure their public, perhaps in a special let-ter or advertisement, of the soundness of their administrative practices and the checkpoints established to foil any misuse of their own solicitation methods or of the funds received. Constant accountability, including open and full disclosure before and after any questionable incidents, is the best policy. Without it, the years and dollars invested in building positive rela-tionships with volunteers, donors, and prospects are placed at risk or wiped out. These consequences are a hundred times worse than a failure to meet an arbitrary dollar goal.

The final component for success with goals and objectives is measurement of performance or results. Goals should be announced early and made clear to volunteers, donors, and prospects. What were the results from last year's campaign? How was the money used? Did the expected public benefit occur? How many people were served or helped? What difference did it make in their lives? First proposed in the case statement, these are the details that need to be verified before any further solicitation is conducted. What were the fundraising results? Was the scheduling workable for each solicitation activity? What were the results of each method of fundraising? How were budgeted dollars spent? How did actual performance compare to the anticipated goals? Is a report on these results available to everyone involved—staff, volunteers, and donors? These answers should be on hand for communication to the public.

Communications about success are important motivators for volunteers and donors. Volunteers who responded to expectations should be asked to help again, in the context of a compliment and a thank-you. Donors should receive a "big picture" report that highlights contributions within the perspective of the organization's overall goals. Everyone should be informed how the performance of each of the solicitation activities is monitored against the organization's own evaluation guidelines and standards. The public benefits achieved through gift support of the organization's programs and services should be stressed. Future direct mail letters can brag about the effectiveness of the group effort that made good things possible. Several of the criteria listed in Exhibit 3-4 can be adapted for use in public reports. If people are told what is being done with their money and how valuable their gifts are, they will be more comfortable with the messages in the case statement and with the multiple annual solicitation activities that follow throughout the year.

WHERE PLEDGES FIT IN ANNUAL GIVING

Many nonprofit organizations encourage pledging as an active feature of their annual giving programs. Pledges encourage lasting relationships with the organizations because pledges are, in effect, long-term commitments that involve frequent contacts (installment payments are spread throughout the year). For some organizations, pledging has become the traditional form of annual giving; for others, it may not work at all. Pledges are especially well-liked by donors, but they place increased burdens on nonprofit organizations. The positive features of using pledges are (1) early commitment and (2) convenience for donors. The negative features are: (1) delayed revenue, (2) recordkeeping costs, (3) defaults by pledgers, and (4) extra administrative costs. Nonprofit organizations should investigate their potential for both the positive and negative features before deciding whether to offer pledges as an option in direct mail and other annual giving programs. Once begun, a pledge program is difficult to terminate.

Pledging can be used positively in several situations. One type of pledge—a payroll deduction to aid United Way campaigns—has become successful nationwide because of its simplicity for employee use and its reliability in collections. Each type of pledge has its merits; each enhances and improves annual giving results. Do the funds actually get collected? Loyalty ranges from low to high, depending on how well the nature of the pledge is matched to the annual giving method (see Exhibit 3-5). Collections rates improve for donors who choose to pay by credit card or who authorize electronic funds transfer (EFT) from their bank checking account or designate payment from their donor advised fund at a community foundation. The value of a pledge can be evaluated for each fundraising method. The pledge option should be explained in the first direct mail acquisition letter of the campaign. Reminders should be inserted in future mailings to encourage use of this option but also to reinforce the obligation of faithful payments.

One Gift a Year

When donors make annual pledges, they are invited to select, early in the year, the total amount of their contribution. Quarterly or monthly installment payments are common, but, as a convenience, they may be allowed to arrange another payment schedule better suited to their resources. This type of pledge should be reserved for an important level of gift support ($500, $1,000, or more). The positive features are early commitment, and recognition as a major participant. On the negative side, a Yes response to a pledge is easy because the payments are put off until later. There is some potential for nonpayment and delinquencies. Recordkeeping, mail-back payment forms for periodic billing, and reminder letters to delinquent donors will be required. In addition, when donors make a once-a-year gift

EXHIBIT 3-5   SCORECARD FOR TYPES OF
ANNUAL GIFT PLEDGES

Pledge Selected	Collectibility Score
One gift a year (Direct mail annual pledge with full payment due by 12/31—or end of fiscal year)	Low/medium/high
Membership dues (Scheduled amount due by deadline to retain membership privileges)	Low/medium/high
Tithing (Fixed total amount with regular payment amounts)	Low/medium/high
Payroll deduction (Employee-authorized direct payments out of regular paycheck)	Low/medium/high
Matching gifts (Employer agrees to match employee gift amount)	Low/medium/high
Upgrade option (Donor to increase pledged amount to qualify for higher recognition and extra benefits/privileges)	Low/medium/high
Introductory offer (Donor commits to a get-acquainted discounted entry into a gift category, with full payment due by a future date)	Low/medium/high
Pledge by phone (Donor replies with verbal intent to make a gift)	Low/medium/high
Pledge by fax (Donor replies on mailed form with gift intentions)	Low/medium/high
Pledge by e-mail (Donor replies on Web page form with gift intentions)	Low/medium/high
Multiyear payment plan (Donor signs pledge form and is allowed more than one year to complete full payment)	Low/medium/high

decision, there is less chance they will agree to any additional gifts during the same year.

Membership Dues

The key feature in any membership program is a fixed dues amount assessed on all members. Payment entitles the member to all of the organization's rights and privileges for a defined period. The payment schedule may have an extended deadline (calendar or fiscal year-end) and may allow quarterly or monthly payments. Use of a firm deadline establishes an anniversary date for annual membership (which simplifies renewal requests) and limits operating costs to the period of the membership drive rather than having them spread throughout an entire year. Retention of status as a member in good standing, entitled to certain benefits and privileges, hinges on payment of dues by the renewal date (or within a reasonable grace period). Chapter 5 will describe membership programs and all their uses and benefits.

Tithing

Possibly the oldest and best known type of pledge used for annual giving purposes, tithing combines the once-a-year gift decision with membership status and gives the donor satisfaction at having fulfilled an important obligation. Tithing has been used most often by religious organizations as testimony of their followers' commitment to a level of annual financial support (sometimes expressed as a percentage of personal income). Tithing's biggest advantage is its reliability of full payments received on schedule. Among its hazards are (1) the tithe stays a fixed amount year in, year out, and (2) the organization may assume faithful payment and spend accordingly, only to find that some tithers have abandoned their financial commitment partway through the year.

Payroll Deductions

In this widespread practice, donors ask their employers to provide a service by taking a portion of their salaries and sending it to a nonprofit organization as payment for a personal gift pledge. The employee stipulates a fixed amount (or percentage) to be taken out, the schedule for withdrawals/payments, and the total amount to be paid during the year. Payroll deduction is an employer's decision and it implies approval of solicitation activity in the workplace, usually performed by employees, not outsiders. The employer also may add a matching gifts program as an incentive for employee participation, a dual benefit to the recipient nonprofit organization.

Matching Gifts

Payroll deduction can also be used by employees who want to make gifts to several nonprofit organizations where their company will match all or a part of their donation. A corporate matching gift program may be available as a separate plan or as a payroll deduction privilege, to encourage employees to be active in their community and to demonstrate civic participation. The amount matched will vary in each company and will usually have a cap on percentage of contribution or dollar amount. Most companies issue a list of generic or specific nonprofit organizations qualified to receive matching funds. The nonprofit organizations selected then receive two annual gifts as long as the employee stays a loyal donor.

Upgrade Option

A scale of increasing annual gift amounts, each offering expanded benefits and privileges, may encourage donors to be progressively more generous. Each larger gift decision achieves greater rewards. Upgrade options can be used in almost every annual giving program described in this chapter; they are most effective when promoted in the solicitation renewal cycle. Evidence of successful use of this technique is twofold: some 10 to 12 percent of current donors will increase their gift amount while the majority of the others will renew at their prior rate.

Introductory Offer

A pledge option is often successful in encouraging a prospect or donor to make a first gift. The offer may allow a discount price (for the initial year only) for access to the benefits and privileges usually reserved for donors who pledge a higher amount. The key is to ask for partial payment up front, with the balance to be paid by a future deadline. This plan requires accurate recordkeeping and other administrative support because overhead costs are incurred. There is some potential for resentment among donors who gave the full amount in their first year of membership but, in the spirit of the organization's purposes, it may be evident only in heavier assignments being given to the newcomers. A membership program can often make the best use of an introductory offer; it may not be as useful to the other annual giving applications. The introductory offer should not be renewable for any donors.

Pledge by Phone

Telephone solicitation relies on a verbal pledge to secure a gift decision. Telemarketing is pervasive in our society and is used in every type of commercial sales and nonprofit solicitation. The public is becoming increasingly irritated with, and even distrustful of, telephone requests. Despite the advantage of a two-way dialogue, use of the telephone for fundraising must be studied carefully (see Chapter 6). Preparations must include solid training and rehearsing for callers, and rapid follow-up to confirm the pledge and ask for payment. Payments spread over several months are not recommended for telephone pledges because of the collections problem. The nonpayment rate is higher for the pledge by phone approach than for other pledge methods.

Pledge by Fax and E-mail

An alternative method for donors to make their annual pledge and have a written record of their intent is to provide a pledge form with a fax number included or have posted one on your Web page with your e-mail address. Pledge forms are easily transmitted using facsimile or e-mail and serve the same purpose as the mail version; in fact, they should look alike. Allow for space for donors to add their credit card number, expiration date, and signature—just in case they wish to make their gift using the pledge form. Donors appreciate all these choices; giving them options makes it just a bit easier for them to get the job done, and there's little or no cost for the transmission.

When the pledge is received, the organization has a choice of how to respond—by mail, telephone, facsimile or e-mail. They should reply as quickly as possible to verify receipt of the donor's intention and to confirm any details when the donor has restricted their gift in any way. Pledge payment experience using the fax and e-mail options should be similar if not slightly better than traditional direct mail pledge collections.

Multiyear Payment Plan

An occasion may arise where a multiyear pledge may be appropriate, but it is not a typical plan. It could be an incentive to achieve a higher level of membership dues or tithing, or as an upgrade option where a two- or three-year payment period would be allowed to achieve the higher donor levels. Multiyear payments are typically reserved for capital campaign gifts from individuals, corporations, and foundations.

Pledges Cost Money

Nonprofit organizations should recognize that their decision to use any type of pledging in support of their annual giving program will be accompanied by extra internal expenses for recordkeeping, billing, collections, and related support activities. The costs to mount a broad-based annual giving program, especially for a new nonprofit organization or one that is introducing new fundraising methods, are already high because of up-front acquisition costs. The addition of internal costs to support pledges counteracts the efficiency and cost-effectiveness of overall annual giving performance. For example, a membership program should be added to overall annual solicitation activities only when it will increase the potential for retaining annual donors already secured by their second or third gift by mail or other means. Members will expect fulfillment of member services, modest membership perks, a members' directory, and possibly an annual meeting for election of officers. They are usually unaware and unconcerned that these operating expenses must be paid out of membership dues revenue. Allowing a pledge payment option for membership dues will spread revenue receipts over several months and further increase recordkeeping and mailing costs. Overall net proceeds to the nonprofit organization may be diminished dramatically.

Pledges can conflict with good fundraising practice. Pressure to meet a goal, a volunteer quota, or a "fair-share" average gift may be offensive. When a solicitation program concentrates too much on reporting how much money was raised, or when volunteers become too enthusiastic about making their assigned goal of gifts achieved, there is a potential for negative effect. Donors may feel an obligation to respond positively to a friend and say yes to a pledge, but remain uncommitted to make payment. Some donors have decided that one way to handle a persistent caller (short of hanging up) is to agree to a pledge they never intend to fulfill. Such practices lead to misleading reports, inaccurate expectancies, displeased donors, and disillusioned volunteers. There is also potential for deceptive practices; an aggressive volunteer or employee may secure a pledge by offering benefits that cannot be fulfilled. As additions to routine annual giving programs, pledges can be a mixed blessing.

Fundraising Costs

Expenses occur throughout the acquisition cycle. The costs to acquire first-time donors are the highest of all fundraising expenses. Reasonable cost estimates to acquire a first-time donor by mail alone can range from $1.25 to $1.50 for each dollar raised; there should be at least a 1 percent response rate and average gift size of $25.00 among those invited to give. Renewal is more cost effective and should perform at 50 percent or better retention rates with increased gift levels at $0.20 to $0.25 per $1.00 raised. These levels of performance are an acceptable standard and can be used as a guideline for acquisition and retention forms of direct mail efforts. As is illustrated in the book's ongoing example of the CCUA Clean Up Cleveland Chapter, all the costs are tracked carefully and measured against the results. It is important to include *everything* involved in finding, motivating, and servicing a donor's first gift. These data are invaluable in making decisions that will continue to build a constituency of faithful, committed donors who can be depended on for generous annual gifts and to be able to do so with demonstrated levels of cost effectiveness and efficiency. Analysis of performance will identify, for the nonprofit organization's management and fundraising team, the acquisition mailing lists and messages that have produced the best results.

ACQUISITION THROUGH MAIL APPEALS

Annual giving means finding new donors each and every year while soliciting all the previous donors again. New nonprofit organizations have no prior donors; they must begin their solicitation activities by communicating their valid needs to lists of previously unaware and uninvolved prospects and suspects. The most effective way to acquire a large number of first-time donors is to reach out broadly, soliciting their interest and support by mail. Any nonprofit organization can begin its fundraising program by mailing a few thousand solicitation letters. However, to have a successful mailing the first time, the fifth time, or the fiftieth time requires strict attention to proven concepts and to details. Using the mail *successfully* is not easy, despite the quantities of appeals that arrive through the mail. The sheer volume of requests is amazing. The reason? Mail solicitation works!

A new organization must start with mailing lists—names and addresses of prospects and suspects. Lists can be compiled from among board members and volunteers; they can also be bought, leased, or rented. Whatever their source, all the entries must be collected together, studied carefully, and made available in some common and usable form. Along with the case statement and the mail package, lists should always be tested (see Chapter 2). The story in the case statement must be converted into letter form. Envelopes, response forms, and any added materials must be designed and their costs estimated; receipt and reply procedures, including thank-you letters, must be firmly in place. Financial controls for handling each gift and depositing the money, recordkeeping of all donors' data and individual gifts, and reports that summarize the results are essential business requirements. Estimated costs for all the printing, computer time, postage, and handling costs of outgoing, incoming, and acknowledgment mail must be reliably tallied. Only after total costs are understood can the final decisions be made about how many letters must be mailed to achieve a level of anticipated results to meet financial goals.

Tom Broce,[3] in his excellent summary of annual giving preparations, lists these as the essential preparation details: A well-defined purpose, extensive planning, an efficient organization, a realistic timetable, meaningful benchmarks, realistic assignments, and logical order. Broce continues:

> Several other factors are considered "givens" in fundraising programs. Remember that the annual program requires
>
> (1) a well-researched prospect pool;
> (2) well-kept records and well-planned solicitors' materials, including brochures and pledge cards;
> (3) an adequate professional and clerical staff to help the volunteers;
> (4) an adequate support budget;
> (5) institutional leadership, including that of the chief executive officer; and
> (6) appropriate gift-acknowledgment and report systems.
>
> The lack of any of these elements may be reason to delay or reevaluate the organization's ability or preparedness to conduct a fundraising program.

These details all must be resolved before committing the funds necessary to prepare the letters to be taken to the post office. Roger Craven[4] explains why:

> Direct mail has been deprecated as a fundraising tool because the gifts it produces are relatively small, costs are relatively high, and, as a rule, the technical and professional skills required to manage a professional mail program are not available on many fundraising staffs. However, the organization that asserts itself in learning the real purpose and proper use of

the medium will reap significant rewards, discover new special-gift and major-gift prospects, educate its constituency, and reach its peripheral constituencies, thus making them more active contributors.

Advice abounds on how to succeed with mail solicitation, whether for commercial or charitable purposes. Expert professional help is necessary to achieve success. "Direct response advertising" is a well-established form of mass communication that is widely used because it gets results—it works! Will it work for everyone? Probably, if used properly. Fundraising by mail alone, however, is not likely to meet all the needs of a nonprofit organization. In the base of the giving pyramid (Exhibit 1-2) mail solicitation has a most important place, but it is not alone. Modern, computerized direct mail solicitation is a complex activity. It can work equally well for smaller and for larger nonprofit organizations. Professional counsel is available to help maximize the potential uses of direct mail, but, by following some basic rules and recognizing that investments of both time and money are required, most organizations can make their programs profitable. Ed Mayer,[5] an early direct mail artist, craftsman, and teacher, created the following seven cardinal rules for success when using the mail:

1. Start with the objective of your program.
2. Reach the right person on the right list.
3. Present the case in terms of benefits to the reader.
4. Use appropriate copy and layout.
5. Make it easy for the prospect to take action.
6. Tell your story over and over again.
7. Research your direct mail efforts.

Direct mail is a primary medium for mass communication; it happens to work well for fundraising. "The direct mail program must clearly and effectively communicate the institution's needs to potential donors."[6] Those who read the letters (1) will be introduced to the cause and the needs it describes, (2) will learn something about community problems and proposed solutions, and (3) will find out about nonprofit organizations that are committed to providing needed services. These are critical objectives, and none of them mentions money.

Where do the financial results fit in, alongside these answers?

	True	**False**
As many as 90 percent of all appeal letters are discarded unopened.	✓	___
Only 10 percent of those who open appeal letters will reply with money.	✓	___

Why bother with direct mail if it is so obviously uneconomical, such a waste of time and money? The answer lies in understanding the multiple values that communication by mail can and does have for nonprofit organizations:

- Exchanging information
- Continuing education
- Building an image
- Forming respect and trust
- Encouraging involvement and commitment
- Making new friends
- Raising dollars for charitable purposes

Cost-effectiveness is another measure of positive performance, but an organization needs some history before it can determine whether its patience and attention to detail have yielded efficiency. Renewal is where profit lies. Most nonprofit organizations are here to stay; through the mail, they can tell their story to a wide audience and then invite any persons who are interested to be part of the solution to problems.

WHY USE THE MAIL?

The chief purpose of any appeal letter—the first, the fifth, or the fiftieth—is to stimulate a reply. Letters are used best as personal, people-to-people communications. When trying to recruit people to action, the steps are: (1) get their attention, (2) explain a need that exists and the organization's competence to provide answers, and (3) invite them to be a part of the solution. The actual letter text is crucial to success, but it must first be delivered to individuals who will open and read it. Selective mailing lists represent the means to find those individuals who will be interested in reading the letter and are likely to reply. By finding and writing to people who have a potential interest, the organization will be using an effective and efficient method for locating those who will respond to the call for action. Those who do not reply are not necessarily wasted potential resources; they may reply to a second appeal. Repeated mailings are valid so long as enough replies with donations enclosed are received. Periodic mailings may convince potential donors that the organization is dynamic, that its need is real and urgent, and that resolution is attainable. They can still help if they choose, and the amount requested is not unreasonable. When acquiring new donors, the organization is making new friends; effort, persistence, and understanding are all needed. Professional mail consultants recommend sending repeated invitations to qualified donors who have not yet responded. People have to be encouraged to take action just as they have to be persuaded that their action will make a difference.

A nonprofit organization can never assume that because it needs money, interested people will respond with a donation. Fundraising is not that simple. Realistic answers to these four essential questions are, in order:

1. Does the mail package work (is it raising money and friends)? If so, is it because of the validity of the need or because of the organization's good image and reputation?

2. What success can be expected right now, based on analysis of the results of the last appeal, the local competition, the time of year, and the economy?

3. How much money will the current mailing bring in?

4. Is investment in another acquisition mailing the best use of a limited budget?

To find its own answers, an organization needs a detailed self-analysis. The following test, prepared by direct mail experts Kay Partney Lautman and Henry Goldstein,[7] has helped many of their clients decide whether to use direct mail for fundraising purposes:

1. Does your organization or cause have broad name recognition?
   (a) in the local community?
   (b) in the state?
   (c) nationally?

2. Does it deal with specific issues rather than broad or abstract ideas?

3. Does it serve or help specific constituencies—for example, minorities, the ill, the elderly, children, handicapped, the poor or disadvantaged, or animals?

4. Are there other organizations performing the same or similar services? If so, how is your organization unique?

5. Does your organization have a demonstrable track record?

6. If your organization is new, does it expect to respond to a critical issue in a dynamic way?

7. Is there a threat to the organization, those it serves, or to traditional funding sources? In other words, is there an issue, a crisis, or an emergency to be dramatized?

8. If yours is a membership organization, are tangible membership benefits offered? If yours is a cause-oriented organization, can you show the donor how his or her gift will make a difference?

9. Would your organization be financially able to survive a loss of 40 percent or more of its investment should the test mailing fail to recoup costs?

10. Do you have the patience (and the investment money) to wait between two and four years before realizing so-called spendable net income?

If you answered "yes" to half these questions, direct mail may be appropriate for your cause and a test mailing can be made a low risk. However, if you answered "no" to questions 9 and 10, think twice. Newcomers to direct mail must not view it as a fix for immediate financial problems, but as a calculated investment in the organization's future.

Readers who have evaluated all these answers and decided, with the blessing of their organization's leadership, to proceed, should reread Chapter 2's discussion of how to test a mailing plan. Testing is how and where direct mail acquisition must begin. Testing is essential; it protects against errors and waste of money. Only after completing an evaluation of its test results should an organization prepare for a full "roll out" of a direct mail solicitation program. Sound testing results promise considerable success in this year and for several to come.

Multiple Acquisition Methods

Preparations should target multiple mailings, not just a single letter. Testing shows which lists, messages, and package elements have the greatest appeal. Beyond money-raising, a successful mail acquisition will yield an understanding of the quality of the lists used and will indicate the investment required to satisfy valid needs and desired community benefits. The plan should project a three-year, multimailing program, a minimum of five to six mailings each year, and a total of between 15 and 18 letter packages to be sent to substantially the same people so long as each segment of the lists being used perform at minimal levels of efficiency and cost effectiveness. From this entire effort, the organization will be able to measure several objectives, including its ability to do the following:

1. Acquire new donors whose future gifts will serve as the foundation for reliable annual income for the future

2. Advance the image and reputation of the organization and its mission

3. Raise the money needed to fund immediate programs and services of public benefit

4. Report the outcomes of their work to donors and prospects alike, to reinforce their decision to support the organization again

After three years, the organization should have a favorable public image. By then, hundreds and perhaps thousands of donors should be committed to support of its mission. A continuing obligation to each of them is *communication*, to preserve their interest and maintain their active support for as long as possible.

The next step is a roll-out, a commitment to mail to the full list or to as many names as prudence and the budget allow. This decision is expensive because all the costs are up-front. The boards and managers of nonprofit organizations are not gamblers; they hate risks of any sort. Test results should give them confidence in the expected rate of returns and may even prove to them that most, if not all, of the funds invested will come back as gifts within 30 to 60 days. If early tests did *not* prove that enough money will come back, another test should seek the lists (or list segments) and the message that will achieve at least a break-even financial return. (The segment of the CCUA Clean Up Cleveland Chapter story that appears at the end of this chapter provides an example.)

MULTIPLE MAILINGS

Any schedule of mailings is conducted in a highly planned sequence; for every first appeal, a follow-up letter is sent within 30 to 45 days. The results of each mailing should be measured before tallying the joint results. To make the sequence work as a single appeal:

- Use the results of each mailing as a basis for decisions about the next mailing.
- Study the replies from each segment of the mailing list used, sifting and sorting the individual responses for each time mailed.
- Count the number of replies received from each list and note the average gift size and total gift revenue.
- Read any comments or letters sent with the replies and respond to all that you can.

The percentage of response illustrates the receptiveness to the appeal. Average gift size shows ability and motivation to give. If the gifts received average only $8.00 per person, the list used may not be a good fit with the cause, or they liked the appeal but did not have much money to give or did not think that more than a token gift was merited. Total gift revenue should be compared with total preparation and mailing costs to measure efficiency and cost-effectiveness. If each mailing produces a 1 percent rate of return, an average gift of $25 and a cost of less than $1.50 for each dollar received, do the following:

- Mail the appeal again to everyone who has not yet replied.
- Keep mailing to the same list, and, after each mailing, cull those list segments that are not producing at least half the results above, or better.
- Use the same list until it no longer meets good performance and profitability standards.
- Retire the list and begin the same procedure with others.

WHEN TO MAIL AND HOW OFTEN

The timing for each mailing deserves careful study. For first-time donor acquisition mailings to lists never before used, the timing is critical. Traditional mailing periods are those times when the competition can be expected to be active as well. As identified earlier in this chapter, the preferred times, in order of preference, are October to December, March to

June, January to March, and July to September. Each organization must settle on the schedule it believes will work best for the people on its lists. One period may work as well as any other, depending on local conditions and many other unique factors. There is enough time in each of these periods for two letters—and possibly for three, if the returns are especially strong. Each of these primary mailing periods can be used to set up the next sequence, prepare to build on the messages already delivered, and add some details about how many other people have replied. Keeping track of what was written to each list in each mailing sequence is an important precaution. People always get the message about being asked for money. If the letters inform them of new facts about the organization, they are more likely to read the text—and, possibly, to respond.

Each nonprofit organization chooses its own mass mailing timetable. The schedule becomes a guide for the frequency and timing of not only its solicitation letters, but all of its other fundraising solicitation activities and all of its other public communications needed during the year. There are limits to what people receiving all this mail can endure. There is also a limit on how much money the organization can afford to spend on all its mail communications. Because results provide guidance for all subsequent mailings, it is essential to measure the results of each mailing by asking:

1. Is it as efficient as possible, especially as measured by its public?
2. How many new donors and how much money has each appeal brought in?
3. What were the net proceeds and expectations for renewal?

Mailings are most successful when designed as a coordinated effort. The messages should complement one another to reinforce the validity and urgency of the appeal. A lot of work is involved but, because of the amount of money invested in these mailings, they must prove they can achieve reasonable performance expectations. Each nonprofit organization's overall marketing, promotion, and mass communications plans should be highly coordinated with its annual giving solicitation messages and timing. After all, the audiences are the same.

The true test of performance for appeal letters and their messages is the length of their run, not how many weeks pass between mailings or how many mailings are planned within a year. Jerry Huntsinger,[8] a current "dean" of direct mail fundraising and one of the most talented and prolific mail experts around, has defined the following critical elements for analysis and future decision making, against which each separate mailing should be measured:

1. Number of pieces mailed
2. Cost of the mailing
3. Total income generated
4. Number of responses received
5. Percentage of response
6. Average gift
7. Net income
8. Cost to raise a dollar

As long as the list is producing acceptable results (usually, a 1 percent rate of response with an average gift of $25), these good people can be asked for their help, on a schedule that works best within the organization. I once kept writing to a start-up list of 200,000 names for 11 mailings over a three-year period. The list shrank each time; some people moved away, others requested to be taken off the list. I kept mailing to this original group because each appeal yielded more than a 1 percent rate of return and maintained an average gift of $50 or more each time it was used. After 11 mail appeals, both the percentage and gift size fell, and it was time to put the original list aside and begin using others.

Careful study of the returns must be performed after every mailing. What geographic areas within each list are doing better than others? (ZIP codes are the link, especially those with nine digits.) Average gift size is a measure of enthusiasm for the message sent and confirms where the quality of the list may be concentrated. If other data are available regarding the list, such as home value, income level, age, occupation, and so on, a more detailed analysis will add clues that can increase performance in future mailings. These studies can also point out lists, or areas within lists, that did not perform well. Any list or segment of a list that does not perform as well as others probably should be discarded or set aside for use only in a final year-end appeal. People are not likely to change their convictions about a cause or a need within a few weeks' time, on the basis of letters alone. The science of direct mail allows each user to establish individual performance guidelines to aid in achieving targeted performance goals. Usually, these are not to waste money needlessly and not to harass the people on the lists. Letters are intended to create friends for the nonprofit organization; to educate the public about the organization's mission, purposes, goals, and objectives; to build respect for the organization and its methods; and to raise the money it needs. The mail should be used to make friends whenever possible; no one needs enemies who will complain to others about the endless mail they receive from the organization or cite it as an example of wasteful management practices.

After the mailing has been "dropped," three additional options may encourage results and may help to preserve the value of the investment in the lists used and in the production costs:

1. Consider adding the words "Address Service Requested" to the outer envelope. Some of the letters will be returned as undeliverable; people move, others die, and mailing lists have errors. The Postal Services will charge $0.55 for each piece of mail that is returned, but it will come back with a correct mailing address to which future appeals can be directed.

2. Evaluate results from the first mailing within three to four weeks, to allow for a few last-minute changes to the next mailing. The materials and letter text are already finished at this point and cannot easily be changed without delaying the next mailing. But there is time to cut back on any list or segment of a list that is obviously failing, or to expand from a segment to the full list if results were outstanding.

3. Prepare to process all the gifts received by sending a "thank-you" letter or an appropriate message of gratitude on the preprinted gift receipt form. Add the IRS-required language for gifts of $250 or more, to substantiate the contribution deduction value. Be ready to write to people who answer the appeal but do not send money; they may need more details before deciding to give. If they request to be taken off the mailing list, honor their request right away.

There will be adequate time between major mail sequences for more detailed evaluation (which parts of the package are in need of revision or can be dropped; what lists or segments of lists should be used again) and for response to anything that received wide public attention during the mailing. Perhaps materials for the next message will be revealed during these catch-up activities.

IMPROVED RESULTS WITH MULTIMEDIA APPEALS

Other communications scheduled to appear within the same time period may help some mailings to succeed. This *multimedia* technique is defined by Huntsinger[9] as follows: "The term 'multimedia' refers to the combination of one or more media to sell a product or promote an organization. . . . So when you venture into multimedia, you venture into an area that has potential for fantastic failure or fantastic success." To illustrate, a notice about an annual giving appeal might appear in reports, newsletters, marketing materials, and other promotions. The widespread coverage keeps the appeal in the public eye. News releases that report on the people helped through the organization's programs and services further reinforce the message. Public service announcements (PSAs) on radio (and, possibly, on cable television) enhance the appeal messages by adding sight and sound. PSAs are inexpensive; by comparison, paid advertising will inflate fundraising costs. Adding all this same information to the organization's Web page is both a reinforcement of the message and a consistent reminder of the organization's commitment to doing good works. The value of these extra messages is in their repetition of the organization's name and the cause; the mail recipients will recognize the appeal when it arrives. "Direct marketing is an interactive system of marketing which uses one or more advertising media to effect a measurable response and/or transaction at any location."[10] "Direct response advertising" has become a major means of communication. The sheer volume of mail appeals has created fierce competition for public attention—and even some public resistance to the medium. The dominant users are for-profit corporations that use the mail to advertise and sell their products. The common nickname for direct mail mass communications is "junk mail." People joke about sorting their unopened and unread mail over the trash basket. In this decisive time span (estimated at five seconds or less), name recognition can be critical. The purpose of multimedia efforts is to save unread appeal letters from immediately becoming recyclable trash.

Nonprofit organizations cannot compete with the large advertising and multimedia communications budgets of for-profit corporations. Maximal results for nonprofit organizations will come from careful use of their limited communications budgets and from coordinated and cooperative multimedia message combinations. The marketing, public relations, and fund development staff should work together to keep the messages in their communications consistent and to place them for multiple and maximum effect with closely coordinated timing (see Exhibit 2-1). Because the audiences chosen for each of these communications are often the same people—community residents—better results will come from coordinating the joint use of shared mailing lists. Working together is efficient, effective, and smart; unfortunately, it is not often attempted. Each department has separate goals and its performance is measured by different results. Even a small effort—such as reference to a current appeal in a regular newsletter, magazine, or report, or in a separate "piggy-back" message that can be inserted in a mailing package for the same postage cost—can improve results.

Change is hard for some people; so are new ideas. Not everyone possesses a cooperative spirit. Some people hold on to textbook theorems about "pure" message delivery or have been warned against the potential for audience confusion from multiple messages. Some have even told me that fundraising appeals might "poison" the audience against their message. Given the precious few dollars available for expensive public communications, perhaps it is time for management-level decisions calling for coordination and cooperation among staff, to eliminate arbitrary barriers or insecurities that handicap the potential for optimum results. Taken from a strategic marketing standpoint, what might be the result of attempting a joint communications effort in the most heavily used mail communications period of October to December? Isn't it worth a test to find out?

OTHER OPTIONS FOR ACQUISITION MAILINGS

Highly coordinated multimedia communications will continue to be a most effective strategy for nonprofit organizations. There may also be other opportunities where these communications can be used to effect the acquisition of new, first-time donors. To continue the speculation just above, referring to the October–December period, what might result from the unexpected, or from a Murphy's law scenario? Suppose a large local retailer proposes a cause-related marketing promotion that will advertise a special sale offer during November and December, the highest sales months in the year. The retailer's offer is 10 percent of all sales proceeds as a gift, in exchange for use of the organization's name and the name of its priority appeal project as benefactor of all funds raised by the arrangement. The marketing strategy is to conduct a blitz of advertising in November, just ahead of the holiday shopping period, using local radio, television, and newspapers, plus posters, bus-back and billboard advertising, and similar spaces. Each advertisement will feature the organization's priority fundraising appeal; the retailer's schedule fits perfectly with the organization's year-end annual giving direct mail solicitation schedule. The expected level of visibility from such a campaign far exceeds what the organization could even hope to afford or accomplish on its own. But how flexible are its marketing, public relations, and fundraising plans? Will everyone (or just the fundraising office) adjust to this unusual opportunity? If the project proves financially successful to the retailer and nets an important gift to the organization, would both be likely to seek a joint promotion again next fall, or perhaps even in the spring of next year?

Other opportunities to enhance a first-time acquisition effort may not be as dramatic as this example but there are many possibilities: news stories about the project during the mailing period; publicized major gifts ($1,000 or more) received from a local corporation or foundation; a human interest story about a family who benefited directly from the service area of the appeal; progress reports announced with proper fanfare at public events. Ideas generate other ideas. The challenge is in making them happen.

Harvey Clout continued with his efforts to form the Cleveland Chapter. In a workbook he had received from the national office were step-by-step instructions on how to start his program. The workbook suggested recruiting a chapter board of directors, hiring a full-time director of development to manage fundraising and communications, and completing plans for the first full year of solicitation and communication activities. Each of these tasks was to be completed before sending out any more appeal mailings.

Chapter Board of Directors

Appointing a local board was easy for Clout. He was already serving on six nonprofit boards, two of which were just concluding successful major capital campaigns. He had also helped Mrs. Clout organize a new board for the Downtown Art Center, and, from his service on the executive committee of the Greater Cleveland United Way, he knew many corporate executives who were actively involved in several other nonprofit organizations. He had already invited a few friends and business associates to help him get the chapter started. These included Sidney Secure, his auditor; Mary Moneybanks and "Ted" Worthy, personal friends; and Titus Brown, his advertising and public relations counsel. A board of 21 members was recommended by the national office. Clout recruited the first board members and gave nearly all of them specific assignments. Two other members, Steve Generous and "Telly" Temple, were added because of their positions as board chairpersons for the Cleveland Orchestra and Cleveland Play House, respectively. Here is how the chapter's initial board of directors looked after these appointments:

Board of Directors, CCUA Clean Up Cleveland Chapter Officers

Chair of the Board	I. Harvey Clout
Vice Chair	Mary M. Moneybanks
Treasurer	Sidney M. Secure, CPA
Secretary	Theodosius ("Ted") Worthy
Assistant Secretary	Titus Brown, APR

Board Members and Committee Assignments

Development Committee Chair	Harold R. Connected
Board Members-at-Large	Steven Generous
	Iris B. Radiant
	Trafalgar ("Telly") Temple

Fundraising Executive

Earlier, Harvey Clout had asked Titus Brown to help him conduct a search for a director of development. Within four weeks, Brown presented three final candidates to Clout, all of whom had been successful at raising money for other organizations in the city. Interviews were arranged to allow new officers of the board to meet all three candidates. Karen I. Anderson, the assistant director in the National Audubon Society's local office, was chosen, accepted, and reported for work two weeks later. Within two weeks, Anderson had hired Alice B. Nice as her executive assistant. They remained in Clout's corporate offices, and Clout continued to meet all the daily operating costs for salaries and benefits, supplies, telephone, mail services, and computers.

First Year's Solicitation and Communications

Karen Anderson studied the results of the initial test mailings (Exhibit 2-6). She began to plan for a follow-up "roll out" mailing to a larger segment of the overall Cleveland population. A few changes were needed, based on her analysis of test results. Anderson chose Letter B (Exhibit 2-5) over Letter A (Exhibit 2-4) and decided to drop List 2 and List 5 (eastern suburbs and sports teams' season ticket holders) for now; the tests showed these two groups were not likely to perform well enough to cover the costs of mailing and production. The four remaining mailing lists, after duplicate-elimination procedures, contained 80,595 names, made up as follows:

List	Definition	Names
1	Shaker Heights residents	28,565
3	Northeast Ohio members, National Audubon Society	17,615
4	Northeast Ohio members, The Nature Conservancy	12,637
6	Subscribers to the Cleveland Orchestra and Cleveland Play House	21,778
	Total names	80,595

Karen Anderson estimated that slightly better than a 1 percent rate of return from these four lists was possible, which would provide 800 new donors. Assuming an average gift of $25, the mailing would yield gift income of $20,000. She also estimated the cost, based on the test mailing, at $.405 per letter. For 80,595 letters, "roll out" expenses would be $32,640.98. Given an income projection of $20,000, this first mailing would suffer a loss of over $12,000, which was not acceptable and could be a major setback to the entire chapter start-up. Anderson knew she had to find a way to increase the number of responses *and* the average gift size in order to achieve a break-even or better response on this first major mailing. Her proposal to Clout was to create a "Circle of Champions," an introductory donor club offer that conferred charter membership for a first-year reduced membership fee of $100. To try to catch the attention of the people who were on the remaining four lists, she proposed an extra benefit to go with the introductory offer—a free pass to some special event or performance by the Cleveland Orchestra or at the Cleveland Play House. She estimated the Circle of Champions idea would close the gap and make this first mailing profitable. Her calculations were as follows: If 5 percent of those who reply to the mailing become charter members at the reduced fee of $100, this will add $4,000 in net income to the bottom line; if 10 percent of those who reply join, $8,000 will be added. Because neither amount would be enough to offset the $12,000 shortfall, she estimated two additional possibilities:

1. Ask Clout to solicit the new board for at least $250 each, which would add $3,500;

2. Offer a variety of giving options, at levels of $100, $250, $500, and $1,000, to the Circle of Champions program, with special benefits for each level.

To reflect all these features and the early commitment from the new board members at $250 each, the text of Letter B and the response form were modified to add charter membership in the Circle of Champions, gift options, and the special event invitation from the Cleveland Orchestra or Cleveland Play House. Draft thank-you letters, for regular donors and for Circle of Champion charter members, also were prepared. The entire package was presented to Clout for the final decision to proceed with the mailing.

The First Full Mailing Is Resolved

Harvey Clout loved the idea of the Circle of Champions. He called Steven Generous, board chair of the Cleveland Orchestra, and "Telly" Temple, board chair of the Cleveland Play House, and asked each if they could arrange a special offer for the charter members, such as an invitation to attend one of their programs. Clout told them that no more than 100 people would be involved. They both reported back in a few days to confirm the offer. Any donor of $100 or more would be invited to a special performance during the coming year. Both asked Clout for $10 from each gift as their share, but Clout convinced them that the CCUA Clean Up Cleveland Chapter needed all the money it could raise during this first year to get the chapter up and running successfully, and then to begin collecting funds for building the new energy plant. Generous and Temple agreed, and Anderson completed the "roll-out" package illustrated in Exhibits 3-6 through 3-10.

Results Analysis

Anderson's analysis of the results is shown below. The figures suggested that a few more modifications would be needed for the spring mailing campaign:

1. A total of 1,156 new donors was acquired.
2. A total of $35,758 was received.
3. An average gift of $30.93 was achieved.
4. Total cost per dollar raised was $0.91.
5. The number of charter members in the Circle of Champions was 118; they gave a total of $12,403, or an average gift of $105.
6. All the other donors (1,038) gave a total of $23,355, or an average gift of $22.50.
7. Net proceeds were $3,117.02.
8. The Circle of Champions made the difference.

The combined performance from the original six-list test mailings (348 donors and $8,527) and the "roll-out" to the surviving four lists came to a total of 1,504 donors and $44,285, at a cost of $44,890. Given the national average for a first-time acquisition mailing ($1.25 to $1.50 to raise a dollar), the CCUA Clean Up Cleveland Chapter was off to a solid start. The next step was to plan a second acquisition mailing in the spring, and, equally important, to prepare to renew the gifts of these first 1,504 donors.

EXHIBIT 3-6   LETTER B: FINAL TEXT WITH "CIRCLE OF CHAMPIONS" ADDED

Letter B (Revised)

THE CAMPAIGN TO CLEAN UP AMERICA
CLEAN UP CLEVELAND CHAPTER

October 15, 200X

Dear Friend for a Trash-Free Cleveland:

Every day as I drive back and forth to work I see a lot of paper littering our streets, along with cans and bottles, boxes, plastic bags, and more.

We all know the City has cut back on trash collections and street sweeping because of the recession, but they are not keeping up with the trash, not at all. And, our city is not the only city in America with this problem.

Earlier this year, I was invited to New York to hear about The Campaign to Clean Up America. I wanted to go for two reasons. First, this is a serious plan to do something about pollution in our country. Second, they've got a great idea. Build a new energy conversion plant and use all the trash to make electricity and cut our energy bills at the same time!

I estimate about 100,000 tons of trash is lying in our city streets and around our buildings and homes right now. With energy conversion in a new plant, this same trash can become 32,000 megawatts of electricity and meet the needs of 18,000 homes in our city for a full year. Further, this plant will reduce all of our electric bills by $12 a month and $144 a year.

Each of us will benefit from this project. That's why I need your help. Here's what I want you to do to support this City-wide effort:

First, stop being a "trasher." Pick up after yourself.

Second, bag all the trash you can find around your house, garage, and yard, and put it out with your garbage next week.

Third, join me as a member of our Clean Up Cleveland Chapter of The Campaign to Clean Up America. Your minimum gift of $12 stays in Cleveland. And $12 is the amount you will get back each month in savings on your electric bill from our new power plant.

Fourth, give $25 if you can. The sooner we raise the money and build the new energy plant, the sooner our new electric bills will go down and our city will be clean.

(continued)

EXHIBIT 3-6   (CONTINUED)

Fifth, join me in the "Circle of Champions," if you can. Your extra generosity at $100 entitles you to a charter membership in this new group of community leaders. Please note too that each charter member will be receiving an invitation to a special event next year to be offered by both the Cleveland Orchestra and Cleveland Play House.

Sixth, spread the word. Talk about what we are doing. Tell your neighbors and the people with whom you work. Ask them to get involved. Ask them to join you in the Clean Up Cleveland campaign. Put your bumper sticker on your vehicle (it's magnetic, not adhesive) and let everyone see you are a supporter of a cleaner Cleveland.

You've heard the old saying, "Every litter bit helps." Each of us can help a bit to make our city a better place to live. Your contribution of $12 or more is what is needed. All contributions will be divided, with 25 percent going to our public awareness and education programs and 75 percent going to help pay for the construction of our new energy plant.

Our proposal for the new energy plant has been approved by the Cleveland City Council. The site has been selected near Perry, Ohio, and the land has been donated by Centurion Energy Corp., who will also operate the new plant. The estimated total cost is $3.5 million. Two-thirds of this cost will be met by federal and Ohio matching funds. What we have to do is raise $1,250,000 in private contributions from the people who live and work in Cleveland.

I hope you will join me and commit yourself to help clean up Cleveland. Your bumper sticker is enclosed along with a response form to be returned with your gift. Let me hear from you soon.

Sincerely yours,

I. Harvey Clout
Chair of the Board
Cleveland Cast Iron Works

P.S. Last week, my son and I picked up three bags full of paper, cans, and bottles around our plant during lunch time, in less than 30 minutes. This coming Friday, our 15 managers will go around this plant, inside and out, and pick up all the trash they can find during their lunch break. The goal is for each of them to match our three bags full. Send me your ideas of what you are doing to help clean up our city.

| EXHIBIT 3-7 | SAMPLE RESPONSE FORM |

THE CAMPAIGN TO CLEAN UP AMERICA
CLEAN UP CLEVELAND CHAPTER

[ ] YES! Count me in the campaign to Clean Up Cleveland. Attached is my gift to help:

   [ ] $12   [ ] $25   [ ] $50   [ ] $_____.

[ ] Yes! I would like to become a Charter Member of the "Circle of Champions" donor club. Attached is my membership gift of:

   [ ] $100   [ ] $150   [ ] $200   [ ] $_____.

[ ] Sorry. I cannot sent a gift at this time. I do support your effort and will use the bumper sticker to help in this campaign.

THANK YOU FOR YOUR SUPPORT!

Name _____

Address _____

City _____ State _____ ZIP: _____ _____

| EXHIBIT 3-8 | RESULTS OF LETTER B: ROLL OUT MAILING WITH "CIRCLE OF CHAMPIONS" OFFER |

Letter B Results

| | | Replies | | | | Cost per |
List Name	Letters Mailed	Number	Percent	Gift Income	Average Gift	Dollar Raised
Cleveland Heights Residents	28,565	414	1.45%	$18,321	$44.25	$0.63
Audubon Society Members (NE Ohio)	17,615	372	2.11	8,916	23.96	0.80
Nature Conservancy Members (NE Ohio)	12,637	158	1.25	3,476	22.00	1.47
Orchestra & Play House Subscribers	21,778	212	0.97	5,045	23.80	1.75
Totals	80,575	1,156	1.43%	$35,758	$30.93	$0.91

Cost of mailing ($0.405 × 80,595) = $32,640.98.

Summary: Among the 1,156 donors, 118 joined the Circle of Champions and gave $12,403, for an average gift of $105.00.

EXHIBIT 3-9   STANDARD THANK-YOU TEXT FOR FIRST GIFT

THE CAMPAIGN TO CLEAN UP AMERICA
CLEAN UP CLEVELAND CHAPTER

December, 200X

Mr. and Mrs. Robert Smith
16210 Shaker Boulevard
Shaker Heights, OH 44120

Dear Mr. and Mrs. Smith:

Thank you for your gift of $25.00 in support of a trash-free Cleveland. Your level of support is most important to this effort and we appreciate your extra generosity at this time.

Welcome to the Clean Up Cleveland Chapter of The Campaign to Clean Up America. I am delighted with the response from our friends and neighbors in this community who want to help.

Your gift stays in Cleveland; no part of it goes to the national effort. Our city has a bright future, thanks to you. And, with your extra help, the new energy conversion plant soon will deliver electricity to you at a lower cost.

I have begun to see our magnetic bumper stickers on cars and trucks all over town. Please be sure to use yours right away and help to spread the word.

Again, thank you for your generous gift and your commitment to support our efforts for a cleaner city and reasonable rates for electricity.

Sincerely yours,

I. Harvey Clout
Chair of the Board
Cleveland Cast Iron Works

EXHIBIT 3-10   CHARTER MEMBERSHIP
THANK-YOU LETTER

THE CAMPAIGN TO CLEAN UP AMERICA
CLEAN UP CLEVELAND CHAPTER

December, 200X

Mr. and Mrs. Phil Anthropy
23350 South Woodland Road
Shaker Heights, OH 44122

Dear Mary and Phil;

Thank you for your gift of $100.00 to support a trash-free Cleveland. I am deeply grateful to you for your commitment to join our Clean Up Cleveland effort. I value your personal support very much.

Welcome to Charter Membership in our new "Circle of Champions" donor club. With your extra help, we will get our city back in shape and build the energy conversion plant all that much sooner.

You will be hearing from the Cleveland Orchestra and Cleveland Play House with your invitation to their special event coming early next year.

I have begun to see our magnetic bumper stickers on cars and trucks all over town. Please be sure to use yours right away to help spread the word. If you would like extra bumper stickers, please give my office a call.

Again, thank you for your generous gift and your commitment to support our efforts for a cleaner city and reasonable rates for electricity.

Sincerely yours,

I. Harvey Clout
Chair of the Board
Cleveland Cast Iron Works

CHAPTER 4

Donor Renewal: A Communications Art

After a first gift is acquired, the new donor should be told about the organization and about how the donated money was used. A pathway is then marked for asking the donor to give again. A first gift begins a relationship between a donor and his or her choice of nonprofit organization; the extra effort to build the relationship must come from the party seeking association and friendship. One of several reasons for expanding the relationship is to achieve a return on the initial investment—a renewal of the new donor's first gift. Nonprofit organizations should *not* look on fundraising as only a one-time, once-a-year cash exchange. If they do, they will fail to receive the full return that is possible on their investment—getting to know their donors, educating them about the good works being performed, and helping to motivate them to give again and again. New donors are like new friends or new customers. If treated properly, they can become part of a lasting friendship and good customer relations. Once a relationship is built, the money will follow. Among the added benefits that will result from the combination of donor relations, communications, and renewal solicitations are:

1. Prior donors are the best prospects for other gifts as well as renewed annual gifts;

2. At least 50 percent of prior donors should repeat their gifts in the same amount;

3. As many as 15 percent of prior donors will increase (upgrade) their gifts, if asked to do so;

4. After the second renewal (third gift), a donor is likely to remain faithful for from five to seven more years;

5. Renewal donors will give from five to eight times more money than new, first-time donors;

6. After five years, renewal donors will provide 80 percent of the money raised each year.

Donor renewal is the means to true success in fund development. Communications with donors between gifts, and invitations to volunteer and to make other gifts, will enhance the annual gift and form a foundation for the desired mutual friendship and respect. Such a friendship can last a lifetime; its value expands over time. The focus must always remain on building the relationship, and the building begins with the first gift. How well it grows and its ultimate return on investment are in the hands of the nonprofit organization. As fundraising competition increases, the strength of the bond between donors and their favored nonprofit organizations will make the difference in retention of donors. Long-term success in fundraising depends on developing positive relationships with the largest possible number of faithful donors. If their confidence and trust are maintained through constant communications, offering added opportunities for information, interest, involvement, and investment, donors can be expected to continue their faithful support for many years, possibly even over their lifetimes.

For any nonprofit organization, its most critical decision in fundraising involves the quality communications, renewal opportunities, and recognition programs that constitute its donor relations. By fostering and preserving friendships with donors, the organization gains benefits far in excess of the costs to secure the first gifts, regardless of their size. Mature fund-development programs (in place five years or more, with broad-based annual giving activities) can expect that 80 percent or more of their annual cash will come from their prior donors. Why? Because these nonprofit organizations have continued to invest in building their relationships with their prior donors. They have also established a firm pattern of multiple and repeat giving. Board members and management staff of nonprofit organizations often place too much emphasis on how much money is being raised in the short term. They should concentrate on who is giving, on the amount of effort needed to maintain their gifts, and on expanding communications and attention to current donors.

The strength of any annual giving program is its ability to expand and renew gifts from its faithful prior donors throughout the year. If motivated to give year after year and to give to many different programs within each year, donors will accumulate a grand total far above what they might have imagined possible. Their potential for support makes it imperative to recognize their continued contributions.

Annual giving is a plan designed to foster the constant renewal of a donor's interest and enthusiasm as well as to encourage and facilitate his or her continuous support. It is the responsibility of nonprofit organizations to guide their donors along this path of multiple giving opportunities, thereby fulfilling their aspirations to do the best they can for the cause they have chosen to support. This guidance is best achieved through (1) communications opportunities, (2) involvement opportunities, and (3) donor renewal, revival, and reward. As with any lifelong friendship, constant effort must be given to building as well as to retaining the relationship. Lacking attention, it will weaken and can quickly be lost. If a nonprofit organization is interested only in the money given and not in the donor as a person who has needs, wants, and desires, the friendship is not likely to last beyond the first gift.

COMMUNICATIONS OPPORTUNITIES

Renewal of donor gifts has the potential to achieve, at a minimum, from five to eight times the original gift value. It is important, therefore, to begin communications with donors immediately after their first gift, using these guidelines:

- Educate them about the organization—its mission, purposes, goals, and objectives.
- Concentrate on the people served or the cause, the quality and effectiveness of the work being done, and the specific benefits it delivers.
- Tell how their money will be used, how their funds make a difference by helping other people, whole communities, or the environment.
- Be creative in selecting the means and methods for communication.
- Be sensitive to the frequency and appearance of the messages.

The following should be decided *before* the communications plan is begun:

- Message—its purpose(s) and content
- Medium to be used (mail, telephone, newspaper, television, Web site, Internet, videocassette, or combinations of media)
- Appearance of the piece (color, size, length)
- Frequency planned for each piece
- Overall objectives (to inform, invite, involve, stimulate to act)
- Estimate of all the costs involved
- Measurement to evaluate results

Donors expect their gift dollars will be used for charitable purposes. They will not react well if they receive expensive and glossy reports, newsletters that arrive too frequently, and other unnecessary (and unwanted) "give backs." Striking the right balance in appearance, content, and length has first priority; choices in frequency and message medium follow closely after. Written communications sent to 200 or more individuals can be mailed at third-class and nonprofit bulk-mail rates, which save money. The message is still delivered, although its arrival may take anywhere from a few days to a few weeks. Most nonprofit organizations have room for improvement in the amount of coordination between staff members who manage public communications and the people assigned or contracted to design and write them. A balance between professional appearance and cost-effectiveness is the goal, and correct English is a must. If the piece looks "too slick," if the several components of a mailing do not look like they were sent from the same organization, if the messages are unconnected, or if the reply requests ask donors for too much too often, the results are confusion and criticism. Coordination on timing alone will help reduce the negative reactions that come from showing up too often in donors' mail boxes.

In today's message-overloaded world, the communications challenge lies in being seen and heard by the people the message is supposed to reach. Mailing list management must select precisely who is to receive each specific message, what each audience is to be sent each year, and ways of making the communications personal and efficient. Broadcast mailings sent to every resident are usually inefficient; they will not communicate effectively with those who should hear the organization's story. Each non-profit organization has to find its own way to speak directly to its donors. Personalized communications—those that look as though they have been individually prepared—are best. Personal mail ("high touch") is recommended as the best way to achieve success in donor communications because it enhances personal giving in return.

Coordinating Messages to Audiences

Nonprofit organizations that achieve the highest level of coordination and cooperation among their marketing, public relations, community relations, and fund development professionals are most likely to be effective and efficient in all their communications. The master mailing lists prepared by these departments for their separate communications can be brought together with the objective of creating one current and viable master list for the organization. Each department would be encouraged to use only a segment of the master mailing list at any one time. Occasionally, there may be a message that the entire list needs to receive. With planning, a well-defined sequence of messages can be accomplished, and the content of each piece can build on the others to transmit the desired information or stimulate the action requested. When donor communications are well-coordinated, responses improve. The most effective messages focus on relevant topics and priorities, are personalized, arrive at regular intervals, and are clearly sent from the same organization. Achieving such coordination among all the staff departments involved may sound like an obvious and simple goal, but it has proven difficult to achieve within many organizations. Each unit must prepare separate goals and strategies for its communications, with performance evaluations based on achieving defined results. Each unit can also participate in setting joint goals and can be measured for its contribution toward achieving multipurpose goals.

There are several good reasons for making the extra effort to define a coordinated communications plan among all the departments that send out messages to the public. Once the plan is established, there will be opportunities to "piggyback" more than one message in a single package, which can achieve cost savings. *Multimessaging* (two or more messages in the same mail package) can provide a variety of interesting materials that are of potential use to donors, friends, and customers. Multimedia packages (more than one message medium are employed) are becoming common. Examples are major public awareness campaigns that include billboard and bus-back announcements, radio and newspaper advertisements, and two or more direct mail packages delivered to select residents—all timed for maximum impact in a two- to four-week period. Newsletters and magazines, while less frequent, can report on the same activities described in the earlier communications. Each message reinforces those before it.

Many nonprofit organizations now advertise special services, timely offers, and the programs and services they make available to the public. They also include helpful details on their program and service activities in their newsletters, magazines, and Web pages, and list phone numbers and e-mail addresses for further information. Telephone, mail, facsimile, e-mail, and other fulfillment services must be prepared to reply promptly to each request, whether for information, service, appointments, giving inquiries, or professional advice. Donors may seek information on how to buy a ticket to a coming benefit event, or may ask about the tax-deductibility of their next gift. A common practice is to insert or bind gift-reply envelopes into the organization's newsletter or magazine, to reinforce the dual message of their nonprofit status and to suggest another gift. The cost of this insert seldom pays for itself in dollars received; its true merit is its subtle message that gifts are always welcome. The envelopes are convenient reminders; some donors will remove them (especially if the postage is paid) and save them for use another day. The envelopes' effectiveness can be tested by printing a code on them, separating them when they are returned, and tallying the number received and their total receipts.

Avoiding Treating Donors as Objects

The primary objective of continuous communications with donors is to educate and inform them about the organization. Every contact need not solicit another gift nor should it always ask for a reply. Some fundraising executives believe donors need to be rehearsed to reply positively to each offer; they seek to "train" donors to continually say yes to each request. I am extremely cautious about using any form of psychology with prospects and donors. Charitable contributions should be willingly made after deliberation; they should not be regarded as a preconditioned or (worse yet) unmotivated response "triggered," like Pavlov's dog, by reflex autosuggestion. This is no way to treat friends! Donors should have the opportunity, each time they are asked for their support, to study the request, ask questions and request details, and, only then, decide freely whether to reply or to send money. Open channels of communication are best; it is always wise to avoid appearing to be too slick in fundraising.

There is real potential that too frequent solicitations will turn off a donor when the next request arrives. People resent being hit on too often. The timing of each communication must be given careful thought. What message preceded this contact and when was it sent? Were any comments or written responses received? Were there any negative reactions that need to be corrected? Support pieces mailed on a regular basis, such as newsletters, invitations, and other materials mailed by other departments of the organization, should be reviewed frequently to avoid repeating the same message over and over without adding new facts or a new twist to the story. Information about results and measurable outcomes should be added when verified and available.

How can all these elements be made to fit together? Which pieces should be sent at the same time solicitations are in progress, and which ones before, during, and after the gift is made? How can the stage be set prior to asking, to create the need and establish its urgency? Each mailing piece that follows should add something to the story—how the funds raised are being used; photographs of people receiving service of attending programs; a brief story about a successful client or patient. Pieces mailed after the gift occurs can report on fundraising results (people like to hear that others joined them in giving) as well as changes in quantity and quality of programs delivered along with details to support outcomes achieved and community benefits delivered.

If messages are carefully planned, donors can benefit in some way from each one. Each mailing piece must be able to stand on its own, be informative and interesting, and retain reader interest. The volume of messages received daily via mail, audio, the Internet, and visual media will only increase; everyone is competing for attention. Being creative is only part of the answer; better coordination and cooperation within the organization and use of strategic techniques and modern technology constitute the communications plan that will probably yield the best results.

What to Say after Receiving the First Gift

When a nonprofit organization receives its first gift from a new donor, it has already achieved several major breakthroughs:

1. It has found an interested person.
2. The message caught that person's attention.
3. The person was stimulated to action.
4. The person acted to send money.

The organization's reply, to be sent back within 48 hours, must report that the money was received safely, express thanks for the gift, and promise to use it to benefit others as described in the appeal. If the gift was large ($1,000 or more), a second, more focused thank-you letter should be sent after a volunteer leader calls the donor. A first-time donor at this level might be testing for a response. They also are sending *two* other messages: "I like you a lot." and "Pay attention to me!" so they deserve some extra attention.

The *next* letter, after the thank-you letter, is possibly the most crucial communication in this new relationship. Before starting to write the message, it helps to imagine the questions within the mind of a donor who has just made a first gift of $50, $100, or $1,000: "What does the appeal propose to do with my money? Why did I send the gift? What response can I expect to receive? Am I supposed to know more about the organization's progress? I wonder, did others give? How much? What was the total received?"

Providing specific answers will take some time and effort, which is why an advance strategy for communications is so necessary. One way to begin is to prepare a one- or two-page narrative in letter form over the signature of the CEO, and mail it third-class, bulk-mail rate every 60 days to everyone who gave $50 or more in the prior two months. Organizations can write about their own programs and services with ease; they achieve results every day. These stories can be told every other month or so. Not much time or money will be required to circulate them, but their value will be significant. After another 60 days, the regularly scheduled communications can continue this contact. A new donor can be overwhelmed with too much information and too many communications received too quickly.

EXHIBIT 4-1	COMMUNICATIONS OPPORTUNITIES IN DONOR ANNUAL ACTIVITY CYCLE

Activity	Timing
1. Acquisition solicitation	1 per year
(-) (First gift received)	(within 1–6 weeks)
2. Thank-you letter	Within 48 hours
3. Bimonthly activity report	6 per year
4. Newsletter	3–4 per year
5. Posted data on Web page	(open info to all)
6. Invitation to public event	1–2 per year
7. Special report	1–2 per year
8. Basic information brochure	1 per year (within 30 days after gift)
9. Reports/updates by e-mail	1–2 per year (minimum)
10. Extra appeal/special campaign	1 per year
11. Invitation to benefit event	1–2 per year
12. Invitation to annual meeting	1 per year
13. Annual report	1 per year
14. Annual gift renewal solicitation	3–4 per year
Total:	21 to 28 mail pieces per year possible

Exhibit 4-1 shows a 12-month activity schedule for donor communications. The cycle begins after the donor's first gift is received in response to the annual giving campaign. Because this schedule takes advantage of existing materials and ongoing activities, a donor could receive between 21 and 28 separate items within the first year! Only one message (the last in the series) is the formal request to renew the annual gift. Some decisions are needed to select what messages to send, which medium to use (newsletter, report, invitation, fax, e-mail, or letter), and when to send them. The best procedure is to decide what must be said to each donor group and then plan the message, medium, and schedule. The objective is to have donors receive the information when it best meets *their* needs, not the organization's.

Newsletters and Annual Reports

Most of the regular communication from nonprofit organizations is carried in their various publications and on their Web page. These publications report briefly on a wide variety of activities and (hopefully) will match one or more interest areas of nearly everyone on the mailing list. Special reports from the administrator or other officials sent by postal or electronic mail allow a nonprofit organization to talk about its priorities, directions, current programs, new services, and future plans, as a way of continuing to inform prior clients, donors, and others. All forms of communication can feature leaders, volunteers, and donors by name and can reproduce photographs showing their interactions with professional and management staff; they can also promote coming activities and events and encourage all supporters to join in. Newsletters and other publications are effective when they are brief (4 to 16 pages), are short on text, include a host of donors' and volunteers' names and pictures, and arrive infrequently (quarterly) but reliably. Frequent references to Web page access to more information should be made whenever possible. Nonprofit editors and writers should appreciate how their audiences (the same people who receive commercial newspapers and magazines) are accustomed to succinct messages delivered in easy-to-read style and enhanced with charts, graphs, and photos that aid their quick understanding of the messages.

Annual reports are more formal documents. They have space for articles that require more than a casual scanning; readers must find the time necessary to concentrate on their content. Annual reports from for-profit corporations have escalated in design, quality, appearance, and expense to the point where they are nearly coffee-table keepsakes. This expensive presentation is not one that nonprofit organizations should imitate. Their annual reports are intended to be read because they report on accomplishments, illustrate financial status, and show how gift dollars were used to achieve some of the organization's most outstanding results. These reports are ideal venues to explain outcomes and speak to the benefits delivered to the community in exchange for their financial and voluntary support.

Some nonprofit organizations believe their annual reports must compete favorably with for-profit and commercial products for the sake of image, not substance. Others have a goal that includes competing for awards. The true objective in preparing annual reports is to communicate effectively with the community served, including volunteers, donors, and prospects. Image impressions and award competitions have their place, but the annual report should concentrate on the substance of the message. Donors are not motivated to make gifts based on receiving prize-winning newsletters or glitzy annual reports. They are more likely to be motivated to give again when they receive a modest presentation that conveys information they can understand about the good works performed by organizations they support. A communication's effectiveness can be measured by counting the number and amount of renewed gifts it stimulates.

Invitations

Invitations are quite different communication tools: they ask for a reply to a specific request for information, for access to a service, for attendance at an event or activity, or for some favor. People do not object to being invited to use some feature of the organization's program or service, or to attend a lecture, public event, or party, even if an admission fee is required. What they appreciate first is being remembered with the invitation, even when they cannot attend. If the service topic, people involved, and event are of interest, they will consider attending. Nonprofit organizations build their relationship with donors each time a reply is stimulated, because another instance of personal involvement and participation has been created. Involvement stimulates increased participation, which is followed by enthusiasm and commitment. Because donors are the backbone of an organization's support, invitations to attend lectures, tours, and open-house days are ideal opportunities for drawing attention to the programs and services of the organization. Lectures and tours open an organization, its professional staff, and its work to the public. Arranging for the professional staff (resident experts) to be guest speakers increases public knowledge of the organization and conveys information. Invitations have the additional advantage of being personal forms of communication, a feature unmatched by newsletters and annual reports.

Invitations also offer donors and prospects privileged access to the organization's programs and services, a way to expand their awareness of the mission, purposes, goals, and objectives. Colleges invite the public to use their campus facilities for lectures, cultural events, and athletic activities, and to return for continuing education classes. These visitors to the campus will help the college to make its case for public support and to communicate its needs when it asks this same public for money. Museums and other cultural organizations exist so that visitors can come to their facilities all the time. Their mission is to encourage people to view their collections, listen to their music, and watch their performances. Attendance increases people's understanding of the value of preserving art and history and their appreciation of where their money is being spent, why it was needed, and how they can help again when asked. Hospitals and national health agencies advocate wellness and promote disease prevention and personal responsibility for self-health. Their invitations encourage people to take action on their own, to follow good health practices (exercise, stop smoking, eat wisely) in order to prevent costly health intervention later on. Health-care facilities are open to visitors of patients, but people are not invited to tour hospitals to look at sick people or to watch surgery. Many other types of nonprofit organizations, especially those involved in direct public services such as feeding the homeless, often invite the public to come and help them to deliver their programs for serving others.

The public expects any activity or event to be worth their time, to present what was advertised, to have other people present, to start and finish on time, to have had advance planning, to provide a memorable experience, and to be carried out with an appropriate level of quality and style. In other words, people want the experience to prove worth the time invested in it. If it does not, they might not attend again. There are more than enough opportunities here for the kind of errors at which people take offense. Given the precarious nature of donor relationships, inviting people to attend activities and events and to visit the organization's facilities can create a minefield of delicate interpersonal relations. Wherever and whenever possible, however, inviting the public to visit the facilities is always good for communications.

Gift Invitations

Gift invitations also seek replies from donors. Those who choose to respond may designate the program or service or other cause within the organization they prefer to receive their gift. When they make such a designation, the organization has an obligation to fulfill their request in detail. The fact that the gift was invited adds an extra dimension to the solicitation. Each person who replies has moved to a new level of donorship, out of personal interest; he or she has a willingness to give something of themselves to benefit others, a wish to act as a good neighbor and be a good citizen. The recipient organization is obliged to use the funds only for the donor's specified purpose or as an unrestricted gift for the benefit of others. If their stipulation is observed faithfully, donors may be inclined to give again when asked—up to a point.

Each gift invitation also is an opportunity for donors to come closer, to become more informed, more involved, more committed and enthusiastic, more actively a part of their favorite organizations. Fulfilling each special gift's requirements to the satisfaction of its sponsor remains the obligation of the nonprofit organization, and this duty must be taken seriously. People have high expectations about being treated correctly, especially when they make the decision to send a large amount of money. Exhibit 4-2 traces

EXHIBIT 4-2   STEPS IN PROCESSING, RECORDING, AND REPORTING GIFTS

1. The donor makes a gift by mail, in person, or by phone, fax, or e-mail (charging a credit card); or sponsors or underwrites an event or gift; or purchases a special-event ticket.
2. Processing begins with the gift processing staff's tasks:
    Data entry
    Update of donor records and donor files
    Journal preparation
    Batch processing
    Transmittal sheets
3. The accounting or business office takes responsibility for:
    Deposit slip
    Deposit of money into the bank
    Revenue entry on the organization's books
4. The bank, upon receipt of the money and thereafter:
    Records the deposit
    Records expenses
    Processes checks
    Pays on account
    Prepares a bank statement
5. The accounting or business office of the organization:
    Receives bank statements
    Reconciles revenue and withdrawals
    Prepares an accounting statement
6. The fund development office:
    Reconciles income and expenses
    Prepares gift reports
    Sends gift reports to the board for review/approval
7. The auditor:
    Reviews all financial activity
    Prepares the annual audit statement
    Presents the audit to the board for review/approval

the pathway and the people involved when a gift arrives from a donor. The numerous tasks listed are elements in the organization's accountability for faithful stewardship of each and every gift received.

Personal Letters

After donors receive a few newsletters, an annual report, log on to its Web page, and event invitations, the next avenue of communication is personal letters. Only telephone calls, e-mail exchanges, and face-to-face meetings are more effective forms of personal communication. Because all these approaches are personal in appearance and style, they have a decided advantage over every other mass communications option. Personal letters can be sent more often (and more cheaply) than invitations, newsletters, and annual reports. They require some writing skill when copies of one letter will be sent to an entire mailing list.

Personal letters, discussing the latest information, can be sent between event invitations and newsletters. They should be brief, personally addressed, and signed by someone whom the recipient may have met or may respect. These letters are likely to be read and appreciated. Nonprofit organizations should keep track of the known interest areas of their major donors and make an effort to send them notes, clippings, progress reports, and other details that are relevant to those areas. Personal letters are made easier by personal computers, word processing software, faxes, laser printers, and Internet transmissions. Used effectively, personal letters can carry a major share of the task of retaining and expanding each donor's personal interest in the organization.

Plan for Donor Communications

Annual giving programs provide a variety of communication opportunities that can be brought to the attention of donors throughout the year. Within reasonable budgetary constraints, a nonprofit organization can be in contact with its donors every 60 to 90 days. Each communication should include, if possible, information about programs that are working, services being performed, people being helped, causes being advanced, and coming events. Most donors are unaware of routine activities going on inside a nonprofit organization; they are usually outside, looking in. People who may have visited the facilities or used one or more programs or services in the past will have a personal experience on which to base their views. Otherwise, most people have limited knowledge about the work done, its value to others, and the results it achieves. Communications are essential because they give nonprofit organizations several opportunities, at minimal cost, to share information with those who are "outside the walls" and are known to be interested. Well-informed and enthusiastic investors (donors) who tell friends and neighbors about "my nonprofit" organization are valuable advocates as its ambassadors-at-large.

A special advantage donors enjoy is access—being "in the know," receiving direct reports, being invited to public and social events, being a part of something of value, perhaps being asked for advice. Donors enjoy knowing about—even bragging about—how their funds are being spent and the results their dollars are achieving. The challenge to each nonprofit organization is in finding ways to encourage such interest by sending donors useful information. Donors do not expect or want their contribution to be spent on brochures, newsletters, and reports sent back to them. However, they are reassured when they hear, from time to time, about the programs and services they are supporting. Some of the best communications methods are inexpensive, which suggests there are no serious barriers to communicating with donors.

INVOLVEMENT OPPORTUNITIES

Donors should be offered multiple opportunities to participate with a nonprofit organization in ways other than giving money. The key opportunity or request is service as a volunteer—giving time, energy, and talents. Most nonprofit organizations should be able to draw benefit to themselves from their volunteers' time and skills (see Exhibit 4-3). Volunteering to help with fundraising is one of several options. Some donors prefer to be involved directly with the actual programs and services provided by the nonprofit organization. A volunteer also can be a spokesperson in the community, help with identification and recruitment of others as donors and volunteers, and help to identify those in need who might benefit from the programs and services offered. Volunteers may be asked, where appropriate, to share their professional and vocational skills in management and operations areas (a major opportunity for cost savings to the nonprofit organization). The more time they give, the more they become personally involved; the more they know and experience first-hand, the more committed and dedicated they will become.

EXHIBIT 4-3   WHAT VOLUNTEERS CAN DO

✔ Help to provide service to others.
✔ Help to staff programs offered to the public.
✔ Identify those who need the programs or services.
✔ Share their skills and talents.
✔ Join a committee.
✔ Bring a friend or neighbor to a function.
✔ Provide access to others—open doors.
✔ Be an advocate.
✔ Identify others who are likely donors.
✔ Solicit others for their support.
✔ Make more gifts.
✔ Become a leader.

Donors, like investors, appreciate knowing about future plans as well as current priorities, because this kind of information reinforces their personal commitment to continue their financial support. When donors who are also volunteers are asked to make an additional special-need gift during the year, they are more likely to be well-informed about the need. It should come as no great surprise, then, that the best donors are volunteers; they are the people most directly involved in "my nonprofit" organization. Most have a good time as well, which is important. Nonprofit organizations benefit from a ripple effect of volunteer participation. Knowledge and experiences are shared with family and friends, business and social acquaintances, and others in the community. They, in turn, may want to share in the same worthwhile efforts; enthusiastic volunteers will encourage others to become involved, too. Their friends and acquaintances may become equally active as informed spokespersons, recruiters of new clients, or volunteers who give time, energy, and skills. These new volunteers will be a source of gifts as well, when asked.

Multiple Solicitations

Annual giving programs are designed to encourage multiple gifts within each 12-month period. Donors and nonprofit organizations have multiple needs that cannot be met with a single gift per person per year. Many people still think one gift is all that is needed or required of them. Donors may choose to give only once, or they can participate in several annual giving activities, such as those described in this book. For example, commemorative giving can be used as a birthday, anniversary, or holiday present to honor a friend or someone the donor respects or wishes to memorialize. In a relationship with a nonprofit organization that offers commemorative or tribute giving, donors can make several of these thoughtful gifts each year to express various messages. Over the years, donors can continue to honor the memory of a family member, business colleague, or personal friend who has passed away. A new gift is made each time. The amounts are usually modest, but they are gestures of praise or remembrance, or thoughtful expressions of sympathy that are of value to the donor and to the family or person honored. The nonprofit organization is responsible for reporting each gift to the honoree or his or her family, and can use the contact letter to describe some uses of the donated funds. Gifts of this kind are quite visible and are perceived as valuable and thoughtful by everyone involved.

Donors expect to receive more than one invitation to special and benefit events during the year. These are other forms of requests for additional gifts. Most nonprofit organizations arrange more than one such annual event, usually of a social or sporting nature. The objective is to encourage personal participation from among the universe of the organization's friends and donors. From each volunteer or donor who participates, additional funds are gained. When they are asked to volunteer a few hours to help plan an event or function in some capacity during its duration, donors can choose to give something other than money. Their participation maintains their involvement and their interest. Donors and prospects should be invited to activities and events throughout the year. If they say no, it means they cannot join in right now; it does not mean they resent being invited.

A corporate matching gift program is another area in which multiple solicitation is possible. Employers offer this program to encourage their employees (and often their retirees) to be active in civic and community service. The company agrees to match their personal contributions with a company gift of an equal or prorated amount to the same nonprofit organization. The donor benefits by causing two gifts to be made to the designated organization. The corporation benefits (1) by fulfilling a corporate objective of encouraging good citizenship among employees, and (2) by placing corporate funds in public support of charitable enterprises in the community. The nonprofit organization benefits most of all because it receives two gifts. Many companies allow their employees to participate in other gift decisions of the company. Employees who are actively involved with nonprofit organizations as donors or as volunteers are eligible to recommend that additional gifts be given to the organization in which they are active.

When donors are offered a variety of giving opportunities each year, their interest and commitment are more easily maintained. Repeated gifts often reveal preferred areas of interest. When these same programs have extra needs or require major support, the nonprofit organization should turn first to these donors to ask for help. From their personal involvement and from regular communications, they may already be well aware of these extra needs. When asked to help, they can probably be counted on to do whatever they can.

Inviting Donors to Be Volunteers

Donors should not be asked, in every communication they receive, to give money. They should be invited to share their professional and vocational skills, too. If they agree to serve by doing rather than by giving, they can save the nonprofit organization the cost of hiring part-time employees to perform the same work. The value of volunteerism is significant when donated services are expressed in financial terms. Apart from counting the hours donated or calculating how much a hired person would have to be paid for the same amount of time, volunteerism is an enormous resource that can take many forms. Within each organization are a host of projects that need attention, not in high-skill areas or in applications that require great preparation or training. They just need someone with the will to see them through.

Volunteers bring several motives with them, and often have specific areas of talent or interest in which they wish to contribute. For example, some might excel in areas that are directed outside the organization, such as advocacy or legislative support on local, statewide, or national issues. They might help via letters, petitions, and attendance (or speaking) at public hearings. Gifts of personal property, as simple as donations of food and clothing in special drives to aid the homeless and the indigent, are another area of interest. Products and merchandise might be available from a donor's employer, at a discount or free, if requested. Among the added benefits is the fact that these services are most often performed in the same community where donors work and live. Volunteerism "feels good," and the good deeds and acts of charity will be seen by others. However personal participation is expressed, it can be beneficial to a nonprofit organization. Some recently expanded activities include tutoring elementary and secondary school students, and teaching English to newly arrived immigrants. An activity may take only two to four hours a week such as driving people with disabilities or senior citizens to medical appointments, social or cultural events or being a "meals on wheels" driver to deliver a nutritious meal to "shut-ins," but the level of satisfaction gained is a high multiple of the numbers of hours worked.

Nonprofit organizations should be prepared to offer each person who wishes to volunteer a well-defined task and organized form of service, a work project with value. Nonprofit organizations thrive because of their volunteers, and the volunteers thrive because of their service. As noted in Chapter 2, satisfied volunteers who have spent time in worthwhile work are more than three times as likely as nonvolunteers to become and to remain reliable annual donors. Volunteering is one of the active ways in which people can draw as close to an organization as they choose. Organizations that plan well for public participation will be well-rewarded. These actions complement one another and, in time, the association produces increased reliability in volunteer duties, a higher level of performance, and faithful annual gifts.

Planning for Donor Recognition

Donors have needs, too. Their generosity must receive the proper response, not just routine thanks. It is important to treat donors with respect at all times. Here are some actions that might be taken on their behalf:

1. Thank donors for each gift they make.
2. Keep track of each gift and its purpose.
3. Write a different personal message in each thank-you letter (this requires some thought and effort).
4. Establish a written policy guide so that everyone in the organization knows how to manage relations with donors.
5. Plan and monitor the valued relationships being built with donors.

6. Ensure that every donor is treated equitably and fairly.

7. Send occasional (1–2 per year) reports to active donors on their donor club level and its benefits, their cumulative gift status and its privileges, and other forms of donor recognition standing.

8. Send occasional reports to donors on how their funds were used and on the progress their nonprofit organization is making in meeting community needs with their help.

Donors have a great interest in the results of their contributions. Their gifts represent being part of something valuable and making a difference. Volunteerism helps to satisfy their need to be involved, even as they implement the funds they have donated. Invitations to public events and activities encourage donors to be active within the organization. Personal letters, e-mail messages, newsletters, reports, and other communications keep them informed. What else can be done? What else do donors want? Attention, respect, and access. Those who give large amounts and those whose faithful giving builds a cumulative gift history over a period of years want to be recognized proportionately. A properly structured donor recognition program takes these differences into account.

Donors who claim their gifts as charitable contribution deductions on their annual income tax returns require supporting documentation from the nonprofit organization for each gift transaction. The Internal Revenue Service (IRS) will accept canceled checks as routine evidence for each smaller gift, but a gift substantiation letter that states details of the amount and date of the gift, any restrictions on its use, when it was received, how much, if any, is not allowed as a gift deduction, and so on, must now be supplied by nonprofit organizations to donors of all gifts of $250 or more. Nonprofit organizations that fail to provide donors with these basic services in a timely manner may lose them to other organizations that will. No extra costs are added when full details are presented in the basic thank-you letter.

A record should be kept of every gift; donor recognition can begin immediately after acquisition of the first gift. A well-defined donor recognition program makes itself visible and well known to the public. Such a program can become written policy approved by the board of directors (see discussion and Exhibit 7-4 in Chapter 7). Extra benefits and privileges are offered to donors who make larger gifts and whose cumulative or historic giving total merits special attention and/or public notice. Forms and materials used (plaques, portraits, memorabilia) should not be confused with direct purchases in exchange for gifts.

The intent of donor recognition is to convey a sincere expression of appreciation for faithfulness in giving as much as for the total amount given. One approach is to invite all donors of $500 or more (or whatever base amount is appropriate for the range of gifts received) during the past year to be guests at a special reception. The invitation can describe the reception as an expression of appreciation and an opportunity to tour the facility and see the results of their gift support. Among this event's added value is the chance to meet others who share the same degree of interest and financial support. New friendships and business contacts might develop from the meeting.

The use of premiums or *give backs* are a visible form of direct exchange for gifts. Premiums, if used, should be selected carefully. They should not cost too much and they must not trigger a reduced deduction on the value of the original gift claimed by the donor for tax purposes. The IRS requires nonprofit organizations to inform donors when the value of benefits and privileges given back *exceeds* "the 2 percent test" (the cost of the item given the donor should not be worth more than 2 percent of the original gift amount or $25, whichever is greater). Possible premiums should be studied carefully *before* they are offered, to ensure that these give backs will not adversely affect donors' tax claims and possibly negate their next gift decision.

METHODS OF DONOR RENEWAL, REVIVAL, AND REWARD

When asking donors for their next gift, the methods of solicitation are often the same as those used to acquire their first or their previous gift. The purposes of donor communications during the past year were: to increase donor awareness of the value of their support and to explain any benefits and privileges donors received. Everything presented and proposed in the interim comes together when it is time to renew the gift. Refinements to the request are worth considering. A small, select group of people is being approached, and the following improvements may help to retain a maximum number of donors and at least a repeated amount of gift dollars:

Previous Annual Gift	Improved Request
1. Form letter	1. Personal letter
2. Personal letter	2. Personal letter plus phone call
3. Personal letter and phone call	3. Phone call to request an appointment
4. Appointment	4. Personal tour

By improving the form and style of the renewal request, the organization shows that attention to the donor is a priority and that his or her continued support is valued. It will help to know: What information was received during the prior year's contacts and activities? What programs, activities, or events did the donor reply to? What other gifts did the donor make? For what purpose(s)? This information will profile the donor's degree of interest and enthusiasm and will point the way to the preferred areas of association with the organization. The donor's replies during the year are a road map for how to maintain present interest while inviting greater participation in the preferred activities.

The primary objective in renewal solicitation is to achieve gifts from as many prior donors as possible. Some will have given to other programs in the organization since their last gift; others will make only one gift, usually at about the same time each year. Some will not give again right now; others will never give again. The second objective in renewal is to persuade donors to give at least the same amount of money as before. Their pattern of giving becomes more valuable at each repetition. Upgrading (donating a larger gift) should be proposed as a way to allow the organization to achieve more of its good work.

Retention performance should recapture at least 50 percent of the prior donors each year. If that percentage cannot be repeated, the organization may never achieve a secure financial base of public support because (1) replacing the funds realized from prior donors is enormously difficult; (2) more costs, in time, multiple requests, and general expenses, are required because the same amount of money must be found among nondonors through acquisition; and (3) the relationship with prior donors may be lost.

It is important to try to understand why the donations were not repeated. A review of the communications and activities of the past year may yield clues. If the prior donors were unresponsive to all appeals and then did not renew their annual gift, it may be fair to assume that their first gift was less of a commitment than an experiment to see how the organization performed. Most of the time, a donor who is unresponsive to the organization's other invitations can be assumed to be uninterested in further giving.

Resolicitation messages should remind donors that their benefits and privileges will expire unless a renewal gift is received. A printer's deadline for the annual report, which will contain the names of all donors who renew their gifts, should be announced early and often. It remains important to stress the value of the support and good works made possible by prior gifts, but human nature is such that retaining privileges and remaining on a published list are strong motivating factors. Every nonprofit organization would like to be able to rely on a core of proven donors whose faithful annual support meets all its current and future monetary needs. Board members, management staff, and employees work hard throughout the year to fulfill their part of the gift exchange bargain; renewal is the donors' part. The renewal request might mention this partnership in a message that enumerates the areas of need that depend on continued giving. People have to *want* to give; there is no requirement that they must do so. All any nonprofit organization can do is put its performance on the line and be sure to ask as well as it can.

Not everyone will give faithfully, year after year. Some attrition should be expected, but it can and should be contained as much as possible. A 50 percent retention rate is recommended as a guide. Donor communications, involvement, and recognition are all pointed toward achieving and exceeding this goal. Resolicitation has the potential to perform *five to eight times* more profitably than acquisition of the same number of equally generous first-time donors. Donors are always better prospects than those who have never given. What may tip the scale is whether donors have heard from the organization more than once since their last gift and how they reacted to the interim communications.

Asking: How Many Times?

When asking prior donors to give again, there comes a point where reasonable propriety blows a whistle. Bombarding people with repeated requests (once a month for six months) can become offensive. Wise fundraisers will review all the other communications, especially requests of any type, that were sent to donors within the past 30, 60, or 90 days. (Exhibit 4-1 will help.) To continue solicitation endlessly is likely to be fruitless, can breed criticism and resentment, and should be discontinued, at least temporarily, when it becomes financially unprofitable. Donor records will report what other gifts these donors have been making during the year, when their last gifts were made, and details about their preferences, timing, and gift amounts. Delinquent donors should not be treated as a group; each has had individual reasons for discontinuing support.

When should the effort stop? The results of prior renewal solicitations will help to indicate when others from the same community felt an appeal had run its course of efficiency and cost-effectiveness. Because prior donors remain from five to eight times more likely to give than nondonors, other opportunities for the same list should be created later on. The final answer lies in good judgment and attention to performance data. The organization's first business is friend-raising.

There is an old theory in fundraising that no name should be removed from a mailing list, no matter what it costs to maintain it there. The reasoning is that donors are always better prospects than nondonors, so they should be kept forever. This assumption is enhanced by the retelling of a tale of a one-time $25 donor who died a decade later and left the organization a large bequest. The organization had kept writing, year after year, without any reply; the rationalization suggested is that the bequest was received because the donor's name was kept on the mailing list. Permanent mailing lists are hard to justify today, when accountability for fundraising expenses (printing, postage, staff time, and so on) must be measured with efficiency and cost-effective results. Accountability, a hard taskmaster, is not sympathetic to mythical and apocryphal stories of fortuitous and unknown bequests. It is not profitable to continue to solicit every living donor of record on the off-chance that these messages enhance the unlikely possibility of an unseen future legacy. Instead, there may be good reason to introduce a planned giving program, given an adequate size and age of the donor pool. Details about planned giving and estate planning options can and should be communicated to all donors easily throughout the year.

Among the important reasons for keeping records of prior donors' gifts is the link between cumulative and historic giving and the donor recognition program. Each gift made—no matter when, for what purpose, or in what form—is added to the donor's permanent gift history. Over time, as the cumulative total begins to build, the donor qualifies for added benefits and privileges, as defined by the donor recognition policy (see Chapter 7). A cumulative history of all gifts has many purposes. It reveals areas of special interest favored by the donor, preferred solicitation methods, responses to event invitations and campaign solicitations, routine levels of annual support, attendance records at benefits and public events, occasional major gifts, planned giving activity, and much more. This same donor profile is a valuable guide to volunteers and staff in assessing key interest areas, gift amounts, and timing for the next renewal solicitation. Should a donor be invited to consider an increase in his or her annual gift to qualify for a gift club? Is a faithful donor ready to undertake a major gift opportunity? Should a long-term donor be approached about an estate planning interview? The donor gift history may hint at the next level of recognition a donor is ready to achieve. Visible recognition can be the extra incentive needed for an increased next gift. Recognition levels can also be used as an incentive to join the next level in the donor club program.

PERFORMANCE ANALYSIS

Why is measurement of donors' renewal performance a must? To monitor how many donors continued, how much they gave, and how many (and what funds) were lost. The following list of performance characteristics should be reviewed after each renewal solicitation:

1. The percentage of prior donors who renewed
2. Their average gift size
3. How many donors renewed
4. How many donors increased, decreased, or maintained their annual gift (gain–loss report)
5. How many donors were asked to increase or "upgrade" their last gifts and what increased amount (if any) was received
6. The total dollars received (all renewal efforts)
7. The detailed results of each renewal program summarizing results of items 1–6
8. What other gifts were stimulated (number and amount)
9. How many donors retained their donor club level, how many increased to a new level, and how many fell below their last level

10. How many failed to renew, and the value of their last gifts

11. How current results compare with last year's

12. What changes are needed before the next renewal

13. The total cost of each renewal solicitation and the cost–benefit ratio comparison with revenue produced

It is also important to review the giving performance of prior donors throughout the year. Are they making more gifts this year compared to last year? To which programs? For how much money? How does this year's total compare to those of prior years? These faithful donors and their multiple gift decisions speak eloquently of their personal estimation of the worth of the nonprofit organization's leaders, staff, programs, and services. Their history also illustrates the level of their commitment, their willingness to be involved, and their confidence and trust that the organization is using their money well. These donors are rare and precious jewels; they are your organization's best friends. How should they be shown appreciation?

Upgrading Annual Gifts

One of the least understood renewal techniques is *upgrading*. Experience has proven that from 10 to 15 percent of prior donors will increase their gift when asked to do so. However, a more telling statistic is that the *other 85 to 90 percent* are more likely to renew their gift *at the same amount*. These favorable results come at no added cost—the upgrade request is included as part of the renewal invitation. An upgrade request should be a regular part of every renewal invitation because of its value to preserve donors' level of giving. The 15 percent who give more are worth extra attention too—membership status or induction into a donor club—especially if they are making other gifts to the organization during the year.

Lybunts, Pybunts or Sybunts, and Locusts

Lapsed donors are individuals who did not make any gifts within the past year. William Grasty and Kenneth Sheinkopf[1] divide them into these categories:

Lybunts	Last year but unfortunately not this year
Pybunts	Prior year but unfortunately not this year

| Sybunts | Some year but unfortunately not this year |
| Locusts | People who give every seven years |

All of these people are prior donors and will remain better prospects than nondonors. How should they be resolicited? Segregation and personal treatment might work. For example, assume that, if asked, they will respond again, at a rate better than nondonors' rate. The guideline for nondonors is response from 1 percent of the list to be compared to donor renewal rates of 50 percent and higher. When lapsed donors' replies fall to low, single-digit levels, the list may be used up. Another measurement is gift amount. The longer the span between the last gift and the most recent resolicitation request, the more the gift will fall below prior levels. Experience will identify each organization's performance measurement guideline. It is not unreasonable to solicit every prior donor at least once a year, usually as part of the regular year-end appeal. Eventually, the organization will maximize whatever retention is possible, and can retire (throw away) the list.

It is always difficult to know whether to retire a list of "old" prior donors. Costs are always involved, and advocates of keeping them need to make some effort to contact them during each year, even if only through newsletters, reports, and similar media. An inexpensive piece might be sent to them a week or two before resolicitation, especially in the first and second year after their last gift. All donors should continue to be informed about the organization and its current priorities; it may be possible to re-stimulate their desire to help. Or, given recent economic conditions, the desire to help may have been constant but the means may not. No suggestion that they have been resistant or stubborn should be allowed entry into thinking or communications. Special handling just might restart their gifts, and it allows room for good reasons for not giving. They may need to be treated differently than before, perhaps welcomed warmly on a lower level of giving. Did they reply to any other invitations or requests? If so, does the amount solicited give any clue to what they can afford now? Some assumptions can be made about why they may have declined to give, but the focus should be on their concerns and on reporting how the organization has improved. All who do respond again, no matter what the gift size compared with prior history, should be welcomed back with a special thank-you letter. There is every prospect now that, with care and sensitive attention, they may remain faithful donors for many years to come.

There are exceptions to the general rule about keeping people on a mailing list. Those who ask to be removed from the list should be deleted immediately. They should not have to repeat the instruction. If they continue to receive appeals, they will become irritated by the insensitivity to and lack of respect for their request. A former friend will become an outspoken enemy. The deleted names should be transferred to a "Do Not Mail" list or a "flush file," against which all future mailings can be cross-checked.

Performance Review

Fund development staff should analyze their own results and confer together about their messages, materials, schedules, and achievements. Some of the specific areas to review are:

1. What were the results of each solicitation activity?
2. How well was each message received?
3. Were any trends seen in the responses?
4. How did the message and performance of each program affect the response to each of the others?
5. Were there any generic or unusual problem areas?
6. What recommendations would be suitable for the next sequence of solicitations?

Staff discussions should include an evaluation of the amount of coordination achieved in areas such as the use of mailing lists, the schedule for special appeals, the underwriting and sponsorship of coming events, the mailing schedule for invitations to benefits and special events, the authorship and distribution of newsletters and annual reports, and the approaches used in mailings, telephone campaigns, telemarketing, facsimile, and Internet activities addressed to donors. Objective analysis of each program's performance will encourage interrelated effort, higher levels of efficiency, and greater cost-effectiveness. The progress of the overall fund-development program is linked to the success of each activity and of the total effort to welcome new friends, renew old friendships, and raise more dollars.

Fund development staff should also confer with their colleagues at nearby nonprofit organizations. They should share data to compare their performance with similar fundraising methods. Attendance figures at activities and events are among the solid data available for comparison. Staff participation in fundraising conferences and workshops encourages learning from the experience of others, helps to interpret the implications of results, and invites other suggestions that may improve both response rates and performance (profitability). Methods of fundraising vary in success among nonprofit organizations, but the practice and performance of traditional annual giving methods and techniques in common practice elsewhere, especially locally, can be instructive. Differences in performance are most often traceable to subjective factors such as geography, type and frequency of common solicitation methods, volunteer training, and length of time each solicitation program has been in operation. Observation of the results of others helps to detect changes in public responsiveness to techniques and to appeal messages. Incoming direct mail is a good barometer of what others, both for-profit and nonprofit, have estimated to be public attitudes about the priorities of community needs. Staff can monitor the following factors and ask about results in data comparison surveys:

- Direct mail packages they receive at home
- Telephone and Internet appeals
- Subtle details such as "teaser" messages on the outer envelope, colors used, signature style, and number of pieces per package
- Urgency and relevance of community needs and their match to the vision and mission of the organization
- Use of one-, two-, or four-page letter texts
- Use of postage-paid versus "your stamp here" return envelopes
- Donor club programs, gift levels, and benefits offered
- Premiums and "give backs" and their link to various gift amounts
- Frequency of all communications methods, linkage of the message, timing of their release, and tracking of all responses
- Results from use of multimedia strategy and tactics

Evaluation of mail samples used by other, established annual giving programs, especially those with experience in the same community, can suggest new options and guide future decisions. Comparisons of the mail packages of both commercial and nonprofit mailers can point to what others have assessed to be working best with local audiences. Commercial mailers are good illustrators of "what's hot" in the direct response advertising business. Their methods may not work for nonprofit organizations (even if they could afford their higher costs), but they remain a solid barometer of what form(s) of sales appeal prompt the best in public responsiveness. Monitoring of other mail users will open up some possibilities and may justify changes in the appeal message's length, design, and content; donor clubs; premium offers; timing; and similar characteristics of the package.

Fund-development staff should also confer often with their colleagues in the planning, marketing, community relations, publications, public relations, and volunteer departments. These internal groups are in frequent communication with members of the same organization's constituency (community residents). Their objectives and their messages have the same origins, even if what they promote or request may be different. Frequently, their goal is to establish a positive image or to stimulate the public's use of the organization's programs and services. A high degree of coordination, cooperation, and communication among staff departments can only improve on the success each will have individually in meeting annual goals and objectives. Critical to fund development in particular is the realization that, if these staff partners and their communications programs are effective, they help the entire fundraising performance. If their efforts are not effective, fundraising success will be hindered. Collaboration should also include sharing the results of everyone's separate measurements and analyses of results. All these data are useful to the entire team's involvement in public communications.

Another internal group to talk with are those on the "front line"—the professional and support staff who provide programs and services directly to the public. Their daily contact gives them a unique sense of what people need and want plus what is known and thought about the organization. They hear firsthand how it is perceived, what are judged to be its strengths and weaknesses, and how it is rated "on the street." Professional support staff have a critical role in advancing the organization's goodwill and positive image: they interact directly with the public at the point of service. They hear about the communications mistakes made, the criticism aimed at the number of appeals received at home, and the rumors and incorrect information their clients may hear and repeat. Direct public contacts are critical input for professional and support staff. An employee can enhance or harm the good image of an organization, multiplying or undoing all the goodwill that countless mailings, messages, and activities have established over many years. Donors and volunteers can offend someone, or become offended enough to speak against the organization. Volunteers and donors are "customers" too, and poor customer relations can hurt the entire organization more severely than good customer relations has the power to repair.

In the intensity of providing service every day, hard-working "frontline" employees and professional staff members can forget that those being served are possibly the same people who have supported their department with personal gifts. Fund development staff should ask to address groups of employees about the public they serve. Everyone within the organization must be aware of the exterior relationships donors have and the need for positive donor relations and good customer relations. Sensitivity to the reality that "the public" is, has been, could be, or will be donors, volunteers, and friends is essential, not optional, among staff members.

Professional Help Is Readily Available

Outside consultants and other professionals are available to assist in interpreting public responses and evaluating every area of annual giving performance. Their experience can help guide decisions to make changes that will improve results and bring variety into future plans. These professionals can help in all the areas of planning, marketing, publications, public relations, community relations, volunteering, and fund development, and usually at reasonable fees. Consultants provide an objective view of present programs and their performance; their broad experience allows them to interpret results based on multiple organizational experiences. Consultants often become working partners with staff and volunteers, monitoring results and guiding future decisions. They have firsthand knowledge of other organizations' performance, and, although professional standards of confidentiality limit the detail they can reveal about other clients, they can give beneficial insights. Because of their length of experience and their concentration and expertise on specific fundraising methods (such as direct mail, telephone, Internet, or special events), they can also provide detailed recommendations on mailing-list choices, list merchants and letter shops, skillful letter writing, package design, added inserts, and audience reactions. They prove their value when their suggestions reduce the cost of mail communications *and* improve net income in a subsequent year.

Other professionals whose knowledge and experience are outside the organization can also be of great use. Local market research firms constantly monitor public reactions, survey public attitudes, and perfect their demographic data. Creative design firms constantly test public responsiveness to the products each of their clients uses. Entry into the fields of telecommunications, television, video messaging, video conferences, the Internet, and other new-age communications also are necessary in order to reach select constituents with reliability. Modern mass communications is an area that nonprofit organizations must learn how to use to their advantage. The days are long gone when highly motivated (and overworked) employees could approach these communication techniques to learn "just enough to achieve adequate results." Without professional guidance in the highly competitive arena of mass public communications, a nonprofit organization will more likely fail to be seen and heard, and will fail to find the donors who might have provided the money to fulfill its mission.

DONOR RELATIONS

Attention to annual donors through recognition and reward should be a proactive part of every nonprofit organization. The budget required to be nice to these best friends is small in comparison to the extent of their current and future generosity. Donors have invested in the organization and should be treated accordingly. Opportunities to be nice are readily available. Some suggestions are:

1. Send them special invitations to regular public events held at or by the organization.
2. Ask them to be guests at a VIP table at one of the benefit events.
3. Invite them to give a testimonial interview about their gift decision for publication.
4. Invite them to tour a new or renovated part of the facilities.
5. Mail their copy of the next newsletter, brochure, e-mail message, or annual report with a brief personal cover note attached.

EXHIBIT 4-4   DONOR RECOGNITION PROGRAMS
FOR ANNUAL DONORS

A. Donors whose cumulative *annual* contributions add to the following gift levels will
be accorded full donor recognition privileges for the following year:

Amounts	*Donor Recognition Level*
$100 to $499	Circle of Champions Club
500 to 999	Ambassadors

B. Donors whose cumulative contributions add to $1,000 or more will be accorded
permanent donor recognition benefits and privileges on the main Donor Wall
as follows:

Amounts	*Donor Recognition Level*
$ 1,000 to $2,499	Friends
2,500 to 4,999	Sponsors
5,000 to 9,999	Patrons/life members
10,000 to 24,999	Benefactors
25,000 to 49,999	Meritorious benefactors
50,000 to 99,999	Honored benefactors
100,000 or more	Distinguished benefactors

C. Donors of future interest, planned, and estate gifts, including irrevocable gifts in
trust, life estates, and gift annuities, will be accorded full donor recognition benefits and privileges as members of the Heritage Society. The names of these individuals will be added to the Heritage Society section of the main Donor Wall.

Because it makes good sense to pay attention to donors, it is reasonable
to define a written policy that provides for consistent treatment to every
donor, fairly and equitably, year after year (see Exhibit 4-4). It also makes
good sense to establish donor clubs that give extra privileges and special attention to larger donors. Well-treated donors will continue to reward their
favorite nonprofit organizations with additional gifts. It makes good sense
to report regularly on the good results achieved with donors' funds and to
speak out about the charitable purposes their funds have helped to provide.
Prior donors are much more likely to continue to give if they receive attention, respect, consideration, and warm, friendly treatment.

FOCUS: CCUA CLEAN UP CLEVELAND CHAPTER

The initial "roll out" letter campaign for the Clean Up Cleveland Chapter produced more than 1,500 donors from last fall's first acquisition mailing. Harvey Clout was disappointed that only 1,500 Cleveland residents had replied with money. Karen Anderson, Director of Development, after clarifying that only one letter had been mailed to 80,000 people, pointed out that a 1.8 percent response was quite good, especially for a new organization and without media coverage to help spread the word. She added that the letters had been effective in informing a select group of key residents first, an important step in this city. When she told Clout that people were talking about the chapter's bumper stickers, he confessed that he had received positive comments about them too, and had seen quite a few around town. He agreed that their message was beginning to be heard after all, and asked Anderson to develop suggestions about what they should do next.

"Roll Out" and First Renewal Mailing Plans

Anderson has studied the results of the test mailings to the six original lists and has compared them with the roll out letter campaign, which was mailed to four of these same test lists. She believes the mailing list should now be expanded to every fifth homeowner in the city of Cleveland and to the ten largest residential suburbs. She also believes she can justify, based on past performance, a mailing budget for a total of 200,000 names. She recommends (1) a two-part acquisition mailing for the spring (drop dates of March 15 and April 30) and (2) a first renewal request using a computer-personalized letter format to resolicit all 1,504 new donors (348 from the July test and 1,156 from the fall roll out). The chapter is now in a new tax year; prior gifts in reply to the test mailings were made between four and ten months ago. The renewal replies are projected to speed up cash flow and help pay for all the mailing costs incurred in the first half of this fiscal year. However, Anderson decides not to resolicit those names on the four test lists that did not respond well to the fall test mailings. In her opinion, after two solicitations within six months last year, they have been tapped out and should be reserved for next fall's mailing sequence. Some of these same residents might be on the new rental lists to be used in the spring roll out mailing, but that is not a problem. Anderson drafts a news story to be released March 15, the drop date of the next mailing. To get additional coverage, she will ask the board to make a few phone calls to local papers and radio stations in an effort to spread the word about the CCUA Clean Up Cleveland Chapter's campaign and to alert the public about the open invitation for them to join.

With all this planning completed, Anderson rents a list of every fifth homeowner in Cleveland and its ten major suburbs through Cleveland Mass Communications, a local mail house hired to prepare the 200,000-piece mailing using the chapter's new third-class, bulk-rate permit. She decides to continue to use the text of Letter B (see Exhibit 3-5) as her appeal letter. She also drafts Letter C (Exhibit 4-5), a follow-up solicitation text to be mailed 45 days after Letter B is dropped.

Her next project is Letter D (Exhibit 4-6), a renewal request to be sent to all 1,504 first-time donors in the fall campaign. This letter will be a combination renewal and upgrade solicitation appeal and will be mailed (first class) on March 14, one day ahead of the drop date for the 200,000 community invitation letters. Anderson then designs a new Circle of Champions information card (Exhibit 4-7), to be inserted into all the spring mail packages. The card will test the idea of an individual membership in the CCUA Clean Up Cleveland Chapter and will encourage larger gifts.

Anderson reviews all these proposals and draft texts with Harold Connected, whom the board has just appointed as chair of the development committee. Connected was a board member at the local Audubon

---

EXHIBIT 4-5   LETTER C: FOLLOW-UP MAILING TO EVERY FIFTH HOUSEHOLD

THE CAMPAIGN TO CLEAN UP AMERICA
CLEAN UP CLEVELAND CHAPTER

April 30, 200X

Dear Concerned Resident:

Last fall, we began our campaign in Cleveland by asking community residents to join with us in cleaning the streets of our city. We had over 1,500 positive replies.

On March 15, we mailed our second invitation and have already received more than 2,000 replies. If you missed our letter, you may want to check us out this time around.

(continued)

EXHIBIT 4-5   (CONTINUED)

I'm sure you have seen the new Clean Up Cleveland bumper stickers around town. They are ours, and if you do not have one, call my office and we'll send you one, free.

All I ask in return is that you join us to help clean up our city streets and, if you can, send us a personal gift to help us in our campaign.

Pollution is a tough problem; I know, because I operate a steel mill and we've invested millions to clean up the air. But, that's not enough.

The Clean Up Cleveland Chapter of The Campaign to Clean Up America aims to remove trash from our city streets and convert it into electricity we can all use. That's a great plan with a bonus. Here's how it will work.

We have to raise $1,250,000 to build the new energy conversion plant; the rest of the money will come from federal and Ohio matching funds. We'll be cleaning up our streets at the same time.

We will use 75 percent of your gift to help build the plant, which will reduce everyone's electric bills by $12 a month and $144 a year. The other 25 percent helps to pay for our public education campaign.

Your gift of $12 will come back to you. If you give us $25 or more, these plans will all happen sooner.

Join us now. Give what you can to help, and spread the word to Clean Up Cleveland.

Sincerely yours,

I. Harvey Clout
Chair of the Board
Cleveland Cast Iron Works

P.S. Charter membership in our Circle of Champions is still open. Please consider an entry gift of $100 or more if you can. Many thanks.

EXHIBIT 4-6   LETTER D: RENEWAL AND UPGRADE SOLICITATION

THE CAMPAIGN TO CLEAN UP AMERICA
CLEAN UP CLEVELAND CHAPTER

March 14, 200X

Mr. and Mrs. Robert A. Smith
16210 Shaker Boulevard
Shaker Heights, OH 44120

Dear Mr. and Mrs. Smith:

Thank you again for your contribution last fall. Your gift helped to launch our campaign on its way to success.

I have three purposes in writing to you today.

First, I can report that more than 1,500 local residents like yourselves heard our call for action. Total contributions were $35,758, an average of just over $30 per person. Ours was a great beginning, thanks to you.

Our plans for use of these funds are that the first 75 percent is set aside to build the energy conversion plant, with the remaining 25 percent used to continue our Clean Up Cleveland public education campaign.

My second reason is to alert you that we are mailing tomorrow more than 200,000 invitations to selected local residents, asking them to join with you in this campaign.

If you have placed a Clean Up Cleveland bumper sticker on your car or truck, friends and neighbors may be asking you what it means. Enclosed is another bumper sticker. Tell our story and ask others to join now.

My third reason is to ask you to consider your next gift to our campaign, perhaps a larger gift this time. Our campaign is far from over, and we need you to continue your support.

Our introductory offer to become a charter member of the Circle of Champions donor club with a gift of $100 or more is still open (see the enclosed card for full details). Charter members will be invited to a special event by both the Cleveland Orchestra and the Cleveland Play House.

(continued)

EXHIBIT 4-6   (CONTINUED)

Thank you again for your first gift last year. I hope you will continue to support our communitywide effort to Clean Up Cleveland. I look forward to hearing from you again soon.

Sincerely yours,

I. Harvey Clout
Chair of the Board
Cleveland Cast Iron Works

Encl. 2

EXHIBIT 4-7   CIRCLE OF CHAMPIONS
MEMBERSHIP INFORMATION CARD

THE CAMPAIGN TO CLEAN UP AMERICA
CLEAN UP CLEVELAND CHAPTER

Circle of Champions
Charter Membership Offer (at $100)

Membership Categories

All active members will receive:
- Quarterly progress reports
- Two complimentary tickets to
  (a) Summer concert at the Blossom
      Music Center
  (b) Premier of a new show at the
      Cleveland Play House
- Annual report

[ ] $100 Active membership

[ ] $250 Family membership

[ ] $500 Ambassador member

[ ] $1,000 Cleveland Clean-up
     Crew (CCC)

For more information, please call the
Clean Up Cleveland office at (216) CLEAN UP.

Society chapter and knows of Anderson's prior success in managing its membership program by mail. He agrees to her plans and invites her to present them at the January board of directors meeting.

At the meeting, the board reviews the project in some detail and approves the entire program. A budget of $150,000 is authorized for the costs of mailing the pieces selected, for analysis of the results (Exhibits 4-8, 4-9, and 4-10), for mailing of a thank-you letter (Exhibit 4-11), and for preparation and release of a news story in support of the spring mailing (Exhibit 4-12).

Results and Analysis

At the May board of directors meeting, Anderson reports on the results of the spring mail campaign. She begins with a review of the two-part acquisition mailing (Letters B and C) to every fifth household in Cleveland and ten residential suburbs:

1. A total of 3,653 new donors were acquired!
2. A total of $116,911 was received!
3. An average gift of $32 was achieved!
4. Mailing costs for Letters B and C were $99,000.
5. Net mailing proceeds were $17,911.
6. Cost per dollar raised was at 85 percent.
7. A total of 76 new donors who joined the Circle of Champions gave a total of $8,550, for an average gift of $112.50.

For Letter D, the combined renewal and upgrade solicitation text that was sent to the 1,504 first-time donors, the results were as follows:

1. The number who renewed was 914 (60.77%)!
2. A total of $31,064 was received!
3. The average gift increased to $33.99!
4. A total of 94 members recruited to the Circle of Champions gave a total of $12,502, for an average gift of $133.
5. The cost of the renewal mailing was $1,827.
6. Net proceeds were $29,237.
7. Cost per dollar raised was $0.06.

Combining all mail results to date, including last July's test letters and the roll out of Letter B, Anderson reports that solicitation letters

EXHIBIT 4-8   RESULTS OF ROLL OUT, LETTER B AND LETTER C

Destination	Letter Sent	Number Mailed	Replies Number	Replies Percent	Gift Income	Average Gift
Cleveland	B	100,000	650	0.65%	$ 16,601	$25.54
City Limits	C*	98,795	605	0.61	17,521	28.96
Cleveland	B	20,000	212	1.06	10,600	50.00
Heights and University Heights	C	19,245	213	1.11	12,985	60.96
Lyndhurst	B	20,000	205	1.03	4,588	22.38
	C	18,985	190	1.00	4,096	21.56
Lakewood	B	15,000	192	1.28	6,365	33.15
	C	14,355	216	1.51	4,005	18.54
Lorain	B	15,000	172	1.15	5,136	29.86
	C	12,995	182	1.40	6,679	36.70
Parma	B	20,000	209	1.05	6,615	31.65
	C	18,887	229	1.21	7,607	33.22
Mentor and	B	12,000	191	1.59	7,031	36.81
Willoughby	C	11,205	187	1.67	7,082	37.87
Total/Average	B	202,000	1,831	0.91	$ 56,936	$31.10
	C	194,467	1,822	0.94	59,975	32.92
Total/Average	(B + C)	396,467	3,653	0.92%	$116,911	$32.00

Costs:		
	List rental (@ $25/1,000 × 200,000)	$ 5,000
	Printing costs (@ $.12 each × 400,000)	48,000
	Outer envelope (.02)	
	Reply envelope (.02)	
	Letters (.06)	
	"Circle" cards (.02)	
	Bumper stickers (@ .01 each × 200,000)	2,000
	Computer services/mail preparations	12,000
	Postage (@ 0.08 each)	32,000
	Total (@ 0.2475 each):	$99,000

*The Letter C list is smaller because of gifts received (donors' names are removed from the list, to prevent future solicitation for the same campaign), undelivered mail, and "Do not mail" replies from Letter B.

EXHIBIT 4-9   RESULTS OF LETTER D: FIRST RENEWAL REQUEST

		First Donor Gifts (Tests)			First Renewal Gifts		
Donor Area	Donor Population	Number of Replies	Gift Income	Average Gift	Number of Replies	Gift Income	Average Size
Shaker Heights							
residents	Test	64	$ 1,407	$21.98	38	$ 879	$23.15
	Full	414	18,321	44.25	308	14,440	46.88
	Total	478	19,727	41.27	338	15,319	45.32
NE Ohio Audubon							
Society	Test	100	3,000	30.00	58	1,880	32.41
	Full	372	8,916	23.96	197	4,950	25.13
	Total	472	11,916	25.25	255	6,830	26.78
NE Ohio Nature							
Conservancy	Test	68	1,500	22.06	36	885	24.58
	Full	158	3,476	22.00	82	1,950	23.78
	Total	226	4,976	22.02	118	2,835	24.03
Orchestra/Play House							
subscribers	Test	50	1,440	28.80	27	950	35.19
	Full	212	5,045	23.80	135	3,450	25.56
	Total	262	6,485	24.75	162	4,500	27.77
Eastern suburbs							
homeowners	Test	30	340	11.33	22	1,200	54.55
Sports tickets	Test	36	840	23.33	19	380	20.00
	Totals	1,504	$44,285	$29.45	914	$31,064	$33.99

Retention rate = 60.77%
Cost of mailing: = ($1.215 × 1,504) = $1,827.36
"Circle" renewals = Started with 118; retained 78
Upgraded 10; added 6 new = 94

EXHIBIT 4-10   NINE-POINT PERFORMANCE INDEX ANALYSIS OF DIRECT MAIL PROGRAM

	Testing		Full Mailing		Renewal		Totals
Participation	1,504	+	3,653	+	914	=	6,071
Income	$44,285	+	$116,911	+	$31,064	=	$192,260
Expense	$38,468	+	$99,000	+	$1,827	=	$139,295
Percent participation	2.00%	+	0.92%	+	60.77%	=	1.20%
Average gift size	$29.44	+	$32.00	+	$33.99	=	$31.81
Net income	$5,817	+	$17,911	+	$29,237	=	$52,965
Average cost per gift	$25.58	+	$27.10	+	$2.00	=	$22.94
Cost of fundraising	87%	+	85%	+	6%	=	72%
Return	15%	+	18%	+	1600%	=	39%

and bumper stickers have now been mailed to more than 280,000 residents. A grand total of 5,127 donor-residents have replied with a total of $192,260 in contributions. With overall costs of $139,295, the net proceeds are $52,965. The success of the Circle of Champions membership introductory offer and the strength of the first renewal response have been encouraging. Overall results in this first year are well above the national standard of $1 to raise $1, using only direct mail. "The reason for our success," Anderson tells the board, "is increased public concern about pollution of the environment. I've talked with the development officers at several other chapters of The Campaign to Clean Up America; they are also reporting good results. It seems the public is ready to respond with action, if given a valid purpose." Anderson concludes her report to the board with two recommendations:

1. The fall mailing campaign should concentrate exclusively on membership in the CCUA Clean Up Cleveland Chapter.

2. Because of the strong community support shown to date, applications should be prepared for submission to local corporations and foundations for grants (a) to support the energy conversion plant as a major capital construction project, or (b) to expand the public education campaign throughout northeast Ohio.

Both recommendations are approved. Anderson is directed to proceed according to the plan she has outlined.

EXHIBIT 4-11   THANK-YOU LETTER TO NEW
CIRCLE OF CHAMPIONS DONOR

THE CAMPAIGN TO CLEAN UP AMERICA
CLEAN UP CLEVELAND CHAPTER

April, 200X

Mr. and Mrs. Robert A. Smith
16210 Shaker Boulevard
Shaker Heights, OH 44120

Dear Mr. and Mrs. Smith:

Thank you for your wonderful gift of $100, and welcome to Charter Membership in our Circle of Champions donor club. I value your personal support very much.

With your extra help, we move closer to our goals of cleaning up our city streets and building the new energy conversion plant.

You will be hearing from the Cleveland Orchestra and Cleveland Play House in the next few weeks about your invitation to each of their entertainment events. Both are planning a special program for all our Charter Members.

By the way, our Clean Up Cleveland bumper stickers are fast becoming a hot item around town. I'm enclosing two more for your use or to share with a neighbor. If you want more, just call my office at 565-9500.

Again, thank you for your generous gift and for your commitment to support our efforts to achieve a cleaner city and lower electric rates.

Sincerely yours,

I. Harvey Clout
Chair of the Board
Cleveland Cast Iron Works

Encl. 2

EXHIBIT 4-12   SAMPLE NEWS RELEASE IN
SUPPORT OF AN EARLY MAILING

FOR RELEASE AT 9:00 A.M., MARCH 18, 200X
CLEVELAND, OHIO

Harvey Clout, head of Cleveland Cast Iron Works, has announced the inaugu-
ration of the Clean Up Cleveland Chapter of America's newest environmental
advocacy group, The Campaign to Clean Up America.

The local chapter is the eighth to be established in the past six months. Others
are in Atlanta, Detroit, Chicago, Los Angeles, Newark, New York, and Pittsburgh.

Mr. Clout also announced a special project adopted by the Clean Up Cleveland
Chapter: To build an energy conversion plant that will turn trash into electricity for
local use. A local fundraising campaign has begun to provide $1,250,000, one-third
of the funds required. The balance will come from federal and state energy grants.

Several public awareness campaigns are in preparation to increase awareness of
every resident's duty to help keep city and neighborhood, streets clean. "A clean
neighborhood is a safe neighborhood," stated Mr. Clout. "Our environment is
made up of more than clean air and clean water. It also includes collecting and
proper use of the trash that litters our streets."

"Clean Up Cleveland" bumper stickers are being mailed to local residents to
encourage public support of this new effort. The local chapter is also inviting
residents to join the new organization. Membership contributions begin at $12.
Charter memberships in the newly formed "Circle of Champions" are available for
a $100 annual contribution.

In addition to Mr. Clout, who is also serving as chair of the board, members of
the local board of directors include vice chair Mary Moneybanks and treasurer
Sidney Secure, CPA. The secretary and assistant secretary are Theodosius "Ted"
Worthy and Titus Brown, APR.

To request a bumper sticker or additional information about giving to support
this campaign, please call (216) CLEAN UP.

CHAPTER 5

Membership and Membership Associations

The effort to acquire and retain donors who will give again this year, next year, and the year after that, takes some creativity and requires personal attention to these individuals. Why not invite them to become part of the organization? Treat them like members of the family so that they are more likely to remain close to the organization. Nonprofit organizations can offer a variety of reasons why people might join up:

1. Members are partners in fulfilling the mission.
2. Members associate with others who have similar interests and share a common cause.
3. Membership makes individuals part of an organized and successful group.
4. Membership offers an opportunity to get involved in voluntary community, service, or civic work.
5. Members become advocates for causes they care about.
6. Members make a commitment for an annual level of giving.
7. Members can give something back to the community.
8. Membership brings the respect of others.

The advantages and challenges in offering a formal membership program to donors should be weighed carefully. Obligations are required of members,

EXHIBIT 5-1　QUALITIES AND CHARACTERISTICS OF MEMBERSHIP PROGRAMS.*

Membership builds loyalty. It gives people a greater sense of ownership or participation in the organization's mission and activities.

Membership builds depth of commitment. People feel they are important beyond simply the amount of money they can give. Their volunteer help, opinions, and, sometimes, voting rights on policy and program matters are also important to the organization.

Membership includes participation as part of the organization's action network.

Members expect to be called on to take certain actions, such as participating in petition drives or writing to elected officials, especially as "hot" issues arise in the public arena.

Membership conceptually prepares people to continue their support through annual membership renewals. When a person becomes a *donor* to an organization, he or she does not necessarily expect to be asked to renew the gift; a *member* knows or assumes that membership renewal will be an annual event.

Membership programs solicit a higher-quality donor. Although it may be more difficult initially to solicit a membership dues gift rather than a one-time donation, supporters who do say yes to the membership option will usually stay with the organization longer. Members are also more likely to respond to appeals for larger gifts.

*Reprinted with permission

and professional staff are necessary to manage the ongoing membership programs. The advantages are many, however. Exhibit 5-1 reproduces Constance Clark's[1] analysis of what membership is, what it does, and why it is important.

There are a variety of civic and service membership associations across America today. Not all are available everywhere. Some restrict their membership; others limit access on the basis of qualification. For example, membership in a college alumni association usually requires a period of formal student status. Every membership association is prohibited by law from discrimination on the basis of sex, race, creed, physical handicap, or national origin. Most of the membership programs offered by nonprofit organizations are open to anyone who is willing to make an annual gift. Other qualifications may be an interest in joining, the annual payment of dues or a requested gift amount, and a willingness to support the mission, vision, values, purposes, goals, and objectives of the organization.

LEGAL AND TAX-EXEMPT STATUS

There can be many forms of membership association. Among the several legal forms of tax-exempt nonprofit organization under the provisions of the Internal Revenue Code (IRC), some forms of membership association may qualify as charitable entities and be tax-exempt organizations. Bruce Hopkins[2] is the best source for an explanation:

> The federal tax law uses the term *charitable* in two ways. The broader definition means all organizations that are eligible to receive deductible contributions. Used this way, *charitable* includes entities that are religious, educational, scientific, and the like, as well as certain fraternal, cemetery, and veterans' organizations. To get technical for just a moment, most of these organizations (not the fraternal, cemetery, and veterans' groups) are 501(c)(3) organizations—they are governed by Section 501(c)(3), probably the most widely recognized provision of the Internal Revenue Code.
>
> In the narrower definition, the term charitable organization is restricted to organizations that match the descriptions of that type of entity under the law.

Any type of nonprofit organization can offer a membership affiliation or operate a membership association. But, because only exempt organizations with IRC 501(c)(3) status can offer its members deductions for their charitable contributions, this threshold question should be resolved before memberships are offered to the public. Tax deductibility for annual dues contributions is an important member service in membership organizations that, on their own, fulfill Internal Revenue Service (IRS) requirements for being fully qualified as tax-exempt. Not all tax-exempt membership groups are able to offer their members a charitable contribution deduction for their dues payment. For example, both AFP and AHP are 501(c)(6) trade associations without the gift deduction privilege. To qualify for their members' gift support, both have established 501(c)(3) subsidiary foundations to assist in fulfilling their mission. The public cannot be expected to know whether deductibility is allowed. Organizations that are qualified should say so; those that are not are required by law to disclose that gifts made to them are not deductible. Hopkins's description[3] of various nonprofit organizations is reproduced as Exhibit 5-2.

The range of fully tax-exempt nonprofit organizations that often feature membership affiliation includes churches, cultural alliances, hospitals,

EXHIBIT 5-2   EXAMPLES OF MEMBERSHIP ORGANIZATIONS.²

- *Advocacy organizations.* These groups attempt to influence the legislative process and/or the political process, or otherwise champion particular positions. They may call themselves *social welfare organizations* or perhaps *political action committees.* Not all advocacy is lobbying and not all political activity is political campaign activity. Some of this type of program can be accomplished through a charitable organization, but that outcome is rare where advocacy is the organization's primary undertaking. In some instances, two nonprofit organizations are used, to have it both ways—a blend of charitable and advocacy activities.

- *Membership groups.* Some nonprofit organizations—associations, veterans' groups, and fraternal organizations—are structured as membership organizations. This is not to say that a charitable organization may not be structured as a membership entity; it can, but there are other categories of membership groups. Frequently, these are *business leagues.*

- *Social or recreational organizations.* Nonprofit organizations may be organized as formal *social clubs* (like country clubs, and tennis and golf clubs), or hobby, garden, or sports tournament organizations. The key factor is their primary purpose; some social activity can be tolerated in charitable groups. There is some overlap with other categories, for example, a social organization can be structured as a membership entity.

- *Satellite organizations.* Some nonprofit organizations are deliberately organized as auxiliaries or subsidiaries of other organizations. Examples of these organizations include title-holding companies, the various types of cooperatives, and retirement and other employee benefit funds. The "parent" organization may be a for-profit entity, such as a business corporation with a related foundation.

- *Employee benefit funds.* The world of compensation is intricate, regardless of whether the employer is a for-profit corporation or nonprofit organization. Various current and deferred benefits for employees are provided, including retirement and profit-sharing programs. When properly organized and operated, these funds are tax-exempt entities.

*Reprinted with permission

libraries, museums, public radio and television stations, college alumni associations, civic and community service groups, and many more. Some membership associations may take on the form of an autonomous or fully independent entity, completely self-sufficient from their parent or sponsoring nonprofit organization. Using the college alumni example again, the association may be separately incorporated, possess its own full tax-exempt status, elect its officers and board of directors from among its members, hire its own employees, and manage all its own financial affairs including the distribution of funds raised to its affiliated college or university. Such an association is guided by its own articles of incorporation and bylaws; its mission, defined in its mission statement, is to support the college or university. If the college had never existed, the alumni association would not exist either. But, should the college cease to function, the association could continue until all its members (former students) were deceased. All of the remaining funds would then have to be directed to a qualified successor college or university.

Membership Options

Membership associations may offer a variety of options for affiliation and for classes of membership. Annual dues or fees are usually personal gifts, are modest in amount, and are paid by each individual member, although membership status in some organizations may also be extended to family members. Categories of membership may use terms such as active, associate, corporate, family, or life, based on the individuals' qualifications, the size of their gifts, or the sources of their membership dues. Membership also may be tied to a specific dues level ($100 for annual membership, $150 for associate or family membership, $500 for a business partner or corporate membership, $1,000 for contributing membership, and $10,000 for life membership). Each membership level often confers detailed privileges offered by the membership association. Members may be asked to serve in a variety of voluntary roles, such as committee member, chairperson, or board member. Normal terms of office are one to three years, with a possible reappointment to another term. Members also may be selected to be representatives to another association such as a local chapter or district; delegates to the parent corporation; or representatives to a related national association or society.

The mission and purpose of a professional trade association is to recruit a broad cross-section of individuals who represent the many qualified professionals in the field. Their related trade partners, affiliated consultants, and vendors are also qualified and invited to join. Although a trade association is partially tax-exempt under Section 501(c)(6) of the Internal Revenue Code and member dues are *not* deductible as charitable contributions, the trade association can establish a fully qualified *related organization* in the form of a subsidiary 501(c)(3) foundation to serve this purpose. Members' annual gifts (not dues) can be made to the related foundation for uses that further the purposes of the trade association. Professional memberships are often paid by an employer, firm, or business, to encourage employees to increase their knowledge of their profession or craft, to meet and talk with others holding similar positions, or to expand business contacts. Memberships also may be offered to employees as a *perk* for management or technical and skilled positions.

Nonprofit organizations can use membership associations as an effective way to invite their constituency to become more active in the organizations. Several forms of affiliation and association can be offered, and any new membership plan should be as flexible in its design as possible. The forms available should be well-structured so that people outside the organization will recognize and respect them. They should attract as wide a following as possible (without becoming unmanageable by the parent nonprofit organization) and should be open to both individuals and businesses. To continue with the example of college alumni associations, many grant memberships to all graduates automatically; dues promote a member to active standing. A university alumni association may divide its members into subgroups that reflect the level of their degrees and the fields in which they were awarded. Individual subgroups may be offered for graduates of the business, education, engineering, law, and medical schools. Memberships in individual subgroups may be formed for science, arts, and physical education alumni; for specialized graduate and professional school alumni—for example, in nursing, foreign languages, social sciences, or fine arts—or for Asian American, Black American, Native American, or Chicano alumni. Former students may be eligible for membership in more than one alumni group and are welcome to join any subgroup for which they qualify. Each subgroup remains affiliated with the parent alumni association but its operating independence may include election of its own board of directors, appointment of planning committees from among the membership, publication of its own newsletters and other communications, fundraising for its priority projects, and scheduling of separate reunions, which may or may not coincide with parent alumni association or college events such as the annual homecoming or class reunions. Each subgroup offers former students a compatible interest group in which they can be active participants. The number and size of all alumni subgroups can become unwieldy and too expensive to manage and support centrally from the parent alumni association. Some institutions are indifferent to where their alumni associations focus their attention and funds, so long as they are active, self-supporting, and deliver net proceeds for use by the college, and consistently gain in the number of long-term members. Active membership is the primary goal to be promoted and retained, the goal that justifies a college's distributing its alumni budget as seed money to each of its alumni groups.

There can be problems. Subgroups may choose activities, goals, and priorities that are not consistent with college policy statements and announced priorities. However, alumni remain a powerful resource to any college or university, and some accommodations and compromises are beneficial to both sides if any controversy arises. Everyone involved may need to be reminded that the primary mission of alumni relations is to support the college. Alumni membership groups can help to accomplish that mission by maintaining active contact and involvement with as many alumni as possible—usually a benefit to both groups. Alumni annual giving represents important and necessary funds coming to the college for annual operating support, scholarships and fellowships, and construction and renovation projects. Alumni activities also encourage and promote use of the library, attendance at athletic and artistic events, community liaison, and legislative and public relations support. Alumni often continue their formal education to receive advanced degrees and to utilize adult education classes in pursuit of personal interests and professional growth. On balance, the college gains through its promotion of nearly every form of alumni activity.

Cliff Underwood[4] has stated four key principles that will determine success in any membership program:

Principle 1   Produce more new members with a successful acquisition program.

Principle 2   Increase the renewal rate of existing members.

Principle 3   Persuade existing members to give more frequently by offering supplemental income and added gift appeals.

Principle 4   Persuade existing members to upgrade their membership levels.

This chapter concentrates on how these four principles apply to memberships and membership associations in their support of the annual fundraising programs of nonprofit organizations. All of the major forms of membership programs and membership associations that are engaged in fundraising will be mentioned. Whatever their solicitation activities and membership programs, their operations must begin with a basic design, must include annual dues and gifts, and must provide benefits and privileges to the members.

BASIC DESIGN

One of the general purposes of a membership program or membership association is to manage a relationship with others who share a common cause. The mission statement defines the purposes to be followed, includes a commitment to public service, and describes the members' privileges. All of these work together toward fulfillment of the mission. Each nonprofit organization offers to its members, in exchange for their annual dues or contributions to the membership program, a variety of services not otherwise available to them. Some benefits and privileges may be reserved for more expensive levels of membership, but most members also are eligible and encouraged to fill a variety of voluntary roles, to serve on committees, and to be elected officers and directors.

Prior to starting a new membership program or new membership association, preliminary market research should be conducted to determine the likely receptivity to the proposal. The alternative, guessing the outcome, could be disastrous. The following series of questions, suggested by Clark,[5] will provide the details necessary to resolve not only how and where to begin, but what results to expect:

1. How many *competitor* organizations exist? How large are their membership rolls? How are they different? Can a smaller niche be carved from a larger organization by offering a more specialized group? Or can the organization serve as an umbrella, gathering members from several smaller groups?

2. How many individuals *share an interest* in the organization's mission? This cannot always be determined; however, figures available from a number of polls and surveys give an idea of how many Americans enjoy certain hobbies, like scuba diving or needlework, and how many are in various demographic categories (the number of parents with college-age children, for example).

3. How many names are available through *list rental* or *exchange*? A reputable list-brokerage firm can be consulted for information on mailing lists that have produced good direct mail results for comparable organizations. Would colleague organizations be willing to exchange mailing lists, for the purpose of membership solicitation?

To become a member often implies active service or a similar level of obligation on the part of the member. Active membership means acceptance of and allegiance to the organization's tenets of ethical conduct or code of professional standards. The group often acts as the voice of its members; it enunciates their views or advocates their position when calling for or taking action. For example, advocacy groups have been formed out of a common concern for the way things are now and the direction events are taking; they promote one group's views and attempt to persuade others to endorse those views. As such, they are effective as active lobbyists at all levels of government. They use the celebrity of members' names and the force of their membership numbers when they speak out. Because their activities are usually highly visible, they are able to market their cause, recruit new members, and retain current members.

Annual membership dues or gifts made represent the primary source of revenue for most membership associations. Annual operations use this income to provide member services (public education, social activities, newsletters, and so on) that keep the members involved with the group and validate the amount paid. To be successful, a membership association must serve its members, whether they choose to be active or passive supporters. Activities, meetings, newsletters, directories, e-mail services, chat rooms, list servers, and reports are member services delivered, and these services are necessary for recruitment and for membership renewal. Member services are available only to members in good standing, a factor the association will use with emphasis when soliciting renewal memberships. Gaining the commitment and loyalty of individual members is as much a goal as advancing the cause everyone shares. Thus, membership transfers the concept of raising the money needed for operations to the members themselves, and they choose to renew their dues in order to continue to receive benefits they value and to achieve the mission, vision, goals, and objectives they support.

ANNUAL DUES AND GIFTS

Annual dues and gifts will vary for each membership program. Most members pay as individuals, through annual gifts; these gift levels are more modest than memberships paid by employers to professional or trade associations. Dues are often offered on a schedule matched to membership standing or position within the organization. Two examples will illustrate.

EXHIBIT 5-3   CLEVELAND ZOOLOGICAL SOCIETY MEMBERSHIP BENEFITS PROGRAM

	Annual Membership Levels						
	$45	$55	$75	$125	$250 Keepers Club	$500 Explorers Club	$1,000 Naturalists Club
Member benefits							
Free admission to Zoo and The Rainforest	X	X	X	X	X	X	X
Discount at Zoo gift shop	X	X	X	X	X	X	X
Discount for Zoo education programs	X	X	X	X	X	X	X
Discounts on special Zoo functions	X	X	X	X	X	X	X
Membership decal	X	X	X	X	X	X	X
Membership card	X	X	X	X	X	X	X
Behind-the-scenes tour					X	X	X
Z magazine					X	X	X
Invitations to category events					X	X	X
Name on plaque on Zoo grounds					X	X	X
Name in *Z* magazine					X	X	X
Name in annual report					X	X	X
Facility rental use discount							X
Subscription to *Wildlife Conservation* magazine							X

The first example is the Cleveland Zoological Society, whose membership grew from 1,784 in 1982 to 24,878 in 1992. Most of this growth occurred between 1990 and 1992, when an aggressive marketing and communications program was built around creative membership concepts using various levels and a wide range of benefits. Annual dues at that time began at $25 for an individual adult. Family memberships for two adults and their children or grandchildren 18 years and under was $40. Senior citizen and senior couple levels were available for those 62 years and older. Other categories were available up to $1,000 and all were tied to a list of member benefits. There also were six corporate membership categories ranging from $100 to $5,000. This large group of optional categories is not unusual for a comprehensive membership program. What was striking about the zoo's approach was the creative benefits granted to all who qualified. At the close of 2001, membership had grown to 36,300 while some annual dues levels had increased, but the roster of member benefits had been enhanced (see Exhibit 5-3).

The second example is the Association of Fundraising Professionals (AFP), a 501(c)(6) professional trade association. AFP membership is open to individuals who are employed by nonprofit organizations and are responsible for managing fundraising activities; to fundraising consultants; and to closely related vendors. AFP's 26,000 members at the end of 2001 were linked together through 150-plus local chapters in communities across America, Canada, and Mexico. Management is directed through an Executive Committee composed of the elected officers and at-large members, plus a National Assembly composed of member delegates who represent the proportional size of local chapters' membership. Metro I Chapters (15 to 49 active or retired members) have one delegate; Metro II Chapters (50 to 149 members) have two delegates, Metro III Chapters (150 to 299 members) have three delegates, and Metro IV Chapters (300+ active and retired members) have four delegates. As shown in Exhibit 5-4, membership classifications and dues are assessed on an individual (not institutional) basis, are paid annually, and include active status in both the local chapter and the national organization.[6] The application process requires completion of the membership invitation form, payment of the appropriate annual dues amount, and the signatures of two voting members of AFP. Each completed application is presented for review and approval by the local chapter's board of directors. Following formal acceptance, the document is forwarded to the national service office.

BENEFITS AND PRIVILEGES

Not all classes of members will have voting rights or equal access to voluntary management of the organization. Such privileges may be reserved for special members ("active" and "retired" members, in AFP) who are the only members eligible to hold office and to serve on the local or national board of directors. It is common practice to provide some public services to members at a reduced fee and to charge nonmembers more for access to the same activity, as an incentive to join. For example, members pay reduced registration fees when they attend annual meetings and conferences; they also receive discount prices for association products and

EXHIBIT 5-4 **EXAMPLE OF PROFESSIONAL ASSOCIATION MEMBERSHIP CATEGORIES (AFP)**

Association of Fundraising Professionals

Member Categories

1. **Active Member.** Full membership in the Association shall be open to individuals (1) who at the time of application have at least one (1) year of experience as fundraisers for organizations or institutions, or as members or employees of counseling firms that are currently engaged in fundraising management, or as self-employed professionals; (2) who, among other responsibilities, hold some degree of accountability for income-generation within the fundraising process; (3) who estimate at least a quarter of their time is spent on fundraising-related responsibilities; (4) who are compensated for their services; and (5) who subscribe to the AFP Code of Ethical Principles and Standards of Professional Practice and promote the Donor and eDonor Bills of Rights.

2. **Retired Member.** Retired membership shall be open to individuals who no longer practice as paid professionals in the field but have been an active member of the Association for the immediate past five (5) consecutive years, and who subscribe to the AFP Code of Ethical Principles and Standards of Professional Practice and promote the Donor and eDonor Bills of Rights.

3. **Introductory Member.** Introductory membership shall be open to individuals newly employed in the field and who have less than one (1) year of experience at the time of application, and who shall meet all the other requirements listed in paragraph B.1 of Article IV of these bylaws. Introductory membership shall be open to persons enrolled as full-time students in a degree-granting, certificate or diploma program; individuals who work for grass roots organizations with an operating budget of $250,000 or less; executive directors who spend less than 35% of their time on fundraising related responsibilities; individuals who are newly employed in the field and who, at the time of their application for introductory membership, have less than one year of fundraising experience; and volunteers who work in the philanthropic process but are not compensated for their services. All must subscribe to the AFP Code of Ethical Principles and Standards of Professional Practice and promote the Donor and eDonor Bills of Rights. Membership in this category is limited to a two-year duration.

4. **Honorary Member.** Honorary membership shall be conferred at the discretion of the board to individuals who have accomplished noteworthy achievements and distinction as philanthropic leaders, or as leaders in the field of fundraising generally.

5. **Affiliate.** Affiliate status shall be extended to individuals who are engaged in fields related to fundraising, or who have mutual interests with fundraising professionals, and who subscribe to the AFP Code of Ethical Principles and Standards of Professional Practice and promote the Donor and eDonor Bills of Rights.

services. Other benefits reserved for active status range from receipt of annual reports to discounts on car rentals, group travel, and health or life insurance plans. The discounts can be an attractive feature when membership renewal invitations arrive. James Brandt[7] warns that the offer of membership or renewal must give members benefits they desire or need, such as the following:

1. *Informational benefits* such as newsletters. These are especially good for advocacy-oriented groups whose members want to be kept up to date.

2. *Token benefits* such as thank-you letters and membership cards. These are important for fundraising-oriented organizations, but they shouldn't be too extravagant.

3. *Prestige benefits* such as photos and certificates. These are effective only for celebrity-endorsed organizations and only when members truly believe that their memberships "entitle" them to be associated with the celebrity.

4. *Throw-away benefits.* Group insurance, car rental discounts and credit cards rarely increase response to marketing promotions, but they rarely hurt response either, if selected carefully and not overused. *Exception:* They can be effective if they relate to the organization's mission or if prospects don't believe they can get them anywhere else.

A similar variety of benefits and privileges can be used in a membership association operated by a nonprofit organization. A college alumni association may require only one qualification for membership—prior student status at the college or university—but may limit service on its board of directors to individuals with earned degrees, or to those who are paid-up active members. Privileges of alumni membership may include discount prices in the campus bookstore or theater, advance opportunity to buy tickets for athletic and other events, access to the library (in person or via the Internet), alumni e-mail addresses, and more.

THE VALUE OF A GIFT MEMBERSHIP

Gift levels and membership standing are often combined because they work well as incentives to join an organization and to remain an active member. Annual giving activities can be enhanced through a gift membership program by offering membership to donors whose existing annual gift levels qualify them to join. Special privileges can be linked to a donation that repeats the prior gift amount, and added benefits can be tied to higher levels of giving. A gift membership plan is often accompanied by offers of perceived or material value described as services in the membership association. These privileges are designed to be incentives to anyone, whether a donor or a prospect, who gives the required amount.

The privilege of association then becomes added to the gift membership. To join and to remain a qualified member is a one-step process: continue to make annual gifts. In time, donors will learn about the other, higher gift levels and their associated benefits, and some will elect to give the amounts required to gain access to these desired levels. Donors are well aware that their gift decision will be seen by others, and some may be motivated on the basis of public image and respectability. Exhibit 5-5 illus-

EXHIBIT 5-5   ANNUAL MEMBERSHIP LEVELS WITH BENEFITS AND PRIVILEGES

Membership Amount	Title	Benefits and Privileges
$ 100	Active member	Membership card Membership directory Newsletter Invitation to annual meeting
150	Associate member or family member	Same as above
250	Individual patron member	Same as above Separate listing in annual directory
500	Business partner Corporate member	Same as above *plus:* Separate listing in annual directory Two free tickets to annual meeting
1,000	Contributing member	Same as above *plus:* Name added to permanent Donor Wall at *Friend* level Invitation to annual donor luncheon
5,000	Life member	Same as above *plus:* Name added to permanent Donor Wall at *Patron* level Permanent member card for member and spouse

trates a typical gift membership plan with escalating privileges for higher annual contributions.

Benefits and privileges are essential to a gift membership program. They act as marketing tools to recruit new members, to encourage member retention, and to increase the total of annual gift revenues received. The membership organization may also provide a variety of opportunities for members to become volunteers and active participants, and to join in one or more active projects the group has undertaken. Because of the great variety of membership associations and operating styles that exist, multiples of benefits and privileges can be defined, all designed to increase the attention and personal involvement of the membership. These options will concentrate on one or more of the following specific features: personalization, orientation of new members, mentoring, access, group projects, retention, recordkeeping, and recognition.

Personalization

With a gift membership, a request for an annual gift to a nonprofit organization is converted into a personal invitation from a membership association to join a group of like-minded and public-spirited individuals. Personalization is quite important to the member candidate who has been nominated, to the current members who have nominated the member, and to the membership association. The invitation attempts to be sincere; a positive reply *will* be welcomed by comradeship. Many of the routine communications prepared and sent by nonprofit organizations to nearby community residents are, of necessity, impersonal and distant. A letter of invitation personally addressed to a prospective member at his or her home or business address is much more likely to be opened, read, and appreciated. This letter is a best effort to reflect a personal message to the invitee; it uses personal pronouns and is signed by someone whose name may be recognized by the recipient. The text of the letter outlines the uses planned for the gift membership and the mission of the membership association. It reports what the association and its members have accomplished as direct community support and defines the commitment to achieve additional public benefits. This letter also explains the specific projects the membership association has undertaken, describes the benefits and privileges of membership, and may include the roster of current officers, board members, and active members. An information card or small brochure may be included to explain the balance of its activities, programs, and services. This letter is accompanied by the membership invitation, which is to be completed and returned to the sender. After the member candidate has replied affirmatively with the required fee or dues amount a personal letter of welcome is sent back with a complete membership packet: a membership card, copies of the most recent newsletter, a schedule of coming events and activities, and other details.

Orientation of New Members

A new member may harbor several anxieties—not knowing many or any of the other members; not knowing the community, if a newcomer to the area; and not being current on the activities, meetings, or events. An orientation program will bring comfort as well as the necessary details and information, will convey a warm welcome, and will provide proper introductions. Newcomers should feel, as soon as possible, that they belong. Exhibit 5-6 lists some activities suggested by Patricia and Daniel

---

EXHIBIT 5-6   SUGGESTIONS FOR NEW MEMBER ORIENTATION[8]

1. Make a special effort to introduce them to other members. You might put a red tab on their name cards and encourage older members to approach them with a special greeting.

2. New members often feel more comfortable if seated with other new members at their first meeting, at a special table perhaps, so that they can compare notes with other people as inexperienced as they. Some groups have a special "New Members Dinner" at which newcomers can be welcomed publicly.

3. Welcome them as well in your publication, including short biographies. Talk them up.

4. Give them something to do as soon as possible. This shouldn't be something too trivial, nor should it be an obvious piece of make-work—that could be perceived as an insult. But it shouldn't be too demanding either—that could be discouraging.

5. Some organizations have a new members' counseling program in which each new member is invited to come for an interview. The main objectives of the organization are explained to him; his interests and reasons for joining are discussed; and he can be taken on a tour and meet the staff.

6. A new member is a source of new ideas—show him you appreciate this potential in him. After he's been with you a short while, ask him his opinion of the group's structure and functions. Ask him if he's getting everything he had hoped for out of belonging.

---

*Reprinted with permission

Gaby[8] to help newcomers get started toward becoming actively involved and valuable members.

Mentoring

A current member may be assigned to a newcomer to assist with introductions. This mentor will offer to escort the new member to the next meeting and arrange to introduce the others present. The mentor will explain current activities, encourage selection of a committee or participation in a work project, and convey an invitation to the next meeting or to an upcoming social event, again in the company of the mentor. Spouses and other guests can be included. This level of personal attention is crucial to newcomers; they immediately feel welcome and will have begun a more rapid integration into the group.

Access

Membership associations offer access to all their members for multiple purposes, particularly for business and personal use. Business contacts and networking are valid activities that add to the attractiveness of membership. The new friendships formed may lead to business and professional opportunities for both parties. If the new member is also new to the community, these new contacts can be valuable for personal references of a church or synagogue, doctor or dentist, banker or accountant, nanny or babysitter, insurance or real estate agent, and for locations of shops and reliable service businesses. Access also should include access to the services of the nonprofit organization the members represent; these may include many "members only" privileges, as defined. Meetings may be held at the institution or agency where its programs and services are delivered and where its professional and management staff have their offices. Access to these additional programs and services, whether the organization is a museum, school, hospital, library, or other interest center, is included as a benefit of membership, and is often an important additional incentive to remain an active member.

Group Projects

The gift membership association may have a special focus of community service or be directed toward support of one or more areas of service at their nonprofit organizations. It may select specific areas for the use of its dues and other funds raised. These areas are often featured in membership recruitment and renewal communications, adding value to the membership gift amount by directing the funds raised toward specific charitable purposes. This focus helps the nonprofit organization to communicate its story about community needs and its capacity to satisfy them, thanks to the members' generosity. The members become associated with each worthwhile project and its success. They are kept informed about public education and awareness projects designed to aid their association in meeting its operating goals and objectives. The membership association can use these visible first-priority projects as effective marketing tools when it is actively seeking and renewing members.

Membership associations that adopt fundraising goals for community benefit will enhance their image and gain the respect of the surrounding community. Their separate identity, reputation, and commitment will also enhance their membership activities. The association will stay highly visible as an active partner of the nonprofit organization it serves, and its successes will reinforce the organization's other annual giving activities. Membership associations can also accept one or more fundraising goals as multiyear projects, such as during a major capital campaign.

Retention

When personalization, orientation of new members, mentoring, access, and group projects are well-managed, recruiting and renewal of active members can be performed with greater effectiveness and efficiency. Annual programs planned and carried out by each membership association should include all the areas of focus in addition to a full schedule of member services. In combination with demonstrated competence, success, and professionalism, these programs achieve their own level of attractiveness for new and current members.

When exciting and valuable activities are in full operation, new candidates will come forward and current members will want to continue their association with these enterprises. Current members also may be encouraged to consider increasing their annual level of gift support or contributing "something extra"—a kind of gratuity at the time of annual dues payment, to assist the association in meeting its financial goals and to express personal support of its priority commitments. Renewal should never be taken for granted. Successful retention of members requires a well-prepared plan for continued communication with new and prior donors after their gifts are made. Invitations to public and benefit events, newsletters, and opportunities for voluntary participation should be sent during the year, perhaps on an every-other-month basis. Richard Trenbeth[9] has pointed out: "A major problem all membership groups have in common is a normal but sometimes shockingly high drop-off rate of first-year members. This is especially true of persons who enroll in response to a premium or free gift offer. The chief reason is the new member's failure to take advantage of the benefits that would weld him or her to the organization."

Membership Records and Other Data

The membership association should retain data on its members and their activities. From its membership records, the association should be able to retrieve

- The names of current members who were active in asking new members to join, how many of those asked joined, and at what levels
- Who was assigned to each new member as a mentor and might approach that member at renewal time
- Which areas individual members chose as their focus for active voluntary support
- Which members attended meetings, social events, and so on
- Which other voluntary activities and gift support each member may choose to provide the parent nonprofit organization

Every member should be asked to help with the annual membership campaign by soliciting new members and asking current members to give again. Volunteer-led personal solicitation continues as the most effective means to maintain a vibrant membership program.

Access to reasonably priced in-office personal computers with highly efficient (and equally inexpensive) software programs permits every fund development office to maintain complete records on all its membership donors. The decision to add computerization should not be based on when there are enough donors on file to justify the expense, but on how long the program can continue to perform without the efficiency and effectiveness that computer recordkeeping provides. Trenbeth[10] acknowledged that several questions need to be assessed in order to resolve the decision on computerization of records:

- Can you afford the cost of complex data collection? Can you staff such a system? Is the right software available for the computer system you plan to use? Or would you have to create your own programs?

- Can your proposed computer system expand to accommodate larger and more complex database information?

- Will the system give you ready access to the information you need? How quickly can you get the segmentation you need for analysis and renewal? Can it generate the reports you need?

- Will the system let you produce mailing labels, dues statements, receipts, and other types of acknowledgments? Will it be able to personalize your communications to your members?

- If you intend to test large mailing lists, can the proposed computer system use a merge/purge program to eliminate duplicates?

- Is the proposed computer system compatible with word processing equipment you may already own?

Recognition

Most cakes can benefit from a little frosting. Adding a few donor recognition features to the list of existing member benefits and privileges will help to sustain member satisfaction and encourage faithful payment of dues. These extra benefits must be valid and consistent within each level of membership. These member benefits also ought to be consistent with the donor recognition policy and procedures of the parent nonprofit organization. Members must get the message that their friendship and support are important to the membership association and to the nonprofit organization that benefits from their funds.

Recognition can be expanded with a *credit system*. For example, dues paid to the membership association can be credited again as annual gift income by the parent nonprofit organization, as part of its overall annual giving program. This linkage permits the parent organization to invite members to participate in other avenues for active participation within its annual giving campaign and special-project fundraising programs during the year. If the parent organization operates a donor recognition policy that keeps track of every contribution it receives, including membership dues, these annual gifts will quickly add up. If the organization then provides one or more visible forms of recognition to donors for their cumulative or life-time giving, members will have an extra motive to continue both their membership affiliation and annual gift support.

A listing in the annual membership directory offers several additional recognition opportunities; the membership level of each active member, the year the member joined, and the number of years of unbroken membership achieved so far. Special membership levels, such as Life Member or Sustaining Member, can be coded on the general list and featured on separate lists. Those who make a "something extra" gift each year might have an asterisk before their names or be gathered on a separate list. Each of these devices can be repeated in the newsletters, Web page, and annual reports of the membership association and its parent nonprofit organization.

Active members can be invited to assist their association in several ways:

- Provide leadership to activities, events, and committees
- Join the membership organization's board of directors
- Qualify as recruits for other voluntary services to the parent nonprofit organization
- Identify and help recruit new members and renew current members
- Respond to support areas where their personal or professional expertise will be of value
- Join in an advocacy effort or legislative support activity

Leadership and volunteerism are enormously valuable resources to any nonprofit organization that is alert enough to ask for help and to stimulate the interest and enthusiasm of all its affiliated members. Active members should be invited to attend the social activities and benefit events conducted by the nonprofit organization outside the community. Commemorative or tribute-giving programs should be offered to them at least annually, and they can be invited to support other annual, capital, and endowment fundraising campaigns. Other responsibilities within the nonprofit organization's total fundraising effort may appeal to them, such as leadership in other annual giving activities and committees. Each member also should be provided uniform information about planned giving and estate-planning opportunities as an added member service.

MANAGEMENT OF MEMBERSHIP ASSOCIATIONS

Member services, the major area of responsibility for most membership associations, may vary greatly among groups. They may be merely a response to competition, or may be tailored to fit the unique needs and desires of the members. Among the member services a membership association can offer are

- Personal standing
- Journals, newsletters, and library resources
- E-mail, list servers, and Internet access
- Leadership on committees and on the board
- Recognition in the membership group and at the parent organization
- Local chapter or affiliate activities
- Membership card and directory of current members
- Invitations to social activities and benefit events
- Advocacy, letter writing, and lobbying opportunities
- Discounts on the organization's programs and services
- Education and training (conferences, workshops, seminars)
- Regulatory activities and instructions
- Research services, studies, and reports
- Personal services (life, medical, dental, and disability insurance)
- Planned giving and estate-planning opportunities
- Travel services

Employee Qualifications and Experience

Nonprofit organizations should hire, as employees for membership associations, men and women who have done prior membership organization work, have fundraising experience, have been trained to manage volunteers and volunteer-led associations, and have served as active volunteers themselves. These employees may be active members of a trade association, such as the Association of Fundraising Professionals (AFP), Association of Lutheran Development Executives (ALDE), Association for Healthcare Philanthropy (AHP), Council for Advancement and Support of Education

(CASE), National Catholic Development Council (NCDC), National Council for Planned Giving (NCPG), Giving Society (PGSA), or others. Their volunteer experience may have come from service in one or more United Way organizations, from a volunteer-intensive annual campaign, or from service to a variety of nonprofit associations or societies.

Personal experience counts greatly in learning the internal and external operating details of membership organizations. Active membership offers exposure to on-the-job professional training that cannot be simulated elsewhere. These staff professionals must become expert in annual recruitment and renewal techniques and in the delivery of membership services in a satisfactory and cost-effective fashion.

The common management features shared by membership associations, whether they are service and civic clubs, trade associations, nonprofit organizations, or other types, include the following:

1. A mission statement (usually for exclusive support of the parent organization)
2. Bylaws or operating rules and procedures
3. Election procedures and fixed terms for service on the board of directors
4. Well-defined committees and their duties
5. Opportunities for leadership, volunteer experience, and personal growth
6. Well-defined volunteer training and orientation program
7. Operating budgets, accounting procedures, expense reports, and audits

Role of the Board of Directors

Voluntary active service in membership associations is open to all the members, but leadership opportunities and positions may be limited to one or more categories of active members in good standing. The members-at-large elect the board of directors, who make long-range and strategic plans, set dues amounts, oversee their organization's financial affairs, and operate their annual activities and services in accordance with their by-laws and approved policies and procedures. The officers of the association are elected from among current board members; each serves a specified term and has assigned duties. The bylaws spell out all the areas where members can be involved—election procedures, terms of office, standing committees and their duties, required meetings, and financial obligations—plus other details for annual operations. Changes to these bylaws must be approved by the membership. In essence, the annual operations of a membership organization, social and civic club, or trade association are much like those of every other nonprofit institution or agency.

Prospective Members: Who Are They? Where Are They?

Each membership association has the potential to appeal to at least one segment of the population. Defining an organization's mission in terms that will match well with the concerns and motives of diverse population segments will contribute greatly to success in membership recruitment and retention, along with its image and reputation, vitality and success. With proper preparations, say Gaby and Gaby,[11] likely membership response can be evaluated from the following sources:

- Published lists of contributors to drives and charitable efforts that are allied to your group's interest
- Membership lists of professional groups (social workers, teachers) in fields related to yours
- Lists of church and community groups
- Nonaffiliated people who have dealt with your group or used its services in the past
- Lists of subscribers to magazines dealing with your area of interest
- Finally, ask all of your members to search their brains for the names of three people they personally know to be likely candidates for membership

Collecting these names and their current mailing addresses is only the beginning. They must all be assembled in a master list, usually on a computer, so that letters, envelopes, mailing labels, and other details can be maintained accurately and used repeatedly during the next membership drive. Personal communications can now begin. Some prospects will respond to the first invitation, but the majority will not. Communications must continue to be sent to the entire list, and increased membership responses can be expected, with the active members engaged in new member recruitment. These recruitment strategies and expected results are similar to those described for direct mail solicitation (see Chapters 3 and 4), especially if membership appeals use only direct mail as their communications channel. Management will be required to keep each list current (as many as 20 percent of the entries on a list may have a change of address or of name each year). Once these lists are assembled, additional work will be required to learn something about who these people are: their professions, gift history, age, active association with the parent nonprofit organization, and other details. This information is helpful in getting to know these candidates and, consequently, in meeting their needs and desires. Their abilities can be a valuable addition to the talent pool.

Recruitment and Renewal of Memberships

Most of the day-to-day activities carried out by a membership association are designed to gain membership recruitment and renewal and to serve the parent nonprofit organization. Membership associations live and die according to how they find and keep members, a rather unique style of annual giving. Membership is a large part of the mission and purpose of the association, club, or society because dues revenue is so vital to financial operations. Considerable attention is given to membership recruitment strategies, which are often carried out at all times of the year. By contrast, membership renewal is often conducted at a specified time in the year, a period either tied to the anniversary date of membership or set aside for an annual renewal drive for all members. Membership goals for recruitment and renewal are set each year (a goal of 80 percent or higher is recommended) and are linked to specific services to be provided from dues revenues.

New-member recruitment must always be carried on to replace those who have retired, left the area, or dropped their active status. Renewal income may account for between 75 and 85 percent of membership revenue in mature associations; new memberships complete the target goal. (These percentages will be reversed in a new group that is building up its membership base.)

Membership recruitment and renewal are also the duty of each member. All members should be prepared and encouraged to act on membership opportunities at all times. Active voluntary participation and involvement is the chief reason most members cite for their own continued membership.

Asking every member to be part of the membership committee and to be active in the annual "every member" campaign is vital to the continued success of the association.

Competition for member attention is always present. Creativity is required when asking people to join or to renew their memberships year after year. The needs and desires of a society can change rapidly; so can its interests in community service. Success in membership renewal activities is important because less time and effort are required than for first-time recruiting. Mature organizations can expect at least 75 to 80 percent of their membership to renew each year; this level of performance can increase over time, with extra year-round effort. One suggestion put forward by Gaby and Gaby[12] was to divide current members into two groups. The control group received the full set of regular renewal materials on the same schedule as prior years. The experiment group received a different mailing package that exhibited new ideas, making renewal more desirable, more vital, or just easier. Renewal percentage rates and net revenues increased for the experimental group. Some of these creative ideas were:

1. A new stuffer emphasizing the benefits of membership in a new way, or one announcing some new action or achievement by the organization.

2. A new invoice permitting payment of dues by credit card.

3. A business reply card offering the option of a new car decal or sticker.

4. A new membership card that says, "Member since _____" and "Valid until _____," instead of "Expires on _____." Perhaps this could be made of plastic instead of paper (though plastic cards can run into money).

5. An insurance company reminder, if applicable in your case, that the holder's benefits will expire at midnight on the date shown on his old card.

6. A change in billing procedures, allowing more or less lead time.

7. A letter to dilatory members from the president, with a message on the left and a blank space on the right wherein the recipient is invited to write any comments or complaints he may have.

Any experiment requires some time to validate the testing methods used. Were there adequate numbers in the survey? Were there enough replies for the results to be statistically sound? The trial should be conducted alongside the regular program throughout the membership renewal cycle, and comparative measurements should be taken when the trial is concluded. Only one variable should be tried at any one time; two might confuse the results so that neither can demonstrate its extra effectiveness. If the evidence points to any one or more improvements that can be attributed to either renewal package or to its contents, further study might determine whether old ways should be abandoned in favor of the new, now proven changes. New ideas also tell members that a good-faith effort is being made on their behalf, which will help their good feelings about their own active standing.

Communications

One or more regular communication pieces are needed to keep the members informed about the association and all of its operations, and to fulfill the many member services. As is true with all other forms of annual giving communications, members (donors) need to hear, between solicitations, from the organizations they support. Meetings and newsletters, which are most often used to report on membership and association activities, can be supplemented with professional journals, special reports, legislative action bulletins, and constant promotions of the special programs and services that the association has promised to its members. Frequent communications give visibility to members who are active as volunteers and in leadership roles. Publishing the names of new members, of recipients of outside professional promotions and awards, and of others who have had notable life changes is well-received. Members need reminders on future social activities, annual meetings, conferences, and workshops they are invited to attend. Advertisements from local business and service enterprises will help to pay for communications costs. Discount prices can apply to members who wish to buy space for their business or professional promotions.

Members as Volunteers

The strength of any association is in members who are active, voluntary participants. Their time, energy, talents, and commitment are all provided free of charge and with the best of intentions. They offer their association an enormous reservoir of human resources. A business or corporation could never recruit a similar group of nonemployees who would volunteer and then work so hard for free. Managing members who volunteer is a skill area that comes from some training and long experience. Volunteers come in with varying degrees of enthusiasm and willingness to perform any task that needs doing. Not all volunteers can be helpful, despite their eagerness and willingness to try; the tasks that are within their capabilities need to be defined. There is always a mix of personalities to be managed. Without causing divisive responses, the manager must be able to identify leadership candidates and committee workers who can work well with others. A multitude of tasks can be accomplished when the members and their leaders are relaxed about who does each task, where it's done, when it gets done, or how well it is performed. The guidelines listed in Exhibit 5-7 represent advice from Arch McGhee[13] on how to effectively manage membership associations.

Recognition (Again)

Recognition is the preferred way to thank each member and to show others (including nonmembers) how members are honored and respected for their decision to join and give faithful service. A variety of membership classes may be offered, and the annual membership fee that is linked to each class can point to the degree of recognition or standing in the association that each member may achieve. The privileges reserved for each class of membership expand with the higher fees; these are important opportunities for the organization to create meaningful benefits. Membership cards, mailing lists, certificates, and directories are available to all members, as are the opportunities to give voluntary service on committees, to gain leadership positions, and eventually to be nominated for election to the local or national board of directors. Recognition can also be offered in the form of invitations to speak at workshops or seminars, to act as a delegate to other organizations, or to perform similar special services. Extra honors should be reserved for those volunteers who have performed prior services or held elected office, or those donors whose cumulative giving has reached higher levels. Formal donor and volunteer award programs conducted before a membership audience are excellent occasions to reward members annually for their achievements in several categories of service. Recognition by one's peers, one of the most valued ways to achieve respect, is an essential

EXHIBIT 5-7   GUIDELINES FOR MANAGEMENT OF
MEMBERSHIP ASSOCIATIONS[13]

⇨ Select assignments that fit the talents and personality of the member. Members will do best those things that they like to do.

⇨ Make assignments definite. Whenever members are given assignments, they should know just what they are supposed to do. Sometimes this might mean consultation to determine the requirements and the limits of the job. Indefinite assignments put members on the spot—they can feel neither quite sure of what they are to do nor when they are finished.

⇨ Set completion dates where specific projects are involved.

⇨ Do not be afraid to ask. A member is complimented, not insulted, by being asked to undertake an assignment. The very worst that can happen is a refusal.

⇨ Never ask for volunteers. It is usually an evasion of administrative responsibility to ask volunteers to select themselves instead of being selected. Those who volunteer might not be those best suited for the project at hand.

⇨ Make sure that each assignment calls for a worthwhile contribution from the member. A member who is given a trivial assignment or is put on a committee with nothing definite to do will not stay interested.

⇨ Never divide responsibility between committees or members. What is everybody's job turns out to be nobody's job.

---

feature of opportunities for honors and rewards. Everything performed in the name of communications, voluntary service, and recognition continuously contributes to both membership recruitment and renewal.

ANNUAL GIVING OPPORTUNITIES FOR MEMBERS

In each membership year, there are several opportunities to ask for contributions beyond membership gifts. However, the members need some understanding and appreciation of the purpose or need for these extra gifts. Most members believe their once-a-year dues payment is all that is required of them. The dues maintain their membership standing in the association, but the nonprofit organization cannot sustain its public benefit programs and services based on dues revenue alone. It is to the association's advantage to be able to offer its members other options for their active participation. There should not be any barriers or hesitancy when the parent organization invites a premier group of its friends and donors to help when financial needs arise and additional support from volunteers and contributors must be requested. For its major capital campaigns, its community relations programs, and its advocacy, legislative, and lobbying agendas, the organization will turn again to these same association members. When estate planning and planned giving opportunities are offered to these members, the offers should be packaged as additional forms of membership services, to be used in conjunction with their own tax and retirement planning.

Supplemental Income Programs

Membership associations need to bring their own and their parent organization's long-range plans and strategic objectives to their members' attention. The focus on member services tends to tilt day-to-day operations toward fulfilling members' needs, but there are larger issues to which members owe some allegiance. Special needs do arise; priorities do change in response to external conditions or internal requirements; and members can benefit from knowing about these other opportunities. Supplemental income programs will attempt to stimulate (1) increased participation by the members and (2) increased income from new and established sources. Exhibit 5-8 offers several ideas that have proved beneficial as supplemental income programs.

Offering a variety of options to individual members is a means of increasing their ties to the association and encouraging better relationships. Satisfied customers, access to additional privileges, improved personal attention, strengthened commitments, and more secure financial support of the parent nonprofit organization—all of these are possible results.

Special offers can be provided within routine annual giving programs or conducted parallel to membership drives. Nonprofit organizations must be committed each year to building up the numbers of their friends and donors by every means available. Those whose donative spirit is greater, or to whom multiple gifts with added privileges are attractive, can consider accepting an invitation to make one or more special gifts, beyond membership dues. It never hurts to ask! The benefits to the member from such additional contributions must be well defined and should be adequately enticing. If not properly explained, these strategies can cause confusion and result in negative impressions among the membership. Each "second ask," which can quickly become as routine as the "second collection" in church,

EXHIBIT 5-8	SUPPLEMENTAL INCOME OPTIONS FOR MEMBERSHIP ASSOCIATIONS
Year-end and holiday appeals	Tax motives and holiday traditions are combined in the calendar year-end solicitation message.
Special gift clubs	Select privileges should be reserved for donors who make extra gifts to one or more gift clubs. These can be directed to children or seniors as special benefit offers.
"Something extra" gifts	Additional amounts can be given at the time of annual membership renewal over and above the normal dues levels, purely out of generosity and respect for the organization and the public benefit purposes it supports.
Special and benefit events	The members stage a social or sporting event for members and for the public. Net proceeds are added to the treasury.
Business and corporate memberships	This separate membership class offers unique programs designed to meet the needs of executives and managers.
Special campaigns	Occasional capital or equipment projects have select fundraising objectives for members' participation; each project has its own goal and special recognition opportunities.
Life memberships	Priced at a value equivalent to 10 or 20 years' membership dues payments, this concept offers a dual convenience: a major, one-time cash payment, and revenue infusion to the operating budget.
Endowment funds	Permanent annual support can be achieved through larger gifts to an endowment fund; the advantage is long-term growth with increased annual earnings.

must be clarified and justified as a special priority or need of the association and as a request reserved for members only.

Various "invitations" to make additional gifts during the operating year are sent by the parent organization. These can include invitations to buy tickets to special and benefit events, or to attend lectures, dedications, receptions, annual meetings, and similar occasions where added admission fees are required. The membership association will be offering its own calendar of activities and events, for its own marketing and recruiting purposes. Options might include first nights at newly opened restaurants, gallery exhibits, or other public and private facilities—events that are primarily advertising vehicles for the host facilities. Members are invited to attend the "opening" for an added-on fee, and the proceeds (or a percentage of the sales) are delivered to the membership association for that year's fundraising project. When the membership association undertakes a special project on behalf of its parent nonprofit organization, such as a multiyear pledge to assist in a major capital campaign, the extra fundraising activity will make a critical contribution. The organization will be attempting to raise funds above its ordinary annual operating levels and will need to find ways to stimulate the membership's attention and excitement and to raise the extra money needed to fulfill its pledge commitment.

Membership Development Strategies

A membership association must give first priority to its own member recruitment and renewal programs. Membership development requires a "battle plan" that has mapped out several primary and alternate strategies to be used throughout the year. A second plan projects the activities and programs that will be carried out over a two- or three-year period in order to achieve growth of membership, increased retention rates, and additional revenue production. Assembled together, these collective activities represent an emerging business plan. Such plans must conform to the membership potential and profile of each organization, but Tracy Connors[14] has found that the following guidelines apply uniformly:

1. Figure out how much a member is really worth to you.
2. Set goals.
3. Keep at it.
4. Use a selling theme.
5. Simplify.
6. Sell the benefits.
7. Don't bore people to death.
8. Use a letter with your membership package.
9. Develop a memorable graphic identity.
10. Try new media.
11. Make it easy to join.
12. Don't be afraid to make mistakes.
13. Be keenly opportunistic.
14. Use your members.

Membership Cards and Affinity Cards

Members are usually presented with an annual identification card acknowledging their standing as active members. This card is often a means to access additional benefits—discounts on purchases (tickets, travel plans, and so on) or lowered rates for routine programs and services (special educational and entertainment programs, reciprocal privileges at other membership associations or other nonprofit organizations, and so on). The card usually states an expiration date, a less than subtle reminder of the obligation to pay their membership fee annually in order to continue to receive these privileges. Each of these benefits is especially useful when annual renewal solicitations are made.

Nonprofit organizations have begun to offer their donors and members affinity card privileges. An affinity card is a charge card or credit card that channels a percentage of the charged expenditure (usually, a prearranged figure of 5 to 10 percent (or less) of the gross or the net amount) to the organization as an additional gift. These new dollars are less a gift than a commercial exchange that benefits others more than it benefits the membership association or the nonprofit organization. Affinity cards may also offer a lower interest rate to members, may display the name and logo of the membership association, and may be substituted for the membership card, further enhancing the value of maintaining current membership standing.

Matching Gifts

Several businesses, corporations, partnerships, firms, and professional corporations now provide corporate matching gift programs to their employees, to encourage civic participation and community support. Most will offer a dollar-for-dollar match, up to a maximum amount, to their employees' contributions to selected nonprofit organizations. Some businesses or firms will offer two-for-one matches, again up to a cap amount, to stimulate higher giving levels among their employees. The intent in matching gift programs is to preserve and increase annual giving by employees. Unfortunately, a fairly common practice among employees with access to such programs is to pay half of the required membership dues or gift amount and tap the matching gift program for the other half. The true goal of increasing or doubling the amount given to nonprofit organizations occurs less often. The membership association or nonprofit organization receives the donations and the matching gift, but the income realized falls short of this special program's intent and potential.

Business and Corporate Membership Programs

Many membership associations and nonprofit organizations offer business and corporate membership programs—either a category of regular membership prorated for businesses or corporations, or a separate program designed to appeal to business and corporate executives. The membership fee is paid by the corporation, which may justify it as part of its annual corporate gift support. The objectives of the membership association are to gain wide notice within the business community, to attract and retain another source of annual membership dues and gift income, and to recruit the attention and active participation of corporate executives, managers, and employees.

When the purposes and goals of the membership association match with one or more of the civic or charitable goals of a business or corporation, memberships are an attractive decision. They add to corporate visibility in the community and help to demonstrate how business leaders perform valuable levels of community service and contribute support. When the product lines of the business or corporation match with the programs and services of the membership association or its parent nonprofit organization, there is ample opportunity for everyone to benefit. For example, local bookstore owners, printers, and publishers may become members of library associations or student bookstore societies in order to further student use of books. In another example, corporate members of an art museum or gallery may be allowed to rent (at discount prices) art works owned by the museum or gallery for display in their offices, a privilege not available to any business or firm that is not a member.

ANNUAL MEMBERSHIP CAMPAIGNS

Considerable effort is required to plan and conduct annual membership campaigns. Membership recruitment and retention are sophisticated enterprises that require experienced and skillful professional managers. When well-defined programs and services are available for the members, including a full range of benefits and privileges, concentration on these features can be a characteristic of all communications during the annual membership campaign. This campaign is a smaller version of the many other forms of volunteer-led annual giving appeals, including the major capital and endowment campaigns. The same preparations, leadership, and expert execution skills are required.

One of the most critical statements in any membership campaign is the "case for support"—a document or paragraph that explains why these members (and their dues) are needed now and what benefits they will provide to others. Most annual giving case statements have had success by addressing new and different projects or priorities that the members have agreed to undertake for that year. The focus on certain projects makes the process of their selection and the annual preparations all the more challenging. A variety of public benefits can be included in the case statement, but membership associations must attach a hefty roster of member benefits and privileges to these other loftier, and perhaps more distant public benefits. For example, membership gifts that will add books to the special collection section of the local college library can be packaged to allow the members private access to these volumes as a members-only benefit. This same project will be of unique interest to the members of the Friends of the Library Association and should be effective in encouraging an annual gift that exceeds the normal amount for membership renewal.

Membership campaigns need to be fully planned, and all the details must be carefully scheduled: materials prepared and printed, mailing lists coordinated with mailing packets and their contents, publicity and promotion scheduled for visible support of the drive, personal solicitations sequenced into direct mail and telephone follow-up (multimedia) activities, full e-mail and Internet applications in place, the kick-off and other support activities planned for maximum impact, and much more. Membership campaigns also require enough volunteers to fill the leadership positions and to provide workers for the jobs required.

One looming challenge is present in every membership campaign: It has been done before. This is not a new activity, for workers or members, and some amount of creativity and innovation may be required to spark some enthusiasm and excitement. In this area, volunteers can make significant contributions. They know many of the members' needs and desires; they know friends and neighbors who can be solicited for an annual membership gift. This type of knowledge is a resource that can be tapped during the selection and training of volunteer solicitors, woven into each year's strategy, sprinkled into the several information packages, and added to all

EXHIBIT 5-9   PLANNING SCHEDULE FOR ANNUAL MEMBERSHIP CAMPAIGN[15]

Event	Weeks before Opening Day
Preliminary organization meeting	12
[Campaign chairperson] and director secured	10
Campaign office set up	10
[Division chairpersons] secured	8
Meeting of [division chairpersons]	6
Team captains secured	4
Prospect list completed, work cards ready	4
Master lists ready	3
Meeting of captains	3
Membership application cards ready	2
Team workers secured	2
Cards divided or selected	$1\frac{1}{2}$
Campaign folder or broadside mailed	$1\frac{1}{2}$
Team lists ready	1
Division rallies; cards distributed	$\frac{1}{2}$ to 1
Second mailing piece, house bulletin, etc.	$\frac{1}{2}$ to 1
Opening meeting of the campaign	

the membership materials. Attention to the campaign schedule is essential. Everyone must know what to do and when it needs to be done, and must be trained in how to perform a particular part. A week-by-week count-down suggested by Gaby and Gaby[15] is reproduced in Exhibit 5-9.

Volunteer Preparations

When all the preparations are completed, the campaign must be carried out according to the plan. Here is where leadership and experience come to the fore. Volunteers have to be prepared for their assignments. Training sessions should be an enjoyable experience so that they will be well attended. The information about this year's campaign objectives, strategy, and available materials (and how to use them) must be transferred effectively so that each volunteer will be successful in solicitation visits with new or continuing members.

Once the campaign is begun, the volunteers will need some encouragement to complete their tasks. Those in leadership positions (board members, committee chairs, management and professional staff) must help by making their gifts first and by motivating the members to complete their assignments. As is true in all other forms of fundraising, the best method for membership solicitation is a face-to-face presentation. A telephone discussion is second best, and sending requests through the mail or by one or more electronic means brings up the rear. Gaby and Gaby[16] have compiled general guidelines for training sessions for volunteer solicitors (see Exhibit 5-10).

Report meetings are scheduled to allow time for any needed remedial action that will bring in the results by the deadline. Members who have completed or exceeded their assignments should be recognized and rewarded at each meeting. Membership drives have start and end dates; the concentrated action causes everyone to give the assignment some priority.

EXHIBIT 5-10   GUIDELINES FOR TRAINING VOLUNTEERS TO BE SOLICITORS[16]

1. Always call beforehand to set up an appointment. This is simple courtesy, since your dropping in unannounced could easily inconvenience your host. He might very well be busy.

2. Tell him exactly why you want to see him while you're on the phone. Downplaying the object of your visit undercuts its importance and therefore the importance of your organization. But don't try to close the deal on the phone.

3. When you see your prospect, thank him for allowing you some of his time before you do anything else.

4. Be sincerely enthusiastic about all the benefits your organization offers him. But don't promise him things it can't deliver. That kind of oversell is one of the prime causes of nonrenewals. You want a member who will *stay* a member.

5. Don't go too fast. Give each point time to sink in.

6. Don't make the mistake of doing all the talking. People who've made up their minds not to buy something generally say nothing. Elicit questions and responses.

7. Try to find the real reasons behind his sales resistance (dues too high? the press of other business too great?) and refer to specific features in your organization to show they don't apply. Counter every objection with a corresponding benefit.

8. Thank him for his time again when you leave. Leave printed matter behind.

9. Always follow up with a call. He may be conferring with associates about joining, and hearing from the salesman again in a week or so can be the final clincher.

---

*Reprinted with permission

Besides, no one likes to fail when the results are so visible. Progress toward the multiple goals—volunteer solicitations completed, number of memberships achieved, and dollars raised—is tallied, displayed, and reported to all members involved in the campaign. The final date on the schedule is the end date of the drive, the deadline for everyone to have completed his or her assignments. This event, usually designated as a victory celebration, is a stimulus for everyone to complete the work in time to be counted in the final campaign results. (Full details on volunteer campaign management are provided in Chapter 11.)

Follow-up activities, after the membership campaign deadline, include the routine duties of collections, thank-you letters with new membership cards enclosed, and recognition activities for the leaders and workers who participated in the drive. It is valuable to perform a campaign critique. The best method is to survey all the volunteers for their comments on the campaign plan, materials used, effectiveness of the case statement, and any other topic of their choice. Final tallies are made of all results, and preparations begin for compiling the new membership directory. In some organizations, the campaign critique takes the form of a brief questionnaire mailed to members. Gaby and Gaby[17] recommend forming a few focus groups among volunteers (new and old members) to ask the following questions:

1. Did you enjoy participating in this campaign?
2. What phases of the campaign did you particularly like?
3. What phases would you criticize?
4. Do you have any suggestions to improve the conduct of future campaigns?
5. Any suggestions about the programs at report meetings?
6. Any suggestions about workers' materials, awards, and so on?
7. What do you consider to be the chief benefits accruing to the association from the campaign?
8. Do you think the campaign had any harmful results?
9. Would you be willing to work in one next year?

Mail and Telephone Campaigns

Why is the volunteer-led, volunteer-staffed annual membership campaign recommended above all other methods? Because it has the highest rate of success, for number of members and dollars, in both new-member ac-quisition and member retention. If volunteers cannot be recruited from among the membership to perform these tasks, the membership organiza-tion may be in distress. The fall-back position is to rely on the mail or to use a combination of letters, telephone calls, facsimile, or Internet means. The results will drop off, and costs to support these efforts will increase, which will reduce net revenues to the membership association and non-profit organization. The whole purpose of membership associations, which is to encourage and facilitate individuals as active members in their own as-sociation, is soon lost. (Details about how to organize and mount tele-phone and Internet campaigns were presented in Chapters 6 and 9.)

Before giving up on members or on personal solicitation, a distressed or-ganization might try taking some creative risks. Fundraising is a relationship business; to get people's attention these days, some inventiveness is needed. How important to the association and the nonprofit organization are the members? When the efforts to acquire new members were adequately high, is it possible that too little attention was given to fulfilling member services? The first year is especially critical. "Once people renew after the first year we keep them around for a long time," says Mike Mueller, who manages renewals for the 370,000-member United States Golf Association. "Re-taining members year after year can also be a tricky affair, often requiring a subtle balance of persuasion, persistence, and humor."[18] Here is an espe-cially effective example from another membership association:[19]

> The Los Angeles County Museum of Art seems to have captured that balance. Membership Director Melody Kanschat recalls that in the past, the museum sent out four direct mail notices to its 80,000-plus members. But in the last year or so, Kanschat began sending out six notices—some with a rather distinct spin.
>
> One of the early notices arrived in the form of an invoice rather than the old personal plea to renew. While some members were no doubt stunned to find a "bill" inside a museum envelope, many responded af-firmatively. Kanschat says the strategy pushed renewal rates up "a couple of points." Another early notice arrived in an envelope featuring a picture of the Madonna staring at a lighted candle. The copy read, "We're still waiting to hear from you."
>
> Those who did not respond received more gentle nudges. The fourth notice offered three months' free membership for renewing within 15

days of receiving the letter. It also featured a photo of an armless sculpture on the envelope, below a headline stating, "We'd give anything to get you back." The fifth notice included an old art catalogue the museum had in stock and wanted to discard anyway. The sixth and last notice went back to a personal appeal from the museum director. In all, the strategy worked, Kanschat says, and last year the museum won awards from the American Association of Museums and the Direct Marketing Association for its efforts.

"It's extremely critical to retain members," Kanschat explains. "The best customer is the one you already have."

Operating Costs for Membership Programs

To review quickly, the chief advantage of a membership association is its ability to define solid reasons for people to join and to remain active supporters of a nonprofit organization. The "linkage" and "connection" are visible through delivery of member services packaged as benefits and privileges; they are the "glue" or *fish hooks* that keeps members close year after year. Members' annual gifts provide crucial dollars for annual operations. Every nonprofit organization needs them. The advantage of a membership association is that members bring their time, energy, and talents, in addition to their dollars. Without all of these, the association could not long survive.

There is a full range of operating costs for membership associations. Delivery of member services requires professional and support staff who receive salaries; paid vacations; health, dental, and life insurance support; pension funding; and other basic employment benefits. The cost of office operations will usually match or slightly exceed salaries and benefits. The biggest budget items are (1) the heavy printing and promotion costs for membership acquisition and renewal and (2) fulfillment of a variety of member services. When all operating expenses are known, they must be measured against anticipated membership gift income. If these costs are charted on a graph, there is a point at which the revenues and expenses lines meet. Above this point, excess revenue is generated; below it, losses occur, just as in any other business. It is essential to know where these two lines meet and whether there will be enough income to exceed the break-even amount. As an example, if membership dues in a 3,000-member association are $100 per year and the operations and member services cost around $50 per member, the "profit" point on the chart is at 1,500 members. The "material value" of the member services delivered causes many membership associations to experience great difficulty in their annual financial operations. A bit of help can come from calculating the members' tax deduction for their annual gift. (The IRS is credited with this solution.) "A museum, for example, has determined that the first $50 of a member's dues must be considered as quid pro quo—for the services a member is provided—and that only what he pays above that amount can be considered a contribution".[20] If the annual membership gift is $100 and half that sum is allowed as a deduction from personal income tax, then all operating costs need to be contained at $50 per member as a matter of operating policy. If membership gift levels are below $100, the association has three options to resolve the situation: (1) raise gift levels, (2) cut member services, or (3) do both of the above. No more agonizing issue will be faced by any membership association than choosing from among these three options.

The course to pursue is the one that will overcome membership instability. It takes a considerable effort each year to maintain a 3,000-member association. If only a 5 percent annual attrition rate occurs, 150 members will be lost each year. To replace them may require recruitment of an average of two to three candidates for every new member signed. Identifying 300 to 450 new member candidates and successfully signing 150 of them is an aggressive recruiting program that will be difficult to achieve year after year. A comparison of the attrition and recruitment rates will help demonstrate this challenge:

Present Size of Membership	Attrition Rate (Percent)	Candidates Required
1,000	@ 5% = 50	100 to 150
	@ 10% = 100	200 to 300
2,000	@ 5% = 100	200 to 300
	@ 10% = 200	400 to 600
3,000	@ 5% = 150	300 to 450
	@ 10% = 300	600 to 900

Renewal at a 90 to 95 percent performance level is exceptionally high. The rate for most membership associations is between 75 and 85 percent, which means a large number of new members will have to be found *each year*. Maximizing membership retention should be the first priority, and, because current members are a control group of modest size, continued membership services with all benefits and privileges must be stressed. These same services, benefits, and privileges must be cost-effective and must meet the 50 percent IRS tax deduction test as well. The mission of the membership association is to fulfill its charitable purposes; at a 50 percent cost of operations, an equal 50 percent goes to programs and services of public benefit. All these calculations are necessary in order to know how many total members (and at what membership levels) are required for the association to achieve a break-even or better financial return on both its 50 percent for operations and 50 percent for charitable purposes. If any new projects or new expenses are suggested, each must be matched with an equal source of new revenue that will contribute to improving the 50 percent break-even minimum.

The lessons from such basic mathematics are clear and illustrate why membership associations are always in search of alternate revenue sources (affinity cards, travel tours, T-shirts, coffee cups, insurance plans, and so on), along with aggressive membership acquisition and retention activities. Their alternative is to consider raising the annual dues, possibly disguised as new (higher) membership levels with added benefits and privileges, which incur increased costs for member services. However, any raise in membership dues is always unpopular, no matter how valid and urgent the reasons. This plan also will result in a bit of attrition and will slow new membership recruitment. The best rule is: Examine all reasonable alternate revenue sources and restrain the value of member services "given away" each year.

One novel answer to the operating budgets problem is joint ventures or purchasing alliances. Allied membership organizations can pool several areas of annual operating expense and achieve higher efficiencies at lower unit costs. Just such a program, the Metropolitan Cultural Alliance, was begun in Massachusetts in 1969 by a half-dozen cultural organizations. Standard services included the following: "Management training workshops and seminars, a monthly newsletter, a library, group purchasing, employment listings, and health insurance plans."[21] Additional benefits can be developed where the members share common operating needs. The arts and theater members, for example, joined together in a central telephone answering service for ticket sales, negotiated with local hotels to get group rates for traveling artists, and contracted for joint use of advertising, graphics, publicity, and printing firms.

The Future for Membership Programs

Every nonprofit organization must commit time and money to building and maintaining a constituency of new and old friends and supporters. Even a cursory review of our fast-paced society reveals that competition for people's time and money will only increase, suggesting that the membership attachment will grow in importance. Budget pressures will tempt reductions in acquisition, donor communications, and retention activities in favor of "easy money" and "quick cash without effort" proposals, which are likely to be poor decisions in the end. What are the trends? Richard Trenbeth[22] forecasts a baker's dozen of changes:

1.   Older people are an expanding market.
2.   More research is being done.
3.   Travel benefits will boom in popularity.
4.   Upscale memberships will increase.
5.   Direct marketing will grow in importance.
6.   Computerization will leap ahead.
7.   More catalogs and merchandise will be offered.
8.   More insurance and investment opportunities.
9.   More newsletters and technical publications.
10. Social events for members will increase.
11. Adult education will grow as a benefit.
12. People want recognition.
13. Accountability will be stressed.

Each membership association must identify the changes that are most significant to its membership program plans for the future and act on them.

Let us return now to the CCUA Clean Up Cleveland Chapter and see how the new membership association, The Circle of Champions, is doing.

FOCUS: CCUA CLEAN UP CLEVELAND CHAPTER

The Circle of Champions program was able to recruit additional members at the $100 gift level. The initial test mailings produced 118 members out of 1,504 respondents (8 percent). However, the first renewal request sent to these donors this past spring succeeded in retaining only 78 of these active members (66 percent), a cause for some concern. In addition, the spring mailing to 1,504 current donors from last fall resulted in only 6 new members of The Circle of Champions at the $100 level (less than 1 percent). The full spring roll out campaign was more successful: another 76 new members were added to the Circle out of 3,653 donors, but this level of response (2 percent) also was a bit disappointing. Total membership stands at 160 as planning for the second fall campaign begins.

In her analysis of all these results, Karen Anderson, director of development for the CCUA Clean Up Cleveland Chapter, has several concerns. Why was the charter membership response to the first test mailing so high (78 out of 1,504 donors, or 8 percent)? Why did 40 of these new members decline to renew their membership in the spring? There should have been more new members at $100 from the 200,000 residents solicited in the spring. In consultation with other fund development professionals around town, Anderson has learned that some of the answers to her concerns might lie in the fact that the initial 118 members had made their first gift during the July test mailing, which was sent to a highly selective prospect list. Their gift decision was that year's tax deduction; the fall resolicitation appeal came in the same tax year. Perhaps other donors who made their first gifts last fall realized that they had given six months earlier; they may have believed their annual membership renewal gift was not due again until the fall, and bypassed the spring appeal. Anderson concludes that the coming fall solicitations should help to resolve these concerns.

Anderson prepares a gift report of total mail results (Exhibit 5-11). A solid response has been achieved from the community at this early point. A total of 3,653 new donors was acquired in the spring roll out mailing, a sure sign that residents have become more aware of the Clean Up Cleveland campaign. Anderson believes that these 3,653 donors will benefit from a progress report from Harvey Clout (Exhibit 5-12), which will be mailed to all donors in late August. She also believes she must intensify the charter membership in The Circle of Champions for each group in the fall mailing cycle. She decides *against* adding any new resident mailing lists for the coming fall program. The current lists appear to have a lot of potential left in them, and some savings can be realized by reusing them. She has already received approval to renew the offer of complimentary tickets to a second Cleveland Orchestra concert and Cleveland Play House show to be held next summer. This offer was well received during the summer; quite a few donors called afterward to ask whether the offer would be repeated.

Anderson's fall mailing program will include three areas of concentration:

1. Continue the charter membership offer in a two-part acquisition mailing (Letter E, Exhibit 5-13), to resolicit the 200,000 residents in the seven select communities of Cleveland who have not yet responded.

2. Stress the charter membership offer in a two-part renewal mailing to all 5,157 current donors (Letter F, Exhibit 5-14), using first-class, computer-generated personally addressed letters and envelopes.

3. Send personal letters to the 160 currently active members of The Circle of Champions, asking them to renew their membership. Follow-up telephone calls from members of the board of directors will encourage their renewal and invite them to upgrade their annual gift, if possible. A sample telephone script is available for board member calls, if needed (Exhibit 5-15).

EXHIBIT 5-11   GIFT REPORT ON TOTAL MAILING PROGRAM RESULTS

Letter	Program	Number Mailed	Replies Number	Replies Percent	Gift Income
Acquisition Phase					
A & B	Test Mailing (July)	30,000	348	1.16%	$ 8,527
B	Full Test List Mailing	80,575	1,156	1.43	35,758
B	Spring "Roll-Out"	200,000	1,831	0.91	56,936
C	Spring Follow-Up	194,467	1,822	0.94	59,975
	Subtotal	505,042	5,157	1.02%	$161,196
Donor Renewal Phase					
D	First Renewal Request	1,504	914	66.77%	31,064
	Total	506,546	6,071	1.20%	$192,260

EXHIBIT 5-12   PROGRESS REPORT LETTER TO CURRENT DONORS

THE CAMPAIGN TO CLEAN UP AMERICA
CLEAN UP CLEVELAND CHAPTER

Summer 200X

Dear Compatriot in the "Clean Up Cleveland" campaign:

Our first year of operations is completed and I want to report to you on all the progress we have been able to make, thanks to you.

First, we have written to over 500,000 Cleveland-area residents to invite them to join in the "Clean Up Cleveland" campaign. A total of 5,157 agreed to our request and sent in a contribution. Total dollars raised to date come to $161,196. Thank you!

Second, our 1,504 earliest donors who gave last summer already were asked to renew their support for a second year. To date, 914 have done so, a marvelous 67 percent performance. Adding their gifts to our total, we have raised $192,260. When you receive your request to renew your gift later this fall, please continue to support our efforts if at all possible.

Third, we have just introduced The Circle of Champions membership association. This new program encourages gifts at $100 or more to help us to finance the energy conversion plant as soon as possible. The first donors who join will be known as "charter members." We will be offering charter memberships this fall; you should think about becoming one of the first members of The Circle of Champions (see the information card attached to this letter for full details).

Fourth, we have been making progress on site selection for the energy conversion plant. Four sites have been identified and are under review. Quite a few federal and state agencies have to be involved in these proceedings, as are a number of citizens' groups including several environmental and conservancy groups. We are proceeding on schedule and hope to be able to announce the final site early next year.

Fifth and last, we are seeing more of our "Clean Up Cleveland" bumper stickers around town every day. Add yours to your car or truck to help spread the word. If you need additional bumper stickers, just call our offices at (216) CLEAN UP and we will send you as many as you like.

(continued)

EXHIBIT 5-12   (CONTINUED)

Have a great summer and thanks again for your support of our campaign. We are making a difference; our streets are looking much cleaner already.

Sincerely,

I. Harvey Clout
Chair of the Board
Cleveland Cast Iron Works

Encl.

EXHIBIT 5-13   LETTER E: SECOND CHARTER MEMBERSHIP OFFER

THE CAMPAIGN TO CLEAN UP AMERICA
CLEAN UP CLEVELAND CHAPTER

Fall, 200X

Dear Concerned Resident,

You will recall our letters last spring. We sent you a bumper sticker and invited you to join in our "Clean Up Cleveland" campaign. More than 3,600 residents replied with a gift to our cause.

We also invited every resident to join in our effort to clean the trash off our city streets. We will use 75 percent of your gift to help build a new energy conversion plant to burn our trash and convert it into electricity for our use. We estimate this new plant can lower our electric bills by *$12 a month* and *$144 a year*.

The other 25 percent of your gift goes to support our public education campaign to ask everyone to stop being a "trasher," and to pick up after themselves. I've noticed a lot of improvement already; our streets are less cluttered; even the areas around our homes and offices are cleaned up. Thank you for helping our cause.

Our campaign is continuing to gain public support. We now offer a charter membership in our new membership association, The Circle of Champions. Every donor of $100 or more will also receive two free tickets to the Cleveland Orchestra and a show at the Cleveland Play House.

Join us today. Put our bumper sticker on your car and help spread the word to "Clean Up Cleveland." Together, we can do it!

Sincerely yours,

I. Harvey Clout
Chair of the Board
Cleveland Cast Iron Works

Encl.

| EXHIBIT 5-14 | LETTER F: OFFER OF CHARTER MEMBERSHIP IN CIRCLE OF CHAMPIONS TO PRIOR DIRECT MAIL DONORS |

THE CAMPAIGN TO CLEAN UP AMERICA
CLEAN UP CLEVELAND CHAPTER

Fall, 200X

Mr. and Mrs. (personal letter; donor name and address printed here)

Dear (donor name):

I want to thank you again for your contribution this past year. Your support has been part of our success. Let's keep up the good work!

Our campaign has begun with a strong reply from our friends and neighbors. More than 6,000 residents are participating in our campaign with their contributions and with their own clean-up activities.

Total funds raised to date are $192,260. The first 75 percent of this money (that's $144,195) has been set aside in our account at National City Bank for construction of the energy conversion plant. Our contribution target is $1,250,000 and we are 12 percent on our way toward our goal.

I hope you will continue your support with a second gift at this time. Please consider a gift of $25 or more if you can; the sooner we reach our goal, the sooner the plant will be constructed and can begin to burn our trash to give us more electricity at lower rates.

Let me also alert you that charter memberships are still available in our Circle of Champions membership association. Gifts of $100 or more are requested. Full details are provided on the enclosed card.

We are off to a great start, thanks to you. Together, we can finish this campaign and clean up our streets at the same time. It's a worthwhile effort.

Please call our offices at (216) CLEAN UP if we can provide you with additional details on our clean-up campaign and about membership in The Circle of Champions.

(continued)

EXHIBIT 5-14   (CONTINUED)

Thank you again for your past support. I hope you will continue to be one of the pioneer contributors to this communitywide effort.

Sincerely yours,

I. Harvey Clout
Chair of the Board
Cleveland Cast Iron Works

EXHIBIT 5-15   TELEPHONE SCRIPT, CIRCLE OF CHAMPIONS RENEWAL FOLLOW UP

Good evening;

This is [___state your name___], a member of the board of directors of the Clean Up Cleveland campaign.

I'm calling to follow up on the letter you received from us last week. You may have noticed that we have raised over $192,000 toward the energy conversion plant, which is 12 percent of our goal. That's a pretty fair start, but we have some work left to do, don't we?

Let me ask if you have any questions about our campaign. Can I answer your questions? [pause]

You were one of our earliest donors and I wanted to call and thank you for your support. We truly appreciate your help on this project. Also, you are a charter member of our Circle of Champions membership association.

By chance, were you able to join us for the Cleveland Orchestra concert at Blossom last summer? How about the show at the Cleveland Play House? I certainly enjoyed both evenings. I am pleased to tell you we will be repeating both programs next summer.

The purpose of my call this evening is to invite you to continue your support of our campaign to clean up our city streets. Can we count on you to renew your membership in The Circle of Champions? [pause]

(If yes, ask) Will it be possible for you to increase your gift at this time? The annual dues remain $100.

(If yes, ask) How much do you think you can give? [pause for reply] That's terrific!

We will send you a confirmation of your renewal pledge tomorrow. It was nice to talk with you. Thank you again for continuing your support of our clean-up campaign. Good evening.

CHAPTER 6

Telephone and
Telemarketing Techniques

Just about everyone knows how to use a telephone. You might think that everyone would be comfortable making and receiving phone calls. Not true, especially when it comes to soliciting on the telephone. Most of us are irked with a call that begins, "May I please speak with Mr. or Mrs. Smith," telling you right away they do not know you at all. Another irritant is the computer call with a prerecorded message that tries to sell you something, but there's no one to talk with.

These and other types of calls have taught us to respond automatically: Hang up! We did not pay for telephone service to get these kinds of calls. For these and other reasons, unwanted and unscheduled telephone calls irritate us. If those are not enough reasons, here are a few more:

- Overuse for commercial purposes
- Insensitivity to calls into the home
- Invasion of privacy
- Overuse of evening hours
- Pressure to respond
- Slick professional callers

These are legitimate reasons why we should react negatively. So, do you think you can raise money using the telephone?

Despite these feelings and their prevalence, direct conversation between donors, prospects, and volunteers on behalf of nonprofit organizations remains an effective and efficient method to raise money. In fact, although our impressions might tell us otherwise, the telephone is underutilized for charitable purposes. There are many positive uses of the telephone for fundraising:

- Donor-relations calls, to maintain close contact with valued donors
- Thank-you calls, to thank a donor for a large gift that has just arrived
- Recognition calls, to thank someone for volunteering, announce an award, or invite to a donor-only gathering
- Service calls, to offer planned giving and estate-planning counsel
- Information calls, to alert donors to a major gift opportunity
- Upgrade calls, to ask for a larger gift than last time
- Renewal calls, to request another, perhaps larger gift
- Recruiting calls, to invite someone to volunteer time and talent
- Support group calls, to stimulate and retain interest, encourage active participation, and retain membership standing
- Donor club calls, to retain interest, stimulate renewal, and explain the added benefits and privileges for a larger gift
- Membership calls, to invite, renew, and upgrade annual memberships
- Follow-up ticket sales calls on mail invitations to encourage attendance at activities, benefits, and special events
- Lapsed donor calls, to recapture prior donors
- Cold calls, to acquire a first-time donor[1]

Anticipate some resistance from board members, management, and volunteers when proposing a telemarketing program. They have heard the horror stories about its intrusion and fraud. You will have to demonstrate that your campaign will be professional, has merit beyond funds raised, and will succeed when fitted into your annual giving programs, whether for new-donor acquisition or renewal and upgrading of current donors, and with positive results, not a public outcry and lots of complaints.

At this point in the book, your direct mail program is now in its second year of renewal and a new membership association is in place. How might the telephone fit each of these established activities? Which group might respond best: those who did not yet renew their direct mail gift or those who just gave again? Should we call our current membership club donors to ask for an upgrade, or will it be more effective to call direct mail donors to invite them to join the club? Should a new telemarketing campaign be tested with each of these two groups first, to see which performs the best? To resolve these options, consider the following requirements to begin a telemarketing program along with the required preparations before you make your decision:

1. Are there enough volunteers who can be recruited and trained to conduct this program?

2. Is there an office site available to make these calls?

3. Should a mailing go out beforehand to alert donors that a call is coming?

4. Do we have the basic research information we need on people who will be called?

5. Should we test our telephone technique on some donors first?

6. Do we have a pledge billing and reminder system ready to follow up?

7. What is the current feeling among people in our community about telephone solicitation calls?

8. Should this telemarketing campaign be prepared as a volunteer activity, or should we hire a telemarketing firm with professional callers?

Given all these tough questions, maybe it will be easier to keep going with our proven direct mail and membership programs. No volunteers or training programs are needed, nor do we need a site or a telemarketing firm. To help resolve so many issues, review the multiple uses for the telephone at the beginning of this chapter. How might your current direct mail and membership programs be improved using one or more of these good telemarketing ideas? If other nonprofit organizations are using telemarketing techniques in your community, call them to ask about their experience as well as their results. With these answers in hand, your evaluations might rest on the final score from the effectiveness criteria shown in Exhibit 6-1. After all this analysis, you will be ready to decide whether to proceed. If you decide to go forward, begin right away with a positive attitude about using the telephone and about telemarketing solicitations.

EXHIBIT 6-1	WHY TELEMARKETING IS EFFECTIVE IN FUNDRAISING[4]

☎ It can be used to personally reach large numbers of donors and prospective donors.

☎ It helps donors better appreciate how their gifts are used, resulting in increased gifts to the organizations.

☎ It increases donor involvement by giving them an opportunity to speak to an organization's representative.

☎ It gathers important donor information about reasons for giving as well as data for keeping records accurate and current.

☎ It allows better communication with donors in times of calm and crisis.

☎ It allows the organization to express its gratitude in person!

☎ It is an excellent way for volunteer callers to become more involved with the organization, see the organization's needs more clearly, and become better donors themselves.

The good news is that when you decide to organize a phone program for your organization, you can turn each of those telephone annoyances into opportunities. *Your* phone program can

⇨ Respect people's privacy and call before or after traditional dinnertimes.

⇨ Call only those individuals you know are interested in your mission and likely to want to help.

⇨ Be attentive to people's responses and engage them without being pushy.

⇨ Care about issues people raise and attempt to address those issues or refer the call to someone in your organization who can.[2]

PREPARING FOR TELEPHONE SOLICITATION

The first lesson everyone involved must learn is to *keep it personal*. A telephone is direct conversation, people talking together. "The more personal the approach, the higher the response rate and the larger the gift."[3] The telephone is the next best thing to face-to-face personal solicitation as the most efficient and effective method of fundraising. However, without a small army of trained volunteers who will meet with your best donors and prospects, the next best method that includes a high degree of personal touch is the telephone.

True, a telemarketing effort also needs a small army of trained volunteers, but each volunteer can call 20, 30, or even 50 people in two hours to discuss making gifts to your organization. The ability of volunteers to "reach out and touch someone" with a personal message is a powerful method to consider on its own because it can reach large numbers of the people you want to contact, and it can be successful.

Volunteers are crucial to a telemarketing effort. Volunteers also have to be recruited, trained, supported, and rewarded for giving of their time and talent, energy, and effort. Volunteers are not always available when you want to stage your telephone calls at times when it fits best with your overall annual giving schedule. Volunteers also take vacations, have emergencies as well as families, jobs, and other duties and responsibilities. The alternative is to hire a professional telemarketing firm that already has experienced and trained callers, that can be scheduled when you prefer, and that can define joint programs that combine using the telephone effectively with your other annual giving methods. Several strengths and weaknesses to these options must be considered when making a choice between these methods, as illustrated in Exhibit 6-2.

Just as testing is essential in good direct mail practice, testing telemarketing as a solicitation method for your organization and its constituency is highly recommended *before* you commit to the full program. One early test is fairly easy and can be done quickly. You and your office staff can each call 20 to 30 of your $100-level donors to contact a total of 100 to 120 people and ask for their annual renewal gift. You also can test their response to making an upgrade gift, giving "something extra" that can support your current priority project, joining your membership club, or making an unrestricted gift. If your test results are better than 50 percent renewal with 20 percent upgraded gifts, you have a potential telemarketing success on your hands. Now test again, this time calling another 100 to 120 individuals who are nondonor prospects (you have mailed them a request but have not yet received a reply to your mail appeals). Select names randomly from your most recent direct mail list. If your test results are 2 percent or higher gifts with an average gift above the minimum that your direct mail program requested (e.g., $25 or $35 or $50), you have another potential telemarketing success on your hands. One more point. These test

EXHIBIT 6-2   COMPARISON CRITERIA BETWEEN VOLUNTEERS AND PROFESSIONAL FIRMS TO CONDUCT A TELEPHONE SOLICITATION CAMPAIGN

Volunteer Callers	Professional Callers
Strengths	*Strengths*
High contact rate (usually 70%–80%)	High contact rate (usually 70%–80%)
Highly interactive and personal	Highly interactive and personal
Ability to contact large numbers of constituents	Ability to contact large numbers of constituents
Response higher than direct mail	Trained and experienced caller ensuring quality
Ability to absorb many indirect costs	High-cost efficiency promoted by technology, techniques, and experienced staff
Direct supervision of calling by staff	High accountability including prompt, detailed reporting
Utilizes and involves volunteers, staff	Low requirement of institutional staff and management
	Return on investment higher than direct mail
	Use of a precall letter reducing phone costs and negative responses and increasing results
	Demonstrated techniques/results
	Experienced senior staff, unique design and application
Weaknesses	*Weaknesses*
Requires careful list selection and data information	Requires careful list selection and data information
Higher investment cost than direct mail	Higher investment cost than direct mail
High demand on professional staff and management	Relatively new approach
High costs in preparation, recruitment, and training	Limited comparable competition
High turnover in part-time callers	Perceptions and experience with other telemarketing firms
Usually requires investment in equipment and facilities	Less commitment to your cause
Telephone charges usually at market rate	No development of volunteers
Results vary widely	
Volunteer attrition likely if calling is on-site	

Source: Adapted from Mark W. Bates, "Advanced Fund Raising Endeavors," in *Getting Started: A Guide to Fund Raising Fundamentals*, The National Society of Fund Raising Executives, Chicago Chapter, 1988, pp. 59–60.

results will provide the information you need to decide the next question, whether you should organize a volunteer telemarketing program or hire a professional telemarketing firm to conduct your program.

THE VOLUNTEER CALLING PROGRAM: PLANNING IS THE KEY TO SUCCESS

Let's assume your choice is to test a volunteer program first. How well prepared are you to launch this telemarketing effort? Quite a lot of work is required to get ready; each of the four elements for success described in Exhibit 6-3 provides excellent guidance.

Planning and Preparation

There can be no substitute for accuracy in current telephone numbers and donor gift records. These are essential data for volunteer callers and should be displayed on a summary sheet or card for each person to be called, along with address, current employer, e-mail address, and recent giving history. This data can be verified during the call. Donor and prospect lists must be sorted into the groups to be called, possibly segregated by locality, gift level, membership status, or other criteria to aid the caller. The letter

---

EXHIBIT 6-3   TELEPHONE SUCCESS IS THE RESULT OF CAREFUL PLANNING[5]

1. *Planning and Preparation.* This means researching phone numbers, preparing prospect cards and report forms, and designing and printing the follow-up mailing pieces. A pre-call postcard is often used to tell prospects that a representative will be calling.

2. *Location.* Calls should be made in a place, preferably free of charge, with ample office space and an adequate number of phones. The type of phone service available helps in making decisions about the wisdom and cost effectiveness of long-distance calling. In some instances, it may be advisable to arrange phonathons on a regional basis.

3. *Solicitors.* A dependable group of capable and enthusiastic callers constitutes the phonathon solicitors. These people may be volunteers or, in some instances, paid participants. Expect them to work four to eight hours total. The training program for these callers should be brief (20–30 minutes) so that their time can be spent on the phone.

4. *Follow-up.* A prompt follow-up mailing confirming each pledge should be sent within a day of the phone call.

announcing the telephone campaign must be written and approved, signed by a board member, senior manager, or volunteer annual telephone campaign chairperson, and mailed on a schedule not more than 10 days prior to when the calls begin. The follow-up pledge confirmation form and reply envelopes must be printed; they should be mailed the day following the calling period.

Location

Selecting the site may not be as easy as it seems, unless you have a board, office area, or conference room at your organization with 20 to 30 phone jacks already installed. What's preferred is a location with the phones within eyesight of all the others so that the callers are together (easier to supervise and support), the tally board can be seen to report results and maintain momentum, and where you can feed everyone before the calls begin. You also prefer a site that includes complimentary phone charges (the donor's "gift-in-kind"), if a lot of long-distance calls will be involved. Other details include parking, access to the building, food service, and clean-up arrangements.

Solicitors

At this point, you will use volunteers. Volunteers have to be identified, recruited, trained, oriented to the project and your organization, scheduled, fed, supervised, motivated, thanked, and rewarded. How many will you need, for how many calling nights, and how reliable can you assume they will be? Next, how capable and enthusiastic will they be on the phone, and will they ask for the gift or just have a nice chat? Will you organize them into teams with team captains to build camaraderie and enthusiasm? What type of performance evaluation will you use; is the focus on the number of calls made or number of pledges secured, or the number of upgrades achieved, or total dollars by caller or teams? Do you also need to know what they thought of your overall program, including how they were recruited, trained, oriented, fed, supervised, motivated, thanked, and rewarded?

Follow-up

At the end of the calling period, you have to be ready to collect all the calling cards with their results, make a quick tabulation so volunteers know the preliminary results, and verify all the pledge details. The next morning, these details must be entered into your donor records system, credit card pledges must be processed, and these donors must be thanked. Pledge notices with the correct amount and project selected must be mailed to each of the other pledge donors. You also need to have your tracking system ready to send reminders in 30, 60, and 90 days to maximize your collection results.

DEVELOPING A TELEMARKETING PROGRAM

All this, just to begin to *think about* how to begin! To prepare and conduct the entire program, examine in detail each of the steps to develop a telemarketing program, shown in Exhibit 6-4 and discussed in detail in the following paragraphs.

Identify Prospects to Call

A few big decisions are needed right away. Are you calling donors or prospective donors? You cannot call both the same evening without running the risk of confusing your volunteers. If you wish to call both, reserve separate evenings to call each group separately. Begin by testing a donor file. Select a group of people who need to be called, such as those who have not

---

EXHIBIT 6-4   STEPS INVOLVED IN DEVELOPING A TELEMARKETING PROGRAM[6]

☎ Identify prospects to call.

☎ Enlist callers.

☎ Find site.

☎ Produce pledge cards.

☎ Produce support materials such as scripts and fact sheets.

☎ Segment pledge cards based on giving history or special affiliations.

☎ Train callers.

☎ Call prospects and ask.

☎ Follow up pledges immediately and through a regular reminder system.

☎ Give appropriate thanks.

☎ Report results.

---

made a gift of $100 or more within the past 12 or more months; these donors are important to you and you need to make this extra effort to keep their interest and support. These donors also are important to you because they have the obvious financial potential for more gifts as well as larger gifts. If this donor list has 200 names, you will need to recruit and train perhaps 10 to 12 volunteers, as each can call about 20 people in two hours or less. If the list has 500 names (you lucky dog!), you will need 25 to 30 volunteers, plus a site with 25 to 30 phone lines. Or, you can ask your original dozen callers to agree to make calls for at least two nights. You also will want to verify that you have home telephone numbers for all these donors. If not, that task of data collection and verification will be the first priority for you and your staff.

Next, consider your prospect file for a second telemarketing test. What do you know about the names in this file? Your best success will likely come from people that live nearby; they are more likely to have heard about your organization and perhaps know something about its programs and services. Sort your list by ZIP code; select those names who live in middle- and upper-class neighborhoods; they are more likely to have incomes to allow added charitable giving. Don't be sensitive or squeamish about being discriminatory in your list making. Your responsibility is to raise money for your organization; this first attempt at telemarketing must prove it can bring in enough money to justify use of the telephone. Last but not least, find out if the source of this mail list can provide telephone numbers for each of these names. If not, find a good list that includes phone numbers; you can't make calls without them. The telephone book is a good and accurate source if you have the time to look up hundreds of names; however, some people on the list may have unlisted numbers.

Enlist Callers

Selecting people to ask to be volunteers requires that you are experienced at identifying, recruiting, training, motivating, and managing volunteer callers. You need a well-thought-out plan as your recruitment strategy. If you have used volunteer callers before, invite them to serve first. Call those who volunteer for your organization in other roles next, to help for one or two evenings. Third, call some of your donors, especially those with three to five years of consistent gifts. By calling to recruit, you also will be able to evaluate how they perform on the phone, a big clue to their potential success with this assignment. Finally, ask to meet with those who agree to volunteer in a face-to-face interview, to finalize your selections. A volunteer who has never done this before will need a lot of help; so will those who have, even if they have been a caller for your organization before. The list of people to be called will be different; the purpose or use of the funds raised will be a different story. Details about their training program will be discussed later on this list, but when recruiting, you must promise you will train them to this task.

Find a Site

Not as easy as it may sound. Certainly, every business office of any size has lots of telephones, but finding one you can use will take some effort. What you seek is a situation, probably a business office setting, that will allow a group of volunteers to come in after hours, sit at workers' desks, eat a catered meal (pizza and salads are always welcome fare), and use the firm's telephones (at company expense) for two hours or more to call their friends. Site candidates can come from your volunteers or board members; a representative of the site selected should be present each time. Accounting firms, banks, insurance companies, and brokerage offices are likely sites; they are convenient locally and safe. It is also possible that the employees may be able to be invited to join in the calls. In any event, the employees have regular work hours so the office will be empty, except for any who volunteer from that employer.

Produce Pledge Cards

Because all replies are verbal pledges, a combination worksheet and pledge record form is necessary. This document provides the caller with data they need to make their calls (name, address, and phone number, prior gift history if any), to each donor or prospect. Other details (see Exhibit 6-5) include details to be recorded as the calls are made; caller's name, date of the call, pledge amount, details about donor's choice for use of their gift funds, charge card account number and expiration date, and comments. This record is important for several reasons:

1. It is your only record of a gift decision.
2. It is your only record of the call's results.
3. It is your only record of the donor's gift restriction.

EXHIBIT 6-5   STATISTICS CHECKLIST[7]

✔ Name of caller
✔ Number of calls made
✔ Number of pledges received
✔ Number of dollars pledged
✔ Number of unspecified pledges made
✔ Number of refusals
✔ Number of noncontacts (bad addresses and telephone numbers)
✔ Average gift
✔ Number of increased and decreased gifts
✔ Number of new gift club members
✔ Number of new gifts pledged

4. It is your only record of any change in data (address, phone number, etc.).

5. It is your only record of the donor's charge card account number and expiration date.

6. It is your only record to tally the results of each evening's calls.

7. It is your only record from which to track payments.

Nonprofit organizations with telemarketing experience prepare the pledge form as a multipart document with donor or prospect data entered from computer records with adequate space for the caller to record the results. Copies are easily available to give to volunteer leaders and staff to tally results, place confirming recalls to donors to thank them for their gift pledge, and to enter into donor record files back at the organization's office the next morning. If the donor authorizes use of his or her American Express, MasterCard, or Visa, a thank-you letter must be sent each donor, along with their credit card receipt the next business day. For all other donors, a separate pledge document is necessary, to be mailed to each donor the next business day with a reply envelope, to begin collections.

Produce Support Materials Such as Scripts and Fact Sheets

Whatever may be their level of enthusiasm to call their friends and neighbors, volunteer callers must be instructed carefully on how to make a solicitation call. They also must be well versed in facts about your organization, the purposes and uses of funds to be raised, how to ask for a specific amount, how to respond to objections, and how to close. Their training must include role-playing exercises to practice, following the script provided them. This script is their most important tool; callers must accept that it must to be followed; they are not to "wing it" with their own version. A telemarketing call is not an easy to call to make; the caller has only seconds to identify himself or herself as a volunteer for a charitable organization; the purpose of their call is obvious. If they cannot establish credibility quickly, the person called will hang up.

Basic elements required in the script include (1) the opening, (2) identification, (3) purpose of the call (the need for their help), (4) the formal "ask" for the gift, (5) a possible second ask for a lower amount, and (6) the closing. The script for a prior donor will be different from that for a first-time prospect. The all-important fact sheet is one page in length and itemizes in bullet points the essential facts about your organization and the priority project. Volunteer callers should be comfortable translating these facts into their own points for brief discussion. As their calls progress, they should use those facts that seem to spark the highest interest and gain the positive gift decision. In the debriefing to follow, every caller should point out those facts that were most acceptable plus where the script might be improved, based on their experience.

Segment Pledge Cards Based on Giving History or Special Affiliations

As donors are the best prospects for telephone solicitation (just as in every other fundraising method), volunteers should receive enough information about each person to be called—especially their prior gifts (dates, amounts, purposes), plus any other relationships with the nonprofit organization (membership organization, donor club, season ticket holder, benefit event participant, and more) that will allow the caller to use these prior experiences in their conversation. Also, given the time constraints of the calling period (usually two hours), and the intent that each caller try to speak with 20, 30, or even 50 people in a two-hour period, calls should be placed to the "best prospects" first. These can be defined as the most faithful donors, largest donors, most frequent donors, or whatever the data suggests as those donors who are most likely to respond positively to the call. Volunteer leaders should instruct their callers to call these best prospects first, so that these candidates are renewed as quickly as possible, to build momentum, and to use the results from early renewals as part of the script with others that follow. Tally boards and broadcast announcements as gifts begin to be recorded also will inspire other callers. Callers can be coached to warm up by calling their best prospects first so as to enjoy these early successes and build their confidence for continued calls.

Train Callers

Proper and thorough caller training is essential and must be repeated every night before callers can begin. The expert advice of Bill Freyd and Diane Carlson, pioneers in nonprofit telemarketing, recommends a thorough agenda plan for caller training, either with volunteers or with part-time employees:

1. Mission and goals of the organization.
2. Case for support—why the organization needs money and how it will be used.
3. Review of any pre-call materials sent in advance of calling to familiarize callers with information the prospect has already received.
4. Training on the script—use role-play.
5. Review of the type of people who will be contacted (alumni, former patients, subscribers, etc.).
6. Key objections the caller may encounter and answers to those objections.
7. Discussion of any public relations problems the organization may have had.
8. Information about the fundraising goals and how caller performance will be measured.
9. Particulars about the job—hours, employment policies, and so on. Follow the laws in your state for part-time employees.
10. Payment of callers. If there are incentives, how they will be used.

When possible, someone who has credibility in regard to the case for support (a physician, a faculty member, a patient, etc.) should participate in caller training. Obviously, an enthusiastic, committed presentation of the case will enable callers to better relate to the need and to communicate it over the phone. Scripts for callers are best when they are *not read* to prospects but are communicated in the callers' own words. The best calling occurs when callers are *listening to prospects* rather than to themselves.[8]

Call Prospects and Ask

Everyone has been trained to the script and fact sheet and has practiced on one another. The pizza and sodas have been consumed. It is time to begin making calls. Here's where the fun can begin, and fun is important. Bring a bell to be rung when each gift of $100 or more is recorded. Put up a chalkboard or flip chart to tally receipts every 15 minutes. Announce the time when a 15-minute midpoint break will be scheduled and when calling will be concluded (all must end before 8:00 or 9:00 P.M., depending on local regulations). Volunteers may group themselves in teams for camaraderie, perhaps even some competition, although contests between teams can lead to pressure tactics in calling, which are not appropriate. Offer prizes to teams as well as individual callers based on number of calls completed, not dollars raised, as the objective is to contact as many donors and prospects as possible. Celebrate the results with everyone and ask everyone for their critique of their experiences, both verbally at the end and on written critique sheets before they leave. Collect all the scripts, fact sheets, and pledge forms to be taken back to your office. Clean up each desk area used and take out the trash (e.g., scrap paper and pizza boxes) so that the office site is left just as it was (or better) when everyone arrived.

Follow Up Pledges Immediately and through a Regular Reminder System

Every pledge must now be confirmed in writing with each donor by mail, usually completed the next business day. This is not a simple task and must have high priority, as each gift must be verified by the staff and pledge notices must be prepared and mailed to each donor. If there are any large pledges that were not confirmed by phone the night before, call them now to thank them. If there were any questionable pledges or unclear volunteer report forms, call these donors now to thank them and to clarify their exact gift intentions. Depending on the donor records system, data entry of these annual gifts as formal pledges ("unconditional promises to give" in accountant's language) is not advised; except for those who authorized credit card payments, their money has not yet arrived. A separate record system is needed to track telephone pledges and to be used in mailing reminder notices. Some experts recommend a reminder system that will continue every 30, 60, and 90 days to those who are yet unpaid; each reminder also is an opportunity to thank the donor again for the commitment, as well as to make clear that payment is now expected in fulfillment of the pledge. Some nonpayment can be anticipated, perhaps as high as 20 percent of pledges from first-time donors. Prior donors are expected to be more reliable with their pledge payments, but both must be pursued.

Give Appropriate Thanks

The thank-you process begins on calling night while the donor is still on the phone. A second call made the same evening is a good idea, to verify the pledge and to provide a second and perhaps more personal thank-you message from someone in official status with your organization, either an administrator or volunteer leader. Pledge billing notices all should begin with a statement of appreciation for the donor's intention of support. When payment is received, a fourth and more formal thank-you opportunity is conducted. For gifts of larger size, depending on institutional policy and practice, a fifth acknowledgment letter from a board member or senior administrator may follow. Every thank-you message will be well received, appreciated, and remembered by your donors.

These acknowledgments will be followed by donor recognition and continued donor communications, according to your organization's established donor-recognition guidelines. These benefits and privileges for telemarketing donors also should follow established policy and procedure for all other donors (see the donor recognition guidelines in Exhibit 4-4); separate recognition programs for telephone donors are not recommended. Your organization needs to be above criticism from even the hint of preference given to one class of donors over another. Once appropriate recognition is in place, added opportunities to acknowledge donors are appropriate and include such standard practices as placing the roster of telephone-campaign participants and the volunteer callers in your next newsletter or annual report, along with a story about how the money is being used. Another option is to publish a list of new gift club or membership participants who joined in the past three to six months. If you received media coverage for your campaign, a paid advertisement in the local paper under a large "Thank-You" banner is a strategic method not only to thank donors and volunteers and tell the story about how the money is being used for community benefit but also to help recruit volunteers and donors for your next campaign. One caution about publishing donor lists using these widely circulated broadcast methods: Some donors are sensitive about such disclosure without their prior knowledge or permission. Always verify permission to publish the name of each of your donors, especially those whose gifts are in higher categories.

Report Results

Two areas merit evaluation—volunteer performance and solicitation results. For volunteers, how well they performed as a *group* is most important. How many calls were made, percentage of calls made to pledges received, how many gifts were received (separate renewals from new, first-time donors), total funds raised, and average gift size are all indicators of a successful telephone campaign. It also is helpful to record how many refusals were received (from both donors and prospects) and how many incorrect telephone numbers prevented any solicitation. It is important to track whether everyone on the donor list was called. If not called, what was the value of their prior gifts, and how will their renewal gifts be solicited now? Final details, including cost–benefit analysis, will have to wait until after pledge collections are completed and expenses tallied (usually within 90 days) to declare the total results. At that point, further analysis of unpaid pledges, along with increases and decreases in donor gift patterns, will be useful to study. All of these details should be segregated for study. Evaluate each calling period and the separate groups called (new and old donors, new prospects, whether their gifts were unrestricted or restricted, average gift size, upgrade performance, estimated value left in uncalled prior donors, and more); all are valuable facts to know, not for competition between groups, but for planning the next telemarketing campaign.

SHOULD YOU HIRE A PROFESSIONAL TELEMARKETING FIRM?

The program described thus far is for a *volunteer* telephone campaign. It is also possible to hire a professional telemarketing firm to conduct this campaign. The details are much the same, except that the firm might hire and train the callers, plus make the calls from its site. You will have to provide the telemarketing firm with the same donor and prospect lists with prior giving details, receive and process all gifts and pledges, send out acknowledgments and pledge notices, enter gifts and pledges in your records, conduct donor recognition, and report the results. The firm can help you with all of these details, if needed, plus prepare the script and fact sheet, design and print pledge forms, track the results, and assist with analysis of the results. If the firm tells you it prefers to receive and process the gifts directly, consider another firm. You cannot give up absolute control of the receipt of every gift. To do so is to beg for trouble. There is no need for a firm to provide this service, other than to set themselves up for potential mischief. All too often, taking the easy route to let the telemarketer do the work leads to abusive practices, high-pressure sales tactics, excessive costs, and other areas of fraudulent behavior with potential lawsuits and a major scandal for your organization.

The process of recruiting and hiring a firm is the same as hiring any other vendor your organization employs. Prepare a *Request for Proposal* (RFP) and send it to a list of professional firms you know about and have researched with the help of other nonprofits who have used these firms. The RFP asks them to submit a plan for how they would provide their telemarketing services, their recommendations for the period of the campaign as well as expectations of the returns, and their compensation plan (which should be fee based, not a percentage or commission based). Exhibit 6-6 provides a series of recommended factors important when selecting an outside telemarketing vendor. Several of the states in the United States have legislated controls regarding telephone solicitation to residents within their boundaries. In hiring a firm, be sure to check first with state authorities for their current regulations on telephone solicitation and on hiring professional solicitors (called *paid solicitors* or *commercial solicitors* in some states). In most states, copies of the contract with the firm and financial results of the telemarketing campaign must be filed prior to starting the campaign. The firm also must be registered each year to practice in the state where your organization operates, to pay the required fees, and to be bonded. These legal requirements are the result of improper conduct by those who have used the telephone for fraudulent solicitations from a trusting public. Observing the highest ethical standards in telemarketing is

EXHIBIT 6-6	CONSIDERATIONS IN SELECTING AN OUTSIDE VENDOR FOR TELEMARKETING SERVICES

1. The program should be custom-designed by the vendor to fit with the mission and goals of the organization.

2. The vendor should be as invisible as possible to the prospects being called so that the charitable organization is presented with a positive image.

3. The callers should be paid a flat hourly rate, not on commission. Incentives for a job well done can be used but should not be a major part of the overall compensation for callers. Commission often leads to high pressure on the phone.

4. Funds collected from the pledges should be sent by the donor directly to the charity rather than to the telemarketing vendor. Most reported abuses have included a violation of this policy.

5. Prospects who prefer not to be called in the future must be tracked and removed from future calling lists so that their wishes are respected. This provision requires database maintenance capability some vendors and charities do not have.[9]

---

critically important to every nonprofit organization and the best answer to negative attitudes from those to be called. It is imperative that charities and their vendors follow the law and observes strict self-regulation to avoid donor embarrassment and disillusion, as well as to prevent damage to the organization's image and reputation and the public's confidence and trust in its fundraising methods. There is no room for error when it comes to observing the law.

There have been legal problems, scandals, and scams resulting from telemarketing abuses. Published reports suggest that solicitation companies hired by nonprofit organizations receive only about 35 percent of the donations collected in their names; the remainder goes to the solicitors for expenses and profits. It is important to add this: "A solicitation company that returns little money to charity is not necessarily acting improperly. But two-thirds of the solicitors that routinely distribute to their charity clients less than 15 percent of donations have been sued by state and federal agencies on charges of engaging in deceptive practices."[10] Smaller nonprofits whose staff support and records systems are minimal, whose cause and organization are lesser-known, and whose location may be rural are higher-risk clients for telemarketing firms. Unscrupulous solicitation companies have thus taken advantage of smaller nonprofit organizations, inflating expenses such as compensation with the excuse that the effort required to raise money was greater.

In truth, larger organizations that integrate telephone usage into an already-established annual giving program have better performance.

> The smallest charities—those with annual revenues of less than $1 million—received a median of only 29 cents for every dollar raised. That means that in half the campaigns for charities of that size, the nonprofit organization received more than 29 cents, and in half it received less. The largest charities—those with annual revenue of $10 million or more—received a median of 42 cents for each dollar raised. Mid-size charities received a median of 34 cents per dollar raised.[11]

It is unfortunate, but there are unscrupulous people who would use the telephone to defraud people of their money in the name of charity. They invent names of charities to sound like established organizations, even religious entities; they add threats for reduced police and fire services when properly or improperly representing law enforcement or fire department causes, usually a "widows and orphans fund." They have runners standing by to come to your home and collect your check, claiming that the cost of printing information about the cause, mailing it, and providing reply envelopes reduces the net proceeds to the charity; their method is more cost-effective. They promise certain levels of net proceeds weekly, which sounds good to the unsuspecting, but results in minimal returns without supervision of all the cash receipts that they control. The means and methods to defraud the unsuspecting are many; those in volunteer and management roles for nonprofits who are gullible or who choose an "easy money" scheme as the fundraising answer to fiscal difficulties, are victims and so are their donors.

It is the duty of nonprofit board members, administrators, and fundraisers to know and to follow the laws relating to public solicitation, including the use of professional solicitors. It also is their duty to perform "due diligence" in selecting a firm. The Internal Revenue Service, the Federal Trade Commission, the U.S. Postal Service, and state attorneys general are serious about preventing telemarketing fraud and are not afraid to prosecute commercial solicitors, their firms, and charities that hire them. Legal recourse to fraudulent telemarketing includes federal mail-fraud and money-laundering charges, along with violations of state registration and reporting regulations. Again, the best advice is to "look a gift horse in the mouth and examine every tooth."

What are the alternatives to using a professional telemarketing firm to make your calls? You can hire a firm to advise and consult with you on your entire program, including how to manage a volunteer telemarketing campaign. You also can retain a firm to manage the campaign with part-time employees hired by your organization. The firm will train and supervise these employees to make the calls and provide all the support required. You need the same preparations as for a volunteer campaign, plus you have compensation issues to address.

Another option is to go it alone and hire a corps of part-time callers yourself. If so, you will need to recruit them more selectively than with volunteers to find individuals whose age, background, and familiarity with your organization will be key assets. Conduct as much of this recruiting as you can over the telephone; use these calls to evaluate how each applicant sounds and how they carry on a conversation. Arrange to see those who pass this test for a formal interview, just as you would any other employee. Colleges and universities have great success with student callers, whose enthusiasm and energy translates well over the phone when calling alumni and parents. A good suggestion is to contact your local college, if they use student callers, to learn when their telemarketing campaign is held and to alert them to your need for experienced student callers for some additional part-time employment. Compensation for every caller should be an hourly wage and never a commission or percentage of funds raised; such business practices may be perfectly ethical and legal in the for-profit business world, but they unfailingly lead to a more aggressive style and high-pressure tactics, neither of which is desired nor appropriate for nonprofit organizations.

BUDGETING FOR TELEPHONE SOLICITATION

The budget required for each option to conduct a telephone solicitation campaign will not be alike. Exhibit 6-7 illustrates sample budgets using volunteers, a professional firm, and the combination of a firm and volunteers. The option of using a firm to be your consultant and to supervise the program using part-time employees hired by your organization is not presented in this exhibit; the budget for that option will be similar to Budget

EXHIBIT 6-7   ESTIMATED BUDGETS FOR
               TELEPHONE SOLICITATION
               (3,000 CALLS)

	Budget A	Budget B	Budget C
			Combined Volunteers and
		Professional	
	Volunteers	Firm	Professionals
Estimated Expenses			
Computer-generated donor selection	$ 500	$ 500	$ 500
Printing donor record cards	400	400	400
Volunteer/staff training meetings (food and beverages)	800	800	800
Telephone equipment fee	-0-	1,000	-0-
Telephone charges			
Local calls (2,500)	300	250	300
Long distance (500)	600	500	600
Printing letters and envelopes	600	600	600
Printing pledge forms	100	100	100
Mail assembly and postage	420	420	420
Gift processing and acknowledgment	200	-0-	200
Donor recognition	300	-0-	300
Miscellaneous supplies	200	200	200
Contingency fund	250	200	200
Firm marketing/advertising	-0-	2,000	2,000
Firm travel expenses	-0-	2,000	2,000
Firm professional fees or salaries for employees	-0-	8,000	4,000
Subtotals	$ 4,670	$16,970	$12,620
Estimated Income (Pledges Paid)	$25,000	$50,000	$35,000
Net income	$20,330	$33,030	$22,380
Cost of fundraising	19%	34%	36%
Return	435%	195%	177%

Source: James M. Greenfield. *Fund-Raising Cost Effectiveness: A Self-Assessment Workbook* (New York: John Wiley & Sons, 1996), 88.

B in the exhibit. Budgets for fundraising programs also should include an estimated income to be received wherever possible.

Accurate predictions of the number of replies, actual expenses and net income are unknown, but estimates are possible based on prior experience.

If the telephone campaign is directed at prior donors, previous experience will be useful for results comparisons, to measure if one campaign was more efficient in recruiting more donors or was more profitable with higher average gifts than another. However, if the campaign objective is to increase the percentage of prior donors who renewed their gifts, or to increase both percentage and amount of increased gift levels from upgrade requests, such comparisons will be more directly beneficial. If the list is not prior donors, performance will be significantly different and can only be compared fairly with other first-time acquisition efforts, such as in a direct mail acquisition campaign.

If this effort is the first telephone campaign held, whether to donors or prospects, budget estimates of cost, income, and net proceeds are still useful as the plan to follow; more accurate forecasts will be possible the next time, based on the first effort's results. After three years of experience (or three separate telephone campaigns), reliable forecasts for costs, income, and net proceeds can be expected. Comparative analysis of telephone campaign results measured against other annual giving methods is useful, to a point. Direct mail response is close to telephone response, as both can be used for acquisition, renewal, and upgrading. In this comparison, the telephone is expected to outperform the mail in each category since personal contact has occurred. In comparing telephone results for membership organizations and donor clubs, you are still comparing direct mail usage, and both should have higher performance levels due to the attractions that these programs have for donors and prospects. The same criteria also are applicable for response rates for charity benefits and special events, again comparing mail invitation responses versus telephone ticket and table sales.

Exhibit 6-8 provides a comparison of direct mail results with telephone solicitation in four separate annual giving programs. In this illustration, not only is gift income higher from telephone solicitations, but the number of donors and average gifts were higher, even after final tallies of paid pledges.

The most efficient and cost-effective use of the telephone is to combine it in strategic ways with other annual giving solicitation methods. A letter to donors and/or prospects announcing a coming campaign sends ahead information on an urgent community need and the expected time when a phone call can be expected to discuss the matter. Follow-up calls must be made when announced, usually within 7 to 10 days after the mail drop date. Any longer delay weakens the recall that anyone will have of the

EXHIBIT 6-8   ANNUAL GIVING DONOR RENEWAL USING DIRECT MAIL COMPARED WITH TELEPHONE SOLICITATION

	Direct Mail	Membership Organization	Donor Club	Support Group	Total
A. Prior Donors					
Solicited by Mail					
Number mailed	3,000	300	300	300	3,900
Mail replies	1,575	211	224	222	2,232
Percentage	52.5%	70.3%	74.7%	74%	57.2%
Income received	$59,850	$21,100	$34,720	$22,200	$133,362
Average gift	$ 38.00	$ 100	$ 155	$ 100	$ 59.75
B. Prior Donors					
Solicited by Telephone					
Number called	3,000	300	300	300	3,900
Calls made	2,250	250	265	254	3,019
Contact percentage	75%	83.3%	88.3%	84.7%	77.1%
Gifts pledged	2,005	225	231	233	2,694
Income pledged	$76,190	$22,500	$35,805	$23,300	$157,795
Average gift pledged	$ 38.00	$ 100	$ 155	$ 100	$ 58.57
Pledge percentage	89.1%	90%	87.2%	91.7%	89.2%
Income received/ gifts paid	$57,038	$18,900	$29,915	$19,700	$136,468
Number paid	1,504	185	201	198	2,209
Average paid gift	$ 37.92	$102.16	$148.83	$ 99.49	$ 61.78
Percentage paid	75%	82%	87%	85%	82%

Source: James M. Greenfield. *Fund-Raising Cost Effectiveness: A Self-Assessment Workbook* (New York: John Wiley & Sons, 1996), 91.

letter and its vital information. It also helps every telephone campaign to have a deadline for responses, adding honest urgency to the message. Examples include the close of a fiscal year, date for an upcoming event, publication of a directory of names of donors, or completed funding of a project with a challenge grant that includes an imposed deadline to qualify for matching funds.

OTHER USES OF THE TELEPHONE

The many uses of the telephone beyond active solicitation begin the moment a gift arrives, to call donors and thank them for their generous support. Many organizations arrange these immediate calls based on gift size ($100 or more, $500 or more, or $1,000 or more), or when they join a membership organization or upgrade their gifts to donor club. What is important about the immediate telephone call is the opportunity for a personal high-touch contact with an important donor. And, at all times, our duty as professionals representing valued community-benefit organizations serving public needs is friend-raising and relationship-building. A call is perhaps the easiest cultivation opportunity to practice that duty. Other reasons to call include this baker's dozen of opportunities for telephone use:

1. To invite donors as your special guests at a future activity, benefit, or special event, in appreciation for their support

2. To ask for consideration of a volunteer assignment, including leadership of a fundraising program

3. To confirm reservations for an activity, benefit, or special event and to discuss who will be coming with them

4. To ask for advice on a donor or prospect being considered for a special project, increased gift, or volunteer assignment

5. To confirm a level of sponsorship or underwriting for an activity, benefit, or special event and discuss what number(s) of their guests and their names who will be participating in the activity, benefit, or event

6. To ask if a donor might make use of a new service, schedule an appointment, or consider a subscription

7. To confirm attendance at an upcoming committee meeting, update with facts to support an assignment, or review the agenda

8. To ask for participation in a market research survey about the organization and its programs and services

9. To confirm acceptance of a volunteer assignment or appointment

10. To ask for nominations for candidates to be recognized in an honors and awards program

11. To confirm a change in cumulative giving total, raising the donor to a new level for donor recognition

12. To ask for nominations for candidates for leadership in voluntary service on the board or at a committee level

13. To confirm an appointment to meet, or to join another volunteer or staff person in meeting with a donor or prospect to discuss a gift for the organization

Add to this list, stimulated most by gifts and focused on donors, any other uses for your telephone you can imagine. There it is, that not-always-silent tool of technology sitting on your desk, that inexpensive, uncomplicated instrument of communication sitting beside your computer. Pick it up; touch someone you haven't spoken to lately, maybe as long as a year ago. You can call a donor or maybe a committee member, even a staff member or someone who helped you and your organization in the past. People are a fundraiser's business; make them feel important by remembering to talk to them. Reach for that phone. Every time you call, you can always begin with "thank you for your support of our organization; we deeply appreciate all that you do for us."

FOCUS: CCUA CLEAN UP CLEVELAND CHAPTER

Karen Anderson had been pleased with the renewal response from her original group of donors, those 1,504 individuals who answered the first test mailings with their 914 gifts and $31,064, for a response rate of 66.77 percent and an average gift of $34. She was concerned that the remaining 590 original donors might be lost unless some added effort for their renewal was made. Karen had been planning to conduct a mini-test of telephone technique by asking her board members to call Circle of Champions members who had not renewed their gift in the fall mail cycle. She also was wondering whether a telephone campaign might be a good idea to renew the 5,157 direct mail donors from the first full acquisition effort, but was unsure how they might respond to a telephone call asking for their first renewal gift. She was intrigued with the idea of using the telephone to conduct a control group test, splitting all the direct mail donors of $100 or more into two control groups, inviting half by mail and the other by telephone to renew their gift, adding a special offer to join The Circle of Champions for each group. The more she thought about it, the more convinced she became to test a telephone renewal strategy first before adding the expenses of another big mailing. She believed her board would agree to this test because the direct mail program had begun to show it was effective at recruiting new donors, with more than 6,000 donors in this first year.

However, they remained quite committed to the goal of increasing participants and were not focused just on the revenue, so long as each solicitation activity also was profitable. So far, all had been.

Anderson called Titus Brown and caught him in his office. "Titus, have you ever used a telephone campaign with any of your clients?"

"You bet," he replied. "Many local companies have been quite successful marketing themselves and their products with telemarketing. Why do you ask?"

Without hesitation, Karen replied: "Because I'm thinking of calling some of our donors who did not respond to our mail campaign last fall as a test; I don't want to lose them and they might respond better if we talk to them rather than send them any more letters. We also will get some feedback from them about our project at the same time."

"Sounds good to me," he replied. "I'll see Harvey tomorrow morning and alert him that you are putting this idea together. Can you have your plans ready for our board meeting next Thursday?"

"Of course," Karen replied. "Thanks, Telly, for your help. By the way, can you put me in touch with someone at the telemarketing company you use? I'll need to ask them for a contract right away."

"Sure thing," said Telly. "Call Bob Yancy at Telecom; he's the president, and a friend of mine, too. Be sure to tell him he owes me one when you call."

"Wonderful," Karen replied, "Thanks again, Telly; you're a peach!"

After she hung up the phone, Karen had to pause. "Here we go again; I just wanted to get Telly's take on the idea, and the next thing you know, I have to make a presentation to the board to spell out the whole program!" She looked up Telecom in the phone book and dialed the number.

Within six weeks, Anderson had recruited 35 volunteer callers, all donors, and had scheduled two separate orientation and training sessions, one a week prior to the two calling nights and the other at the start of both evenings. Micky Edwards, director of training at Telecom, was assigned without any charge by Bob Yancy to provide the training and to guide Anderson through all the necessary preparations. He also told Karen he had now paid off Telly's obligation "in full."

A random selection of donor names was made by computer for this test, choosing 200 donors from the direct mail lists used this past year, plus 250 names from the more recent spring acquisition and renewal series. All 138 charter members of the Circle of Champions were called for their first renewal. Harvey Clout agreed to send out the letter alerting donors about the call (see Exhibit 6-9); it was mailed to all 1,639 donor prospects on Monday the week before the calls were scheduled.

EXHIBIT 6-9   SAMPLE LETTER NOTICE OF SCHEDULED VOLUNTEER TELEPHONE CALL

The Campaign to Clean Up America
Clean Up Cleveland Chapter

April, 200X

Mr. and Mrs. (personal letter; donor name and address printed here)

Dear (donor name):

Again, it is my personal pleasure to thank you for your early support of our special campaign to clean up our city streets. Our efforts this first year are making good progress, but we have much yet to do.

You will receive a phone call from one of our volunteer callers in about a week. It is our hope to be able to provide you, as one of our early contributors, with the opportunity to share more information about our project and its progress. At the same time we also will be asking for your thoughts on how our campaign is going, whether you are using our bumper sticker on your car, and a few other brief questions.

Also during our call, we will invite you to consider renewing your first contribution as part of our spring fundraising campaign. Our Circle of Champions program may be of interest to you; enclosed is a brochure that describes this new donor club and its many benefits for your contribution of $100 or more. Be sure to ask about this program when our volunteer calls you. I hope you will consider joining the Circle of Champions as so many other Cleveland residents have already.

Let me thank you again for your first gift to our campaign. We look forward to your continued support of this special effort; only with your help can we make our city the great place to live that we all desire.

Sincerely yours,

I. Harvey Clout
Chair of the Board
Cleveland Iron Works

Enclosure

Micky drafted the script for the callers and provided both their training sessions on its use (see Exhibit 6-10). The calls were all local and were made on the next Tuesday and Thursday evenings from Telecom's outbound calling headquarters in Solon, just south of Cleveland, between 6:00 and 8:00 P.M. For both Karen Anderson and Alice Nice,

EXHIBIT 6-10	SAMPLE SCRIPT FOR A VOLUNTEER CALLING A PRIOR DONOR

Greeting: Good evening. Is this Mrs. Robert Smith? Mrs. Smith, my name is Valerie Adams and I'm a volunteer calling on behalf of our "Clean Up Cleveland" campaign. We are so grateful to you for your early support of our efforts to improve our city streets. Did you receive a letter from our chairman, Mr. Harvey Clout, in the last week? Good, I'm glad you did. I'm the volunteer he said would be calling you.

Purpose: May I ask you for your opinion about our project? I only have four questions. Thank you; I'll be brief. First, did you receive your bumper sticker? (If yes, reply "That's great!" If no, offer to send another and go to question #3.) Second, did you place it on your car? It's a magnetic sticker, not a permanent one with glue. That's right, you can put it on and take it off anytime. Mine stays on even in the car wash. My third question, what do you think about our campaign to clean up our city streets?

The Upgrade Ask: We appreciate all your thoughts; they are very helpful. My fourth and last question is to invite you to continue your support of our project—can you consider a gift of $100 to join our Circle of Champions this year? (If yes, reply, "Thank you so much. Do you wish to pay by credit card? I can take the information this evening and we will process it tomorrow." If yes, but not by credit card, say: "I will be happy to record your pledge and send you a confirmation notice and reply envelope right away. Let me verify your mailing address right now. Thank you so much for all your help. Goodbye.")

The Back-Up Renewal Ask: (If unable to give at the Circle of Champions level, proceed.) I can understand that $100 is too much right now. Can we count on you for the same amount as last year; your gift was for $35 last fall? (If yes, reply: "We can; thank you so much. That's wonderful! Do you think you could increase it to $50 this time? Yes, that's really generous. Thank you. Would you like to pay by credit card? I can take the information this evening and we can process it tomorrow." If yes, but _not_ by credit card, say: "I will be happy to record your pledge and send you a confirmation notice right away. Let me verify your mailing address right now. Thank you again for all your help. Goodbye.")

her assistant, this was their first experience with a volunteer telephone solicitation and a telemarketing exhibition. Thanks to Micky's help, both evenings went quite well. The evaluation sheets from the volunteers showed they were pleased with their new and exciting roles and almost all were willing to volunteer again.

Friday morning, Karen and Alice mailed all the pledge notices (see Exhibit 6-11) and processed all the credit card gifts. They then tallied the results and began to wonder if this program was really all that successful (see Exhibit 6-12). The response rate at 43 percent was surprisingly good, as was the average gift at $52 much better than their direct mail results, with an average gift of $34 (see Exhibit 5-11). Somewhat mysterious was the comparison between the 66.77 percent re-

---

EXHIBIT 6-11   SAMPLE TELEPHONE PLEDGE THANK-YOU RECEIPT AND PLEDGE NOTICE

Official Gift Receipt

Campaign to Clean Up America   Receipt #: 00045272

Clean Up Cleveland Chapter   Pledge Date: ___04/16/02___
12345 Superior Avenue
Cleveland, OH 44020   Gift Pledge: ___$ 250.00___

                                               Purpose: Unrestricted

Thank you for your recent gift of ___$ 250.00___ to support our efforts to clean the streets of our lovely city. Your generous pledge in support of our telephone campaign is greatly appreciated. Please send us your gift with this reply form as soon as possible.

                                               I. Harvey Clout, Chair

Name: _____

Address: _____

_____ ZIP: _____

[ ] *Yes, send me a "Clean Up Cleveland" bumper sticker.*

[ ] *Yes, I am interested in membership in The Circle of Champions; send me your application.*

EXHIBIT 6-12 GIFT RESULTS: TELEPHONE TESTS FOR CLEVELAND CHAPTER

Original Series Mailings	Donor Pool	Calls Made	Gifts Made	Percentage	Gift Income	Average Gift
A & B Test Lists	348	200	32	31%	$ 1,155	$ 36
B Fall Roll Out	1,156	200	87	38%	$ 2,340	$ 27
B Spring Roll Out	1,831	200	57	40%	$ 2,080	$ 35
C Spring Follow-Up	1,822	200	69	47%	$ 1,518	$ 22
D First Renewal	914	200	71	60%	$ 3,788	$ 53
Subtotal	6,071	1,000	478	48%	$16,881	$ 35
Second Series Mailings						
E Acquisitions (2)	4,192	250	58	23%	$ 3,175	$ 55
F Renewals (2)	3,383	250	77	31%	$ 5,050	$ 66
Circle of Champions	138	138	98	71%	$12,120	$124
Subtotal	7,713	638	233	37%	$20,345	$ 87
Grand Total	13,784	1,638	711	43%	$37,226	$ 52

sponse rate from their first renewal mailings and the telephone tests, at only 43 percent. Karen and Alice had to admit they were delighted to see the average gift grow to $52 compared to $34 from the mail but wondered, why was the telephone response rate lower, and why had not more donors joined the Circle of Champions?

Micky Edwards had offered to meet with Karen on Monday afternoon to review how this first telemarketing test went and to evaluate all the results. In her analysis, Micky believed the mail response rate was higher in part because of the combination of the arrival of this unique cause plus the offer of the bumper stickers, which were an instant hit. Micky, too, was disappointed at the response rates from donors who had already renewed their first gift—the E and F lists at 23 and 31 percent—but these gifts were made only six months earlier. However, their average gifts had gone up nicely, to $55 and $66. The Circle of Champions renewal rate of 71 percent was quite good for a first renewal, as was their average gift at $124, although both Karen and Alice had hoped to renew more donors at $250, the next gift level. Both were disappointed at the average gift size responses from every list, but Micky suggested this might be because the volunteer callers were not experienced in how to make a successful upgrade offer.

CHAPTER 7

Groups, Guilds, and Support Organizations

There are a multitude of affiliation models for donors and volunteers in addition to membership associations. The purpose of each is to help the parent nonprofit organization and its annual giving programs, using different methods and techniques designed to provide for higher levels of annual gift support, higher levels of personal involvement, or both. The overall plan for an annual giving program, as outlined in this book, begins with identifying and acquiring first-time donors in order to expand and enhance their relationship with a nonprofit organization through volunteerism and gift renewal year after year. Creativity, persistence, and reward are required when asking volunteers and donors to continue to give their time and personal resources again and again. One of the best such methods is through a membership affiliation, as described in Chapter 5. Other methods are offered through groups, guilds, and support organizations, the next plateau in annual giving.

Groups, guilds, and support organizations offer opportunities to become personally involved in the daily life of a nonprofit organization. Each individual should be invited and encouraged to expand the relationship in any of several directions that will help the organization to succeed in meeting its mission. An active relationship may feature one or more of the following characteristics:

- Concentrates on friend-raising along with fundraising
- Personalizes the relationship

- Invites and encourages active participation
- Invites and encourages additional gifts during each year
- Offers a variety of voluntary assignments and active roles
- Defines leadership positions and develops leadership candidates
- Communicates progress in meeting priority projects of annual need
- Trains volunteers to solicit others and to conduct support activities
- Identifies candidates for major and planned gift opportunities
- Provides for special recognition to encourage continued support

This expansion of interest, involvement, and participation is made possible through a variety of forms, vehicles, or models that are distinguishable from membership and membership associations by their concentration on higher levels of annual gift support, their emphasis on personal involvement through voluntary service, their semiautonomous nature and self-management style, and their extra recognition opportunities. The operating style of these models is for its members to be active (not passive), and to take, as their own enterprise, responsibility for the welfare and success of their voluntary organization. They can and do provide advice and counsel from time to time, but their primary energies are directed toward managing activities that promote and enhance their own image and that of their parent nonprofit organization.

In their official names, these formal and informal voluntary organizations use a variety of words and terms, most of which appear to have similar meanings (see Exhibit 7-1). Their overlap can be confusing to someone attempting to understand the purposes of these entities and how they are distinguishable from one another. The words available for their names are close to synonymous, but the name chosen is important as an indicator of the degree of separateness from the sponsoring nonprofit organization. Each group, guild, or support organization is distinguished by the degree of its dependence on the parent or sponsoring nonprofit organization for routine operating support.

Regardless of their names or their degree of independence, most of these entities will share one or more of the following objectives:

1. They have a single purpose or mission.
2. They ask for a commitment of time, money, or both.
3. They offer enhanced benefits and privileges.

4. They offer contacts and networking opportunities with select audiences.

5. They feature recognition and reward.

6. They operate in a semi–independent style.

7. They are more volunteer–led than staff–directed.

8. Their image enhances that of their parent or sponsor.

This chapter describes how these objectives are pursued in four distinct but typical entities: (1) the auxiliary, (2) the guild, (3) donor clubs, and (4) support group organizations. A variety of features may be incorporated into each entity's routine operating programs, as indicated in Exhibit 7-2.

EXHIBIT 7-1   COMMON NAMES FOR SUPPORTIVE ORGANIZATIONS

Alliance	Any union or connection of interests
Association	A society of members united by mutual interests or for a common purpose
Auxiliary	A group that is subordinate to another organization, helping or aiding, and giving support
Circle	A group of persons or friends who have a common tie
Club	1. A select group of persons who are in the habit of meeting for the promotion of some common objective such as athletics, literature, science, or politics
	2. A group of persons who participate in a plan wherein they agree to make regular payments or purchases in order to secure some benefits
Coalition	A voluntary union of individual persons, parties, or states for a common objective or cause
Company	A number of individuals assembled or associated together; a number of persons united or incorporated for joint action
Fraternity	A group of people gathered for a common purpose
Group	A number of persons, as in a community, who are united by common ties or interests; a number of persons or things ranged or considered together because they are perceived as being related in a scientific, natural, or other way
League	A combination of parties for promotion of their mutual interests and goals; the covenant or compact by which these parties are joined
Organization	A body of persons united in working toward some end or purpose
Society	A group of persons united for the promotion of a common aim, typically literary, scientific, political, religious, benevolent, or convivial

EXHIBIT 7-2 COMMON PROGRAM FEATURES FOR SUPPORTIVE ORGANIZATIONS

Active Programs	Auxiliary	Donor Guild	Supportive Club	Group
1. May operate with separate tax-exempt status	X	X		X
2. May maintain separate financial records	X	X		X
3. Requires staff and operating support from parent	X		X	X
4. Accepts annual fundraising goals from parent	X	X		X
5. Is focused on friend-raising	X	X		X
6. Is focused on fundraising		X	X	X
7. Is focused on recognition and reward	X		X	
8. Is focused on benefits and privileges			X	X
9. Is focused on volunteerism and service	X	X		X
10. Requires annual membership dues or gift	X	X	X	X
11. Requires active participation	X	X		X
12. Prefers self-management style	X	X		X
13. Elects its own board and officers	X	X		X
14. Appoints its own committee chairs and members	X	X		X
15. Trains its volunteers in their assigned duties	X	X		X
16. Trains volunteers in personal solicitation		X		X
17. Conducts performance evaluation of volunteers	X	X		X
18. Keeps track of hours of service	X			
19. Conducts annual membership recruitment and renewal drive	X			X
20. Maintains active leadership development program	X	X		X
21. Conducts its own fundraising benefit events	X	X		X

(continued)

EXHIBIT 7-2   (CONTINUED)

Active Programs	Auxiliary	Donor Guild	Supportive Club	Group
22. Publishes its own newsletter and membership directory	X	X		X
23. Conducts its own annual meeting	X	X		X
24. Conducts member activities to enhance participation and renewal	X	X		X
25. Performs legislative advocacy and lobbying support	X	X		X
26. Performs community education programs		X		X
27. Performs community service activities	X	X		X
28. Participates in parent's marketing and promotion activities		X		X
29. Promotes direct involvement with parent's delivery of programs and services	X			
30. Permits fundraising events in its name by others		X		X

The adoption of one or more of these features will depend largely on local preferences for operating style, the priority of needs and wishes of the parent nonprofit organization, and the personalities of the charter members.

THE AUXILIARY

An *auxiliary* is a volunteer-led association of members whose principal activities assist the parent nonprofit organization in the delivery of its programs and services to the public. In its management style, this model features a board of directors and as many operating committees as there are programs and services within the parent where volunteer workers can be used. The primary purpose is to recruit, train, and develop men and women who will take it as their personal obligation and responsibility to assist with the actual delivery of programs and services to the public. Their acceptance of this level of responsibility is the essential feature that distinguishes them from members of other groups because it requires a commitment to be present at assigned times to perform their service, whether day or night, weekend or holiday.

This personal style of direct service to others is the key attraction to the volunteer, the chief motive for active participation. The result is a higher level of personal "high touch" than staff can offer, which adds to the competence and quality of the service provided. For example, hospital auxiliary members can be found in nearly every area of hospital service where their primary attention can be directed toward support of hospitalized patients and their families. Hospitals could never afford to hire enough employees to perform these same assignments, much less be able to motivate them to be as caring and friendly. In another example, auxiliary members in a rehabilitation center will "work directly with patients through physical therapy, occupational therapy, or therapeutic recreation. These activities include assisting with patient exercise and wheelchair skills classes, adapting patient clothing by sewing adaptations for easy dressing, and accompanying patients on recreational outings and in leisure time activities."[1] These extra services are possible only if the hospital is able to organize the auxiliary model of voluntary participation and offer it to local residents as an opportunity to help. Improved and enhanced support services that assist patients and their families to regain self-confidence and to maximize their remaining skills despite health-imposed limitations are the very visible result.

The essential feature of an auxiliary is its ability to provide a variety of volunteer assignments that offer a large amount of personal satisfaction in return for a few hours of service each week. People helping people is the attraction and the chief reward. An auxiliary may also be able to offer a variety of subgroups, each with their own leadership and committee system, that can appeal to a wide array of volunteers' interest areas. Again using a hospital as an example, its auxiliary may offer one group of committees linked to a specific area of health-care service. A favorite is the modern childbirth center with its labor-delivery-recovery (LDR) rooms and accompanying neonatal intensive care and well-baby units. Who can resist the opportunity to help a new baby feel loved? Another group of auxiliary volunteers may be interested in supporting the special needs of preschool-age and adolescent patients and their families. Whatever the area of service, a sensitive volunteer with extra time to spend with each patient is enormously welcome and valuable. Other auxiliary volunteers may prefer to work in the coffee shop or gift shop, take the book-and-game cart around, staff the information or customer service desk, perform escort and transport services, or donate their clerical skills in administrative office support. Many volunteers contribute professional skills that the nonprofit organization would otherwise have to pay employees or consultants to perform. Other volunteer-led areas of activity may include planning and conducting the auxiliary's membership recruitment program, giving orientation and training to new volunteers, conducting tours of the facility, participating in the speakers bureau, or assisting with the newsletter's design, writing, and preparation for mailing. Some members, after appropriate active service and experience, aspire to committee leadership and membership on the board of directors. To satisfy their needs, volunteers should be placed in assignments that are well-matched to their interests and competency. Just about every area of hospital activity offers opportunities for trained volunteers to lend a helping hand for a few hours each week, which may explain both the popularity of hospital auxiliary work and its remarkable success. When hundreds of volunteers are involved, the effect on the quality and quantity of care provided is enormous.

Training

Auxiliary members find it attractive to be able to work within a nonprofit organization. Most come with preferences of where they want to spend their time. When multiple areas within an institution need support, auxiliary leadership and institution staff must prepare and offer a well-defined orientation program that will encourage members to consider several worthy areas where their time will be equally valuable and rewarding. Not everyone can play with the new babies! Comprehensive training programs are needed for all areas of service. Included in the curriculum will be details about the operating rules and procedures, the policies and guidelines of the nonprofit organization, and the protocols of the assigned work area. Each auxiliary volunteer must understand and observe these parameters. Treating volunteers the same as employees has great merit in building their loyalty for faithful service, reinforcing their commitment to their assigned tasks, and enhancing the personal satisfaction they receive in return. The employees in nonprofit organizations may need to be reminded that volunteers are *not* employees, that personal circumstances may limit their available time, and that they will not always be there when expected. Well-defined orientation sessions and professionally conducted training programs will go far in ensuring the nonprofit organization that its auxiliary volunteers are a reliable and satisfactory work force.

Dues and Other Revenue

Annual dues for auxiliary membership and payment of a uniform fee may be required, but these amounts are usually modest ($10 to $25 per year). A life membership plan may be offered as a one-time gift option at $100 to $150. Fundraising is not an auxiliary's chief purpose. All funds raised from dues, fees, and other sources should be delivered directly to the parent nonprofit organization. If the auxiliary is a separately incorporated tax-exempt entity, its income in excess of expenses, as reported in its annual financial statements, is transferred to the parent organization. A variety of fundraising activities may be organized to provide additional revenue, but raising money is usually a secondary goal. The volunteers' preference for hands-on participation in direct service comes first. When a fundraising program is defined, it is often accompanied by a formal process that allows the auxiliary board to select a project for sponsorship after evaluating several current priorities of need identified by the nonprofit organization. This procedure enables the volunteer members to decide where the money they raise will be used. Their decisions are commonly directed toward areas where the public receives programs and services, because auxiliary members often work in these areas and are knowledgeable about the value of services provided there. The role of professional and support staff (when required) is largely administrative: facilitating the scheduling of volunteer assignments, conducting or supervising orientation and training programs, keeping the records of each member's hours of service, assisting in management and clerical tasks, and engaging in "other duties as assigned." Service is recorded faithfully in half-hour increments, for proper recognition of accompanying honors; volunteers' time is valuable, no matter where they give their service. A failure to recognize, honor, and reward volunteers for the services they provide is a huge mistake. Volunteers may decide to give their time and energy to another organization that will be more appreciative of their many contributions.

THE GUILD

The chief difference between an auxiliary and a guild may be that guild volunteers often do not work inside the organization. They prefer to support the organization through activities conducted outside, away from its direct programs and service facilities. A guild and an auxiliary are alike in asking volunteers for their time and service, but the guild will direct this energy toward preparation and management of social activities, educational programs, or public service. A guild may define specific tasks for its volunteers and focus their activities in support of one or two major areas of activity rather than try to cover the breadth of services an auxiliary is committed to fulfill. Volunteer satisfaction is derived from the faithful completion of a mission or an assigned task each year and from the amount of visible recognition received. For example, a theater or orchestra guild may set annual goals that include each member's promotion and sale of a certain number of season passes or series tickets. Members may also take responsibility for an assignment in one or more fundraising activities, such as a benefit event that has a goal of $50,000 or $100,000 in net proceeds. The guild may define all of its annual goals and decide how these net proceeds will be used— for general operating purposes, for a specific area of theater or orchestra activity that the guild "adopts," or for seeding and growing a permanent endowment fund to ensure that activity's future financial security.

A guild membership recruitment and renewal program may include an annual gift of perhaps $25 to $100. Emphasis may be placed on each member's buying at least one ticket to the guild's benefit event, accepting one active volunteer assignment in one of the guild's programs or committees, and attending one or more of the professional programs offered by the parent nonprofit organization. New members may be required to visit and tour the facilities of the sponsor within a year of joining. All members are invited to an annual meeting (which often features a speaker from the nonprofit organization) at which officers and directors are elected and recognition awards for volunteerism and service are conferred. A guild may circulate a membership directory, prepare newsletters, and offer other amenities. The members will work hard to obtain media coverage for their events and activities, their financial success, and the specific programs and services their funds support. They may not require any administrative or staff support from the parent nonprofit organization, preferring to manage their own affairs.

Guilds can be organized in a variety of ways, using either a social or a business format. They may develop subgroups or chapters composed of select professionals (doctors, lawyers, accountants, and so on) or of people who are living in a specific area of town or in a geographic area that is separate from the sponsor's principal location. The overall mission is to develop a reliable group of men or women (sometimes both) who share a willingness to commit their time to the sponsor's cause, who value the friendship and company of the other guild members, and who will act together to complete the mission and goals assigned. Guild members often select their leaders and board of directors from among their more active members (and those who aspire to leadership). The board will elect the guild's officers, appoint all committee chairpersons and members, set annual goals, and oversee routine operations, including financial affairs during each year. Rotation of the members to serve in board and committee positions is expected and often aspired to. Support provided by the parent nonprofit organization may be on an "as-requested" basis and can take the form of management, clerical assistance, or direct financial support. Often, such support is minimal because guilds may prefer (and take pride in) being independent and self-sufficient. They may choose to maintain their own membership lists, perform their own volunteer recruitment and renewal efforts, and provide all their own communications—a newsletter, contact letters, e-mail addresses and members directory, use of and entry on the organization's Web page, and the invitations and reservations required for attendees at the annual meeting and at benefit events. The guild will provide its roster of volunteers and members to the parent nonprofit organization so that every guild member will receive all the regular communications sent to other volunteers and donors. Funds raised through membership fees, activities, and benefit events should be delivered directly to the parent nonprofit organization unless the guild is a separately incorporated tax-exempt entity.

DONOR CLUBS: THE BENEFITS OF ORGANIZING DONORS

Faithful donors appreciate recognition and respect for their generosity; they place a value on the courteous and consistent treatment their gifts have earned for them. They are not offended when offered opportunities for increased personal activity or association with their chosen nonprofit organization. Many organizations group their faithful donors together in order to manage the relationship optimally. A society of donors or a donor club enhances the association, confers a special identity on each qualified donor, and provides donors with the added opportunity of associating with others whose levels of commitment and generosity match their own. It is a courtesy and a privilege to be invited to join such a distinguished and select group.

> The first purpose of donor clubs and associations is to convey gratitude for higher contribution levels; they must then perpetuate a privileged association with the organization in order to encourage faithful participation each year. Donor clubs represent one of the best means to demonstrate an institution's commitment to expressing honest gratitude. Offering a list of benefits and privileges to donors whose annual gifts begin at $1,000 gains their appreciation, helps to retain their interest, and cultivates the potential for other gift opportunities in the future.[2]

Donor clubs (often called gift clubs) possess several unique features that can be offered to their participants and to the nonprofit organization they support. For annual donors, the chief attribute is increased benefits and privileges based on a higher level of giving or on the cumulative total of all gifts received in one year (see Exhibit 7.3). Thomas Broce calls donor clubs "the fastest way to increase the annual gifts total and is also the best method of raising donors' giving levels. Each year the gift evaluation should automatically encourage each donor to move up to the next category. No one has ever been offended by being asked for too much (though by the same token few donors have suggested that the solicitor didn't ask for enough!)."[3] A donor club encourages annual donors to give at higher levels and offers them recognition and rewards in the form of extra benefits and higher visibility. Those who respond by giving at these higher levels may qualify for extra recognition and reward from the parent nonprofit organization. Donor clubs also can request higher levels of active personal involvement and voluntary participation to retain full standing. Most are designed to reinvest the recognition and reward given to donors based on the amounts they give each year. Whenever possible, nonprofit organizations should tie the uses made of these gifts to the highest-priority needs, especially when the gifts support a program or service that is highly visible

EXHIBIT 7-3   DONOR CLUB ANNUAL GIVING BENEFITS AND PRIVILEGES

Gift Amount*	Club Name	Benefits and Privileges
$ 100	Circle of Champions	Quarterly newsletter Annual report Invitations to benefit events
500	Ambassadors	All of the above *plus:* Name listed in annual report donor roster
1,000	Friends	All of the above *plus:* Name added to main Donor Wall VIP identification card with 10 percent discount in gift shop Invitation to annual meeting
2,500	Sponsors	All of the above *plus:* Name added to Sponsors plaque at main entrance Invitation to annual recognition luncheon Subscription to *President's Letter*
5,000	Patrons and Life Members	All of the above *plus:* Name added to Life Member plaque at main entrance Two tickets to annual black-tie ball Personal gift

*Multiple gifts within the same year will be counted together in order to qualify the donor at the highest level of donor privileges achieved through cumulative giving. The donor will be honored throughout the following year at this cumulative total.

to others outside the organization. This added element of urgent need helps to preserve the relationship, especially when the success of the programs and services funded is attributed to the principal donors. Donor recognition honors the contributor and, in so doing, lets others witness how faithful and generous donors are treated. The maxim "It pays to advertise" can be put to good use in recognition programs used for donor clubs.

Many donors will welcome the association and status connoted in belonging to a donor club. Formalization of their association with donor gift levels (and their related privileges) adds the appearance of a membership relationship. Membership status can be defined to include the usual array of member services and benefits, all designed to hold the attention of the donor and to secure continuous commitment of faithful annual support. However, a donor club can be more aggressive about the level of gift support required and the direct relationship of gift size to membership status. A clear focus on higher gift levels will help to preserve the special attention given to those who participate at these prescribed rates.

A lesser known fact about donor clubs is their exceptional record of cost-effectiveness and high profitability. Broce[4] comments:

> One of the most successful means of soliciting significant annual gifts is through donor clubs. First let me say that in today's economy few organizations can afford to make solicitations for gifts of less than $100. All gifts below that amount should be solicited by mail. Even telephone solicitations should be for $100 and above. We should not waste valuable manpower on small gifts; moreover, most organizations should set their minimum gift level at $100 (though many prospects may respond with less than $100). This is difficult for many people to accept, but it makes good business sense.

Donor clubs are profitable to operate because they require only limited amounts of direct budget support for annual solicitation and maintenance. The costs of recognition elements are typical budget items: sending members copies of newsletters, annual reports, invitations to annual meetings, and the like; purchasing paperweights, certificates, plaques, and other mementos of appreciation. With advance planning and wholesale buying, these articles can be acquired at reasonable expense. The IRS rule on *give backs* (recognition to donors) limits them to 2 percent of the original gift value and is a helpful guide for how much to spend on recognition gifts.

Nonprofit organizations can and should maintain one or more areas within their facilities for donor recognition displays. Annual maintenance costs of such areas, once established and furnished, are reasonable. Designated donor recognition areas also serve as active advertising space for the importance attributed to larger gifts from donors and for the cumulative giving history of faithful contributors. Inquiries about the amount required to add a name to a donor recognition display are usually followed by new gifts of just these amounts, and a steady stream of new gifts more than offsets the costs of maintaining the display programs. Other recognition elements, such as citations and plaques, also are important to donors and to the organization. In offices and homes, they are often displayed with pride.

The wider public sees these symbols of giving as a statement on how each nonprofit organization treats its more important donors.

> Tell your members that you love them. Tell them as often as possible and in as many ways as possible. Let them know your plans and ideas. Involve them in these activities. Use them on your committees and programs. Herald their accomplishments in your publications. Remember their birthdays and anniversaries. Send them invitations to special programs and events. Show how easily, and at what little cost, the needs to feel important, appreciated, and loved can be satisfied through membership in your institution's gift club, and your contributors should become your best friends.[5]

An association of donors or the members of a donor club may well become the most committed friends a nonprofit organization can hope to have. Their faithful generosity will attempt to attain levels of giving that are well above the average gift size required in every other annual giving program and activity. Their faithful support represents the source for the largest percentage of annual gift income received each year. These VIP donors are important financial security for any parent nonprofit organization. They should be given extra good care at all times.

Donor Records

Keeping records of donors' prior gifts is important for many reasons; primarily, their annual and historic (lifetime) giving is linked to a formal donor recognition program. Each gift made—no matter when, for what purpose, or in what form—should be added to the donor's permanent gift history. Over time, each donor's cumulative total can build to an amount that qualifies him or her for the extra benefits and special privileges defined in the donor honors and recognition policy (see Exhibit 7.4). Cumulative tallies are not at all difficult to maintain today, thanks to reasonably priced office computers and software. The data stored may indicate the areas of special interest favored by each donor; the preferred solicitation methods (where, when, and to what type of appeal this person responds best); other invitations extended and the responses received each time; giving levels and interests preferred, as indicated by annual support; participation at benefits and public events; special project and major campaign gifts; pledge his-

EXHIBIT 7-4   SAMPLE DONOR HONORS AND RECOGNITION POLICY

Qualifications: All donors whose cumulative contributions add to $1,000 or more will be recognized on the main Donor Wall as follows:

Category	Amounts		
Friends	$ 1,000	to	$ 2,499
Sponsors	2,500	to	4,999
Patrons/life members	5,000	to	9,999
Benefactors	10,000	to	24,999
Meritorious benefactors	25,000	to	49,999
Honored benefactors	50,000	to	99,999
Distinguished benefactors	100,000	to	999,000
Preeminent benefactors	1,000,000	or	more

Types of Gifts:

1. Donations of cash, bonds, securities, and real estate will be included. The value of each gift to be recognized will be based on the charitable contribution deduction amount.

2. For planned gifts and estate planning arrangements, donors whose gifts are in the forms of pooled income funds and future interest gifts (irrevocable gifts in trust, life estates, and gift annuities) will be included. The value of each gift to be recognized will be based on the charitable contribution deduction amount. Individuals who present documentary evidence of a future gift will be listed on the Endowment Society section of the main Donor Wall.

3. Gifts of life insurance will be recognized at cash value until maturity of the policy. Individuals who provide a copy of a policy with a minimum value of $10,000 directed to this nonprofit organization will be listed on the Endowment Society section of the main Donor Wall.

Commemorative Gifts: The names of those individuals in whose memory or honor a gift of $1,000 or more has been received will be listed on the Commemorative Gifts section of the main Donor Wall.

Recognition: Other forms of appropriate recognition will be given to qualified donors by action of the Board of Directors in accordance with the Donor Honors and Recognition Policy.

tory and record of payments (including assets used); and estate planning interests and activity.

This type of donor profile is a valuable guide to staff and volunteers when they must assess likely candidates for ability to manage areas of need and new and changing priorities; for volunteer assignments; for positions that require a record of training and proven experience; or for leadership. All these data help the organization and its volunteer fundraising leaders to determine the interests and aspirations of their best donors. Each such donor deserves an annual evaluation of how well his or her interests are being served, and should be considered for any opportunities that may offer expanded ways to fulfill his or her preferences. Additional enhancements through the benefits and privileges in a donor club should be part of these analyses. One donor might be prepared to consider a major gift opportunity; another, who is approaching retirement, might be interested in an estate-planning interview. Donor records and gift histories reveal all the information necessary to help guide the nonprofit organization in selecting options to offer its major donors. What will assist them in fulfilling their long-term preferences, even their life-time aspirations, and yield a maximum level of financial support to their favorite nonprofit organization?

The most practical use of a donor club is in helping to retain as many prior donors as possible each year. Current donors should be encouraged to increase (upgrade) their annual gift whenever possible. Donor clubs provide substantial advantages to all who can give or who choose to give at higher levels. Every current participant should be rewarded equally. A recognition plan that is tied to uninterrupted annual giving should recognize those who have been faithful over many years. Other advantages from a well-defined donor club program are

- Increased potential for continued (secure) gift income
- Identified and qualified prospects for major gift support when a special-project or capital campaign gift is needed
- Likely candidates for volunteer and leadership duties
- Active community advocates and ambassadors for the organization
- Likely candidates for estate and planned giving opportunities

Donor club members may have a variety of reasons for choosing to continue their current level of support. Feeling good about being treated well, being part of a valued group, and enjoying special benefits and privileges are important incentives, but these might not be their motives for giving. One way to understand motives is to picture a $1,000 donor standing outside the front door, waving both arms, and yelling, "I like you a lot! Pay attention to me!" These should be the steps taken in response:

- Get to know these people
- Meet with them and listen to their thoughts about why they give so much to the organization and what they would like to receive in return
- Find out what else they might be willing to do
- Introduce them to volunteers, management and professional staff, and board members
- Continue to offer them privileges, such as access to the organization and benefits they can use in exchange for their generous level of support
- Invite them and their spouses, plus any special friends they might choose, to be guests at the next major benefit event or public meeting
- Show them appreciation in a personal way at least once a year: call on them or give them a telephone call, or send them a birthday or anniversary card

William Grasty and Kenneth Sheinkopf[6] gave this summary:

The basic purposes of gift clubs are to:

- Involve a very special group of institutional friends who will give mainly unrestricted funds, which are the most difficult to get, and the most useful to have;
- Encourage an increased level of giving by current donors;
- Attract a high level of annual support;
- Upgrade donor gifts;
- Recognize and honor the individuals who have supported the institution financially;
- Attract new contributors who are influenced by the individual recognition given the more generous donor;
- Inform and involve the membership in the purposes and plans of the institution;
- Develop volunteers for their effective use as ambassadors, advisors, and fundraising leaders in support of many important projects . . . .

Support Group Organizations

What exactly is a support group organization? It combines many of the features of a membership association, an auxiliary, a guild, and a donor club, all put together in a single entity. It is a highly structured program designed to facilitate constituency building, to conduct friend-raising, to offer a membership affiliation, to enhance and invigorate volunteerism, to develop leadership candidates, to market and promote a cause, to facilitate community relations, to prepare and produce fundraising activities and benefit events, to undertake major fundraising objectives, and to identify, recruit, and develop major gift candidates. A support group organization will include all of these features in a volunteer-led, self-management style that provides multiple opportunities for and direct benefits to the nonprofit organization that is its sponsor. Harold Seymour[7] cited a famous college alumni association as an example of a successful support group organization:

> Our oldest alumni fund is at Yale, where in 1890 they agreed on these principles: that the funds should be unrestricted; that the appeal should be universal; that emphasis on numbers would actually encourage larger gifts; and that the primary objective should be to persuade the alumni to give annually, with such a steady flow of contributions that the alumni themselves might properly be regarded as an endowment, with the fund's yearly receipts as the income.

Now, more than 100 years later, not much has changed from this original prescription for success. Funds raised are for annual operating purposes and for promoting growth in the number of donor participants; these remain the priority objectives. The funds raised *each year* are equal to the investment earnings achieved by an operating endowment worth more than twenty times the annual gift total.

Support groups are usually formed under the tax-exempt umbrella of privileges granted to their parent nonprofit organization. Separate tax-exempt status is not required or recommended. As a semi-independent organization, each support group will need to operate within written guidelines (called "Operating Rules and Procedures" instead of "Bylaws") that are approved by the parent, to whom they owe their allegiance. Funds are raised in the name of the parent and should be delivered directly to it. (The procedure is the same for an auxiliary, guild, or donor club.) The uses made of these funds can be determined jointly with the parent, according to its current roster of priority needs. The project or program selected becomes that year's or that period's official objective for the support group. All its activities are dedicated to the successful completion of the assignment; all funds received (membership fees, benefit event net proceeds, "something extra" annual gifts from members, and so on) are counted toward the support group's annual gift. Acceptance of these responsibilities each year is one of the distinguishing features of support groups, chiefly because of their self-management style and their ability to undertake important tasks on behalf of the parent nonprofit organization. Such independence fosters, among the members, greater pride in their past accomplishments as a group working together and in their continuing commitment.

The key feature for successful operation of a support group organization may lie in a combination of self-management and volunteer-led participation. Support groups offer varied opportunities for public service, from board membership to a great variety of active committees (see Exhibit 7-5). Every function and every activity can be facilitated through one or more of the group's active committees. Most committees also offer a variety of subcommittees to support their overall assignment. A benefit event committee can maximize its potential to raise funds by delegating several assignments to subcommittees on sponsor and underwriter gifts, on ticket sales, on in-kind contributions (food, beverages, decorations, flowers, printing, entertainment, linens), and on recruiting auction and raffle prizes (see Chapter 10).

The balance of committee members can be organized to help with the design, printing, and addressing of invitations, with creating and tasting the menu, with planning the program and entertainment, and with putting up the decorations. The list of assignments is purposely made long so that as many people as possible will have a responsible task to perform. A committee work plan requires a host of volunteers, with several volunteers in leadership positions. Several months will be required to organize and produce this event, but the work is spread around so that no one person has too heavy a burden. If any volunteer senses that he or she has too much to do, help should be requested from other volunteers. Among the results of this operating style are: high attendance at the function (all volunteers will, of course, be expected to attend), and the enormous value each support group organization can offer to its parent nonprofit organizations. Large

EXHIBIT 7-5   SAMPLE SUPPORT GROUP
ORGANIZATION CHART

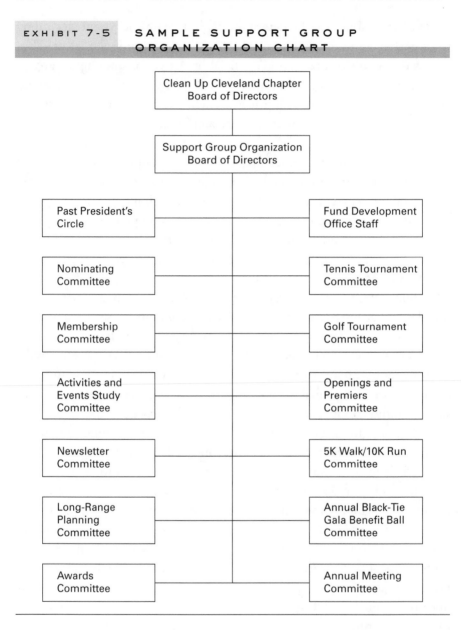

nonprofit organizations may sponsor more than one support group, with each support group designed to match the needs of several standing programs or service areas within the institution. Because of their visibility in staging public activities considered beneficial to others in the community, support groups provide substantial marketing, promotion, and communications enhancements to the programs and services they sponsor.

Operating styles may vary, but most support groups prefer to have a major voice in managing their own affairs. They conduct all their activities within a prescribed set of "Operating Rules and Procedures" (see Appendix A for complete sample text), recruit new members and renew prior members, plan their many activities and events, critique their performance, publish their newsletters and annual membership directory, study and make comprehensive plans for their own future, recruit and train new volunteers to their methods and style of operation, identify and prepare future leaders for larger assignments, handle cash and other forms of contributions, and conduct annual business meetings for the orderly transfer of leadership to their successors. They utilize many if not all of the features previously described in this book for (1) how to identify and recruit new friends by mail, (2) how to recruit and renew annual donors, (3) how to prepare and conduct successful membership activities, and (4) how to operate in a semi-independent style endorsed by the sponsoring nonprofit organization. Support groups may augment some or all of these features in their own operation, and may explore and adopt others completely new to the parent nonprofit organization.

Support group organizations may be asked to take an active role in community service, similar to that of a civic or fraternal association, depending on local conditions and circumstances. In times of community need, the organizational skills plus the strength and caliber of support group members may be needed for broader purposes, such as collaborative activities with other nonprofit organizations and civic associations. Where such additional efforts also serve to advance the mission and purpose of the parent nonprofit organization, they are undertaken willingly. Support groups remain alert to community relations opportunities that will promote their own activities and those of the parent nonprofit organization. They may engage in legislative action and lobbying from time to time, especially when there is a need to address issues, laws, and regulations that affect their ability or their sponsor's ability to fulfill their mission. They also remain conscientious about being visible in the community through media coverage of their activities and events. Their members are a constant example to others of the spirit of volunteerism, leadership, personal commitment, and gift support of the mission, purposes, goals, and objectives of their own organization and of their parent nonprofit organization.

Activities Other Than Fundraising

Support groups need to offer their members several opportunities for personal participation in addition to voluntary service and personal gift support. These might include activities sponsored by the parent nonprofit organization, such as public tours of facilities, lectures on topics of public interest by professional staff, and invitations to public events (an annual picnic, ground-breaking ceremonies, new-building dedications, and so on). Any routine activity open to the general public should be offered to support group members in a personal, VIP manner. The purpose of these invitations is to permit those members who prefer a less active role than voluntary service to participate at a level where they are most comfortable. Other forms of activity may be included as routine membership benefits. These types of offerings—affinity credit cards, supplemental insurance plans, group travel tours, and estate planning seminars—are designed to encourage members to remain active participants in the support group each year, no matter what their level of personal participation or giving may be.

Throughout each year, a volume of information is sent to all members— their own and the institution's newsletters and annual reports, plus other materials selected for all other donors and active volunteers. The purposes are: to offer direct education in areas where the sponsor has expertise, to increase the members' information about the charitable good works their gift dollars help to provide, and to report on all the activities and events the support group has completed and is planning for the future. Special activity reports, newsletters, membership directories, and annual reports are forwarded on a steady schedule to maintain member awareness of all these activities, to continue to invite their active participation, and to honor and reward those who choose to participate.

Independence

The basic mission of a support group organization is to enhance the image and reputation of its parent and to raise friends and funds that will assist in the fulfillment of its sponsor's mission. Good communication, coordination, and cooperation are necessary to both entities, but a support group may be more capable of undertaking broader areas of responsibility than an auxiliary, guild, or donor club could perform. Support groups are designed to develop and retain their own membership, manage their own activities (including financial transactions), reward those whose voluntary service has been distinguished, undertake new as well as routine programs and services, and recruit and train volunteers who will move on to other roles on behalf of the sponsor. Their flexibility is one of their greatest assets, alongside the talent and commitment of their members.

They are given fairly extensive amounts of responsibility for their own conduct; for the choice of their officers, board members, and committee chairpersons; for the quality and success of their activities, events, and publications; for their relations with the media; and for charting their own destiny and future plans in concert with their sponsor. To fulfill these responsibilities, they require defined amounts of independence. Autonomy is a double-edged proposition; it includes tests of accountability and performance evaluation while it shares the image and reputation of its sponsor. Independence requires an ability to make tough decisions when necessary, and a flexibility that can respond to changing economic conditions while still fulfilling the purpose of helping its sponsor to meet changing priorities. Changes to the group's well-made plans may be required when the priorities of the parent organization conflict with those of the group. Support groups must (1) be exacting in their management of all funds entrusted to them in the name of their sponsor; (2) ensure that no member uses an appointment or position for self-promotion or derives personal financial gain from the funds received for charitable purposes; (3) ensure their own continuity through continuous dedication to enhancing friendships and gift support that will benefit the parent nonprofit organization.

Important legal and accounting requirements need to be honored voluntarily by each support group organization.

> Separate from these legal and accounting requirements, every person and every entity involved, no matter how independent it is from the parent corporation, must operate within the purview of the board of directors, chief executive officer, and fund development office of the parent corporation. The controlling factor is the use of the official name of the parent, which holds the original charter and without which all the others would have no reason to exist. Internal or external fund-development operations by any subsidiary organization, whether related to the parent's purposes or not, must be within the administrative control of the parent. The control is even tighter for funds raised in the parent's name.[8]

There are two important reasons to faithfully observe such a close relationship on behalf of all donors:

1. A donor who makes a contribution to a support group organization assumes that the funds will be delivered to the parent nonprofit organization and will be used for charitable purposes. An official acknowledgment of each gift from the parent is essential to preserve this bond of trust.

2. Each donor may be entitled to a tax deduction for his or her contribution. Tax advantages are an important motive for continued giving; they reinforce the need for proper acknowledgment and record-keeping of all gifts received by the support group organization.

(For additional details on the cooperation and coordination necessary to manage ownership and authority, setting goals and objectives, financial accounting and reporting, and donor relations in related organizations, see pages 343 to 347 in my earlier text.)[9]

Recognition

Support group organizations offer a variety of extra opportunities to honor, recognize, and reward volunteers and donors for their work and for their gifts. It is important to acknowledge as many of these valued participants as can be qualified for rewards. Considerable pride builds up within support group organizations, and they should be showcased by the parent nonprofit organization. Just as the loyalty that donors develop for the parent and its cause can be strong and enduring, volunteering and contributing through a support group can inspire similar "warm feelings" toward the group itself, toward its mission, which all who join can share, and toward the charitable purposes that their efforts help to fulfill.

The benefits that gifts achieve each year need to be published. Gift levels and historic giving also should be recognized by the parent organization in accordance with its official policy and procedure (see Exhibits 7-3 and 7-4). These same benefits and privileges can be extended to qualified support group members and to participants in the activities and events. A range of membership levels and gift sizes can be keyed to correspond to the donor club gift levels. Consistency in the benefits and privileges provided to all donors by the parent nonprofit organization is paramount. Support group members should be accorded the same benefits and privileges that donor club members receive. These benefits can be marketed as "double the value" opportunities—additional features that will encourage the members to continue their active levels of participation. Benefits offered to donors for their gift of $100 should be equivalent to the benefits of annual membership in the support group organization (see Exhibit 7-3). With proper coordination, the parent nonprofit organization can arrange to have its honors and recognition policy administered to all its donors on a fair and equitable basis. Support group members will receive all of these privileges in addition to the special benefits arranged for support group participants only.

In some circumstances, special treatment of gifts made through support groups is appropriate in addition to recognition opportunities for volunteerism and leadership service. For example, special handling is required in the area of contribution value and donor "credit" for the specific tax deduction amount allowed for event tickets. The amount of contribution "credit" (the same as charitable contribution deduction value) must be clearly defined and explained in all of the event literature because the contributions credit and gift deduction value of tickets purchased for benefit events are not the price paid for the ticket. The IRS has published a guide instructing nonprofit organizations to advise each purchaser of special-event tickets that the price paid for the ticket is not the amount that can be claimed as a charitable contribution. The donor must deduct the "material value" of the cost of goods and services (food and drink) consumed at the event[10] to arrive at the gift deduction value the donor may claim at income tax time. This same value is the correct amount that can be credited to the donor's gift records. The net proceeds from the event, or the profit delivered to the parent nonprofit organization, is credited as a separate gift from the support group organization, and the amount is added into its tally of total contributions provided each year.

Recognition for Volunteerism

Honors and recognition for voluntary and leadership service are additional features that can be offered to members, volunteers, and leaders of support group organizations. The chairperson of each event committee should be recognized following the successful completion of the event. This ceremony can be scheduled for the time and place where the net proceeds check is presented or for the annual meeting. The form of this recognition may be a personal gift, such as a clock, glass figurine or memento, or similar gift or favor. Board members are usually honored at the conclusion of their term, and special awards are reserved for the elected officers. Another awards program may be held by the parent nonprofit organization. For example, each auxiliary, guild, donor club, and support group organization can be invited to nominate a candidate from among its distinguished members for a volunteer service award to be presented by the parent. The occasion may be the nonprofit organization's annual meeting, at which distinguished donors are also recognized for their accomplishments. A combined event for these awards for volunteerism and generosity sends a message that the parent institution values its volunteers and its donors with equal merit and distinction.

Management of Groups, Guilds, and Support Organizations

This chapter began with a suggestion that auxiliaries, guilds, donor clubs, and support group organizations are valuable because they can concentrate on the promotion of individual donors into more active levels of both personal involvement and gift support. Each of these entities has its own separate style and structure, as it should. Yet each must be sufficiently modified in style and structure to "fit" within the overall program of annual fundraising of the parent nonprofit organization and within the voluntary and giving styles of the local community. Professional management of these programs is required and should be provided by the parent nonprofit organization; they will not be able to achieve their maximum levels of productivity and efficiency if they are operating alone and outside the institution. They are part of an overall program designed to develop reliable annual contribution support for the parent nonprofit organization. Their activities must be coordinated with those of all of the organization's other annual giving programs. Participants will benefit from communications from the parent that keep them well-informed of its progress, its concerns, and its future plans. Their professional direction, which must take into account the somewhat separate nature of each entity, will require routine support features that should be provided by the Fund Development Office, as follows:

1. A professional staff member assigned responsibility to supervise their daily operations, to provide professional guidance and direction, and to provide whatever clerical support is required.

2. Maintenance of up-to-date and complete mailing lists of current and past participants.

3. Gift acknowledgment and appropriate posting to each donor record.

4. Preparation of gift reports and analysis of results, by event, activity, and group.

5. Advice and counsel to all volunteers in leadership positions, to assist in their success.

6. Inclusion on invitation lists for institutional public activities and events.

7. Inclusion on mailing lists for institutional newsletters, marketing pieces, e-mail, Web page access, and annual reports.

8. Inclusion in the institution's honors and recognition program for all who qualify as distinguished volunteers or as generous donors.

These routine functions can be centralized in the Fund Development Office, but it is important for each auxiliary, guild, donor club, or group to maintain a strong sense of its separate and independent nature. Individual activities and programs should retain their separate identity, represented in the use of unique logos, graphics designs, stationery, invitations, newsletters, and so on. For many auxiliaries, guilds, donor clubs, and support group organizations, their separate image and reputation are among their main assets in the community. To many of their leaders, volunteers, and members, this identity *is* their cause, their association. All that the parent nonprofit organization need insist on is that the affiliation with their sponsor be visible at all times. A unique partnership is at work here; both sides benefit from public awareness of the relationship. The parent nonprofit organization should always give proper credit to each of its supportive organizations for all that they do, including the public-recognition opportunities that they make possible. Neither the public nor the individuals affiliated with any of these groups benefit from being confused about how the nonprofit organization is related to or benefits from these separate entities.

Competition among groups must remain friendly and positive. Generally speaking, each group has its own record of prior performance to measure itself against. It is normal for this year's board and committee chairs to want to do a better job than their predecessors. This point of view is not a negative report card on prior years' performance; wanting to do as well or better is a valid objective. However, it is important to guide these comparisons into areas where performance is measured positively and no individual member is embarrassed. A positive approach would be to count the increases in the following:

1. Number of new members recruited
2. Number of prior members retained
3. Number of lapsed members reacquired
4. Number of prior members who upgrade to higher levels
5. Public attendance at activities and events
6. Number of volunteers who participate on committees
7. Number of members who attend activities and events
8. Training and experience for future leadership candidates
9. Attention to budgets, to achieve greater efficiency and productivity
10. Total in net revenue delivered to the parent nonprofit organization

When more than one auxiliary, guild, donor club, or support group organization is active in support of the same nonprofit organization, there can be circumstances that cause friction, but there are more opportunities for the groups to work together, in a spirit of coordination, cooperation, and communication. For example, all the entities could adopt the same fundraising goal or program area as their objective for the next year. From the organization's point of view, this concentration may greatly increase public awareness of the designated program area and may attract new clients.

However, one group could feel unsuccessful if its results are not equal to or greater than those of the other groups. Competition can be healthy if the teams are fairly equal, but the last thing a parent nonprofit organization wants to encourage is an unfair or unequal situation where one or more of its auxiliaries, guilds, clubs, or support organizations become discouraged because they were unsuccessful or inadequate to the challenge. Most nonprofit organizations have a long list of program and service areas that need attention and support from these entities; they also have a variety of fiscal needs that can be defined as annual goals and objectives. Each of these program areas and service needs should be reviewed for its added value as a marketing opportunity and evaluated for one or more recognition opportunities to be used when the project is fully funded by the entity. Most of the time, each entity has a preferred area that it chooses to sponsor. Once these choices are established, other groups will need to respect the stated wishes and commit their support to other parts of the nonprofit organization.

Management skill is required to engage volunteer groups in accepting guided self-direction. Their founding purposes and their operating rules and procedures will spell out their basic mission, which is to provide support to the parent nonprofit organization. Armed with that statement alone, volunteers in leadership positions have the duty and the responsibility to preserve and enhance the relationship, not redirect it away from this mission. New and revised mission statements can and should be prepared so that supporting organizations are always in step with changes in direction made by their parent nonprofit organization. Group management is possible only through the active cooperation of the volunteers who are in leadership positions. At times, individuals may come forward and seek these positions in order to achieve a personal goal or to espouse a new or different point of view. Controversy seldom makes friends, and although democratic procedures are valid to address questions of change or redefinition of mission, the overriding objective should not waver from faithful support to the parent nonprofit organization.

Because auxiliaries, guilds, donor clubs, and support groups bring a wealth of talented people into active roles within the family and life of nonprofit organizations, they are of enormous value. Several additional objectives can be achieved through this joint relationship:

1. Improved communications, image enhancement, and understanding within the community of the parent nonprofit organization and its mission

2. Increased marketing opportunities and market penetration

3. Improved community relations and public participation in the life of the nonprofit organization

4. Increased media awareness and responsiveness

5. Improved volunteer participation and training

6. Increased avenues for leadership development to meet future institutional or agency needs

7. Improved public relations with corporations, business executives, community residents, and government officials at all levels

8. Increased contributions revenue

Another important area where support entities contribute positively to the parent nonprofit organization is in reduced cost of operations. Volunteers who bring time and talent to work areas may substitute for paid employees, and they may be equally efficient and effective in carrying out the work assignments. Volunteer support to nonprofit organizations may allow salaried staff to spend more time in directing programs and providing services. Volunteers can improve the overall quality of programs and services rendered. They can also add contributions of revenue not otherwise available, especially when they become involved in soliciting their friends, neighbors, business colleagues, and fellow club members. As a result, the costs to provide programs and services and to raise funds are lowered. Improved cost–benefit ratios may occur in every program in which volunteers are actively involved, which means more gift dollars are available for programs and services.

Auxiliaries, guilds, donor clubs, and support group organizations, when teamed with a mature annual giving program, can be a much broader area of public influence than most people appreciate. Volunteer solicitors can approach many more people than fund-development staff can hope to see, and they often are more successful in their solicitations. In addition, volunteers can identify new candidates for other annual giving activities and can achieve corporate and foundation solicitations, special project efforts, major gift campaigns, and estate and planned giving programs. Further, and perhaps most important, volunteers can motivate others to join them in active support of the parent nonprofit organization. They can conduct orientation and training programs for newcomers and communicate their enthusiasm. They can help newcomers to integrate their time, talent, and energy into the activities of the organization.

Leadership development is one of the more important areas of volunteer support to nonprofit organizations. The experience that volunteers gain through a variety of roles within auxiliaries, guilds, donor clubs, and support group organizations greatly enhances their visibility to others. These activities serve to demonstrate their ability and skill to work within organizations and to lead others. Such volunteers are being prepared to become the future leaders of nonprofit organizations. Their knowledge of annual giving and fund development programs, activities, principles, and practices will aid them if they rise to a senior management level. Their background and training will greatly enhance their ability to be influential and effective when major fundraising objectives need to be planned and carried out successfully.

FOCUS: CCUA CLEAN UP CLEVELAND CHAPTER

It is now mid-January and the fall annual giving activities have been completed. Karen Anderson is tallying final year-end giving results for a report to the board later in the month. Three main programs were held this past fall:

Program A. The original roll-out list of 200,000 prospects solicited for the first time last spring was contacted twice more (minus those who had made a gift), to ask for a first gift. Anderson used Letter E (Exhibit 5-13, page 208) and included a second invitation to charter membership in The Circle of Champions donor club.

Program B. All 6,071 prior donors to the program who had given under $100 (she excluded only the 160 who had given over $100 and were already members of The Circle of Champions) received Letter F (Exhibit 5-14, page 209), encouraging them to upgrade their gifts to $100 and to join The Circle of Champions.

Program C. The board conducted a personal letter-and-telephone follow-up campaign to ask each of the 160 first-time members of The Circle of Champions to renew their important annual gifts at $100 or more; this appeal was their first renewal opportunity.

The results of all these activities were as follows:

Program A. Letter E to 200,000 community residents. (See Exhibit 7-6 for complete details of all these results.)

1. A total of 4,192 new donors was acquired!
2. A total of $106,396 was received!
3. An average gift of $25.38 was achieved!

EXHIBIT 7-6   GIFT REPORT 2, CUMULATIVE
PROGRAM RESULTS

Letter	Program	Number Mailed	Replies		Gift Income	Average Gift
			Number	Percent		
E	Fall second mail acquisition	192,116	2,216	1.15%	$ 54,276	$ 24.49
E	Fall follow-up mail acquisition	191,012	1,976	1.03	52,120	26.38
Subtotal/Average		383,128	4,192	1.09	106,396	25.38
F	Second renewal request	6,661	1,864	27.98	81,872	28.58
F	Second renewal follow-up	3,797	1,519	40	44,664	29.40
Subtotal/Average		10,458	4,383	66	126,536	28.87
Circle of Champions renewal (letter + phone)		160	138	86	16,836	122.00
Fall Mail Total/Average		393,746	8,713	2.21%	$249,768	$ 28.66
*Cumulative Total/Average		900,292	14,784	1.64%	$442,028	$ 29.90

*Includes figures brought forward from all prior mailings, described in Chapters 2 through 5.

4. A total of 226 persons joined The Circle of Champions; they gave a total of $28,250, for an average gift of $125.
5. Mailing costs for Letter E were $94,824 ($0.2475 × 383,128).
6. Net acquisition mailing proceeds were $12,574 ($106,396 − $94,824).
7. Cost-per-dollar-raised ratio was 0.89 percent.

Program B. Annual donor renewal and Circle of Champions first renewal request.

1. The number who renewed was 4,383 (66 percent).
2. A total of $126,536 was raised.
3. The average gift was $28.871.
4. The cost of these renewal mailings was $12,707 ($1.215 × 10,458).
5. Net proceeds were $113,829 ($126,536 − $12,707).
6. Cost-per-dollar-raised ratio was 0.10 percent.

7. A total of 78 persons agreed to join The Circle of Champions; they gave a total of $8,979, for an average gift of $115.

8. The first Circle of Champions renewal mailing and telephone follow-up resulted in 138 out of 160 renewal gifts (86 percent), for a total of $16,836 and an average gift of $122.

Program C. Combined and Total Gift Report. Combining all the fall mailing results, both acquisition and renewal, as of year-end, Anderson will report that a grand total of 14,784 community residents are now active participants in the Clean Up Cleveland campaign. Also, a total of $249,768 was received this fall; added to all other prior gifts received, the grand total is $442,028 (see Exhibit 7-6).

As part of Anderson's summary report, she plans to recommend that the board of directors consider two new solicitation programs in the first half of the new calendar year. Although these assignments will increase her workload along with that of Alice Nice, her assistant, both the direct mail and membership programs are running smoothly now and she believes they can go to the next level. They also know they will need more help from board members and perhaps will need help from a consultant, just as they received in their first telephone campaign. Their proposed budget also will need to demonstrate a hefty net profit from these additions. The new programs will be quite separate activities but will operate in somewhat similar fashion and require similar staff support.

Anderson also believes she must respond to her board members' repeated request that she start asking local corporations and foundations for support of this campaign. Once this area has been addressed, she can consider her second set of new program ideas. Quite a few large corporations and foundations are based in Cleveland. Anderson knows a few of the professional staff from her previous jobs; she also knows this project is a bit nontraditional as clean city streets might not be on the radar screens as priorities with these corporations and foundations. She tells Alice, "Lets get ready to lay out our plans to start work on local corporations and foundations at the next board meeting."

CHAPTER 8

Soliciting Annual Gifts from Corporations and Foundations

At this point in your new fund development program, you have built a constituency using direct mail, renewed and upgraded their annual gifts, created a membership organization to increase their involvement and re-tention, and organized donors and volunteers into effective teams in groups, guilds, and support organizations. The CCUA Clean Up Cleve-land Chapter has processed 14,784 gifts from new donors! Terrific! But for months now, your board and management staff plus your donors and vol-unteers have encouraged you to start raising money from corporations and foundations. "Make a list and send them letters; the mail has worked so far," they tell you. No! Please don't do that! First, understand that corpo-rations are vastly different from foundations. Second, raising money from either is vastly different from anything you have tried yet. Here's why:

1. These are institutions, not individuals; they think and act differently.

2. Institutions make gift decisions based on established policies and follow firm grantmaking procedures with lots of restrictions; if you cannot "fit" their prescription almost exactly, you should not even apply.

3. They receive more applications than they can fund (like 100 to 1!).

4. Everyone on their current gift list fought hard to get there; your proposal will likely have to knock someone else off to get on an in-stitution's list.

5. They prefer specific projects with well-defined plans.

6. They require firm evidence of relevant community needs matched to your organization's mission and ability to make a real difference.

7. They require written proposals, often with extensive details, of truly big ideas as projects with impact and visibility.

8. Staff do not always welcome visits to their office; check first before you call for an appointment.

9. Staff especially do not like direct contact with their board members, seeking to go around the staff or to bend established procedures.

10. They take their own time to make decisions; the money may come months later, even next fiscal year.

11. Together, they represent only 12 to 15 percent of all gifts made in American each year.

12. They are *not* a reliable source for continuous annual gifts.

Prepare yourself for lots of work and for limited success in raising annual gifts from corporations and foundations. Approach them only after careful research and with a project that fits closely with everything you can learn about them. Verify that your projects "match" to their current priority preferred area(s) of funding. They will prefer to see other corporations and foundations involved in your project, and do not welcome being asked to be the only source of funding. It is your obligation, once you have identified qualified prospects for your current priorities of need, to make your first and best effort for the largest gift possible from your absolutely best source, because the others respect their colleagues' process to decision but will give only as much and probably less. But, once you have one or two of these leadership gifts, you can use their decisions to great advantage to leverage the others to join the cause.

This chapter will examine the nature and process of annual solicitations from corporations and foundations, ending with some experiences as first-time efforts by our friends at the CCUA Clean Up Cleveland Chapter.

SECURING ANNUAL CORPORATE GIFTS

Milton Friedman has said, "The business of business is business!" Corporations exist to make money for their stockholders. That's their primary purpose; they do this by offering products and services to customers who chose to buy them. Why do corporations give money to charity? Why would they even consider doing this? Doesn't that defeat their primary purpose? Yes and no. Yes, stockholders do have a strong voice in how corporations spend their money, but also no—they don't give away much money, either. Corporate stockholders, board members, and executives also are community-minded citizens who believe business has a civic duty to be a good community citizen, and should give back for one or more good reasons (see Exhibit 8-1).

Each of the motives listed in Exhibit 8-1 represents a rational process that has been adopted, in part, for appearances' sake. Most gift decisions will represent all of them in one form or another. The first, corporate social responsibility, is a current corporate theme that has evolved over time into a common tune. Reality, however, is that corporate giving is most often guided by the answer to this question: "What's in it for us to make a gift to your organization?" Call it by whatever tune you choose, if you

---

EXHIBIT 8-1   WHY DO CORPORATIONS GIVE?

1. *Good corporate citizenship.* Many companies think that it is important to present a positive image in the communities in which they operate. Such an image can be maintained or heightened through charitable gifts to local not-for-profits that provide community service.

2. *Enlightened self-interest.* Most fundraisers subscribe to the notion that companies make charitable gifts because it is basically in their best interest to do so. Because companies hire local employees, they want to maintain an educated and healthy work force. This often can be accomplished by supporting the work of local charities such as colleges, hospitals, and cultural organizations.

3. *Individual leadership initiative.* Companies are also likely to support not-for-profit organizations simply because of the interest and clout of those in charge. This is often the case in family businesses in which the founder may direct help to a favorite charity without a committee vote. This will also happen in large corporations where the CEO or president uses his or her clout to direct gifts to selected charities.

4. *Civic participation.* Most often a company will restrict its support to not-for-profits in the communities in which the company operates and has an employee base.

5. *Quid pro quo interests.* Many companies use quid pro quo interest (that is, they ask, "What's in it for us?"). Such a company wants to see a tangible return on its charitable investment. Such a direct relationship between making a gift and obtaining something in return (other than general satisfaction) is not always easy to delineate. Some people, however, argue that seeking such a connection diminishes the spirit of philanthropy. Still many companies continue to look for such linkages.[1]

cannot answer this basic *return on investment* question by credibly demonstrating that a donation is worthwhile to company interests, it is not likely to make a gift.

Is this philanthropy? No, and it never has been. "Despite the fact that there are several newsletters and books with the title *Corporate Philanthropy*, and despite the fact the term is widely used in other ways, the reality is there is no such thing."[2]

In choosing to support charitable organizations, businesses consider these factors:

- Will the activity increase company revenues?
- Will the activity reduce overall costs?
- Will customers know more about company products?
- Will the image of the company be improved?
- Will the activity improve employee morale?
- Will the activity lead to greater success by the company?
- Will shareholders consider the activity important?[3]

If nonprofit organizations want corporate donations, they will have to convince the company that the answer to most—if not all—of these questions is yes.

Another set of answers will be found in the four models illustrated as the Four Paradigms of Corporate Giving (see Exhibit 8-2). You are likely to find the motive(s) for every corporate or business gift decision contained in one, even two of these models, although it is unlikely that just one will be a "pure" example. Giving programs, those that are formally organized within a company, also differ from company to company. Although any company, business, partnership, or firm can establish a contributions program of its choosing (often considered a "community relations" initiative), the vast majority have no organized, written guidelines, process, or procedure to respond to the many requests they receive from nonprofit organizations.

Corporate giving also has gone through periods of changing focus or fads, rallying around the arts, the environment, community revitalization, and other popular topics in turn as, for altruistic or public pressure reasons, local and national business leaders agreed that such causes were worthy of their coordinated giving enterprise. Within individual companies, change also occurs as a result of new leadership at the board and CEO levels, local

EXHIBIT 8-2   **FOUR PARADIGMS FOR CORPORATE SUPPORT TO NONPROFIT ORGANIZATIONS**

1. **"The Neo-Classical/Corporate Productivity Model** [is designed] to contribute to the ability of the firm to make profits. . . . [Its] ultimate measure of success is increased corporate productivity and enhancement of the financial bottom line." [Students of corporate economic theory will readily associate this paradigm with the early research and continuing influence of Milton Friedman, and the Chicago School of Economics.]

2. **"The Ethical/Altruistic Model** [is] based on the assumption that corporations generate financial surpluses that are used by corporate leaders to do what is right for society. . . . [This model] conceives of corporations as citizens and corporate executives as societal leaders . . . [who] allocate some of their surpluses according to criteria of social value and ethical and moral precepts not tied to bottom line considerations."

3. **"The Political Model** [is rooted in a corporation's desire] to preserve corporate power and autonomy by building private initiatives [among nonprofit grantees] as an alternative to the growth of governmental authority and by limiting government interference in the free enterprise system. . . . In this view, corporate philanthropy is not driven by profits or by social good per se but by the desire of the corporate giving community to bolster its position in the environments in which it operates."

4. **"The Stakeholder Model** posits that the corporation is a complex entity that affects, and is affected by, various significant groups—stockholders, managers, workers, customers, suppliers, community groups, and so on. . . . In this view, managing a corporation is an exercise . . . guided by the desire of corporate leadership to steer a clear path through the shoals of stakeholder interests."[4]

and national marketplace positions, competition, product lines, legislation and regulation, taxes, and, above all else, profits. Corporate philanthropy is itself dependent on the global economy for solid, sustained growth in productivity and products to generate profits. Business success means profits, which means employment, growth, and prosperity—which means philanthropy can share in this success. Without profits, corporate giving cannot continue. It's nothing more than a pure business decision every time.

Corporate giving also performs differently in cities and towns around the nation as local conditions such as need, population size, culture, history, and so forth are different. Further, a family-held business might act more like an individual giving source than a public company. In similar fashion, a company that is a major employer in town will likely have been involved over many years with several nonprofit organizations, providing them with

volunteers and leadership by senior officers, managers, and workers, because of its employees' dependence on these programs and services.

Corporations also give differently depending on their size.

> McElroy and Seigfried have perhaps done the most extensive research on
> the relationship of firm size and corporate contributions. Three interest-
> ing results emerged from their work. First, medium-sized firms (based on
> number of employees) contribute proportionately more than larger and
> smaller firms. Second, as the firm size increases, contributions to health
> and welfare organizations decrease because most giving is done through
> the United Way, which is considered a fixed rather than proportionate
> obligation. Third, larger firms are more apt to contribute to education
> and national organizations.[5]

Despite these conditions that affect their decisions, corporations also have
a variety of means where giving can occur.

What kinds of support might a nonprofit organization expect from a
corporation? Keep in mind that they are not obligated to give at all; giving
is as voluntary for them as it is for everyone else. But, unlike individuals
and foundations, corporations have a variety of fiscal sources to draw upon
to make annual gifts. Cash is available from several different budgets within
the company—advertising, human resources, marketing, research, as well
as the formal corporate Contributions Committee or Community Relations Committee. There also might be a corporate foundation, which
functions just like the Corporate Contributions Committee but might have
its own funds from investments (stocks and bonds, real estate, oil wells, and
more) as well as receiving corporate distributions from annual profits. This
gives it more fiscal stability. Also, company employees are community residents who use nonprofit services for themselves and their families. Several
companies utilize employee managed giving committees for their local distribution purposes. Employees are also encouraged to participate in civic
affairs as company representatives, to offer their professional skills and talents along with their time and energy to nonprofit organizations. Furthermore, any company that has products and services can use these as annual
contributions (see Exhibit 8-3 for a full list of corporate giving sources). Finally, companies can change their policies and procedures from time to
time, as a result of internal changes, new product lines, buying and selling
subsidiaries, or being acquired by another corporation. An example of a

EXHIBIT 8-3   BUDGET SOURCES FOR CORPORATE GIFT SUPPORT[6]

Source	Description
Outright gift	A direct contribution or grant
Matching gift	A gift to match an employee's personal gift to a qualified not-for-profit organization
Advertising and marketing budgets	A gift for public visibility or for a cause-related marketing campaign
Research and personnel budgets	A grant to support company product development or to benefit the employee relations program
Corporate partnerships	Joint ventures or contracts where programs and services are arranged for employees or customers
Employee volunteers	Time, talent, and expertise shared by employees
Equipment and service donations	Use of facilities, equipment and professional services on a pro bono basis
Facilities	Access to buildings, telephones, or printing and copying machines
In-kind donations	Delivery of products without charge or purchase
Corporate foundations	Separate granting vehicle for gifts and pledges

corporate contributions program description is the DaimlerChrysler Corporation Fund, a newly defined program described in Exhibit 8-4.

One set of conclusions about corporate giving can be stated clearly: There is no single motive, no single pattern, no single source, no single avenue, no single guideline that can be followed to secure corporate gifts. Each company is different in how it approaches charitable giving; to succeed, you need to learn (and keep up with) each preference and priority for each company you qualify as a valid prospect for annual gift consideration for your organization.

TAX DEDUCTIONS AS A MOTIVATION

What about the corporate income tax deduction as a motive? In two words, "not hardly." Corporations have long been encouraged by government tax policy to make charitable contributions and claim their deductions. That

EXHIBIT 8-4   **EXAMPLE OF A CORPORATE CONTRIBUTIONS PROGRAM DESCRIPTION**

The DaimlerChrysler Corporation Fund is the philanthropic arm of the company created when U.S. automaker Chrysler Corporation merged with Germany's Daimler, the maker of Mercedes-Benz automobiles. The Fund seeks to improve the community and business environments in which the DaimlerChrysler Corporation conducts business. Grantmaking is focused on the following areas:

- Develop a skilled work force
- Support responsive, healthy, and attractive communities
- Encourage employee participation and involvement
- Support public policy and marketplace issues

The fund values programs that demonstrate the following:

- Leadership
- Innovation
- Model of effective change
- Organizational self-sufficiency
- Empowered people
- Involved employees
- Teamwork
- Continuous improvement
- Results

Applicants are encouraged to submit a brief (two- to three-page) letter outlining the proposal and responses to questions found on the Fund's Web site. The letter should include a copy of the organization's 501(c)(3) letter and the most recent annual report or other available information about the organization. National, international, and southwestern Michigan inquiries should be sent to: Ms. Lynn Feldhouse, Vice President and Secretary, DaimlerChrysler Corporation Fund, CIMS: 485-02-46, 1000 Chrysler Drive, Auburn Hills, MI 48326y-2766. Ph: (248) 512-2502. Web site: *http://www.fund.daimlerchrysler.com*. Groups serving communities where Daimler-Chrysler has a facility with a large number of employees should address materials to the local DaimlerChrysler management. Applicants also may apply online. Requests and proposals are accepted and reviewed on a continuing basis.

privilege was first introduced into law in Texas in 1917, the same year contributions to charity by individuals were allowed as an income tax deduction from federal taxes. In 1935, amendments in the Internal Revenue Code added the corporate deduction from business income tax.

For years since, stockholders have challenged the company's right to make gifts to charitable causes, but this issue too was resolved in favor of corporate giving in the landmark *A.P. Smith* case in 1953.[7] Today, companies can claim gift deductions for charitable contributions up to 15 percent of pretax income. That's the good news. Unfortunately, the bad news is that their average has not even been close to 2 percent since 1986, when it hit the all-time high of 2.3 percent.[8] Corporate giving has since sunk to between 1.1 to 1.3 percent a year for the past decade, despite the greatest growth in corporate profitability ever seen in history. This performance is inconsistent with the fact that Congress enacted two increases in deductibility during the same period: to 10 percent in 1981, and to 15 percent in the recent 2001 tax act.

Why is corporate giving at such a low level? In part, the answer is Congress and politics. When Congress raised the percent deductibility limits, it also deflated this incentive by lowering corporate tax rates. This reduced the tax benefit derived from corporate contributions. In one example, the same 1986 tax reform act that increased deductibility also lowered corporate tax rates from 46 to 34 percent. The net effect was *to increase* the after-tax cost of giving money from \$0.54 to \$0.66 per dollar given, an increase of 22 percent—poor encouragement by government indeed.[9] Nonetheless, corporations have continued to make contributions (see Exhibit 8-5 for the list of largest corporate foundations by total giving).

Separate from charitable contribution deductions for gifts of cash, corporation income tax law allows other areas where business tax deductions can occur, such as marketing and promotion expenses and in giving away their products and services. The performance of these forms of gifts, called "gifts in kind," is hard to track on a national or local scale but the practice has increased substantially in recent years to the benefit of both corporations and charities. Gifts of products are especially valuable in support of activities, benefits and special events where direct contributions of auction and raffle prizes, decorations, entertainment, flowers, printing, wines, and more reduces these otherwise budgeted event costs and increases net proceeds (see Chapter 10 for added details on "in-kind" gifts as well as sponsorships and underwriting gifts for benefit events).

Corporate volunteerism is another area of substantial growth. "According to a study conducted by the Points of Light Foundation and the Conference Board (1993), 92 percent of the 452 corporations that responded to

EXHIBIT 8-5 LARGEST CORPORATE FOUNDATIONS BY TOTAL GIVING[10]

Rank	Name (state)	Total Grants	Fiscal Year End Date
1.	Ford Motor Company Fund (MI)	$97,769,429	12/31/99
2.	Bank of America Foundation, Inc. (NC)	90,999,532	12/31/99
3.	SBC Foundation (TX)	64,047,020	12/31/99
4.	Wal-Mart Foundation (AR)	62,617,641	01/31/00
5.	AT&T Foundation (NY)	39,626,024	12/31/99
6.	BP Amoco Foundation, Inc. (IL)	36,944,795	12/31/99
7.	Verizon Foundation (NY)	35,332,818	12/31/99
8.	The Chase Manhattan Foundation (NY)	35,227,314	12/31/99
9.	GE Fund (CT)	35,126,991	12/31/99
10.	Fannie Mae Foundation (DC)	33,926,500	12/31/99
11.	The UPS Foundation (GA)	32,838,108	12/31/99
12.	General Motors Foundation, Inc. (MI)	30,482,845	12/31/99
13.	The Procter & Gamble Fund (OH)	30,430,962	06/30/00
14.	Hoeshst Marion Roussel Health Care Foundation for the Ill (MO)	28,650,012	12/31/99
15.	Lucent Technologies Foundation (NY)	27,738,988	09/30/99
16.	DaimlerChrysler Corporation Fund (MI)	27,487,427	12/31/99
17.	The Prudential Foundation (NJ)	25,045,110	12/31/99
18.	The Merck Company Foundation (NJ)	24,281,664	12/31/99
19.	FleetBoston Financial Foundation (MA)	24,200,000	12/31/00
20.	The First Union Foundation (NC)	23,249,643	12/31/99
21.	ExxonMobil Foundation (TX)	21,388,379	12/31/99

a national survey indicated that they encourage their employees to become involved in volunteer activities. In addition, 72 percent of top corporate executives affirmed the success of corporate volunteer programs in helping companies meet strategic goals and community needs. Most importantly, the study documented the following as evidence of this rapid and substantial increase in corporate volunteerism."[11]

In over 70 independent Corporate Volunteerism Councils nationwide, 1,048 companies share their volunteer experiences. New programs are added every day. The growth from 600 such member companies in 1985 represents a recognition that volunteer programs are one of the best ways for corporations to support their involvement in the community. Forty-five percent of contributions/community relations managers in 100 Fortune 500 companies anticipated expanding their employee volunteer programs over the next two to five years, in spite of downsizing.[12]

However, as of yet, there is no tax deduction to a corporation or business for the time their employees take during working hours to volunteer at nonprofit organizations. Furthermore, employees may claim as charitable deductions on their individual income tax returns only those specific expenses (i.e., mileage, parking, and uniform costs), for voluntary work at nonprofit organizations. The tax deduction motive for companies and their employees is negligible if not altogether invisible.

THE ROLES OF RESEARCH, RELATIONSHIPS, AND REQUESTS

The good news here is that there are good sources for research on corporations, more all the time, and they include useful details on corporate contributions programs. The bad news is that less than 20 percent of all companies have formal contributions programs. Of those that do, many describe their community involvement program on their corporate Web page or will send you these details on request. *Please note:* Companies prepare this information so that nonprofit organizations will read their guidelines and observe their procedures. Far too many requests show a lack of respect for this most basic fundraising practice, which does nothing to warm the hearts of corporate contributions officers. The first, most important step in obtaining corporate or foundation funding is to do your homework.

To understand how corporations make gift decisions, use the following criteria to judge whether a company would qualify as a prospect:

- The number of years of previous support
- The level of involvement by company personnel
- The degree of benefit to the company
- The size of gifts being made by other companies
- Importance of the project to community welfare
- Whether the company makes one-time gifts or annual support[13]

If you determine that your organization and the corporation or foundation are a good fit, you will need to proceed to the next level: build relationships, respect the corporation's guidelines and processes, submit well-prepared and relevant projects, be persistent but not aggressive, and look for multiple opportunities for involvement together in community work.

What information do you need to qualify a company or business for your annual gift request? A better question is, how much background work should you do before you qualify a company as a potential gift prospect? Not much, if you will observe the following:

> As with any fundraising approach, potential corporate donors should be carefully researched, screened, and cultivated prior to requesting gifts. No matter how compelling the need, gifts are invariably larger and extend over longer periods of support when a relationship has been carefully nurtured with corporate donors.[14]

Research must focus first on finding a match between corporate giving guidelines and your project; without a close match, there will be no gift. Next, establish whether any local relationships are possible with staff at the branch office, within the sales or service geographic area, as home to corporate employees and major suppliers, and so on. Third, capture only the basic data you need or will use: company name, corporate executives including contributions manager, headquarters and local office mail addresses and telephone numbers, Web page address, prior giving in your area, and application requirements and deadlines. Fourth, learn whether anyone in your organization—board members, volunteers or donors, management, or professional staff—have linkages with any employees or the business itself. Based on all these data, assemble a logical plan that is built on the match of your project to one or more areas of current corporate priority that has the potential for personal access through your contacts, and the probability of a likely working relationship into the future.

Sources for information on U.S. corporations are extensive. However, finding information about their corporate giving programs is just about impossible, as they do not reveal these details in their annual reports, stock prospectus, or other public documents. You have to dig it out. Fortunately for all of us, others have done a lot of the digging. Much of what you need to know about the executives in any company will be found in the reference books published by Marquis' *Who's Who* and *Who's Who in Business and Industry*. To learn about each company's line of business, financial performance, number of plants and office sites, employee size, and much more, seek out the directories published by Dun & Bradstreet, Moody's, and Standard & Poor's, all available at your local public library. Annual 10-K reports filed with the Securities and Exchange Commission (SEC) by all publicly traded corporations are available from local SEC offices and online through Lexis/Nexis (www.lexis-nexis.com) and Dialog (www.dialog.com). A host of other online sources also are available, but it takes a trained research person to not only locate these sources but also verify key data with at least a second source.

Information about corporate contributions programs *is* hard to get (see Exhibit 8-6 for examples of how companies limit their information), but even brief descriptions provide clues. For example, whatever areas are

EXHIBIT 8-6	EXAMPLES OF CORPORATE CONTRIBUTIONS PROGRAM DESCRIPTIONS[15]

Reynolds Metals Company Foundation: "Foundation's grantmaking is heavily focused on education, specifically to encourage middle and secondary schools, colleges and universities in the development of business, engineering and science curricula and on efforts to prepare students in those fields. The Foundation also supports health and social services organizations, culture and arts agencies, and civic groups, particularly those in which Reynolds employees serve in leadership positions or organizations that Reynolds customers support or employees endorse. Grants are awarded to organizations in communities where Reynolds Metals operates."

General AMR/American Airlines Foundation: "The Foundation works to help meet the needs of organizations in the communities that the airline serves, especially the hub cities of Dallas/Fort Worth, Chicago, Miami and San Juan. The Foundation focuses its grantmaking on the following areas: community development, arts and culture, education, and health and welfare. Proposals are reviewed on an ongoing basis and grants are awarded throughout the year."

ExxonMobil Company: The Company focuses its grantmaking on the following areas: education, environment, health, minority- and women-owned service organizations, public information and public research, arts, museum, historical associations, civic and community service organizations. Support for local organizations is only in ExxonMobil communities."

Rohm and Haas: "The Company, a leader in specialty chemical technology, invests in programs and activities to improve the communities where its employees live. The Company's grantmaking priorities are health and human services, education, civic and community improvement, and culture and the arts—with special emphasis on health and human services and education programs. The Company seeks new ways to use its resources to address old and new societal problems."

listed first are usually a company's priority focus; those listed last are least likely to receive much support. Once you have determined that a company might become a qualified prospect, make direct contact with it and ask for copies of its contributions policies, procedures, and guidelines, along with the name(s) of the appropriate staff person(s) to contact, their telephone and fax numbers, and more. Two sources provide details on contributions with amounts, to whom, and for what purpose. They are the directories published by The Taft Group (www.galegroup.com/taft) and The Foundation Center (www.fdncenter.org). Both offer data in print or in online form. Any company with a Web page might provide some details on its community relations programs: this is about your final source.

With good data in hand, the next step is to establish a relationship with those who make decisions. Individuals to cultivate include top executives, board members, local office officials, and the managers of community relations, human resources, marketing, research, or whatever department it is that supervises the corporate contributions program.

Why all this effort if the potential for corporate giving remains at 1 percent of net income before taxes? And, if corporate giving is "flat" at 1.3 percent during the most profitable years in corporate America, and remains at only 5 percent of annual contributions made in America, why pursue such a limited source? Two fair questions. Part of the answer lies in the ability of nonprofit organizations to manage the relationship between any company, business, or firm. Annual gifts from companies are like annual gifts from individuals in that they are opportunities to begin a relationship, in this case a business relationship. Whatever potential lies in such a relationship depends largely on the nonprofit organization. What does your research suggest as honest potential beyond an occasional annual gift? If answers include volunteer leadership, event sponsorship, a major gift for a future capital campaign, even a joint venture such as a cause-related marketing program, then investing in building a relationship using one or more annual giving vehicles to grow the relationship will be worth the time and effort involved.

There is both art and science in cultivating relationships. Business relationships are built around common needs. Manufacturers need reliable suppliers; suppliers need reliable buyers. You don't have to like a person to do business with him or her, but you do need to rely on the person, sometimes with a formal contract to bind both to the task. A level of respect and trust is involved. Nonprofit organizations seldom have a sufficient business relationship (amount of money involved) with any single company to give them any leverage at all, so this relationship has to be personal, and it has to emphasize respect and trust. Is this why nonprofits invented committees? So we could seek out prospective donors, involve them in the organization's work, build a sufficient business relationship based on respect and trust, gain some advantage and some leverage, then ask them for money. Well, it does work, and has for lots of nonprofit organizations, but it also takes a lot of time.

Keep in mind that every corporation thinks and acts differently when it comes to making contributions. Prepare a strategic plan to guide the cultivation and solicitation process for each corporation you qualify as a prospective donor. Recruit help from your board members, donors, volunteers, former clients, staff, and so on to establish personal contact with corporate officials. Gather data on where, how often, and how many employees and their families have used your organization's programs and services. In one example, a hospital, in preparing its presentation to a local company, tabulated employee use of its services to demonstrate not only the extent of employee use with demographic details not likely to be known to the company but also highly favorable to the hospital's leverage in demonstrating a relationship of some significance (see Exhibit 8-7).

The next step might be to investigate whether any current programs and services might be brought to company offices and plant sites, as an added employee benefit and to provide increased visibility for the organization. Once a working relationship has been established with value-added benefits to the company, ask company officials to help you do the same with their suppliers and vendors in the area. The net effect is an honest relationship, a partnership with value-added benefits to both parties. Now you are doing business together; now you can ask for support.

Whatever priority project you wish to bring forward, for whatever purpose, always prepare it as a formal proposal to the company. Never assume your relationship will allow you to simplify or shortcut the process. Follow the company's guidelines to the letter, including any request for brevity (see Exhibit 8-8 for guidelines for preparing corporate proposals). Your relationship should be strong enough that you do not need to provide a detailed history, copies of brochures, plus your most recent newsletters and annual report, and more, unless specifically directed to do so.

EXHIBIT 8-7   CORPORATE EMPLOYEE HOSPITAL USE STATISTICS

Patient Types	1998 No.	1998 %	1999 No.	1999 %	Jan–June 2000 No.	Jan–June 2000 %	All Years Combined No.	All Years Combined %
Inpatient visits	54	7.8%	60	7.6%	28	7.8%	142	7.7%
Emergency care unit visits	32	4.6%	50	6.3%	24	6.7%	106	5.8%
Outpatient visits	605	87.6%	681	86.1%	305	85.4%	1591	86.5%
Totals	691	100.0%	791	100.0%	357	100.0%	1839	100.0%

Patient Sex	1998 No.	1998 %	1999 No.	1999 %	Jan–June 2000 No.	Jan–June 2000 %	All Years Combined No.	All Years Combined %
Male	342	49.5%	430	54.4%	199	55.7%	971	52.8%
Female	349	50.5%	361	45.6%	158	44.3%	868	47.2%
Totals	691	100.0%	791	100.0%	357	100.0%	1839	100.0%

Age Groups	1998 No.	1998 %	1999 No.	1999 %	Jan–June 2000 No.	Jan–June 2000 %	All Years Combined No.	All Years Combined %
0–18	16	2.3%	27	3.4%	19	5.3%	62	3.4%
19–35	39	5.6%	55	7.0%	27	7.6%	121	6.6%
36–55	170	24.6%	185	23.4%	88	24.6%	443	24.1%
55+	466	67.4%	524	66.2%	223	62.5%	1213	66.0%
Totals	691	100.0%	791	100.0%	357	100.0%	1839	100.0%

Centers of Excellence	1998 No.	1998 %	1999 No.	1999 %	Jan–June 2000 No.	Jan–June 2000 %	All Years Combined No.	All Years Combined %
Women's	7	29.2%	11	42.3%	3	25.0%	21	33.9%
Heart	10	41.7%	9	34.6%	5	41.7%	24	38.7%
Ortho	4	16.7%	6	23.1%	4	33.3%	14	22.6%
Cancer	3	12.5%	0	0.0%	0	0.0%	3	4.8%
Totals	24	92.3%	26	100.0%	12	100.0%	62	100.0%
% of Inpatients	44.4%		43.3%		42.9%		43.7%	

EXHIBIT 8-8   GUIDELINES FOR PREPARING
CORPORATE PROPOSALS

1. Summarize the request concisely.

2. Grab the reader's interest quickly (do not be afraid to use modifiers to make your concepts sparkle; however, avoid using words like *unique*).

3. Link the not-for-profit's request to the company's expressed interests (determine those interests through careful research, reading its published guidelines, telephone and personal contacts, and discussions with others familiar with those funding sources, especially agency board members).

4. Do not ramble on any of the issues addressed in the proposal.

5. Confine the request to one page and *never* exceed two.

6. Address the request to a person, not to "Dear Friend" or "Dear Corporate Director" (reference sources should be consulted to obtain the names of contacts *and* accuracy should be confirmed by telephone).

7. Reference previous telephone or personal contact with the addressee.

8. Cleanly type the proposal on agency letterhead using correct grammar. Proofread for typos. If the agency letterhead does not include a telephone number, it must be included in the cover letter.

Source: Lester A. Picker, "The Corporate Support Marketplace," in *The Nonprofit Handbook: Fund Raising*, 2d ed., edited by James M. Greenfield (New York: John Wiley & Sons, Inc., 1997), 389–390. Reprinted with permission.

Brevity is considered a big plus with corporate contributions staff. Define your project in terms of its value to the company first and then to the community; offer a proposed solution to a community problem that is or may affect employees, outline your methodology for success, list other funding sources, and that's about all you need. Any formal documents requested (e.g., IRS determination letter, recent audit, and roster of board members) will complete the proposal. It should be two to five pages in length (10 at the most), including a to-the-point cover letter citing the amount of money requested. Include all the required attachments. For other tips for success, see Exhibit 8-9. As you can see, without a solid relationship in place, any hope for a corporate gift is slim indeed!

You prepared your best proposal to your best corporate prospects, followed their guidelines to the letter, and, after weeks pass, you receive a rejection letter! You are crushed, disappointed, even a bit angry. What happened? Why was your request denied? Good questions, and the answers

EXHIBIT 8-9   TIPS FOR SUCCESS IN CORPORATE SOLICITATIONS

1. Plan ahead when making a corporate solicitation. Consider submitting a proposal on the first day after a deadline has passed to give the prospect ample time to review the request. Proposals received on or near a deadline typically receive less attention.

2. Always read the funding guidelines carefully. Read between the lines to determine what is not being mentioned. Guidelines usually state clearly what is and is not eligible for funding, but some programs or projects may not be specifically excluded or included, thus falling into a gray area. Consult with the funding prospect to determine whether a project may be of interest and thus worth a proposal submission.

3. Administrative assistants in a corporate-giving office can provide valuable advice by telephone that sometimes is more comprehensive than what a director will provide on a company's philanthropic program.

4. When approaching a company for the first time, it might be easier to develop a long-term relationship by making an initial request for a small annual gift. A larger grant will be more likely if cultivation is successful and annual support is given each year.

5. Where possible, develop a relationship with corporate-giving consultants who advise corporate funders.

6. Seek out companies with new corporate-giving programs or new personnel. In the early phases to a corporate-giving program, funding guidelines are usually broad and unfocused. It may be easier to obtain support early in the cycle.

7. Utilize corporate employee matching-gift programs where appropriate. A good source for information on matching-gift programs is the Council for the Advancement and Support of Education in Alexandria, Virginia.

8. Determine what professional groups corporate-giving officers belong to and look for ways to become involved with those groups. A not-for-profit may wish to host a meeting for one or more of them.

9. A not-for-profit should invite corporate-giving officers to visit the organization's facilities. Solicitation success rates jump dramatically when funders can see first-hand what not-for-profits seek to accomplish.

Source: Reprinted with permission from K. Scott Sheldon, "Foundations as a Source of Support," in *Achieving Excellence in Fund Raising* by Henry A. Rosso and Associates (San Francisco: Jossey-Bass, 1991), 241–242.

are at the company. Here is Scott Sheldon's prescription for turning a corporate no into a yes.

1.   First, call the company. You may learn it was simply a timing decision, or you should apply again in the next budget cycle.

2. Thank the company for turning you down. You did appreciate their taking the time to review your proposal.

3. Make sure your request matches their stated interests; confirm their guidelines.

4. Consider another of the doors of entry into a large corporation, such as the marketing, sponsorship, or employee contributions committee.

5. Review your agency's relationship with the company; any board member work for the company? Any matching fits? Any services provided to the company? Any company services provided to your agency?

6. Invite company representatives to your annual dinner or benefit event; if a list of donors is printed in the program, their absence might prove to be a stimulus to making a gift.

7. Look for ways to strengthen the bond between your organization and the company. Is there any opportunity for volunteers at your agency, especially by senior company executives?

8. Consider recruiting gifts from CEOs of other companies and enlist their help in soliciting others.

9. Solidify your case for support in terms of why their gift can make a difference for the company.

10. Always maintain a positive image; keep up all your contacts and communications and continue to build your relationships.[16]

THE UNITED WAY CORPORATE CONNECTION

Without question, the largest national corporate engagement with philanthropy is through their local United Ways—all 1,400 of them across the United States. It is also one of the largest fundraising enterprises in the world, with 1999 to 2000 contributions of $3.77 billion, an increase of 5.4 percent ($190 million) over the 1998 to 1999 campaigns. Employees of corporations and small businesses were the largest source of United Way revenue, at $1.864 billion (49.4 percent of the total campaign). Direct corporate giving, apart from employees and small business contributions, was

$837.3 million, or 22.2 percent of the 1999 campaign.[17] The Tocqueville Society, a leadership gifts program asking for annual gifts of $10,000 and higher, provided 25.1 percent to a recent campaign. The balance of funds comes from public support sources including planned gifts, government grants, and investment interest. The brilliant concepts that yield these levels of annual giving are their partnership with corporations for community benefit, a shared objective of mutual benefit. United Ways also can "brag up" their administrative expense ratio—an average of 13 percent of all funds raised, thanks to their vast network of volunteers and the simplicity of corporate payroll–deduction programs.

The United Way movement reaches into nearly every community in America. Its mission is "to respond to, support and serve local United Way member organizations to help increase the organized capacity of people to care for one another." The concept of a community campaign for local charities was founded in Denver, Colorado, in 1887. The identification of the "community chest" combined campaign originated in Cleveland, Ohio, at the beginning of the twentieth century. Today there are 1,900 community-based health and human service organizations served by 45,000 United Way agencies and chapters. To be accepted as a United Way agency, the organization must (1) have nonprofit, tax–exempt status, (2) be governed by volunteers, (3) receive an annual, independent financial audit, (4) provide services at reasonable cost, and (5) maintain a policy of nondiscrimination. Community volunteers appointed by the agencies themselves make distribution grants to member agencies.

The role of the national headquarters, not established until 1918, is to provide advertising, training, corporate relations, research, networks, and government relations. The national service center does not compete with its local affiliates for funds. Governed by a 45-member board composed of 15 local United Way and six AFL-CIO representatives, the national office has 11 board committees for governance and operations: Community impact, compensation and human resources, diversity, executive, ethics, finance and audit, marketing, membership, nominating, public policy, and resource development. Despite its visibility and name recognition, "the action" is at the community level, where true annual giving programs reside.

The current popularity of United Way is due in no small part to their 50-year-plus partnership with the American Federation of Labor and the Congress of Industrial Organizations (AFL-CIO) and with their 25-year-plus partnership with the National Football League (NFL). These are not casual relationships; the members of the AFL-CIO and the NFL are personally engaged with their local United Way agencies. Union members are trained for the decision-making requirements of volunteer service on health and human service organization boards and committees, as well as with information about available local services for referral in need. Affiliated union groups, such as the National Association of Letter Carriers' (NALC), hold additional annual fund drives; letter carriers collect nonperishables from customers on their mail routes for distribution to community food banks, pantries, and shelters. This is the largest one-day food drive in the world. The NFL partnership includes television spots that reach more than 113 million viewers per week, a gift value estimated at $30 million annually and provided to United Way without cost. Each team member in the NFL is personally involved in community projects such as building homes for low-income families and new playgrounds for agency kids, conducting junior training camps, and serving food to the homeless, as witnessed on their TV spots throughout the year and especially throughout the NFL season.

Among United Way's coordinated programs across the nation is the new "Outcome Measurement Activities" effort. Several manuals and guides for agencies on measuring their program and service outcomes were issued in 1996, and many agencies are already demonstrating the effectiveness of reporting performance measurement results back to the communities who funded these programs and services (see Exhibit 8-10 for several progress reports).

CORPORATE MATCHING GIFTS: UNTAPPED GOLD?

For many years, companies have provided a matching-gifts program as an incentive for employees to participate actively in their communities. Most match dollar for dollar; a few match three to one. "This has an immediate and long-lasting effect on employee morale and retention, while benefiting social causes."[19] Because employee satisfaction is the chief goal of this program, some companies have begun to place increased emphasis on employee-directed corporate gift committees. This strategy has increased employee participation to the extent that matching gifts have begun to

EXHIBIT 8-10   SELECTION OF OUTCOME
MEASUREMENT ACTIVITY
REPORTS[18]

Camp Fire Boys and Girls

Camp Fire Boys and Girls (CFBG) reports that outcome measurement is becoming a topic of focus for many of its members. In 1997, CFBG held its biannual national conference at which outcome-measurement workshops were held. CFBG also sponsors a national initiative called *Extending Our Reach*, a four-year grant program that incorporates training on outcome measurement.

CFBG announced publication of UWA's outcome manual to its members through its national newsletter and circulated copies of the manual to members around the country. The national office communicates new resources and information on outcome measurement to local members on a regular basis. Tools for measurement of outcomes specific to CFBG's programs are presently under development.

Catholic Charities USA

Catholic Charities USA (CCUSA), the nation's largest private network of independent social service agencies, has taken an active interest in encouraging and leading its members toward developing outcome measures for their programs and services.

The issue of outcome measurement has been addressed in *Charities USA*, the association's quarterly magazine to the network, and is an integral part of Catholic Charities USA's strategic plan, Vision 2000. Newsletters to various sections of the organization are also being initiated and will focus on specific issues such as accreditation, quality assurance, and outcome measurement.

In developing training and providing support to member agencies using or developing outcome measurement, CCUSA strives to strike a balance between the requirements of the Council on Accreditation of Services to Families and Children, which accredits many CCUSA agencies, and UWA recommendations on the development of outcome measures. Workshop sessions on outcome measurement, managed care, total quality improvement, and accreditation will be offered at CCUSA's spring sections meeting in April 1998 and at its annual conference in September.

A new task force will be formed in 1998 to offer information, assistance, and models to Catholic Charities agencies as they develop outcome measures for their programs and services.

Child Welfare League of America

The Child Welfare League of America (CWLA) believes in the necessity of assessing the effectiveness of its programs. For this reason, workshops on outcome measurement are held at its regional and national conferences, and resource materials focusing on the importance of measuring program outcomes are published, including *Outcome Measures for Child Welfare Services*.

CWLA also utilizes several measurement tools to monitor the effectiveness of the programs and services its members provide, including those designed for family assessment and child well-being. These tools help determine the type of services required and how they can be most beneficial to the people who receive them.

(continued)

EXHIBIT 8-10 (CONTINUED)

Corporation for National Service and the National Senior Service Corps

The Corporation for National Service and the National Senior Service Corps reports that all of its agencies are currently involved with outcome measurement. Outcome evaluation for a sample of program models takes place on an annual basis. This year, the Corporation for National Service anticipates that from 15 to 20 new studies will be undertaken to assess the effectiveness of its programs. The Corporation provides technical assistance and training on outcome measurement to local staff members as needs are identified.

The Corporation for National Service is currently working with a contractor to create an evaluation tool kit for agencies to use in developing their evaluation plans. The tool kit will present examples of specific outcome-measurement tools based on particular program models. Other outcome-measurement tools and instruments will be developed as needed by contract and corporation staff.

Member agencies may obtain information on a variety of topics, including outcome measurement from the National Clearing House. Best-practice monographs are distributed periodically to programs and will soon be posted on the Internet for agencies to review.

National Mental Health Association

Nearly all affiliates of the National Mental Health Association (NMHA) are involved in measuring program outcomes. NMHA's involvement was prompted first by requests from affiliates, then by contacts from UWA. The association recognizes the magnitude of the movement and its implications for the mental health field. It announced publication of UWA's outcome manual to affiliates in multiple issues of its national newsletter. It also purchased a quantity of the manuals to provide them to its affiliates for shipping and handling costs.

NMHA offered workshops on outcome measurement at its 1996 and 1997 annual conferences. Regional training held in Kansas City in November 1997 included an orientation to outcome measurement. A similar workshop will be delivered at the June 1998 annual conference.

NMHA has provided affiliates with prototype logic models for four core program areas: advocacy, community education, information and referral, and self-help/support groups. The prototypes, based on UWA's materials, are intended to give affiliates a starting place for developing logic models appropriate to their own programs. There also will be an appendix to a 25-page guidebook being developed, *It's About More Than Money: Building Partnerships With Your United Way*.

NMHA provides limited technical assistance to affiliates by phone. The emphasis is on referring callers to other affiliates that are undertaking outcome measurement successfully. The association has both a private list-serve for affiliates and a public Web site. Use of the list-serve to disseminate outcome information is being considered.

reflect a significant percentage of overall corporate cash gifts in some major national corporations.[20]

However, this program adds an administrative burden to the corporate contributions office in processing volumes of annual gifts to long lists of charities, many of which receive under $100 each. Company policy also might include an upper limit, but this could be as high as $10,000.[21] Matching gifts might also be restricted to charities that do not qualify under current corporate policy. Although each matching gift program is praise-worthy, the actual dollars received by any single nonprofit organization is limited to the number of employees with whom they have a relationship. All too often, a scattering of gifts from any single company is all that may occur. The exception appears to be local colleges and universities where lots of alumni go to work at a single corporation nearby. Lastly, while the potential exists to increase annual gift amounts is implied, employees often decide to give the same net amount, splitting the gift with the company.

On the receiving side, nonprofit organizations have some processing requirements after each employee's gift. Employees must get a copy of the company form, complete the details on their own gift, and send it to their chosen charity along with their contribution to trigger the matching gift response. The organization completes and returns the form, verifying the amount of the employee's gift and date received, and then sends a matching gift.

How shall the gift be recorded? Add the value of the company gift to the donor's gift history (they made the gift happen) or to the company's gift history (the source of the money), or both? Internal accounting for matching gifts requires a consistent handling procedure to prevent dual credit for the same gift dollar.

Companies believe nonprofit organizations have not made enough effort to promote matching gifts; organizations point to the few gifts and few dollars that each receives. Nonprofit organizations should encourage matching gifts by asking their annual donors if they work for a matching gift company, inviting them to use this added opportunity to increase their support. Reminders can be printed on just about everything that goes out to donors and volunteers, direct mail response forms, event invitations, memorial or tribute gift cards, telemarketing calls, newsletters, and more. If you make the effort, some gifts will come your way, and most will result from one or more of the routine solicitations in your annual parade of gift requests. Once you receive a matching gift, recognize that you now have *two* annual fund donors to cultivate for future gifts; check them both out. One last thought: When company profits decline, cutting the matching gifts program may be the last area to suffer. Why? Because it's the employee's money!

CAUSE-RELATED MARKETING: YES, IT'S MONEY, BUT IT IS NOT PHILANTHROPY

Cause-related marketing has become popular with several companies as an alternative to annual contributions. The world of business is highly competitive, and any advantage will be considered. A nonprofit organization may find it advantageous to partner with a corporation, not only for the money it may receive in return but also for the value of the high public exposure it receives, usually much more than it could ever afford. The amount of money an organization might receive is unknown at the start of the marketing campaign; in fact, only the company will know the financial results in detail, since the amount the charity receives is a percentage of total sales or a fixed amount agreed to in advance. When considering this option as a corporate fundraising strategy, ask the following five questions before making your decision:

1. Can a corporate giving relationship be established with this company, separate from the marketing program?
2. Are donors or dollars being recruited?
3. Is the organization exploiting its name, or is its name being exploited?
4. Will a full accounting summary of all dollars raised in the organization's name be received?
5. Is this method of fundraising regarded as a completely ethical program within the organization?[22]

Any corporation seeking a cause-related marketing strategy will look for a match that fits their goals and objectives, beginning with increased sales and new markets, followed by their evaluation of whether the reputation of the nonprofit organization is sound and is a logical fit with the corporation's product line to be marketed. In this way, a company seeks the same type of "match" that nonprofits look for when qualifying a corporation for potential gift support.

A company also will want to verify that this agreement has the support of the organization's board of directors, meets all applicable state regulations, and specifies how the funds will be used for charitable purposes. There is some evidence that consumers will switch brands "based on a good cause, provided price and quality were the same."[23] But, above all else, they will assess whether this plan has the ability to generate sufficient numbers of new customers and new sales along with improving its image and reputation in the community. In other words, will it be worth it? From their financial and marketing point of view, it might be. Whether it is also worth it for the nonprofit organization is worthy of a similar risk-reward analysis. In the end, if both parties agree on its mutual benefits, they should formalize their plans with a written agreement to clarify all the details. Two areas are important for organizations, in particular. First, how will their name be used, including advance approval of all promotional materials? Second, what portion of the sales revenue will be due the charitable organization and the method by which it will be calculated? Observing good judgment about a business decision may be somewhat new to nonprofit managers but it is not new to business executives who are their volunteer board members. Following a cautious approach to a corporate invitation to join in a cause-related marketing strategy is good advice (see also Exhibit 8-11 for one set of guidelines).

How does cause-related marketing fit your organization's annual giving program plans? The other methods you use (e.g., direct mail, membership programs, donor clubs, special events, and more) all involve direct exchanges between donors and your organization. Cause-related marketing does not directly result in gifts to your organization, nor does it provide a list of donors to thank and to integrate into your regular solicitation programs for repeat gifts. However, you do receive the cash proceeds, your organization does receive public relations value, and you do have the opportunity to build a broader relationship with your corporate partner, which is likely to be the more lasting benefit from this experience. Cause-related marketing is a pure business arrangement between two or more parties; it is not philanthropy. And, because it is such a clear business transaction, the IRS enters the picture as the nonprofit organization may be obliged to pay an unrelated business income tax (UBIT) on the proceeds it receives. To qualify to be taxed, the "business" must be "regularly carried on," produce revenue, and be conducted with a profit motive. Most such campaigns will qualify. Further, if this type of promotional campaign

EXHIBIT 8-11 GUIDELINES FOR CHOOSING AND EVALUATING A CAUSE-RELATED MARKETING PROGRAM

- **Good company citizenship is good business.** It has been proven time and again that those companies exhibiting conscience are consistently the most successful. The recent Cone/Roper Benchmark Survey found that 75 percent of all questions expressed the importance of buying from companies that make charitable contributions.

- **Check references.** Corporations and charities should check each other out with the same due diligence as hiring a new employee. Corporations need to analyze how a charity spends its money, and they should talk with other corporations who have worked with the charity to determine its credibility. Charities need to take the time to study a corporation to determine its reputation in the community.

- **Target audience.** A successful cause marketing campaign must match the cause to the desired target audience of a corporation. An alcohol company would typically not look toward a children's charity; obviously, a tobacco company would not either.

- **Lead time.** One of the most important elements of a successful cause-related program marketing effort is lead time. Packaged goods manufacturers were some of the first to use cause marketing, and have reaped the most benefits, in part because they have more time to work on a campaign than other corporations.

- **Timing.** The timing of the program itself is important. Companies often try cause-related marketing when sales are low. This type of approach almost always fails. The best programs should not be run in the best months or worst months for a company. Somewhere between is the best.

- **Involve employees.** The best cause marketing programs are team efforts that involve all levels of employees. When the CEO of a corporation stands shoulder-to-shoulder with employees in a program, it makes for a winner.

- **State your goals.** Do not merely announce a cause-related tie-in. Say what it is for. The promotional message should state the amount of money trying to be raised, and what it will be used for. This will help people identify with and develop empathy for the cause.

- **Dominate a cause.** Corporations will see the most benefit if they can be the pre-eminent benefactor. If you are splitting your efforts among several charitable organizations, you tend to lose exposure.

Source: Sylvia Allen, "Cause-related Marketing and Sponsorship," in *The Nonprofit Handbook: Fund Raising,* 3rd ed. ed. James M. Greenfield (New York: John Wiley & Sons, 2001), 650. Used with permission.

is not "substantially related" to the achievement of charitable purposes (and most are marketing and sales promotions linked to direct product sales), it meets another test for taxation, further reducing the net proceeds for charitable purposes.[24]

There are several states where a cause-related marketing program also will qualify as a *commercial co-venture* since a "charitable sales promotion" is involved. In these instances, the company sponsor might be required to register with the state authority (usually in the Attorney General's office), file a bond, submit a financial report of the outcome, and other details.[25] The nonprofit organization also has its legal obligations such as board approval for a signed contract, the compensation arrangement and how it will be computed, and other details. Due diligence is recommended by both parties to be certain to investigate these legal requirements before entering into a cause-related marketing partnership. As the saying goes, "Look a gift horse in the mouth and examine every tooth."

Securing Annual Foundation Gifts

After being challenged by the quest for corporate gifts, the good news about foundations is—they exist to give money away! They give away at least 5 percent of their asset value each year. But, just like corporations, the match of their priorities with your annual priorities will be your key to success. The same attention to homework is required. In-depth research must establish your qualification, formal policies, procedures and guidelines to follow, deadlines, review committees and professional staff, and (for them) more applications than they can hope to fund, qualified or not (nearly a 500 to 1 ratio and higher!).

Finally, foundations are not annual giving prospects; they are funding prospects for programs and services that have high priority for expansion or improvement, initiation or redirection, and with quality enhancements. If you do not have a specific project to match with a foundation's priority interests, including any activity with a one- to two-year open timetable from start to finish, you may not qualify. If that is the situation, you should not even apply to this foundation but to others where the match is more likely a perfect fit with their primary interests.

Foundations are great prospects but how can your organization meet their qualifications and compete successfully with others for its share of their required annual grant decisions?

There are a lot of foundations today, more than 50,000 in the United States alone. The majority are personal and family foundations, created by individuals who choose to make annual gifts to their own foundation for maximum income tax deductions and then make gifts to selected non-profits out of that foundation's annual 5 percent distribution requirement. The asset value varies with market performance throughout the year, like all foundations, and represents some 15 to 20 percent of all foundations grant funds. They reflect their founders' personal giving preferences, may or may not have professional staff, and act pretty much like individual donor prospects. They just happen to have a foundation with their name on it as an alternate means of making annual gifts. And, these are good prospects for annual gifts because they make personal giving decisions more often than formal decisions for approval by a foundation board.

A smaller group in numbers but largest in terms of assets are called *private* or *public foundations*. Their names are household words, such as Annenberg, Ford, Gates, Getty, Hewlett, Kellogg, Kresge, Lilly, Robert Wood Johnson, McArthur, Mellon, Mott, Packard, Rockefeller, Soros, Woodruff, and others. They are big (see Exhibit 8-12; the top 20 each have assets valued above $2.5 billion), have high-quality professional staff, make grants in every segment of the nonprofit sector, and even invite organizations to submit proposals for projects they choose. They are often looking for innovative, imaginative, and nontraditional purposes within their guidelines, along with collaborative programs with proven track records of measurable benefit. If you find that your biggest and best ideas match any of these interests of a major foundation, major gifts and grants will be your reward.

Corporate foundations are listed among the types of foundations that are prevalent as potential gift and grant sources. As discussed earlier, they are dominated by their corporate owners, mirror the corporation's priorities when making gift decisions, and prefer opportunities that benefit them in some significant way.

Community foundations are both grantmakers and fundraisers. They can give to the full spectrum of local community projects; they also ask for and receive direct gifts from community residents to be distributed to local community projects. Because of their flexibility, each is a highly valuable community asset. They also are seen increasingly as an attractive means for individuals to use just like a personal foundation with their own *donor-advised fund*. A donor may establish a fund with the community foundation who are responsible to invest and manage their asset. The donor directs annual gifts from the investment earnings to whatever causes they prefer each

EXHIBIT 8-12   TOP U.S. FOUNDATIONS BY ASSET SIZE

Rank	Name (state)	Assets	Fiscal Year End Date
1.	Lilly Endowment (IN)	$15,591,738,808	12/31/00
2.	Bill & Melinda Gates Foundation (WA)	15,515,454,543	12/31/99
3.	The Ford Foundation (NY)	14,659,683,000	09/30/00
4.	The David and Lucile Packard Foundation (CA)	13,144,241,646	12/31/99
5.	J. Paul Getty Trust (CA)	10,929,809,811	06/30/00
6.	The Robert Wood Johnson Foundation (NJ)	8,640,408,000	12/31/99
7.	The Pew Charitable Trusts (PA)	4,894,417,637	12/31/99
8.	W.K. Kellogg Foundation (MI)	4,853,383,875	08/31/00
9.	John D. and Catherine T. MacArthur Foundation (IL)	4,629,518,668	12/31/99
10.	The Andrew W. Mellon Foundation (NY)	4,615,683,000	12/31/99
11.	The Starr Foundation (NY)	4,486,499,157	12/31/99
12.	The Rockefeller Foundation (NY)	3,837,542,000	12/31/99
13.	The Annie E. Casey Foundation (MD)	3,626,229,530	12/31/99
14.	The California Endowment (CA)	3,490,256,407	02/28/00
15.	Charles Stewart Mott Foundation (MI)	3,229,256,496	12/31/99
16.	Robert W. Woodruff Foundation, Inc. (GA)	3,114,438,206	12/31/99
17.	Casey Family Programs (WA)	2,810,531,925	12/31/99
18.	The Annenberg Foundation (PA)	2,755,835,168	06/30/00
19.	The William and Flora Hewlett Foundation (CA)	2,738,945,087	12/31/99
20.	The Kresge Foundation (MI)	2,575,424,556	12/31/99

year. If there is a community foundation in your area, check them out for a variety of annual gift opportunities.

RESEARCH, RELATIONSHIPS, AND REQUESTS

You have to do your homework to find just those few foundations whose interests match those of your organization's mission and vision and whose current grants are nearly identical to your priority needs. Just as with corporations, it begins first with eligibility. The good news is that foundation information is public knowledge and readily available in several places. These include their own offices, in a variety of directories, in their IRS Form 990PF (annual return), and on the Internet. There is no excuse for a nonprofit organization to fail to first ensure that it can qualify to meet a foundation's grantmaking criteria and priorities *before* it submits a proposal. Not only will you get a quick rejection letter pointing out this lack of courtesy, but the foundation will open a file on your organization with a negative entry. Relations with foundations ought to be directed to their professional staff, not their board members. Both prefer that organizations work with their professional staff; that's the job they hired them to perform. Direct contact with board members is considered off limits, although some volunteers do not heed this advice. Concentrate your attentions on their professional staff who are quite helpful, will guide you through their process, help you with your application, and (if you handle them right) serve as your project's advocate to the board.

Foundation board meetings follow an agenda prepared by its staff, review proposal assessments prepared by the staff, and vote on grant awards in amounts recommended by the staff. If the operating guidelines invite qualified applicants to visit the foundation, you meet with the staff. If they include site visits to your organizations, their staff will make the visit. You can, of course, include your board members and your own staff in these visits, but you are not likely to meet with foundation board members in either case. The one exception is the many personal and family foundations where the founders, their children, and other family members are both staff and board.

Researching foundations is much easier than corporations because foundations make a considerable effort to circulate, promote, publish, add a Web site, and more, all to communicate their policies and procedures, guidelines, and preferences, in every way possible. They encourage direct contact so they can provide these details. Why? For two reasons. First, they seek applications that match their priorities and purposes; otherwise, they can't give their money away. Second, they receive far too many applications that cannot hope to qualify because of their published priorities and restrictions. Inattention to this first level of research by applicants is an entire waste of effort. Lists of foundations are not like direct mail lists, to be used in mail broadcast solicitations. You have to do your homework on each and every one; when you do, you will be rewarded with grants.

One way to conduct research is to use a filtering process. You begin at the top of this long filter with the names of perhaps 65 foundations that your first level of research suggests are possible candidates, but only suspects at this point. This level of the filter with its series of wide openings will only allow those to pass through whose area of support includes your project. The next level, with slightly smaller openings, is the geographic limitation; you will qualify here simply if your organization or project happens to be in the right location. The third level (already, 32 foundations have been eliminated) will block additional candidates because the purpose or use requested does not fit their guidelines (i.e., no grants to individuals, no capital or equipment grants, and no grants to endowment). The next level is grant size limitation (i.e., no grants are made above $2,500). If the project has survived to this level, it is not disqualified here, but these foundations are not the best candidates because their limited dollars are unable to fully fund the project; set them aside for a second round of applications after you have secured larger grants from others. The remainder (now 14 from your original list) must pass the final test, organizational preference. Have any of these 14 foundations made recent grants to organizations like yours? Each of the final 10 foundations who fall out the bottom of the filter is a valid candidate for high expectations for a good match.

Research sources abound, beginning with The Foundation Center, its comprehensive files in multiple offices around the nation, its frequently published group of directories, copies of annual IRS tax returns, its CD-ROM series with full directory data on larger foundations, and its Foundation Associates program that provides subscribers with access to all of the above (see Exhibit 8-13 for the list of top U.S. foundations by total giving). Information in great detail is available, such as asset values, lists of grants made to organizations, and the amounts and the projects they supported. To build a data file on your best candidates from the filtering process, capture the name of the contact person to write or call for current application procedures and priority funding policies. Dig into the other foundation sources available, if they can provide additional details. Study each foundation's material and follow its instructions to the letter. If you need to, don't hesitate to call the contact person with questions to clarify any detail you do not understand. Many foundations will require a preliminary letter that will allow their professional staff to review the project prior to submitting a proposal; if this review is positive and a proposal

EXHIBIT 8-13   LARGEST FOUNDATIONS BY TOTAL GIVING

Rank	Name (state)	Total Giving	Fiscal Year End Date
1.	The Ford Foundation (NY)	$652,091,000	09/30/00
2.	Lilly Endowment Inc. (IN)	583,890,521	12/31/00
3.	Bill & Melinda Gates Foundation (WA)	549,432,864	12/31/99
4.	The David and Lucile Packard Foundation (CA)	391,568,231	12/31/99
5.	The Robert Wood Johnson Foundation (NJ)	290,249,646	12/31/99
6.	The Pew Charitable Trusts (PA)	211,053,071	12/31/99
7.	Robert W. Woodruff Foundation, Inc. (GA)	191,355,356	12/31/99
8.	The California Endowment (CA)	189,663,220	02/28/01
9.	W.K. Kellogg Foundation (MI)	186,605,961	08/31/00
10.	The Andrew W. Mellon Foundation (NY)	161,501,133	12/31/99
11.	John D. and Catherine T. MacArthur Foundation (IL)	158,582,350	12/31/99
12.	Open Society Institute (NY)	152,974,312	12/31/99
13.	The Rockefeller Foundation (NY)	149,343,068	12/31/99
14.	The Starr Foundation (NY)	143,822,676	12/31/99
15.	The Annenberg Foundation (PA)	133,487,973	06/30/00
16.	The New York Community Trust (NY)	130,680,652	12/31/99
17.	Charles Stewart Mott Foundation (MI)	116,137,110	12/31/99
18.	California Community Foundation (CA)	113,449,501	06/30/00
19.	The Kresge Foundation (MI)	112,710,216	12/31/99
20.	Arthur D. DeMoss Foundation (FL)	104,283,341	12/31/99

is invited, both applicant and grantmaker are in agreement and can proceed further.

The next challenge for every applicant, because of competition with the multitude of applications received daily by foundations, will be in the craftsmanship of the proposal itself. When you begin its preparation, strict observance of application guidelines is essential. Your proposal, moreover, must present its case that this project is an indisputable use of the foundation's funds; the better the fit, the better the chances for a grant. More than a fit is required, however. Your proposal on its own must meet an even stricter test. To quote one experienced source, "In short, you will answer all of the subquestions posed in this mega-question: *who will do what, for whom, with what, at what cost, by when—and how will we know it is done and how effective it was?*[26] The contents of your proposal are quite straightforward, as shown in the following list. It provides all the answers to the mega-question that will win the day for your project.

1. Cover letter with succinct description of the project, its match to current priorities, how it has fulfilled all guidelines, and amount of funds requested

2. Introduction to the project and summary of its projected outcomes

3. Brief history and background of the organization to demonstrate qualification to perform the work as proposed

4. Statement of the problem and how the project will address it

5. Your management plan; personnel assigned and their qualifications, timetable, and estimated outcomes

6. Evaluation criteria and progress report schedule

7. Budget required, other funding sources and funding plans

8. Attachments (as defined by the foundation)

The project description must be clear, concise, and honest. The management plan must be sound and able to stand serious scrutiny. And your budget must reflect good accounting practices, as well as be sound and reasonable. The project budget is one of the more difficult elements to prepare. Most foundations are quite specific about what can and cannot be included. Overhead costs (heat, light, insurance, rent, etc.) are areas that foundations choose not to fund. They want to know, in detail, just how you are going to secure full funding for this project; their participation will be only partial support, at best. Although these restrictions might seem harsh, even unfair to applying organizations, reality is that foundations have limited funds and want their money spent only on the project's direct costs.

This means that every proposal must either describe how the organization will use its own resources to provide the necessary support required or describe how it intends to raise the rest of the money from other sources. These plans cannot be pipe dreams either; they must be realistic and have a deadline for receipt of support funding. Do not even think about being creative with the budget; foundations can read between the lines of your budget better than your chief financial officer and your independent auditor together. They have seen hundreds of applications, many with highly creative accounting attempts, all of which resulted in a single response—rejection, based on disqualification.

How does the foundation evaluate your application? Every foundation has its own guidelines, but most will consider the following factors:

1. Does the project match our interests?

2. Does the project fit into our budget?

3. Does the project duplicate programs or services already being provided by another agency?

4. Does the project promise results that could be important enough to warrant an investment by the foundation?

5. Does the project appear feasible on the basis of the quality of the organization's leadership and other resources?

6. Does the project have sufficient appeal (in the view of the foundation executive doing the initial appraisal) to win the approval of my staff, colleagues, and the governing board?[27]

You complete the proposal exactly as required, deliver the 10 copies in a nice folder yourself, and then you wait. One day, weeks later, you receive a letter from one of these foundations. It doesn't look like all the rejections you received before because the envelope is thicker. You open it to find a letter that announces a grant will be made to your organization, based on your proposal. The amount of the grant is less than requested, but rather than follow a suggested payment schedule to be spread over the next two calendar years, the foundation has given you a lump-sum donation (see Exhibit 8-14 for a sample announcement letter). The bulky enclosure is a legalistic formal agreement that your executive director must sign and return in 10 working days, accepting the grant with all of its terms, conditions, and reporting requirements. The cover letter and agreement spells out the details of what must be included in each progress report, the quarterly filing dates for these reports, and a financial report form for all expenses. You are asked to draft a news release announcing the award, to be approved by the foundation prior to release, with the release date to be set by the foundation. This is all good news, but it is going to require a lot more work to fulfill the administrative instructions contained in the agreement letter.

EXHIBIT 8-14   SAMPLE GRANT AWARD LETTER[28]

May 12, 200X

Mr. I. Harvey Clout
Chair of the Board,
Clean Up Cleveland Chapter
The Campaign to Clean Up America
c/o Cleveland Cast Iron Works
4555 Rust Avenue
Cleveland, OH 44120

Dear Mr. Clout:

The Sample Foundation is pleased to enclose our check for $2,000 in full payment of a grant for your campaign to improve the City of Cleveland and convert trash into new energy for its residents, as described in your formal proposal dated March 16, 200X.

As a private foundation, we must document that our grant is expended for a charitable or educational purpose. We must ask that you use our funds exclusively to carry out the project described in your proposal. You must not use any of our funds to influence legislation, to influence the outcome of any election, or to carry on any voter registration drive.

We are required by the Internal Revenue Service to ask for proof that your organization continues to be exempt under section 501(c)(3) of the Internal Revenue Code and is still classified as a public charity pursuant to section 509(a)(1), (2), or (3) of the Code. Please send us a copy of your most recent IRS tax determination letter along with a copy of your annual budget, your most recently completed audited financial statement, and your most recently submitted IRS Form 990.

Attached are two copies of our Formal Agreement with information regarding our requirement for interim progress and financial report deadlines and other details of your administration of this grant. Finally, we require that any funds not expended for the purposes for which this grant is made be returned to us. Please indicate your agreement with these conditions by returning signed and dated copies of this letter and our Formal Agreement as soon as possible; we will return one copy to you with our signature for your files.

With all best wishes for every success with your project.

Sincerely yours,

Anastasia B.S. Verbatim   _____
Executive Assistant to the President   Acknowledged by I. Harvey Clout

Encl: Formal Agreement (2)   _____
                                            Date Signed

Grant administration is a necessary part of every grant proposal you submit. Many do not require all the details in Exhibit 8-14 and will be satisfied with an appropriate thank-you letter confirming that your use of their funds will be just as your proposal outlined. They might require a summary report on the project when completed, along with prior notice of any public announcements of their involvement (use of their name in donor lists or public recognition plans). Whatever is required, it is recommended that formal accounting and reporting procedures be established and followed for all grants, to include the following:

1. Formally acknowledge the grant with a letter from the executive director, with any additional thank-you letters from volunteers and professional staff who were listed in the proposal as directing the project.

2. Establish a separate fund account to which all expenses will be allocated.

3. Resolve internal approvals for expenditures to the account including assigned personnel with signature authority.

4. Establish a project report deadline, including financial status at least every six months unless more frequent reporting is required.

5. Resolve approval procedures for all public announcements of the grant, including press releases, internal newsletters, annual reports, and more.

6. Resolve what level of public recognition is acceptable, including adding the foundation's name to donor walls, lists of project donors at public events or in print materials, and more.

7. Resolve the interest and extent that foundation staff will entertain receiving routine publications, event invitations, and other documents.

8. Resolve the interest and extent of staff's continued involvement with the project, site visits, internal reports, dedications, news releases, newsletters, and more.

9. Establish a summary review date near the end of the project to assess the potential for applying for additional grant support, and when.

10. Monitor all the above actions to ensure that each is completed successfully.

DONOR RECOGNITION FOR CORPORATIONS AND FOUNDATIONS

Both corporations and foundations appreciate a considerate response from those they choose for their annual gift support. Depending on the nature and size of the gift, the intent of the project and their other relationships with your organization, a measured amount of attention is quite appropriate. Just how much, in what form, at what time, and how visible to make it will vary. You should consider what is appropriate out of respect for each grant and the overall level of support the company or foundation already has achieved with the organization. The best advice is to keep the level of recognition and its benefits and privileges consistent with other donors at this same level or range. Each grant is eligible to receive what others at that level also receive in the form of benefits and privileges; the same donor-recognition guidelines that apply to a single-gift donor should apply to donors who make cumulative gifts. For guidelines, see Exhibit 4-4, Donor Recognition Programs for Annual Donors. Foundation staff will appreciate the invitation to respond to their grantees on what levels of recognition they can or cannot accept; these are to be observed faithfully.

There can be exceptions, enhancements, and modifications in the recognition arena. The advantage of a consistent donor-recognition policy is the practice that the basics are applied to everyone. If added features are reasonable and appropriate and consistent with the donor's relationship with the organization, some additional courtesies do not upset the fair and equitable treatment other donors receive.

As an example, a corporation or foundation commits to a two-year pledge of $20,000 to underwrite 25 percent or more of the operating budget of your new project, with the funds to be used to introduce a new service to the community. This is a Benefactor-level gift, and all the other recognition benefits will also be fulfilled. Given the significance of the grant, however, it is appropriate to invite representatives of the company or foundation to be special guests at the organization's annual meeting, to make an announcement of their grant during the program, even to introduce those from the foundation or corporation who are present. Further, if a corporation, it is not unfair to others that one or two corporate officers or a foundation board member or two might be evaluated for future board-level consideration (foundation staff will always decline any such duty). Not only are these actions a courteous and proper way to convey a sincere appreciation in front of the best audience possible, they also signal to everyone present how your organization respects important donors who make a significant gift or grant (plus, it might help attract other major gifts). Such actions also show others how they might be treated if they make a similar gift or grant.

FOCUS: CCUA Clean Up Cleveland Chapter

It is now April. Karen Anderson and Alice Nice, her assistant, have managed another series of follow-up acquisition mailings to the original four lists used in the first roll out, a two-part renewal mailing to all current donors including the Circle of Champions membership offer at $100 or more. They also have tested a telemarketing strategy to improve donor retention, invite donors to join the Circle of Champions, and ask all for an upgrade gift above their last contribution. Now, in response to board urging, they have identified nearly 70 local corporations and foundations as likely candidates for giving to the Clean Up Cleveland Campaign. Of this group, board members knew several of the officers and directors but told Anderson they had been warned before not to approach these people.

Anderson did call 35 of these prospects and has received written guidelines from each. Just last week, she completed the last of her two-page letter proposals to the 17 prospects in this group that she believed would accept direct applications if the request was for $2,500 or less. No replies yet, but she is hopeful that the majority of her requests, adding to just over $45,000, will receive favorable consideration. Her letter did request gift decisions this year with payment before December 31, the end of her current fiscal year. Anderson also has selected 12 other prospects, all foundations, whose application procedures require a much more detailed proposal but who were likely candidates for larger grants payable over two years. She has confirmed appointments to meet with program officers at seven of these foundations in May and early June. All have proposal deadlines in July, with decisions to be announced in September and October. These seven appointments will be critical both to the revenue needed in this year and next and also to leverage these gift decisions with other prospects. Anderson appreciated the fact that her cause will be a challenge because it is outside the mainstream of traditional giving areas for each of these foundations. These first meetings will be most revealing to her entire strategy for corporate and foundation support.

It was noon on Friday, and Anderson and Nice were preparing gift reports on the spring mail campaigns along with an activity report on

EXHIBIT 8-15   ACTIVITY REPORT ON CORPORATION AND FOUNDATION SOLICITATIONS

Research Activities	Number	Gift Ranges
Prospects identified	68	$0 to $25,000
Application forms requested	52	(16 did not respond)
Research in progress	35	$0 to $25,000
Research completed as qualified prospects	17	$0 to $25,000
Cultivation plan written	17	(all are written)

Phone Calls or Meetings Scheduled	Number	Phone Calls
Corporations	19	12
Foundations	16	5

	Number	Meetings Scheduled
Corporations	3	2
Foundations	14	5

Proposal Activity (delivered or mailed)	Number	Request Values
Corporations	12	$2,500 to each
Foundations	5	Up to $25,000

Gifts and Grants Received	Number	Gift
Corporations	3	$ 7,500
Foundations	3	$15,000

their first foray into the corporate and foundation grantseeking arena (Exhibit 8-15), when the phone rang. It was Titus Brown, who had just had lunch with Sidney Secure. They both wanted to know if Anderson had checked out creating a Web site for the chapter. She said they had not, but added that she had seen a report that the national office of the Campaign to Clean Up America was preparing one that all the affiliate chapters could use. "Good," said Titus. "We need to be online soon. Keep your eye on them and let me know when they go live. I want to see how we can use it here in our annual campaign." After he hung up, Anderson thought to herself: "Here we go again; another new adventure before we have both feet on the ground."

Internet Solicitation

We have had a national tragedy. Two airplanes have crashed into the World Trade Center in an apparent terrorist attack on our country.

George W. Bush, 9:30 a.m., September 11, 2001

No more shocking news has ever been broadcast in America. Only President Roosevelt's announcement that "December 7, 1941, will live forever as a day of Infamy," following the Japanese attack on Pearl Harbor, Hawaii, was as stunning. Our world, as we knew it then, had been changed.

For philanthropy, the terrorist attack resulted in the largest outpouring of relief and recovery contributions ever seen in our nation. Within five weeks, more than $1.04 billion had been raised. The Red Cross received $452 million, of which $64 million was received online.[1] Several other charities, including those newly formed to support families and other victims of the World Trade Center and Pentagon disasters, received substantial numbers of gifts via the Internet. It is fair to state now that fundraising on the Internet has been accepted by donors; now nonprofit organizations must apply this option to their own solicitation programs.

This chapter was reviewed after September 11, 2001, by Ted Hart and Mal Warwick, authors along with Nick Allen, of *Fundraising on the Internet: The ePhilanthropyFoundation.Org's Guide to Success Online*. Their generous contributions to its accuracy are gratefully acknowledged.

Even as this chapter is being written, changes are being made as to how the Internet works; new uses are being made available among its many options. A new provider goes into business, adds software features, or invents new options that refine and improve utilization. At the same time, despite adequate venture capital funding, another provider's advertisers pull out or a key link fails, and that venture flops. The dot-com you pick today as your service provider could be tomorrow's dot-gone.

The Internet is still new. It is growing rapidly—too rapidly, as it has gotten ahead of itself and its users. Such is the way of any new technology. Nonprofit organizations, conservative by nature, have moved slowly into active use of online fundraising. Something so new in technology is first an experiment, then an adventure. The learning curve and up-front costs are steep. Early reports about a slow public response, along with a few flops, raised a caution flag. And, while the business world is years ahead in its use and continued experimentation, society has been pulled into this adventure on a global scale, but they have had problems and more than a few flops, too.

The question to ask about the Internet today is not, "Does it work?" It does. The question is, "How do I use it well?" People who have begun to use its multiple features in their daily lives often consider Internet access a necessity—right up there with phone service. The Internet is, above all else, a superb means of communication. As a research tool, it is an inexhaustible resource. As a new fundraising method, it has been a disappointment, but that's not the fault of the Internet. "Online fund raising over the last few years has been passive. Nonprofit organizations have been content to build giving forms, hope donors find their way to the form, and then count the unsolicited gifts that trickle in."[2] Yes, the potential to raise money exists, but that has not been a sufficiently good reason for nonprofit organizations to make the investment required. The commitment required of any organization, large or small, to purchase and maintain a computer system is much smaller today and no longer a hindrance. Access to the Internet also appears to be no longer a hindrance. One estimate is that in 2001, 100 million Americans have access to the Internet, out of 265 million people.

Fundraising professionals, especially those responsible for annual giving activities, can and should prepare to use the Internet in concert with their direct mail, membership, donor club, telephone, corporate and foundation, benefit events, and volunteer-led solicitation programs. They also should give preference to the Internet for use in communications, whether for thank-you letters, event invitations, or online newsletters, reports, or news releases. Just how, when, and in what way is an experiment in progress. "Fundraising on the Internet is a pioneer adventure. There are few experienced guides, the trails are rough and unmarked, and the technology can be as creaky as a wooden wagon wheel."[3] That was Nick Allen, Mal Warwick, and David Stein's view in 1996. Their view today is: "By 2001, there were dozens of experienced guides. The trails are better marked, thanks to the experiences of thousands of organizations that have toiled to acquire and cultivate donors online."[4] Fundraising professionals need to learn a lot about Internet technology to know how to integrate it into their active and/or passive annual giving practice. For guidance, the rules still apply as in all of fundraising: friend-raising and relationship-building are required first. The good news is that both can be enhanced, thanks to the personal communications features possible on the Internet.

Prior to September 11, 2001, the giving public had only just been introduced to active solicitation on the Internet. Organizations and their donors now are likely to want to rethink just how, when, and where it fits with their annual giving, which is the focus of this chapter. But first, we must prepare our victory garden for a brand new vegetable, to be known by the label of *ePhilanthropy*. How much direct sunlight can it take? What are its fertilizer, watering, and other labor needs? When should it be planted, when will it ripen, what is its estimated yield?

Some suggest that ePhilanthropy will "reshape philanthropy," even suggesting that one of every four dollars raised will come via the Internet by 2010.[5] Using the *Giving USA* data for 2001, with total giving at $203 billion in 2000,[6] that's an estimated $50 billion to $68 billion to be given via the Internet each year. However, following the September 11, 2001, tragedy, the American Red Cross *alone* achieved this level of online support. Nonprofit organizations now have to catch up to this "jump-started" use of the Internet.

Internet fundraising, using its new identity of *ePhilanthropy* coined by the ePhilanthropy Foundation, has been defined as follows:

> **ePhilanthropy** is the building and enhancing of relationships with supporters of nonprofit organizations using an Internet-based platform.
>
> **ePhilanthropy** is the online contribution of cash or real property or the purchase of products or services to benefit a nonprofit organization.
>
> **ePhilanthropy** is the storage of and usage of electronic data or use of electronic methods to support fund raising activities.[7]

Look to the Internet as the total package, a medium of exchange for interest and information, a channel for communications of all kinds with e-mail correspondence being its chief asset, designed to lead to increased involvement and participation. "The greatest value of this important new communications channel lies in its ability to provide donors with increased access to information and more consistent, timely details regarding the stewardship of their charitable support."[8] Being online provides a two-way communications channel open 24 hours a day, 365 days a year for anyone to visit your Web site for information, to send and receive messages, to make appointments, to make contributions, and more. A list of some of the active Internet uses that nonprofit organizations can consider for their own purposes and that of their constituents follows:

- Advocacy of their cause
- Branding their identity for public trust
- Collaborating to meet community needs
- Communicating their mission, vision, and values
- Distance learning to share knowledge
- Electronic commerce to facilitate support
- Fundraising to invite support
- Information access for open and full disclosure
- Marketing to those in need
- Promoting their programs and services
- Research to understand
- Stewardship of past gift support

- Surveys to learn
- Testing to become effective and efficient

Internet applications to annual giving practice can be quite extensive. Acquiring new donors and renewing and upgrading current donors can be performed easily. Consider a multimedia message as used in direct mail and telephone with letters followed by phone calls. An e-mail message in advance of a letter or phone call—or following it—adds a form of personal conversation, definitely a "high-touch" extra contact. Membership organizations and donor club involvement can be enhanced by a donor's access to full information on the organization's Web page using members-only passwords. Research access to corporation and foundation information helps to find the necessary "match" with priority programs that both seek to fund; it also allows corporations and foundations to search each applicant's Web page to aid in their proposal evaluations. Invitations and reservations for activities, benefits, and special events are only the click of a mouse away. Volunteer recruitment, training, supervision, motivation, coordination, and recognition are all available online. Enhanced donor relations with instant thank-you messages can engage donors in recognition activities, including access to donor benefits and privileges. The multiple uses of this remarkable technology and all its applications require nonprofit organizations to apply professional practices from the moment they enter this field. To maximize its effectiveness for developing an online Internet presence that includes active fundraising, follow "The Ten Rules of ePhilanthropy Every Nonprofit Must Know" guidelines provided in Exhibit 9-1.

An organization should understand that its own Web site is the most important first step when adding this technology to its fundraising capacity.

> A charity's Web site has to provide the opportunity for relationship-building. It must provide communication. It must be entertainingly interactive, and it must provide an opportunity to give. The site must provide many avenues for that gift and for information that could eventually lead to major gifts and planned giving. That's right—planned giving. That new demographic includes people who were computer-phobic, were forced to learn how to use a computer at work, and now can't live without one. Here is the translation—they are in their 50s and have money and are starting to think about estate planning.[9]

EXHIBIT 9-1 TEN RULES OF ePHILANTHROPY EVERY NONPROFIT SHOULD KNOW

- Rule 1: Don't become invisible

  If you build it, they won't just come. Building an online brand is just as important and just as difficult as building an off-line brand.

- Rule 2: It takes "know how" and vision

  Your organization's Web site is a marketing and fundraising tool, *not a technology tool*. Fundraisers and marketers need to be driving the content, not the Web developer.

- Rule 3: It's all about the donor

  Put the Donor First! Know your contributors; let them get to know you.

- Rule 4: Keep savvy donors; stay fresh and current

  Make online giving enjoyable and easy. Give the donor options. Use the latest technology. Show your donor how their funds are being used.

- Rule 5: Integrate into everything you do

  Your Web site alone will do nothing. Every activity you have should drive traffic to your site.

- Rule 6: Don't trade your mission for a shopping mall

  Many nonprofit Web sites fail to emphasize mission, instead turning themselves into online shopping malls, without even knowing why.

- Rule 7: Ethics, privacy, and security are not buzzwords

  Many donors are just now deciding to make their first online contribution. They will expect your organization to maintain the highest standards of ethics, privacy, and security.

- Rule 8: It takes the Internet to build a community

  Many nonprofits (particularly smaller ones) lack the resources to communicate effectively. The Internet offers the opportunity to cost-effectively build a community of supporters.

- Rule 9: Success online means being targeted

  The Web site alone is not enough. You must target your audience and drive their attention to the wealth of information and services offered by your Web site. Permission must be sought before you begin direct communication via the Internet.

- Rule 10: ePhilanthropy is more than just e-money

  ePhilanthropy is a tool to be used in your fundraising strategy. *It should not* be viewed as quick money. There are no shortcuts to building effective relationships. But the Internet will enhance your efforts.

Note: Copyright © 2001 by the ePhilanthropyFoundation.Org. Reprinted with permission.

A Web site has enormous potential for a myriad of services that can be ordered from its menu, images so visitors can "see" the organization and its people, video tours of facilities and programs in action at the organization, even links to other Web sites with related information and/or services. A fair amount of attention and care must be given to basic site design (or its next redesign) to address the many uses likely to be used by visitors. There also must be easy access and directions for donors, volunteers, and others on how they can give, how to expand their relationships, and how to search for the details they seek. Among design considerations, think about this starter list of how a visitor might use your site to do the following:

- Tell you their views (via surveys or e-mail forms)
- Get updates on your work, your successes, upcoming media interviews, and events
- Order books, videos, T-shirts, or anything else, and pay with a credit card (and member discount!)
- Change addresses and perform other housekeeping tasks, or request a call from one of your staff
- Renew their membership or make special contributions
- Correspond with other members who share their interests and are members of the same chapter.[10]

Consistent monitoring of the site provides ample clues to what visitors are seeking. Designate one or two staff members to serve as "Content Manager" with responsibility for day-to-day management of the site. Their role will be to measure the number of hits received, the ease with which visitors navigate the site, and areas they frequent, so as to respond quickly with information, guidance to other services, and more. Performance evaluations include counting requests for information, appointments made, and e-mail exchanges—all measurable indicators of an active site and successful site management. Response times by the organization also are important to track; a Web site is a two-way communications link as well as a significant area for interactive public service. A separate analysis of contributions and pledge details, either as a direct response to the site or from multimedia annual fund solicitation tactics, should be compared with other fundraising results for future solicitation purposes. All in all, the upfront investment in Web site development and management will pay off with maximum results only if the site is handled as professionally as every other program and service within the organization.

> Years of experience in the offline world have taught fundraisers that attention to detail, privacy, security of information, honesty in reporting, and building a case for support will yield success in fundraising—because they help to build trust. While the use of the Internet for philanthropic purposes is in its infancy, building trust in that new medium is equally vital. It's essential, then, that professional fundraisers pursue clear, ethical principles for the use of the Internet. To fulfill the promise of the ephilanthropy revolution, the Internet must be viewed as a way to enhance the philanthropic experience. The greatest value of this important new communications channel lies in its ability to provide donors with increased access to information and more consistent, timely details regarding the stewardship of their charitable support.[11]

ARTFUL USES OF THE INTERNET FOR ANNUAL GIVING

Testing Internet use with current annual giving programs is a great place to begin. Start with two or three tests with current constituents (always test donors before testing nondonors), just as in direct mail (see Chapter 2), to get support systems ready to evaluate responses clearly. Collect e-mail addresses from as many current annual giving donors as possible; contact at least 2,500 to 5,000 names with three different tests at the time of their next normal renewal cycle, each with the upgrade option.

The three tests are (a) direct mail letter with e-mail follow-up, (b) telephone call with e-mail follow-up, and (c) straight e-mail request alone. The results of each test will guide the next steps to take, beginning with what percentage of current donors are online and have an e-mail address. Compare prior renewal statistics from the last two to three years to test results for percent that renew, average gift size, percent that upgrade, and upgrade increases. If any test method outperforms prior performance, test that combination again with a larger group before using it with the entire list. If these three tests perform worse or no better than prior years' experience, keep the e-mail option visible as a regular feature. Continue to monitor usage over the next two years. If online giving is going to improve, you will want to be fully ready while you educate your donors to the advantages of its use. Provide guidance and encouragement in every other communication sent to donors to promote e-mail as the preferred contact medium.

One special note of importance, whether using online solicitation in an active or a passive mode: Design the response form to meet every giving situation possible. Each reply is only a click of a mouse away. Arrange a format that donors will recognize and can complete easily (look to your current response forms for a good example). Use drop-down windows to guide donors in options they can select to make their gift (use of credit card, whether restricted or unrestricted, the commemorative gift option, etc.), the same choices as are available on the response forms used in mail, event, and telephone appeals. Also, be sure to ask for their e-mail address each and every time; some people change addresses frequently.

Finally, prepare the organization's response to every e-mail gift and be ready to go the day the first e-mail gift arrives. That includes being ready to meet all the following gift acknowledgment objectives:

- Use the name of the donor in the reply.
- Mention the gift amount.
- Use complete sentences. Do not make it seem like a computerized receipt. Make it as personable as possible.
- Include the contact information for the nonprofit organization.
- Thank the donor.
- Ask the donor to print out the thank you and receipt as a temporary receipt.[12]

The following sections describe how Internet solicitation may be applied to each annual giving method covered in this book.

Direct Mail and Telephone

The Internet has tremendous outreach, allowing organizations to define their audiences for acquisition strategies by geographic, demographic, and/or ZIP code sorting and selection. However, just as with lists selected for direct-mail and telephone solicitation, e-mail address lists allow you to communicate just about anywhere you wish. You also can get the same result as with direct mail and the telephone—instant resentment! People get upset with unwanted mail and unsolicited telephone calls during the day and on weekends; let them "opt in" to provide you with their e-mail addresses as a signal that they welcome online communications.

How will you use the Internet for acquisition of new donors? The testing rule is the same: Begin by testing at least 2,500 to 5,000 e-mail addresses and follow the testing examples discussed in Chapter 2. Decide ahead of time how to target potential prospects and donors, just as in direct mail and telephone solicitation, including three multimedia options: letter and e-mail, telephone call and e-mail, or e-mail alone. Avoid broadcast solicitations (contact with large list-serves and message boards). This practice is called *spamming* (as is the use of rental e-mail lists!) and is not welcomed by recipients. It will receive the identical response as unwanted direct-mail letters and phone calls, this time using the "delete" button. There are good guidelines for Internet use (see Rule 9 in Exhibit 9-1).

State solicitation regulations apply to the Internet as well, just as with other forms of public solicitation using mail and telephone. In states where a nonprofit organization chooses to solicit broadly, the organization must be registered in advance in each state where it intends to solicit on the Internet; they also must file annual reports in these same states with overall financial details and program activities. Guidelines on Internet solicitation have been prepared by the National Association of State Charity Officials (NASCO), the state regulatory officials, most of whom are assistant attorneys general. Called the "Charleston Principles," these guidelines outline best practices for Internet solicitation. To review their helpful text, go to *www.nonprofits.org/library/gov/urs*. See also the section on Cyberspace Law later in this chapter for more details on public solicitation regulations.

Memberships and Donor Club Programs

Use of the Internet in solicitation for membership associations and donor clubs begins with prior donors from direct-mail and telephone activities, provided you have requested and received their e-mail addresses. This renewal invitation is to current donors who know something about the organization as they are currently supporting it. This opportunity also allows for verification of as many current e-mail addresses as possible. With e-mail invitations to these donors, asking them to become more involved in a membership and/or donor organization can and should be personalized, just as would a direct-mail letter or telephone call. The message is similar:

They are being invited to join with others, to upgrade their current gift and receive added benefits and privileges, to become a volunteer, or to attend public and members-only events and more—all possible messages over the Internet conducted in a personal manner and at a fraction of the cost of mail and telephone invitations. Prepare a reply form for their use, one that resembles the current mail and telephone text they have used previously, to be easily completed whenever the donor chooses, including credit card data. It should be instantly returnable with the "send" button. Once donors have used the e-mail option, encourage them (by e-mail again) to invite others from their personal e-mail address list to join, extending the organization's reach well beyond its own capacity. Qualified members now will receive members-only information (again via e-mail), including past and future newsletters, a membership directory, coming events schedule and invitations, and more. The directory should encourage members to correspond with one another (by e-mail, of course) or, if a members-only list serve is provided, to enter live discussion groups and "chat rooms." Staff must monitor appropriate use of discussions to benefit the organization; the privilege is provided to support its mission and is not a private medium for unlimited or inappropriate personal use.

A "best use" technique is to link members to the organization's home page, where full access to available programs and services is conveniently available. Other member benefits now can be defined within this link, based on the scope of technology available. For example, using their members-only password, donors can access programs and services on the organization's Web site, make appointments, request specific information, and more. From the organization's point of view, members can be receiving news releases regularly, before they read or hear about news in the papers, or on radio or television. They also can be offered routine publications, such as newsletters and annual reports, saving organizational printing and postage expenses. Members whose computers have the capacity, when linked to the organization's home page, can download directly any variety of the "new media" data storage and transmission devices that may be offered, such as "DVDs, interactive television, video tours, touch-screen kiosks, and CD-ROMs."[13] They can be sent direct reports in their choice of format from the nonprofit's management and professional staff as personalized communications that report on how their funds are making a difference in the lives of others. They also can be sent copies of grateful client or patient letters and other details, all designed to maintain a positive relationship, increase the members' own involvement and ensure their continued interest and support. The nonprofit organization that makes this effort has opened an active link with its most valuable asset of today and for its future—its donors.

Pledging Online

Online pledge forms for membership and donor club renewals are just as useful and valid as when used in direct-mail and telephone solicitation. Again, you need to request and maintain current e-mail addresses to use this technique effectively. Donors have the option to add their credit card details on the reply form, which already is established as the most popular form for use (just ask Amazon.com). Or, they can authorize an electronic funds transfer (EFT) with their bank for automated payment, or download the pledge form from the organization's Web site, then attach their check and return both the pledge form and their gift by regular mail. Although there is limited experience to date with online pledging, early experience suggests fulfillment rates will approximate that of telephone pledge fulfillment rates, which may be 70 percent or higher, depending on whether it is a pledge resulting from an acquisition or renewal solicitation. Improved results will follow by combining telephone and e-mail to follow up collection notices using regular mail, but these efforts require staff and volunteer time, plus daily coordination with the donor-records staff as pledge payments are received.

Activities, Benefits, and Special Events

The activities, benefits, and special events organized and produced by nonprofit organizations (see Chapter 10) are designed to recruit participants, whether or not an admission price is charged. The great variety of lectures, open houses, tours, public ceremonies, dedications, benefit fundraising events, and so on each require printed invitations and notices to be prepared and sent out by mail. The combined cost of printing, envelopes, paper, and postage, along with other forms of event promotion, is significant. A "save the date" notice, plus the formal invitation package, is normal practice; so is the ratio of four to five invitations required for each attending participant. Some activities and special events, such as annual meetings, inaugurations, graduations, and the like are open to the public, but guests still have to be invited and the event promoted widely to gain the audience needed for the program. Consider the cost savings if it is possible to add e-mail communications. First, the e-mail addresses of board members, management, support staff, volunteers, and donors, who are already on nearly every invitation list, can be used for most if not all the organization's activities, benefits, and special events. However, until these members become comfortable with receiving and replying to e-mail notices and invitations, both mail and telephone might still be required to secure the desired audience. When they have demonstrated consistency in responding to e-mail notice alone, then the cost savings will mount up quickly; many organizations host a minimum of one or two invitational activities a month throughout the year.

Commemorative and Tribute Giving

One of the donor conveniences on your Web page will be to provide instructions about how to make an "In Memory" or "In Honor of" gift. Currently this form of giving is reported by way of direct mail, telephone, newsletters, annual reports, and other routine communications. Current donors and others who have not given before do not see these routine vehicles, but will make commemorative or tribute gifts on such special occasions as "a birth, an anniversary, a promotion, at graduation, or at death. Tribute is paid to someone by making a gift to a charity in his or her honor or name. The majority of commemorative gifts are made in memory of an individual after his or her death, as an expression of sympathy to the family and of honor to the deceased."[14] Basic instructions are needed for this type of gift, which also allows family or friends to specify the use of the funds by the organization. The donor also is asked to identify the person being honored, along with name and mailing address of the person or family to be notified that a gift has been made (but not the amount). The Web site response form also asks the donor to provide mailing information, including e-mail address, for gift acknowledgment purposes. All these donors can be thanked by e-mail and their gifts added to their cumulative giving history, but it is good practice also to send them a printed receipt or formal acknowledgment letter, especially if any gift is $250 or more, in accordance with IRS gift substantiation regulations.

It is important to note, however, that if the donor is new to the organization as a first-time donor, he or she might not be a candidate for other solicitation programs because the motive for this first gift was unrelated to the charity itself; only to the person honored. However, it is valid to invite continued support. To renew a one-time commemorative donor will take extra communications after the thank-you notice that follows the first gift. Both the Internet and regular mail can be used to stimulate added gifts. It is important to include these occasional donors in annual, end-of-year renewal solicitations for perhaps a year or two, after which they can be dropped from the list if they do not respond.

Volunteers

Volunteer recruitment and committee work now use letters of appointment, meeting notices, and telephone calls for their communications. How can this work be improved using the Internet? Routine notices can be followed by e-mail messages to confirm scheduled work times and assignments, training meetings, new information about the organization, its programs and services, activity reports in areas where the volunteer is assigned, and more. Volunteers also can be encouraged to correspond with each other, to ask for any information they need, to resolve scheduling difficulties, to track their hours and assignments, and more, all by e-mail. Because volunteers are so necessary and so valuable to nonprofit organizations in fulfilling their mission, there is good reason to provide them with extra care and attention. Volunteer activity is a local action program. Nonprofit organizations can concentrate their recruitment and retention activities nearby, investing their efforts in asking for e-mail address lists from churches, service and social clubs, Chamber of Commerce membership rosters, and more. Two online recruitment services, *www.servenet.org* and *www.volunteermatch.com*, might be of assistance. It is recommended to use new e-mail address lists as backup to routine mail and telephone contact at the outset. Further, each organization's regular online and Web site communication programs available to donors also can be made available for sharing with volunteers. There is nothing quite like a merry band of well-informed advocates telling stories all over town about their active roles and responsibilities in working at their favorite charities.

Committees and Meetings

Operating committees composed of staff and volunteers at all levels of annual giving program support can correspond via e-mail between meetings to carry out their work, set up and conduct task force assignments, research topics, schedule future meetings and agenda, distribute minutes and reports, and otherwise conduct a wide range of support operations, all over the Internet, perhaps on the organization's list serve. Benefit event committees, with their hundreds of details and dozens of volunteers required to manage these complex activities, also can use e-mail to keep everyone well informed of progress, along with reminders of their assignments, reports on ticket sales and attendance, remaining options for sponsorship and in-kind gifts, arranging table seating, and more, all saving volunteer and staff time for other work instead of scheduling endless meetings for these same purposes. The organization's Web site also should promote each event and include a copy of the invitation and response form to help ticket sales to all interested participants. Internet services, such as *www.groups@yahoo.com* and *www.bluestep.com* also can assist with efficient software for committee communications and events management.

Fundraising Campaigns

Can the Internet be used for campaign purposes? Yes, it can be used for multiple forms of annual giving campaign techniques, as well as with advocacy efforts and emergency solicitations. Instant communications capabilities make the Internet highly attractive for advocacy campaigns to raise public awareness and to motivate action. The rapid response following the September 11, 2001, attacks has already demonstrated the capacity of the Internet to assist with charitable work. The combination of an active e-mail address list with an informative Web site allows for all of the following:

- Effective and accurate information about the nonprofit organization and its campaign
- A list of contact information for institutions and individuals the campaign is targeting
- A place for campaigners to exchange information
- A way for supporters to contact the nonprofit

- The ability to send faxes and emails to decision makers directly or in- directly from the Web site
- Campaign materials ready for printing
- A way for supporters to sign up for the campaign
- An outreach system for sending campaign materials to supporters via email
- Interactive and animated elements to appeal to visitors
- Online civil disobedience[15]

Emergency situations, such as the tragedy of September 11, 2001, called for rapid and widespread communications, a natural function for the Internet and e-mail response services. The best results occur when using mail and telephone reinforced by radio and television news coverage, coupled with the convenience of Internet contributions, to permit the public to make instantaneous contributions. The best example of maximum multimedia notice is the American Red Cross, where pre-event planning and prepa- ration for active solicitation in times of emergency has added widespread notice of e-mail contact points and 800 telephone numbers for informa- tion. The extent of its ability to communicate with the general public, along with its own entire network of donors and volunteers, all within hours of a disaster, has proven its value for public service as well as for the Red Cross.

CYBERSPACE LAW: ONLINE FUNDRAISING RULES AND REGULATIONS

Among the 50 states, 43 have passed laws to regulate public solicitation for charitable purposes within their boundaries. Several counties and cities also have solicitation regulations for local activities. Each employs a system of preregistration requirements for charities and commercial firms they hire to assist in their fundraising. Most also have annual reporting requirements for nonprofits that solicit their citizens. The nonprofits must disclose their fi- nancial activity, including their fundraising expenses, usually with a copy of the organization's most recent IRS Form 990. These laws and regulations were enacted to protect the public from fraud and other abuses. There are no specific regulations at this time that address the unusual aspects of Internet solicitation; electrons flying through space or speeding through wires do not respect the boundaries of any state or nation. As a result, a nonprofit organization based in any city or town that buys, rents, or leases an e-mail address list and uses the Internet to engage in *active* direct solicitation is acting the same as if it was conducting a multistate direct-mail or telemarketing campaign. It must meet all of the required registration, fee payments, reporting obligations, and so forth for each jurisdiction where its message will be received, whether or not anyone gives. However, if the organization has a Web site that is *passive* about giving and does not actively solicit the public, this organization is not required to preregister, pay fees, or fulfill differing fundraising regulations of every state on the off chance that some resident might find this Web site and make a gift. This explanation is but one interpretation of the current situation; already it is not uniformly true in every state. In particular, California, Minnesota, and Pennsylvania have passed new laws that require any soliciting charity receiving funds over the Internet to be registered in their jurisdiction.[16] Whether this more aggressive practice will be adopted across the nation is unknown, but a major scandal or fraudulent use will certainly stimulate public opinion and legislation response.

Several areas of annual fund solicitation uniformly practiced by nonprofit organizations also may qualify the organizations for specific registration and reporting requirements. The most common form of this activity is auctions and raffles. There are specific legal rules and regulations associated with forms of charitable gambling that may qualify as such (see "Charitable Gambling" in Chapter 12).

Auctions and Raffles

Any form of public solicitation that encounters local regulation should first know and follow these legal requirements. They also should consider whether improved results would result from adding them for Internet use. Annual giving practices have included auctions, raffles, bingo, and other games of chance, plus the lotteries that sometimes accompany them. The use of the Internet for these forms of online solicitation is quite new; it might be an open field for more experimentation and adventure, but might also be full of briar patches and thorn bushes. It is not necessary to stage a benefit event to hold an online auction, raffle, or bingo game. Several states and local jurisdictions consider an auction, raffle, or bingo activity to be a form of charitable gambling; certainly Las Vegas and Monte Carlo games always qualify. Gambling regulations are strict, even when used for charitable purposes, and include severe penalties for all involved.

Auctions are less likely to run afoul of the law than raffles or bingo, but all have potential to come in harm's way, especially if they choose to use commercial auction sites in partnership with a for-profit company. Such public services are available with eBay and others (go to: *www.pages.ebay. com/charity/Index.html*). This partnership arrangement is best designed when guided by a formal contract as a *commercial co-venture* or *charitable sales promotion*. As such, it may be qualified to conduct public solicitations in one or more legal jurisdictions. This commercial function also may qualify for unrelated business income taxes (UBIT) on the gross revenue received. It is important to note that occasional auctions, raffles, bingo, and other forms of games of chance conducted by nonprofit organization may *not* qualify as charitable gambling if they are not "regularly carried on," a legal phrase that defines an occasional (once or twice a year) activity from one that is conducted more frequently (most bingo nights occur weekly). If regularly held, they could qualify for both charitable solicitation and local gambling or lottery regulations and the income subject to UBIT. It is good advice to seek legal counsel whenever auctions, raffles, or bingo games are to be used for fundraising purposes. Remember that any form of active Internet solicitation can be global in its reach and may encounter other forms of legal qualification under local regulatory authority outside the United States (see Exhibit 9-2 for 10 points of sage advice in this young field).

WORKING WITH APPLICATION SERVICE PROVIDERS

An Application Service Provider (ASP) can be a commercial company or another nonprofit organization acting as its online agent and offering a full range of Internet services. The ASP may be in the form of an affinity portal, such as the local chapter of a national organization that "hosts" its affiliates for convenient and less-expensive access to a full array of Internet services. The ASP is an outsourcing option to provide a direct link to the organization's Web site and appears to any visitor to be part of that same site. Two of the more important advantages in this partnership are (1) the

EXHIBIT 9-2 SAGE ADVICE ON ONLINE AUCTIONS[17]

1. The first thing any not-for-profit organization needs to do is decide what items it is going to sell and then visit an index site like www.bidfind.com to see what auction site might be most appropriate for its auction items.

2. Once a not-for-profit has found an auction site that looks suitable, it needs to contact the owner/managers of the auction site.

3. The not-for-profit needs to find out if the auction site will reduce its sales commission for the not-for-profit. Commission fees range from 2.5 percent with *www.keybuy.com* to 5 percent for *www.ebuy.com*. *www.keybuy.com* offers a 50 percent reduction in commission fees, and that is what every not-for-profit should fight for as a minimum reduction.

4. A number of auction sites also charge a listing fee. Every not-for-profit organization should ask that the listing fee to be waived for its items. Often a listing fee is a minimum fee (e.g., 10 cents) that helps to reduce the number of items that are posted with outrageously high beginning bids. Online auction sites that charge listing fees are trying to have only serious online sellers post items.

5. Every not-for-profit organization should be prepared to provide the following for each auction item:

   a. A short, one-paragraph description of the item. The description should include the brand/make or specifications of the item (especially for computer goods). This is important. For example, if a not-for-profit organization is selling a computer, then the make of each component is vital in getting the item sold. Some organizations provide a link to a manufacturer's Web site from the description of the item, but often this drives people out of the auction item Web page, and many will not come back to buy.

   b. A picture should almost always be included. It boosts sales and final price.

   c. It is often effective to include a hypertext link from a description of the auction item to the not-for-profit's home page to find out more about the organization.

   d. It is also effective when the not-for-profit includes a hypertext link to a list of other auction items the organization has for sale.

   e. A one-sentence explanation of the mission and mandate of the not-for-profit organization, included in the description of the auction item, is also important.

   f. To receive a reduction in commission or listing fee, most on-line auction houses need a letter, on the not-for-profit's letterhead, asking for the fee reduction. In addition, a brief explanation of the organization's work is helpful.

   g. Many online auction houses will shy away from more controversial advocacy not-for-profits because showing favor to a group representing one side or another may upset some of their repeat customers.

   h. Studies by *www.keybuy.com* have shown that on-line bidders spend an average of $80. However, the value of the item will dictate the final bid—if a $1,200 antique is offered, the final bid will be higher than for a $12 computer part.

(continued)

EXHIBIT 9-2   (CONTINUED)

6. Not-for-profit organizations need to think carefully about a starting price for their online auction items. According to Erman, starting every item at $1 is a successful strategy for online auctioneering. A psychology major in college, Erman has been carefully tracking online buyers' motivations. He has found that online buyers are afraid to make the first bid. They are wary of bidding too high for an item with an initial high bid amount because other online bidders will ridicule their bid. Others will say, "That bid is too high, is this person a sucker or what!" By starting at $1, individuals are not afraid to begin bidding, and in Erman's experience, once people make that first bid they are hooked.

7. Furthermore, people are even more hooked into the bidding process online when they get an e-mail notice telling them they have been outbid. That means every not-for-profit organization should make sure that the online auction house they are going to use, or their own system, includes such an e-mail notification system that tells bidders if they have the highest bid.

8. Not-for-profit organizations should think carefully about how long they would like to offer items. According to Erman, a 7-day bid period is usually the most effective. His service offers 3-day, 5-day, 7-day, and 14-day auction periods to choose from.

9. Not-for-profit organizations must understand standard activity during that bid period. Usually almost all of the activity is on the first and the last days of the 7-day bid period. If a not-for-profit is thinking about bumping up the bidding, it may want to state that the bidding might be cut off at any time during the 7-day period if a high enough bid is received. This termination threat may be enough to get bidders to be active before the last day of bidding and help drive up the selling price.

10. Not-for-profits that are going to use an online auction house must make sure the site has been around for at least one year.

Source: Michael Johnston, Chapter 25 in *The Nonprofit Handbook: Fund Raising*, 3rd ed. (New York: John Wiley & Sons, 2001), pp. 526–527. Used with permission.

means for an organization to offer an interactive, fully functional Internet service that also is integrated with its marketing and communications programs on what appears to be its Web site, and (2) avoiding the high costs and need for skilled technical employees required to develop and maintain an array of online programs and services. ASP services can be quite broad and include:

> secure donation forms, shopping carts, event registration, and community-building features like bulletin board and chat rooms designed to plug in to an organization's existing Web site. Usually there will be a set-up fee, which will include some customization work to make the ASP pages look and feel like the rest of the organization's Web site.[18]

User fees for ASP services can be leased for a period of months or years. Careful selection of the ASP partner is recommended to define what will be the level of services and fee structure in the contract. The contract also should provide many more services than online fundraising. It should be of direct benefit to the marketing and communications needs of the organization for its clients, customers, and patients. In addition, it should meet its internal requirements for privacy, security, access, data storage and management, fiscal controls, and more. Exhibit 9-3 provides good advice in selecting an ASP partner, beginning with choosing one that fits the organization well in its current style of communications and working relationship with its constituents.

Each ASP also must have several paying customers to meet its operating expenses and compete for survival; more than a few have appeared and disappeared all too quickly, leaving their customers with no service at all and sometimes no records of any transactions. If fundraising support services are to be included in the contract, arrangements must be in place to handle

---

EXHIBIT 9-3   GUIDELINES FOR SELECTING AN APPLICATION SERVICE PROVIDER

1. It provides support to online donating, e-mail campaigns, and other links to the Internet and you understand how the data are transmitted to your system.
2. It easily provides data output in a format consistent with your organization's accounting package.
3. It can support multiple campaigns and appeals at the same time.
4. It can export all data for reports, labels, and mailings in a format familiar to your organization (i.e., Microsoft Word).
5. You understand all the cost variables for use of the system, and you understand how you can access online and telephone support.
6. It allows you to assign multiple security levels for users, and you understand the security protocols for data input into the system.
7. It allows you to create custom user-defined fields.
8. All data elements are available for reporting and query purposes, and it allows you to create custom reports for all data sets if required.
9. You know who technically owns the data input into the system.
10. You know the typical hardware and software requirements for full utilization of the system, not just the recommended requirements.

Source: ePhilanthropyFoundation.org. 2001. Used with permission.

actual online contributions. This area begs for trouble because of the financial security required for handling money, response forms that come back with personal information, bank and credit card identification, and occasional correspondence as to donor restrictions for the use of gifts. In addition to considering fiscal controls on deposit, receipt, and accounting for every gift, you must decide up front whether fees or a commission will be the basis for charges for these services. A straight fee structure is recommended; whenever commissions or percentages tied to gift income are involved, they are the source of fraud and abuse. It is for this reason that compensation is the most sensitive area of professional fundraising ethics and why any form of commission or percentage fundraising is prohibited. Several good questions should be asked and answered when negotiating for management or support services of any outsourcing arrangement to protect the organization as well as all of its online participants. (See Exhibit 9-4 for guidelines on working with ASPs.)

ETHICS CODES AND STANDARDS OF PROFESSIONAL PRACTICE

There is a continuing necessity for strong and effective measures to protect the privacy of donors and volunteers and to ensure the security of all information held by a nonprofit organization. The relationships that exist between nonprofit organization and their clients, customers, and patients is built almost entirely on trust—trust to provide quality services, to be honest and truthful, and to be stewards of the public's funds at all times. Without this high degree of confidence and trust, contributions of time, talent, and treasure so essential to nonprofit organizations from their communities would be lost. Professional trade associations whose members are fundraising executives have developed complete guidance for themselves and their employers for observing ethics codes and professional practice standards. The Donor Bill of Rights (see Exhibit 9-5) provides added guidance on the continuous obligation of every nonprofit organization to honor its privileged relationship with those who provide the necessary funds and volunteer support. Ethics codes are now common for professional consultants, fundraising executives, research staff, planned giving practitioners, and others.[19]

The advent of Internet fundraising requires a separate set of guidlines for ethical professional practice (see the ePhilanthropy Code of Ethical Online

EXHIBIT 9-4   GUIDELINES FOR WORKING WITH APPLICATION SERVICE PROVIDERS

✔ *Is there a contract*, and does it guarantee that the affinity dot-com will not use the not-for-profit's name without permission—in every instance?

✔ *Are there hidden requirements for consumers (donors/members) who come to use a dot-com service because of participation in the dot-com's affinity service?* Can the not-for-profit ensure that those hidden requirements are made explicit?

✔ *Are all common questions clearly outlined on the Web site?* Donors need to have a clear explanation of what a dot-com is offering to them and to the participating not-for-profit organization.

✔ *Will proceeds from the affinity relationship be delivered in a timely and transparent manner?* Any not-for-profit organization deserves to get the proceeds of the dot-com relationship within 30 to 60 working days (or sooner). If that is not the case, then that should be stated on the dot-com site.

✔ *What kinds of not-for-profits are allowed to participate with a particular dot-com?* Every not-for-profit organization needs to know what other organizations are a part of the same service.

✔ *Does the dot-com believe in an open-book policy?* Every not-for-profit organization should be able to review its proceeds and results through the dot-com 24 hours a day, via a Web interface that is presented in a clear, understandable manner.

✔ *Are prices inflated in product affinity relationships?* Every not-for-profit organization wants to be in a dot-com product relationship that gives the consumer a fair price, the dot-com a profit, and money back to the not-for-profit. The price of the product should not be inflated beyond principles of profit and fairness. Nothing could be worse for a not-for-profit than to be seen as a price gouger!

✔ *Is the transaction/information secure?* Every not-for-profit organization needs to know that the dot-com has security systems in place that protect the not-for-profit, the dot-com, and the donor.

✔ *Does the not-for-profit get access to supporter information in a timely and transparent manner?* Does it have access to the online donor information 24 hours a day? Is it Web-interfaced? Can it be easily downloaded into any database? Is it a real-time database of online donors?

✔ *Does the dot-com have a list of happy clients?* There are so many new dot-coms that it is hard to know if the service is effective. Ask for not-for-profit client references. If there are none, or very few, then drive a very hard bargain.

✔ *Is the dot-com well capitalized?* Will it be a dot-com that appears one day and is gone the next? Is it committed to improving its applications? Does it have a system in place for taking not-for-profit experiences and comments and working them into the applications?

Reprinted with permission from the ePhilanthropyFoundation.org © 2001

EXHIBIT 9-5   A DONOR BILL OF RIGHTS

Philanthropy is based on voluntary action for the common good. It is a tradition of giving and sharing that is primary to the quality of life. To assure that philanthropy merits the respect and trust of the general public, and that donors and prospective donors can have full confidence in the not-for-profit organizations and causes they are asked to support, we declare that all donors have these rights.

I.

To be informed of the organization's mission, of the way the organization intends to use donated resources, and of its capacity to use donations effectively for their intended purposes.

II.

To be informed of the identity of those serving on the organization's governing board, and to expect the board to exercise prudent judgement in its stewardship responsibilities.

III.

To have access to the organization's most recent financial statements.

IV.

To be assured their gifts will be used for the purposes for which they were given.

V.

To receive appropriate acknowledgement and recognition.

VI.

To be assured that information about their donations is handled with respect and with confidentiality to the extent provided by law.

VII.

To expect that all relationships with individuals representing organizations of interest to the donor will be professional in nature.

VIII.

To be informed whether those seeking donations are volunteers, employees of the organization or hired solicitors.

IX.

To have the opportunity for their names to be deleted from mailing lists that an organization may intend to share.

X.

To feel free to ask questions when making a donation and to receive prompt, truthful and forthright answers.

(continued)

EXHIBIT 9-5　(CONTINUED)

DEVELOPED BY	ENDORSED BY
American Association of Fund Raising Counsel (AAFRC)	Independent Sector
	National Catholic Development Conference (NCDC)
Association for Healthcare Philanthropy (AHP)	
Council for Advancement and Support of Education (CASE)	National Committee on Planned Giving (NCPG)
	Council for Resource Development (CRD)
Association of Fundraising Professionals (AFP)	United Way of America

Philanthropic Practices in Exhibit 9-6).[20] These texts should be adopted as best-practice guidelines by every nonprofit organization with either an active or passive Web site that allows for online contributions. These statements also serve as an excellent primer to this entire area; they address privacy and security, open disclosure, how to address complaints, and the variety of transaction media available for online giving.

Donors have just begun their first online contributions; they have the right to expect that the organizations they support will be as well prepared to receive, process, and safeguard their funds and their personal information

EXHIBIT 9-6　ePHILANTHROPY CODE OF ETHICAL ONLINE PHILANTHROPIC PRACTICES

The ePhilanthropy Foundation exists to foster the effective and safe use of the Internet for philanthropic purposes. In its effort to promote high ethical standards in online fundraising and to build trust among contributors in making online transactions and contributions with the charity of their choice, this code is being offered as a guide to all who share this goal. Contributors are encouraged to be aware of non-Internet related fundraising practices that fall outside the scope of this Code.

ETHICAL ONLINE PRACTICES AND PRACTITIONERS WILL:

Section A: Philanthropic Experience

1. Clearly and specifically display and describe the organization's identity on the organization's Web site.
2. Employ practices on the Web site that exhibit integrity, honesty, truthfulness and seek to safeguard the public trust.

(continued)

EXHIBIT 9-6 (CONTINUED)

Section B: Privacy and Security

1. Seek to inspire trust in every online transaction.

2. Prominently display the opportunity to have their names removed from lists that are sold to, rented to, or exchanged with other organizations.

3. Conduct online transactions through a system that employs high-level security technology, to protect the donor's personal information.

4. Provide either an 'opt in' or 'opt out' mechanism to prevent unsolicited communications or solicitations by organizations that obtain email addresses directly from the donor, and require the "opt in" mechanism before the donor's email address may be sold, transferred or otherwise distributed to a third party for communication, advertising or promotion purposes.

5. Protect the interests and privacy of individuals interacting with their website.

Section C: Disclosures

1. Disclose the identity of the organization or provider processing an online transaction.

2. Guarantee that the name, logo and likeness of all parties to an online transaction belong to the party and will not be used without express permission.

3. Maintain all appropriate governmental and regulatory designations or certifications.

Section D: Complaints

1. Provide protection to hold the donor harmless of any problem arising from a transaction conducted through the organization's website.

2. Promptly respond to all customer complaints and to employ best efforts to fairly resolve all legitimate complaints in a timely fashion.

Section E: Transactions

1. Insure contributions are used to support the activities of the organization to which it was donated.

2. Insure that legal control of contributions or proceeds from online transactions are transferred directly to the charity or expedited in the fastest possible way.

3. Companies providing online services with charities will provide clear and full communication with the charity on all aspects of donor transactions including the accurate and timely transmission of data related to online transactions.

4. Stay informed regarding the best methods to insure the ethical, secure and private nature of online ephilanthropy transactions.

5. Adhere to the spirit as well as the letter of all applicable laws and regulations, including but not limited to charity solicitation and tax laws.

6. Insure that all services, recognition and other transactions promised on a Web site, in consideration of a gift or transaction, will be fulfilled in a timely basis.

7. Disclose to the donor the nature of the relationship between the organization processing the gift or transaction and the charity intended to benefit from the gift.

Source: ePhilanthropyFoundation.org, *ePhilanthropy Code of Ethical Online Philanthropic Practices.* Used with permission.

on the Internet as they are through every other means and at the same high level of ethical and professional conduct. Many more years will be required to develop the public's complete trust in online giving, and it is essential at this early stage of Internet use that the highest ethical standards are fully in place and in wide practice throughout the nonprofit fundraising industry. No single incident has more potential to upset the public's confidence and to cause them to lose faith in every other form of online service than fraud and abuse of the public's trust. It is certain that a major scandal arising from some abusive practice or scam on the Internet will receive extensive media attention, just as do direct-mail and telemarketing fraud today—this brush paints every organization with the same stroke.

INTELLECTUAL PROPERTY, COPYRIGHT, PRIVACY, AND SECURITY

Space in this book is not available, nor is it the author's intent, to provide a comprehensive presentation on all the details associated with use of the Internet. It has been established as one of the newest and most creative forms of personal communication and solicitation. Nonprofit organizations are being encouraged to get online and join the Internet Age without, as of yet, a full understanding of its implications to the organization and to the communities its mission is dedicated to serve. Excitement abounds at the prospects, the efficiencies, and the opportunities (be they explorations and adventures still). The resources listed in the End Notes and Selected References on this subject represent qualified experts; their advice and counsel will be of great assistance to any who wish to enter this arena or, having already jumped aboard this train, require guidance to know where they should be going next. Four other areas remain to be discussed in this chapter: intellectual property, copyright issues, privacy, and security (see section B of Exhibit 9-6). We close with a look to the future of cyberspace and its applications to professional fundraising practice.

Intellectual Property and Copyright Issues

Because communication on the Internet is so open and convenient, just about anything can be sent anywhere. Technology can "scan" a book, download a music video, and copy a painting or photograph and send its encrypted electrons anywhere at any time. Digitized reproductions are nearly perfect and it is difficult to know whether the print or copy in your hands is an original. Protection of items of intellectual property are embedded in copyright laws, an area of great concern since most of what can be sent on the Internet is text or image files, software and/or recordings, all of which is copyright-protected material. There also are issues about patent law, trademark, and trade secret laws in cyberspace. The overall issue is how to protect original works of authorship, no matter the medium of expression used. To be technical, even an e-mail message is the property of its author, whether or not a copyright notice was attached to the message declaring its ownership. The boundaries on property that is protected by copyright law include "literary works; musical works, including any accompanying words; dramatic works, including any accompanying music; pantomimes and choreographic works; pictorial, graphic and sculptural works; motion pictures and other audiovisual works; sound recordings; and architectural works."[21]

Why are intellectual property and copyright laws and regulations important to fundraising practice? Because of open use of the Internet for solicitation purposes, the content of every message should be verified as owned by the sender and none other. If a legal challenge arises by an author or property owner over material that was used by a nonprofit organization without written permission in advance, the organization could be subject to statutory damages up to $100,000 per infringement plus legal fees. When creative juices are flowing and quotes, pictures, or sounds are easily copied from books, magazines, newspapers, or even on-air and on-line sources, in an effort to be as effective in soliciting as possible, the potential for improperly using another's property arises.

Privacy Issues

There are two main areas where privacy issues can affect fundraising practice. The first is the traditional area of each donor's contribution history and any personal information gathered through electronic prospect research techniques. Also included is personal data relating to professional services provided by the organization to any of its clients, customers, and patients. Security of the organization's Web site is a matter for serious attention; privacy and security are important to all phases of fundraising practice, including security for personal bank or credit card details.

Staff and volunteer solicitors should be instructed carefully regarding donor privacy issues and the need to protect the confidentiality of information collected and maintained by the fundraising department. Any details regarding use of the organization's programs and services should be treated at all times with sensitivity and security. Privacy is an especially sensitive issue for hospitals, health care, and social service and welfare organizations that counsel and treat their clients, customers, and patients on matters that need be shared only with their caregivers.

The efficiency of computers allows electronic access to institutional records by authorized individuals in performance of their professional duties. This includes fundraising staffs whose access to name, address, telephone number, and perhaps employer data are needed to conduct efficient and effective annual giving programs with their clients, customers, and patients. Nonauthorized personnel have no need to know things that any client, customer, or patient is entitled to keep confidential or that are otherwise of a sensitive nature. In the same vein, nonprofit organizations should not use any personal information other than in direct support of their professional relationships with these same clients, customers, and patients.

Security Issues

Security of sensitive information begins with protecting access via any electronic means, a requirement nonprofit organizations must meet with flying colors every day. Online vandalism and computer hackers can break in and download sensitive information, interfere with current operations, destroy data, inject misinformation, "bugs" and viruses, alter an existing site with embarrassing images, text, and other infringements, and more. Ask the obvious fair question: "Why would anyone want to do any of these acts to a nonprofit organization?" Not every organization is popular or free from controversy. For example, here are just a few organizations that deal with issues that foster strong emotions: the American Civil Liberties Union (ACLU), the National Rifle Association (NRA), and Planned Parenthood, each of which must take extra precautions to provide added security to their property, employees, and customers, as well as their Web site. In America, our personal freedoms are protected by the Bill of Rights in the U.S. Constitution, including our precious right of free speech.

So how do you protect a Web site? First, pay attention to security regarding use of the Internet and its related partners, your Web page, and your computer staff. Professional help is available from many sources, but you can take some important initial steps: Monitor your Web site, protect your passwords, choose an ASP carefully, and make backup copies of any data needing protection. Be wary of downloading any data you do not know about, including offers of access to interactive free "upgrades" to enhance or speed up your computer service; they may be improvements but they also may degrade your internal security.[22]

Second, look out for the donor, beginning with protection of detailed personal information. Giving history, preferred areas for support, volunteer records including any evaluations, personal history, and credit card numbers, are all entrusted to the fundraising staff. Here is a quick but effective list of safeguards for Internet security to use as guidelines, whether you prepare these yourself or use a third-party vendor or ASP:

( ) Have you made sure that only the Web pages that are gathering sensitive information are using a secure, encrypted format?

( ) Have you made every effort to get your ISP to provide free or close to free secure service by presenting your donation form as a chance for the ISP to highlight this security option to its commercial customers?

( ) Have you made sure that your e-mail address that receives sensitive credit card or banking information is secure?

( ) Have you ordered your Digital Certificate for your secure online donation/membership form?

( ) Have you made sure that your certificate is still valid and has not expired?[23]

Sensitive or personal data should not be accessible to anyone entering the organization's Web site. Security for personal data in office computers should observe the same rules as hard-copy material in a donor's paper file; keep only what is necessary to the donors' or volunteers' relationship with the institution. Donors have the right to visit the fundraising office and ask to see their personal records and files. Out of respect for each individual's rights to privacy—whether a donor or volunteer, prospect or suspect—no personal information should be kept that does not relate directly to a donor's business relationship with the organization in any capacity. The fundraising department must keep these records secure from any other use. Some nonprofit organizations trade their house lists (names and addresses in donor files); others will rent their lists to outside agencies as an alternative revenue source. Make sure you have established clear limits about what level of detailed information about donors and volunteers can be released to any other organization or person.

Lastly, all electronic systems of fundraising donor records should be protected with at least two passwords. Access to these records should be restricted to those staff members whose job requires them to deal with this service area.

THE FUTURE OF INTERNET SOLICITATION

Internet solicitation has arrived. Prior to September 11, 2001, it had gotten off to a slower start than some would have expected. Following the tragedy of terrorist attacks, use of the Internet to make gifts is now front and center as a viable option—along with mail, telephone, facsimile reply forms—and is likely to grow rapidly. It is a safe prediction that the Internet will not replace any of the traditional methods of annual giving described in this book; however, it can and should be used to add layers of personalized e-mail contact to each communications opportunity within these traditional, time-tested techniques. It is also safe to predict that as donors and volunteers become more trusting of the Internet for all their affairs, including financial transactions, they will become more confident in using it for monetary exchanges with nonprofit organizations.

What is important for nonprofit organizations today is that they actively use the Internet to recruit and engage their constituents in their mission, vision, and values. This can only be done if they prepare and maintain active e-mail address lists and provide interactive Web sites that are user friendly, allow easy access to information people seek, and work at building people's confidence and trust in what organizations say and what they do with their money to benefit others.

Titus Brown asked Karen Anderson to keep calling the Campaign to Clean Up America (CCUA) national office for information on development of its Web site. Karen also had received requests from the national office for details on the Cleveland Chapter program, the new energy generator plant, and the Circle of Champions program, for insertion onto the new Web site. She reported back to Titus with updates on design and preparation of the new home page for the Cleveland Chapter. The process was taking longer than expected and was costing more money than anticipated because improvements in Internet technology seemed to occur daily. The CCUA chapters were not going to be asked to provide any of the funding needed; Michael Activist, the national chairman, had raised all the necessary funding. In another report, Karen told both Titus Brown and Sidney Secure that one reason for the delay was CCUA's investigation into an ASP site, which was rejected in favor of the decision to build its own. Titus agreed. "I've heard that so many of those 'charity channels' have folded in recent months, and I agree that option was not too reliable. Keep me posted, Karen; I'm anxious for us to tap into the Internet to help tell our story and boost our fundraising results."

Two weeks later, Anderson received a packet that announced the CCUA Web site would go "live" in two weeks. The package contained five copies of the instruction manual on how the Cleveland Chapter was to be linked up with the national site for a full variety of services. Fortunately, as Karen was still in office space provided by Harvey Clout, she had a desktop computer with Internet access. The new services included access to information on the overall national campaign, profiles of all 16 national chapters, and more. The manual fully explained security of the site, privacy provisions for all donors, and the pathway by which funds received by the national office would be accounted for and transmitted to the chapters. Bi-weekly reports on all fundraising activity were to be sent via e-mail to each chapter, along with summary results of the national campaign. Each chapter was assigned a unique password to access its site for the number of hits, e-mail messages, and daily gift reports on contributions received. Donor records required a second password, selected by each chapter. Karen quickly went to her computer and looked up the site, found the icon for the Cleveland Chapter, and was delighted to find all her information presented in a clear and user-friendly manner, including an icon called "How to Make A Gift" to the Clean Up Cleveland Campaign, plus a separate response form page in the chapter's name to be downloaded. Complete instructions on how to make a gift were provided, including a credit card transaction, electronic funds transfer authorization, pledge form, and payment schedule—even an introduction to planned giving and estate planning options.

Karen called upstairs to Harvey Clout's office to report receipt of the package, only to learn that both Titus Brown and Sidney Secure were in a meeting with Harvey on Cast Iron Works business. Harvey's secretary interrupted their discussion and Karen relayed her news. "That's great, Karen," boomed Harvey into his speakerphone. "You should be here to see Titus and Sid; they're on their feet, dancing around the room! You had better deliver copies of that manual to them today; drop one off for me, too. Keep the fifth copy for now. You say the Web site will be active in two weeks? We better add a discussion on the Web site to our next board meeting agenda. Thanks for your call, Karen. Now, I've got to try to get these two guys to focus on my business." After Karen hung up, she said to herself: "There are some pretty high expectations for this Internet program. Let's see; it's 11:30 now. I'll deliver the manuals after my lunch meeting at the Cleveland Foundation. Hang onto your hat, girl. Ready or not, here we go into the wild blue yonder of the Internet!"

Two months later, Karen submitted the following results received from the national Web site:

National Web Site Results

Number of hits to the site:	42,789
Number of hits for the Cleveland Chapter:	8,775 (20.5%)
National gift activity report (all chapters):	

	Number	Gift Values	Avg. Gift Size
Gift response forms	5,979	$215,044.00	$36
Credit card payments made	1,953	$ 94,360.50	$48
EFT gifts authorized	217	$ 9,775.00	$45
Pledges outstanding	3,909	$110,909.50	$28
Planned gift inquiries	21	-0-	-0-
Totals:	5,990	$215,044.00	$36

Cleveland Chapter Results

	Number	Gift Values	Avg. Gift Size
Gift response forms	198	$6,139	$ 35
Credit card payments made			
Circle of Champions	16	$1,950	$122
Other payments	56	$1,792	$ 32
Subtotal	72	$3,742	$ 52
Circle of Champion pledges	26	$3,042	$117
EFT gifts authorized	17	$ 595	$ 35
Pledges outstanding	83	$3,427	$ 41
Planned gift inquiries	11	-0-	-0-
Totals	209	$6,139	$ 29

Karen's performance analysis revealed that the average number of gift response forms received by the national office was 2.2 percent compared to total hits, while the Cleveland Chapter response rate was 3.4 percent. The average gift to all chapters was $36, compared to Cleveland's $35. The Circle of Champions program, the only donor club in operation across the country, acquired 26 new members for $3,042—an average gift of $117. Credit card use was encouraging; CCUA received 1,953 payments for $94,360.50—an average gift of $48. The Cleveland Chapter received 72 payments for $3,742—an average gift of $52, thanks to the 16 new Circle of Champions members. Electronic fund transfers produced 217 gifts for the national office at an average of $45 each; Cleveland's response was 17 gifts and $35. Overall bottom-line figures were $215,044 with an average gift of $36 received from 5,979 new donors; the Cleveland Chapter received 209 gifts for $6,139, an average of $32, a promising start for the entire Internet program.

Karen thought the Internet report was to be the main focus for fundraising at the board meeting until she heard about the proposed special benefit event that Iris Radiant introduced next on the agenda. "Oh my goodness," thought Karen. "I had hoped this idea might not come up for at least another couple of months. We're right in the middle of our late spring direct mail and telephone campaigns, and I've got those corporate and foundation proposals to complete! I wanted to wait a bit longer before entertaining any benefit event plans; this idea is going to take a lot of staff time and we have so many other annual giving activities already in full swing. I wonder what special event ideas Iris has in mind?"

CHAPTER 10

Activities, Benefits, and Special Events

Activities, benefits, and special events are what many people think fundraising is all about. After direct mail, these functions and occasions are the most pervasive forms of public solicitation in current practice. Visibility appears to be their primary objective; raising money for charity is the excuse to have a party. They are popular with the many volunteers who plan them and with the people who attend. We read about them in the papers and see photographs of the dedicated people who planned them and the celebrities and distinguished guests who attended. We read and see less about why they were held or what the funds raised will do.

Why are activities, benefits, and special events held? Nonprofit organizations seem to favor them a great deal; they conduct many of them during each year. What are their advantages, their values? Do they actually raise any money? Are they worth all that effort? There are several good answers that validate keeping these activities and occasions on the annual calendar of events; there are also several good reasons why nonprofit organizations should cross some of them off. This chapter will discuss activities, benefits, and special events, defining their many purposes and describing their many forms. They are a rich and valuable addition to a comprehensive annual giving program. They are an asset because of their ability to enhance and reinforce direct mail and membership acquisition and renewal objectives and to further the goals of auxiliaries, guilds, donor clubs, and support groups. Each of these annual giving methods is repeated again and again, year after year. Activities, benefits, and special events can add spice, vigor, and zip to these repetitious programs while they each may serve many other valid purposes on their own.

A complete list of all the types of activities, benefits, and special events that can be held would be long and not especially enlightening, except as proof of the human creativity and experimentation invested in gathering people together. Examples range from camel races to rat races, from auctions to raffles, from Las Vegas nights to Monte Carlo nights, from chili cook-offs to cotillions, from 10K runs and 5K walks to golf and tennis tournaments, and (saving the best for last) from pancake breakfasts to fashion show luncheons to black-tie, gala dinner dances. This brief list is ample evidence of how men and women can invent activities, benefits, and special events and offer them to other people as exciting "fun things" to do, especially if they are held for "a worthy cause." Exhibit 10-1 illustrates some of the primary purposes for nonprofit organizations' use of these functions.

I have chosen to segregate activities, benefits, and special events as three distinct entities for presentation in this chapter. The terms are similar, and

EXHIBIT 10-1	PRIMARY PURPOSES FOR ACTIVITIES, BENEFITS, AND SPECIAL EVENTS	
Method	**Primary Purposes**	**Examples**
Activities	Communication	Lectures
	Information	Tours
	Support	Memberships
	Advocacy	Lobbying
	Awareness	Community services
Benefits	Friend-raising	Grand openings
	Marketing and promotion	Ground-breaking ceremonies
	Media relations	Sporting events
	Donor relations	Victory parties
	Community relations	Fairs/open houses
	Volunteer involvement	Social events
	Leadership development	Campaigns
	Fundraising	Every benefit
	Fun	Every benefit
Special Events	Contacts	Retreats
	Required business	Annual meetings
	Honors and recognition	Dedications
	Public activity	Convocations
	Tradition	Public ceremonies

some people use them interchangeably. By distinguishing among the three types, the chapter can cover all of their multiple purposes and their separate utilization in the comprehensive annual giving program.

Activities, benefits, and special events can be staged by nearly every form of organized human enterprise, whether held for a business, governmental, or philanthropic purposes. They attract attention; they bring people together; they convey a message; they promote a purpose or cause; they encourage people to action. Here are twenty of the purposes that activities, benefits, and special events can accomplish for nonprofit organizations:

1. They can increase visibility and improve public image.
2. Volunteers have an opportunity to participate.
3. Community relations are increased.
4. There is opportunity for leadership development.
5. Market penetration increases.
6. Market response can be tested.
7. The events raise cash for current purposes.
8. There is an opportunity for honors and recognition.
9. Media coverage is possible.
10. Activities, benefits, and special events energize donors and volunteers.
11. Corporate contacts and participation increase.
12. These functions showcase the organization's leadership.
13. Ongoing programs and services receive more attention.
14. These functions provide an opportunity to recruit new donors.
15. Multiple annual gifts increase.
16. There is an opportunity to cultivate major gifts.
17. The professional staff is more visible.
18. There is an opportunity to promote the mission or cause.
19. There is an increase in public awareness and general consensus.
20. Activities, benefits, and special events provide an opportunity to have fun.

Given all of these potential attributes, is it any wonder that activities, benefits, and special events are held so frequently? No single activity, benefit, or special event could hope to accomplish all of the above purposes, but, like every other endeavor planned by the organization, there should be a list of defined objectives against which an activity, benefit, or special event will be measured. Planning for an activity, benefit, or special event should begin with the selection of several purposes; the greater the number, the greater the value of the activity, benefit, or special event in opening up its nonprofit sponsor to its community of friends, neighbors, clients, and potential clients. Public activities invite people to come inside, to see the facilities, to learn about the programs and services being provided to others in the community, and to consider joining with other volunteers to help the organization accomplish its urgent and necessary goals and objectives. Activities, benefits, and special events serve philanthropy best as means to an end rather than ends in themselves.

VOLUNTEER DEVELOPMENT

Activities, benefits, and special events are exceptional opportunities for volunteerism. To be successful, they need and can use hundreds of hours from hundreds of people working together. They offer opportunities for community liaison, volunteer participation, and leadership identification and development. Converting suspects, prospects, and donors into volunteers is one of the best ways to help an organization to grow and to attract those who will support its needs today and in the future. Active volunteers also become more faithful donors, according to a national survey published by Independent Sector:

> The incidence of volunteering has a direct relationship to the amount of contributions. In 1991, respondents who reported household contributions but did not volunteer (26 percent of all households) reported contributions averaging $477, or 1.4 percent of household income. Respondents who reported household contributions and volunteering (46 percent of all households) reported contributions averaging $1,155, or 2.6 percent of household income.[1]

Involvement increases personal awareness and knowledge of nonprofit organizations and their many charitable purposes. To volunteer is to begin to learn about an organization's mission and purposes, its need for volunteers, and its methods of fundraising. Successful nonprofit organizations explain exactly how volunteer services make a difference and how the funds raised by volunteers are used to carry out programs and services that meet public needs. The personal experience of volunteerism should be rewarding, even if it is sometimes hard work begun at the end of a regular workday. It serves a high purpose by helping to make the community, the nation, and the world a better place to live. People want to help; they want their good efforts to make a difference. Satisfaction increases their enthusiasm for volunteerism and sustains their commitment to continued support of a nonprofit organization. When a nonprofit organization asks for volunteers from among the residents of its community, it is serving the public interest and creating a valuable community benefit. Every nonprofit organization needs volunteers to fulfill its mission; it cannot fulfill it alone.

Because volunteers are essential to the success of each activity, benefit, or special event, it is important to review what is involved in finding and training them. Each nonprofit organization must identify and recruit volunteers, inform and train them, carefully select their early assignments, supervise their development, support all of their efforts, evaluate their performance, and honor and recognize them for all they have done. These steps are summarized in Exhibit 10-2. For some volunteers, their capacity for responsibility will predict their later roles as volunteer leaders; they will take a turn at planning and directing nonprofit organizations. Every organization needs volunteers who like to be involved with public activities, who can organize and manage a group, whether friends or strangers, and who will support an organization's need to conduct necessary and useful special events.

Identification

Despite its great need for volunteers, a nonprofit organization must be selective about whom it invites to work for it. People who are already active in community work and experienced with activities, benefits, and special

---

EXHIBIT 10-2   STEPS IN VOLUNTEER AND
LEADERSHIP DEVELOPMENT

1. Identification
2. Recruitment
3. Orientation and training
4. Assignment
5. Leadership development
6. Staff support
7. Performance evaluation
8. Honors and recognition

events are the best choices. The first criterion to measure is a candidate's ability to join with others and, by working together, to accomplish a common purpose. People with a record of responsibility and performance in support of activities, benefits, and special events at other organizations might be asked to do the same job here.

I recommend calling other nonprofit organizations where a leadership candidate has been active, and asking about his or her performance. Was it characterized by cooperation and coordination with the volunteers and professional staff in place, or did the candidate insist on bringing in "my own people" and subordinating those already active on the organization's behalf? Some well-intentioned people have a personal style that drives people away. Will the candidate raise friends and build relationships in the community, and make a successful cadre of volunteers into an enthusiastic unit? If not, no matter what the candidate's credentials or past successes, it might be wise to look for someone else. Friend-raising and relationship-building remain the prime directives of the annual giving program.

Do any board members have experience in directing activities, benefits, or special events? If so, they were probably not board members at that time. Board members may not be eager to take on a major project unless they have absolute assurance that the professional and support staff know what they are doing. Given their position as board members, neither they nor the organization can risk any failures. They can, however, be asked to serve as information resources during the planning of an activity, benefit, or special event, and as advisers if problems develop during implementation of the plans. Do they know others who have worked on similar functions? Can they assist in recruiting experienced volunteer leaders, or serve on the committee that will manage the project? How, in their opinion, should the organization proceed with planning each of its activities, benefits, and special events? What functions do they think the public will support? Which ones should be avoided? The experience and intuition of board members who have observed many social activities and benefit events held in the community can be invaluable when choosing the type of function that will be held. Can they nominate or help to recruit people who are experienced and reliable volunteers? The new project will need a few individuals who have succeeded in managing similar functions. Board members will be sensitive to the possibility that the nominees for this function might help to meet other needs of the organization in the future.

The next resource might be current volunteers. Have any of them demonstrated the talents needed for this more demanding assignment? Whose faithful service has gained recognition and earned a new opportunity to serve by leading? Their commitment to a working relationship may warrant turning over to them the staging, producing, and directing of this important new project. Volunteers in current leadership positions are often looking for their next assignment. Who among them has a proven ability to organize and manage both people and the complex components of a financial and social success? These are the organization's own qualified candidates!

Donors might also be tapped. There are always people in the donor files who have not come forward because no one has asked them. Donors with faithful giving histories are telling the organization that they care about it a lot. Consistent performance is the clue here, not how much they have given. Donors come in many sizes and shapes. One donor may have access to others and may be willing to call on them to help the activity, benefit, or special event. Donors who are well placed in business and commerce and are already active in community and civic projects will have established contacts that can be used in the organization's behalf. Some donors' businesses or professions may bring them into frequent contact with a suitable audience for the planned function—and may illustrate their leadership ability. Any donor who is in an executive position has the necessary knowledge and experience to accomplish goals by set deadlines. For example, any donor in a sales position is a good candidate to serve on the subcommittee charged with recruiting sponsors and underwriters and soliciting table hosts and individual ticket sales.

Among the new people nominated for service to the organization, are any candidates reported to be well-qualified? These individuals may have already emerged as highly placed volunteers with other nonprofit organizations. Some research will indicate whether these nominees might agree to serve in some voluntary capacity. Motives are still important. Are these people inclined to participate in charitable work only to advance themselves and expand their business and professional contacts? If so, they may have only a minimal interest in the mission and purposes of the nonprofit organization and may abandon a committee or an event if it does not fulfill their personal objectives.

In suspects, or newcomers already identified as probable annual givers, an active interest in the nonprofit organization is already stirring. An invitation to serve in a volunteer role on a committee responsible for a major function will acquaint them with other volunteers and donors and start them at a good pace toward personal involvement with the organization. Their progress can be a gauge of their potential for continued service. Their immediate interest and their willingness to skip the preliminaries and go right into the main event should be appropriately recognized.

The remaining search criteria are tied to the type of activity, benefit, or special event that is being considered. If entertainment is essential, people who are close to the entertainment industry should be contacted. For a social function, the help of men and women who are well-versed in local social customs and possess local social standing should be enlisted. For a sporting event, sports celebrities will give a great lift to the party, although their schedules are uncertain and they might not have time to help beyond their appearance at the event. When the call goes out for nominees, people will submit names of friends who have connections, of public figures who are "politically correct," and of themselves if the community service will look good on their resumes. Not everyone nominated may know or care about the nonprofit organization or its mission. The perspective, knowledge, and political sense of the board members, the president/CEO, and the volunteer leadership deserve some trust here. Meeting these unique needs is part of their leadership obligation. The organization's name and reputation are inside the package when an activity, benefit, or special event is handed over to a volunteer committee.

RECRUITMENT

After a roster of qualified volunteer candidates has been assembled, the volunteers nominated should be evaluated against the plan for the activity, benefit, or special event. Do they have the skills that will be needed to manage this project to success? How many of the primary purposes identified in Exhibit 10-1 can be realized with their assistance? Some names may be on the roster only because removing them would send out negative shock waves. Politically correct favorites will also need to be invited. Some candidates may be more valuable to other annual giving programs and should be set aside for those duties. Others, especially candidates who are not well known, can be coded for possible selection on a second pass through the list.

The best approach is to identify at least three leadership candidates first: an overall chairperson plus two (or more) nominees for vice chair. The positions of chairperson and vice chair are crucial, and board members and other key volunteers close to the organization can be enormously helpful in resolving this choice. They should be asked to review the leadership candidates identified for each project and to assist in their recruitment. Each of these candidates should be personally interviewed before being asked to serve as chairperson or to take responsibility for a high-level duty on the committee. The candidates' capabilities, interest, and willingness to commit the time required should all be thoughtfully assessed.

> The ideal fundraising leader is influential in the community, resourceful, creative, and ambitious; has a strong sense of order and is a good administrator; is interested in people and attentive to their ideas; gives others a feeling of involvement; delegates easily and wisely; has a contagious sense of commitment; possesses excellent communication skills; is accessible and discriminating; and is willing to take on a tough challenge for the right cause.[2]

Each candidate should evidence some interest in the organization and prior experience with the type of activity, benefit, or special event being proposed. The names of others who have made a firm commitment to participate and the extent of staff experience and support personnel that will be available should be communicated during the interview.

Careful consideration of vice chair candidates is also required. Where possible, these candidates should be from among the top leadership group of current volunteers and donors, as proved by their commitment and record of service. This position should not be conferred; it should be earned by dedicated work and given as a reward. Each vice chair candidate should understand that selection for this assignment carries the possibility of nomination to chair the activity, benefit, or special event the following year or the year after that. The time spent as vice chair will assist the chairperson in leading the event successfully and will be preparatory for a future term as chair.

Those who nominated the final leadership candidates are usually the most qualified persons to assist in the recruitment process, which can take as long as the candidate search. Securing the nominees' acceptance is crucial; success is riding on their saying yes. Recruiting leaders and key volunteers is like soliciting important annual gifts. Personal contact will be the most successful method and is highly recommended. Telephone calls might work if a personal meeting is not possible. However, sending a letter to someone qualified for a leadership position is the least persuasive way to gain a commitment of his or her time, energy, and talent.

After the chairperson and one or two vice chairs have been recruited their work can be launched with a few basic steps:

1. Bring them together, outline the project fully, and identify all the other areas of responsibility that will need their attention

2. Provide this new leadership team with the list of all the other qualified candidates so that they can review them against the suggested tasks that remain.

3. Supply them with sound background information, and then let them make their own choices for whom they want to recruit and how best to sign up the balance of their committees.

In advance of recruiting volunteers, each role should be defined, and a brief job description should be written for each assignment area. Summary information should explain the overall purposes of the activity, benefit, or special event and its specific goals—in dollars, attendees, or similar measures of success.

As volunteers are recruited, a thank-you letter should be sent to each person who agrees to serve. This letter will serve as an official appointment, an acknowledgment of the commitment expressed, and a designation of an official assignment on the committee. Those who cannot serve should receive another letter thanking them for considering the request and expressing the hope that they may be able to join in next time. (This exchange is good cultivation; when asked again, they might be more willing to join.) Each of these letters should come from the chairperson of the activity or event, from another volunteer who has overall responsibility for annual giving, or perhaps from a member of the board of directors.

You should also plan an initial meeting of the new committee, which should be scheduled for a day close to the completion of recruiting. If you provide the date, time, and place of this first meeting at the time of invitation, these details will need to be ironed out ahead of time. Further preparations might include setting an agenda, providing light refreshments, and designating a moderator.

Some candidates might ask for a specific assignment or express a clear preference to avoid being asked to work in certain areas. For example, some volunteers love to work on designing the invitations and official program, preparing and tasting the menu and making the wine selections, or choosing the decorations and flowers. These tasks should be diplomatically placed in a perspective that centers on the more significant contribution made by helping to sell tickets, recruiting sponsors and underwriters, searching out donations and auction and raffle prizes, and meeting the essential fundraising assignments by a set deadline. Volunteers are needed in all of these capacities; the volunteer leaders must be trusted to sort out who will best serve in each area and to help them with completion of their duties as quickly as possible.

Orientation and Training

For all volunteers, including the leadership team, orientation and training are always valuable. The focus should be on the objectives of the activity, benefit, or special event and on the organization and committee structure needed to achieve success. Early projections of the budget, estimates of revenue sources, likely ticket sales volume, expected attendance, calendar openings and dates of competing events, staff capabilities and resources the nonprofit organization will provide, and other details requiring attention should all be ready for presentation at the first meeting. These early details help to identify areas of strength and weakness that need to be resolved, and where, how many, and at what levels of competence volunteers will be needed. Some volunteers may have prior experience that can benefit the planning stage. Others may not have had the opportunity to work with the organization before.

When these preliminaries have been presented, both the leadership and the organization are prepared to invite others to join in this affair. Everyone can help with the basic design of the activity, benefit, or special event, and it is always valuable to invite volunteers to help with planning a new activity from the beginning. Everyone's prior experiences will be highly useful as this new activity is designed for success. Experienced volunteers can (1) warn where likely problem areas and mistakes might occur, (2) clarify what pitfalls are to be avoided, and (3) offer realistic advice on operating details. Volunteers will begin to identify the activity as theirs and will take ownership of it.

Committee leaders will want these planning sessions to arrive at an early version of a fundamental action plan directed toward meeting the desired objectives. This preliminary plan will be shared with the nonprofit organization for review and approval. The orientation of volunteer committee members should begin with a general overview of the nonprofit organization and its mission and purpose. It should clarify the specific primary purposes or aims, the goals (in dollars or numbers), and the objectives (the features that can be achieved) that this activity, benefit, or special event seeks to accomplish, the plan of action and master schedule (time line) to be followed, and the planned use of any funds that will be raised. Typically, once these preliminary details are introduced, everyone is invited to add thoughts and suggestions. The activity, benefit, or special event is then ready to be turned over to the volunteer committee, which will proceed according to an agreed-on schedule.

Assignments

All the possible areas of support need to be identified early. Some tasks stand alone, but most are interrelated. Some completed assignments (for example, the design of a printed program) may remain in limbo for weeks because other work (the written content of the program) has not been done. A master schedule or time line is essential for each activity, benefit, or special event. Deadlines are a firm reality (see Exhibit 10-3), and certain tasks must be completed on time if others are to meet their deadlines. Support tasks are usually assigned to subcommittees, each of which has its own appointed chairperson, a vice chair or two, and a team of worker-assistants. Given the numerous details associated with an enterprise of this sort and the possibility that the chair or vice chair might not be present during hours when volunteers are working and have questions, a brief written description of each assignment is recommended. A simple paragraph can specify exactly what will be required, when the work must be done, and where the assignment fits into the time line.

Before volunteers accept assignments, they will want to know what they are being asked to do, who else is available to help them (or if they can recruit their own team), when their task must be completed, and what support they can count on from the committee, its leadership, and the staff at the nonprofit organization.

EXHIBIT 10-3 MODEL LIST OF DEADLINES FOR MASTER SCHEDULE

Assignment/Task	Deadline	Date Completed
1. Goals and objectives (set by board)	9 months prior	
2. Leadership selection	9 months prior	
3. Vice chair selection	8 months prior	
4. Subcommittee chairs	8 months prior	
5. First organizing meeting	7 months prior	
6. Training and orientation	7 months prior	
7. Budget completed/approved	7 months prior	
8. Sponsor/underwriter lists	7 months prior	
9. Resolution of critical details	6 months prior	
a. Date/time	6 months prior	
b. Place/space	6 months prior	
c. Theme	6 months prior	
d. Program plan	6 months prior	
e. Entertainment	6 months prior	
10. Begin monthly committee meetings	6 months prior	
11. Sponsor/underwriter letters	6 months prior	
12. Site inspection conducted	6 months prior	
13. Notice to area master calendar	6 months prior	
14. Invitation list	5 months prior	
15. "Save the Date" notice mailed	5 months prior	
16. Invitation design	5 months prior	
17. Sponsor/underwriter gifts/pledges	4–5 months prior	
18. Invitations delivered	4 months prior	
19. Invitations addressed	3 months prior	
20. Decoration/flower plans resolved	3 months prior	
21. First invitations mailed	2 months prior	
22. Media/press invitations sent	2 months prior	
23. Menu/wine tasting and resolution	2 months prior	
24. Second invitations mailed	5 weeks prior	
25. Program text/design finalized	5 weeks prior	
26. First draft agenda plan/script	4 weeks prior	
27. Phone-bank invitation follow-up	3 weeks prior	
28. Site plan walk-through	3 weeks prior	
29. Second draft agenda plan/script	2 weeks prior	
30. Media kit plan resolved	2 weeks prior	
31. Volunteer on-site duties confirmed	2 weeks prior	
32. Final program text completed	1 week prior	
33. Critique meeting held	1 month after	
34. Critique report sent to board	1 month after	

Subcommittee chairs and vice chairs should be members of the organizing committee or the executive committee. Subcommittee members need not attend these larger sessions, but the chairperson, a vice chair, or another representative should be present at each meeting to make a report on ongoing activities and the progress of the overall activity or event. Coordination of all the necessary details is an essential function of the project's leadership; monitoring progress, an assignment that usually belongs to professional and support staff, also requires attention. The risk in failing to maintain good communications with everyone is that duplicate efforts, mistakes, failures, and other errors will surface after it is too late to head off their harmful effects.

Regular meetings of the organizing committee should begin six to nine months in advance of the date of each activity, benefit, or special event. The committee's purposes are to organize leaders and teams to handle all of the assignments (see Exhibit 10-4) and to be able to monitor everyone's progress according to the master schedule. One meeting of the full committee each month is usually adequate; subcommittees will establish their own work schedule, as necessary. Teamwork is the preferred method to manage a large group of tasks assigned to various volunteers. Committees, holding regular meetings, are necessary to keep everyone informed and motivated, to spread the work among many volunteers, and to keep everything and everyone moving forward on schedule. It is much harder to manage an event if there are not regular opportunities to bring everyone together to review progress and make decisions on the issues that require resolution. Within the group, consensus on major decisions is important, as is agreement on style, price, location, time of day, time of year, and a host of other important details regarding the activity, benefit, or special event. Once these details are resolved, the work will go forward more easily.

Leadership Development

Managing an enterprise with many volunteers, each with a different assignment, demands that someone be in charge. Leadership of a committee of volunteers is a unique skill. The all-important duty of the chairperson is to be able to orchestrate different individuals toward a common objective, giving everyone room to play a part, managing to get everyone to complete an assignment on schedule, and directing everyone's enthusiasm

EXHIBIT 10-4   SAMPLE ORGANIZATION CHART
FOR VOLUNTEER-LED COMMITTEE
TO PREPARE AN ACTIVITY,
BENEFIT, OR SPECIAL EVENT

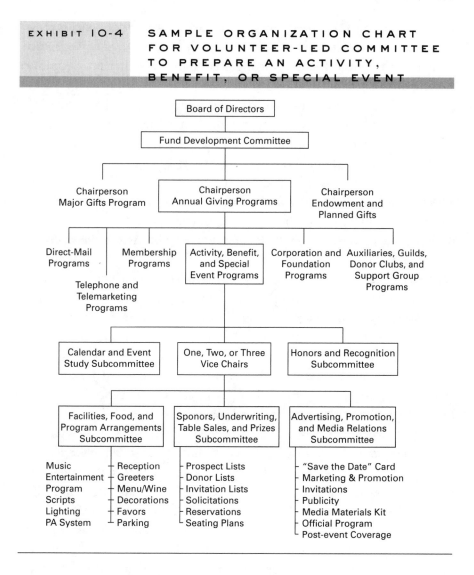

and motivation toward achieving a success. Leading and managing a committee that is responsible for putting on a public activity, benefit, or special event might be compared to being a conductor of a symphony orchestra. Between 40 and 80 musicians will be recruited to play, but each plays a separate instrument and has a different level of experience and knowledge about the music. Each player wants an opportunity to play a solo part that will feature his or her talent. Rehearsals are required to bring the group together, to practice the music, and to learn to play with perfect synchronization so that they can achieve the best quality of concert possible. Everyone must follow the conductor's direction and play the parts as written in the musical score. Making great music together is a far greater challenge than playing a solo to perfection. The group preparation takes practice, patience, and hard work. The live performance gives immediate results. The public will express appreciation of all the hard work by buying tickets to fill the house and with their applause after each piece on the concert program and when the performance is concluded.

Committee work is one of the best ways to identify and train future leaders of volunteers. Each volunteer who accepts a committee assignment has an opportunity to learn how to be an integral part of a voluntary work project, how to perform new tasks, and how to work with others. Volunteers do not come to an organization pretrained in exactly the fashion each organization needs or with mastery of the skills with which assignments must be performed. Many people willing to give their time will be satisfied being working members of the team, doing their assigned part, and sharing in the results. They enjoy the project and the company of the other volunteers, and they believe in the cause they are serving. A few others are willing to provide leadership and direction to their assigned area, to delegate the work to others who wish to learn, and to supervise these assignments. Experience is a great teacher; leadership skills can be learned.

Those who enjoy the work they are asked to perform and are willing to take some responsibility for its completion should be invited to serve again. Those who work well with others and demonstrate that they can encourage others to perform their tasks as required are leadership candidates. They should be asked again and perhaps given more responsibility. A leadership development program, with a variety of job assignments for those who are qualified and eligible, should be formulated and offered to selected people. Without a follow-up assignment, the most competent and experienced volunteers are likely to leave the organization and seek one that has a greater need for their talents and willingness to work.

Staff Support

Volunteers will require some level of staff support. The exact amount and extent depend on their prior experience with the organization; their knowledge of its culture, style, and history, their training and orientation to their specific assignment; and their understanding of the purpose and objectives of the activity, benefit, or special event. Prior experiences in these assignments have taught volunteers where they need assistance and what kind of help they will require to succeed with their tasks. Staff must remain flexible in their response to the variety of support volunteers may require. They must be experienced and knowledgeable enough to be able to assist volunteers with the specific area assigned, without performing the duties for them. In a successful committee of team players, the support staff are identified as advisers to the project. Volunteers can expect to receive the staff support they require, and the staff can expect volunteers to conduct their assignments with energy and independent effort. For a volunteer to accept an assignment and then expect the staff to do the work is not acceptable. The staff may have little choice but to fill the work gap because the task has to be met. Committee leaders should be made aware of this kind of nonperformance; they should not be led to believe that the volunteer is fulfilling all the assignments independent of staff help.

Performance Evaluation

Everyone performs better when someone else will be measuring the results. Volunteers in nonprofit organizations do not expect any degree of personal performance evaluation, which is correct. Their task will be evaluated by their peers, who will also review the overall success of the activity, benefit, or special event. Judgment of one's peers is an adequate motive that can be pointed out to volunteers when they accept their assignments. Other forms of analysis also can assist everyone involved. The objectives are to be fair, to not embarrass anyone personally, and to identify areas where the task or project can be improved. All members of the committee should be asked to participate in a critique meeting following the project's completion (see Exhibit 10-3). This final meeting is an excellent time to express praise for individual and collective accomplishments.

Volunteers who judge their own results are usually honest and fair in suggesting areas for improvement, especially when the suggestions come from the volunteer in charge of a function. Each assignment area should be reviewed in turn, and suggestions about future roles and the desired performance should be welcomed. This review should also be forthright in assessing all the purposes and attributes for the activity, benefit, or special event, including whether the function should be continued and, if so, what recommendations are valid for its goals next time and for its volunteer leadership candidates. Agreed-on recommendations should be recorded for use by the next committee (and shared with the next group of volunteers assigned to these tasks), and the critique report should be forwarded to the board of directors.

Honors and Recognition

It is essential to provide proper recognition and reward for volunteers who support activities, benefits, or special events. This duty is so important that an honors committee should be created for every project. The multiple purposes and attributes that can be accomplished through activities, benefits, and special events are of enormous value to a nonprofit organization, which can never produce or achieve these results on its own. The board of directors should establish suitable guidelines for honors and recognition for each project in which volunteers are invited to participate. As has been mentioned earlier in this book, the certificate, plaque, or personal gift that is presented to a volunteer is not what counts the most, although these gifts are appreciated. Of true value to volunteers are the proper occasion at which they are recognized for what they have done, the people (especially the organization's leadership) who are present and express thanks, and the honest feelings of appreciation and gratitude that are conveyed. For example, if each volunteer received a letter of appointment to an assignment from a board member when the project began, that board member should now participate in the honors and recognition ceremony. The board should also send a special thank-you letter to each volunteer who served in a leadership position.

Everyone likes to be thanked for work done, especially when it has been done for others and done voluntarily. Volunteers will not return if they believe their efforts have not been appreciated. The challenge to nonprofit organizations is to thank their volunteers properly and thoroughly. When honors and recognition are established as a visible part of each activity, benefit, and special event, volunteers know that their efforts were seen and were honestly appreciated, and they will be more than willing to serve again and again.

DEFINITIONS AND DIFFERENCES

Before beginning the separate examination of activities, benefits, and special events, I offer here the two approaches that I have chosen to distinguish these types of functions from one another. The first approach is to separate them based on their definitions and purposes. What are activities, benefits, and special events, and why are they held?

	Definition	Purpose
Activities	Occasions whose chief goals are to communicate person-to-person, to convey a message, or to demonstrate a worthwhile charity. These goals are carried out in lectures, meetings, rallies, tours, and other forms of public gatherings. There is no charge or fee to participants who attend and receive the information or service provided.	To gather people together to inform them or provide them with a service. There may be no fundraising goal other than to further good relationships.
Benefits	Occasions that request attendance, for a fee or ticket charge, but offer in exchange some form of entertainment.	To stage a function for public enjoyment and to provide financial support to the organization's cause.
Special events	Occasions for which no admission fee is charged because the official business to be conducted needs a crowd.	To convene people for business or official endeavors such as an annual meeting or school graduation.

Nonprofit organizations often stage several versions of all of these functions during each year. Guests who attend, and others who receive invitations, are likely to interchange the terms activity, benefit, and special event. All three types of function share similar goals—to communicate, to entertain, and to conduct some business (which may include fundraising). I distinguish them from one another according to their primary purposes, which is a decision made by their sponsors. Most of their other features are added to help attract a crowd.

The second approach I use to distinguish activities, benefits, and special events from one another is to pose four questions about each:

1. What details are required for success?
2. How can each aid annual giving?
3. How and where can volunteers help?
4. How can success be measured?

The replies will address how each function contributes to the annual giving program. Whatever they may be called and however these similar functions may be put to use, activities, benefits, and special events possess different features and attributes that make them useful to an annual giving program's continuous success.

ACTIVITIES

The primary purpose of an activity is to achieve public participation. Attendance at an activity is encouraged through invitations, advertisements, promotions, and the like. Potential guests may learn about an activity from their family, friends, business associates, and social contacts. Activities should be scheduled at times when those invited are likely to be able to attend. The sponsor has a message to share or something to offer every person who attends; the activity should get right to the point as soon as it begins. Those who respond make a decision to attend so that they can hear the message, an important fact to consider when attempting to understand and to forecast public response. Why will people attend? To hear the message, to be seen, to learn something, or to receive something (a public service) that is promised.

As an illustration of how a variety of activities can be used, hospitals' message of AIDS prevention can be communicated through multiple channels. Information about AIDS prevention must be transmitted repeatedly, in various forms, in an effort to reach all of the hospital's targeted audience. This objective is too massive for one activity or message medium; multiple means of transmission are needed, to handle constant repetitions of the same message. The next objective, influencing human behavior, is even more difficult. Mass communication techniques, even in this age of instant news traveling everywhere on the Internet, are dedicated to trying to motivate people and stimulate them to action. Influencing human behavior is much like a crusade. To be effective, hospitals must first prepare a variety of activities that will help to communicate their messages about AIDS prevention—lectures, meetings, videos, speakers bureaus, rallies, perhaps even tours of hospital areas where AIDS treatment is provided.

Delivering health care to any community involves more than taking care of those who get sick. To be maximally effective, hospitals must become proactive, taking on ancillary activities and expanding the available channels and modes of communication. Parents-to-be, preparing for their new arrival, might be offered classes on how to care for their newborn. The hospital might set up mobile clinics in shopping centers to administer flu shots, screen for diabetes or glaucoma, or hand out skin cancer prevention advice and free sunscreen lotion. Hospital staff might visit offices, plants, and schools to lecture about the risk factors in heart disease (to pick only one topic). They might conduct tests for high blood pressure, excess weight, cholesterol levels, and stress, and provide instruction and information materials on early warning signs of heart disease. Exercise, smoking cessation, healthy eating habits, and proper rest can be promoted in continuous running videos and in posters and handouts. All of these activities, repeated over months and years, are necessary to get the attention of the public.

One such campaign is having success: the incidence of heart disease in America has decreased within the past 25 years. The consistent message, warning of the risk factors in heart disease, has been heard. Conversely, consistent and widespread messages about the dangers and risks of smoking have yet to reduce either the incidence or attractiveness of cigarettes to teenagers. Such an enormous overall effort is expensive, but making people healthier is worth the cost. One might wonder why it is so difficult to get people to pay attention to their own lifestyle and to protect their own health. Preventing disease contributes to increased productivity, a longer and happier life, and less need for expensive health-care intervention (hospitalization) later on. Message-delivering activities are now second nature to hospitals and other health-care institutions across the nation, because they do raise people's awareness. But hospitals had to learn how to use these activities for best effect.

When a nonprofit organization must reach selected audiences, it has to rely on the same communication channels it uses for all of its other messages. An invitation is reliable for getting people's attention and stimulating the desired response because an invitation is a personal message. Nonprofit organizations offer community benefits to the public, but lack the financial resources to get all their messages to everyone intended to receive them. Some well-known activities will attract a high response without much extra work. Examples are the rich variety of classes, lectures, exhibits, and cultural and athletic events that are held by colleges and universities, galleries, libraries, museums, performing arts centers, theaters, and similar organizations. These activities are known to be open to the public and to have value for those who attend. Except when an admission fee may be required, there are no restrictions or special qualifications to attend. A person has only to decide to go and arrive in time to participate. For galleries, libraries, and museums, attendance fulfills their very purpose. All who choose to attend these activities receive the information prepared for everyone. Those who do not attend are aware that the activity remains open to them at another time; they have only to decide when they wish to attend.

Activities with larger attendance can become more complicated to plan and execute than others. Reservation forms may be needed when a location's capacity limits how many people can attend at any one time. Popular activities may require extra planning for parking, crowd control, refreshments, and other details. Expenses will be incurred, and some prior experience with these detailed arrangements may be needed to achieve the desired objectives for the activity.

Activities are opportunities to improve a nonprofit organization's public image and to enhance public understanding of its mission to fulfill charitable purposes. Activities showcase the programs and services offered for public benefit and help to improve an organization's reputation among the people invited to attend. These same people may eventually choose to support the organization in other ways beyond attendance. Media attention is an important priority because extended communications offer the bonus of spreading the message to those who were unable to attend the activity.

When so many positive attributes will result, early planning must not neglect the time and attention needed to develop a well-planned, well-coordinated publicity campaign to support each activity. The objective is twofold: (1) to advertise the activity in order to deliver the primary message about the need, cause, or charitable purpose the nonprofit organization espouses, and (2) to spread the word widely about the activity itself, promoting interest and attendance while letting the public know the organization is alive and kicking and is working on their behalf.

> Press, radio, and TV coverage will give you credibility and legitimacy. Most radio stations and many TV stations are willing to broadcast public service announcements of community events. Ordinarily, these announcements are 15-, 30-, or 60-second spots resembling commercials; therefore, the announcement must be brief. When writing the announcement for the station, include only the who, what, why, where, and when. . . . In addition to media coverage, other ways to publicize an event include posters, flyers, handbills, buttons, balloons, marquee messages, and store counter displays in banks, cafes, and other viable outlets. Excellent publicity can also be obtained by getting banks, utility companies, and department stores to let you include a "statement stuffer" in their monthly statements.[3]

Activities can expand rather easily. A once-a-month lecture series that features interesting speakers can grow overnight into a major activity if the speaker, who may have been selected months earlier, suddenly becomes famous. An auditorium with multiple audiovisual aids may be needed, and the speaker may be asking for a generous honorarium plus travel and living expenses. Such good fortune is a nice advantage; a routine activity has the potential to achieve several extra attributes as bonus values—wider media coverage, a larger audience, evidence of the urgent need for volunteer help, major image enhancement, donor cultivation potential (especially if selected donors are invited to a private pre- or postlecture reception with the speaker), improved market position, new member recruiting, and much more.

What Details Are Required for Success?

For starters, common courtesy. The people invited should be treated as guests in the organization's "home." Advance arrangements for their participation must include adequate parking, door attendants, comfortable seating, refreshments, a program with an agenda, and information about the organization. Every activity requires planning, preparation, personalization, and attention to a myriad of details; makes good use of volunteers; and needs a bit of luck to be carried off without a hitch (see Appendix B for a master checklist). Attention to these details will make guests feel welcome and allow them to fully appreciate the activity. Invitation lists, an important detail, must be guided by the selection criteria. Checking the calendar carefully for religious holidays and other sensitive dates also is required so as not to offend any potential guests, sponsors, or underwriters. Anyone who is interested may be welcome at a public activity, but a number of others deserve to be invited as special guests, whether or not they can be present. Friend-raising begins with personal invitations that are designed to lead to involvement; involvement results in participation and can yield gift support.

How Can Activities Aid Annual Giving?

Donors are more inclined to make annual gifts to organizations they know something about. After an organization has invited people to be guests at several of its activities, it will know how they replied to each invitation and whether they attended. If they did attend and found the activity worthwhile, their willingness to consider financial support has multiplied. Activities communicate effectively to all those who participate. Because the guests are often people who live nearby, they can return again and again. To convert interested people into donors may require only asking them for a gift. All the annual giving methods presented in Chapters 2 through 9 can then be put to use. The request can be tied to the activities they have attended or have been invited to attend, with a few simple messages:

- Tell them how these programs are linked to the mission of the organization.
- Explain the programs and services in terms of what the organization has accomplished for others and its commitment to continue to do so.
- Tell them how gift money is a way to achieve improvements in the volume and quality of programs and services delivered to the community.
- Using as an example the type of activity they just attended, show how funds received can be used to repeat the activity, to improve on the quality of speakers, and to maintain the facilities used.

When personal invitations are involved, the mailing list becomes a reasonable prospect list for annual gift solicitation *after* the activity. A bit of homework will reveal something about who is on the invitation list, and an appeal message matched to their interests can be prepared. It helps to re-

move from solicitation lists the names of those who are already donors—
and the name of anyone who has asked *not* to be solicited. One to two
weeks should pass between the activity and the gift appeal. Solicitation timing is always a delicate judgment call. The memory of the activity must still
be fresh, but the activity should not appear to have been staged just to set
up guests for a money touch! If the activity is successful in building a faithful following, the invitation list can become the heart of a new membership association. Common courtesy is the best guide; people who are
treated well will respond with friendship and support for years to come.

How and Where Can Volunteers Help?

A variety of tasks and a multitude of details are involved in arranging and
carrying out activities for the public. Most nonprofit organizations cannot
afford to hire professional and support staff just to manage activities; employee positions are fully committed to providing programs and services.
Employees who have paid responsibilities, however, can be asked occasionally to volunteer some of their personal time to help their employer.
Requests to employees to volunteer their time must be carefully limited, or
the employees will feel they are being put upon. If they believe these tasks
are within their job descriptions, they may correctly ask to be paid for these
extra hours at an overtime rate; volunteerism should not be, legitimately,
extra work for them.

Volunteers who believe that their time, energy, talents, and contacts are
of value must be entrusted with duties and responsibilities that require a
high level of performance—actual leadership and direction of an activity,
selection of other volunteers who will help, and delegation of specific duties to perform. Other volunteer tasks may be less demanding or may appear to be minor work projects; all must be identified as necessary for the
event to be successful.

A committee system is recommended to provide some order and structure to any activity (see Exhibit 10-4). A committee is a democratic system
for planning, preparing, and conducting activities. People are quite comfortable with committee work; it is a normal experience. They also understand that working together as a team is how a committee functions best;
committee members join together and share a sense of true responsibility
for their overall performance. A committee system also helps a nonprofit

organization to use its volunteers well. Activities allow volunteers to manage themselves toward accomplishing a valued assignment in support of "their" organization. The tasks volunteers may identify for themselves include all of the following:

- Assist in planning the activity
- Assist in making all the arrangements
- Provide names for the invitation list
- Prepare and address the invitations
- Promote attendance in the community
- Contact the media and enlist their coverage
- Bring friends and colleagues to the activity
- Greet all guests on arrival
- Evaluate the results
- Assist in planning the next activity

To succeed with volunteers in any assignment, a nonprofit organization must be willing to entrust to them the work it asks them to perform. The organization is also entrusting them with its good name and reputation, which volunteers respect and will honor. Some volunteers come with a lot of experience in performing these assignments; these are primarily the people an organization seeks. Volunteers who are trained, motivated, and well-led will perform well. A nonprofit organization's professional staff provides guidance in identifying, recruiting, training, managing, and supporting volunteers who can lead and direct others. Working through a committee system, volunteers can plan and carry out a variety of activities with high success each year.

The organization must identify the goals and objectives for each of the activities it will ask volunteers to conduct, and provide clearly stated policies and guidelines to be followed by everyone involved (see Exhibit 10-5). The board of directors, professional and administrative staff, and employees should appoint volunteers to their assignments, identify and often select those who will be chairpersons, ask for progress reports during the preparation stages, and require a critique report after the activity is concluded. Volunteers must understand that clear accountability is their obligation to the organization. In their working partnership, both parties must appreci-

EXHIBIT 10-5   POLICIES AND GUIDELINES FOR
ACTIVITIES, BENEFITS, AND
SPECIAL EVENTS

New Activity, Benefit, or Special Event

1. Primary purpose(s), goals, and objectives
2. Availability of volunteers; number required
3. Identified volunteer leadership
4. Marketing and communications attributes
5. Community relations and community benefits attributes
6. Conflicts with known calendar of local functions
7. List of sponsor and underwriter prospects
8. Estimate of attendance and ticket sales revenue
9. Preliminary budget (revenue and direct costs)
10. Staff support required; prior staff experience
11. Potential for conflict with ongoing annual giving programs
12. Review and approval by board of directors

Approved and Existing Activity, Benefit, or Special Event

1. All of the above criteria *plus*
2. Critique report from previous function(s)
3. Final report on prior budget, net proceeds, and name of project funded with proceeds
4. Marketing and communications assessment
5. Community relations and community benefits assessment
6. Preliminary operating budget with estimate of net proceeds
7. Priority project for use of net proceeds identified
8. Potential for new leadership and volunteer development
9. Potential advantages of ongoing annual giving programs
10. Potential for volunteer and donor honors and recognition

ate that close coordination, cooperation, and communication are required for success in working together.

How to Measure Success

Nonprofit organizations should set the standards of performance for all their activities. The board of directors should establish and clarify expectations for each activity to be carried out in the name of the organization. The criteria to be used for performance evaluation should be prepared and approved by the board, identified and expressed as specific goals to be achieved, and made known to those who will be evaluated. Unrealistic expectations neither encourage nor inspire volunteers. A balance must be struck and a consensus achieved in order for appropriate measurement criteria to be accepted.

Because activities are directed at people and intended to elicit their response in some way, measurement should focus on how the process performed as well as on the numerical results. Evaluations should never be punitive exercises. They are held after the fact; they are most valuable for future planning purposes and as learning experiences. Here are some measures that can be used in performance analysis of an activity:

1. Were the goals and objectives clearly stated?
2. Were leadership candidates recruited early enough?
3. Were committee members trained for their tasks?
4. Were adequate staff and budget support provided to the committee?
5. Were there a communications channel between volunteers and the organization's leadership?
6. Was the date selected in conflict with any religious holiday or the established calendar of other, similar activities in the community?
7. Were advertising and promotion communications adequate in relation to public response and attendance?
8. Were the names and addresses on the invitation list accurate?
9. Were the invitations mailed on schedule?
10. What percentage of invited guests attended?
11. Was a record made of attendance by the special guests who were invited (name, address, telephone, e-mail address) and their sponsor?
12. Were the facilities adequate to support the speaker, the program, and the audience?
13. If media coverage was important, what results were achieved?
14. Were postactivity assignments completed as planned?
15. Did the committee hold a critique session after the activity?
16. Was the committee's critique report delivered to the board of directors?

Success can be measured in many ways. A complete list of appropriate evaluation criteria should be prepared in advance for every activity, to clarify for everyone involved the areas that have been identified as important goals.

BENEFITS

Benefits are best known for their popularity with participants and volunteers, their high visibility, and the money they raise for charity—usually in that order. They share some of the primary objectives of activities: they communicate widely and they motivate people to respond with attendance. Benefits add monetary goals for worthy purposes. A money goal requires (1) considerably more attention to fundraising techniques and (2) exact financial management of all expenses so that maximum net proceeds can be delivered to the nonprofit organization. Marilyn Breutlinger and Judith Weiss[4] expressed their opinion of benefits this way:

> [T]he only way to determine the degree of success a benefit attains is to establish clearly defined financial and promotional goals in advance. If we have one message to convey, it's that benefits are indeed a business. Unless you approach them in a businesslike manner, your charitable intentions may go out the window. Therefore, to further refine the definition of a benefit, our "special occasions" must also meet the following requirements:
>
> 1. *They make significant amounts of money.* Net profits (from ticket sales, contributions and other income, minus expenses) should be no less than $50,000 or 10 percent of the organization's annual fundraising budget. An event that earns less than this is not worth the time, effort, and expense of putting it on.
>
> 2. *They have a high ticket-price structure,* relative to the actual cost of food, entertainment and incidentals. These costs should be reduced by underwriting and by the donation of professional managerial and clerical services by volunteers.
>
> 3. *Tickets are presold,* through personal solicitation by committee members. Walk-ins or box-office sales are not anticipated, except for those benefits that offer a large number of "performance only" tickets at considerably lower price than the complete package.
>
> 4. *They are deliberately targeted to a well-defined market segment* that includes those individuals who can afford and are willing to pay a premium for an evening out in order to demonstrate a high level of support for a worthy cause.
>
> 5. *They promote community involvement and continuing support for the sponsoring organization,* not only through publicity surrounding the event, but through a planned campaign that includes follow-up contact with individuals introduced to the organization through the benefit.

6. *They are carefully planned and executed, right down to the last detail,* so that the event itself goes smoothly and nothing is left to chance. Those who attend have a satisfying experience, those who hear about it afterward wish they had been there, and all concerned go away with a favorable impression of the sponsoring organization.

Careful planning is essential to selecting the kind of benefit that has just the right style to inspire contributions and attendance from the people who can afford to participate. Benefits have an inherent potential to expand as preparations progress, chiefly because of the energy and enthusiasm of the volunteers who become truly involved. Committee leaders must be alert to the effect new ideas can have on the overall plan, especially on the budget. Clear guidelines will help to keep everyone focused on the plan (see Exhibit 10-6). To be successful, benefits must appeal to some of the people all of the time. Benefits can be planned, prepared, conducted, and evaluated in weeks, months, or years, depending on their history, tradition, magnitude, and complexity, and on the availability of adequate numbers of trained and dedicated volunteers. Once a benefit is held, most organizations begin preparations for the next one, which is why benefits fit well in the overall program for annual giving.

> No event should be undertaken without careful thought. Every angle should be considered. This is best done by a planning committee composed of dedicated individuals who understand the organization's needs and objectives. They should know that almost every fundraising event takes a lot of work, many transactions, and a lot of volunteer help. Since volunteers have a limited amount of time to spend on any organization, the goal is to maximize the dollar return per every volunteer hour expended. For example, if the need is for $10,000, it may be a better investment of time to ask ten prospects for $1,000 each than try to sell 400 dinner tickets at $25 each.[5]

Benefits are much more challenging to conduct than activities because of the financial obligation to produce a profit. More time and attention must be paid to the invitation and the invitations list, to the choice of facilities and their decoration, to having a program that entertains enjoyably, to the menu and beverages, and so on. (See Appendix B for a master checklist.) Activities are a function to be carried out; benefits are a performance to be staged. Employees may be asked to plan and stage a benefit

EXHIBIT 10-6   THIRTEEN RULES TO GUARANTEE
SUCCESS WITH BENEFITS

1. Do no benefit that will net less than 50 percent of gross income.
2. Eighty percent of the tickets should be sold before the invitation goes out.
3. Do not expect the invitation to sell the benefit. Mailing to a list of people who know and like the organization will produce a response of about 2 percent. A mailing to people unfamiliar with the organization (a purchased list) probably will not produce enough income to pay for the mailing.
4. Plan to sell about five tickets for every volunteer who is actively selling tickets through personal solicitation.
5. The vast majority of people who will attend the benefit will come from the organization's family, so:
   (a) Make sure the benefit is within the means of the majority of them.
   (b) Make sure it will be of interest to most of them.
   (c) Make sure it will take place at a location and a time that are convenient for them.
6. Do not mimic another organization's traditional benefit. A traditional benefit sells itself; the new benefit will not, and a comparison will make the new benefit appear to be a failure.
7. Never hire a promoter who charges a percentage of gross receipts as a fee to conduct a benefit.
8. Never ask a sponsor or underwriter to subsidize attendance (i.e., reduce the price of the benefit tickets because some expenses are being underwritten).
9. Never say something is tax-deductible if it is not. Seek the advice of a tax accountant or tax attorney on how to explain to purchasers of benefit tickets the IRS regulations that limit the charitable deduction amount to only a portion of the price of the benefit tickets.
10. Always prepare a detailed budget in advance, and stick to it. Do not guess what the expenses will be; ask for quotations on prices and hold vendors to them.
11. Make the benefit fun so that people will want to attend next year. To do so:
    (a) Do not try force people to spend more money than they expected.
    (b) Do not belabor them with speeches about how great the organization is.
    (c) Do tell them how great they are for participating actively.
    (d) Do tell them how the proceeds will be used and what good works are expected.
12. Design the benefit to make friends first, then raise funds.
13. Do not decide unilaterally what the organization needs money for. Ask the organization about currently urgent needs, then raise funds for that priority.

Source: Adapted from Frank R. Hall, "Guidelines for a New Special Event," St. Joseph Health System, Orange, CA, with permission.

alone, but complete success can be achieved only through volunteer leadership and participation. Benefits, more than either activities or special events, are public enterprises and attractions because their primary goal of raising money demands that they fulfill high public expectations.

Financial goals aid the participants in defining success, and in achieving a sense of reward and accomplishment at the termination of the event. Specific goals stimulate and challenge participants to stretch imagination and efforts beyond their intended limits. If the committee has invested themselves in the benefit effort, they will desire the esteem associated with a job well done, and will "get" or "give" the resources required to meet that goal.[6]

Benefits are also more of a business venture and require commercial decisions not usually needed for activities or special events. Benefits require negotiating for prices and contracts; recruiting in-kind gifts and donated services; seeking contributions of products to be used in direct support of required budget expenses or as prizes and auction items; sales effort to secure sponsorships, underwriting, and table sales; and astute expense management.

Certain costs are highly specialized. For example, you may want to take out liability insurance on an event to protect your organization from unavoidable accidents. Other costs often are not normally considered, but should be. For example, rarely will an organization identify costs of a regular employee's time. If a salaried staff person devotes half time for a 3-month period in planning an event, it is the unusual organization that earmarks this portion of the staff person's salary as an expense of the event. If this were done more frequently to reflect actual costs, many organizations probably would not undertake fundraising events, because costs would appear to be excessive.[7]

Benefits are intense fiscal projects from start to finish. There is no room here for inappropriate fiscal management, inattentive accounting, or private inurement practices; to permit any of these is to encourage failure and the potential for IRS "Intermediate Sanctions."

Benefits also offer a variety of business promotion opportunities that can be shared with local area businesspeople, companies, partnerships, and firms. These expanded contacts, which build relationships that can aid other annual giving and major-gift fundraising goals, are a result of the commercial nature of benefits. Company executives can be asked to serve as volunteer leaders on the benefit planning committee. The businesses, corporations, and firms receive *quid pro quo* exchanges from advertising, marketing, public relations, and promotions, plus the civic and community-relations visibility that corporate sponsorship and underwriting gifts can deliver in exchange. When business and corporate leaders are involved, expectations for professional management of benefits are higher because company names and the names of their executives are going to be widely broadcast. These features are all on the plus side. To examine the potential negatives, only a look at the law is required.

Laws, Regulations, Licenses, and Permits

Because soliciting money from the public is a part of every benefit, every such function must observe local ordinances. Legal requirements vary among the several states, counties, and cities, and time and patience are needed to search them out. Most authorities require the sponsoring organization to file an application in advance of conducting the benefit. A permit is issued after providing certain details about the planned benefit and paying a filing fee ($25 to $50 for each benefit). Some jurisdictions may add specific requirements for traffic control and police security, site inspection and approval by the fire marshal, and on-site paramedics. If alcohol is to be served or sold, a one-day liquor license might be required from the local alcohol and beverage control authority. If the benefit will involve any form of sweepstakes, lottery, or other game of chance, or will be a Las Vegas or Monte Carlo night, more than one regulatory authority may specify operating procedures. They will have a keen interest in fiscal control procedures in particular. A complete financial statement showing all income and expenses will need to be filed following the benefit. A tax may be assessed on a percentage of the net proceeds.

The federal government becomes an invited guest at every benefit because a charitable contribution deduction may be allowed for a portion of the price of the ticket. The nonprofit organization is responsible to inform donors *on the invitation* what amount of the ticket price is deductible (the rest cannot be claimed as a tax deduction).[8] This deduction figure is the difference between the amount of "material value" received by the donor who attends the event (cost of food, beverages, and favors such as taking home the floral centerpiece) and the price of the ticket. Federal tax rules on deductions for auctions are clear: No deduction is allowed except where the value of the auction item is exceeded by the bid price. No tax deduction is allowed for raffle tickets and door prizes.

Another area of increased legal sensitivity is the use of professional (also called paid or commercial) solicitors who can be hired to conduct fundraising benefits (see Chapter 5). Several court cases have resulted when state authorities pursued fraudulent and deceitful solicitors whose operating method was to conduct benefits in the name of a nonprofit organization. These solicitors often propose to make all of the arrangements for a benefit—sell the tickets, book the talent, sell the advertisements, print the program book, handle all the money, pay all the bills (including their fee for marketing, promotional, and professional services)—and deliver a check for the net proceeds to the organization. There are several problems with such a proposal; chief among them is the amount of the net proceeds, which is usually less than 20 percent of gross revenue.[9]

More than a few nonprofit organizations have experienced benefits conducted as illegal enterprises or scams. The public is increasingly suspicious of high-pressure sales techniques (telephone "boiler rooms" for ticket sales with "runners" to collect the money). This kind of benefit activity hinders all the efforts of sponsors of legitimate benefits. The nonprofits' volunteer or part-time paid callers may use the phone to encourage public participation, only to be met by suspicion.

Several states and local jurisdictions have well-defined regulations just for this narrow area of fundraising practice: They require annual registration of any organization, business, firm, or private contractor who engages in professional, "paid," or commercial solicitation of the public. A registration fee, posting of a bond, and a copy of each contract for service to a nonprofit organization will be required before a "paid" solicitor may begin to solicit the public on behalf of a charitable organization. The contract, signed by an officer of the nonprofit organization, must disclose details about the benefit, such as how the solicitor will be paid (straight fee, a commission for each sale, or a percentage of net proceeds). The contract must also specify where the money will be received and deposited, who has approval authority for expenses, and who can sign checks. A complete financial statement must be filed within 30 days after the benefit, and all these details must be made public upon request. Behind such extensive regulations are abusive practices by entrepreneurs who trade on the public's confidence and trust in charitable giving. To be fair, a number of legal and legitimate professional fundraising firms and solicitors provide complete services to stage a benefit. However, suspicions about their trustworthiness persist because of others' illicit practices.

The board of directors has the responsibility to be certain that every legal and regulatory requirement associated with benefit fundraising is fully and completely observed. Much is at risk, beginning with public confidence and trust in the name of the organization. No board member, volunteer, donor, or staff member wants to read in the morning paper or see on television that a lawsuit has been filed against their nonprofit organization or against the firm they hired to conduct a fundraising benefit. The media appear to have a high interest in reporting scandal and abuse, and will put special focus on the fees paid to solicitors whose purposes appear to be more directed at attempting to defraud the public of its money than at raising money for charitable purposes. If illegal acts are proven in a court case, the subsequent legal action could result in IRS intermediate sanctions, fines, or even the loss of the nonprofit organization's tax-exempt status. The public loses, the charity loses, and a valid fundraising method loses; only the paid solicitor wins. As a general rule, when looking this gift horse in the mouth, one should examine every tooth!

What Details Are Required for Success?

Strict financial management that will produce the highest net proceeds possible for charity is essential. If a benefit does not possess the ability to yield *at least* 50 percent of its gross revenue after direct costs to the nonprofit organization, it should be challenged to prove it can do so or be discarded. Each new benefit should not be held immediately accountable to this level of success; a minimum of three years should be adequate to achieve this goal. The 50 percent standard requires that budget be prepared, approved, and used to manage the benefit (see Exhibit 10-7). The budget will help keep everyone's attention on the primary objective. This fiscal requirement also helps to achieve a clear understanding that each benefit should be able to document its potential to achieve the 50 percent level of performance after three years. If it cannot, it should be set aside for another benefit that can deliver at that level.

An organization's officers should pay close attention to benefits sponsored by other organizations in the community and to those sponsored by outsiders to benefit other organizations. Many civic, community, and service organizations that conduct benefits for charitable purposes are committed to civic improvements that will help to meet community needs and are led by responsible community residents, but there are others that are in business for themselves. (See Exhibit 10-8 for professional guidance[10] on

EXHIBIT 10-7   BENEFIT EVENT BUDGET WORKSHEET

Sample Budget Worksheet for an Activity, Benefit, or Special Event

		Approved Budget	Actual Expenses
A.	*Projected Cash Receipts (Revenue)*		
	Ticket sales (400 at $100/couple)	$40,000	$42,000
	Sponsor gifts ($250, $500)	6,750	7,500
	Underwriter gifts ($1,000, $2,500)	10,000	8,000
	Auction receipts	4,000	4,350
	Raffle receipts	1,500	1,250
	Contributors	1,000	500
	Donated materials (gifts-in-kind)	(3,500)	(2,250)
	Subtotal	$63,250	$63,600
B.	*Projected Cash Expenses (Costs)*		
	Cash expenditures (itemized list)		
	Printing	$7,650	$7,880
	Postage	450	365
	Facility use fees	1,000	1,000
	Food and beverages	9,500	10,555
	Decorations	2,500	1,800
	Flowers	1,000	‹800›
	Favors	1,000	‹1,000›
	Entertainment	3,500	3,500
	Miscellaneous costs	1,000	350
	Auction/Raffle prizes purchased	1,000	‹450›
	Temporary staff hired	-0-	600
	Consultant fees	-0-	-0-
	Subtotal	$28,600	$26,050
C.	*Projected Net Proceeds (A minus B)*	$34,650	$37,550
D.	*Percent Proceeds (Cost of fundraising)*	55%	59%

Guidelines and Instructions

The Budget Worksheet is designed to assist benefit committees in achieving *successful fiscal management*, which is defined as achieving net income for a benefit equal to at least 50 percent of the gross proceeds for the benefit, after excluding contributions and donated materials, in-kind gifts, and so on, from gross income.

Definition of Terms

Benefit budget   An estimate of all planned income and expense categories, prepared and submitted for approval by the board of directors, to represent projected income and expenses required for the benefit to function successfully.

Cash receipts   Direct income from ticket sales plus donations from those unable to attend.

EXHIBIT 10-7   (CONTINUED)

Sponsors and underwriters	Donors who make a special-level gift and qualify for visibility in the official program, on the invitations, at the benefit site, and so on. The benefit committee sets the levels (there can be several), and this revenue counts in the 50 percent test.
Auction receipts	Auction revenues shall be reported in the amount of actual receipts at the auction. The purchase of auction prizes is not recommended.
Raffle receipts	Tickets purchased for raffle sales shall be reported as raffle revenue. If raffle prizes were purchased (which is not recommended), these costs shall be treated as expenses. Donated prizes shall be treated as donated (gifts-in-kind) materials.
Contributors	Donors who "purchase" an item on the expense budget as their special contribution, either with cash or an in-kind gift. The value does *not* count as gross revenue.
Cash expenses	Items bought or directly paid for out of the benefit expense budget, in direct support of the benefit.
Temporary staff	Benefit chairpersons and committees may require direct staff support that exceeds the time available from employees to support the benefit. The decision to hire temporary staff will be considered by the board and development officer. If approved, staff will be hired by the development officer and all expenses for their employment will be added to the benefit budget as an expense.
Consultants	If professional experts should be required to supplement volunteer and staff talents in order to succeed with a benefit, the hiring of any consultant shall be with prior approval of the board and the development officer, and shall be engaged in a written agreement (fee payment basis only), with all costs added to the benefit budget as an expense.
Miscellaneous costs	Staff time (salary, benefits, and so on) and other expenses incurred by the organization in support of benefits are considered "indirect costs" and are not billed against benefit budgets. These hours and costs will be applied to the annual productivity analysis of all activities, benefits, and special events.

how to work with outside organizations in sponsorship arrangements.) Some of these service organizations plan only to stage promotions at their place of business and to attract a crowd who will buy their products. A percentage of sales is advertised to be assigned to the nonprofit organization, which has agreed to use of its name in the promotion. These "cause–related marketing" efforts have raised money for a few nonprofit organizations,

EXHIBIT 10-8   COUNCIL OF BETTER BUSINESS BUREAUS (CBBB) GUIDELINES FOR SPONSORSHIP INVOLVING CHARITIES AND COMPANIES[10]

Participants in joint-venture marketing should include the following elements in their campaigns if they wish to ensure the charitable organization's compliance with the voluntary CBBB Standards calling for charities (1) to establish and exercise controls over fundraising activities conducted for their benefit and (2) to include certain information in solicitations made in conjunction with the sale of goods or services:

1. A written agreement that gives (a) the corporation formal permission to use the charity's name and logo and (b) the charity prior review and approval of all joint-venture solicitations that use the charity's name, and

2. Joint-venture advertisements that specify (a) the portion of the product or service price or the fixed amount per sale/transaction to benefit the charity and, if applicable, the maximum amount the charity will receive, and (b) the full name of the charity, (c) an address or phone number to contact for additional information about the charity or the campaign, and (d) the term of the campaign.

The additional suggestions listed below are not required to meet the CBBB Standards. However, in the interest of full disclosure and public accountability, PAS [Philanthropic Advisory Service] recommends that corporations consider the following questions:

- Some states now have specific guidelines for sales made in conjunction with charities. Does the promotion follow these suggestions?
- Does the written agreement: (a) indicate how long the campaign will last, (b) specify how and when charitable funds will be distributed, and (c) explain any steps that will be taken in case of a disagreement or unforeseen result with the promotion?
- Does the corporation have financial controls in place to process and record the monies received to benefit the charity?
- Will the corporation issue a financial report at the end of the campaign (or annually, if the campaign lasts more than a year), which identifies: (a) the total amount collected for the charity, (b) any campaign expenses, and (c) how much the charity received?

Reprinted with permission.

---

but their purposes are neither charity nor relationship-building. They yield only increased sales for the business. Commercially sponsored benefits depend on the public's confidence and trust that some of the money will go to charity; a typical promotion offers 5 to 10 percent of all sales. Because these benefits are conducted outside the management control of the nonprofit organization, accounting for all the money exchanged is difficult. The preferred method for managing a benefit is to organize it in-house and invite volunteers to help with achieving a 50 percent profit margin.[11]

With agreement and acceptance of the financial objectives, the details required for success are now quite clearly stated. The names of prospects and prior donors for sponsorship and underwriting gifts are the first priority, as are candidates for in-kind gifts and donated services. The invitation list must include current and past donors plus qualified candidates for contributions, especially those who seem capable of strong support of the nonprofit organization. Attention to detailed planning and management of the benefit will achieve a balance between appealing to those invited at a reasonable expense and being sure that everyone has a good time at the party.

How Can Benefits Aid Annual Giving?

Successful benefits add revenue to meet annual operating needs. They also draw attention to nonprofit organizations because of their high visibility. Benefits can help to promote the same priority of needs for which other annual giving appeals are soliciting public support. No single solicitation program is likely to produce all the funds needed each year. Prospects for other annual giving programs, if they live nearby, can be invited to attend benefits; a portion of their ticket price becomes an annual gift to the organization, and this amount may be a larger gift than the organization would have received in response to a direct mail letter or a membership invitation. Corporations that are frequent prospects for other areas of annual giving will be prime candidates for sponsorship, underwriting, table sales, and "in-kind" gifts to benefits. Current and prior-year annual donors should also be invited to benefits. Many donors are likely to attend because they are already aware of the organization and have begun to invest their money in its current needs and future plans. A few may object to another solicitation, but when everyone is being invited to the party, they cannot be left off the invitation list. This "extra" solicitation only asks them to attend a social or sporting occasion that they might enjoy and that helps to support the organization; they do not have to attend. A selection of current and past major-gift and planned-gift donors should be invited and treated as special guests; a portion of the program might be set aside to honor and recognize their exceptional support. This highlight will send an important message to everyone present: "To those who are able to do more for us, we are pleased to give recognition and reward before their friends, neighbors, colleagues, and peers." The *brief* official program should not be expanded with a detailed "message" of why the benefit was held and the good uses intended for the money raised. This message should be transmitted in the printed program given to every guest and included in press releases and media coverage. The media should be encouraged to report on (and photograph) the party, the names of those who attended, what they were wearing, and the cause they were supporting.

How and Where Can Volunteers Help?

A benefit is one of the most popular forms of volunteerism available to nonprofit organizations. A benefit realizes the most intensive and extensive use of volunteers among all the annual giving fundraising methods available today. Volunteers can do it all for a benefit, start to finish (see Exhibit 10-9). To the extent that they can and do plan and execute successful

EXHIBIT 10-9   SELECTED FUNDRAISING BENEFITS THAT NEED VOLUNTEERS

Anniversary of founding
Art show/exhibition
Auction (live and silent)
Bake sale
Ball/banquet/cotillion/dinner dance/gala
Bingo
Breakfast/luncheon/dinner
Car-wash
Concert
Contest
Fashion show
House party
"Kick-off"
Las Vegas/Monte Carlo night
Opening night/premier
Picnic/BBQ
Race/run/walk
Raffle
Rally
Roast
Sporting event (fishing, golf, tennis, etc.)
Testimonial
Tournament
Travel tour
"Victory celebration"

(profitable) benefits year after year, volunteers' willingness is of enormous value. Nonprofit organizations are not expert in staging social or sporting functions; in contrast, most volunteers began and have developed their community service career through benefits. They bring real experiences and strong views based on working with other organizations. They choose to support organizations that have the capability to assist them in these duties; no one wants to run the risk of being associated with a failed benefit.

A committee of volunteers supported by professional staff is the recommended method for managing and conducting benefits. All of the details required can be organized around subcommittees (see Exhibit 10-4), and the work can be delegated for performance according to a master schedule (see Exhibit 10-3). To succeed with benefits year after year, the nonprofit organization must provide volunteers with adequately trained and experienced professional and support staff and a reasonable budget for necessary indirect and overhead expenses. It should also provide policy guidance and direction on the functions preferred and the results desired. A benefit committee is a marvelous vehicle for the identification, recruitment, and training of volunteers for all the duties and assignments that make a benefit successful—organization and planning, teamwork, attention to detail, list building and friend-raising, corporate and major-gift solicitation, fiscal responsibility, marketing and promotion, honors and recognition, and attention to other details. Benefit committees are also exemplary training grounds for future leadership at all levels. Hard-working volunteers one year should be asked to take charge of another area the next year. Volunteers need to know they can work their way up to the chairperson role. Some may prefer just to be involved and to help make the benefit a success; others will want to take on more responsibility. Both groups of volunteers are essential, and both need to be recognized and rewarded.

There may be circumstances where access to volunteers, especially those with prior experience and training, is limited. New nonprofit organizations require a year or two of operation to build a reputation for validity and successful management that will attract friends and donors as well as volunteers. Some history is also required before the new organization can expect to marshal enough volunteers to support activities, benefits, and special events. The organization's current and future management plans must be defined well enough to be able to hire professional fundraising staff (either as consultants or as employees) during these early years. No matter how honest their assessment, the leaders of every nonprofit organization should be aware that a conclusion that "We can do it alone" can be a trap leading to poor decisions. Fundraising is not only an expertise in holding benefits that produce money. Each of the other methods and techniques of annual giving described in Chapters 2 through 9 possesses greater efficiency and effectiveness at raising money than do benefits. Benefits *add to* the annual giving program; they are not a substitute for mailings, memberships, and volunteer-led groups that contribute to the primary objectives of friend-raising and relationship-building for a new organization.

> Small, new organizations may complain that they cannot raise money without hiring outside help in the form of a professional solicitor who is not a fundraising executive or a professional consultant. One of the primary responsibilities of every board member in any nonprofit organization is to initiate professional fiscal methods and controls. Hiring out this responsibility is a mistake and a lapse in stewardship.
>
> Special and benefit events, like every other method of fundraising, take time and expertise. There are no easy dollars or quick fixes. Poorly run events will not build a quality reputation for an organization nor will they motivate a cadre of committed volunteers and donors to return for another event next year.[12]

The ability of the community to support annual giving programs by nonprofit organizations in the future may well depend on the cooperation between community residents who are willing to volunteer their time and talent and nonprofit organizations that can provide the means to utilize the volunteers' commitment well. Benefits and committee work offer multiple ways to accomplish all these objectives, especially if the organization remembers to recognize and reward those who freely give so much of their time to serve.

How Is Success Measured?

Because one of the primary areas of emphasis for benefits is their financial success, several measurements can be made of their monetary performance. The board of directors should set up fiscal signposts, such as the need to achieve 50 percent net proceeds within three years of operation. The board also needs to define a firm policy on the use of the official name of the organization for any benefit purpose, internal or external. Performance measurement is not intended for punitive reasons; it distinguishes the factors that led to success from those that did not. Measures that can be applied to benefits include the following, all of which can be compared with prior years' performance:

1. Was the budget prepared in advance and approved?
2. Was recruitment of sponsors and underwriter gifts successful?
3. What percentage of total revenue did sponsors and underwriters represent?
4. Were the materials used in sponsor and underwriting sales valuable to volunteers making these solicitations?
5. Were the sponsors and underwriters satisfied with the visibility their higher gifts promised?
6. What was the number and estimated value of in-kind donations and auction or raffle prizes received?
7. What was the amount of auction (live and silent) and raffle income?
8. Were the invitations mailed on schedule?
9. Were the marketing and promotion materials timely and accurate?
10. What percentage of those invited purchased tickets and attended?
11. What percentage of those invited did not attend but made a gift to the organization anyway?
12. What was their average gift size?
13. Were acknowledgment letters sent to all who purchased tickets and did they specify the income tax contribution deduction value?
14. How many guests did those invited bring with them?
15. How many tables were sold?
16. Who were the people who sat at the sold tables? Were the names of all these guests recorded?
17. Were all bills for services paid quickly? Were expense levels according to budget?
18. What were the unexpected costs?
19. What were total net proceeds and their percentage of gross revenue?
20. Was the net proceeds check delivered to the nonprofit organization?
21. Was the critique report delivered to the nonprofit organization?

Many other areas of performance measurement described in this chapter should be studied to understand the overall performance of each benefit. Those listed above focus on items related to fiscal results. Every detail of the benefit should be reviewed to learn from the experience and to recommend improvements for the future. Benefit evaluations should also try to establish how the guests enjoyed the affair. Benefits are a form of market research to survey fundraising attitudes in the community. If sponsorship, underwriting, in-kind gifts, donated services, table gifts, or individual ticket sales declined from prior years, the cause of such losses must be learned. The committee and staff should analyze every factor in an attempt to understand this change in response. The economy may be in recession, but this excuse is too easy. More serious issues may be a lack of proper training for solicitors, late delivery of invitations, no telephone follow-up to personally encourage those who attended in prior years, no media coverage, rising prices, poor financial controls, or inadequate staff and budget support from the nonprofit organization. All of these will affect overall performance and should be understood.

Other less quantitative areas to measure for success include the extent to which invitations, media coverage, and the messages about the nonprofit organization and its needs were communicated through this benefit. Each invitation to an activity, benefit, or special event is another means of communication to the community and should add to the fundraising ability of other requests for gifts during the year. Was there good coordination with the other annual giving programs regarding the invitation and sponsor lists? Was there any follow-up to the benefit by another annual giving area; for example, were membership applications mailed to nonmembers who were attending? Is there any evidence that the benefit siphoned off important gifts from other annual giving programs? How well did the advertising, promotion, and media relations plans work to communicate the priority needs these funds will support? What effect will these efforts have on the next request to the media for their attention and coverage? These questions about the value of benefits are worth exploring in depth. A great effort was required to produce the benefit, and it is important to measure as many of its attributes as possible. Only with a full understanding of the potential of benefits to communicate needs and establish warm feelings can they achieve their full potential to succeed on their own and to assist the other annual giving programs.

SPECIAL EVENTS

Most special events are conducted for an official business or ceremonial purpose. This purpose may be their primary objective, but the special events can be quite flexible in their design and useful to the overall annual giving program. The most common example of a special event is the annual meeting. Nonprofit organizations are required in their bylaws to conduct, each year, a meeting at which they elect the board of directors, amend the bylaws (if needed), and conduct such other business as may come before the organization. This agenda of necessary business usually does not require much time, but the program is deadly dull for the public. The remedy is usually a dual-purpose program plan. The annual business meeting is held first and, after adjournment, the board of directors invites the public to join in an expanded annual event.

This affair often emerges as a social occasion (luncheon or dinner) to which spouses and several groups of guests are invited. In a brief program planned for this segment, the board of directors, chief executive officer, and others may present their annual reports. The accomplishments reported should inspire confidence and instill enthusiasm for continuing these good works. The program part of the annual meeting is also the perfect occasion to honor retiring board members and introduce newly elected ones, and to recognize donors and volunteers. Annual meetings are anniversary celebrations, and extra features can be added at five- and ten-year milestones of the organization's history.

Convocations, dedications, ground-breaking ceremonies, employee picnics, planning retreats, and certain public presentations are other examples of special events. These special occasions in the life of an organization offer the opportunity to celebrate accomplishments; to thank volunteers, donors, and employees for their services; and to announce the beginning of major new initiatives. Invitations to attend these events are often extended, even though they are convened so that the public may join in the festivities. Dedications and ground-breaking ceremonies are public events because they represent major accomplishments in the life of an organization that were made possible with public support. Convocations and retreats have an additional purpose: to bring decision makers and members together to achieve consensus on major issues and future plans. Special events may also be used to inaugurate a new board chairman or chief executive officer;

military organizations conduct change-of-command ceremonies to formalize such transitions. Religious organizations, colleges, and universities possess long traditions of special events celebrated through public ceremonies, such as religious holidays, charter days, and graduation exercises. Most of these ceremonies reflect decades-old, or even centuries-old, traditions of pomp and circumstance that are reenacted and observed. Whatever their primary purposes, special events are superior opportunities to invite wide public participation that will further the objectives of annual giving programs.

What Details Are Required for Success?

The first decision is whether a special event is required or optional. If required, what demands must it accomplish? If optional, what purposes and extra attributes does the organization wish to accomplish? In either case, the special event becomes an opportunity. With the primary purpose clarified, the next group of decisions relates to date, time, place, featured speakers, size of the invitation list, other agenda items that can be accomplished, and estimated cost. These details and the process to accomplish them are the same as for activities and benefits, and will not be repeated here. (See Appendix B for a master checklist.) Often, a committee of employees is formed and charged with planning all of the event's details. However, when a volunteer advisory committee is appointed instead, the nonprofit organization can profit from the volunteers' experience in staging successful public affairs. Most special events are not designed to serve as fundraising benefits, although close attention to budget planning and financial controls is certainly appropriate. Some special events may lend themselves to sponsorship and underwriting as well as in-kind gifts and donated services, but they may then compete with other appeals to the same donors for funds needed to support scheduled benefits.

One area of detail that always deserves special attention is the invitation list. Friend-raising and relationship-building continue to be the list's prime directives. Because special events are more open to public participation (especially when no admission fees are required), the regular invitation list may need to be expanded. Many segments of the community, including employees, are not regularly invited to many of the activities and benefits that an organization may sponsor for a fee during the year. A special event is an opportunity to balance their access to the nonprofit organization's official functions. Invitations lists for special events must be attuned to political issues and to a wide selection of elected officials, many of whom are accommodated at other public activities and benefits as well. Compiling invitation lists and maintaining them accurately to support all of the organization's activities, benefits, and special events is a major responsibility. This duty can be assigned to the fund-development office because of its ongoing attention to the maintenance of other lists of volunteers, donors, and prospects. When this department keeps the master mailing list, all of these resources for friend-raising and relationship-building purposes can be used throughout the year.

Despite all the careful planning and preparation, something can be expected to go wrong. The wine may have been ordered weeks before but, just days before the event, the vendor calls to say that the supplier has delivered a different wine. The invitations are delivered late, which leads to late mailing and reduced attendance. These mistakes are comparatively easy to live with; few people will even know they were made. Other things that can go wrong are true disasters. The speaker fails to arrive, the electricity (lights, air conditioning, and PA system) goes off, and (worst of all for outdoor events), it rains all day! In the events business, being prepared will avoid preventable errors and mistakes, but natural disasters and "acts of God" require back-up plans. Grasty and Sheinkopf[13] compiled this list of ruin-preventing guidelines for special events:

- Proper insurance
- Receipts
- Cash boxes with cash in proper denominations for each box
- Emergency numbers for police and fire departments
- First–aid kit
- Pens, tape, poster board, and markers
- All phone numbers for key participants, including band, speakers, master of ceremonies
- Fire extinguisher
- Enough bags, if you are selling something
- Sound system that works
- Runners for emergencies and all things forgotten

How Can Special Events Aid Annual Giving?

Any occasion in which suspects, prospects, donors, and volunteers can be involved as active participants is a positive opportunity for one or more of the traditional annual giving programs. It is essential to be able to invite people to respond to an organization in other ways besides donations— perhaps to answer a call for advocacy, attendance, giving, or volunteerism. Special events are valuable in much the same way as activities: they communicate information and raise awareness of the mission and purposes of the organization; they offer a balance for the fundraising invitations extended to the public. The more opportunities offered to the public to be active participants, the better. Activity leads to information, which leads to education, which leads to commitment. The annual giving continuum moves on.

How and Where Can Volunteers Help?

The use of volunteers in support of special events may be limited when these functions are organized and carried out by the nonprofit organization itself. Several special events (convocations, dedications, and ground-breaking ceremonies) are highly appropriate for joint committees with volunteers, particularly when volunteers have been involved in the project that is being celebrated. Ground-breaking and dedication ceremonies tied to fundraising campaigns are special events for which both donors and volunteers should be asked to assist in the planning and preparation. Voluntary advisory committees are valuable to other types of special events as well. A good rule of thumb is: Whenever the public will be invited to participate in a function, it is wise to call on the organization's friends in the community to assist in planning in order to maximize the occasion for the public's active participation.

How to Measure Success

Because most special events do not have any direct financial objectives, performance evaluation should be focused on the areas where qualitative analysis will be useful. How did the mailing list, invitations, and reservation system work? What improvements can be suggested? Annual business meetings usually need remedies for their length, a lack of sparkle or humor, and failure to inspire people with their message. Retreats and convocations should be measured on their ability to conclude with a plan of action that is an agreed-on vision, for both the coming operating year and the next three to five years. Dedications and ground-breaking events should be measured on how well they serve to honor and thank all those volunteers, donors, and staff who contributed to their accomplishment. Public ceremonies also should be measured on how they acknowledge the accomplishments of others and how well they confer rites of passage on those around whom the event was centered. Other approaches to qualitative evaluation might include these questions:

1. Were the support arrangements well prepared and conducted on time?

2. Were accommodations for guests (parking, access, greetings, seating, public address system, refreshments, bathrooms, exiting, and so on) suitable, and did they perform satisfactorily?

3. Were accommodations for speakers suitable? Was each speaker adequately prepared regarding his or her role in the special event?

4. Did the planning committee include enough people for all the detailed tasks required?

5. Did other employees cooperate with the extra demands the special event placed on them?

6. Were media objectives attained, and was the coverage evaluated?

7. Were the ceremonies filmed or audio or video taped, and were the comments of featured participants recorded for use in the future?

8. Did the committee complete its tasks within budget?

9. Did the committee conduct its critique and evaluation?

10. Was the critique report submitted to the board of directors?

One important area that is difficult to measure is the level of interest (or tolerance) of the public for all of the activities, benefits, and special events offered each year. Attendance and participation are valid measurement criteria of response, but more information may be needed for assessment in the future. Everyone invited is not expected to attend everything, but when these functions are prepared in the belief that they offer value to those who participate, it is important to learn the public's opinion on the outcome. During times of economic stress, the price to attend any activity may need to be lowered, so that as many people as possible may still attend. At times, board members and staff grow weary of the burden of being required to participate in everything. They may raise critical questions about the need for special events, especially those that are not well-managed and well-executed. The board is correct to question the value and worth of every activity, benefit, and special event held, and should be reading the critique reports submitted after each affair. Performance measurement is designed to document the number of attributes attained as well as the problems encountered. If special events are not contributing to the mission of the organization and cannot be kept fresh and exciting to the public, they may be discontinued.

MANAGEMENT AND PERFORMANCE MEASUREMENT

Knowledge, experience, and skill are required to manage activities, benefits, and special events. Professional and support staff in marketing, public relations, fund development, and other offices cannot achieve maximum results working alone; there is a need for volunteers to assist in preparing public functions. Performance measurement is a valid method of evaluating each activity, benefit, and special event; each should be able to demonstrate its effectiveness and efficiency in achieving its own goals and objectives and in contributing several attributes of benefit to its nonprofit organization. Functions that involve fundraising should be able to demonstrate their cost-effectiveness in their delivery of profits as net proceeds for charitable purposes. Final judgment turns on this question: Does everyone want to do it again? Several areas of management and performance measurement have been examined in this chapter. This final section assesses the factors that contribute to the success of activities, benefits, and special events.

Nonprofit organizations should set goals for their use of activities, benefits, and special events. They should also support adequately any occasions that will serve their purposes. Budget and staff resources are required if activities, benefits, and special events are to be successful, but these resources will be limited. Because restraint is necessary, decision on which functions to approve, and at what financial levels, must be based on how they demonstrate their potential to assist the organization in achieving its mission, purposes, goals, and objectives. To do so, they must be able to meet performance standards set by the board of directors. The board, the source of the organization's goals and objectives, should define goals and objectives for each activity, benefit, or special event it approves. The board should also establish the standards of performance against which each function will be measured. The plans proposed for each activity, benefit, or special event, repeated or new, must begin with a statement of goals and objectives (see Exhibit 10-10) and be accompanied by a preliminary budget (see Exhibit 10-7). To evaluate actual performance, the board must receive and read a postfunction critique report that includes recommendations from those closest to the function—its volunteers and participants. Among the areas of emphasis for evaluation are

- Progress in volunteer recruitment and training
- Progress in leadership development
- Success in prospect and donor identification
- Financial performance against the approved budget
- Benefit net proceeds of at least 50 percent of gross revenue

Planners of activities, benefits, and special events should analyze in their postmortem the potential for burn-out among volunteers and staff if aging activities, benefits, and special events are repeated too often. It is not easy to remove a function and it certainly should not be done without adequate documentation. Each public affair will have its proponents and faithful followers whose goals and analysis of their achievement may differ from the more objective view of the board of directors. Performance evaluations and critique reports document how and why each function is successful and reveal where others need to be fixed. Steps to revise or freshen those that can become more successful should be given active consideration and, if viable, be allowed to be implemented once more and should be given the support needed to achieve the newly projected potential for success. If performance does not improve sufficiently, there is documented reason to retire the event. Keeping a public event on the calendar for sentimental reasons may be its worst sentence. If it must be retired, it is best to let it go. Another function should not be allowed to take its place on the calendar *unless* it can demonstrate the potential to attract a wider public audience, achieve more attributes that benefit the organization, *and* deliver increased

EXHIBIT 10-10   SAMPLE PROPOSAL FORM FOR GOALS AND OBJECTIVES FOR VOLUNTEER-LED ACTIVITY, BENEFIT, OR SPECIAL EVENT COMMITTEE

Name of activity/benefit/special event: _____

_____

Current chairperson/vice chairs: _____

_____

Proposed next chairperson/vice chairs: _____

_____

A. Description of activity/benefit/special event:

B. Primary purposes/goals/objectives of the function:

C. Proposed date and schedule for planning, preparation, and implementation:

D. Estimate of volunteers and staff required:

E. Estimated budget worksheet (attached):

_____

financial support to meet priority needs. If any function cannot achieve all three of these critical criteria, there is no good reason to offer it to the public in the name of the organization.

Conducting performance measurement can be as easy as counting the number of people attending. Evaluating how many (and who) were there is evidence of the public's confidence that the organization will conduct satisfactory functions. Raising friends and building relationships can be traced through public participation in every annual giving program offered. Gathering the direct opinions of this same public is essential and easy: People just need to be asked what they think. Gathering opinions from guests, which is well worth the nominal time and expense involved, can begin with placing addressed postage-paid evaluation post cards in their seats or distributing them randomly in the crowd.

The assessment of the public's reaction needs to separate their enjoyment of the affair from the committee's ability to manage the benefit so that it passes the 50 percent test. If a benefit does not have strong public support (comparing prior-year attendance figures will yield the answer), it is consuming precious resources that other annual giving programs can use to increase their profitability and their achievement of other measurable attributes. Volunteers' opinions are valuable, but their enthusiasm has been known to cloud their judgment. If they are tired, lack enthusiasm for a function, and do not come back to help next year, there must be a method to hear that message. It is just as important to achieve volunteer satisfaction as it is to realize a successful event. No activity, benefit, or special event is worth keeping at the risk of losing the enthusiastic commitment of volunteers.

Activities, benefits, and special events can prove their value in many quantitative and qualitative performance areas. More than 65 specific criteria have been listed in this chapter. These public functions have the ability to cement positive relationships with people (volunteers and donors) and to stimulate those who support the organization to do so again and again. That's why nonprofit organizations hold public-participation functions! Tracking the performance of each annual giving method over many years will chart its progress in providing the additional attributes the organization needs, beyond friend-raising, relationship-building, and financial support. A combination of well-defined plans, carefully defined attributes, and realistic goals and objectives can supply quite satisfactory tools for monitoring progress and demonstrating effectiveness, efficiency, and profitability.

As first outlined in Chapter 1, the prime directive for the entire annual giving program is raising friends and building relationships and then raising money for annual operating needs. Activities, benefits, and special events have the potential to contribute to this directive. Direct mail was advocated in the acquisition and renewal of new, first-time donors in Chapters 2 through 4. Invitations to activities, benefits, and special events can enhance the responsiveness of these new friends and donors. The membership associations discussed in Chapter 5 used activities, benefits, and special events to maintain members' interest and enthusiasm, which aided membership renewal gifts. Chapter 6 discussed use of the telephone for renewal purposes and to confirm attendance and guests' names in order to aid seating and meal planning details. The auxiliaries, guilds, donor clubs, and support groups described in Chapter 7 could serve as active sponsors and provide the volunteers needed to conduct activities, benefits, and special events. How to engage corporations in active support was presented in Chapter 8 and the variety of Internet options discussed in Chapter 9.

Opportunities for personal participation add to these volunteers' self-worth and enthusiasm and encourage their active support. Every annual giving program can be made more successful through a wise and balanced use of activities, benefits, and special events. The conclusion is overwhelming: Activities, benefits, and special events are among the most effective means for nonprofit organizations to make friends, build relationships, invite participation, deliver information, achieve involvement, and realize commitment and loyalty from the public. With meticulous management, they can make money, too.

FOCUS: CCUA CLEAN UP CLEVELAND CHAPTER

Following the board's approval of a plan to combine the first annual meeting and the first benefit event into a "Gala Benefit Evening," Karen Anderson began planning the balance of the chapter's spring fundraising activities. The resident mailing list for Cleveland and six of its suburbs has continued to respond well and will be used again for a two-part letter that includes a final offer for charter membership in The Circle of Champions. Anderson has also made a list of previous donors who did not renew their prior gift before December 31. She knows that she has to make an extra effort to encourage these important donors to renew their first gifts to the Clean Up Cleveland Chapter; their next gift decision will be critical to their willingness to continue their support for several years afterward. She makes plans to invite some active donors who served earlier as telephone volunteer solicitors to make telephone calls to as many of these nonrenewed donors as possible; personal contact is most important at this point.

Solicitation messages will highlight the combined first annual meeting/gala benefit evening, to help spur results and ticket sales. Anderson plans to close out the charter membership feature after these spring appeals; this introductory offer has been in place for a full year. She also adds a proposal for a "discount plan"—a special sale offer of two complimentary tickets to the gala for any charter membership gift of $100 or more received *prior to* the date of the benefit. This discount offer will be announced in all of the promotional activities and publicity releases for the gala.

With her solicitation plans in place, Anderson begins work on the combination annual meeting and gala benefit evening to be held sometime in June. After calling to check available dates against the Women's City Club community calendar and the Greater Cleveland Convention and Visitors Bureau, Anderson discovers that every major hotel and auditorium, including the Cleveland Convention Center, is already heavily booked for every weekend, a weekday evening will have to be considered. Anderson believes that if the program begins at 6:00 P.M. and is over by 9:30 P.M., the choice of a weekday will work out. She calls Harvey Clout and Harold Connected about their availability to attend the gala on weekday dates in June; several dates are good for both of them. They both ask her to call Mary Moneybanks right away; it seems that Moneybanks and Trafalgar ("Telly") Temple have talked with the owners of Cleveland's three professional sports teams and have come up with a "fabulous idea" for the gala's entertainment program. Neither Clout nor Connected will say anything more about this idea and, with more than a little fear in her heart, Anderson calls Moneybanks but is forced to leave her name and number on Moneybank's message machine. Anderson resumes studying the benefit master checklist in the manual from The Campaign to Clean Up America (see Appendix B).

Moneybanks calls back within the hour and is quite excited. "All three teams have agreed to join our gala and we have the greatest idea for the entertainment—a variety show." Moneybanks tells Anderson about a breakfast meeting she and Temple had two days ago, adds that she has called the executive director of the Play House Square Foundation, and reports that she has a tentative "hold" on the large reception hall and dining room at the State Theater for Thursday evening, June 15. Moneybanks then returns to telling Anderson about the variety show idea. Moneybanks believes the combined annual meeting and benefit is the perfect opportunity to ask Cleveland's professional athletes to get involved in the Clean Up Cleveland campaign. "Let's have a variety show!" Moneybanks told Temple. "Let's ask each of our three Cleveland professional teams to prepare at least one act apiece, and to compete against one another for the best performance, like the old-time vaudeville acts but in a live contest with the audience serving as judges. With so much television today, we never get to see live acts any more." The deal was struck. Anderson's summary to herself, later that evening, was that the future of the first annual meeting and first benefit event for the Clean Up Cleveland Chapter now rested on the thespian talents of professional ball players.

By 10:00 A.M. the next morning, Anderson had heard from Clout, Connected, Temple, and Moneybanks again; each asked her what she thought of the variety show suggestion. Anderson had to admit that her leaders were certainly excited about the idea. Moneybanks told Anderson that she and Temple were having lunch at the Union Club on Thursday, and asked Anderson to join them. Moneybanks added: "I forgot to tell you earlier that Telly and I saw Iris Radiant at the orchestra concert two nights ago and asked her to join us to co-chair the gala. You know Iris; first it's 'No, I don't have the time.' Then it's 'Maybe, because I owe you both for all you've done for my charities.' Well, we waited to hear her out, then dropped the idea of the variety show on her, and she went for it like a trout! I'm so glad she liked our idea; she can get a lot of sponsors and underwriters as well as corporate executives to buy tables and to fill them, too! Oh yes, Iris will be joining us for lunch on Thursday, too. Do you think we could see a preliminary budget and program agenda? Can you piece together a few details for the luncheon? Thanks so much, Karen. See you Thursday. Bye." Anderson thought to herself, this train is out of the station already!

The Thursday luncheon was one of those rare moments, Anderson realized afterward, when the right people were matched perfectly with the right idea at the right time. Moneybanks began, as soon as everyone had arrived, with all the reasons she knew why the variety show would be a big hit. She had talked with the majority owners of each of the three teams; all were enthusiastic about the idea but raised questions about the date. "The Cavs could be in the NBA playoffs with Chicago, the Indians could be out of town for a game, and the Browns are on vacation," Temple added, "but I assured them it would work out fine. The NBA division championships should be decided by the first week in May, and flying a few baseball players home for a day between games is easy enough." Moneybanks added that she had the Play House Square Theater on hold for June 15, a Thursday evening, from 6:00 P.M. until 10:30 P.M. Moneybanks asked Anderson to show everyone her draft budget and program plan (Exhibits 10-11 and 10-12). Anderson reported that she had e-mailed copies that morning to both Clout and Connected, but had not heard from them before the luncheon. The budget plan showed a potential gross revenue of $104,500, expenses of roughly $45,000, and an estimated net profit of $59,500 (57 percent). Radiant commented on how ambitious these figures were for a new event, especially with the gold and silver medalist levels set at $2,500 and $1,000, respectively. After discussion, the group agreed that sponsorships and underwriting at these levels were essential to a financial success. They also agreed they had a good case for keeping general admission at $25 per person. Everyone next offered suggestions about where to get many of the expense items at good prices and named some candidates for in-kind donations. They next reviewed Anderson's draft agenda plan. They were concerned about the length of the program but agreed that each of the agenda items was necessary. They also agreed with Anderson's list of five goals and objectives for this first public function of the chapter:

1. Attract a minimum of 700 people as paid attendance
2. Achieve a better than 50 percent net profit
3. Achieve newspaper, radio, and local television coverage
4. Announce the early campaign results
5. Significantly heighten public awareness of the mission and purposes of the Clean Up Cleveland Campaign

Anderson articulated her conviction that the success of this first public event would depend on the people present at this luncheon and on the number of their friends they could recruit to assist as volunteers. Everyone agreed this was a personal obligation. "That's why we're here today," said Radiant. They also agreed the ticket price for general admission must be kept at $25 per person so that nearly everyone could afford to attend. They also agreed to recruit a good auctioneer along with some choice auction and raffle items. They thanked Anderson for her preparations, and the luncheon adjourned in solid agreeme

EXHIBIT 10-11   BUDGET WORKSHEET FOR FIRST ANNUAL MEETING AND GALA BENEFIT EVENING

	Estimated Budget	Actual Budget
A. *Projected Cash Receipts (Revenue)*		
Ticket sales (500 @ $25)	$ 12,500	$
Charter member sales (150 @ $100)	15,000	
Gold medalist sponsor gifts (8 @ $2,500)	20,000	
Silver medalist underwriter gifts (15 @ $1,000)	15,000	
Bronze medalist gifts (35 @ $500)	17,500	
Auction receipts	12,000	
Raffle receipts	8,000	
Other revenue	2,000	
Contributors (sent gifts; did not attend)	2,500	
Donated materials (in-kind)	‹1,800›	‹ ›
Subtotal	$102,700	$
B. *Projected Cash Expenses (Costs)*		
Cash expenditures list:		
Printing (5,000 invitations/tickets/programs)	$ 12,500	$
Postage		
VIP (@ $0.34 ea)	390	
Donor list (@ $0.08 ea)	320	
Theater fees:		
Sets/backdrop	8,000	
Stage crew	2,500	
Concessions	‹1,800›	
Clean-up	2,000	
Food and beverages (postreception)	6,000	
Decorations/signs	2,500	
Certificates (350)		
Printing	2,500	
Caligraphy	1,750	
Frames/boxes	700	
Rental tables/chairs	2,500	
Valet parking (VIP only)	1,000	
Police (2 @ $100)	200	
Committee meetings	250	
Contingency	2,000	
Subtotal	$43,310	$
C. *Projected Net Proceeds*	$59,390	$
(B minus A)		
D. *Percent Proceeds*	58%	%

EXHIBIT 10-12 PRELIMINARY PROGRAM AGENDA FOR FIRST ANNUAL MEETING AND GALA BENEFIT EVENING

Preliminary Agenda Plan

Welcome and Introductions	Mrs. Mary M. Moneybanks Mistress of Ceremonies
Invocation	Rev. William Smith Pastor, Cleveland Community Church
In Appreciation	Michael M. Activist National Chairman, The Campaign to Clean Up America
Convene Annual Meeting of the Clean Up Cleveland Chapter of The Campaign to Clean Up America	Mr. Harvey Clout Chair of the Board
Treasurer's Report	Mr. Sidney M. Secure, CPA
Election of Directors	Mr. Theodosius Worthy Secretary
Adjourn Annual Meeting	Mr. Harvey Clout
Recognition Program	Mr. Harold Connected Chairman, Fund Development Committee
Charter Members of The Circle of Champions	with Mr. Activist and Mr. Clout
Entertainment Program	Mrs. Mary M. Moneybanks Mrs. Iris B. Radiant
Cleveland Browns Cleveland Cavaliers Cleveland Indians	Mr. Trafalgar Temple
Adjournment to the Reception	Mrs. Mary M. Moneybanks

Driving back to her office, Karen now understood why Moneybanks, Radiant, and Temple were so successful; they had enthusiasm and clear thinking. She wondered how she and Alice Nice, her assistant, could hope to keep up with these three energetic volunteers. When she returned to her office, she called Titus Brown, president of Clout's public relations firm, to brief him on the entire plan and to ask for his help with the promotion and printing, as the luncheon group had suggested. "Harvey already called me last night," said Brown. "He asked

THE CAMPAIGN TO CLEAN UP AMERICA
CLEAN UP CLEVELAND CHAPTER

April 2, 200X

Dear Concerned Resident:

Thanks to the help of many of our friends and neighbors, our campaign to Clean Up Cleveland is working quite well. There is less trash on our streets than one year ago.

The Campaign to Clean Up America (CCUA) is making progress, too. Each one of us wants to be proud of our country, and we want it to be clean.

After just our first year of operations, the CCUA Clean Up Cleveland Chapter has received more than 14,500 gifts and $442,000. That's 36 percent of our overall goal of $1,250,000! My personal thanks to each and every one of you, our generous donors.

To celebrate our progress, I am inviting you to our first annual meeting and gala benefit evening to be held on *Thursday* evening, *June 15*, beginning at *6:00 P.M.* in the State Theater in Play House Square. And, do we have a show for you!

Our program will have two parts. First, every charter member of our Circle of Champions donor club will be honored on stage. Second, a variety show will feature entertainment by team members from the Cleveland Browns, Cavaliers, and Indians. You won't want to miss this show or the great dessert-tasting reception that follows the program.

Tickets are only $25 per person. Your income tax deduction is $12.50, exactly what goes toward our project.

Special Discount Offer: Any donor of $100 or more whose gift is received *before June 15* will (a) receive *two* tickets to our gala celebration and (b) be inducted into The Circle of Champions as a charter member. Act now; the State Theater has only 700 seats.

The new energy conversion plant will give each of us more electricity at less cost, just from collecting and burning our own trash. Join us on June 15 to celebrate a cleaner Cleveland; I look forward to seeing you.

Sincerely yours,

I. Harvey Clout
Chair of the Board
Cleveland Cast Iron Works

me to assign one of my account executives to this project for the next three months, and charge it to his company. You know Susan White on my staff? Good. I've asked Susan to set up a meeting for the three of us early next week." When Anderson hung up, she had a growing conviction that the combined first annual meeting and first gala bene-fit evening was going to work out just fine. She turned to her com-puter and composed the spring appeal letter (Exhibit 10-13) for Clout's signature.

CHAPTER 11

The Volunteer-Led, Personal Solicitation Annual Giving Campaign

The slogan, "It doesn't get much better than this!" applies fully to the volunteer-led, personal solicitation annual giving campaign. All of annual giving is a yearly campaign, and personal solicitation is the best method to invite volunteers and donors to ask others to *renew* (and possibly *increase*) their annual gifts. Of all the several methods and techniques of fundraising practice to develop annual gift dollars, the volunteer-led, personal solicitation campaign is "as good as it gets!"

If volunteer-led, personal solicitation is so great, why is it discussed so late in this book? The answer is that it cannot begin until *after* the other forms of annual giving are up and running. There must be donors at levels where their continued involvement and support is so valuable that personal contact is mandated. For a volunteer-led, personal solicitation campaign to succeed, these elements must be present:

1. Donors who need to be seen

2. Trained volunteers who have experience in asking

3. Volunteer leaders who can organize and motivate other volunteers

4. Experienced staff who can guide and direct a volunteer-led campaign

5. Board commitment, based on the conviction that an intense, personal solicitation campaign is necessary

A volunteer-led, personal solicitation annual giving campaign is the *culmination* of the overall annual giving program, not its source. There are several advantages and attributes to be realized from the successful introduction of a volunteer-led, personal solicitation annual giving campaign:

1. It tells current donors that they are appreciated for who they are and valuable for what they have done.

2. It identifies and recruits volunteers who will ask their friends for money.

3. It identifies and recruits leaders who are able to direct others to perform a specific assignment by a deadline.

4. It asks current donors to increase their level of annual support.

5. It invites current donors to become volunteers and actively help the nonprofit organization.

6. It identifies major gift and planned gift prospects among individuals.

7. It identifies corporate and foundation prospects and donors who can and should be seen for new major gifts and grants.

8. It proves that personal solicitation is 16 times more effective than direct mail and 8 times more effective than use of the telephone.

9. It proves that personal solicitation, at $0.05 to $0.10 to raise a dollar (or less), is the most cost-effective method of annual giving available.

To establish and manage a volunteer-led, personal solicitation campaign every year is not an easy task. Each campaign must follow a strategic plan grounded on well-documented and well-publicized priority needs. The strategic decision to use a campaign model, which is an intense experience for everyone involved, must be fully supported by the board of directors. Board members also must agree to be the first donors to this campaign, with personal gifts that are large enough (as a group) to inspire others to follow their example of giving and their personal endorsement of this annual giving effort with their 100 percent participation. Further, one or more board members must serve as committee leaders and active volunteer solicitors in the campaign; if the board expects others to work in their behalf, the board must show the way. Several components are required, and all of them are critical to the success of each annual giving campaign:

1. An adequate supply of current donors with a known potential for increased levels of participation and support.

2. An adequate supply of well-trained volunteer solicitors to represent the nonprofit organization while acting as its public solicitors.

3. A few identified leaders who are experienced in organizing and directing volunteers and in motivating them to complete their assigned duties on schedule.

4. A well-prepared campaign plan managed by experienced fundraising professionals in whose advice and counsel leaders and volunteers will have confidence.

5. A tracking and reporting system to evaluate the campaign's performance and to keep everyone informed of progress.

6. A recognition program that will honor donors for their achievements and reward volunteers for their accomplishments.

DEVELOPING QUALIFIED DONORS

Even the smallest of nonprofit organizations, if it has begun its annual giving program by using the mail for acquisition and renewal solicitations as described in Chapters 2 through 4, should develop at least 1,000 donors *after* three years. Among these 1,000 donors will be some 10 to 15 percent who have upgraded their original gift amount by the third year. Most of the others (40 to 50 percent) will maintain the same gift level each year. If gifts to donor clubs or membership associations have been requested, some of these donors (10 to 15 percent) will have added another gift or switched from being mail respondents to the donor club or membership program. Another 10 to 15 percent of donors will have bought tickets to one or more benefits within three years. Other donors may have begun to volunteer in some capacity (the final 10 to 15 percent), taking assignments and proving their willingness to help in other ways. Given all these opportunities during the first three years, the majority of donors will have invested between 5 and 10 separate gifts in the organization for a total of $100 to $300 or more. They will have received newsletters and three annual reports and will have a fairly good idea of the progress made and the needs that remain to be addressed. They have proven their loyalty and are prepared to answer the next request.

These donors and volunteers are well-prepared to ask their friends for donations. They have made an extensive personal commitment with their personal investment decision to the organization. They continue to give because they believe in the mission and purposes of the organization. They remain positive about the value of their investment and have become ambassadors for the cause, perhaps without knowing it. How much more qualified can they be? What can the organization ask them to do next? The answer is: Join the volunteer-led, personal solicitation annual giving campaign and solicit *other donors* (not strangers) for their annual gifts.

> If donor development has been well planned, a series of naturally progressing steps brings donors to this decision point. They believed in the organization's services enough to aid it with repeated contributions. They gave their time and talents to help with projects and to serve on committees. They may have been directly involved in a project, taken a leadership role in organizing others, and brought their friends to a benefit event or open house. Their involvement increased without much prodding on the part of the organization, but all according to the development plan.[1]

Despite their qualifications, they may not be willing to ask their friends for money. Some will say they are willing to do *anything* else, even to give five times the amount of time and effort in any other assignment, no matter what it may be. Others will be reticent to solicit anyone, even another prior donor, because they are shy or uncomfortable with the idea. A few may never have "sold" anything before (so they think) and are not sure how to do it. Perhaps they have asked others for gifts before, were turned down, and came away with bad feelings of what they thought was rejection of them. Any volunteer wants to succeed and fears failure most of all, especially in front of friends and for an organization they care about. Each of these attitudes, good or bad, can be addressed during orientation and training, if these donors will first agree to serve.

Assume that at least 250 of the 1,000 donors developed by an organization after three years might be eligible to become volunteer solicitors. What criteria can be used to find 250 prospective volunteers from among 1,000 donors? Eight sure indicators are the following past actions:

1. Gave repeated personal gifts each year
2. Gave additional gifts, or increased annual gift levels, or joined the donor club, or asked about commemorative gifts

3. Attended one or more activities, benefits, or special events in each year

4. Brought friends to activities, benefits, and special events

5. Requested additional information, whether asking for themselves or "for a friend who wants to know"

6. Volunteered for service to the organization outside the fund development program

7. Volunteered for service at another organization, possibly in a fundraising assignment

8. Was nominated by a board or staff member or by another donor

"Donors make the best prospects," an old maxim in fundraising practice, applies as much to volunteers as it does to donors. The next step, *how* to ask them to be solicitors, is all-important; a lot is riding on this request. Summarizing the advice in the first nine chapters of this book: *Do not* write them a letter! What will come back is another check. If they are being asked to perform personal solicitation, the only way to invite them is by *personal solicitation*—by board members, administrators, volunteer leaders, and fund development staff. Without volunteers, there will be no volunteer-led, personal solicitation annual giving campaign.

RECRUITING AND TRAINING VOLUNTEER SOLICITORS

Each volunteer who accepts the invitation to serve as a member of the volunteer-led, personal solicitation annual giving campaign should receive a letter of appointment from a high-ranking officer of the organization (chair of the board, chair of the development committee, president, or CEO). A copy of the letter should be sent to the person who asked the volunteer to serve. The appointment letter should specify the assignment, verify the importance of the work to the organization, identify who is in charge of the project, specify the period of service (the planned length of the annual campaign), and conclude with an offer to be available at any time for assistance. The appointment letter should announce the date(s) and time(s) for the orientation and training sessions and stress that every volunteer should attend (see Exhibit 11-1). It is important to preserve the personal style that is essential to every phase of this project. A confirmation notice with de-

EXHIBIT I I-I **LETTER OF APPOINTMENT TO VOLUNTEER-LED, PERSONAL SOLICITATION ANNUAL GIVING CAMPAIGN COMMITTEE**

August XX, 200X

Dear _____;

Thank you for agreeing to join our annual giving campaign committee this year. We are highly dependent on volunteers such as yourself who are willing to meet with our most faithful annual donors to ask them to renew their annual gift for our continuing efforts to improve our city.

Please plan to attend one of our volunteer orientation and training meetings next month. These one-hour sessions will provide you with complete information about our campaign plans, the projects needing funds this year, and how to solicit a gift. You will also meet the other members of our committee. The schedule for all sessions, to be held in our conference center at 1234 Main Street, is as follows:

7:30 A.M.	Wednesday	September 22
5:30 P.M.	Thursday	September 23
7:30 A.M.	Friday	September 24

Enclosed is an RSVP card to sign up for one meeting; please reply by September 15. If you cannot attend, we will schedule another time for one of us to meet with you.

Enclosed is a roster of annual donors. Please circle the names of each person you are willing to see about a gift this year. Return the list to us *prior to* September 15. Each volunteer will be assigned *five* donors to see during the campaign period, from October 1 to November 15. You will receive your assignments at the training session.

Please give either of us a call if you have any questions. Thank you again for joining our committee; we look forward to working with you to benefit our community through this, our favorite charitable organization.

Sincerely yours,

Timothy Brown   Rachel Smith
Campaign Chairman   Team Captain
897-6655   545-3211

Encl.

tails about the orientation and training session should arrive shortly after the appointment letter and should come from the annual giving campaign chair or vice chair or from a team captain. The volunteer is now enlisted in their effort and will be asked to follow their direction from this point forward.

Each volunteer comes to this assignment with an individual background and varied experience. Not all volunteers will have the same level of knowledge of or comfort with this assignment. Most are likely to have been involved with the organization in some entirely different capacity, especially if recruited from among the roster of donors. A few may have had prior experience in a campaign and may have attended orientation and training sessions. Their new role is being part of a personal solicitation campaign committee. Annual giving campaigns are not military operations, but orientation and training sessions are a command, not an option, for every volunteer, especially in the first years of volunteer participation. Experienced volunteers may be excused from the instruction sessions but should attend to communicate their enthusiasm and experience to the newcomers. Each volunteer needs to be brought up to date on current priorities and to renew his or her enthusiasm for this task.

Orientation and training meetings should be scheduled at a time of day and on a day of the week when most volunteers can attend. People who are unable to attend any session will have to be seen separately by a committee member or staff employee, to be sure they receive the instruction they need to fulfill their assignment. Attendance implies acceptance of the accountability to perform as requested. Volunteers will not want to have to explain their lack of performance to others on the committee. It is usually much easier to do the work than to try to explain why it was not done. Completing the assignments is all they are asked to do; the results (each donor's gift decision) are a separate matter and are not always within the volunteers' ability to control. Their jobs are to meet with each of their assigned donors and to invite his or her continued support.

The orientation and training session is an important part of *every* personal solicitation annual giving campaign. To help stress this point to everyone involved, leaders from the board of directors should attend; some should be included on the agenda (see Exhibit 11-2) as speakers, and others can be introduced and participate in the discussion. Their attendance will count greatly with the volunteers present. Each session should be conducted as a

EXHIBIT 11-2 **SAMPLE AGENDA FOR ONE-HOUR TRAINING AND ORIENTATION SESSION**

1. Welcome and introductions	Chair, Annual Giving Campaign Committee
2. Importance of annual gift support	Chairman of the Board or President/CEO
3. The project that needs support	President/CEO or senior professional staff member in charge of the project
4. Prospect assignments	Chair, Annual Giving Campaign Committee
5. The campaign plan, timetable, visit reports, gifts reports, staff support available; introduction of team captains	Chair and Vice Chair, Annual Giving Campaign Committee
6. The art of asking for money (role-playing exercise)	Chair, Annual Giving Campaign Committee with successful volunteers from last year's campaign
7. Discussion: Questions/answers	Chair, Annual Giving Campaign Committee plus all other speakers
8. Adjournment to refreshments	

seminar or workshop, using an adult education model. Informality will encourage audience participation. To be effective, each session should be limited to 25 or 30 people; extra meetings can be held if more volunteers are involved. The time span should be one hour, with only 30 to 40 minutes planned for actual presentation. Audiovisual aids should be used and refreshments should be provided. The site should be conducive to training purposes and devoid of distractions. Where possible, training should take place at the site of the project or within the nonprofit organization. A successful session will cover the following:

- It begins as soon after the announced time as possible.
- It encourages questions.
- Board members and other representatives from the organization should be available to answer questions.
- It should be conducted professionally.
- Volunteers should be thoroughly prepared for all facets of this assignment.

The key reasons that orientation and training sessions are valuable to volunteers can be described by what they accomplish:

1. They provide complete instructions on the project and on how the funds will be used, how those served will be helped, and how the cause will be advanced.

2. They explain the benefits to the community that will result from meeting these needs.

3. They explain the recognition program planned for donors at all levels.

4. They explain why volunteers' own personal gift decision must be made *before* they ask someone else for their annual gift, and why they should secure the gifts as soon as possible.

5. They explain how to present the project fairly, without overstatement, and how to ask for a gift without implying any coercion (giving is voluntary).

6. They explain how to invite others to join in support of a project whose value is expressed in terms of helping those in need and fulfilling the mission and purposes of the organization.

7. They explain how the campaign is organized, who are the people in charge, which team captain they will work with, how they are to conduct their assignment, and when the campaign begins and ends.

8. They review the contents of the "worker's kit" to show how the information and materials can be used.

9. They explain how the results will be reported, how the overall program will be evaluated, and how their performance will be measured.

10. They provide encouragement and praise for volunteers and describe how they will be recognized and rewarded for their service.

All that remains is to assign each volunteer the names of the prior donors and prospects he or she is to see and solicit. Assignment is a crucial part of the orientation and training session. Personal solicitation is a delicate and, for many people, a somewhat confrontational experience. Everyone should be asked to take a minimum number of donor candidates (between three and five) and should be provided with basic information on each donor assigned. The information is *confidential* but necessary to the task of asking for the next gift (see Exhibit 11-3). At the orientation, the value of reporting the contents of the discussion with each donor should be stressed; this information is an essential portion of each donor's permanent record. Because annual giving campaigns are scheduled to last only one to two months, it is not unreasonable to ask a volunteer to meet with three to five donors within four to eight weeks. Some volunteers will ask for more than five assignments. Their enthusiasm is commendable, but they should begin with three to five. After these visits have been completed, their results can be studied before they are given additional assignments.

> No formula for determining how many prospects an individual can handle will be applicable to every situation. In an intensive campaign, however, solicitors should seldom be asked to make more than five calls. This is especially true in the campaign that is operating on a genuine deadline (and without a deadline it is not a campaign!). Many well-meaning persons accept too many assignments with the result that, while they may make all the calls, they usually do so perfunctorily and without enthusiasm and determination. Some people can handle only one or two calls well.[2]

After a year or two of experience, those volunteers who can secure more gifts from prior donors can take more than five assignments. Most volunteers prefer to select the names of people they know because they have a higher comfort level when asking their friends or business colleagues for donations. They expect to see these people once or twice in the course of their normal activities during the campaign period. Other volunteers prefer to take the names of people they do not know; they become embarrassed when confronting their friends. Some may take new names for an opposite reason: They want to make new contacts and acquaintances, either for personal or business reasons. Whatever the choice or motive, everyone should accept an assignment of three to five donors to see and to resolicit for their next gift.

The next step is to educate the volunteers about who and what they are representing. One way to get this message across is to weave the information into a monologue that illustrates what the volunteer might say or how the project or cause might be explained to someone the volunteer will call on. A short video or CD provided for laptop presentations in which sight and sound are used together, or a role-playing exercise, will help volunteers

EXHIBIT 11-3   SAMPLE PROSPECT ASSIGNMENT
CARD AND CONTACT REPORT
SUMMARY

Donor Name:	Mr. and Mrs. Allen B. Constant
Address:	23456 Chagrin Falls Blvd. Gates Mills, Ohio 44022
Telephone:	Office: 123-4567 Residence 765-4321

Giving Summary:	Annual Gifts	2000	$100.00
		2001	150.00
		200X	150.00
		Total:	$400.00

Suggested Renewal/Upgrading/Gift: $200.00

Other Gifts:	Date	Amount	Purpose
	3/10/XX	$ 50.00	Memorial gift
	5/12/XX	100.00	2 tickets to BBQ
	9/15/XX	50.00	Memorial gift
	2/21/XX	100.00	Membership
	5/15/XX	200.00	4 tickets to BBQ
	7/27/XX	25.00	Memorial gift

Possible Areas of Priority Interest:

1. Commemorative giving

2. Western BBQ committee

Comments from Prior Contact Reports:

1. Appears from address to have money.

2. Annual gift renewed by phone last two years; has not been called on.

3. Ask Mary Moneybanks if she knows them and what their interests might be.

Contact Report Summary

Date of meeting: _____ Time: _____

Place of meeting: _____

Comments on visit:_____

_____

Question areas: _____

Annual gift renewed?	[ ] Yes Amount: $ ____	[ ] No
Upgrade requested?	[ ] Yes Amount: $ ____	[ ] No
Overall assessment:	[ ] Major gift candidate	[ ] Planned gift candidate
Follow-up required:	[ ] Yes	[ ] No

to remember details. Speakers might stress only two or three key points for volunteers to remember and use in their conversations with donors. Each speaker must be carefully prepared on the topic, project a positive and optimistic attitude about soliciting, and convey enthusiasm about what the money raised will accomplish. Other information volunteers may find useful should be placed in their information kits (see Exhibit 11-4). Each document should be reviewed briefly to explain what it contains and how to make use of it.

Volunteers will be anxious to learn how they should ask for money. There are two parts of this section of the meeting: (1) assignments from the donor list and (2) training on how to ask for a gift. Volunteers should have an opportunity to review the list of donors prior to the orientation and training session. For example, a volunteer who has agreed to serve should be sent the list of qualified donors and requested to return it by a set date—after they have identified all the names (not just five) of donors they would be willing to accept as their solicitation assignments. Confirmation of their actual assignments, made by campaign leadership and staff, will be completed prior to the date of the orientation and training session. This open session is not the place or the time to air everyone's assignment preferences. Assignments can be changed, but if each volunteer is assigned a few of the names requested, he or she is more likely to call on those prospects first, then see other donors who were not requested. Volunteers who ask for substitutes should be willing to accept the next donor(s) assigned to them;

EXHIBIT 11-4	CONTENTS OF A VOLUNTEER SOLICITOR'S INFORMATION KIT

Left Side	**Right Side**
1. Table of contents	1. Table of contents
2. Project fact sheet/key points	2. Giving history and brief personal profile for each assigned prospect
3. Question/answer sheet	3. Supply of contact/visit report forms
4. Basic fact sheet on the nonprofit organization plus short video or CD	4. Roster of members and organization chart of annual giving campaign committee
5. Most recent annual report and last two newsletters	5. Roster of annual giving committee members
6. Supply of stationery and envelopes	6. Supply of postage-paid reply envelopes

if they don't, there can be doubt whether they want to solicit anyone. Each donor who is returned or exchanged for reassignment to another volunteer should be reassigned as soon as possible.

Training in how to solicit prior donors is the last topic on the agenda. This "moment of truth" can be a stumbling block for many volunteer solicitors. They need to know how to guide the discussion, what approach to use when asking for a gift, and what vocabulary is acceptable. They must be told that every solicitation will be unique; people are different, and there is no "one way" that will work every time. How they approach each donor and what they say can be the same; how to read each donor's response is hard to teach. Here are some basic facts to stress with volunteers at the outset:

1. Each person they will see is already a donor, just as they are.
2. Whether the donor knows the volunteer or not, both have positive feelings about the organization they are supporting.
3. The face-to-face meeting is essential for success
4. Each donor has thoughts and opinions; invite comments to be shared with the organization.
5. There is no "easy way" to get this job done; other ways are never as successful as face-to-face meetings.
6. The organization cannot hope to talk with all of its donors; only volunteers can complete this important contact each year.

Each volunteer also should be instructed on how important each prior donor is to the organization. Meeting with them is important, but continuous support is the true objective. Donors are investors; like clients or customers, they deserve to be treated well, which includes taking the time to meet with them at least once a year. If these annual visits are held faithfully, there can be every expectation that financial support will follow.

Donors are always interested in learning what the organizations they support are doing and planning. They will look forward to talking with someone who knows the plans firsthand and will be quite receptive to a chance to meet. Volunteers should take a moment to think about how they will make their initial approach to each donor. Among the options they should be encouraged to consider are: (1) call to ask for an appointment, (2) write a brief note to introduce themselves and say they will be calling for an appointment, or (3) try to intercept the donor in public to ask for an appointment. None of these options should be used for actual solicitation unless it is impossible to make the desired arrangement and meet with the donor. After the appointment has been made, here are some basic suggestions for how to prepare for the meeting with each donor.

1. Be yourself.

2. Remember that this is a social call and is voluntary by both parties.

3. Keep the appointment; donors deserve respect.

4. Select a time and place comfortable to the donor, not the solicitor.

5. Give the donor the choice of where and when to meet (safe at home, or in public).

6. Give the donor the deference due a host, but pick up the tab.

7. Prepare for the meeting; study the donor's giving history in particular.

8. Concentrate on requesting a repeat of prior support.

9. Begin by thanking the donor for the meeting and for his or her previous support.

10. Allow time to get acquainted, catch up on other topics, and develop a comfort level.

11. Discuss key points about the organization and the targeted project; be informative, not boring.

12. Do not rush into the "pitch."

13. Explain your own interest; explain (briefly) your involvement and why you believe the cause is worth your time and money.

14. Explain that your assignment is to meet with other donors, to share information, and to answer questions.

15. Welcome any questions; try to answer those you know, and promise to get any answers you do not know (always a good follow-up opportunity).

16. Explain the project succinctly; again, invite questions; share campaign materials if there is interest in having them.

17. If asked, tell how much you have given.

18. Ask whether the donor is willing to consider continuing his or her important level of support again this year.

19. Explain the separate giving levels offered and the donor-recognition benefits and privileges.

20. If the donor is willing to give again, extend warm thanks.

21. Depending on the context of the answer, ask whether the donor might consider adding "something extra" to the prior gift amount; explain why a little more is needed and how it will make a difference.

22. If the donor is not ready to give, accept the indecision and allow time for further consideration; try to set a date for a call-back to receive the decision.

23. Thank the donor for his or her commitment and generosity and for the time spent with you.

24. Report the donor's decision to the fund development office; if a gift was made, deliver it as soon as possible; pass along any requests for follow-up action.

25. If it is your personal practice and style, send a brief, handwritten note within a few days to thank the donor for the gift decision and for the meeting.

The list of things "not to do" is brief and easy to remember:

1. Don't push.
2. Never hustle.
3. Don't overstate the need.
4. Never promise something you can't deliver.
5. Don't think any donor is easy.
6. Never meet with a donor unprepared.
7. Don't forget to say thank you.

Are there magic words to use? Because solicitation is a request, it can be put in the form of a question: "Is it possible you will be able to support us again this year?" or "Can you consider a gift of $1,000 at this time?" or "Can you see your way clear to join us with your gift again this year?" Phrases that assume a gift is forthcoming or that imply a bit of pressure (such as "Can we count on you again this year?" or "I hope you will agree to support us") can work against a favorable gift decision. Donors must decide whether they want to give again; nothing should be assumed. Here are some guidelines for reacting to their answer:

- ✔ If they reply with the same gift as last year (and upgrading was mentioned), accept their decision.
- ✔ If they decide to increase their gift, thank them twice: (1) for giving again and (2) for giving more than before!
- ✔ If upgrading was not mentioned, ask about it now.
- ✔ If they decide on a smaller gift, thank them.

Donors may have a reason for reducing their support; more than likely, the reason will be revealed during the discussion. If the reason relates to any unhappiness or dissatisfaction with the organization, the project, or how they have been solicited or treated since giving their prior gift, these facts should come out during the discussion. If no reason has been mentioned and there is no evidence of hardship, the donors might be asked gently if they want to share any comments with the organization. Note taking may be necessary, and all the details should be reported to the team captain or office staff.

CAMPAIGN LEADERSHIP: THE KEY TO SUCCESS

Leadership is absolutely critical to a volunteer-led, personal solicitation annual giving campaign. Leadership adds legitimacy and brings credibility to the campaign; exhibits passion and a caring attitude about the organization and those who benefit from its programs and services; inspires volunteers to join and to perform; sets the tone and creates the spirit for the campaign; insists on deadlines being met; sets the performance levels expected; and fully accepts being accountable for the results. Leaders actively participate in decisions on campaign purposes, design, and goal setting. Leaders conduct the identification, recruitment, and training of volunteers and provide personal direction from start to finish. If the individuals chosen to provide leadership also possess some of the following capabilities—visibility, respectability, clout, wealth, and a willingness to take responsibility for the work of others—and are fearless when it comes time to ask for money, the volunteer-led, personal solicitation campaign can be assured of success.[3]

The role of volunteer leaders and their identification, recruitment, training, and other operating details have already been discussed (see Chapters 2,

7, and 10). The focus here will be on their role in organizing and managing volunteers who agree to be part of a personal solicitation campaign. The basic leadership talents needed include knowing how to conduct meetings, preserve order, keep to deadlines, be conscientious about the budget, delegate authority, create teamwork, and motivate others. There will be times when a problem may arise or something may not be going well. Corrective action must be taken, or a volunteer or donor may require a bit of "extra attention." Leaders must be willing to address these issues and sensitivities.

The most effective way to manage a volunteer-led, personal solicitation campaign is with a committee (see Exhibit 11-5). Experienced fundraising executives know how to direct a program through a committee, and volunteers understand how to perform as members of a committee. There is a degree of comfort in the formal structure and procedural style that committees observe and in the ready access to others for help when needed. Committees spread the work around fairly and equitably; no one

EXHIBIT 11-5   ORGANIZATION CHART FOR VOLUNTEER-LED ANNUAL GIVING CAMPAIGN COMMITTEE

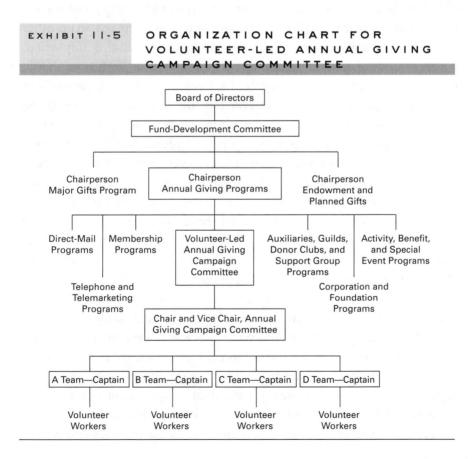

person is asked to bear too great a responsibility for the overall campaign. The duties for each of the various tasks, like job descriptions, can be explained so that each participant knows what to do, what others are doing, and where everyone's assignment fits into the overall committee design. Annual giving committees need only a minimal structure to support their assignment of solicitations of prior donors.

> The organization must not be cumbersome or get in the way of the goal. It should be streamlined, utilizing just the forces needed for a successful program and no more. An overlarge organization requires a lot of care and feeding and does not ensure success. A compact group of compatible, effective, involved leaders representing the community or the organizational power structure can perform miracles.[4]

Each committee layer represents a rung on a ladder that volunteers can use to advance to greater responsibility. Because annual giving campaigns must be repeated every year, committees represent a training ground and a promotion sequence for those who choose to move up and share other areas of responsibility. A committee is the superior method to implement a leadership development program. In its simplest form, each layer should be required to have a chairperson and a vice chair. The chairperson is in charge this year and maybe next year too; the vice chair is assisting the chairperson as required and is in training to take over next year or the year after. Training volunteers to be successful as leaders of other volunteers is a significant step in the growth to maturity of every nonprofit organization.

Volunteer-led, personal solicitation annual giving campaigns will require several areas of management. The board of directors and the nonprofit organization depend on the annual giving campaign as a major source of operating revenue. Leaders who take responsibility to organize the campaign and direct the volunteers to produce these funds are also managers of the friend-raising and relationship-building inherent in this process. Most of the volunteer solicitors will not be involved in campaign details such as decisions about appointment letters, agenda planning, budgets, notices, printed materials, orientation and training sessions, speaking appearances, thank-you letters, and donor and volunteer recognition and reward. Added to the responsibilities of campaign leaders are executive committee meetings, expense approvals, contract and liability requirements, progress reports to higher authority, and similar tasks. These levels of responsibility are significant and require some prior experience with previous campaigns.

The fund-development staff will support the campaign leaders in all of these activities, but will not make these decisions.

Shared responsibility is a key part of committee design and operation. The annual giving campaign chairperson who delegates authority along with responsibility is giving volunteers a larger role to play in the entire process and a greater stake in its success. Volunteers will then develop a better sense of how important their assignment is to the success of the overall campaign. As an example, team captains have to (1) be sure their volunteer workers attend orientation and training sessions, complete as many of their assignments with personal visits as possible, and report back on their experiences with their assigned donors; (2) evaluate the volunteers' and their own performance; and (3) identify likely candidates for added responsibility next year. The postcampaign critique session will invite everyone to offer suggestions for improvements. Capturing these suggestions and passing them along to the campaign leadership will be the final entry on the team captains' job description.

The assignments accepted by a volunteer solicitor are important to the overall campaign and to each volunteer's experience because they concentrate on meetings with prior donors. Nearly every other annual giving activity concentrates on acquiring new, first-time donors and then securing their second and third annual gifts. The volunteer-led, personal solicitation campaign is designed to invite and train volunteers to meet with only selected prior donors. The annual contributions of these donors often represent as much as 60 to 80 percent of actual cash income received in each year. This campaign and its performance should receive major attention from the nonprofit organization's board of directors and management.

Several performance areas will be monitored during and after the campaign. Each of these evaluations and their criteria will be defined in positive terms. Routine gift reports will provide basic details such as the number of donors who have made gifts to date, their gift amounts, and the average gift size. These results should be compared with prior campaigns at the same point in time. Much more data will be needed before the performance of a volunteer-led, personal solicitation campaign can be evaluated. How many prior donors qualified to be seen at the start of the campaign? How many of these donors were assigned to volunteer solicitors, how many were seen, and what gift decisions resulted?

To understand the total campaign, this performance evaluation should also provide details on the number who were *not* assigned and *were not* seen,

1. Number of qualified prospects and volunteers available	Prospects	=	250
	Volunteers	=	50
2. Number and percent of prospects assigned to volunteers	Number	=	225
	Percent	=	90 %
3. Number of calls made, number of gifts received, and ratio (percent) of calls to gifts	Calls made	=	200
	Gifts made	=	175
	Percent	=	88%
4. Average gift size for all prior donors and average gift size for all new donors	Average gift (prior)	=	$ 525
	Average gift (new)	=	$ 580
5. Number of upgraded gifts received, percent of donors who upgraded, and average gift size	Number	=	35
	Percent	=	20 %
	Average gift	=	$ 650
6. Number of prior donors assigned who did *not* make a gift, percentage, and value of their lost gifts (total made in prior year)	Number	=	50
	Percent	=	22 %
	Value	=	$ 25,000
7. Number of prior donors who were *not* assigned and did make an annual gift last year, percentage, and average gift size	Number	=	25
	Percent	=	40 %
	Average gift	=	$ 250
8. Number of prior donors who were *not* assigned and did *not* make an annual gift last year, percentage, and value of gifts *not* received	Number	=	50
	Percent	=	20 %
	Value	=	$ 25,000

and the value of their prior gifts *not received* as a result. The form shown in Exhibit 11-6 provides a comprehensive analysis and helps to illustrate what the personal solicitation campaign was able to accomplish. It is not reasonable to expect volunteers to be able to see every donor within a short campaign period, and there is no value in trying to assess what the no–visit problem may have been. Volunteers should believe they succeeded in their assignment if they met with each of their assigned donor prospects or *made every effort* to do so.

The overall campaign evaluation should address the positive opportunity that remains: How, when, and where can these faithful donors be asked to give again? The answer is to try again, perhaps later in the year during a second volunteer-led, personal solicitation campaign. If a second campaign is not possible, alternate solicitation methods can be used. The same volunteer or team captain can try to call the donor in a few months. If that fails, a personal letter can be sent. The final objective is to be sure that every prior donor receives an invitation to continue to make his or her annual gift sometime within each year.

MANAGEMENT OF THE ANNUAL GIVING CAMPAIGN

The annual giving campaign will require a lot of attention from everyone who is part of it. The overall campaign schedule (see Exhibit 11-7) illustrates the extent to which planning and attention to detail must be provided by the fund-development staff. Campaign leadership must stay on top of each deadline as the schedule progresses. The vice chair and team captains must be in touch with volunteer workers throughout their period of training and actual solicitation. Once the campaign is begun, volunteers will be contacting their donor prospects to set up face-to-face meetings. Each gift they secure will require a proper thank-you letter—a personal text to be drafted, approved, prepared, and signed. A lot of follow-up is needed to keep everything moving and to complete everything by the established deadlines. A four- to eight-week campaign covers a brief period of time that passes all too swiftly.

Campaign report meetings are the best medium for maintaining momentum and keeping the campaign on schedule. Report meetings motivate volunteers to complete their assignments, to share their progress and their success, and to alert leaders and staff of any problems they have encountered. The meetings also offer opportunities to recognize and reward those volunteers who have completed their assignments: seen all of their assigned prospects and secured an annual gift from each one. Scores can be posted for each of these "100 Percent Club" performers; their example is for everyone to imitate. Additional scoreboards can keep track of other volunteer and team performance details, the number of donors who increase their gifts, the total gifts achieved compared to prior years, and other encouraging information. When a spirit of competition enters the

EXHIBIT 11-7   STAFF SCHEDULE FOR ANNUAL GIVING CAMPAIGN

April 15	Begin analysis of last year's effort.
May 15	Hold budget meetings; identify project to be funded, and set goals and objectives for the campaign. Begin identification and recruitment of campaign leadership.
June 15	Complete leadership appointments; draft text and design for all campaign documents to describe the project and its need for funds.
July 15	Complete recruitment and appointment of leadership team; hold first meeting to plan campaign. Resolve campaign dates, including kickoff function date and site; reserve facility for kickoff event.
August 15	Complete approval of all campaign plans and support documents. Begin volunteer identification and recruitment, beginning with team captains. Schedule orientation and training sessions; resolve contents of volunteers' information kits.
September 15	Complete recruitment and appointment of team captains, followed by recruitment and appointment of volunteer solicitors. Prepare donor prospect cards; circulate to entire committee to select preferred assignments. Complete preparation of orientation and training sessions. Expect delivery of all campaign documents for volunteers' information kits.
October 1	Begin campaign promotion and publicity. Complete assignments to all volunteers. Conduct volunteer orientation and training sessions before October 15.
October 15	Conduct campaign kickoff event. Begin all solicitations.
November 1	Conduct first report meeting for all volunteer solicitors. Report gift results. Recognize those who have completed their assignments.
November 15	Conduct second report meeting. Report gift results. Recognize those who have completed their assignments.
November 30	Conduct third report meeting. Conclude active solicitation campaign. Report all campaign results, including overall volunteer performance. Recognize those who have completed their assignments.
January 15	Complete preparation of all reports for gifts received as of December 31. Complete donor recognition. Conduct victory celebration and reward leaders and volunteers.
January 30	Complete thank-you letters to all volunteers. Publish results. Prepare final accounting report. Conduct critique meeting with campaign leadership. Prepare and submit critique report with all performance details to board of directors. Include nominations for next campaign's leadership.

annual campaign, it can spark enthusiasm and help to motivate volunteers to finish their assignments. Team captains and their team members will work together to achieve 100 Percent Club status for their percentage of calls completed, total dollars raised, highest average gifts, and other categories (see Exhibit 11-8).

There can be a danger, however, in too much focus on team competition in annual giving campaigns. Some volunteers may forget that the

EXHIBIT 11-8   TRACKING SYSTEM FOR VOLUNTEER SOLICITATION TEAMS

Team	Volunteer Number	Donors Assigned	Donors Seen	Percent of Response	Value of Gifts	Average Gift Size
A	1	5	4	80%	$ 325	$ 81
	2	4	4	100	450	112
	3	5	5	100	500	100
	4	5	5	100	525	105
		19	18	95%	$1,800	$100
B	5	5	5	100	$ 235	$ 47
	6	5	5	100	750	150
	7	5	5	100	315	63
		15	15	100%	$1,300	$ 87
C	8	5	4	80	$ 425	$106
	9	5	5	100	550	110
	10	5	4	80	450	112
		15	13	86%	$1,425	$110
D	11	5	3	60	$ 325	$108
	12	5	5	100	450	90
	13	5	5	100	575	115
	14	5	5	100	450	90
	15	5	5	100	500	100
		25	23	92%	$2,300	$100
Team Summary:						
A	4	19	18	95	$1,800	$100
B	3	15	15	100	1,300	87
C	3	15	13	86	1,425	110
D	5	25	23	92	2,300	100
Total/Average	15	74	69	93%	$6,825	$ 99

purpose of their assignment is to meet with prior donors who have sincere commitments to the organization and the cause; campaign goals and team competitions are of little or no interest to donors (they may even be offended by the concept's application to the cause) and should not be discussed when meeting with donors to ask for their annual gift.

Campaign details that need leadership attention include the action steps to be taken if any deadline is missed, personal attention to prompt thank-you letters for each gift, separate meetings or telephone calls with other campaign leaders, and early planning on how to thank volunteers for their good efforts. Campaign leaders should talk one on one with any reluctant volunteers who need encouragement or a verbal "boot in the tail" to complete their calls on time. Leaders may be asked to join a volunteer and form a dual-visitor team for an important solicitation. Leaders themselves are often assigned to visit important prior donors, usually those with higher giving levels. Campaign leaders should screen for important gifts as they come in. They offer opportunities for a phone call to thank a special donor, a personal note to thank someone who has upgraded a prior gift, praise for a volunteer's performance of persistence, or a personal note attached to each progress report that is sent to all volunteer workers. Campaign gift reports with details on volunteer performance (see Exhibit 11-9) are presented to the board committee on development and perhaps to the board of directors. As the campaign moves into its final scheduled days, campaign leaders will need to be in touch with team captains and volunteers to encourage them to make their final calls by the campaign deadline. Once the campaign is over, they will give their attention to the victory celebration and then the critique session. These final meetings must be well prepared so that everyone who participates can contribute to all areas in the performance evaluation, including a review of all campaign support activities by fund development staff. A personal solicitation campaign is a personal "contact sport" from start to finish.

Evaluating the performance of a volunteer-led, personal solicitation campaign will require detailed analysis. A summary report on overall performance—what worked well, who performed well, who should be considered for leadership positions, what areas need attention next year—should be prepared and delivered to the board of directors. The board and management should join in assessing how the campaign fulfilled several objectives besides raising funds. Because this campaign is the only time

EXHIBIT 11-9	SAMPLE GIFT REPORT FOR SOLICITATION TEAMS IN PERSONAL SOLICITATION ANNUAL GIVING CAMPAIGN

Team	Number of Volunteers	This Time Last Year			Results This Year		
		Donors	Amount	Average	Donors	Amount	Average
A	4	14	$ 1,350	$ 96	18	$ 1,800	$100
B	3	14	1,075	77	15	1,300	87
C	3	12	1,320	110	13	1,425	110
D	5	18	1,740	97	23	2,300	100
	15	58	$ 5,485	$ 95	69	$ 6,825	$ 99
E	5	22	$ 2,350	$107	24	$ 2,550	$106
F	4	18	1,850	103	18	1,900	106
G	5	21	2,000	95	22	2,050	93
H	4	19	1,700	90	21	1,900	91
I	5	21	2,200	105	23	2,450	107
	23	101	$10,100	$100	108	$10,850	$101
J	4	18	$ 1,500	$ 83	18	$ 1,600	$ 89
K	4	15	1,250	83	16	1,300	81
L	5	22	2,300	105	24	2,800	117
M	4	17	1,800	106	18	2,150	119
N	5	21	2,350	112	22	2,550	116
	22	93	$ 9,200	$100	98	$10,400	$106
O	5	22	$ 2,450	$111	24	$ 2,650	$110
P	4	22	2,200	100	24	2,400	100
Q	5	18	2,150	119	20	2,450	123
R	4	17	1,550	91	16	1,400	88
	18	79	$ 8,350	$106	84	$ 8,900	$106
S	4	18	$ 1,500	$ 83	18	$ 1,400	$ 78
T	4	16	1,300	81	18	1,450	81
U	3	13	2,350	181	14	2,550	182
V	4	12	1,200	100	13	1,000	77
W	3	15	1,800	120	15	1,800	120
	18	74	$ 8,150	$110	78	$ 8,200	$105

Summary: Last Year versus This Year

23	96	405	$41,285	$102	437	$45,175	$103

Improvement in Results This Year | | | | | +32 | +$ 3,890 | +$122 |

during the year when the organization's best donors are actually seen, feedback on these meetings will be of critical interest to the board of directors, the campaign leadership, and the fund-development staff. What do these donors think about the organization in general or about its direction, its progress, its problems, its fundraising style? Suppose these donors' gifts were to decline. Unless they had made it a priority to ask for and to read visit reports from volunteers as part of the overall campaign performance evaluation, the board and management would have no clue to explain the cutback.

Considerable effort is invested in planning and executing the volunteer-led, personal solicitation annual giving campaign. Each volunteer will give an average of 15 to 25 hours to the campaign during its four to eight weeks of intensity. Campaign leadership will give twice that number of hours and will work a minimum of four to six months on the project. If 50 to 100 volunteers are involved in the campaign, their overall commitment represents a huge investment in the nonprofit organization. The board of directors and management can acknowledge this commitment by attending and participating in the victory celebration. The postcampaign celebration is an essential part of the overall campaign plan and the strategy to develop experienced and committed volunteers.

The victory celebration is the final campaign report meeting; its primary purposes are to report all the results, to honor volunteers and teams who achieved 100 percent Club status, and to thank the staff and volunteers for their hard work. After the campaign is over, a celebration of these good efforts is valuable to each volunteer's self-confidence. Everyone involved should feel good about what was accomplished by working with others on behalf of the nonprofit organization. Asking people for money was not an easy assignment for most volunteers. Taking the time to recognize and reward each volunteer for his or her contributions of time and effort is just as important as thanking each donor for a gift of money during the campaign. On a more pragmatic level, these are the volunteers who will be invited to serve again next year.

The campaign critique session is the final campaign activity. Volunteer solicitors may also be invited, but the campaign leaders need to perform this evaluation session for their own purposes. The role of professional and support staff throughout any campaign is to do everything possible to enable the volunteers to carry out their assignments. Staff efforts should be reviewed by all campaign volunteers and leaders, and their critique comments on staff support should be included in the summary report to the board. What ideas will volunteers have that would make their job more successful? The purpose of each critique session is to review and study what happened; its goal is to learn from experience and to improve next year's performance, not to find fault or point fingers at anyone or anything. If errors were committed, they should be noted alongside suggestions on how they can be prevented next time. The critique meeting will concentrate on volunteer and donor performance (using data from Exhibit 8-7), but should also examine all other areas of operations, perhaps separated into subgroups as follows:

1. Preparations (goals, leadership recruitment, documents)
2. Recruitment (identification, appointment letters)
3. Orientation and training (time, place, agenda, speakers, workers' kit contents)
4. Volunteer support (donor profiles, team captains)
5. Campaign operations (budget, gift reports, report meetings)
6. Donor relations (contact reports, thank-you letters)
7. Staff support (to leaders, volunteers, and donors)
8. Recognition and reward (donors and volunteers, victory celebration)

RECOGNITION AND REWARD

During the campaign and immediately afterward are the best times for recognition and reward. As soon as possible after receipt of a gift, the donor should receive a proper acknowledgment letter. IRS rules, following Congress's 1993 tax law changes, require nonprofit organizations to provide "substantiation" for each gift of $250 or more; a canceled check is no longer adequate evidence that the gift was made. Sending a substantiation letter creates an opportunity to initiate a series of positive experiences for a donor. There is more to gift acknowledgment than simply writing a letter of substantiation. Another factor is speed of delivery. If today is Friday and a donor mails a gift today, Monday will be the earliest the U.S. Postal Service will deliver it to the fund-development office. If routine gift processing executes a 48-hour turnaround for all acknowledgment letters, a thank-you letter will be in the mail by Tuesday afternoon and received by

Thursday, a full seven days after the gift was made. This sequence is about as quick a turnaround as is possible. The 48 hours may be shortened to 24 hours by saving one day in-house, but the fact remains that a week will pass from the day the donor sends a gift and the day a thank-you letter is received in acknowledgment. Can this performance be improved?

A number of thank-you letters are possible. Personal solicitation campaigns offer different options and allow a variety of personal alternatives. Here are some thank-you possibilities:

1. The volunteer receives the check during the solicitation meeting and acknowledges the donor's generosity the next day, in a personal note.

2. The volunteer calls in the gift decision to the team captain, who may call or write the donor to express the organization's appreciation.

3. The donor receives a formal acknowledgment letter from the non-profit organization one week later.

4. The donor's standing, or the size of the gift, warrants a second acknowledgment letter sent from the campaign chair, a board member, or the president/CEO.

5. If the gift size qualifies the donor for donor club status (see Chapter 5), another letter announces the donor's eligibility for the benefits and privileges of the donor club.

Are there other opportunities? Yes. Is there a need for more? Yes, if these good practices can be consistently applied to all donors who qualify because of the amount of their annual gifts. Some organizations send multiple letters to express their appreciation for gifts of $100 or $1,000; others reserve their enthusiasm for higher amounts. Whatever the practice, a number of thank-you opportunities are available and should be used when justified. The IRS may question the material value of "give backs" to donors when they receive umbrellas, tote bags, and coffee mugs, but no questions are raised over the number of thank-you letters a donor may receive.

Formal recognition policies and procedures are linked to giving levels and to cumulative giving histories (see Exhibits 4-4 and 7-3). These same guidelines should be used to support each method of annual giving that an organization uses. Additional features can be applied to the volunteer-led, personal solicitation campaign, beyond the thank-you notes sent to acknowledge the gift. They may pay off later when these same donors are invited to give again. Formal recognition practices provide opportunities for continued attention to *all* qualified donors, regardless of which annual giving program(s) developed their contribution. As an example, the benefits and privileges of donor club standing might be extended to every qualified donor in the personal solicitation campaign. To qualify for the full range of benefits and privileges provided to all donor club members, the only requirement would be the size of the gift ($100, $500, or $1,000). This recognition program maintains communications with donors through newsletters, annual reports, and other written documents, and sends courtesy invitations for a variety of activities, benefits, and special events held by the nonprofit organization. Some of these communications may arrive with a roster of major donors enclosed; people appreciate being thanked in public as well as privately. By tracking cumulative giving throughout each year (from any annual giving program to which donors respond), additional donors may qualify for donor club benefits. A complete program of honors and recognition should be made available to every donor, especially those whose gift size and history of support are largest, longest, and strongest.[5]

Some nonprofit organizations, in their effort to do right by their most faithful and generous donors, may overlook recognition and reward for their volunteers. Opportunities to acknowledge the extra efforts of each annual giving campaign volunteer arise during the campaign, at report meetings, and at the victory celebration. Because campaigns are repeated year after year, recognition procedures should be *consistent* from year to year. If there are a hundred ways to say thank you to volunteers, each one should be considered. Most volunteers will have already received several types of recognition in their career of service. Outstanding volunteers might share in some of the benefits and privileges reserved for donors. Finding novel ways to recognize volunteers year after year is a challenge, but good volunteers are worth this extra effort. Some unique and special reward should be reserved just for them, to add stature to what they do for the organization and to mark their special standing in the community. Plaques, certificates, and other objects are adequate, but a personal gift such as a watch, a clock, or an attractive paperweight will more accurately represent the appreciation and respect they are due. If the gift selected has space for engraving, the person's name and year of service can be inscribed.

Each gift should be nicely wrapped, an inexpensive touch. How and where these symbols of recognition and reward are presented, and by whom, may offer the best way to show appreciation to volunteers. Thoughtfulness is what counts the most.

The final opportunity for recognition is to nominate donors *and* volunteers for honors and award programs sponsored by other organizations. Being nominated is a special form of recognition in itself, regardless of whether the nomination wins an award. For example, annual National Philanthropy Day celebration programs are held across America, and donors and volunteers are honored by their communities for service to nonprofit organizations. Major donors and campaign leaders for your annual giving programs are logical candidates to nominate for these awards and are richly deserving of such public recognition. A nonprofit organization does not have to depend on others to define its donor and volunteer recognition program. Each annual meeting is a splendid and highly visible "family" occasion at which to confer awards, honors, and other forms of recognition to those donors *and* volunteers whose generosity and service have distinguished them above all others during the year.

FOCUS: CCUA CLEAN UP CLEVELAND CHAPTER

A week after the combination first annual meeting and first gala benefit evening, Karen Anderson called Mary Moneybanks and asked her to invite Iris Radiant and Trafalgar ("Telly") Temple to lunch at the Union Club. The purposes of this meeting were to be a private celebration of the successful affair, a consensus critique, and a pooling of all the "lessons learned" from this first experience. Anderson added, "This evaluation will be crucial, especially because it was a first-time event; the decision to repeat it again next year depends on our critique report to the board of directors." Moneybanks agreed, and the date was set two weeks away—time enough for Anderson to collect and pay all the bills and to complete her financial analysis.

During lunch, everyone was still "high" on the success they had achieved. A lively discussion of all the details resulted. In appreciation of their leadership, Anderson presented each of the others with a small album of photographs taken during the gala evening.

Their critique began with agreement on the outcomes of their five primary goals and objectives:

1. Of the 700 tickets printed, 680 tickets were sold, and 668 people attended.

2. Net proceeds were 56 percent of gross revenue ($56,775 of $101,500), slightly below the 58 percent projected ($59,490 from $104,500) in the approved budget.

3. News coverage was adequate before the event, but it did not help ticket sales as much as had been expected. Postevent coverage was better, chiefly because of media coverage of the variety show performances by the professional athletes.

4. The report on fundraising success was warmly received, but all were surprised when Harvey Clout's announcement of a $1.5 million federal grant toward the energy conversion plant received a standing ovation.

5. The event was clearly successful in heightening public awareness about the Clean Up Cleveland Campaign.

The group completed discussion of all aspects of the benefit. Anderson was asked to summarize their comments in a critique report to be presented at the next board of directors meeting (see Exhibit 11-10). All agreed to recommend that the combined annual meeting and gala benefit evening (and variety show) be continued next year, with a goal of $65,000 in net proceeds.

Anderson's next task was to prepare, for the next board meeting, a summary gift report on all fundraising results to date. She also wanted to report her plans and recommendations for the fall fundraising season. The spring mailings had again performed well, no doubt because of the gala and its media coverage. It was too early to know if the telephone and Internet calls and messages were going to be effective. And, all the corporate and foundation proposal work was still waiting for their replies. The final charter membership offer of two gala tickets for a gift of $100 appeared to work well. Considerable progress had been made over the past two years: 19,137 gifts had been received for a total of $714,118 (see Exhibit 11-11). Following the 75/25 split of all receipts, the construction fund for the new energy conversion plant had achieved $535,589; operating funds for marketing and fundraising purposes were $278,529. Adding the $1.5 million grant from the federal government, the overall goal of $3.5 million for the plant was now 58.2 percent complete, with $2,035,589 in the bank.

Although these figures represented considerable progress, Anderson expected the board to press for completion of all funding. Membership in The Circle of Champions now exceeded 288 individuals. There would

EXHIBIT 11-10   GALA BENEFIT EVENING CRITIQUE REPORT

First Annual Meeting and Gala Benefit Evening Critique Report

1. *Summary/Recommendations:* In this first-time effort, 668 people attended, $56,775 were the net proceeds (56%), entertainment was enjoyable and received good coverage, and public awareness of chapter mission was advanced. The combined annual meeting and gala benefit evening is recommended for continuation.

2. *Leadership/Volunteers/Staff:* The "triumvirate" (Moneybanks, Radiant, Temple) embodied enthusiasm, optimism and commitment to a quality program; they also divided responsibility, recruited volunteers, delegated duties, and supervised details. Need to add volunteer training and to develop future leaders for all areas.

3. *Invitations/Print Materials/Promotion/Publicity:* With more time next year, all printed and collateral materials will benefit from single graphic design (logo). Better coordination with media should improve pre-event coverage.

4. *Sponsorship/Ticket Sales:* Charter membership offer will have expired but offer of two seats for $100 Circle of Champions membership should continue. Gold/ Silver/Bronze medalist sponsors can be improved and will help profits, as should some corporate sponsors and underwriters.

5. *Registration/Facilities/Arrangements/Decorations:* Need more volunteers at all entrances and in aisles to aid seating. Add staffed displays on project, membership booth, information desk, seating charts in lobby area. Postevent booths worked well; increase lighting and heating; larger signs for food vendors; add 10 tables/100 chairs to seat guests. Add valet parking as option for all guests.

6. *Program/Agenda/Entertainment:* Need to start on time (more volunteers to aid seating will help). Crisp business meeting was a blessing. Hard to repeat Clout's $1.5-million surprise announcement. Presentation of certificates took too much time; may not be necessary again as charter memberships are concluded. Competition between teams unnecessary; drop judging. Encourage more athletes to remain after and join in postevent reception.

7. *Food/Beverage/Service:* Pre-event refreshments can be limited to light beverages at theater concession stands; no food. Postevent reception can be promoted better; concentrate menu on desserts and "finger food" tastings of vendors' wares. Wine and beer bar only. Keep everything free.

8. *Added Fundraising Events/Prizes:* While revenue was solid, raffle ticket sales and drawings took time. Consider silent auction only; open theater lobby 90 minutes ahead of program to facilitate bidding; close 10 minutes before program to move crowd into theater. Winners posted on signs at entrance to postevent reception where prizes are paid for and picked up.

EXHIBIT 11-10   (CONTINUED)

9. *Acknowledgment/Recognition:* Tickets are costly and unnecessary. Thank-you letter can verify reservation and assigned seats; volunteers and ushers can assist entry and seating. Printed program is ideal for sponsor/underwriter recognition. Brief mention during meeting of lists, if large posters listing all medalist groups are displayed in lobby and at postevent reception. Can we link medalists with food vendors as partners?

10. *Budget Management:* Superb efforts by leadership and volunteers provided medalists' gifts plus in-kind gifts and donated services for many expense areas, which aided profits; may be hard to duplicate next year. Auction prizes can be fewer but of better quality. Solid staff work kept other expenses in line.

be a growing need to personalize the renewal solicitation of these $100-plus annual donors; letters and telephone calls would not be enough to hold most of them for another year. She also was confident that several of their corporate and foundation proposals would be successful with funds received in the next fiscal year. Anderson planned to recommend that the coming fall campaign season would be an ideal time to initiate the first volunteer-led annual giving campaign. She estimated that between 35 and 50 Circle of Champions members would volunteer if asked. If each volunteer called on five prior donors, between 175 and 250 personal contacts could be made.

Anderson prepared a complete plan. It began with recommendations on candidates for a campaign chairperson, a vice chair, and five team captains. Anderson also defined plans to prepare: donor lists with giving histories, orientation and training meetings, volunteer information kits, a budget for printed materials and meetings, and other campaign details. With the addition of personal solicitation to the overall annual giving plan, Anderson believed that the chapter's fund development program was now in place. She intended to expand her use of direct mail, plus use of the telephone and Internet, for acquisition and renewal and to continue to market memberships in The Circle of Champions as a combined membership association and donor club package. The annual gala would be offered as the major benefit event each year with better opportunities for corporate sponsorship and underwriting. With this balanced fundraising program in place, Anderson believed that the Clean Up Cleveland Chapter of The Campaign to

EXHIBIT 11-11   **TWO-YEAR TOTALS AND CUMULATIVE GIFT SUMMARY**

Letter	Program	Number Mailed	Replies Number	Replies Percent	Gift Income

Acquisition Phase (Chapters 2 and 3)

Letter	Program	Number Mailed	Number	Percent	Gift Income
A & B	July test mailing	30,000	348	1.16%	$ 8,527
B	Fall: Full test mailing	80,575	1,156	1.43	35,758
B	Spring 1—"Roll out"	200,000	1,831	0.91	56,936
C	Spring 2—Follow-up	194,476	1,822	0.94	59,975
	Subtotal	505,051	5,157	1.02%	$161,196

Donor Renewal Phase (Chapter 3)

Letter	Program	Number Mailed	Number	Percent	Gift Income
D	Spring renewal: Introduce charter membership	1,501	914	66.77%	$ 31,064
Year 1	Cumulative totals	506,555	6,071	1.20%	$192,260

Acquisition and Renewal Plus Donor Club Offer (Chapters 3–5)

Letter	Program	Number Mailed	Number	Percent	Gift Income
E	Fall: Second acquisition mailing plus charter membership offer	192,116	2,216	1.15%	$ 54,276
E	Fall: Follow-up letter	191,012	1,976	1.03	52,120
	Subtotal	383,128	4,192	1.09%	$106,396
F	Renewal 2 plus charter membership offer	6,661	1,864	27.98%	$ 81,872
F	Renewal 2 follow-up	3,797	1,519	40.00	44,664
	Subtotal	10,458	3,383	32.35%	$126,536

Circle of Champions: Renewal (Letter and Phone Follow-up)

	Program	Number Mailed	Number	Percent	Gift Income
	Fall renewal	160	138	86.25%	$ 16,836
	Fall totals	393,746	7,713	1.96%	$249,768
	Cumulative totals	900,301	13,784	1.53%	$442,028

Spring Campaign: Telephone, Corporate and Foundation (Chapters 6 to 10) plus Spring Acquisition & Renewal Direct Mailing Results

	Program	Number Mailed	Number	Percent	Gift Income
	Telephone Test Results	13,784	1,638	11.88%	$ 37,226
	Corporate and Foundation Results*	27	-0-	-0-	-0-

*17 proposals submitted for between $210,000 to $250,000; replies pending.

EXHIBIT 11-11   (CONTINUED)

G	Spring acquisition mailings (2)	187,334	1,835	0.97%	$ 97,665
G	Spring renewal mailings (2)	6,339	1,838	28.99%	$117,650
	Subtotal	207,484	5,311	2.56%	$252,541

Spring Campaign: Acquisition, Renewal and First Gala (Chapter 10)

G	Spring acquisition mailings (2) plus gala	187,334	1,835	0.97%	$ 97,665
G	Spring renewal mailings (2) plus gala	6,339	1,838	28.99%	$117,650
	Subtotal	193,673	3,673	1.90%	$215,315

Spring Acquisition and Renewal Mailings with Internet Results from Chapter 9 (CCUA Gift Reports) plus Gala Benefit Evening Net Results

G	207,484	5,311	2.56%	$252,541
Internet	8,775	188	2.14%	$ 6,139
Gala	3,800	680	17.89%	$ 56,775
Spring Campaign Results Totals	220,059	6,179	2.81%	315,455
First Year Cumulative Totals	900,292	14,784	1.64%	$442,028
Second Year Cumulative Totals	220,059	6,179	2.81%	$315,455
Grand Total	1,120,351	20,963	1.87%	$757,483

Distribution	Public education (25%)	=	$ 189,621
	Energy plant (75%)	=	$ 568,862
	Federal grant award	=	$1,500,000
	Subtotal	=	$2,258,483
	Plant construction cost	=	$3,500,000
	Percent of goal raised	=	64.53%

Clean Up America would continue to make steady progress toward fulfilling its mission.

Clout called Anderson the next week, after returning from The Campaign to Clean Up America's national board meeting. He realized that it was time for the board to begin to address the chapter's plans following completion of the energy conversion plant's construction. The first phase in the overall strategy of The Campaign to Clean Up America would end with the completion of a visible project that had major economic as well as environmental impact. Phase two was scheduled to begin before the plant was completed and producing new electricity; it was to address one of three issues: (1) air, (2) land, or (3) water pollution. "Thanks to the ecology of Lake Erie and the decline of smokestack industries in the area, air quality around Cleveland is much improved," Cloud said. "Even Lake Erie water is making a comeback, but the water level is rising and causing erosion of the shore line. Perhaps land should be our next project, especially if we can begin to reclaim land sites where industrial waste burial jeopardizes the value and use of the property. We had best begin to study our options," added Clout. "Karen, can you call some of the other chapters and learn where they are with planning phase two? I'll also think about whom to appoint to a planning committee to begin work on our next project. Many thanks." To Anderson, there seemed to be several purposes for the chapter to continue with its mission for years to come.

12

■

Other Ways to Raise Money Every Year

Nonprofit organizations invest their annual fundraising budgets in a variety of mailings and memberships; telephone and telemarketing techniques; auxiliaries, guilds, donor clubs, and support groups; corporate and foundation grant seeking plus the Internet, activities, benefits, and events; and volunteer solicitation programs. Their combined purpose is to be able to raise friends and build relationships with a constituency of donors on whom they can depend for reliable annual support and, when necessary, for major and estate gifts as well. To establish and operate a comprehensive annual giving program requires (1) a major investment of time and money and (2) professional management to achieve maximum efficiency and profitability. Among the benefits to be realized are committed donors, volunteers, and leaders who will provide reliable gift support to meet the priority needs of the nonprofit organization.

If raising money were the *only* objective for annual giving, most of the fundraising programs described in this book would not be worth the time, cost, or trouble that must be invested in them. Money-raising is *not* concerned with friend-raising, relationship building, donor renewal, volunteer and leadership development, donor recognition, and all the rest; it is focused only on cash. Many nonprofit organizations may begin their fundraising programs with a need for cash (starting at the bottom of the pyramid in Exhibit 1-2), but they must grow beyond a mercenary use of fundraising methods if they hope to realize the potential that a comprehensive annual giving program can deliver. To grow beyond money-raising and to build a reliable base of support requires using the annual giving programs described in this book to attain several other objectives as well as reliable sources of cash (see Chapter 3). Fund development is a strategic plan for managing every fundraising method toward achievement of a nonprofit organization's mission over multiple years. All of these programs are coordinated in a complex process toward the larger objective of enabling the institution to advance according to its own plans to provide services to the public at the highest level of quality possible. Money-raising alone can never fulfill these larger requirements.

The objectives of annual giving programs should be designed to *Acquire* donors, *Renew* donors, and *Maximize* donors' relationship with the organization. To fully ARM a nonprofit organization, each annual giving method of fundraising should be selected not just to produce cash but because of its ability to fulfill most of the following objectives every year:

1. Develop the image linked to the mission.
2. Obtain friends to support the mission.
3. Identify and acquire new donors.
4. Continue to renew most prior donors.
5. Build relationships with donors.
6. Identify and involve volunteers.
7. Develop and train future leaders.
8. Raise money in a cost-effective manner.
9. Communicate with and inform donors.
10. Recognize and reward donors.
11. Develop major and estate donors for the future.
12. Build confidence and trust in the organization.

As with a script for any stage play, the organization must first set the stage for why annual giving is necessary (its mission). "Star" players are selected from among the most experienced and successful performers (the annual giving techniques presented in Chapters 2 through 11). To complete casting and crew assignments, legitimate roles for the supporting cast and tasks for the stage hands are identified (other ways to raise money every year). The completed production team is then rehearsed in their roles to present a great story (the case for support). A successful production will attract an audience who will provide, night after night and year after year, the funds needed to continue and to expand.

The fundraising techniques described in this chapter are the legitimate roles reserved for the supporting cast and the tasks assigned to the stage hands. Many of these methods might function well enough alone and be offered to the public year after year, but their potential is more likely to be realized when offered in concert with a comprehensive annual giving program. These programs are best used as "extras," especially when they can fulfill only one or a few of the 12 primary objectives just listed. Acting alone, they are less reliable for producing faithful donors, developing volunteers and leaders, and (most important) building confidence and trust in the organization. There may be times when these alternative fundraising methods will be chosen because of competition for donors and dollars, or a lack of resources and volunteers to raise the money needed. Competition alone may not justify choosing what many donors and prospects will consider a less than professional or even a questionable fundraising method, just to get money. Properly used as options and enhancements to ongoing annual giving programs, other ways to raise money every year can spark enthusiasm, capture attention, and add variety and spice. None is able to carry the full load of providing all the funds a nonprofit organization needs each year. In alphabetical order, these legitimate other ways to raise money every year are

1. Advertising and coupons
2. Commemorative and tribute giving
3. Commercial sales, cause-related marketing, and affinity cards
4. Door-to-door and on-street solicitation
5. Federated campaigns
6. Gambling and games of chance
7. Multimedia options
8. Premiums
9. Television and telethon solicitation
10. Various other annual giving ideas of merit

ADVERTISING AND COUPONS

Among the media options for solicitation messages are newspapers and magazines, billboards and bus-backs, radio and television. Within these outlets are opportunities that may include news and feature articles, paid advertisements, and coupon cards. Achieving news cover age in the papers, in magazines, or on radio or television is quite difficult for nonprofit organizations. When a story does appear, it can increase public awareness and foster public confidence and trust—valued and coveted tangible results. Given these communication avenues, "good news" stories could be delivered daily, but they are not.

Media executives believe routine good works, "people helping people," are not newsworthy material most of the time. It is true that good works are soft news that cannot compete with crime, disasters, and politics, but stories about people helping people are valid news stories. Media readers, listeners, and viewers *are* people who volunteer at and give money to organizations that help people. To succeed in the news market, an organization must treat media representatives in the same manner as prospects or donors, and bring them only story ideas that they can use. They need to hear what nonprofit organizations are doing to combat hunger and poverty, illness and disease, abuse and cruelty, homelessness and illiteracy—all newsworthy topics. They will appreciate how the human spirit can be crushed, how polluting the environment affects everyone, why access to culture and the arts has value, what the rewards of volunteerism are, and how nonprofit organizations can make a difference. There are plenty of news ideas; they just have to be communicated more effectively.

Paid advertisements that will deliver the message are available to every nonprofit organization. If the primary goal is to communicate a message to a large number of people, to market a program or service, or to increase public awareness, advertising can be bought. However, it is budgeted as an expense. As a fundraising method, advertising has never worked well to produce numbers of donors or substantial income. Commercial advertisements with clip-out product discount coupons work for retail stores and food markets because the customers are buying products, not giving their money away to store owners. The expense of advertising can be a double barrier: (1) because of its cost and (2) because the public's reaction may be, "If they can pay for advertisements in the papers and on television, they obviously don't need my money." Whether this conclusion is true or not, nonprofit organizations must remain conservative by nature and sensitive to public criticism.

The expense-of-advertising question requires further analysis. If a quarter-page newspaper advertisement for one week costs $5,000 and is circulated to 100,000 people, how does that expense compare to the postage required to mail a letter to the same 100,000 people? The third-class, non-profit enhanced carrier route, high density, presort bulk rate will be $0.066 × 100,000 = $6,600. Added costs are for rental of the mailing list, printing of the letter and envelope, and mailing house charges to affix the labels, sort, tie, and bag the letters, and deliver the entire shipment to the U.S. Postal Service. The lower cost makes paid advertising appear to be the clear winner, but advertisements alone do not raise money. When used together with a direct mail program or benefit event, they can boost the number of mail responses and ticket sales. The bottom line reads: The use of paid advertising increases the cost of fundraising. Placements of paid advertising should be measured just as carefully as direct mail, telephone, and event results, to verify whether an adequate increase in responses was realized and whether the dollars raised exceeded their added expense.

The alternative to paid advertising is a public service announcement (PSA) for radio and television use. The Federal Communications Commission (FCC) used to require, as part of its licensing procedures, that stations reserve a portion of their on-air time for public service programs and announcements. This requirement was discontinued for radio in 1981 and for television in 1984. Each station has the option to air as much public service programming as it chooses. Two steps are recommended: (1) Meet with station representatives to learn their preferences, community relations objectives, and on-air styles, and (2) prepare and submit PSAs in 15- and 30-second segments (audiotaped or videotaped) for their use. In practice, 15-second tapes are likely to be played more often.

Exceptions to any rule are always possible. News stories and advertisements asking for gifts to aid victims of fires, floods, hurricanes, or earthquakes will achieve impressive results. A need is clear, people want to know how they can help, and the media provide the names and mailing addresses for responses. Nonprofit organizations cannot expect misfortune to be the source of motivation for their annual gifts. Those organizations whose mission is to support victims of emergencies will be prepared in advance to get their message to the media immediately. Because of the pace of news and the number of disasters reported almost daily, there is little time for the other means of annual solicitation to be communicated to the public in as timely a manner as the news.

News stories, magazine articles, advertisements, coupons, and PSAs can all be used by nonprofit organizations to enhance their annual giving programs, but they should not hope to meet all of their annual cash requirements through these media alone. Their best use is in combination with traditional methods, as part of a "multimedia" program plan. Two key decisions are needed to achieve maximum effect with multimedia messages: (1) control of timing and (2) choice of medium. The ability to control when a soft news story will be used is next to impossible to achieve. By contrast, paid advertisements and PSAs on local radio and television (cable or commercial) can be scheduled to run during a week when mailings, invitations, or telephone solicitations are delivered. Multimedia messages will help to improve public awareness of the need, which, in turn, will help increase responses. There are no limits to the use of advertisements and coupons in the newsletters, magazines, and annual reports produced by nonprofit organizations. Each of these communications outlets should be used at all times to reinforce the message that annual gift support is requested and welcome at any time.

COMMEMORATIVE AND TRIBUTE GIVING

Several nonprofit organizations receive a regular number of commemorative and tribute gifts each year. Each gift may be reasonably modest ($10 to $25), but their volume can produce an impressive sum of money each year. Commemorative and tribute gifts are used most often to recognize special occasions—birthdays, anniversaries, promotions, graduations, confirmations, and weddings. They are also used to honor individuals by making a gift to charity in their name, as a tribute. Through the gift, the donor expresses both respect and generosity. There are many positive occasions for such donations, but most commemorative gifts to nonprofit organizations are made in memory of an individual after his or her death. These memorial gifts express sympathy to the surviving family and a desire to perpetuate the memory of the deceased. Families often designate a beneficiary of memorial donations, usually a nonprofit organization that the deceased or other family members have actively supported. Many obituary notices announce family preferences for a gift to a named charity in lieu of flowers.

A nonprofit organization's proper response to commemorative and tribute gifts consists of two acknowledgments: (1) a thank-you letter, receipt, or card sent to the donor, and (2) a notice forwarded to the honoree or family to announce that a gift has been made in an individual's name. The name and address of the donor (*never* the gift amount) are added to the second notice, for convenience, in case the honoree (or his or her family) wishes to send a personal acknowledgment.

Some of the donors who use commemorative and tribute gifts will be new to the nonprofit organization. Few of these people are likely to become candidates for other annual giving programs, including donor renewal solicitations, because their motive in making their first gift was to show respect for the person honored, not to support the designated organization. They probably will not give again, even if asked. The best hope for converting these donors into annual givers begins with properly acknowledging each donation, regardless of its size. A postage-paid reply envelope, to be used for a future commemorative or tribute gift, should be enclosed with the acknowledgment. This form of solicitation cannot be pushed on people; it must be treated as a special service offered to donors who choose to use it. An exception will be the prior donor who designated the organization to receive the memorial gifts and regularly makes commemorative and tribute donations. Supplying commemorative gift forms and postage-paid envelopes is a considerate and supportive service that will encourage repeat gifts. The cumulative gift history of these donors should reflect each additional contribution, especially when counting up the total for annual giving recognition purposes.

Every nonprofit organization can receive a commemorative or tribute gift and should be prepared to respond with the dual acknowledgments. National health agencies and health-care organizations tend to receive memorial gifts; colleges and universities, museums, and arts organizations receive commemorative and tribute gifts. Organizations that are frequent recipients encourage this practice by preparing packets with multiuse forms and reply envelopes. The packet, usually a combination "turnaround" envelope that has detailed information printed on the preaddressed return envelope's back and flap, can be contained in a $3'' \times 9''$ brochure describing the many forms of commemorative and tribute gifts. The brochure may also describe the optional uses made of such gifts, illustrate the reply cards and quote their messages, and provide a supply of reply envelopes in a pocket flap. Displaying these brochures in lobbies and waiting rooms and near donor recognition walls will draw public attention to this gift option.

Administrative details to support this program include hand-addressed envelopes and cards, records of all gifts received, separate accounting for each fund, communication of donors' names and addresses to the honored individual's family, assignment of the funds received, and special recognition. Most gifts received are retained within a special fund established in the honoree's name; each new gift received in that name is added to the special fund account. After the gifts are declared to be concluded, the funds are released to the purpose or project identified with the honoree or by the family. If significant funds ($2,500 or more) are involved, they may require additional consideration as to their use. They might be invested and preserved as an endowed fund for named scholarships or assigned to a priority purpose of the organization.

Recognition of commemorative gifts should be part of the nonprofit organization's honors and recognition policy (see Exhibits 4-4 and 7-4). The policy's guidelines may specify a minimum amount of funds needed to qualify for a named fund or for display within the donor recognition system (for example, $2,500 for inscription on the donor wall or on a plaque). Commemorative or tribute funds raised to establish an endowment fund—often to honor a retiring professor at a college or university—are likely to include several recognition components. The named endowment fund will carry the individual's name forward whenever the fund or the recipient is mentioned. Its complete title will appear in faculty rosters, catalogs, and publications. If a scholar-recipient publishes a research paper, the notation "Supported in part by the XYZ Research Endowment Fund" will be carried as a credit.[1] Prior to any announcement of the establishment of this form of recognition, commemorative and tribute gifts of considerable magnitude must be received by the nonprofit organization, and the naming and recognition must be approved and granted by the board of directors.

The names of honorees, the purposes of the funds, the gift levels offered, and the roster of participating donors may be published in institutional newsletters, magazines, on the Web page, and in annual reports and may help to promote additional commemorative and tribute gifts. Apart from the visibility these named projects will enjoy, the name of each honoree and an updated list of those who have recently made gifts to the named fund should be a regular feature in the organization's newsletters, annual reports, and other publications.

Nonprofit organizations must be willing to invest the time and overhead needed to handle commemorative and tribute gifts properly. The effort and costs involved are minimal and will be repaid, but these gifts are not a predictable source of annual giving dollars. When a new commemorative or tribute fund account is first established, a rush of giving usually follows; after a few weeks, the intensity often dwindles. Family members and honorees who expected more donors and larger gifts may be disappointed with these results. The reality is that most commemorative and tribute gifts are expressions of courtesy and respect, not investment decisions. The solicitation methods available are direct mail or obituary notices in the newspaper, certainly not the most effective ways to ask for gifts. In practice, commemorative gifts tend to have a short life; the period of intense giving lasts only several weeks at most. These gifts are also unpredictable for their ability to attract either a volume of donors or large donations, but each gift must be handled with care. Estimates of the annual results of commemorative and tribute gifts should always be conservative.

COMMERCIAL SALES, CAUSE-RELATED MARKETING, AND AFFINITY CARDS

These methods of raising money also are unpredictable options. To understand what they are and what they can or cannot accomplish, some definitions are given here in alphabetical order:

Affinity cards. [Programs] in which an exempt organization is paid a portion of the revenues derived from the use of the cards by the consumers who make up the affinity group. The position of the IRS [Internal Revenue Service] is that the revenues from affinity card programs are taxable because they arise from the exploitation of mailing lists, and that the special exception for these lists is not available because the lists are provided to noncharitable organizations.[2]

Cause-related marketing. Fundraising techniques used to generate nongift revenues, involving related and/or unrelated activities; the term usually includes charitable sales promotions and other forms of commercial co-ventures.[3]

Commercial co-venture. An arrangement between a for-profit organization and a charitable organization (sometimes more than one),
whereby the for-profit entity agrees to make a contribution to the charitable entity, with the amount of the contribution determined by the
volume of sales of products or services by the for-profit organization
during a particular time period.[4]

The application of these options introduces three entirely new and complex questions that the board of directors and CEO must weigh at the outset:

1. May a commercial business be allowed to use the name and reputation of this nonprofit organization in advertising and selling its products?

2. What negotiations are required to resolve the amount to be received, or to verify the accounting for the sales of products or services that will provide income to this nonprofit organization?

3. Will this transaction qualify the nonprofit organization as carrying
   on an unrelated trade or business, for which it will be subjected to
   income tax on the revenue received?

The answer to the first question is "Yes, but only after this gift horse has
had a total body examination." Any nonprofit organization may enter into
a written contract with a commercial business for sales and/or marketing
purposes. State and local regulations, where applicable, will specify the
details to be contained in the contract, the filing of copies with state and
local authorities (which makes the details public knowledge), the financial
reports due within a stated time following the campaign, and much more.
All of these details demand additional investigation and complete observance. The contract should be signed by at least a senior officer of both
parties (see Chapter 8).

Particular attention should be paid to (1) how the name of the nonprofit
will be used and its link to the product or service to be advertised, (2) the
methodology used to resolve the amount of money due to the nonprofit
organization, (3) the specification of who is obligated for any expenses incurred, and (4) the time period of the promotion campaign, all contained
in the written contract.

The third question could be answered yes or no, depending on the
product sold and the extent to which the nonprofit organization is in-

volved in the product prior to and after a sale is made. One such marketing effort, a charitable life insurance program offered to members of the American Bar Endowment, lost its court case:

> Despite the findings of the lower courts, the U.S. Supreme Court held that the provision of group insurance policies, underwritten by major insurance companies, by the American Bar Endowment (ABE), a charitable organization, to its members constitutes the carrying on of an unrelated trade or business. The Court noted that the organization negotiated premium rates with insurers, selected the insurers that provided the coverage, solicited its membership, collected the premiums, transmitted the premiums to the insurer, maintained files on each policyholder, answered members' questions concerning insurance policies, and screened claims for benefits.[5]

To some board members and CEOs of nonprofit organizations, commercial sales, cause-related marketing, and affinity cards may appear to be ways to produce "easy money with little effort on their part." (Those words telegraph a warning; beware!) These methods are not reliable sources of annual gifts, for two reasons:

1. When sales fail to meet expectations, the company may withdraw from the program.
2. No record of the buyer/donor is captured; there is no opportunity to renew the "gift" nor build any lasting relationship.

An understanding of why these programs appeal to companies might come from standing in their shoes. They want to trade on the public image and reputation of a nonprofit organization to sell their products; they believe the public will be more inclined to purchase from them because they are donating a portion of the sales price for a well-known and respected charitable purpose. What's on the line for the company? Sales volume and profits. What's on the line for the nonprofit organization? Image and reputation! If a nonprofit organization wants to build a strong and lasting relationship with any local business, corporation, or firm, it should do so for reasons other than a windfall "easy money" gift opportunity.

Affinity cards are a more recent arrival among creative products used for annual giving. A common example is a bank credit card offered by a nonprofit organization to its donors. The organization enters into a joint venture with a bank and negotiates a competitive interest rate to offer donors for Mastercard or Visa credit card privileges. Most donors may already use more than one bank credit card at any one time, but they probably will not yet own one with their favorite nonprofit organization's name and logo on the face. The special added offer is that a percentage of the value of items purchased via card use will be returned to the organization as a "contribution." Affinity cards appear to overcome many of the objections lined up against other ways to raise money every year, as discussed at the beginning of this chapter. They build relationships with donors, encourage annual giving, raise money in a cost-effective manner, recognize and reward donors, and build confidence and trust in the organization. Of concern are the issues raised regarding commercial sales and cause-related marketing, including unrelated business income tax (UBIT) on the revenue delivered to the nonprofit organization.

Can commercial sales, cause-related marketing, and affinity cards be used by nonprofit organizations in their annual giving programs? Yes; but only after due diligence and full disclosure by both parties of their dual objectives and their ability to meet IRS and state regulations without potential damage to the nonprofit organization.[6]

Door-to-Door and On-Street Solicitation

Friend-raising and relationship-building can seldom be achieved using these "cold-call" approaches. As methods of annual giving, both have diminished in use by all but a few nonprofit organizations over the past decade. The reasons for this decline may include:

1. Loss of volunteer workers who would solicit
2. Distaste for the confrontational style required
3. Public resistance and suspicion
4. City and state regulations; police enforcement
5. Poor results; raising only "what's in my pocket at the time"
6. Too much of a money-raising-only tactic; no time or opportunity to present the case or consider the merits of the cause
7. Names and addresses not retained for renewal requests

8. Lack of an adequate public response

9. Concern for the safety of volunteer workers

10. Other more efficient and profitable methods now readily available

Only a few successful practitioners of door-to-door and on-street solicitation remain. The best known are the annual cookie sale by the Girl Scouts of America and The Salvation Army and Volunteers of America holiday appeals, which feature musicians, singers, bell ringers, and "kettles and red pots." Many of America's national health foundations conducted door-to-door solicitations in the past but most of these have been absorbed into other causes or have adopted other media. The charity coin canisters that continue to be displayed, for example, in McDonald's restaurants, for Ronald McDonald houses, are usually linked with a corporate sponsor that accepts the responsibility to monitor the money and channel it properly. One national firm, Taco Bell Corp., collects about $1 million annually for the Muscular Dystrophy Association using "Jerry's Kids" canisters. Young people are obliged to use door-to-door and on-street solicitations as fundraising methods for their school or camp projects.

Offers of magazine subscriptions, specialty candy products, and car washes, which are actually commercial sales disguised as fundraising opportunities, are common. Homeowners have developed sales resistance to door-to-door cold-calling solicitations. Telephone callers may be the last to pursue the strategy of cold calls to homeowners (see Chapter 6), whose resistance to this method is growing as well. It seems fair to state that most door-to-door and on-street solicitations have become quite commercial in nature. The public has become confused about whether they are buying products or making gifts for charitable purposes. The media have given better than usual coverage to scams and con artists whose fraudulent and abusive practices originated from door-to-door and on-street charitable solicitations that defrauded the public. These criminals have hurt the overall image of nonprofit organizations, reduced volunteer effectiveness, increased public resistance and suspicion, and damaged the public's underlying confidence and trust in making gifts when invited to do so, whether at their home or business or on the street. Perhaps it is better for everyone that door-to-door and on-street solicitation is diminishing.

FEDERATED CAMPAIGNS

The annual operating budgets of many nonprofit organizations depend on being an approved institution or agency in a federated campaign. This style of annual solicitation is a combined or joint appeal held in the workplace once a year on behalf of all the members in the federation, who share in the results. Two of the most famous of these, United Way of America and the Combined Federal Campaign, have developed the workplace solicitation, payroll deduction, and corporate annual gift with a high degree of success. Because of the success of United Way of America and the Combined Federal Campaign, many nonprofit organizations that were not members of either group (and are denied access to the participating companies and their employees during campaign periods) have petitioned successfully to be allowed into the workplace at other times to solicit. Corporations and their employees are a proven source of reliable annual gifts, but the designated charities will not receive all of their annual gift support from workplace campaigns. Dependence on any single source of funds can become a liability when that source falters. Following the William Aramony scandal at United Way of America headquarters in 1992, contributions declined dramatically, including allocations from member United Way chapters across the country. The member organizations affiliated with these chapters received between 20 and 30 percent less money as their allocation, a large amount to make up in one year through other annual giving methods. The public confidence and giving levels have returned after five years.

Most recently, the historic outpouring of emergency contributions to the American Red Cross, in excess of $550 million following the September 11 terrorist attacks on New York's World Trade Center towers and the Pentagon, resulted in public outrage over disclosure that some of the funds were to be held and others redirected to separate Red Cross purposes. Although this was corrected weeks later with the promise of full distribution to the victims, as donors had been led to believe, this incident itself is likely to hinder future emergency giving. A further concern is how this revelation—apparently common practice to set aside some funds for other priority needs—might affect the hundreds of Red Cross chapters across North America that received none of these funds for their local needs. The main issue is public trust: Will the spirit of giving be as forthcoming the next time there is a national disaster?

Federated campaigns appear to have established "turf" ownership of the corporation, its employees, and, to a degree, the fall campaign period. For member organizations, any other corporate solicitation and employee solicitation at home is "off limits" throughout this period. Nonmember organizations are completely free to solicit both groups, but the competition is keen and the phrase "I gave at the office" is a frequently heard response. I am unaware of any major study that has demonstrated whether public giving has been diminished for nonmember organizations as a consequence of this practice. The fall months remain the prime period for every nonprofit organization to conduct its annual giving campaigns. The results seem to suggest that the public also prefers to make most of its gifts during this time period.

GAMBLING AND GAMES OF CHANCE

Gambling is a strong word, but it is accurate to describe a select group of fundraising activities when they are used for annual giving purposes by nonprofit organizations. In alphabetical order, gambling activities include auctions, bingo, Las Vegas or Monte Carlo nights, lotteries, raffles, and sweepstakes. At issue here is not whether they can raise money; they do. The fact is that they are forms of gambling as defined by law in most states, as well as in county and city jurisdictions, and may not be charitable giving opportunities at all. At best, they can be used only occasionally by nonprofit organizations to raise money for charitable purposes. Greg Gattuso[7] reports: "Lawmakers in a number of states are considering legislation that would ban charitable gambling. . . . A bill in the Rhode Island state legislature proposes a ban on all poker, slot machines, and other casino games in the state. . . . Recently, the state of Arizona banned all casino gambling, including all fundraising gaming." Gambling has a limited ability to develop faithful annual donors; what it appears to develop is faithful gamblers. Advocates espouse the philosophy that gambling is OK because they will "clean the tainted money by its good works." Gambling in any of its forms is a risky business for any nonprofit organization to use for fundraising purposes. Most states limit its use and a few outlaw it altogether. When and where permitted, gambling and games of chance may operate only under strict supervision and are limited as to their frequency. Several cities and counties have enacted additional local ordinances in an attempt to regulate and supervise most of the forms of gambling and games of chance, including bingo, within their jurisdiction. Exhibit 12-1 lists charitable gambling's games.[8] They can be a serious problem, especially for the uninitiated, unaware, and unthinking.

Auctions and raffles are included in these regulations because money is exchanged for goods bid on and purchased. Auctions may be the most benign of gambling forms; raffles can easily run afoul of state lottery laws. Even U.S. Postal Service regulations are involved, if raffle tickets are sold through the mail. Volunteers who espouse these methods often cite the fact that they have never heard of a nonprofit organization being prosecuted for holding an auction or raffle—yet. How much comfort should the board of directors and CEO take from that fact? Very little, according to Hopkins.[9]

> Players were charged a fixed amount for the use of bingo cards, the games were held on three nights each week, and the receipts from and expenses of the games were substantial. The IRS concluded that "the bingo games constitute a trade or business with the general public, the conduct of which is not substantially related to the exercise or the performance by the organization of the purposes for which it was organized other than the use it makes of the profits derived from the games." [The organization was unable to utilize the exemption from unrelated income taxation afforded by IRC § 513(f) because, under the law of the state in which it is organized (Texas), the bingo games constituted, at that time, an illegal lottery.]

All but four states allow one or more of the forms of charitable gambling. Permits for nonprofit organizations to hold a Las Vegas or Monte Carlo night, the most obvious form of gambling, as a fundraising activity may be obtained (usually from city or county police departments), but they contain restrictions on the types of games allowed and the hours of operation, and they require strict financial controls (no "real money" is permitted; only script or chips). Local authorities will require at least one uniformed police officer to be present at all times (at the organization's expense), usually stationed at the "cage" where cash is exchanged for chips or script. No patron can win any money; winnings must be converted into prizes, which can be purchased, auctioned, or raffled off using chips or script. A complete financial report must be filed following the event, and the city or county may exact an excise tax on the proceeds.

EXHIBIT 12-1   FROM BINGO TO TIPBOARDS:
COMMON CHARITABLE-GAMBLING
GAMES

Bingo: Players buy cards printed with a grid containing letters or numbers, and cover the symbols that match those selected at random and announced to people in the bingo hall. The first player to cover all symbols arrayed in a certain fashion, usually in a row, wins a prize.

Calcuttas: Players bet on which participant in a sports event (a rodeo or golf tournament, for example) will be victorious. The size of the wager varies according to each participant's perceived skill—for example, a golfer's handicap. The bets are pooled, then divided based on the outcome of the event.

Casino Nights: Also called Las Vegas nights, Nevada nights, Monte Carlo nights, or millionaire parties, these are temporary mock casinos, featuring games like blackjack, craps, and roulette. In some states, players wager play money after paying an entrance fee; in others they buy chips as in regular casinos.

Charity Game Tickets: Available in hundreds of versions, known variously as pull-tabs, jar tickets, break-opens, pickle tabs, paper roulette, criss crosses, and so on. Players buy a sealed bit of paper and unfold it, lift up the perforated tabs on a card, or otherwise reveal hidden numbers or symbols—like those on a slot machine. If the numbers of symbols disclosed match the winning array, they win a prize. The tickets are often sold at bingo games, in taverns or restaurants, or even in the offices of some charities.

Keno: Players bet on combinations of numbers. Those whose picks come closest to the ones drawn at random win a prize. Often played during casino nights.

Paddlewheels: Players bet on which number, color, or symbol will be selected when a large vertical wheel stops spinning.

Punchboards: Players punch a hole through a face sheet of a cardboard playing board to obtain a folded bit of paper. If the number or symbol on the paper matches the winning combination displayed on the board, the player wins a prize.

Raffles: Players buy numbered tickets, each of which represents a chance to win a prize of cash or merchandise. From the pool of all entrants, a number is selected at random, and the holder of the matching ticket wins the prize.

Tipboards: Players buy and remove game tickets affixed to a board and see if the number printed on the ticket matches a number printed on the board. If players have a match, they put their names on the board next to their number. When all the tickets have been purchased, a seal on the board is opened and an underlying number is disclosed. The player whose number matches the winning one takes the prize, which can be cash or merchandise.

Other Games: Games permitted in some states include video versions of bingo or poker; fish ponds, crane games, and other activities where the object is to capture a particular prize; sports pools, in which players bet on professional sports contests; and simulcast horse racing (or off-track betting). Alaska has spawned unusual variants like dog-mushing contests or fish derbies, in which players bet on whose dog sled will finish first along a certain course or on who will catch the first or the largest fish.

Reprinted with the permission of *The Chronicle of Philanthropy*.

Where they are allowed, they are closely regulated, involve high fixed costs for equipment rental and operator fees, and require fees of from 5% to 10% of income to city or county authorities, along with filing of a full financial statement of all income and expenses. They incur all the overhead costs of any special and benefit event and are hard to manage for a minimum goal of 50% net profit to the charity. If their only real benefit seems to be appeasement of those few volunteers and donors who just want to gamble, an organization must evaluate whether gambling is the type of activity it should be known for in the community.[10]

The amount of money involved in charitable gambling is staggering. In a report compiled by the National Association of Fundraising Ticket Manufacturers, more than $5.9 billion was wagered in 26 states during 1991, the latest year for which information is available. The figure is nearly double the $3.05 billion reported by 23 states in 1989. The amounts delivered to charity were not this total sum; the highest was 35 percent of gross revenue (in only two states). Most proceeds were in the 10 percent to mid-20 percent range, and five were below 10 percent. The final figure of note was the amount provided to the 26 states in 1991 in tax revenue: over $200 million.[11]

The board of directors and CEO should exercise their stewardship responsibilities and be certain that whatever type of gambling or games of chance are offered, they will be conducted fully within the law. Volunteers may fail to recognize, in their well-intentioned enthusiasm to raise money for charity, that much more is at stake than staging a bingo party or a Las Vegas night, or that adding an auction or raffle to a black-tie dinner dance actually adds many complications. The tax-exempt status of the nonprofit organization may be put on the line.

Can any of the forms of gambling be used in an annual giving program, perhaps as a feature of a benefit? Yes, because the activity is held only once or twice a year by the sponsoring nonprofit organization. If the event were held weekly, the purpose would clearly change: gambling would become the chief reason for holding the event. Local regulations governing auctions, raffles, bingo, and Las Vegas or Monte Carlo nights, when followed meticulously and without deviation, can be used to enhance traditional annual giving methods—chiefly, activities, benefits, and special events. Lotteries and sweepstakes, where allowed, are in a different class because they use the mails; the U.S. Postal Service and the Treasury Department (income taxes are due on money raised from gambling) join state and local authorities as interested parties to these activities.

> The United Cancer Council (which was one of the charities involved as a recipient of Watson & Hughey sweepstakes) had its tax exemption status pulled by the IRS, which said that the charity operated for the nonexempt purpose of operating sweepstakes games through its fund raiser (Watson & Hughey) to which it paid 93 percent of its total gross income in 1986 and 1987.[12]

Lotteries and sweepstakes are not recommended unless careful prior analysis of every layer of law and regulation is completed first. With so much at risk and with more efficient and profitable annual giving methods available to every nonprofit organization, the board of directors is well-advised to avoid gambling and games of chance as a "regularly carried on" portion of their annual giving programs.

MULTIMEDIA OPTIONS

Today's technology allows instant and effective communications with nearly everyone. Consequently, the public is deluged with instant worldwide information on every subject imaginable, visually, audially, on the Internet, and in writing. The challenges to nonprofit organizations are:

1. What is their message; what is it about their cause and appeal that will be heard?
2. Whom should they be trying to reach?
3. What media must they use to reach those whose help they seek?

For most nonprofit organizations, broadcast, telecast, Internet, or other mass communications will not be necessary in order to carry out their annual giving programs. A selection of national and international agencies (for example, UNICEF and World Vision) will engage in massive multimedia forms of communications because of their mission. A few other nonprofit organizations, using "televangelist" messages or "infomercials," will be able to deliver their programs and services directly into the home using live telecasts via satellite and telephone line. In advance of a telecast, an information packet and videotaped message promoting the program are received by mail, possibly followed up by a telephone call to encourage watching the telecast. The telecast makes the case and invites contributions. A solicitation letter arrives within days to secure the gift. Such a level of "high touch" using multimedia "high tech" is available to only a few among even the largest and best funded of nonprofit organizations.[13]

Being able to talk with or write to prospects and donors requires effective communication within an available segment of the total market. Market segmentation is the essential first step, as it is in direct mail solicitation, when the lists to be used for acquisition must be selected carefully to build a constituency (see Chapters 2 and 3).

The key to success with nonprofit organizations is in keeping close to donors and prospects.

> Our focus must become one of understanding our donors, their needs, beliefs and attitudes. We need to get close to donors to aid their trust in our organizations and our programs. To succeed, we must master computers and the art of talking in the style of one-on-one dialogue with everybody.[14]

The five means available for audio and visual communications, each of which can be used with one or more annual giving fundraising methods, are advertising, radio, television (including cable channels, videocassettes, and DVDs), the computer, and the telephone. Budget will remain the single largest constraint on how much each of these (or more than one) will be put to use by nonprofit organizations. Creativity can overcome many fiscal constraints. Computer access to the Internet and its information highway offers multiple ways of using alternate forms of multimedia techniques in support of annual giving communications. For those who do find a way to access the airwaves, improved results will likely occur.

PREMIUMS

A premium is a gift returned to a donor in exchange for the gift amount requested. The quality of the premium and its uniqueness or distinctive nature are advertised to encourage the gift. Premium objects appear to be "for-sale" items, except that the value of the premium is well below the amount of the gift required to qualify for or "purchase" the premium. If any object or "gift" is given back to a donor as a token of appreciation or as a recognition award after the contribution is received, it may not be a premium because it was not a condition for a gift; the exchange or "sale" of the object was not advertised or known to the donor prior to the gift decision. The types of objects often used as premiums range from bumper stickers, decals, calendars, and coffee mugs to caps, tote bags, and umbrellas, all bearing the nonprofit organization's logo and message. The theory behind the practice of offering premiums is that the object is a desirable commodity, or the promise of a "give back" is enticement enough for the donor to make the gift.

Premiums and donor recognition "presents" work quite well when the product can somehow be related to the exempt mission and purpose of the nonprofit organization. For example, public radio and television stations offer tapes of popular programs already aired or CD collections featuring artists who performed during the special broadcast when the appeal was made. They are known to be of high quality and are not available in stores or from any other source. Likewise, museums offer reprints and art books picturing their special collections; colleges offer graduation rings and a wide array of "stuff" bearing their logos, mascots, or names; the U.S. Olympic Committee offers patches and pins; environmental groups offer bumper stickers, decals, and wildlife stamps; veterans groups send key chains and return address labels; the list is endless. Other nonprofit organizations may not have (as of yet) objects to match their purposes. Soup kitchens, for example, probably could not sell their soup even if markets gave them counter space. For these organizations, an alternative is to purchase objects they can offer as premiums or "gifts" for donors.

Some donors look forward to receipt of the premium product they purchased, if that was their motive in giving. Many other donors are less interested in what is offered in exchange for their gift. If premium objects are considered trinkets or the type of "stuff" people already possess in excessive supply (how many bumper stickers will one car hold? how many coffee mugs will fit on one shelf?), the incentive has less effect. More favorable results may be attained from premiums or "give backs" offered as incentives for donor renewal rather than for acquisition of first-time donors, especially when they represent a reward for upgrading to higher annual gift levels. Considerable creativity is required to find the right object, one that is appealing and has a low unit cost. Once premiums and "gifts" are introduced to annual donors, objects of equal attractiveness and appeal must be found *every year*. Many donors do not react well when the annual "extra" is discontinued.

For guidance when considering the use of premiums, the advice of the Disabled American Veterans, which has been using premiums since 1942, is valid:

1. Use premiums which have a logical tie-in with your organization.

2. Use premiums with the highest perceived value at the lowest cost.

3. Feature premium offer in copy.

4. Use premiums which require periodic replacement.

5. Provide quality premiums.

6. Use premiums only when cost-effective.[15]

Premium objects provided in advance, at the time of solicitation, are called *unsolicited merchandise* and are used only occasionally today (return address labels may be the current exception). The intent behind this practice is to engender guilt in the recipient, who might feel that the object should not be kept and used without making a gift to the organization that sent it. The cost of such objects must be added to the already high mailing expense; with rising postage and materials costs, this practice may soon disappear altogether. Veterans groups and a few others continue shipping return address labels and decorator stamps as part of their direct mail solicitations; environmental groups offer holiday greeting cards (printed with soy ink on recycled paper or stickers with their logo). Most recipients use the cards and address labels without making a gift, and they decorate their personal and business mail with the Wildlife and Easter seal stamps (insinuating to recipients that the sender supports these nonprofit organizations). For the sake of those who *are* faithful donors, sending out unsolicited merchandise *after* a gift is made would seem a fairer (or more honest) protocol to follow.

Donor recognition gifts are part of the donor relations and donor communications program. Donors are worth extra attention and even a "gift" now and then to acknowledge the importance of their support. Guidelines for donor recognition gifts should be well-defined and tied to the amount(s) of the annual gift, the cumulative gifts made throughout the year (see Exhibit 5-5), and the cumulative giving history (see Exhibit 7-4). As an example, the names of donors who gave $1,000 within one year might be displayed on a special plaque throughout the following year. They also might receive a certificate attesting to their status as members of the "Millenium Club." Donors who achieve higher levels, such as $10,000, $25,000, or $100,000, either with a single gift in one year or from cumulative gifts after many years, may receive a donor recognition "gift" of a glass paperweight or quartz clock displaying the logo of the nonprofit organization. The IRS will be interested in the actual value of these objects if they exceed 2 percent of the original gift value. Most organizations buy these objects in bulk to keep the unit price down, but there is potential for an IRS challenge to the amount a donor may claim as a charitable contribution deduction. If the premium or "give-back" object exceeds the 2 percent test amount, the material value of the object will reduce the value of the original contribution.

Donor recognition is an important part of annual giving, especially in renewal communications. Caution should be exercised when offering recognition that may more accurately be defined as customer relations or benefits purchased in exchange for premiums, "gift" objects, and services. Will a donor "switch" products (and nonprofit organizations) if a nicer premium or a lower interest rate is offered? The "commerciality test" is a valid measurement of whether premiums, "gift" objects, and services are more accurately benefits and privileges extended to donors in recognition of their generosity, or commercial products and services in exchange for gift amounts. The variety and value of donor recognition programs, benefits, and privileges seem to outweigh the commercial exchange, especially when building with donors relationships that need to last for many years.

TELEVISION AND TELETHON SOLICITATION

Much of the information and advice that applies to telephone use and telemarketing to enhance annual giving (see Chapter 6) also applies to television as a medium for sales and solicitation, except that television costs more. Several nonprofit organizations are already using television, notably churches and *televangelists*, a word coined out of their preference for this most personal of mediums. Other well-known users are public television stations, for their pledge campaigns; the Children's Miracle Network (a consortium of children's health-care causes); and the Muscular Dystrophy Association, for its traditional Labor Day telethon starring Jerry Lewis and "Jerry's Kids." There are other, mostly local, users, and they have proportionately similar results. How strong is television as a fundraising medium? Each of the national appeals raises millions each time it goes on the air. These productions are maximum efforts, but they yield maximum returns. A telethon is a major benefit, a membership drive, and a personal appeal— all rolled into one powerful communications channel. Well-known, occasional telethons have larger followings than most hit TV series. Cable systems and transmission via satellite offer an increasing array of access channels as alternate outlets for television use. With FCC regulations endorsing every radio station and television (including cable) channel to offer some hours of PSAs each week, an array of prepared programs, "infomercials," and PSAs can be effective for nonprofit use. If "the medium is the message," then fundraising has begun to build a home in television.

Only a few nonprofit organizations currently have access to television or can afford to purchase air time, but the other use of this visual medium is becoming widespread—videocassettes. They are no more expensive than newsletters, magazines, or annual reports, and they are far more able to "make the case" eloquently and succinctly and stir a donor to action. With over 80 million videocassette recorders (VCRs) sold in the past decade, and millions more DVD players, nearly every homeowner can play a cassette or a DVD disc received in the mail and may be moved to reply. The proper name, mailing address, and telephone number of the charity should be provided in the mailing packet and repeated frequently on the screen. Again, multimedia strategies appear to work best.

The problems with television use are not as great as those with telephone use. By controlling transmission, the medium thwarts most fraudulent schemes, although a few scams and con-artist schemes do occur, usually in the form of copyright infringements on pirated videos. One problem area for annual giving programs is in building a constituency that cares about the mission of the nonprofit organization as much as the "show" that sparked the gift. The exception here appears to be religious organizations' telecasts; donor renewal is pursued vigorously, and the programs are on the air constantly. For other organizations, donor renewal rates can be improved using better donor relations communications between broadcasts, but these represent added expenses. Television reaches hundreds of thousands, even millions, of people instantly. The frequency with which TV donors will move into other annual giving categories and upgrade their annual gifts is about the same as for any other fundraising method. A special problem is TV pledge collections: Defaults may run as high as 20 to 25 percent, the highest in fundraising practice.

VARIOUS OTHER ANNUAL GIVING IDEAS OF MERIT

The best use of all these other ways to raise money every year is in partnership with ongoing annual giving programs. When they are offered alone, they may perform well only once or twice. Usually, their performance peaks at the beginning because they offer something new to the constituency; they may fade when they are seen as just another way to ask for money each year. Using them intermittently and coordinating them with ongoing programs will help to keep them fresh. The same criteria used to measure the annual giving methods described in Chapters 2 through 11 should be applied: How well can they raise new friends, build new relationships, and renew and upgrade annual gifts from prior donors? There are some higher tests to pass: Do they enhance the image and reputation of the nonprofit organization? Do they inspire greater public confidence and trust in its mission and purposes as well as its ability to use their money well? Some of these other forms of raising money every year may not meet these final standards. If not, that is reason enough to give them a second look or to divert their investment of time and budget to already proven annual giving programs.

In what other ways can an organization raise money every year? Art shows, bake sales, sports tournaments, travel tours, and other fundraising ideas are conducted as activities, benefits, and special events (see Exhibit 10-9 for a list). No doubt there are quite a few others. The other ways to raise money discussed in this chapter may find a good home in one or more of the broad-based annual giving programs of mailings, memberships, clubs, and volunteer solicitors. Some may be usable in combinations, emerging as creative fundraising concepts for annual giving purposes. The final assessment is whether any other ways can pass the CARE test:

1. **C**omfort for the donor in the cause, the solicitation method used, and how the approach is made

2. **A**nticipation of the request and preparedness with adequate information that encourages a decision to give

3. **R**eadiness to give because of a conviction that the money will be well used for charitable purposes that serve the public good

4. **E**njoyment in the act of giving and a welcome to the invitation to give again

Scams and Con Artist Fraud and Abuse

Unfortunately, ours is not a perfect world. There are a few people who would use all of the annual giving fundraising methods presented in this book (and the other ways to raise money every year described in this chapter) to defraud the public and put the money raised to personal use. The public is not easily able to distinguish between a legitimate nonprofit organization that is soliciting via mail or telephone, or offering a coupon or premium, from another that acts, looks, and sounds exactly alike, but is not legitimate. Public confusion is increased when look-alike and sound-alike names are given to bogus organizations. The American Cancer Society is the official name of the largest public health agency in the United States, and its name is well-known to most people. Dozens of other legitimate cancer support organizations use the word *cancer* in their titles but are not as well known. A name for a fictional organization may include *Cancer* and add, at the beginning or end, *American, National, Coalition, Friends, Association, Institute,* or other imaginative choices. Why do scams, run by con artists, engage in fraud and abuse the public's good intentions in giving to charity? To keep the money for themselves. Harvey Dale[16] described the impact on the independent sector:

> [A]buses hurt the sector. In the wake of the televangelist scandals, dona-
> tions to almost *all* television ministries fell dramatically. When Father
> Ritter came under criticism, Covenant House was severely and adversely
> impacted. Although government can raise funds by forced exaction, and
> business can tempt investors with profits, the nonprofit sector has noth-
> ing to offer except its good image, good purposes, and good activities.
> We should be vigilant to seek out and eliminate undesirable conduct be-

fore it corrodes and tarnishes the luster of our activities. We should be concerned, then, when an inadequate level of supervision and scrutiny leaves an enlarged scope for undetected abuses.

One role of government is to protect the public from fraud and abuse. Because it is difficult and expensive to do so, problems arise. State governments have the police powers to provide consumer protection services and to enforce antifraud activities. David Ormstedt[17] warns:

> There will always be fraud and other misuse of charitable assets. There is fraud and abusive conduct in every segment of society. Government cannot eradicate it. The best government can hope for, and the most the public should expect of government, is that efficient regulation will keep problems reasonably under control.

Government's limited resources to pursue illegal activities have hindered its effectiveness. A locked door or safe can be picked, but at least entry is delayed. A door that is open just a crack offers no protection at all. When criminals choose to use annual giving and other recognizable fundraising methods to defraud the public of money in the name of charity, nonprofit organizations and their donors have cause for concern. Ormstedt[18] gives this summation:

> To maintain a strong charitable sector and to foster confidence in charitable institutions, fraud in the name of charity must be minimized. The public needs reasonable assurance that their donations and the donations of others, as well as their tax dollars that are, in effect, used to subsidize charities, are being used in a manner consistent with their expectations. Thus, government needs to be able and prepared to ensure the due application of charitable funds. This means not only prosecuting fraud. It also means ensuring that restricted donations are used for the restricted purpose. A person who donates money in response to an appeal for money for financial assistance to victims of a disease has every right to expect that the donation will be used for that purpose and not some other purpose, even if the alternate purpose serves a charitable objective.

One of the most difficult challenges to prospects and donors, to nonprofit organizations, and to state and local regulators, is the use of annual giving fundraising methods by professional solicitors. Many of these "paid" or "commercial" solicitors operate within the law, but some do not and others appear to teeter at the very edge of legality and legitimacy. Anyone is entitled to conduct a business and to provide qualified professional solic-itation services to nonprofit organizations. Some nonprofit organizations, however, hire paid solicitors because they believe they cannot raise money (or they do not want to), and they will accept the offer of a sizable gift in return for "no-effort-on-your-part" services (warning!). Some commercial solicitors have been allowed considerable freedom in the use of organiza-tions' names and in the methods chosen for public solicitation. The orga-nizations appear to be willing to look the other way in order to receive the money promised.

The solicitation practices that have caused much public criticism and regulatory pursuit include telephone requests from a police or firefighter "widows and orphans fund." The caller, implying that he or she is a police officer or firefighter, appeals to the public's concern for the families of de-ceased public servants, and offer to come to the home or business within a few hours to pick up the money. (Legitimate appeals of this origin remind the prospect, on the telephone, to ask for the solicitor's identification and to accept a receipt and perhaps a window sticker that carries the organiza-tion's seal. Checks made out to the organization are requested rather than cash.) Another scam is a ticket sales campaign to take hospitalized or handi-capped children to a circus or sports event, again using a runner to come and get the money. A third example is a request for advertising in a pro-gram book for a special veterans benefit, to which the caller is also selling tickets. Each of these appeals may actually exist (or the event may have been recently held). The caller may be operating in its wake and pocket-ing the funds collected. The "runner" may even arrive wearing a uniform but is not a police officer or firefighter. A few circus tickets may be deliv-ered, but the circus may never come to town. The program book never gets printed and the benefit event to honor veterans is never held. Each contact was a deception to defraud the public of money.

Additional clues to fraudulent behavior include: the caller has no litera-ture to send out, pledges cannot be paid later, and the organization has no mailing address. The excuse will be that by not incurring these expenses, more money can be delivered to the charity. A tax ID number will be vol-unteered as a supposed verification of legitimacy (the number can be ficti-tious). Another clue to fraud is an offer to take care of all money matters, including deposits and payment of expenses, and bring the nonprofit orga-nization the net proceeds. These con artists will open a bank account and gain complete check-writing authority, and will indeed pay all the bills plus their own salaries, commissions, and marketing and promotion fees. Is it any wonder that little money is left for the charity when all this is over? All too often, scams and con artists operate for one or two weeks, collect a surprising amount of money from an unsuspecting public, and leave town before authorities can respond. To prevent or at least reduce fundraising traps, how should nonprofit organizations proceed? By drafting a comprehensive, well-considered, properly worded agreement and not allowing any involvement with the outside agent until it is signed and the agent's credentials are verified. A contract can be the best protection, says Errol Copilevitz,[19] provided each of the following elements is dealt with effectively:

1. When an organization is working with a direct-marketing company or a telemarketing company, a competitive bidding process should be utilized.
2. There should be a clear description of the relationship of the parties and the functions that each will perform.
3. Provisions dealing with donor file ownership and use should be clear and in accordance with industry standards.
4. The use of the nonprofit postal rate should be addressed in accordance with the standards of the U.S. Postal Service.
5. The receipt, control, and distribution of proceeds should be set forth with specificity and in accordance with various state laws.
6. The issue of state registration should be addressed and compliance assured, where applicable.
7. An addendum to comply with the various state laws should be a part of the contract.
8. The provisions dealing with the fees to be paid should be clear and concise.
9. The responsibility for project expenses must be unequivocal.
10. The organization should have direction and control over creative and program service material used.
11. The activity, where applicable, should make a distinction between donor acquisition and donor renewal fundraising with appropriate provisions dealing with contacts, content, and costs.

Responsible nonprofit organizations and regulatory authorities are frustrated in their efforts to reduce scams and con artists' fraud and abuse.

Harm occurs when the organization abrogates its fiduciary responsibility in favor of the promise of "easy money." Also harmed are the legitimate police, firefighter, and veterans groups that seek public gift support. Constant efforts are made to educate the public about "wise giving" throughout the year and especially during the end-of-the-year holiday season. The news media do give coverage to fraudulent and deceptive solicitation techniques such as "fake" Santas and phony religious impersonators, and will describe how the scam was operated or the con was perpetrated. However, the effect is limited. The public has some responsibility to ensure that any solicitation to make a gift is legitimate and that the donation will actually be delivered to a nonprofit organization for charitable purposes. Victims must do more than complain loudly when they have been hoodwinked.

The problem of scams and con artists' fraud and abuse is complicated by misconceptions and overreaction by legislators. In Colorado, when a legislative regulation was proposed, the situation was described by Hopkins as follows:[20]

> [F]raudulent charitable solicitations are a widespread practice in this state, which results in millions of dollars of losses to contributors and legitimate charities each year. Legitimate charities are harmed by such fraud because the money available for contributions continually is being siphoned off by fraudulent charities, and the goodwill and confidence of contributors continually is being undermined by the practices of unscrupulous solicitors. [The law enacted is] necessary to protect the public's interest in making informed choices as to which charitable causes should be supported.

The final area to discuss here is the abuse of funds raised. Donors who restrict the use of their gifts to any purpose are asking the nonprofit organization to use their money only for that specific purpose. In most solicitations, the purpose is a project or priority identified by the nonprofit organization; the funds are requested for exactly this use. Once the money is received, it may be used only in fulfillment of that purpose. If a donor makes a gift for a purpose that is unacceptable or cannot be fulfilled, the nonprofit organization has the right to refuse the gift. Once a gift is accepted, the organization is bound by law to retain the money until the purpose can be fulfilled. Among the problems that can occur within nonprofit organizations regarding the use of restricted funds are: a lack of proper accounting for all restricted funds received and spent, a lack of knowledge and appreciation (even by board members and managers) of correct accounting procedures, and legal complications associated with changing donor restrictions or using funds raised for purposes other than those intended by donors.

A highly publicized example of improper use of funds raised was the fraud perpetrated by James and Tammy Fay Bakker and their colleagues on donors to the PTL Ministries. The trial of James Bakker revealed several fraudulent practices. One area of activity was overselling the accommodations promised to the PTL's "lifetime partners" (a number of free days and nights at the PTL Grand Hotel, Towers Hotel, Bunkhouse, and 1100 Club in exchange for gifts of $1,000). These offers, by mail and during PTL television programs, raised in excess of $158 million. Many of the partners could not get a reservation as promised; portions of the facilities were never completed, although more than enough money had been raised for their construction. A second area of fraud was in the use of PTL "construction" money to purchase expensive homes for the Bakkers. Third, numerous (and quite generous) bonuses were paid to both James and Tammy Fay Bakker, as well as to David Taggart. Bonus payments paid to James Bakker, which the court found to be excessive and qualified as "private inurement," were in amounts from $10,000 to $300,000. In the final days of PTL Ministries, between June 1986 and March 1987 (just prior to bankruptcy), the Bakkers, David Taggart, and Richard Dortch together received more than $2 million in bonus payments.[21] Bonus payments in *any* amount were not the intent of the donors; construction of the named facilities was the restriction that was abused.

Fraud and abuse are major problems, especially when they occur within nonprofit organizations and involve contribution dollars. Good and sufficient laws are in place to protect the public from most of these practices. Despite the best efforts of public servants, however, illicit activity continues. Scandals will occur from time to time, and they are especially harmful to the public's willingness to continue to place confidence and trust in nonprofit organizations, in charitable giving, and in the many board members, volunteers, and employees who work on behalf of nonprofit organizations for charitable purposes.

CHAPTER 13

Managing the Comprehensive Annual Giving Program

Annual giving programs are the foundation of every organization's structure. Each annual giving method is like a cut stone: It has shape and size, color and weight, presence and function, stability and supportive strength even when it is standing alone. When several of these stones are assembled together with skill, they can form the foundation, the most essential part, of a structure. The quality of the stones selected for the foundation is all-important because the entire structure will rest on them.

In the pyramid of giving (Exhibit 1-2), the entire structure of the giving process has been presented graphically. When the process is successful, donors will move from annual giving to major gifts and then to estate or planned giving, but only if the foundation of the pyramid is firmly in place, well-aligned, and able to carry the added weight placed on it. A nonprofit organization builds upward as it prepares for its future. Annual giving programs are an important element of the organization's foundation; each stone is needed to make that upward structuring possible.

The primary and continuing objectives of every annual giving program are as follows:

1. Identify and recruit new friends and donors.
2. Build lasting relationships through gift renewal and volunteerism.
3. Raise the money needed each year for priority projects.
4. Expand the relationship between community and organization.

5. Improve public understanding of the mission.

6. Increase public confidence and trust in the organization.

7. Fulfill the promise to make maximum use of gifts received by rendering quality services for public benefit.

8. Provide honors and recognition to faithful donors and volunteers.

A comprehensive annual giving program will make several contributions to the image and reputation of the nonprofit organization. By its nature to reach outside, it is actively marketing and promoting the organization's programs and services and by communicating its vision far and wide, the comprehensive annual giving program will attract and keep donors and will provide opportunities for any person who chooses to become an active participant in its accomplishments.

No organization is complete and no charitable purpose is fulfilled while unmet needs remain. A generous, caring public is prepared to assist to the extent that personal means allow. Such charitable motives are reinforced by government's advocacy of giving and its granting of privileges of tax-deductibility for qualified donors. Public needs are many; resources are inadequate. Annual giving programs invite the public to join a cause and participate to the extent that time, talent, and treasure will permit. Society's unmet needs are mirrored in the mission statements of nonprofit organizations whose purposes are to respond to the best of their ability. A nonprofit organization's ability to meet public needs depends on its acquiring the public's support. This entire process begins with, is sustained by, and is dependent on the comprehensive annual giving program.

BALANCED PARTICIPATION: A KEY TO SUCCESS

This final chapter will discuss the support features necessary to the management of annual giving programs. The several fundraising methods and techniques described in this book provide the means to accomplish the annual priorities identified by the organization's board of directors and CEO. Responsibility for fundraising is shared among the board of directors, management, volunteers, donors, and staff. Fundraising guidance and direction, training and materials, and management of all the internal support details required are the responsibilities of the fund development staff. When leaders lead and volunteers carry out their assignments, and when plans are solid and supplies are adequate, there can be every expectation that the annual goals and objectives of a nonprofit organization will be achieved with reliability. Facilitating that success is another responsibility of the fund development staff.

The annual giving process might be compared to an election campaign: Comprehensive plans are made; options are examined and counterplans are resolved; the district is studied to identify areas of opportunity and strategic value; campaign workers are recruited and trained for assigned missions; supplies are acquired, timetables are coordinated, and a campaign launch date is set. The campaign begins on schedule, and progress reports communicate results, reactions, and any problems encountered. When the campaign is over, a critique is performed to communicate the lessons learned and to prepare for the next campaign. The role of the fund development staff is to enable each of the parts of the annual giving campaign to succeed, year after year. Every campaign begins with leadership, is carried out by volunteer workers, and is sustained throughout by the rear guard, the fund-development staff. When it is over, the leaders, volunteers, and donors share the glory.

The Role of Leadership

All leaders are volunteers, and volunteerism *is* philanthropy. Robert Payton calls philanthropy "voluntary action for the common good";[1] volunteerism is action where "people helping people" "brings out the best in all of us." Volunteerism is a powerful concept; it continues to be a vital part of developing America as a unique nation. Alexis de Tocqueville,[2] commenting on the use of public associations in America, wrote in 1835:

> I met with several kinds of associations in America of which I confess I had no previous notion; and I have often admired the extreme skill with which the inhabitants of the United States succeed in proposing a common object for the exertions of a great many men and in inducing them voluntarily to pursue it.

Leadership brings people together, builds on their skills and talents, and motivates them to address the needs of others. The spirit of "people helping people" exists everywhere in the world. Following the breakup of the former Union of Soviet Socialist Republics during the past decade, numerous public support organizations emerged among the people at both local and national levels. Most recently, the tragic events of September 11, 2001, the terrorist attacks on New York's World Trade Center and the Pentagon, resulted in the largest outpouring of contributions of money (more than $1 billion) from a generous public. In addition, volunteers came from throughout the entire country, a philanthropic phenomenon never seen before. Traditional relief organizations like the American Red Cross and The Salvation Army were well prepared to provide immediate help; they also were ready to organize and encourage public participation and gift support. At the same time, new relief organizations were established overnight by local leaders, in particular, New York City's Mayor Giuliani and New York's Governor Pataki. Leadership sets the example that others follow. When trusted leadership acts to address basic human needs, people everywhere follow.

Leadership in annual giving begins with the board of directors and the CEO. Their vision of the mission, purposes, goals, and objectives of a nonprofit organization is the source of inspiration and motivation for annual giving's leaders and volunteers, prospects and donors. Together, the board and CEO interpret the vision and formulate a statement of the organization's annual priorities of need. They serve as stewards of all of the organization's resources—employees, finances, and facilities—and supervise the delivery of its programs and services to the public. Visionary leaders and top executives will guide their craft through calm and stormy waters to safe harbors of quality programs and improved benefits to all whom they serve.

> When annual contributions from regular supporters are the life-blood of an organization, the appeal deserves the full attention of board members. Remember that annual giving is not the same as mass mailings to unknown prospects; rather, it is the solicitation each year of a first or repeated donation from preselected individuals who already know, or know about, the organization. But annual giving must be more than mere reminders to members that their dues are due. Annual giving solicitations are carried out primarily by mail, although churches in their "every member canvas" try to have all parishioners asked in person for donations to match or increase their previous year's contributions. Three cardinal elements count heavily in annual gift solicitations: the *mailing list*, the *appeal letter*, and the *personalized approach*.[3]

Nonprofit organizations with strong and effective leadership will be able to attract and maintain the levels of public support they need each year. Others, especially those whose vision appears to be concentrated on financial survival or job security, are not as likely to realize such an ill-defined mission, nor will they succeed in delivering quality services to those in need; they will, moreover, be forever begging for whatever public gift support they can find.

The Value of Volunteers

Volunteerism is next in importance to leadership, if nonprofit organizations are to achieve their vision, mission, annual purposes, and goals. Volunteers must be identified and recruited, oriented and trained, encouraged and rewarded each year. Volunteers are the arms and legs of annual giving and the force that enables each of the methods and techniques described in this book to blossom to its potential. Without the active involvement of volunteers at all levels of annual giving, nonprofit organizations will not make as many friends, will be limited to fewer people for quality relationships, and will spend more of the money raised to hire staff to do what volunteers could do better and for free. The best way to build a base of committed and loyal volunteers is to imitate the steps for building a base of committed and loyal annual donors. To develop volunteers in numbers and to utilize their time and energy productively each year requires a commitment to invest time and budget by the nonprofit organization. Each volunteer has the opportunity to enjoy a lifetime relationship with several nonprofit organizations. Along the way, the volunteer will need preparation, training, experience, promotion, and recognition, all of which are begun in the comprehensive annual giving program (see Exhibit 13-1). The organization that invests in its volunteers will achieve their life-long commitment and loyalty, plus their willingness to continue to give of their time, talent, and treasure. Some nonprofit organizations favor hiring employees to do the fundraising work of volunteers, believing that, although they cause extra expense, employees are more reliable, can be told what to do, and can be held more accountable for their performance. Where volunteers are full partners with "their" nonprofit organization, they will remain while employees will come and go. Volunteers, who should *never* be treated as employees, are an invaluable extra resource that allows an organization to

EXHIBIT 13-1   BEGINNING SERVICE CYCLE OF A VOLUNTEER: PREPARATION, TRAINING, EXPERIENCE, PROMOTION, AND RECOGNITION

Year 1   Invited by mail to make first annual gift; sends $25.
Invited by friend to public function (free); attends with spouse.
Invited to visit facilities; visits East Wing.
Receives two newsletters, one annual report.
Asked to renew (and upgrade) annual gift; sends $35.

Year 2   Invited to join the membership association; sends $100.
Invited to membership "mixer" to meet others; no charge. Attends with spouse.
Invited to serve on a committee; selects membership. Attends orientation and training session. Renews own membership at $100 and brings in two new members at $100 each.
Invited to a public activity, one benefit, and a special event (annual meeting). Attends the activity and buys two tickets to benefit at $100/couple.
Takes second tour of facility (Main Wing); spouse joins tour.
Receives two newsletters, one annual report with name on membership roster.
Asked to renew (and upgrade) annual gift; sends $50.

Year 3   Invited to work on membership committee again; accepts and attends orientation and training session. Renews own membership at $100 and brings in five new members (three from office) at $100 each.
Invited to a public activity, one benefit, and a special event (annual meeting). Attends the activity; buys two tickets to benefit and invites two new members and spouses who attend.
Attends annual meeting.
Becomes tour leader after two training sessions.
Receives two newsletters, one annual report.
Asked to renew (and upgrade) annual gift; continues at $50.

Year 4   Invited to serve as vice chair of new-member drive; on membership committee; helps plan orientation and training sessions; on agenda to report on successful solicitation techniques. Recruits five more new members.
Invited to serve on benefit planning committee; accepts. Attends orientation and training session. Agrees to serve on ticket sales committee. Invites four couples, to sell table of ten; calls members recruited to encourage them to join as well.
Accepts appointment as vice chair of tours program; defines two new tour areas.
Attends annual meeting; is recognized for new-member recruiting services.
Asked to renew (and upgrade) annual gift; sends $100 and joins Century Club.

Year 5   Invited to serve as chairperson of new-member campaign.
Invited to serve on benefit ticket sales committee.
Serves one-year term as chair, tours program. Recruits five new guides.
Receives two newsletters, one annual report.
Attends annual meeting; is recognized for leadership in voluntary service.
Renews annual gift at $100 again (has not been asked for larger gift).

achieve quality relations with people. Volunteers are also willing and able to add a wide variety of extra benefits and can raise *and give* more money than employees ever will. Volunteers exemplify the following attributes:

- Participate publicly in the life of the organization
- Act as committed and loyal ambassadors and spokespersons
- Advocate with pride "their" organization to friends and neighbors, co-workers and business contacts, family and relatives
- Give of their time, talent, and treasure annually
- Lead prospects and donors into giving
- Lead other volunteers into service
- Enhance the image and reputation of the nonprofit organization by their visible association
- Prepare to become future leaders as well as future donors

The Role of Fund Development Staff

Vision and mission are translated by staff into a "case statement" for all to hear and read. Communicating the case is carried out jointly by the external relations team of employees in the planning, marketing, public relations, and fund development offices:

- *Planning* documents the vision and mission and describes its annual components in terms of product lines (programs and services).
- *Marketing* identifies to whom the case is addressed (target markets) and prepares a strategy that will bring the organization and the markets together.
- *Public relations* creates the image and describes the availability and quality of the programs and services for those who need them.
- *Fund development*, because of the good advance work done, is positioned to raise the friends and funds to carry out the programs and services that fulfill the mission.

In order for each of these objectives to be realized, employees who do the planning, marketing, public relations, and fund-development work must come together in a spirit of *cooperation, coordination,* and *communication*. By joint scheduling of all their activities (*calendar control*) they can achieve a *comprehensive* effort that will be *competitive* with others. *Collaboration* is the road to success for everyone involved.

The public, to whom the care is addressed and for whom the programs and services are intended, is often the same people—community residents living near the organization. Given the volume of messages to deliver and the diversity of audiences who receive them, a high degree of *cooperation* and *coordination* is needed among the external relations team. Each *communication* should improve and expand public understanding and respect in order to reinforce confidence and trust in the organization. *Calendar control* helps to guide internal decisions (and budgets) on when each message is to be sent, to whom it will be addressed, what purpose it intends, and how its effectiveness will be measured. Without calendar control, messages can rain down on people, causing them to wonder, "How well managed is this organization?" and "Is this how they spend my money?"

To be maximally effective in public communications requires a *comprehensive* effort by all parties working together. *Competition* for leaders and volunteers, for prospects and donors, and for clients will intensify; organizations will not survive if they fail to gain the public's acceptance and gift support. There will be new opportunities for *collaboration* among organizations in the community. Joint efforts will become more desirable than unnecessary duplication and expensive competition. The continued success of the organization and its annual giving program depends on the successful implementation of these concepts of integrated management.

MANAGING ANNUAL GIVING PROGRAMS

When competent professional and support staff are matched with solid plans and effective and efficient communications systems, they will be able to meet the needs of leaders and volunteers, prospects, and donors, and will realize success in annual giving. Continuing success will build everyone's confidence in the nonprofit organization and in each of its annual giving programs. Thomas Broce[4] described the delicate balance that is involved:

> Much of the success of the annual campaign depends on good staff work, including the professional, clerical, and record-keeping staffs. The professional staff members should do everything possible to set the pace, maintain momentum, and create the sense of urgency and excitement that is vital to the campaign. Each meeting and special event must be

planned with precision and conducted in good taste. A poor meeting will ensure a low turnout for the next one. The staff members must maintain pressure on volunteers without offending them. The visibility of the professional staff is higher in annual fund campaigns than in any other kind of fundraising.

The variety of functions performed by the fund-development office is a daily challenge, a joy of association, and a source of affirmation to those of us who work there. Development work is never done; there are too many people to talk with and listen to, too many details to be resolved, and too many deadlines. Conflicting directions do arise because of too many "bosses" and too many priorities. Expectations set by others not closely involved with annual giving performance (and without consultation with more active and informed leaders and volunteers) can add unproductive stress.

> Organizations and their volunteer boards have high expectations, sometimes too high for the individual charged with meeting them, or fail to support an effort themselves, or are impatient with the time required for results.[5]

Unrealized expectations are not thoughtful statements of multiyear goals and objectives for annual giving programs; they are short-term measurements of cash-only results. They also are a frequent cause of the rapid turnover in fund-development staff. One of the duties that should be written into the job description of every fundraising professional is to educate the organization in how fundraising works. This book provides a structured and logical presentation of what steps to take and in what order to take them to realize the potential that annual giving offers. Each method contributes to the maximum efficiency and effectiveness of the others. Too often, the board of directors and CEO, who have defined the vision and mission after extensive studies, will, without much reflection, assign annual giving goals to achieve these purposes. Fundraising professionals who cannot explain what they do, cannot educate others on how annual giving performs, and cannot communicate what the expected results from the budgets invested will be, may soon be in another line of work. Fund development staff are assumed to possess these articulation abilities; they are hired because of their knowledge and experience and should be able to explain annual giving concepts and explain their results to board members and volunteers, prospects and donors. They are also expected to provide guidance and direction in how to use these proven, reliable, tested annual giving methods to achieve success.

Annual giving, like every other fund-development program, does not operate in a vacuum. The letters mailed today may not get a quick response, but the second letter, or a telephone call, or the next event invitation may stimulate a reply. When donors and prospects receive other communications about the organization, whether they are promotions for services, news stories about results, or advertisements of coming events, these communications will help keep the organization in the public eye.

The primary duties of the annual giving program remain

Acquisition (identify and recruit friends)

Renewal (build relationships)

Maximization (involve as many people as possible in the life of the organization)

Because similar messages are being sent by the same organization to the same people, annual giving programs, through their own added communications, will contribute to the objectives that advertising, marketing, promotion, and publicity are trying to achieve for the organization. Annual giving performance will be measured against separate objectives, including how many people responded to each solicitation and how much money was received from them. Success should be measured by the overall rate of *growth in giving* (see Exhibit 13-2) that the comprehensive annual giving program is achieving. Other questions to use in measuring annual giving performance are:

1. By how much did each program increase the number and percentage of prior donors renewed compared to last year and two years ago?

2. How many different solicitations were offered to prior donors, and how many acquisition efforts were made to prospects in the past 12 months?

3. Did the total number of donors and the value of all their gifts increase this year?

4. How many volunteers were recruited and trained and how did they perform compared to last year's volunteers?

5. Have volunteers identified any ideas about how to increase public participation and gift support?

6. How many volunteers and donors were identified as having leadership ability that the organization can look to for direction in the future?

Evaluations of these results and of other areas will verify whether a comprehensive annual giving program has been achieved. To accomplish many of the program's potential objectives, the fund-development staff will be required to carry out several functions beyond solicitation. Ten support areas will be necessary to complete their management responsibility:

1. Board, CEO, and employee relations

2. Management of changing annual priorities

3. Gift reports

4. Budget preparation and management

5. Cost–benefit standards and guidelines

6. Program performance measurement

7. Office functions, operating procedures, and computer support

EXHIBIT 13-2	REPORT ON OVERALL RATE OF GROWTH IN GIVING USING NINE-POINT PERFORMANCE INDEX					
	Two Years Ago	Last Year	Annual Rate of Growth (%)	This Year	Annual Rate of Growth (%)	Cumulative Rate of Growth (%)
Participation	1,355	1,605	18	1,799	12	31
Income	$448,765	$507,855	13	$571,235	12	26
Expenses	$116,550	$123,540	6	$131,850	7	13
Percent participation	39%	44%	13	52%	18	31
Average gift size	$331	$316	−4	$318	0.4	−4
Net income	$332,215	$384,315	16	$439,385	14	30
Average cost per gift	$86.01	$76.97	−11	$73.29	−5	−15
Cost of fundraising	26%	24%	−6	23%	−5	−11
Return	285%	311 %	9	333%	7	16

8. Training for all staff members

9. Financial accounting and reporting

10. Donor relations

BOARD, CEO, AND EMPLOYEE RELATIONS

Members of the fund-development office enjoy a unique association with the board of directors and the senior management staff. They must be able to develop a working relationship with them and enjoy their confidence and trust. The CEO and other senior management staff may have concerns about the extent of the fund-development office's personal contact with the board. The purposes and results of this contact must be communicated to the CEO and senior management, not just to allay their fears but to keep them fully informed of plans and proposals arrived at in all of the discussions at which they were not present. Few employees other than the CEO and fundraising staff rely on board members' direct participation to carry out their work. The job descriptions of fund development staff are quite unlike those of other employees in many areas, just as the programs and services provided to the public by the fund development staff are quite different from those delivered by other employees. No CEO would permit his or her employees to ask board members for money!

Fund-development staff are involved almost exclusively *outside* the organization; their business is different from that of the employees *inside* the organization. Fund-development staff are seldom involved in program and service delivery—a separation of function that can cause misunderstanding and even tension from time to time, when other employees see the fund-development staff spending their time in activities that do not appear to be "work." It is the responsibility of the fund-development staff to go to their fellow employees and explain what their job is and how they do it, to bridge the gap between perception and reality. My own experience has been that, after other employees learn more about fund-development tasks, they confess that they would never want to ask people for money. Fund-development employees must integrate themselves into the culture and lifestyle of their organization and not hold themselves apart, as though they were different (or better). We are employees too, just like everyone else; only our jobs are different.

Management of Changing Annual Priorities

By nature, annual giving depends on the annual operating needs of the nonprofit organization. These needs change at least annually, and sometimes within the same operating year. The messages in each annual appeal are designed to achieve public understanding of these needs and encourage a decision to support the project. Each new project requires time and effort to establish the level of public understanding needed for a decision to participate as a donor or a volunteer. Annual giving communications are necessary and may be sent as often as two dozen times a year (see Exhibit 4-1). These messages are most effective when the projects "for sale" are part of a well-defined, multiyear plan that has been explained many times before; the basic story has not changed, only the details of how it will be continued in this year's projects are different. The projects promoted each year are the next steps in the overall plan. Previous projects completed (with donors' help) have been fitted into the plan like pieces of a mosaic. The next priority is explained as the next component to the picture; with donors' help again, the plan will keep moving forward on schedule. Consistency is critical in annual giving communications, especially when the message must be repeated many times to the same audience. In their messages, some organizations express their plans only in terms of the annual operating budget; their objective is financial survival for another year. Which organization will donors want to give their money to today, and for the next five years?

Gift Reports

The results of annual giving are of interest to everyone involved in this yearly effort. Donors want to know that their money was received and has been spent as they were promised. Volunteers want to know whether all their hard work paid off and the level of their success. The board and CEO want to know how much money has arrived so they may proceed with their programs and plans. Regular gift reports are recommended to convey information in three basic areas: (1) sources of gifts, (2) purposes or uses of funds raised, and (3) annual giving methods used to raise the money. Frequent reports will help maintain momentum for each annual giving program and will give incentive to donors and volunteers alike. Another benefit of gift reports is that they help everyone to understand how annual giving works, how the separate methods are performed, and what can be expected based on previous performance. Gift reports take the guesswork out of annual giving and allow volunteers and staff to begin to feel comfortable in forecasting how each of these methods will continue to perform. Each method will possess flexibility for adjustment and room for improvement; these can be enlisted next time, to achieve the results that are needed. These recommendations should be presented when the next year's budgets are prepared and when reliable gift revenues are being forecast.

Budget Preparation and Management

A nonprofit organization should expect a reliable level of annual gift support from a reasonable investment of its operating budget. The amounts for both should be based on performance during the past three years, not just the past year. The results seldom are dramatically different from year to year, but steady growth can be expected unless new methods are introduced or new performance levels are established. The several methods of annual giving described in this book perform at different levels of net income and operating costs. It stands to reason that if it cost $100,000 to raise $250,000, the organization should not expect to be able to reduce the budget by $10,000 and increase the results by $25,000 unless dramatic and detailed information is on hand to justify these expectations.

The relationship between fundraising cost and results is linked to each method used, the maturity of each program, and its previous performance. If the same or slightly increased results are needed, the investment must total the same amount or a bit more, not less. When needs are increased substantially, the most profitable annual giving method should get most of the added budget. Most annual giving programs are not limited by a lack of prospects and donors, but by a lack of enough volunteers and enough resources to carry out the most efficient methods of asking that are required. Performance measurements conducted for each annual giving method will provide reliable details for assessing the quality of the method's performance and estimating its future revenues and the budget to be invested to achieve them. Using only "bottom line" figures of total revenue and total budget from the previous year can be a misleading and an inaccurate way to forecast future results. To develop accurate projections and to study productivity and efficiency, the following seven measurements should be applied to *each* annual giving method in use (see also Exhibit 3-1):

1. Percentage rate of return

2. Average gift size

3. Net income

4. Average cost per gift

5. Program cost percentage

6. Overall "bottom line" cost percentage

7. Return on investment (ROI)

Percentage Rate of Return

Counting the number of donors who respond validates the quality of the prospect lists chosen, the effectiveness of the solicitation package, and the consensus about the needs (and the message) that prompted a reply. Each method of annual giving will perform with a different rate of return each time it is used, even when the method is the same. For example, the direct mail acquisition program seeks first-time donors; if it achieves a response rate of 1 percent after each mailing and from each list used, it should be judged as quite successful. In practice, each list does not often yield a 1 percent rate of return each time. By comparison, a donor renewal effort, which also uses the mail, should achieve a 50 to 60 percent response rate, because it is asking previous donors to repeat (and upgrade) their last gift.

> *Method:* Divide the number of responses received by the number of solicitations made; the result is the percentage rate of return. Using the CCUA Clean Up Cleveland Chapter as a familiar continuing example, 5,157 replies from a first mailing to 506,546 prospects = 1.02 percent; 914 replies from 1,504 prior donors = 60.77 percent. (See Exhibit 11-11 for other illustrations of annual giving performance.)

Average Gift Size

How much people give is a strong clue to their level of respect and confidence, as well as their financial ability. Direct mail replies may average between $25 and $50. If the average falls below these levels, the mailing lists, package, message, and timing should be examined. When a variety of gift levels is offered, people tend to choose the minimum amount. The number of people who give at each level is an indicator of how carefully the list was segmented and how well the "case for support" is being received.

Method: Divide the total amount of contributions ($192,260) by the number of gifts received (6,071) = $31.67.

Net Income

Net income is sometimes neglected in fundraising reports because when attention is focused on gross revenue, the results look more successful. This practice is often seen in reports on direct mail and benefit events. True success is the net income the nonprofit organization can use to support its programs and services after deducting the costs of solicitation. Focus on net revenue underscores profitability along with effectiveness in managing the prospect list chosen, solicitation method used, the timing of the ask, and more. Renewal mailings are more profitable because they resolicit donors so their efficiency as well as their effectiveness (percent participation) is greater than acquisition mailings that must reach out to hundreds or thousands to secure the same number of new donors at greater expense with lower participation and average gift size rates plus a higher cost per gift.

Method: Subtract total contributions ($116,911) from solicitation expenses ($99,000) = $17,911.

Average Cost per Gift

Cost–benefit ratios are the relationships between gross revenue received and net revenue available after expenses. Fundraising costs are not well understood; reasonable cost levels to be used as generally accepted standards or guidelines are needed. For example, the net results achieved by the CCUA Clean Up Cleveland Chapter in its first series of roll-out mailings were 3,653 replies from 396,467 letters mailed (a 0.92 percent response rate), which produced $116,911 and an average gift size of $32 (see Exhibit 4-8). The average cost per gift was $27.10, and a "profit" of $4.90 per gift was achieved in the first year—a higher-than-average achievement. How else ought these results to be interpreted?

Method: Divide the total fundraising costs ($99,000) by the number of gifts received (3,653) = $27.10.

Overall "Bottom Line" Cost Percentage

This evaluation looks at the results of the comprehensive annual giving program for overall profitability, productivity, and ROI. *Bottom-line* analysis is useful here because comparable data from prior years are available. These results can be misleading if they are not accompanied by the details of each solicitation method, which allow comparison with each program's results in previous years. The CCUA Clean Up Cleveland Chapter received 6,071 gifts and $192,260 in its first year, a 1.20 percent rate of return, and a $31.67 average gift. In its second full year, with more prior donors to renew, more emphasis on charter memberships in The Circle of Champions, and the addition of net profits from its first gala benefit evening, the results increased to 13,066 gifts and $521,858, a 2.21 percent rate of return, and a $43.25 average gift. The increased performance came mainly from the four renewal mailings and the gala, not from the four acquisition mailings still looking for new, first-time donors. Both were necessary and successful, but their performance was markedly different.

> *Method:* Divide the total fundraising costs for the first year of operation ($100,827) by the total gifts received ($192,260) = $0.52; multiply by 100 for the overall "bottom line" cost percentage of 52.44 percent or $0.52 to raise $1, and a 191 percent ROI.

Program Cost Percentage and Return on Investment

Each of the several acquisition and renewal mailings conducted by the CCUA Clean Up Cleveland Chapter performed with slightly different results. Analysis of the mailings' individual performance levels helped the board and fund development officer decide how to proceed each time. Some acquisition lists performed better than others; donor renewal fluctuated in the spring and fall months. Introducing a $100 donor club, charter memberships, and tickets to a summer concert and a theater performance were effective in sparking a higher response from both lists. When the year was over, 7,713 gifts had been received yielding $249,678 (see Exhibit 11-11). Comparing these results with the first acquisition efforts, which produced 6,071 gifts and $192,260, there were 1,642 more gifts worth an added $57,508. The individual program cost percentage and return on investment percentage for an acquisition and a renewal mailing must then be determined. (See Exhibits 4-8 and 4-9.)

Method: Divide first-year acquisition program total costs ($99,000) by total contributions received ($116,911) = $0.85; multiply by 100 for a program cost percentage of 84.67 percent, or $0.84 to raise $1 and 118 percent ROI. Divide the costs of the first renewal request ($1,827) by total contributions received ($31,064) = $0.058; multiply by 100 for a program percentage of 5.88 percent, or $0.58 to raise $1 and 1,700 percent ROI.

COST-BENEFIT STANDARDS AND GUIDELINES

Efficiency and productivity in fundraising results will require more analysis than percentage rate of return, average gift size, bottom line, and return on investment percentages, valuable as they are. How well do these results compare with those of other nonprofit organizations of the same type and in the same community? National standards published by the Philanthropic Advisory Council of the Council of Better Business Bureaus and the National Charities Information Bureau examine several management and operations performance areas, advocate a fundraising cost–benefit ratio of 35 percent as a minimum guideline. No other guidelines are available at this time. It is generally accepted that comparative analysis should begin *after three years* of continuous annual giving operation, when each of these solicitation programs has begun to achieve a level of performance maturity. Again, *each* fundraising method should be evaluated separately and completely. To do so requires that all direct expenses, plus indirect and overhead costs, be applied against gift results. This is the correct principle to advocate, but the fact remains that organizations do not count their results or tally their expenses using any available commonly accepted accounting procedure. This inadequacy has been raised several times in the past decade with the Financial Accounting Standards Board (FASB)[6] and the American Institute of Certified Public Accountants (AICPA). The reasonable cost guidelines suggested in Exhibit 13-3 can be applied for two purposes: (1) to measure cost-effectiveness of current programs and (2) to forecast future results based on continued budget investment.[7] Attempting to predict fundraising results for annual giving methods from one year to the next is an uncertain exercise. There are too many variables that can influence results—economic conditions, volunteer and staff performance, and Murphy's law. The variables that can be controlled, such as list management (segmenta-

EXHIBIT 13-3	REASONABLE COST GUIDELINES FOR SOLICITATION ACTIVITIES

Solicitation Activity	Reasonable Cost Guidelines
Direct mail (acquisition)	$1.25 to $1.50 per $1.00 raised
Direct mail (renewal)	$0.20 to $0.25 per $1.00 raised
Membership associations	$0.20 to $0.30 per $1.00 raised
Activities, benefits, and special events	$0.50 per $1.00 raised (gross revenue and direct costs only)*
Donor clubs and support group organizations	$0.20 to $0.30 per $1.00 raised
Volunteer-led personal solicitation	$0.10 to $0.20 per $1.00 raised
Corporations	$0.20 per $1.00 raised
Foundations	$0.20 per $1.00 raised
Special projects	$0.10 to $0.20 per $1.00 raised
Capital campaigns	$0.10 to $0.20 per $1.00 raised
Planned giving	$0.20 to $0.30 per $1.00 raised

Sources: For direct mail guidelines—Direct Mail Marketing Association. For planned giving—Norman S. Fink and Howard C. Metzler, *The Costs and Benefits of Deferred Giving* (New York: Columbia University Press, 1982). For capital campaigns—American Association of Fund Raising Counsel, New York. The balance are derived from the author's direct experience, research, and publications.

Reprinted from James Greenfield, *Fundraising Cost Effectiveness* (New York: John Wiley & Sons, 1996), 281. Reprinted with permission.

*Benefit event cost allocations: To calculate bottom-line total costs and net proceeds from a benefit event, calculate and add the indirect and overhead support expenses to direct costs incurred and subtract from gross revenue.

tion, merge–purge, letter copy, amounts requested, benefits offered, address corrections), meeting deadlines for mailing dates, and others, require considerable discipline and some expense. To predict likely expectations, one must study prior results in detail, followed by execution of each solicitation activity as efficiently and effectively as possible.

PROGRAM PERFORMANCE MEASUREMENT

Performance measurement includes assessing the rate of growth in giving (see Exhibit 13-2), evaluating the support systems, and testing options for alternate action. It is also necessary to evaluate and to score (using a range of opinions in a low to high score) consistency of messages, personalization, and the effects of each method on community relations, volunteerism, and leadership development (see Exhibit 13-4). With more understanding, it is possible to define fundraising potential and to gauge each method's capacity. There is a difference between potential and capacity in annual giving: *Potential* is raising as much money as is needed; *capacity* is raising as much money as can be raised. Performance measurement must begin with an internal analysis of how the following elements are performing individually and how well they interact:

People	Systems
Leadership	Prospect identification
Volunteers	Office systems/operations
Training	Donor relations
Performance	Budget management

Annual giving program managers must be willing to consider alternatives to their current practices. Neither change nor risk is a popular concept in fundraising management. There are many opportunities to test alternate

---

EXHIBIT 13-4   AREAS FOR ANNUAL GIVING PROGRAM ASSESSMENT

	Score				
	Low				High
1. Comparison with prior-year results	1	2	3	4	5
2. Growth in donor universe	1	2	3	4	5
3. Penetration of new markets	1	2	3	4	5
4. Quality of effort	1	2	3	4	5
5. Leadership development	1	2	3	4	5
6. Consistency and personalization of messages	1	2	3	4	5
7. Regular reports and analysis of the results	1	2	3	4	5
8. Staff training and development	1	2	3	4	5
9. Matching institutional needs (dollars delivered on schedule)	1	2	3	4	5
10. Forecasting future income and each program's performance	1	2	3	4	5
Median Score: _____					

ideas, to experiment with different packages, and to use multimedia and other creative techniques. Any change to annual giving practice should first be tested (see Chapter 2); the results will be known immediately. The following roster of options to current practices should be considered; some of them might be exercised each year:

1. Keep using what is working, especially if it is effective and efficient.

2. Study all the performance data to learn where improvements may lie.

3. Report current results to others and explain what they mean.

4. Define options for improvements based on results, not speculation.

5. Define a business plan each year for every annual giving activity, and review the results at quarterly intervals.

6. Propose changes based on performance plus improvements, and be willing to forecast likely results.

7. Forecast a three-year plan for each activity, stating the performance standards to be achieved; integrate these plans into the overall annual giving program.

8. Ask for more budget to implement the total program of annual giving activities, including improvements; base the requested amount on the forecast of increased net revenue that will result.

OFFICE FUNCTIONS, OPERATING PROCEDURES, AND COMPUTER SUPPORT

Many activities are conducted in the fund-development office and, like any group of office procedures, they are largely taken for granted. A review of a few of the orientation instructions provided to new clerical assistants who have no prior experience with fundraising operations will reveal the details involved. They may include the following:

1. How telephones are answered (the preferred wording of a friendly greeting)

2. The names of board members, volunteers, and important donors

3. The assigned duties and how they relate to what others are doing

4. How to handle mail, especially when checks are enclosed

5. How every gift received must be recorded, deposited, added to the donor's records and files, and thanked

6. The capabilities of the computer and the preferred (or required) format of reports

7. How to process reservations for all activities, benefits, and special events

8. How address changes are entered and communicated

There are many subjects to learn and procedures to master. Quality office operations are reflected in gift results, effective volunteers, and satisfied donors. Annual giving involves large numbers of people every year. They will call to report their address changes, ask for information, offer suggestions, and make complaints. Membership associations require priority attention to member services. Volunteer solicitors, who are worth their weight in gold, also require priority attention to help them succeed with their assignments. These duties require the personal attention of everyone in the fund-development office. Friendships and close working relationships will develop among the donors and volunteers and everyone who works in the office. Taking the time to have meetings, to visit with people over the phone, and to exchange personal notes in the mail may, to some observers, seem unnecessary or unproductive if they think staff should only be asking for money! A study of donor renewal behavior often proves the value of personal attention. Those who are actively in touch with office staff are usually the most frequent and generous donors and the most reliable and effective volunteers.

Management of annual giving methods has been a recurring topic throughout the book, and some details have been given on the basic office functions that support each program. Exhibit 13-5 illustrates common office activities and staffing assignments for a three-person and a 13-person department. Teamwork is essential; so are telephone coverage and etiquette, cross-training, a discipline regarding accuracy, and a respect for confidential information. Office procedures grow up over time and can become fixed in stone; they should be broken open at least every two years to examine whether all the steps being followed remain necessary. To increase office efficiency and improve morale, the people who work in the office should be asked what improvements are needed.

Computers have added greatly to the efficiency of annual giving operations; it is hard to imagine how the fund development office ever func-

EXHIBIT 13-5   BASIC FUNCTIONS OF THE FUND DEVELOPMENT OFFICE

	Office Staff Assignments	
General Duties	Three-Person Office	Thirteen-Person Office
Leadership and direction	Fundraiser	Fundraiser/leader
Fundraising solicitations	Fundraiser	Fundraisers (3)
Office supervision; budget and personnel management	Secretary	Office manager
Secretarial tasks	Secretary	Secretaries (3)
Gift processing, donor records, pledge billing, gift records	Gift records clerk	Gift records clerks (2)
Thank-you letters and cards for all gifts received	Gift records clerk	Gift records clerk
Research and files control	Gift records clerk	Research clerk
Computer records, data input, and data control	Gift records clerk	EDP coordinator
Mail, phone, visitors	Secretary	Receptionist
Supplies, equipment, storage	Secretary	Office manager
Mail-list preparation, changes, maintenance, control	Secretary	EDP coordinator
Personnel training and skill development	Secretary	Office manager
Fund-development training	Fundraiser	Fundraiser
Activities, benefits, and special events	Everybody	Everybody
Plaques, awards, honors, and donor recognition	Fundraiser	Fundraiser and secretary
Donor clubs and membership associations	Fundraiser	Fundraiser and secretary
Volunteer-led, personal solicitation committees	Fundraiser	Fundraiser and secretary

tioned without them. They maintain infallible records on everything, which is a major asset when the numbers of prospects, donors, and volunteers keep growing. Although accurate historical records are valuable, the sophistication of today's software is able to provide data management functions relating to annual giving programs. As an example, assuming the information has been entered correctly into the database, the computer can sort and print out (on envelopes or mailing labels) a list of all the donors who gave $50, $75, and $100 as of a certain date, match them to a letter text, and produce personally addressed individual letters with prior-gift and suggested upgrading amounts inserted in the text—all within a few hours. To attempt such a task for hundreds or thousands of donors without a computer would be excessively expensive today, and the gift results would be the same. Computers also assist with budgeting and cost–benefit ratio analysis, gift reports, accounting and management of funds raised, investment management, donor recognition, and almost every other routine office procedure. They also provide a host of word-processing tasks, and, with laser and inkjet printers, they produce a high-quality product. To make the best use of computers and data management, three things are required: (1) modern equipment, (2) current software, and (3) well-trained employees who are genuinely interested in using their machines for time-saving tasks that will increase productivity.

TRAINING FOR ALL STAFF MEMBERS

Professional staff employees in for-profit companies usually have academic degrees in fields that relate to their job descriptions. People may assume that professional staff in the fund-development office of a nonprofit organization have been equally prepared. Few people realize that a fundraising degree is not available except in a few colleges and universities. Most staff have earned a bachelor's or master's degree, but not in fundraising. The primary training comes from on-the-job experience, and national trade associations provide most of the instructional opportunities. Training programs are offered at local, regional, and national conferences and workshops; through journals, newsletters, and special reports; in an increasing number of books; and by networking. Nonprofit organizations should not hesitate to budget the modest amounts needed for memberships and attendance at one or two professional fundraising association conferences each year. Accreditation and certification programs are also offered; they will help both employers and fundraising professionals to validate their knowledge and experience against established concepts and best practices. Fund development remains an experience-driven field and, with patience and investment in training, employers and employees will benefit. Training should not stop at the professional level. The information gained should be shared with volunteers in the form of improved orientation and training programs. The entire office staff will not attend conferences, but those who do should conduct minisessions after they return, to pass on to others what they have learned. Local meetings and workshops are also learning opportunities for support staff, who should be encouraged to attend when possible. Improving the entire staff's knowledge of how fundraising works will increase the efficiency and productivity of the entire fund-development program.

FINANCIAL ACCOUNTING AND REPORTING

Because annual giving raises money, exemplary financial accounting and reporting procedures are required. Internal accounting procedures for receipt, deposit, and use of annual gifts require meticulous recordkeeping and reports prepared for internal and external use (see Exhibit 4-2). Internal summaries should contain details such as cost–benefit ratio analysis and performance measurements, to illustrate efficiency as well as effectiveness. External reports should fulfill the accountability due to donors on the use of their money, especially where restricted gifts are involved. Reports of annual giving results must be correct for each program in operation; they should present details clearly and in a form that is easy to read and understand. When annual giving results are success stories, they will serve to motivate volunteers and donors. They will also help everyone to appreciate how results were achieved and how improvements can be made. Withholding the "bad news" about a program that was not able to make its goal is unwise, for two reasons:

1. Several volunteers were involved and many donors gave as requested; all these personal efforts remain worthwhile.
2. Failure may bring to light a method or technique that is not working well for volunteers and staff; by finding and correcting it, the expectations for next year may be secured.

DONOR RELATIONS

Investing time and budget dollars in donor communications, recognition, and reward is as valuable as investing in donor acquisition and renewal. Everyone agrees that "donors are the best prospects," but not everyone pays as much attention to keeping existing donors as they do to acquiring new ones. As long as the focus of annual giving is on raising money and not donors, donor relations will suffer. Donors are the source of most of an organization's income, and maximum efficiency is realized by working toward their giving again. The second-year results of the CCUA Clean Up Cleveland Chapter annual giving program, when there were donors to renew, showed 3,383 prior donors giving $126,536 in the fall, and 1,838 prior donors giving $117,650 in the spring; a total of 5,221 donors renewed and gave $244,186 (see Exhibit 11-11). By comparison, the results from acquisition mailings in the same time periods were 4,192 gifts and $106,396, and 1,835 and $97,665, respectively, for a total of 6,027 new donors and $204,061. Both groups used only direct mail solicitation. There will be better results from continued attention to current donors, although acquisition efforts should not stop.

An important statement is worth repeating one more time: Donor relations begins with the first gift. The cost required to achieve a first gift is high (between $1.00 and $1.25 per dollar raised). When such an investment has already been made, it is certainly worth a bit more expense to maximize continued giving. Follow-up begins with personalized acknowledgment letters. The fund-development office is responsible for processing each gift and sending a thank you. Donors also can be offered honors and recognition. These benefits are usually reflected in increased communications from the organization, which will keep them informed in an effort to stimulate their interest and will invite their future involvement. Donors want to know (1) whether their gift was received safely, (2) how it will be used, and (3) whether it made a difference. If satisfied on all three concerns (and if they hear again from the organization), they are more likely to repeat their gift when asked. Repeat contributions can become a habit among donors. The annual giving methods described in this book permit many ways to ask a donor to participate and to give more than once a year; repeat gifts create an opportunity to begin building relationships with donors. A friendship can start on the first day a donor calls and is addressed by name before he or she has said who is calling.

Wise nonprofit organizations establish and announce guidelines for how donors who make substantial contributions, especially those who make major gifts, will be recognized and rewarded. Donors of $1,000 should receive more attention than donors of $100, but everyone who gives $100 should be treated equally. A cumulative donor records system linked (via computer) to a donor-recognition program will allow donors who are faithful givers to qualify in time for a cumulative level of recognition. Written guidelines help everyone to understand how much is required for the promised benefits and privileges (see Exhibits 4-4 and 7-4). Uniformity of treatment is a major factor in an honors and recognition policy.

Rewards to donors, including the privileges and benefits of donor clubs, are part of donor relations. Material objects reflecting the organization's appreciation for a donor's dedication and generosity can be added as tokens. As stated before, the object given is treasured far less than the recognition—the ceremonial occasion when the gift was presented, who was present, and the compliments paid. Donors deserve sincere attention; they are more than their gifts reflect, and donor relations is more than a gesture.[8]

ISSUES AND CHALLENGES FOR THE FUTURE OF ANNUAL GIVING

This second edition concludes with a review of several issues and challenges already affecting philanthropic practice. By nature, annual giving is quite sensitive to environmental changes because of its instant response style; if you want to know how your public thinks about an issue, ask. You *will* get responses! Because change is pervasive in our society, keeping pace with those that affect philanthropy and its annual giving methods is a challenge in itself. Some issues are subtle; others are more direct. Tax law changes (even discussion about them in Congress) cause many donors to hesitate about giving, not because their gift deduction may be affected but because tax laws affect their sense of spendable cash. For nonprofit organizations, an increase in postal rates means increased costs to their operating budgets, including the cost of raising money. This increase results in fewer resources available for programs and services and might force budget cuts to fundraising activities, decisions made in obvious conflict with one another.

Most issues and challenges described in this forecast are outside the control of nonprofit organizations themselves (see Exhibit 13-6). Those they can control, such as the quality of their programs and the ability to manage operations with a positive financial performance, are in themselves subject to external forces such as the cost of goods and services they must purchase,

EXHIBIT 13-6	ISSUES THAT AFFECT ANNUAL GIVING
Accountability	Leadership
Community benefits and outcomes measurement	New philanthropists
Dot-com wealth	Privacy rights
Ethics in fundraising	Research on philanthropic practice
"High tech, high touch"	Vision and values
Internet usage	Women in philanthropy

again outside their control. Being aware of these internal and external forces is more helpful than being ignorant of them. Awareness is directly related to preparedness; a planned response without loss of service or quality of care is the objective. There is little room for defending ignorance or inattention.

In fundraising practice, there is always a delay between changes in societal response and implementation of a new or revised method of professional practice. To minimize this delay and avoid negative perceptions caused by changes in societal trends, nonprofit organizations must monitor the community's mood and interpret societal changes. If the fund-development office senses such a shift, it will need to create and test alternative courses of action. Alternate fiscal sources will have to be developed, and this takes time and new money. If, for example, the response to a new dynamic is to increase the number of donors participating in any annual giving program, more effort will be required to reach out to more people. If the decision is to increase the amount of net proceeds using another, perhaps new, program, it will take time to organize and implement the program, including both increasing donors and their gift amounts while controlling expenses to realize increased net proceeds. This process can take a year or more.

Growth in annual giving is never fast—there are no sure-fire quick fixes or easy-money schemes. This is true not because of a lack of ability or resolve to make change or try new methods, but because changing people's attitudes and perceptions takes time. It will require a preponderance of targeted communications to justify the need as well as validate the new direction.

Lastly, annual giving is a direct involvement with hundreds, thousands, and, in some cases, hundreds of thousands of people, most of whom make relatively small gifts each year. To effect a major shift in how many will participate and how much they will give is akin to trying to move a thirsty elephant away from water. It will take time to get the elephant to move, and then you have to be equally persuasive about the new direction you want it to take.

Management of a nonprofit organization is a lot like herding elephants, made more difficult because of limited incentives to offer their elephants. Revenue sources are limited, while demands for services are greater than the ability to provide them. When forecasting the future, nonprofit organizations cannot add any new revenue-producing options beyond these five:

1. Excess of revenue over expenses
2. Profits from for-profit enterprise
3. Investment earnings
4. Cash from fundraising
5. Borrowing money

Of these five, good managers cannot generate much profit from their annual operations or their for-profit enterprises, which leaves investment earnings and fundraising results as their best options for new revenue. (Borrowing money for annual operations is not recommended!) Of these two, only fundraising is within an organization's direct control. (Playing the stock market is not an option, either!)

When you measure these five options against ever-present pressure for cash, realizing only fundraising is the alternative revenue source they can control entirely, annual giving strategies are far too limited to meet these demands. However, if a comprehensive annual giving program has been in place with reliable donors matched with volunteer leaders and experienced solicitors, you have exactly the foundation for growth that is needed. Such an organization is poised and ready to reap the rewards in the next tier of the Pyramid of Giving—major-gift solicitations, capital campaigns, and planned-giving strategies. A solid foundation in quality annual giving programs is the ticket to greater gift support; without making this investment first, annual giving can never meet the operating needs that will be placed upon it.

Accountability

More than a passing fad in the 1990s, accountability has become a consistent demand from board members, donors, and volunteers alongside the media and regulatory officials; they want to see measured performance and demonstrated results from their investment in nonprofit organizations. The claim of "doing good works" is no longer sufficient in exchange for the privileges of tax-exempt status. As public benefit corporations, the need is for greater visibility of the actual "public benefit" the community receives; greater transparency to the daily operations providing programs and services is requested, along with increasing demands for open and full disclosure.

Result federal law made the IRS Form 990, an organization's annual tax return, widely available to increase disclosure. These information requests for results in operating areas and fiscal management are not the result of media coverage of fraud and abuse or scandalous behavior by nonprofit executives. They come from community residents who have become increasingly skeptical about the value of the nonprofit sector and want to see measurable outcomes. Volunteer statistics are in decline. Giving continues to grow but at a slower rate, barely on pace with inflation. Full implementation of IRS "intermediate sanctions" regulations grants the government the authority to impose fines and assess fees for misconduct, including personal liability for board members and senior managers. In truth, nonprofit organizations and the people who work for them, plus those who volunteer their time to support them, are each called to a higher standard.

Most accept this responsibility with the confident assurance they are doing the right thing, but public scrutiny has imposed an increasing discomfort with the burden of honest responsibility that accompanies election to a volunteer board or a senior management appointment. To answer, the leaders of nonprofit organizations must be willing to step forward and explain their decisions as well as report on their activities and future plans. If guidelines will help, here are three necessary steps to the process: First, they must begin to analyze, assess, and audit their results in order to be able to evaluate their own effectiveness and efficiency. Second, they must be able to manage, measure, and monitor their performance to evaluate their productivity, progress, and profitability. And third, they must disclose their results through public reports and other avenues to demonstrate their success. With all three in place, they are well prepared to describe how they used the resources given to them by a generous public. Those who do all this will be rewarded with continued public support, plus increased public confidence and trust in what they propose to do in the future.

Community Benefits and Outcomes Measurement

A significant challenge for all nonprofit organizations is to show, with measurable outcomes, how their programs and services have made a difference to the lives of the people and the communities they serve. It may sound simple, but it is especially difficult to do. Nevertheless, serious effort must be given to prepare and report on results in some detail.

Colleges recruit large freshman classes, count those left at graduation four or five years later, and report on their success in bringing students through their rigorous curriculum. Do they measure how each student was prepared to be a member of the community along with the work positions they hold? Hospitals perform life-saving procedures, offer public health education, and run free clinics to test for risk factors of diabetes, heart disease, and more. Do they measure any change to the overall health of their communities? Cultural organizations make art, music, and theater available for those who visit their museums, hear their concerts, and see their plays. Do they measure the difference these activities made in people's lives? Social service and welfare organizations are better equipped to document how they make a difference to the lives of those they serve. Do they measure themselves against the challenge of reducing the incidence of broken families, abused children, unemployed workers, rehabilitated drug users, and more?

In each example, good works are being performed; it's the quantitative measurement of the results that is difficult. Let stewardship be the guiding principle here; stewardship in philanthropy is defined as "a process whereby an organization seeks to be worthy of continued philanthropic support, including the acknowledgment of gifts, donor recognition, the honoring of donor intent, prudent investment of gifts, and the effective and efficient use of funds to further the mission of the organization."[9] Those last few words point to the issue and the challenge—how well were the entrusted funds used to further the mission of the organization? How does an organization measure its own activity? Help is on the way.

United Way of America has committed itself to a uniform performance measurement yardstick with its 1995 *Strategic Direction for United Way: Charting a Path for Building Better Communities*. This master plan is designed to measure the outcomes of health and human services and allocate funds accordingly.[10] Their workbooks and supporting documents provide complete instruction for this targeted "building better communities" initiative. How does United Way measure its outcomes?

> Outcomes may relate to knowledge, skills, attitudes, values, behavior, condition, or status. Examples of outcomes include greater knowledge of nutritional needs, improved reading skills, more effective responses to conflict, getting a job, and having greater financial stability.[11]

Further, stewardship is a personal objective for each board member. The level of responsibility as guardian of the public's trust is to be directly responsible for all the actions of the organization, its management, professional staff, and employees in serving the mission for the benefit of the community. In many states, nonprofit organizations are incorporated first as "public benefit corporations;" their very existence is to serve. Determining how well they perform means measuring the benefits they deliver back to their communities.

Several state, county, and city authorities have taken action against local nonprofit organizations that, according to their measurements, have not done enough community benefit to justify their tax exemption. These organizations have been fined or assessed fees based either on a percentage of their annual operating budget judged appropriate for community benefit or based on their real estate's value.

The Commonwealth of Pennsylvania has been especially aggressive in this arena in observance of its new regulations that measure nonprofit organizations against a scale of "pure public charity" (see Exhibit 13-7). When these regulations were enacted in 1997, part of the motive was to recover funds from hospitals and other health-care providers in lieu of their property exemption privileges, to help rectify state, county, and city deficits associated with fire and police services (without property tax as-

---

EXHIBIT 13-7   CHARACTERISTICS OF A "PURE PUBLIC CHARITY"[12]

- Advance a charitable purpose
- Render gratuitously a substantial portion of its services
- Benefit a substantial and indefinite class of persons who are legitimate objects of charity
- Relieve government of some of its burden
- Operate entirely free from private motive

sessments, hospitals made no contribution to these expenses but used them). In part, the five characteristics listed in Exhibit 13-7 were designed so that nonprofit organizations would fail this community benefit test and have to pay the fines or assessed fees. Enforced accountability, perhaps, but on point with accountability for what every nonprofit organization claims as its stated mission—measurable benefits returned to the community. To what extent this concept, under challenge in the Pennsylvania courts, will spread to other states, counties, and municipal jurisdictions is unknown. Suffice it to say that nonprofit organizations have been given notice to begin to gather their data, measure their results, and report their accomplishments to their communities.

Dot-Com Wealth

Here is an issue and a challenge about which everyone has an opinion. "Why haven't you brought us any big gifts from these super rich people?" is one that's common. Remember where this book talked about friend-raising and relationship-building? This book is only about annual giving, not about major gifts or capital campaign gifts, the playing field for the dot-com wealthy. But, since all this new wealth is around—and some of it survived the plunge in the technology sector in 2000 and 2001—let's ask ourselves about the inclination of a newly rich person to make a gift to charity.

Put aside how they made their money, their age, where they went to school, marital status, and how many cars or homes they already own. Why would anyone want to give away newly acquired wealth? How liquid are they, really? What was their preparation for instant wealth? What are their values, their awareness of community needs, their civic engagement? Just because they now have money does not mean they inherited all the fine attributes their parents and grandparents exemplified. Are there exceptions? Yes, of course.

Indeed, many newly rich individuals have come forward to share their good fortune with causes they care about. What is still big news is the size of their gifts. We are not used to reading and hearing about these "mega-gifts" as contributions to churches, arts organizations, social and welfare groups and others who are grass-roots and lesser-known organizations. We are not accustomed to hearing about gifts in the millions of dollars, or even hundreds of millions when you move up to the Bill Gates and Ted Turner level of giving. The flip side to these megagifts is whether they have changed philanthropy. Perhaps it is still too soon to know with certainty. They have caused quite a stir with board members and administrators, who keep asking that persistent question—"Why haven't you brought us any big gifts from these super rich people?"

Nonprofit organizations have the daily task of taking care of people. Windfall megagifts are like winning the PowerBall lottery or the Irish Sweepstakes—you can play the game, but you never really think you're going to win. You have to keep your focus on your mission and do the best you can with what you have. That means getting back to basics—but with some new thinking about paying attention to your annual donors. They are your future, your "wealth reserve" investment for when the need arises. It would be a good idea to prepare yourself for the day that might never come, when you might win with a surprise phone call. If that day should come, you will want to be ready for this call: "I was reading about your organization last night and would like to do something important with you. What is your current biggest priority of need, whom does it serve, and what will it cost to make it fly? I'd like to be involved in making something important happen. Think large; I'm willing to consider a seven-figure gift."

Do you have such a project ready to go, maybe even two? Will it truly make a measurable difference in people's lives? Will it have immediate impact on a community need? Will it allow the donor's personal involvement? Will your "best big idea" have prior consensus and board approval? You will not want to delay a minute in answering this call, other than to say, "Yes! Here's my idea, and we can begin tomorrow."

Ethics in Fundraising

One thing about ethics, the meaning never changes. Standards remain high, public awareness is strong, watchdogs are alert, enforcement is active, and the penalties are high. But a few individuals continue to think they will not be caught. Well, they do get caught, and everyone else shares in their shame because scandals, fraud, and abuse hurt everyone, especially all those in philanthropic practice because the public's confidence and trust in charitable purposes is what is at risk. If you study the codes of ethics and standards of professional practice of associations and trade groups whose members serve the U.S. nonprofit sector, you will find they are all similar in what they advocate as high ethical standards for their professional roles, especially when it comes to the public's money given as charitable contributions. The Donor Bill of Rights is designed to protect the donor's intentions, as well as ensure a respectful relationship with the organization (see Exhibit 9-5 in Chapter 9). Accounting guidelines are strict about requiring arms-length ties among those who receive gifts, those who deposit them, and those who spend them. Fundraisers in annual giving assignments are vulnerable because their activities involve money, including assets in the form of stocks and bonds. Some of their activity involves cash, such as exchanges for raffle tickets at benefit events, or script and chips at a Monte Carlo evening.

The courts today are full of cases brought against direct mail, telephone, and benefit-event vendors who, acting on behalf of a charity (real or imagined) attempt to defraud the public for their own gain. Ethics codes do not prevent people from breaking the law; they can serve only as a guide for the level of quality performance that is required. To break an ethics tenet is to break the bond of trust with the public. The challenge for board members is to fulfill their role as the public's trustees for their organizations. Fundraising professionals are out in public representing the highest ethical standards of their organization. Public confidence and trust are absolutely essential to the reputation of every nonprofit organization; even the hint of impropriety can cause not only lost gifts but also lost volunteers who turn away and lost clients who refuse to use the services intended to help them.

"High Tech, High Touch"

At issue here is the degree of impersonalization resulting from modern technology's use of mass communications with volunteers, donors, and the general public. This is a major challenge since it also includes competing for public attention using commercial message channels where for-profit businesses have larger advertising and communications budgets as well as knowledge and experience in using them. They also have access to every media arena (television, telephone, radio, and the Internet), and they have saturated the airwaves.

The downside of "high tech" has been increased public resistance to these communication avenues, no matter the source or the message. Nonprofit organizations have neither the money nor experience to compete for public attention here. Because annual giving is a social exchange medium, it depends on highly personal communications methods. To succeed, nonprofit organizations must learn how to use paid advertising selectively, how to target their markets and their messages strategically, how to use cable and commercial television efficiently, and how to use the Internet wisely. If they are going to participate in high tech, such as the Internet, they need to invest in continuous maintenance of their Web page; it has to be active and it must be current or it will be largely useless. They also need to prepare marketing and communications strategies to guide how they present themselves and their programs, including their annual giving programs.

Competition for public attention is difficult and it is increasingly difficult to achieve any level of personal association using high-tech communications. Personal messages can and should be delivered using methods that people are accustomed to receive—first-class mail, telephone calls, fax messages, and e-mail—"high touch" styles for contact and conversation. Additional features such as videocassette tapes, CDs, list servers, and more hold high promise for nonprofit use to advertise their programs, promote their services, send helpful information, and encourage the public to support their cause. In combination, each of these communications elements can be joined together for increased efficiency and produce good results with one objective—personal interaction between people. Fundraising remains a people business; that's why it is a successful investment by nonprofit organizations, because fundraising will always be a "contact sport."

Internet Use

Best-use practices are still in the future as organizations continue to learn how to integrate the distinct advantages of Internet communications. The forecast for global use is here already; we have access to every kind of information and service "at the click of a mouse." Public confidence and trust in using the Internet is lagging, but more people are using its conveniences to shop, arrange airline tickets, plan vacations, pay their bills, invest their money, take classes for academic degrees, and manage more of their lives by electronic means. It is unfortunate that all these good uses also are ripe for those who would abuse them in charity's name. Technology is tough to regulate when it is designed to be open to everyone, and even harder to prosecute those who use it improperly and illegally.

At risk for nonprofit organizations will be public confidence and trust in using the Internet to make their personal contributions. Existing state rules and regulations along with enforcement authorities could not anticipate electronic giving when their laws were written. As a result, attempting to use the same rules and regulations previously successful in regulating mail and telephone solicitation is ineffective at present. The challenge for state authorities is to enact new laws to govern electronic solicitation with the following elements. First, they need to be consistent in registration and reporting of results among the several states. Second, they need to protect the public from scam artists and crooks who would defraud the public. And third, they need to permit legitimate nonprofit organizations to utilize the advantages of Internet solicitation for their needed public gift support. To confuse this issue further, there also is the likelihood that Congress and the federal government, acting in response to growing public complaints, will attempt to pass legislation that is likely to strip existing state authorities of their proven ability to address this issue. No clear solution either way is available at this time.

Leadership

There is never enough that can be written about the importance of leadership. Whether to run a government, guide a nation, lead an army, or just rally a group of friends to help neighbors down on their luck, it all starts with leadership—someone taking charge and motivating others to follow.

> Many people do not realize it, but the largest number of leadership jobs in the United States is in the nonprofit, social sector. Nearly one million nonprofit organizations are active in this country today, and they provide excellent opportunities for learning about leadership. The nonprofit sector is and has been the true growth sector in America's society and economy. It will become increasingly important during the coming years as more and more of the tasks that government was expected to do during the last thirty or forty years will have to be taken over by community organizations, that is, by nonprofit organizations.[13]

Leadership of nonprofit organizations requires being a dedicated advocate, making personal gifts and soliciting others, and serving as an example to all involved. At the board level, members also are asked to advocate the cause, make strategic plans, hire and fire the CEO, and be responsible for the fiduciary affairs of the organization. Few who are called to top leadership, no matter their passion or commitment, are adequately prepared to serve as the organization requires; they learn their job on the job.

Leaders are not born to this work any more than they are born to it elsewhere. True leadership is rare; it is a gift to the world. "In the field of human endeavor, leaders are indeed rare.[14] Nonprofit leaders are volunteers first and foremost. They have to be recruited, informed, and involved before they can be invited into an organization in a beginning capacity and before they can be invited to serve in a position of responsibility. To assume that elevation to the board of directors comes with a brain implant of knowledge and understanding of nonprofit management is an unfortunate expectation for men and women of good and caring hearts.

The qualities desired for a leader of an annual giving program are quite clear: "visibility, respectability, clout, wealth, and a willingness to take responsibility over others—and fearless when it comes time to ask for money."[15] Annual giving programs offer a great variety of leadership training opportunities. Because annual giving has one-year terms, performance can be evaluated and accountability for future reliable service can be measured quite readily. Good service may be rewarded with a new appointment next year, quite possibly with expanded areas of responsibility. A *career ladder* for nonprofit leadership, like all others, is based on consistent fulfillment of voluntary duties that merit recognition and promotion. For some, the ladder is their goal in order to give more of themselves to benefit the organization. For others, finding the right spot where they can serve with distinction is the goal. Both are welcome additions to the volunteer leadership ranks; bless them, one and all.

The New Philanthropist

When you stop and think about it, it is novel to combine the words *entrepreneur* with *philanthropy*, but that time has arrived, and we have *entrepreneurial philanthropists* living among us. These two words (not the people) are strange bedfellows. Traditional definitions of an entrepreneur include an individual "who commits resources in the face of financial risk, at times even personal financial risk, to pursue an opportunity," which does not appear to fit well with philanthropy, "an effort to increase the well being of humankind." What has brought these two together is the rapid rise in the number of entrepreneurs and entrepreneurial business characteristics, which has led to entrepreneurial giving. Entrepreneurs have several fascinating characteristics, beginning with this list:

- Entrepreneurs recognize opportunities and constantly seek to leverage resources for maximum use.
- Entrepreneurs are interested in addressing issues and causes, not in supporting institutions.
- Entrepreneurs focus on performance and want the projects they support to be self-sustaining.
- Entrepreneurs are action oriented, not process oriented.
- Entrepreneurs are most interested in addressing root causes and making permanent changes.
- Entrepreneurs want to use market-based approaches to solving society's challenges and problems.
- Entrepreneurs are convinced that innovation, constant change, and reassessment of circumstances are crucial to progress.
- Entrepreneurs expect a return on their investment.
- Entrepreneurs do lots of research before making charitable gifts but are impatient to implement them.
- Entrepreneurs want to be hands-on, a tendency to direct or restrict their gifts to ensure that their dollars are leveraged to the maximum.
- Entrepreneurs have no patience with process or paperwork.
- Entrepreneurs prefer immediate decisions, not group-think gatherings and committee deliberations.
- Entrepreneurs believe in the capacity of a single individual to make a difference.
- Entrepreneurs make snap decisions with limited information in their business and expect the same quick response time from nonprofit organizations.
- Entrepreneurs view their gifts to charity as an investment that is expected to yield results in public good not dollars.
- Entrepreneurs who lack liquidity often make gifts-in-kind or services, again leveraging their resources for maximum use.
- Entrepreneurs are extremely busy, lack liquidity, and are rarely motivated by a primary goal of making money for money's sake.

- Entrepreneurs give on their own time, not an organization's timeline.
- Entrepreneurs are motivated to give back to a community or organization that has been good to them.
- Entrepreneurs make philanthropic decisions as highly personal and individualized actions, often influenced by their peers.
- Entrepreneurs became rich without compromising their integrity; they credit their integrity with their success and expect the same of nonprofits.
- Entrepreneurs know very little about philanthropy and philanthropic decisions, but are interested in receiving more education about philanthropy.[16]

If you encounter an entrepreneur, be prepared for a new (and exciting) experience.

Privacy Rights

Individual privacy rights are related to protecting personal information about an individual. Electronic access to vast sources of information is widely available. Access has made privacy rights a sensitive issue, one that is now gathering legal protection. Just because someone has access to volumes of personal details does not give them license to use that information in an unethical manner or without the person's permission. A prime example of sensitive personal information is a medical record. Hospital patients have the right to keep details about their health from their employer, family members, banks, credit card and mortgage companies, and others. Recent government regulations now restrict hospital use of patient data only for purposes directly related to hospital operations, restricting what information is available and how it may be used by doctors and nurses and for marketing and fundraising purposes. Gift details are another privacy issue. Annual donors have the right to ask to be anonymous; they also can ask for no further contact by mail or telephone.

Every facet of a nonprofit organization's fundraising program depends on respect; it is united in a bond of trust between donors and their chosen charitable causes, as expressed in the Donor Bill of Rights (see Exhibit 9-5). This respect is also due to board members and employees, with clients, patients, and customers, and must be accompanied by respect for the personal and private information now accessible from public sources. What information does an annual giving volunteer or staff member really need in order to succeed? Name, address, telephone number, e-mail address, and recent gift history of those who are, have been, or will be donors and/or volunteers. Nothing more.

Research on Philanthropic Practice

Professional studies on philanthropy have only begun. More than 200 colleges and universities have formal nonprofit management and philanthropic studies programs, offer degrees and certificates, and sponsor research projects led by academicians. Outside these formal educational settings, other organizations, notably the Urban Institute, Independent Sector, the Foundation Center, the Conference Board, the National Center for Nonprofit Boards, and others are sponsoring research projects to study the functions and services provided by nonprofit organizations and the relationships between organizations and those who support their cause. Several publishers and professional associations have invested resources in a stream of textbooks, resource manuals, and workbooks in this field where, prior to the 1980s, little was available. Quality reporting demands quality information based on sound principles of investigation. Quality research is more than an indicator of correctness; it adds confidence and trust to what organizations say about themselves, including how they use their resources for community benefit. In combination, professional research efforts have added substantially to the body of knowledge of the nonprofit world. Much more remains to be done. The challenge is to provide guidance to the process so that basic theory and ethical issues can be combined with professional practice to be used to further public policy decisions that support these vital enterprises.

Vision and Values

Most nonprofit organizations focus a lot of attention on their mission statement, review it as part of their long-range planning process, and use it as a concise descriptor of their purpose. Most mission statements are too long, lack precision about why the organization exists and what it really does, and are too cumbersome to be memorized or quoted without a copy in hand. One of the best examples of a mission statement that both encompasses accuracy of purpose and is easily quotable is from Mothers Against Drunk Driving (MADD): *"To prevent drunk driving and care for its victims."* Not only is this statement precise and crystal clear, but also it has only nine words in all! Most people may know only about the first four words, not the last four. Together, these nine words are an impact statement of mission, vision, and values.

Partners to a good mission statement are its vision and values statements. A vision statement provides a direction for the future, a set of aspirations an organization is striving to achieve with noble and notable goals. Values statements cite the virtues that the organization and its employees strive to attain in order to achieve their mission and vision. Values describe the culture the organization chooses to live by in serving its clients, patients, and customers with personal attention and respect. Vision and values reflect the expectations of all who choose to work there.

The challenge to every nonprofit organization is to prepare and approve both vision and values statements consistent with its mission. Further, since customer relations have become increasingly important as an internal strategy for nonprofit organizations, these three statements will guide them in serving their clients, patients, and customers. It is these same clients, patients, and customers who are the potential advocates for their cause as well as their services to others. Advocacy is a key ingredient for success in their involvement in the organization's annual giving programs, today and in the future. In combination, the mission, vision, and values statements of an organization explain why they exist to serve their communities, what they believe is their future, and their commitment to quality service. What better background for the "case for giving" could an annual giving program hope to have?

Women in Philanthropy

The nonprofit world has become feminized. So has philanthropy. Women represent the majority of employees, of volunteers, and of employed fundraising professionals. They make most of the gifts. Fundraising work offers opportunities for satisfaction with career options that contain the flexibility necessary for women who work and maintain a home and family. Fundraising work matches well with a woman's natural ability to engage people in social settings, to cope with diverse personalities, and to nurture relationships. The field also is open equally to women and men with no formal training or prior experience, although women more often have had direct experience as volunteers in similar duties and responsibilities. Equity in compensation is not yet the reality. The nature of fundraising also brings with it the challenge of dealing with frequent travel, flexible hours including evenings and weekends, and the necessity of changing jobs to gain wider experience and increased levels of responsibility.[17]

Women as donors and as volunteers will continue to be significant in the future of nonprofit organizations and their fundraising programs. Women as the inheritors of wealth now control or will control decisions on the distribution of the bulk of an estimated $46 to $136 trillion in the next 50 years, of which an estimated $6 to $25 trillion may be directed to charitable organizations.[18] Women as philanthropists have established themselves by their personal leadership and their major gifts. They are dedicated, passionate advocates for a mission or cause and are capable of asking others for money. Their participation is best defined as guided by six precepts: Create, Change, Connect, Collaborate, Commit, and Celebrate. Both men and women need to understand these attributes in detail and appreciate them in full.[19]

CONCLUDING THOUGHTS

The realm of annual giving is a splendid victory garden filled with fruits and vegetables to sustain the daily activities of every nonprofit organization. The methods and techniques described in this book have been time-tested in hundreds of thousands of circumstances and settings with audiences of every type and description for more than 100 years. There may be new ideas, other ways to achieve the same ends, but these basic tools have proven themselves time and again to be effective and efficient, as well as reliable; they should not be abandoned or disregarded without serious commitment to first invest in them and allow them to perform at their best levels of productivity and profitability. Annual giving is a numbers game; how many donors have been recruited, how many retained, how many upgraded. How many volunteers have been recruited, how many trained, how many are effective? Money follows people. Lots of people are necessary to be successful in fundraising.

And, after you have completed an entire year and successfully managed multiple annual giving programs, celebrate! Tomorrow, you get to do it all over again. Take courage pills; annual giving is like a fine wine, it gets better with tender care and age. Among your courage pills take a few from these final thoughts:

There are no secrets to success. It is the result of preparation, hard work, and learning from failure.

Colin L. Powell (1937–)

The proper aim of giving is to put the recipients in a state where they no longer need our gifts.

C.S. Lewis (1898–1963)

Give with no strings attached, no expectation of return. Give because it is right for you to give.

Arthur Caliandro (1934–)

In the United States, one can seldom pass a day without benefiting directly or indirectly from some present or past philanthropic act.

Robert L. Payton (1926–)

If our entire society is to be revitalized, it will depend on what we as individual Americans are willing to do on our own, in association with others, and how willing we are to extend ourselves beyond our own personal interests.

John D. Rockefeller III (1906–1978)

We should place a higher value on what we contribute to society rather than on what we accumulate.

Senator Ben Nighthorse Campbell (1933–)

Philanthropy flows from a loving heart, not an overstuffed pocketbook.

Douglas M. Lawson (1936–)

Philanthropy is almost the only virtue that is sufficiently appreciated by mankind.

Henry David Thoreau (1817–1862)

We make a living by what we get, but we make a life by what we give.

Winston Churchill (1871–1947)

The best thing to hold on to in this world is each other.

Linda Ellerbee (1944–)

The vineyards of philanthropy are pleasant places, and I would hope good men and women will be drawn there . . . if these vineyards are to thrive and bear their best fruit, they must always have first-class attention.

Harold J. Seymour (1894–1968)

If you want happiness for an hour—take a nap.
If you want happiness for a day—go fishing.
If you want happiness for a month—get married.
If you want happiness for a year—inherit a fortune.
If you want happiness for a lifetime—help someone else.

Chinese proverb

Operating Rules and Procedures for a Support Group Organization

WHEREAS, the [name of parent nonprofit organization] is a corporation organized under the [state name and title of state code identified for nonprofit public benefit corporation law];

WHEREAS, the Board of Directors of [name of parent] is authorized under the [state name and title of state code] to establish committees and support groups that do not exercise the authority of the Board of Directors of the [name of parent];

WHEREAS, the Board of Directors of [name of parent] has established a support group to solicit property to be received, administered and disbursed by the [name of parent] and to carry on other related tax-exempt purposes in accordance with the [name of parent]'s articles of incorporation; and

WHEREAS, the Board of Directors of [name of parent] has adopted the following Operating Rules and Procedures for the governance of the following support group.

ARTICLE I. Name

The name of this support group of the [name of parent] shall be

_____.

ARTICLE II. Affiliations and Operations

Section 1. Affiliation:

The _____, sometimes referred to herein as the "_____," shall be a support group of the [name of parent], but shall not be a committee of the Board of Directors of [name of parent] and shall not exercise the authority of such Board. The activities and affairs of the [name of parent] shall be managed and all corporate powers of the [name of parent] shall be exercised under the ultimate direction of the Board of Directors of the [name of parent].

Section 2. <u>Title of Property</u>:

Any and all property solicited by the "_____" shall be and shall remain the property of the [name of parent].

<u>ARTICLE III.</u> <u>Principal Office</u>

The principal office of the _____ shall be located at [full description of the location and mailing address of the support group].

<u>ARTICLE IV.</u> <u>Purposes</u>

Section 1. <u>General Purpose</u>:

The "_____" seeks to build understanding, appreciation, and long-term commitment by individuals, corporations, and foundations of the work of the [name of parent].

Section 2. <u>Specific Purposes</u>:

1. The "_____" shall provide financial support for [name of parent] through membership dues, benefit events, and other fundraising activities;

2. Any such property so received shall be administered and disbursed by the [name of parent] in accordance with [name of parent]'s articles of incorporation. Property solicited by the "_____" and the income therefrom shall be disbursed by the [name of parent] solely to, or for the benefit of, the [name of parent] which is operated at [full mailing address]. Such disbursements by the [name of parent] shall be used at the [name of parent] for only the following purposes and no other purposes, mainly related to [cite specific restricted purposes, if funds are directed to one or more programs or services of the parent] in the form of (a) capital expenditures; (b)renovation of the buildings and facilities; (c) equipment purchases; (d) education; and (e) research;

3. The "_____" shall increase public awareness of the facts about [name of parent and specific restricted purposes, if any], through ongoing community education;

4. The "_____" shall seek to build public understanding of [cite restricted purposes, if any] through a publication program, including its newsletter and other communications;

5. The "_____" shall endeavor to stimulate personal involvement toward the common goal of promoting the highest quality of [cite parent's mission and restricted purposes, if any] in this region through [name of parent].

ARTICLE V. Members

Section 1. Voting Member:

The only voting member of this organization as defined in [state name and code] shall be the [name of parent] which shall have sole voting control over the final election of the Board of Directors of "_____." There shall be only one class of voting membership.

Section 2. Nonvoting Members:

The nonvoting members of this organization shall be those persons who have applied for membership in the "_____," been approved by the Membership Committee, and have, from time to time, paid annual dues to the "_____."

There shall be four classes of membership, based solely on the amount of dues paid by the nonvoting members, as follows:

(a)   Life Members

(b)   Gold Members

(c)   Silver Members

(d)   Bronze Members

The amount of dues for each level of membership shall be determined, from time to time, by the Board of Directors of the "_____." All such nonvoting members shall have the same rights and privileges regardless of the amount of dues paid.

Family Membership: When a married individual becomes a member, his or her spouse shall automatically be deemed a member, be entitled to the same privileges as a nonvoting member, and be known as a Family Member. Each such couple shall be deemed to be (1) member on the records of the "_____." At "_____" membership events where admission is charged, *each* individual shall pay an admission charge except as modified by the Board of Directors.

ARTICLE VI. Board of Directors

Section 1. Number and Qualifications:

The Board of Directors shall consist of _____ (_____) elected directors.

Of that number, _____ (_____) shall be members of the professional staff who are serving as employees of [name of parent] in the following capacities:

(a) Director of the _____.

(b) Director of the _____.

(c) A delegate appointed by the _____.

If Co-Directors of any of these professional services are acting, either or both such Co-Directors may attend the "_____'s" Board meetings and vote thereon but they shall have only one (1) vote between them.

The remaining directors shall be lay individuals selected from the community. Their minimum qualification shall be current membership standing of the "_____."

No more than 49 percent (49%) of the persons serving on the Board may be interested persons. An "interested person" is (a) any person compensated by the "_____," or by the [name of parent] for services rendered within the previous twelve (12) months, whether as a full-time or part-time employee, independent contractor, or otherwise, excluding any reasonable compensation paid to a director as a director; and (b) any brother, sister, ancestor, descendent, spouse, brother-in-law, sister-in-law, son-in-law, daughter-in-law, mother-in-law, or father-in-law of such person. However, any violation of the provisions of this paragraph shall not affect the validity or enforceability of any transaction entered into by the "_____" or its Board of Directors.

Section 2. Terms of Office:

A total of _____ (_____) lay directors shall be elected each year, each for a three (3)-year term. Lay directors may be reelected for a second consecutive three (3)-year term but may not be reelected thereafter until the expiration of at least one (1) year following the completion of his or her last term on the Board of Directors.

Professional staff members who, by reason of office, possess membership on the Board of Directors, shall serve during such time as they hold the staff position set forth in Section 1 above.

Section 3. <u>Election of the Board of Directors</u>:

The lay members of the Board of Directors shall be nominated by the Nominations Committee at the regular meeting prior to the annual meeting.

The slate of candidates selected by the Nominations Committee shall be voted on by the Board of Directors at the annual meeting. Such slate, if approved by the Board of Directors, shall then be submitted to the [name of parent] for confirmation.

Any lay director may be removed at any time by the [name of parent] by vote of its Board of Directors.

The professional staff members of the Board of Directors shall be selected as provided in Section 1 of this Article.

Section 4. <u>Powers of the Board of Directors</u>:

Subject to the provisions and limitations of [state name and code section] and any other applicable laws, as well as subject to the policies and procedures of the [name of parent], the "_____" activities and affairs shall be managed, and all powers shall be exercised, by and under the direction of its Board of Directors.

The Board of Directors shall:

(a) Perform any and all duties imposed on them collectively or individually by law, by the [name of parent], or by these Operating Rules and Procedures.

(b) Elect the officers of this organization.

(c) Approve all activity and event plans.

(d) Establish committees and ratify the appointment of committee members.

(e) Supervise all officers, committees, and volunteers of the organization to ensure that their duties are properly performed.

(f) Develop an activities plan for submission annually to the Board of Directors of [name of parent].

(g) Make recommendations periodically to the [name of parent] as to the application of funds raised by the "_____."

(h) Set membership dues for all levels of nonvoting members.

Section 5. <u>Vacancies</u>:

Any vacancy as to a lay director on the Board of Directors shall be filled by election of a new director for the unexpired term in accordance with the provisions of Section 1 and 3 above.

Section 6. <u>Meetings of the Board of Directors</u>:

(a) Regular meetings of the Board of Directors shall be held at least quarterly at the time and place specified by the Board of Directors.

(b) The annual meeting of the Board of Directors shall be held in the month of _____ each year.

(c) Written notice of the time and place of meeting shall be delivered personally to each Director or sent to them by United States Mail, postage prepaid, at least seven (7) days prior to such meeting.

(d) Special meetings of the Board of Directors may be called by the President, or, if he or she is absent or is unable or has refused to act, by the Vice President or by any two (2) Directors, and such meeting shall be held at the place designated by the person or persons calling the meeting.

(e) One (1) more than half the number of directors then serving shall constitute a quorum of the Board of Directors for the transaction of business, except to adjourn.

(f) The transactions of any meeting of the Board of Directors, however called and noticed or wherever held, are as valid as though the meeting had been duly held after proper call and notice, provided a quorum, as hereinabove defined, is present.

(g) Every action taken or decision made by a majority of the Directors present at a duly held meeting at which a quorum is present shall be the act of the Board of Directors, subject to the more stringent provisions of the [state name and code section] including, without limitation, those provisions relating to (i) approval of transactions in which a director has been a direct or indirect material financial interest, (ii) approval of certain transactions between organizations having common directorships, (iii) creating of and appointments to committees of the Board of Directors, and (iv) indemnification of Directors.

(h)   A meeting at which a quorum is initially present may continue to transact business, despite the withdrawal of directors, if any action taken or decision made is approved by at least a majority of the required quorum for that meeting.

Section 7. Action without a Meeting:

Any action that the Board of Directors is required or permitted to take may be taken without a meeting if all members of the Board consent in writing to the action, provided, however, that the consent of any Director who has a material financial interest in a transaction to which the organization is a party and who is an "interested Director" as defined in Section _____ of the [state name and code section] shall not be required for approval of that transaction. Such action by written consent shall have the same force and effect as any other validly approved action of the Board. All such consents shall be filed with the minutes of the proceedings of the Board.

ARTICLE VII. Officers

Section 1. Appointed Officers:

The officers of this organization shall be a President, a Vice President, a Secretary, a Treasurer, and an Immediate Past President. An officer of the "_____" shall not be an officer of the [name of parent] unless he or she has otherwise been appointed an officer of the [name of parent] in accordance with the Bylaws of the [name of parent].

Section 2. Election of Officers:

The officers shall be nominated by the Nominations Committee at the regular meeting of the Board of Directors prior to its annual meeting. The officers shall be elected by the majority vote of the Board of Directors at its annual meeting.

Section 3. Term of Office:

The officers shall serve a term of one (1) year, or until their successors have been elected and qualified or until removed by majority vote of the Directors.

Section 4. Vacancies:

A vacancy occurring in any office shall be filled by election of a new officer for the unexpired term by majority vote of the Board of Directors.

Section 5. <u>Duties</u>:

The duties of the officers shall be as follows:

(a)   <u>President</u>:

The President shall be the executive officer of the organization and, subject to the control of the Board of Directors, shall have general supervision, direction, and control of the affairs of the organization. The President shall preside at all meetings of nonvoting members and at all meetings of the Board of Directors. The President shall appoint the committee chair of all standing committees (other than the Long-Range Planning Committee and the Nominating Committee) in accordance with these Operating Rules and Procedures, subject to the approval of the Board of Directors, and shall be an ex-officio member of all committees.

(b)   <u>Vice President</u>:

The Vice President shall, in the absence or disability of the President, perform all of the duties of the President, and when so acting shall have all of the powers of, and be subject to the restrictions on, the President.

(c)   <u>Secretary</u>:

The Secretary shall keep at the principal office of the organization a book of minutes of all meetings of the Board of Directors and of the nonvoting members prepared by the Secretary or by the support staff of the [name of parent]. The Secretary shall maintain a membership book showing the name and address of each nonvoting member. The Secretary shall serve as parliamentarian at all meetings of the Board of Directors and shall perform such other duties as may be designated by the Board of Directors.

(d)   <u>Treasurer</u>:

By virtue of the relationship between this organization and the [name of parent], all funds generated by the "_____" are paid directly to the [name of parent], which shall furnish regular reports of income and expenses to the Treasurer for submission to the Board of Directors of this organization. The Treasurer shall, in conjunction with the Chair of each Events Committee and appropriate support staff of the [name of parent], review the budget for each event prior to submission of that budget to the Board of Directors.

(e)   Immediate Past President:

The Immediate Past President, by reason of his or her prior experience, shall act as Chair of both the Nominations Committee and the Long-Range Planning Committee.

ARTICLE VIII. Committees

Section 1. Executive Committee:

The Executive Committee shall include the five (5) elected officers who shall conduct such day-to-day affairs of the Board of Directors as may be required in the absence of meetings or between regularly scheduled meetings of the Board of Directors. Actions taken by the Executive Committee shall be presented to the Board of Directors at their next meeting for approval.

Section 2. Other Standing Committees:

The following committees shall be considered standing committees of the Board of Directors. The Chairperson of each standing committee shall be appointed annually by the President and ratified by the Board of Directors. The Chairperson shall be invited to attend meetings of the Board of Directors. All committee members asked to serve shall be non-voting members of the "_____" and their appointment shall be approved by the Board of Directors annually.

The other standing committees are:

(a)   Membership Committee:

The Membership Committee shall be responsible for recruitment and renewal of nonvoting members annually at all dues levels. Activities of this committee shall include membership recruitment and renewal activities including the solicitation of friends of present nonvoting members and their friends, and all orientation events for new members.

(b)   Event Committees:

Each event committee shall be responsible for definition and operation of its designated benefit event held, and shall observe the [name of parent]'s budget guidelines to achieve a goal of at least fifty percent (50%) net profit for each event held. Each event committee shall also advise and assist, where appropriate, those other activities that will support annual membership solicitations, other benefit events, and such additional fundraising activities as may be defined as the priority of the [name of parent].

(c)   Long-Range Planning Committee:

The Long-Range Planning Committee shall monitor implementation of the existing long-range plan and shall conduct any continuing or new long-range planning process at the request of the Board of Directors.

(d)   Communications, Public Relations, and Marketing Committee:

The Communications, Public Relations, and Marketing Committee shall be responsible for assisting [name of parent] in the plans for and the use of the "_____" publications, invitations, membership directory, membership brochure, and other materials for public consumption and for use of the roster of members of the "_____."

(e)   Fundraising Committee:

The Fundraising Committee shall be responsible for such special projects and campaigns among the members where the "_____" can be of special help to the [name of parent] in meeting its identified needs. The Chairman shall also be invited to participate in any campaign committee of the [name of parent] where the goal includes projects of benefit to the [restricted purposes of the "_____"] so that maximum coordination in fundraising activities will occur between the "_____" and the [name of parent].

(f)   Policy and Procedures Committee:

The Policy and Procedures Committee shall be responsible for periodic review of these Operating Rules and Procedures so that they remain current and correct regarding the operating policy of the [name of parent] as well as federal and state law and regulation. In addition, the Committee shall conduct such reviews of its policy and procedures as requested by the Board of Directors and develop recommendations for action by the Board of Directors.

(g)   President's Circle:

The President's Circle shall be composed of all previous Presidents of the "_____," who shall be responsible for preparation and conduct of the annual meeting and for the nomination of candidates for any awards program of the "_____" or [name of parent]. The President's Circle shall make itself available to periodically advise the Board of Directors and the Officers of this organization.

(h)   Nominations Committee:

The Nominations Committee shall be chaired by the Immediate Past President. Members shall also include the current President and two members selected and appointed by the President from the President's Circle. The Nominations Committee shall perform their duties as defined in Article VI, Section 3, and Article VII, Section 2, of these Operating Rules and Procedures.

Section 3. Other Committees:

The President, with approval of the Board of Directors, shall appoint and define the duties of such special committees and advisory groups as may be necessary from time to time to achieve the objectives of this organization and which shall serve ad hoc at the pleasure of the Board of Directors.

ARTICLE IX. Rules of Order

Robert's Rules of Order, Revised, shall govern the deliberations of this organization and all procedures not expressly covered in these Operating Rules and Procedures.

ARTICLE X. Limitation on Political Activities

None of the activities of this organization shall consist of the carrying on of propaganda, or otherwise attempting to influence legislation, nor shall this organization participate in or intervene in (including the publishing or distributing of statements) any political campaign on behalf of any candidate for public office.

ARTICLE XI. Insignia

The Board of Directors may adopt, use, alter, or cancel an insignia for the "_____" and by rule shall prescribe the time, manner, and place in which such insignia may be worn or used.

ARTICLE XII. Amendments

These Operating Rules and Procedures may be amended at any time by written approval of the Board of Directors of the "_____." These Operating Rules and Procedures, and any amendments thereto, shall not become effective until their being adopted by the Board of Directors of the [name of parent].

RESOLUTIONS. Adoption

We, the undersigned, being the directors of the "_____" of [name of parent] as well as the directors of the [name of parent] hereby consent to and do, adopt the foregoing Operating Rules and Procedures as the Operating Rules and Procedures of the "_____."

Dated: _____, 200X

Board of Directors of "_____"	Board of Directors of [name of parent]
_____ (name of Director)	_____ (name of Director)
_____ (name of Director)	_____ (name of Director)
_____ (name of Director)	_____ (name of Director)
_____ (name of Director)	_____ (name of Director)
etc.	etc.
etc.	etc.
etc.	etc.

Certificate of the Secretary:

I certify that I am duly elected and acting Secretary of the "_____," that the above Operating Rules and Procedures, consisting of _____(_____) pages, are the Operating Rules and Procedures of this organization as adopted by the Board of Directors of the [name of parent] on _____, 200X, and that they have not been amended or modified since that date.

EXECUTED, this _____ day of _____, 200X, at [name of city and state].

_____

[Name of Secretary]

Master Checklist for Activities, Benefits, and Special Events

[*Author's Note*: Each activity, benefit, or special event will require preparation of a separate master checklist to aid leadership, volunteers, and staff to schedule and monitor progress of all the details required to execute the function without error or serious mishap. There is no single checklist or master schedule complete enough to fit every conceivable form of activity, benefit, or special event; the following roster of details represents one guide. There is no order to the list of details needed to help plan a function, assign responsible parties, establish costs and expenses, and monitor progress to meet established deadlines, as illustrated below. This same document can be used to guide the postevent critique evaluation and as a pre-planning tool for the next activity, benefit, or special event.]

Function Name or Title: _____

Name of Sponsor: _____

Location or Site: _____

Day, Date, and Time(s): _____

Requirements: ☐ New function   ☐ Existing function
                                   (Prior Critique Report attached)

               ☐ Activities, goals, and objectives form submitted

               ☐ Proposed budget (revenue and expenses) submitted

Part A: <u>Approvals</u>

1. Sponsor: _____

   Name: _____   Date: _____

   (Signature)

2. Fund Development Officer: _____   Date: _____

   (Signature)

3. Fund Development Committee: ☐ Yes ☐ No   Date: _____

4. Board of Directors: ☐ Yes ☐ No   Date: _____

Part B: <u>Prefunction Planning Details</u>

  1. <u>Leadership and Volunteer Committee Status</u>

Date/Deadline

☐ Chairperson or co-chairs recruited and accepted on   _____

☐ Leadership orientation conducted on by _____   _____

☐ Leadership approval of function plan, committees and
subcommittee structure, and master schedule on   _____

☐ Leadership approved master schedule/time line on   _____

☐ Committees and subcommittees identified with
leadership candidates   _____

☐ All committee leadership recruited by   _____

☐ Leadership orientation conducted on by _____   _____

☐ Honorary chair/co-chairs identified on   _____

☐ Convene first general meeting by   _____

☐ General meeting schedule established by   _____

☐ Volunteers recruited and appointed to all committees
and subcommittees on   _____

☐ Volunteer orientation conducted on by   _____

☐ Committees and Subcommittees began planning and
preparations for their duties and responsibilities on   _____

☐   _____

  2. <u>Program Plan, Agenda, Principal Speakers,
and Entertainment</u>   _____

☐ Master of ceremonies accepted on   _____

☐ Required/courtesy speakers accepted on   _____

☐ Date and time confirmed with each speaker on   _____

☐ Speaker biographic data/photos required by   _____

☐ Main speaker or entertainment confirmed on   _____

☐ Speaker references checked on _____

☐ Talent interviewed/auditioned on _____

☐ Recording/taping requirements agreed to on _____

☐ Verified site can provide stage support on _____

☐ Contract negotiated and signed on _____

☐ Advance to be paid on _____

☐ Balance of fee is due on/by _____

☐ Escorts/local transportation resolved by _____

☐ Auction/raffle/door prize plan approved on _____

☐ Committee for auction/raffle prizes appointed on _____

☐ Program or "ad book" decision approved on _____

☐ Sales committee leadership appointed on _____

☐ Volunteer sales force recruited and trained by _____

☐ Other honoraria/travel/accommodations set by _____

☐ _____

3. Mailing Lists and Invitations _____

☐ Mailing lists resolved and total count by _____

☐ Graphics designer/printer selected by _____

☐ Save-the-date notice/card to be mailed by _____

☐ Invitation graphics design package approved by _____

☐ Donors' contribution deduction resolved by _____

☐ Invitation/ticket texts approved by _____

☐ Invitations to be addressed by _____

☐ Invitations to be mailed by _____

☐ Reservation/acknowledgment system ready by _____

☐ Second invitation to be addressed/mailed by _____

☐ _____

4. Facilities _____

☐ Location/room inspection conducted on _____

☐ Parking (access, valet, number of spaces) verified on _____

☐ Special needs/modifications identified on _____

☐ Speaker/entertainer audiovisual needs resolved on _____

☐ Audiovisual requirements resolved on _____

☐ Notification of authorities completed on _____

☐ All required permits received on _____

☐   Medical and security needs resolved on   _____

☐   Concessions and other service needs resolved on   _____

☐   Catering or food service decision on   _____

☐   _____

5. Food/Beverage Requirements (Reception, Function, Postfunction
    Party)   _____

☐   Preliminary budget estimate to determine deduction
    value and to set ticket prices resolved by   _____

☐   Facility/function seating capacity resolved on   _____

☐   Equipment rentals identified and resolved by   _____

☐   Menu plan complete and tasting performed by   _____

☐   Full beverage plan completed by   _____

☐   Linen, tableware, service resolved by   _____

☐   Budget for decorations approved by   _____

☐   Centerpieces resolved by   _____

☐   Preliminary floor plan approved by   _____

☐   Favors or special gifts approved by   _____

☐   _____

6. Collateral Printing and Official Program   _____

☐   Graphics designer and printer resolved by   _____

☐   Sponsor/underwriter materials needed by   _____

☐   Stationery, envelopes needed by   _____

☐   Print advertisements/posters needed by   _____

☐   Advance banners/flags/signs needed by   _____

☐   Official program design approved by   _____

☐   All copy for program text needed by   _____

☐   Program delivery required by (time and date)   _____

☐   Tickets, place cards, drawing tickets due by   _____

☐   On-site banners, signs, posters, displays due by   _____

☐   Badges, identification ribbons due by   _____

☐   _____

7. Advertisement, Promotion, and Publicity   _____

☐   News conference decision needed by   _____

☐   Promotion and publicity plan approved by   _____

☐   Press release texts approved by   _____

☐   Media release mailing list completed by _____

☐   PSA/Advertising materials completed by _____

☐   Media invitation list completed by _____

☐   Press kit prepared for advance promotion by _____

☐   Press kit prepared for function needed by _____

☐   Press room/equipment/materials resolved by _____

☐   Photographer(s) and assignments resolved by _____

☐   _____

8.   Support Details at the Function _____

☐   Extra invitations, RSVP forms, tickets due by _____

☐   Event site ticket sales/will-call desk resolved by _____

☐   Cash box/credit card machine/receipts needed by _____

☐   Raffle ticket sales/trained salespersons resolved by _____

☐   Raffle ticket bin for drawing needed by _____

☐   Display tables for auction prizes needed by _____

☐   Ushers, table hosts appointed and trained by _____

☐   Reservation lists/table seating charts needed by _____

☐   Name tags prepared with table numbers needed by _____

☐   Parking validation stamp/ink pad needed by _____

☐   Adequate staff and trained volunteers resolved by _____

☐   Volunteers as official greeters at all doors resolved by _____

☐   American and state flags visible to all guests due by _____

☐   _____

9.   Final Function Checklist: What Not to Forget _____

☐   Phone numbers for critical personnel needed by _____

☐   Extra supply of invitations and programs due by _____

☐   Copies of all speakers' scripts due by _____

☐   Adding machine, hand calculator needed by _____

☐   Supplies (pens, markers, name tags, easels, tape, poster board, etc.) needed by _____

☐   Informational literature about organization due by _____

☐   Locations for restrooms and public phones needed by _____

☐   Appointment of clean-up committee due by _____

☐   Foul weather and disaster plan resolved by _____

☐   _____

10. <u>Critique Meeting and Performance Evaluation</u>   _____

☐ Invitation lists and performance; analysis   _____

☐ Advertising and promotion results; analysis   _____

☐ On-site coverage; press requirements   _____

☐ Postfunction coverage evaluation   _____

☐ Sponsor and underwriting sales results; analysis   _____

☐ Attendance (how many, who, guests' names, seating)   _____

☐ Table placement, seating plan evaluation   _____

☐ Program evaluation (speakers/A-V/timing, etc.)   _____

☐ Facilities and staff evaluation   _____

☐ Food and beverages evaluation   _____

☐ Service and courtesy evaluation   _____

☐ Arrival (greeters, ushers, table hosts)   _____

☐ Registration table (name tags, guest lists, ticket sales)   _____

☐ Parking; access and egress evaluation   _____

☐ Print materials, deadlines, and use   _____

☐ Collateral materials, deadlines, and use   _____

☐ Raffle and auction performance   _____

☐ Quality of prizes, awards, auction items   _____

☐ Budget review and final approval on all bills   _____

☐ Thank-you letters prepared for all volunteers   _____

☐ Complete master file of all materials   _____

☐ Critique report prepared and delivered to Board   _____

☐   _____

Glossary of Internet Terms

This glossary of terms has been compiled from a variety of sources (noted in parentheses) by the ePhilanthropyFoundation.org.

Acrobat (Source: Adobe.com). Acrobat® is a program made by Adobe that allows you to convert any document to a Portable Document Format (PDF) file (a type of file that is commonly posted on the Web for download). Anyone can then open your document across a broad range of hardware and software, and it will look exactly as you intended—with layout, fonts, links, and images intact.

Applet (Source: Sun.com). An applet is a small program that can be included in an HTML page, just like an image is included. Java applets can perform interactive animations, immediate calculations, or other simple tasks without having to send a user request back to the server.

ASCII (Source: Learnthenet.com). ASCII is an acronym for American Standard Code for Information Interchange, a seven-bit code that represents the most basic letters of the Roman alphabet, numbers, and other characters used in computing. ASCII characters allow us to communicate with computers, which use their own language called binary, which is made up of zeros and ones. When we type ASCII characters from the keyboard (which look like words to us), the computer interprets them as binary so they can be read, manipulated, stored, and retrieved.

ASP (Source: ASPNews.com). Application Service Providers (ASPs) are third-party entities that manage and distribute software-based services and solutions to customers across a wide area network from a central data center. ASPs may be commercial ventures that cater to customers or not-for-profit or government organizations that provide service and support to end users.

Bandwidth (Source: Webopaedia.com). Bandwidth is the maximum amount of data that can travel a communications path in a given time, usually measured in seconds. For digital devices, the bandwidth is usually expressed in bits per second (bps) or bytes per second.

Banner (Source: SearchWebManagement.com). Depending on how it's used, a banner is either a graphic image that announces the name or identity of a site (and often is spread across the width of the Web page) or an advertising image. Advertisers sometimes count banner "views," or the number of times a banner graphic image was downloaded over a period of time.

Bookmark   (Source: Whatis.com). Using a World Wide Web browser, a bookmark is a saved link to a Web page that has been added to a list of saved links. When you are looking at a particular Web site or homepage and want to be able to get back to it quickly later, you can create a bookmark for it. Netscape and some other browsers use the bookmark idea. Microsoft's Internet Explorer uses the term *favorite*.

Bounce   (Source: Computeruser.com). An electronic mail message returned with a notice indicating the transmission failed, either because the message was misaddressed or a connection failed.

Browser   (Source: Webguest.com). A software program that allows you to surf the Web. The most popular Web browsers right now are Netscape Navigator and Internet Explorer.

CGI   (Source: Instantweb.com). Common Gateway Interface (CGI) is a standard for running external programs from a World Wide Web HTTP server. The CGI program can, for example, access information in a database and format the results as HTML. A CGI program can be any program that can accept command line arguments.

Cookie   (Source: Webguest.com). A small piece of information that a Web server sends to your computer hard disk via your browser. Cookies contain information such as log-in or registration information, online shopping cart information, and user preferences. This information can be retrieved by other Web pages on the site so that the site can be customized.

CRM   (Source: 1to1.com). Customer Relationship Management (CRM) is the same as one-to-one marketing. This customer-focused business model also goes by the names *relationship marketing*, *real-time marketing*, *customer intimacy*, and a variety of other terms. But the idea is the same: Establish relationships with customers on an individual basis, and then use the information you gather to treat different customers differently. The exchange between a customer and a company becomes mutually beneficial, as customers give information in return for personalized service that meets their individual needs.

Digest   (Source: Instantweb.com). A periodical collection of messages that have been posted to a newsgroup or mailing list. A digest is prepared by a moderator who selects articles from the group or list, formats them, and adds a contents list.

EDI   (Source: Instantweb.com). Electronic data interchange (EDI) is the exchange of standardized document forms between computer systems for business use.

Encryption   (Source: Learnthenet.com). A way of coding the information in a file or e-mail message so that if it is intercepted by a third party as it travels over a network it cannot be read. Only the person or persons that have the right type of decoding software can unscramble the message.

ePhilanthropy   (Source: ePhilanthropyFoundation.Org). The building and enhancing of relationships with supporters of nonprofit organizations via an Internet-based platform, the online contribution of cash or real property, or the purchase of products or services to benefit a nonprofit organization, and the storage of and usage of electronic data or use of electronic methods to support fundraising activities.

Firewall (Source: Learnthenet.com). A firewall is a combination hardware and software buffer that many companies or organizations have in place between their internal networks and the Internet. A firewall allows only specific kinds of messages from the Internet to flow in and out of the internal network. This protects the internal network from intruders or hackers who might try to use the Internet to break into those systems.

FTP (Source: Instantweb.com). File Transfer Protocol (FTP) is a client-server protocol that allows a user on one computer to transfer files to and from another computer.

HTML (Source: Learnthenet.com). An acronym for Hypertext Markup Language, HTML is the computer language used to create hypertext documents. HTML uses a finite list of tags that describe the general structure of various kinds of documents linked together on the World Wide Web.

HTTP (Source: Learnthenet.com). HTTP stands for HyperText Transfer Protocol, the method used to transfer hypertext files across the Internet. On the World Wide Web, pages written in HTML use hypertext to link to other documents. When you click on hypertext, you jump to another Web page, sound file, or graphic.

Hyperlink (Source: Webguest.com). A highlighted word (or graphic) within a hypertext document (Web page). When you click a hyperlink, it will take you to another place within the same page or to another page.

IP Address (Source: About.com). An IP (Internet protocol) address is the thirty-two-bit numeric address that serves as an identifier for a computer; informa-

tion is routed based on the IP address of the destination. The IP address is written as four numbers separated by periods. For example, 207.158.192.40 could be an IP address. Each of the four numbers (which can be from zero to 255) is used in different ways to identify a particular network and a host on that network.

ISP (Source: Webopedia.com). Internet service provider (ISP), a company that provides access to the Internet. For a monthly fee, the service provider gives you a software package, username, password, and access phone number. Equipped with a modem, you can then log on to the Internet and browse the World Wide Web and send and receive e-mail.

Listserv (Source: Searchvb.com). Listserv is a small program that automatically redistributes e-mail to names on a mailing list. Users can subscribe to a mailing list by sending an e-mail note to a mailing list they learn about; listserv will automatically add the name and distribute future e-mail postings to every subscriber. (Requests to subscribe and unsubscribe are sent to a special address so that all subscribers do not see these requests.)

NGO (Source: UN.org). A nongovernmental organization (NGO) is any nonprofit, voluntary citizens' group that is organized on a local, national, or international level. Task-oriented and driven by people with a common interest, NGOs perform a variety of services and humanitarian functions, bring citizens' concerns to governments, monitor policies, and encourage political participation at the community level. They provide analysis and expertise, serve as early warning mechanisms, and help monitor and implement international agreements. Some are organized around specific issues, such as human rights, the environment, or health.

OPX (Source: OPXInfo.org). Open Philanthropy Exchange (OPX) is a specification for data transfer between institutions in the philanthropy industry. The purpose of the OPX standard is to help philanthropic institutions communicate in a common language. Through seamless transmission of data, OPX removes technical barriers and allows data to flow seamlessly from one organization to another.

Perl (Source: Instantweb.com). Practical Extraction and Report Language (Perl) is a general purpose language, often used for scanning text and printing formatted reports. The use of Perl has grown significantly since its adoption as the language of choice of many World Wide Web developers.

POP3 (Source: Instantweb.com). Post Office Protocol, version 3, is a publication that standardizes the way computers on the Internet send and receive e-mail messages. The computers that do the sending and receiving are called servers.

RGB (Source: Instantweb.com). Red, Green, Blue—the three colors of light that can be mixed to produce any other color. Colored images are often stored as a sequence of RGB triplets or as separate red, green, and blue overlays. The term is often used as a synonym for color, as in "RGB monitor" as opposed to monochrome (black and white).

Search engine (Source: Learnthenet. com). A search engine is a type of software that creates indexes of databases or Internet sites based on the titles of files, keywords, or the full text of files. The search engine has an interface that allows you to type what you're looking for into a blank field. It then gives you

a list of the results of the search. When you use a search engine on the Web, the results are presented to you in hypertext, which means you can click on any item in the list to get the actual file.

SQL (Source: Instantweb.com). An industry-standard language for creating, updating, and querying relational database management systems.

SSL (Source: Instantweb.com). Secure Sockets Layer is a protocol designed by Netscape Communications to provide encrypted communications on the Internet.

TCP/IP (Source: Whatis.com). Transmission Control Protocol/Internet Protocol (TCP/IP) is the basic communication language or protocol of the Internet. It can also be used as a communications protocol in the private networks called intranets and in extranets. When you are set up with direct access to the Internet, your computer is provided with a copy of the TCP/IP program just as every other computer that you may send messages to or get information from also has a copy of TCP/IP.

Top-level domain (Source: Network-Solutions.com). .COM, .NET, and .ORG are top-level domains in the hierarchical Internet Domain Name System. These top-level domains are just underneath the "root," which is the start of the hierarchy. Anyone may register Web Addresses in .COM, .NET, and .ORG.

URL (Source: Instantweb.com). Uniform Resource Locator (previously "Universal"). A draft standard for specifying the location of an object on the Internet, such as a file or a news group. URLs are used extensively on the World Wide Web. They are used in HTML documents to specify the target of a hyperlink, which is often another HTML document (possibly stored on another computer).

WWW (Source: Webopaedia.com). A system of Internet servers that support specially formatted documents. The documents are formatted in HTML, which supports links to other documents, as well as graphics, audio, and video files. This means you can jump from one document to another simply by clicking on hot spots. Not all Internet servers are part of the World Wide Web.

XML (Source: W3.org). Extensible Markup Language (XML) is a simple, very flexible text format. Originally designed to meet the challenges of large-scale electronic publishing, XML is also playing an increasingly important role in the exchange of a variety of data on the Web.

Notes

Notes to Chapter One

1. Henry A. Rosso, *Achieving Excellence in Fund Raising* (San Francisco: Jossey-Bass, 1991), 4.
2. Robert L. Payton, *Philanthropy: Voluntary Action for the Common Good* (New York: Macmillan Publishing Co., 1988).
3. Brian O'Connell, *America's Voluntary Spirit: A Book of Readings* (New York: The Foundation Center, 1983), xx.
4. Bruce R. Hopkins, *A Legal Guide to Starting and Managing a Nonprofit Organization*, 3rd ed. (New York: John Wiley & Sons, 2001), 38. Details on formation and operation of nonprofit organizations will be found in this readable text. Complete legal details are contained in Hopkins's basic textbook, *The Law of Tax-Exempt Organizations*, 7th ed. (New York: John Wiley & Sons, 1997).
5. Hopkins, 3.
6. John Gardner, as quoted in Hopkins, *A Legal Guide*, 4.
7. Gardner, as quoted in O'Connell, *America's Voluntary Spirit*, xv.
8. John D. Rockefeller III, "America's Threatened Third Sector," *Across the Board*, The Conference Board (March 1978), as reprinted in *Reader's Digest* (April 1978).
9. Payton, 40.
10. Robert L. Payton, Henry A. Rosso, and Eugene R. Tempel, "Toward a Philosophy of Fund Raising," in *Taking Fund-Raising Seriously*, ed. Dwight F. Burlingame and Lamont J. Hulse (San Francisco: Jossey-Bass, 1991), 11 and 41.
11. Harold J. Seymour, *Designs for Fund Raising: Principles, Patterns, Techniques* (New York: McGraw-Hill, 1966), 43. (A second edition of this exemplary text was reissued in 1988 in paperback by The Fund Raising Institute, Ambler, PA.)
12. "Giving in America: Toward a Stronger Voluntary Sector," Report of the Commission on Private Philanthropy and Public Needs, John H. Filer, Chairman, 1975.
13. Harvey P. Dale, "Tax-Exempt Organizations: Winds of Change," Distinguished Norman A. Sugerman Memorial Lecture sponsored by the Mandel Center for Nonprofit Organizations at Case Western Reserve University, Cleveland, Ohio, May 20, 1991.
14. Internal Revenue Service, as reported in *The Chronicle of Philanthropy* (August 9, 2001).
15. Payton, Rosso, and Tempel, 7.
16. Jon van Til & Associates, *Critical Issues in American Philanthropy* (San Francisco: Jossey-Bass, 1990), 226–227. Reprinted with permission.
17. Seymour, 115.
18. Payton, Rosso, and Tempel, 16.
19. Peter F. Drucker, *Managing the Nonprofit Organization: Practices and Principles* (New York: HarperCollins Publishers, 1990), 56.

20. Hopkins, 102–103.

21. Payton, Rosso, and Tempel, 4.

22. Ibid., 7.

23. Financial Accounting Standards Board, *Statement of Financial Accounting Standards No. 116: Accounting for Contributions Received and Contributions Made* (Norwalk, CT: FASB, June 1993), 7–8 (pars. 22–26), and 30–38 (interpretations, pars. 87–117).

24. Ibid., 3 (pars. 9 and 10); 38–40 (pars. 118–124).

25. Thomas E. Broce, *Fund Raising: A Guide to Raising Money from Private Sources*, 2nd ed. (Norman: University of Oklahoma Press, 1986), 17–25.

26. William K. Grasty and Kenneth G. Sheinkopf, *Successful Fund Raising: A Handbook of Proven Strategies and Techniques* (New York: Charles Scribner's Sons, 1983), 61.

Notes to Chapter Two

1. Virginia Ann Hodgkinson and Murray S. Weitzman, *Nonprofit Almanac 1996–1997: Dimensions of the Independent Sector*. Washington, DC: Independent Sector, 1996, 69–71. Also, Virginia Ann Hodgkinson and Murray S. Weitzman, *Giving & Volunteering in the United States: Findings from a National Survey 1994 Edition*. Washington, DC: Independent Sector, 1994, Table 1.1, 16.

2. James M. Greenfield, *Fund-Raising: Evaluating and Managing the Fund Development Process*. 2nd ed. (New York: John Wiley & Sons, 1999), 60.

3. Robert L. Torre and Mary Ann Bendixen, *Direct Mail Fund Raising: Letters That Work* (New York: Plenum Press, 1988), 1.

4. Ibid., 1–3.

5. Mal Warwick, *You Don't Always Get What You Ask For: Using Direct Mail Tests to Raise More Money for Your Organization* (Berkeley, CA: Strathmoor Press, 1992), 25.

6. Kay Partney Lautman and Henry Goldstein, *Dear Friend: Mastering the Art of Direct Mail Fund Raising*, 2nd ed. (Rockville, MD: Fund Raising Institute, 1991), 292.

7. Warwick, 32.

8. David J. Harr, James T. Godfrey, and Robert H. Frank, *Common Costs and Fund-Raising Appeals: A Guide to Joint Cost Allocation in Not-for-Profit Organizations* (Pittsburgh, PA: Frank & Company, p.c., 1991). This book was published in conjunction with the Nonprofit Mailers Federation.

9. Lautman and Goldstein, *Dear Friend*, 288.

10. Jerry Huntsinger, *Fund Raising Letters: A Comprehensive Study Guide to Raising Money by Direct Response Marketing*, 3rd. ed. (Richmond, VA: Emerson Publishers, 1989).

11. See note 6.

12. Huntsinger, 11.

13. Lautman and Goldstein, 10.

14. Ibid., 141–171.

15. Ibid., 10–11.

16. Huntsinger, 23-3, 23-5.

17. Ibid., 23–11.

18. The Campaign to Clean Up America was invented by Bruce R. Hopkins to illustrate principles contained in his text, *A Legal Guide to Starting and Managing Nonprofit Organization*, 3rd ed. (New York: John Wiley & Sons, 2001). Permission to link the examples in this book to his fictional organization is greatly appreciated.

Notes to Chapter Three

1. Edith H. Falk, "The All-Important Annual Campaign," in *Getting Started: A Guide to Fund Raising Fundamentals* (Chicago: The National Society of Fund Raising Executives, Chicago Chapter, 1988), 45–46.

2. Kay Partney Lautman and Henry Goldstein, *Dear Friend: Mastering the Art of Direct Mail Fund Raising*, 2nd ed. (Rockville, MD: Fund Raising Institute, 1991), 5–7.
3. Thomas E. Broce, *Fund Raising: A Guide to Raising Money from Private Sources*, 2nd ed. (Norman: University of Oklahoma Press, 1986), 86–88.
4. Roger M. Craver, "The Power of Mail to Acquire, Renew, and Upgrade the Gift," in Henry A. Rosso and Associates, *Achieving Excellence in Fund Raising* (San Francisco: Jossey-Bass, 1991), 65.
5. William K. Grasty and Kenneth G. Sheinkopf, *Successful Fundraising: A Handbook of Proven Strategies and Techniques* (New York: Charles Scribner's Sons, 1982), 130–133.
6. Robert L. Torre and Mary Anne Bendixen, *Direct Mail Fund Raising: Letters That Work*, 2nd ed. (New York: Plenum Press, 1990), 267.
7. Lautman and Goldstein, 3–4.
8. Jerry Huntsinger, *Fund Raising Letters: A Comprehensive Study Guide to Raising Money by Direct Response Marketing*, 3rd ed. (Richmond, VA: Emerson Publishers, 1989), 47–9.
9. Ibid., 35–1.
10. Mary Lou Roberts and Paul D. Berger, *Direct Marketing Management* (Englewood Cliffs, NJ: Prentice-Hall, 1989), 2.

Note to Chapter Four

1. William K. Grasty and Kenneth G. Sheinkopf, *Successful Fundraising: A Handbook of Proven Strategies and Techniques* (New York: Charles Scribner's Sons, 1982), 48–49.

Notes to Chapter Five

1. Constance Clark, "Membership Development," in *Nonprofit Management Handbook: Operating Policies and Procedures* ed. Tracy Daniel Connors (New York: John Wiley & Sons, 1993), 486.
2. Bruce R. Hopkins, *A Legal Guide to Starting and Managing a Nonprofit Organization*, 3rd ed. (New York: John Wiley & Sons, 2001), 37–38.
3. Ibid., xi–xii.
4. Cliff Underwood, "Building Donor Relationships Strengthens Zoo's Membership," *Fund Raising Management* (January 1984), 36.
5. Clark, 489.
6. AFP membership invitation details are provided courtesy of the Association of Fundraising professionals. For full information, write to AFP at 1101 King Street, Suite 700, Alexandria, VA 22314, or call (703) 684-0410 during normal business hours.
7. James A. Brandt, "Five Rules for Getting Started on a Membership-Development Campaign," *Non-Profit Times* (March 1991), 23.
8. Patricia Gaby and Daniel Gaby, *Nonprofit Organization Handbook* (Englewood Cliffs, NJ: Prentice-Hall, 1979), 53.
9. Richard P. Trenbeth, *The Membership Mystique: How to Create Income and Influence with Membership Programs* (Rockville, MD: Fund Raising Institute, The Taft Group, 1986), 200.
10. Ibid., 264.
11. Gaby and Gaby, 34.
12. Ibid., 55.
13. Arch McGhee, "Why Members Volunteer. . . . and . . . Work Harder," *Association Management* (August 1971), 85, as quoted in *The Nonprofit Management Handbook*, 2nd ed., edited by Tracy Daniel Connors (New York: McGraw-Hill, 1988), 21.4.
14. Tracy Daniel Connors, "Membership," in *The Nonprofit Management Handbook*, 2nd ed., ed. Tracy Daniel Connors (New York: McGraw-Hill, 1988), 21.9–21.11.
15. Gaby and Gaby, 35.
16. Ibid., 38–39.
17. Ibid., 44–45.

18. Mike Mueller, as quoted in Sean Mehegan, "Keeping Members: The New Priority," *Nonprofit Times Special Report* (April 1993), 21.
19. Mehegan, 21.
20. Maurice Gurin, *What Volunteers Should Know for Successful Fund Raising* (New York: Stein & Day, 1981), 71.
21. Joan Jeffri, *Arts Money* (Minneapolis: University of Minnesota Press, 1983), 187.
22. Trenbeth, *The Membership Mystique,* 268–278.

Notes to Chapter Six

1. Used with permission by James M. Greenfield, *Fund-Raising Cost Effectiveness: A Self-Assessment Workbook*, The NSFRE/Wiley Fund Development Series (New York: John Wiley & Sons, 1996), 82.
2. John Mutz and Katherine Murray, *Fundraising for Dummies* (Foster City, CA: IDG Books Worldwide, Inc., 2000), 229.
3. William Freyd and Diane M. Carlson, "Telemarketing," in *The Nonprofit Handbook: Fund Raising, Third Edition*, ed. James M. Greenfield, The NSFRE/Wiley Fund Development Series (New York: John Wiley & Sons, 2001), 564.
4. Used with permission by Barbara Kushner Ciconte and Jeanne G. Jacob, *Fund Raising Basics: A Complete Guide*, ed. James P. Gelatt, Aspen's Fund Raising Series for the 21st Century (Gaithersburg, MD: An Aspen Publication, 1997), 93.
5. Freyd and Carlson, 565.
6. Used with permission by Ciconte and Jacob, 93.
7. Ibid., 95.
8. Freyd and Carlson, 571.
9. Ibid., 573.
10. Harvey Lipman, "Calling Solicitor to Account," *Chronicle of Philanthropy*. vol. XIII, no. 12 (April 5, 2001), 24.
11. Ibid., 1.

Notes to Chapter Seven

1. Marlene Cassini, "The Craig Hospital Auxiliary—Making a Personal Difference in the Lives of the Disabled," article in brochure produced by Craig Hospital, Englewood, Colorado, 1989.
2. James M. Greenfield, *Fund-Raising: Evaluating and Managing the Fund Development Process* (New York: John Wiley & Sons, 1999), 145–146.
3. Thomas E. Broce, *Fund Raising: A Guide to Raising Money from Private Sources*, 2nd ed. (Norman: University of Oklahoma Press, 1986), 92.
4. Ibid., 91.
5. William K. Grasty and Kenneth G. Sheinkopf, *Successful Fundraising: A Handbook of Proven Strategies and Techniques* (New York: Charles Scribner's Sons, 1982), 76–77.
6. Ibid., 76.
7. Harold J. Seymour, *Designs for Fund-Raising: Principles, Patterns and Techniques*, 2nd ed. (Ambler, PA: Fund-Raising Institute, 1988), 145.
8. Greenfield, 343.
9. Ibid., 343–347.
10. Internal Revenue Service, *Deductibility of Payments Made to Charities Conducting Fund-Raising Events*, Revenue Ruling 67-246 (June 1988), Publication 1392.

Notes to Chapter Eight

1. Reprinted with permission from K. Scott Sheldon, "Foundations as a Source of Support" in *Achieving Excellence in Fund Raising* by Henry R. Rosso and Associates (San Francisco: Jossey-Bass, 1991), 247.

2. Hayden W. Smith, "Corporate Contributions to the Year 2000: Growth or Decline," in *The Future of the Nonprofit Sector: Challenges, Changes, and Policy Considerations*, ed. Virginia A. Hodgkinson, Richard W. Lyman, and Associates (Independent Sector. San Francisco: Jossey-Bass, 1989), 316.

3. Dwight F. Burlingame, "Corporate Fund Raising," in *The Nonprofit Handbook: Fund Raising*, 3rd ed., ed. James M. Greenfield (New York: John Wiley & Sons, 2001), 641.

4. Dennis R. Young and Dwight F. Burlingame, "Paradigm Lost: Research toward a New Understanding of Corporate Philanthropy," in *Corporate Philanthropy at the Crossroads*, eds. Dwight F. Burlingame and Dennis R. Young (Bloomington: Indiana University Press, 1996) x–xi and 158–163. See also Burlingame, "Corporate Fund Raising," 642–644.

5. Dwight F. Burlingame and Patricia A. Frishkoff, "How Does Firm Size Affect Corporate Philanthropy?" in Burlingame and Young, 87.

6. Reprinted with permission from James M. Greenfield, *Fund-Raising Cost Effectiveness: A Self-Assessment Workbook* (New York: John Wiley & Sons, 1996), 150.

7. *A.P. Smith Manufacturing Co. v. Barlow*, 98 A.2d 581 (Sup. Ct. N.J. 1953).

8. American Association of Fund-Raising Counsel, *Giving USA*, 2001 report (New York: AAFRC Trust for Philanthropy, 2001), 77.

9. American Association of Fund-Raising Counsel, *Giving USA*, 1989 report (New York: AAFRC Trust for Philanthropy, 1990), 70.

10. Reprinted from The Foundation Center, *Fifty Largest Corporate Foundations by Total Giving*, World Wide Web page http://www.library@fdncenter.org.

11. Alice Korngold and Elizabeth Hosler Voudouris, "Corporate Volunteerism: Strategic Community Involvement" in Burlingame and Young, *Corporate Philanthropy at the Crossroads*, 24–25.

12. Cathleen Wild, "Corporate Volunteer Programs: Benefits to Business" (New York: Conference Board, 1993), 9.

13. Sam Sternberg, ed. *National Directory of Corporate Charity* (San Francisco: Regional Youth and Adult Project, 1984), 17.

14. Lester A. Picker, "The Corporate Support Marketplace," in *The Nonprofit Handbook: Fund Raising*, 3rd ed. ed. James M. Greenfield (New York: John Wiley & Sons, 2001), 624.

15. From The Society for Nonprofit Organizations, "Nonprofit World Funding Alert" (August Funding Alert, 2001).

16. Scott Sheldon, "Don't Take No for an Answer," in *Contributions* (January/February 2001), 38.

17. United Way of America. http://national.unitedway.org/campres_99.cfm.

18. United Way of America. "Outcome Measurement Activities of National Health and Human Service Organizations" (April 1998).

19. Picker, 623.

20. Debra E. Blum and Susan Gray, "Big Business Means Big Philanthropy," *The Chronicle of Philanthropy* 10, no. 18 (1998): 20.

21. Elizabeth Greene, "Making the Most of Matches," *The Chronicle of Philanthropy* (April 19, 2001), 28.

22. James M. Greenfield, *Fund Raising: Evaluating and Managing the Fund Development Process*. 2nd ed. (New York: John Wiley & Sons, 1999), 233–238.

23. Yankey, "Corporate Support of Nonprofit Organizations: Partnerships across the Sectors" in Burlingame and Young, *Corporate Philanthropy at the Crossroads*, 13.

24. Bruce R. Hopkins, "Federal Regulation of Fund Raising" in *The Nonprofit Handbook: Fund Raising, Third Edition*, p. 1067–1069. See also Hopkins "The Tax Law of Charitable Giving." New York: John Wiley & Sons, 1993, 155–163.

25. Seth Perlman, "State Regulation of Fund Raising," in *The Nonprofit Handbook: Fund Raising*, 3rd ed., 1085, 1088.

26. Susan L. Golden, "The Grant-seeking Process," in *The Nonprofit Handbook: Fund Raising*, 3rd ed., 673.

27. Robert L. Krit, *"The Fund-Raising Handbook,"* *Society for Nonprofit Organizations* (Dubuque, Iowa: Kendall/Hunt Publishing Company, 1993), 96.
28. Adapted from Bruce R. Hopkins and Jody Blazek. *Private Foundations: Tax Law and Compliance.* (New York: John Wiley & Sons, 1997), 264.

Notes to Chapter Nine

1. Ian Wilhelm, "September 11 Donations Hit $1-Billion," in *The Chronicle of Philanthropy.* October 16, 2001.
2. Michael Johnston, "Fund Raising on the Net," in *The Nonprofit Handbook: Fund Raising, Third Edition,* ed. James M. Greenfield (New York: John Wiley & Sons, 2001), 519.
3. Nick Allen, Mal Warwick, and Michael Stein, eds., *Fundraising on the Internet: Recruiting and Renewing Donors Online* (Berkeley, CA: Strathmoor Press, Inc., 1996), i.
4. Mal Warwick, Ted Hart, and Nick Allen, eds., *Fundraising on the Internet: The ePhilanthropyFoundation.Org's Guide to Success Online* (San Francisco: Jossey-Bass Publishers, 2002), xvii.
5. James E. Austin, "The E-Philanthropy Revolution is Here to Stay," Report of the Harvard Social Enterprise institute, in *The Chronicle of Philanthropy* (March 8, 2001).
6. American Association of Fund Raising Counsel, *Giving USA* (New York: AAFRC Trust for Philanthropy, 2001), 18–20.
7. Theodore R. Hart, *ePhilanthropyFoundation.Org.* 2001. Used with permission.
8. Mal Warwick, Ted Hart, and Nick Allen, 3.
9. Paul Clolery, Editor-in-Chief, *The NonProfit Times,* Foreword in Michael Johnston, *The Fund Raiser's Guide to the Internet.* The NSFRE/Wiley Fund Development Series (New York: John Wiley & Sons, 1999), xii.
10. Allen, Warwick, and Stein, 1.15.
11. Warwick, Hart, and Allen, 3.
12. Michael Johnston, *The Fund Raiser's Guide to the Internet* (New York: John Wiley & Sons, 1999), 108.
13. Jason Potts, "New Media and Direct-Response Fund Raising," in *The Nonprofit Handbook: Fund Raising,* 3rd ed., 537.
14. James M. Greenfield, *Fund Raising: Evaluating and Managing the Fund Development Process,* 2nd ed. (New York: John Wiley & Sons, 1999), 168.
15. Johnston, *The Fund Raiser's Guide to the Internet.* 165.
16. Johnston, "Fund Raising on the Net," 528–530.
17. Ibid., 526–527.
18. Ibid., 532.
19. For full details on ethics codes and standards of professional practice, see Albert Anderson, *Ethics for Fundraisers* (Indiana University Press, 1996); Marianne G. Briscoe, ed., "Ethics in Fundraising: Putting Values into Practice," *New Directions for Philanthropic Fundraising* (San Francisco: Jossey-Bass, 1995); Marilyn Fischer, *Ethical Decision Making in Fund Raising* (New York: John Wiley & Sons, 2000).
20. ePhilanthropyFoundation.Org., *ePhilanthropy Code of Ethical Online Philanthropic Practices.* Used with permission.
21. Robin Zeff, *The Nonprofit Guide to the Internet* (New York: John Wiley & Sons, 1996), 157. For a full description of Internet legal issues, see also pp.149–163.
22. See these recommendations in "Security: Safeguarding Your Homestead" in Michael Johnston, *The Fund Raiser's Guide to the Internet,* 122–138.
23. Ibid., 138.

Notes to Chapter Ten

1. Virginia A. Hodgkinson and Murray S. Weitzman, *Giving and Volunteering in the United States: Findings from a National Survey* (Washington, D.C.: Independent Sector, 1992), 2. (See also pp. 21–33 for complete details on volunteerism and charitable giving statistics.)

2. Sara H. Skolnick, "Special Appeals," in *The Nonprofit Management Handbook: Operating Policies and Procedures* ed. Tracy Daniel Connors (New York: John Wiley & Sons, 1993), 590.

3. William K. Grasty and Kenneth G. Sheinkopf, *Successful Fund Raising: A Handbook of Proven Strategies and Techniques* (New York: Charles Scribner's Sons, 1983), 165.

4. Marilyn E. Brentlinger and Judith M. Weiss, *The Ultimate Benefit Book: How to Raise $50,000-Plus for Your Organization* (Cleveland: Octavia Press, 1987), 20.

5. Grasty and Sheinkopf, 160.

6. Lee Katz, "Vital Ways and Means in Planning a Major Benefit," *Fund Raising Management* (December 1988), 52.

7. Ralph Brody and Marcie Goodman, *Fund-Raising Events: Strategies and Programs for Success* (New York: Human Sciences Press, Inc., 1988), 64.

8. Internal Revenue Service, *Deductibility of Payments Made to Charities Conducting Fund-Raising Events*, Revenue Ruling 67–246 (June 1988), Publication 1392.

9. Office of the Attorney General of Connecticut, special report, as reprinted in *The Chronicle of Philanthropy* (May 2, 1989), 25.

10. Philanthropic Advisory Service, Council of Better Business Bureaus, New York, 1982, as reported in *The Chronicle of Philanthropy* (June 1, 1993), 29.

11. For additional information on cause-related marketing and commercial sales, see James M. Greenfield, *Fund-Raising: Evaluating and Managing the Fund Development Process*, 2nd ed. (New York: John Wiley & Sons, 1999), 168–170, 233–238, 408–410.

12. Ibid., 136.

13. Grasty and Sheinkopf, 163.

Notes to Chapter Eleven

1. James M. Greenfield, *Fund-Raising: Evaluating and Managing the Fund Development Process*, 2nd ed. (New York: John Wiley & Sons, 1999), 150–151.

2. Thomas E. Broce, *Fund Raising: The Guide to Raising Money from Private Sources*, 2nd ed. (Norman: University of Oklahoma Press, 1986), 87.

3. Irving R. Warner, *The Art of Fund Raising* (New York: Harper & Row, 1975), 24–25. For additional leadership characteristics, see Sara H. Skolnick, "Special Appeals," in *The Nonprofit Management Handbook: Operating Policies and Procedures*, ed. Tracy Daniel Connors (New York: John Wiley & Sons, 1993), 590

4. Broce, 86.

5. Greenfield, 396–399 (Policy on Honors and Recognition).

Notes to Chapter Twelve

1. James M. Greenfield, *Fund-Raising: Evaluating and Managing the Fund Development Process*, 2nd ed. (New York: John Wiley & Sons, 1999), 396–399. (Appendix A, Policy on "Honors and Recognition"). See also James M. Greenfield, "Appendix" in "Fund-Raising Management," in *The Nonprofit Handbook: Management*, 3rd ed. (New York: John Wiley & Sons, 2001), 419–421.

2. Bruce R. Hopkins, *The Law of Fund-Raising*, 2nd ed. (New York: John Wiley & Sons, 1991), 414.

3. Bruce R. Hopkins, *A Legal Guide to Starting and Managing a Nonprofit Organization*, 3rd ed. (New York: John Wiley & Sons, 2001), 282.

4. Ibid., 284.

5. *United States v. American Bar Endowment*, 106. S. Ct. 2426 (1986), as quoted in Hopkins, *The Law of Fund-Raising*, 474.

6. This debate has proponents too; see Jay L. Vestal, "Hitch Your Wagon: Cause-Related Marketing Works," *NAHD Journal* (Spring 1986), 35–38. The author's opposition can be found in Greenfield, *Fund-Raising*, 168–169, 233–238, 372, 408–410.

7. Greg Gattuso, "Charity Gambling on the Way Out?" *Fund-Raising Management* (May 1993), 8.

8. Stephen G. Greene and Grant Williams, "Charities' Big Gamble," *The Chronicle of Philanthropy* (May 18, 1993), 27.

9. Hopkins, *The Law of Fund-Raising*, 402

10. James M. Greenfield, *Fund-Raising: Evaluating and Managing the Fund Development Process* (New York: John Wiley & Sons, 1991), 98.

11. Robert L. Krit, "Sweepstakes—A Benefit for Whom?" *Fund-Raising Management* (August 1991), 35. See also Carol M. Gibbons, "The Sweepstakes Appeal: Friend or Foe?," *Fund-Raising Management* (July 1988), 48–49.

12. For additional discussion on multimedia options, see Greenfield, *Fund-Raising*, 126–130.

13. John R. Groman, "Fund-Raising in the 90's: Five Key Changes to Make or Break Success," address to Breakfast Plenary Session, NSFRE Orange County Chapter Conference, Anaheim, CA, October 16, 1989.

14. Max L. Hart, "How Premiums Can Help Your Organization," *Fund-Raising Management* (July 1988), 32–38.

15. Harvey P. Dale, "Tax-Exempt Organizations: Winds of Change," Distinguished Norman A. Sugerman Memorial Lecture sponsored by the Mandel Center for Nonprofit Organizations at Case Western Reserve University, Cleveland, Ohio, May 20, 1991.

16. David E. Ormstedt, "Government Regulation of Fund Raising: A Struggle for Efficacy," in James M. Greenfield, Editor, *Financial Practices for Effective Fund Raising* (San Francisco: Jossey-Bass, 1994), 129–141.

17. Ibid.

18. Errol Copilevitz, "Avoiding Fund-Raising Traps," *Fund Raising Management* (June 1993), 39.

19. Bruce R. Hopkins, "Charitable Solicitation Acts and Fund Raising: Part Two," *Fund Raising Management* (September 1990), 70.

20. For a detailed account of the documents and court proceedings in the James Bakker trial, see Gary Tidwell, *Anatomy of a Fraud: Inside the Finances of the PTL Ministries* (New York: John Wiley & Sons, 1993). For the bonuses paid, see this source's Exhibit 5-2.

Notes to Chapter Thirteen

1. Robert L. Payton, *Philanthropy: Voluntary Action for the Public Good* (New York: Macmillan Publishing Co., 1988).

2. Alexis de Tocqueville, "Democracy in America," in *America's Voluntary Spirit: A Book of Readings*, ed. Brian O'Connell (New York: The Foundation Center, 1983), 54.

3. Fisher Howe, *The Board Member's Guide to Fund Raising* (San Francisco: Jossey-Bass, 1991), 27.

4. Thomas E. Broce, *Fund Raising: The Guide to Raising Money from Private Sources*, 2nd. ed. (Norman: University of Oklahoma Press, 1986), 96.

5. James M. Greenfield, *Fund-Raising: Evaluating and Managing the Fund Development Process*, 2nd ed. (New York: John Wiley & Sons, 1999), 317.

6. In June 1993, the Financial Accounting Standards Board (FASB) released two new statements that address these concerns: Statement of Financial Accounting Standards No. 116, *Accounting for Contributions Received and Contributions Made*, and Statement of Financial Accounting Standards No. 117, *Financial Statements of Not-for-Profit Organizations* (Norwalk, CT: Financial Accounting Standards Board, 1993).

7. There are only limited cost guidelines based on empirical research. Generally accepted performance standards allow a range of 20 to 25 percent as the "bottom line" cost–benefit ratio for broad-based and mature fund development programs (three years' continuous experience) and up to 35 to 50 percent for annual giving programs collectively. America's colleges and universities reported (*Chronicle of Philanthropy*, September 4, 1990) a 16 percent cost-effectiveness ratio (a 525 percent return on investment), while hospital studies revealed a 12

percent performance factor in the same year. For details on how these data were developed, see Council for the Advancement and Support of Education, *Expenditures in Fund Raising, Alumni Relations, and Other Constituent (Public) Relations*, (1990), and Association for Healthcare Philanthropy, *USA Report on Giving, FY 1990*.

8. A sample policy on donor recognition is found in Greenfield, *Fundraising*, 396–399.

9. Barbara R. Levy, ed. *The NSFRE Fund-Raising Dictionary*. The NSFRE/Wiley Fund Development Series (New York: John Wiley & Sons, 1996), 160.

10. *Focusing on Program Outcomes: A Guide for United Ways* (Alexandria, VA: United Way of America, 1996), iii.

11. *Measuring Program Outcomes: A Practical Approach* (Alexandria, VA: United Way of America, 1996), xv.

12. Commonwealth of Pennsylvania, "Institutions for Purely Public Charity Act" (November, 1997).

13. Peter F. Drucker, "Not Enough Generals Were Killed," in Frances Hesselbein, Marshall Goldsmith, and Richard Beckhard, *The Leader of the Future* (San Francisco: Jossey-Bass, 1996), xiv.

14. Harold J. Seymour, *Designs for Fund Raising* (New York: McGraw-Hill, 1996), 4. (Paperback edition: Ambler, PA: Fund Raising Institute, 1988).

15. Irving R. Warner, *The Art of Fund-Raising*, 3rd ed. (New York: Harper & Row, 1990), 24–25.

16. Adapted from Kay Sprinkel Grace and Alan L. Wendroff, *High Impact Philanthropy: How Donors, Boards and Nonprofit Organizations Can Transform Communities. Wiley Nonprofit Law, Finance, and Management Series* (New York: John Wiley & Sons, 2001), and Paul Schervish, *Millionaires and the Millennium: New Estimates of the Forthcoming Wealth Transfer and the Prospects for a Golden Age of Philanthropy* (Boston College, MA, 1999).

17. See Kathleen S. Kelly, *Effective Fund-Raising Management*. Mahwah, NJ: Lawrence Erlbaum Associates, 1998, 89–102, for a thorough presentation on the feminization of philanthropy. See also Margaret A. Duronio and Eugene R. Tempel, *Fund Raisers: Their Careers, Stories, Concerns, and Accomplishments* (San Francisco: Jossey-Bass, 1997), 24–43, 61–68, 178–180, for details on career options, demographics, salary, titles, work weeks, and more.

18. Schervish.

19. See Sondra C. Shaw and Martha A Taylor, *Reinventing Fundraising: Realizing the Potential of Women's Philanthropy* (San Francisco: Jossey-Bass, 1995), 83–100. See also Shaw and Taylor, "Women as Philanthropists: Leading the Transformation in Major Gift Fundraising," in *Developing Major Gifts*, ed. Dwight F. Burlingame and James M. Hodge. New Directions for Philanthropic Fundraising, no. 16 (San Francisco: Jossey-Bass, 1997), 66–69.

Selected References

Philanthropic Concepts

Anderson, Albert. *Ethics for Fundraisers*. Bloomington: Indiana University Press, 1996.

Brakeley, George A., Jr. *Tested Ways to Successful Fund Raising*. New York: AMACOM, 1980.

Bremner, Robert H. *American Philanthropy*, 2nd ed. Chicago: The University of Chicago Press, 1988.

Briscoe, Marianne, ed. *Ethics in Fundraising: Putting Values into Practice*. New Directions in Philanthropic Fundraising, no. 6. San Francisco: Jossey-Bass, 1994.

Burlingame, Dwight F. *The Responsibilities of Wealth*. Bloomington: Indiana University Press, 1992.

———, ed. *Critical Issues in Fundraising*. The NSFRE/Wiley Fund Development Series. New York: John Wiley & Sons, 1997.

Ciconte, Barbara Kushner, and Jeanne G. Jacob. *Fund Raising Basics: A Complete Guide*. Aspen's Fund Raising Series for the 21st Century. James P. Gelatt, ed. Gaithersburg, MD: Aspen Publishers, 1997.

Cutlip, Scott M. *Fund-Raising in the United States: Its Role in American Philanthropy*. New Brunswick, NJ: Rutgers University Press, 1990 (reprint of a 1965 work).

Duronio, Margaret A., and Eugene R. Tempel. *Fund Raisers: Their Careers, Stories, Concerns, and Accomplishments*. San Francisco: Jossey-Bass, 1997.

Fisher, Marilyn. "Ethical Fund Raising: Deciding What's Right." *Advancing Philanthropy* 2 (Spring 1994): 29–33.

———. *Ethical Decision Making in Fund Raising*. The NSFRE/Wiley Fund Development Series. New York: John Wiley & Sons, 2000.

Grace, Kay Sprinkel. *Beyond Fund Raising: New Strategies for Nonprofit Innovation and Investment*. The NSFRE/Wiley Fund Development Series. New York: John Wiley & Sons, 1997.

———, and Alan L. Wendroff. *High Impact Philanthropy: How Donors, Boards, and Nonprofit Organizations Can Transform Communities*. New York: John Wiley & Sons, 2001.

Hall, Peter Dobkin. *Inventing the Nonprofit Sector and Other Essays on Philanthropy, Voluntarism, and Nonprofit Organizations*. Baltimore: Johns Hopkins University Press, 1992.

Hicks, John. "Grass-Roots Fund Raising" in *The Nonprofit Handbook: Fund Raising, Third Edition*. Ed. James M. Greenfield. The AFP/Wiley Fund Development Series. New York: John Wiley & Sons, 2001.

Hodgkinson, Virginia A., and Associates. *The Nonprofit Almanac 1996–1997: Dimensions of the Independent Sector*. Washington, DC: Independent Sector, 1996.

——— and Murray S. Weitzman. *Giving & Volunteering in the United States: 1994 Edition*. Washington, DC: Independent Sector, 1994.

Howe, Fisher. *The Board Member's Guide to Fund Raising*. San Francisco: Jossey-Bass, 1991.

Joseph, James A. *The Charitable Impulse*. New York: The Foundation Center, 1989.

Magat, Richard A. *Philanthropic Giving*. New York: Oxford University Press, 1989.

Marta, Armaud C. *Philanthropy's Role in Civilization: Its Contributions to Human Freedom*. New Brunswick, NJ: Transaction, 1991 (reprint of a 1953 work).

Martin, Mike W. *Virtuous Giving: Philanthropy, Voluntary Service, and Caring*. Bloomington: Indiana University Press, 1994.

Nichols, Judith. *Changing Demographics: Fundraising in the 1990s*. Chicago: Precept Press, 1990.

———. *Targeted Fund Raising: Defining and Refining Your Development Strategy for the 1990s*. Chicago: Bonus Books, 1991.

———. *Pinpointing Affluence: Increasing Your Share of Major Donor Dollars*. Chicago: Bonus Books, 1994.

———. *Growing from Good to Great: Positioning Your Fund Raising for BIG Gains*. Chicago: Bonus Books, 1995.

———. "Demographics: Our Changing World and How It Affects Raising Money." In *The Nonprofit Handbook: Fund Raising*, 3rd ed. Ed. James M. Greenfield. The AFP/Wiley Fund Development Series. New York: John Wiley & Sons, 2001.

O'Connell, Brian. *America's Voluntary Spirit: A Book of Readings*. New York: The Foundation Center, 1983.

———. *Philanthropy in Action*. Washington, DC: Independent Sector, 1987.

———. *Civil Society: The Underpinnings of American Democracy*. Hanover, NH: University Press of New England, 1999.

O'Neill, Michael. *The Third America: The Emergence of the Nonprofit Sector in the United States*. San Francisco: Jossey-Bass, 1989.

Payton, Robert L. *Philanthropy: Voluntary Action for the Common Good*. New York: Macmillan, 1988.

Salamon, Lester M. *American's Nonprofit Sector: A Primer*. New York: The Foundation Center, 1992.

Schervish, Paul G., Virginia A. Hodgkinson, Margaret Gates, and Associates. *Care and Community in Modern Society: Passing on the Tradition of Service to Future Generations*. San Francisco: Jossey-Bass, 1995.

Schwartz, John J. *Modern American Philanthropy: A Personal Account*. New York: John Wiley & Sons, 1994.

Annual Giving: General

Broce, Thomas E. *Fund Raising: The Guide to Raising Money from Private Sources*, 2nd ed. Norman: University of Oklahoma Press, 1986.

Burlingame, Dwight F., and Lamont J. Hulse, eds. *Taking Fund Raising Seriously*. San Francisco: Jossey-Bass, 1991.

Council for Advancement and Support of Education. *Case Management Reporting Standards: Standards for Annual Giving and Campaigns in Educational Fund Raising*. Washington, DC: Council for Advancement and Support of Education, 1996.

————. *Fund-Raising Standards for Annual Giving and Campaign Reports for Not-for-Profit Organizations other than Colleges, Universities, and Schools*. Washington, DC: Council for Advancement and Support of Education, 1998.

Flanagan, Joan. *The Grass Roots Fundraising Book*. Chicago: Contemporary Books, 1982.

Grasty, William K., and Kenneth G. Sheinkopf. *Successful Fund Raising: A Handbook of Proven Strategies and Techniques*. New York: Charles Scribner's Sons, 1983.

Gurin, Maurice G. *Confessions of a Fund Raiser: Lessons of an Instructive Career*. Washington, DC: The Taft Corporation, 1985.

Lord, James Gregory. *The Raising of Money*. Cleveland: Third Sector Press, 1987.

Rosso, Henry A., and Associates. *Achieving Excellence in Fund Raising*. San Francisco: Jossey-Bass, 1991.

Rowland, A. Westley. *Handbook of Institutional Advancement*, 2nd ed. San Francisco: Jossey-Bass, 1986.

Seltzer, Michael. *Securing Your Organization's Future: A Complete Guide to Fundraising Strategies*. New York: The Foundation Center, 1987.

Seymour, Harold J. *Designs for Fund-Raising*. New York: McGraw-Hill, 1966. (Paperback edition: Ambler, PA: The Fund Raising Institute, 1988.)

Taylor, Bernard P. *Guide to Successful Fund Raising for Authentic Charitable Purposes*. South Plainfield, NJ: Groupwork Today, Inc., 1976.

Warner, Irving R. *The Art of Fund Raising*, 3rd ed. New York: Harper & Row, 1990.

Williams, M. Jane. *The FRI Annual Giving Book*. Rockville, MD: Fund Raising Institute (a division of The Taft Group), 1981.

Direct Mail

Bendixen, Mary Anne, and Robert L. Torre. *Direct Mail Fund Raising: Letters That Work*. New York: Plenum Press, 1988.

Huntsinger, Jerry. *Fund Raising Letters: A Comprehensive Study Guide to Raising Money by Direct Response Marketing*. Richmond, VA: Emerson Publishers, 1985.

Jones, Susan K. *Creative Strategy in Direct Marketing*. Chicago: NTC Business Books, 1990.

Kuniholm, Roland. *The Complete Book of Model Fund Raising Letters*. Englewood Cliffs, NJ: Prentice-Hall, 1995.

Lautman, Kay, and Henry Goldstein. *Dear Friend: Mastering the Art of Direct Mail Fund Raising*, 2nd ed. Englewood Cliffs, NJ: Prentice-Hall, 1991.

Lautman, Kay. "Direct Mail." In *The Nonprofit Handbook: Fund Raising*, 3rd ed. Ed. James M. Greenfield. The AFP/Wiley Fund Development Series. New York: John Wiley & Sons, 2001.

Roberts, Mary Lou, and Paul D. Berger. *Direct Marketing Management*. Englewood Cliffs, NJ: Prentice-Hall, 1989.

Warwick, Mal. *Revolution in the Mailbox*. Rockville, MD: Fund Raising Institute (a division of The Taft Group), 1990.

————. *You Don't Always Get What You Ask For: Using Direct Mail Tests to Raise More Money for Your Organization*. Berkeley, CA: Strathmoor Press, 1992.

————. *999 Tips, Trends and Guidelines for Successful Direct Mail and Telephone Fundraising*. Berkeley, CA: Strathmoor Press, 1993.

Telephone and Telemarketing

Balthaser, William F. *Call for Help: How to Raise Philanthropic Funds with Phonathons*. Rockville, MD: Fund Raising Institute (a division of The Taft Group), 1983.

Blimes, Michael E., and Ron Sproat. *More Dialing, More Dollars*. New York: American Council for the Arts, 1985.

Carlson, Diane M., and William Freyd. "Telemarketing." In *The Nonprofit Handbook: Fund Raising*, 3rd ed. Ed. James M. Greenfield. The AFP/Wiley Fund Development Series. New York: John Wiley & Sons, 2001.

Schultz, Louis A. *Telepledge: The Complete Guide to Mail-Phone Fund Raising*. Rockville, MD: Fund Raising Institute (a division of The Taft Group), 1987.

Warwick, Mal. *999 Tips, Trends and Guidelines for Successful Direct Mail and Telephone Fundraising*. Berkeley, CA: Strathmoor Press, 1993.

Membership Associations

Gaby, Patricia, and Daniel Gaby. *Nonprofit Organization Handbook*. Englewood Cliffs, NJ: Prentice-Hall, 1979.

Trenbeth, Richard P. *The Membership Mystique*. Ambler, PA: Fund Raising Institute (a division of The Taft Group), 1986.

Corporations and Foundations

Allen, Sylvia. "Cause-Related Marketing and Sponsorship." In *The Nonprofit Handbook: Fund Raising*, 3rd ed. Ed. James M. Greenfield. The AFP/Wiley Fund Development Series. New York: John Wiley & Sons, 2001.

Belcher, Jane C., and Julia M. Jacobsen. *From Idea to Funded Project: Grant Proposals That Work*. Phoenix, AZ: Oryx Press, 1992.

Burlingame, Dwight F. "Corporate Fund Raising." In *The Nonprofit Handbook: Fund Raising*, 3rd ed. Ed. James M. Greenfield. The AFP/Wiley Fund Development Series. New York: John Wiley & Sons, 2001.

————, and Dennis R. Young, ed. *Corporate Philanthropy at the Crossroads*. Bloomington: Indiana University Press, 1996.

Carlson, Mim. *Winning Grants Step by Step: Support Centers of America's Complete Workbook for Planning, Developing, and Writing Successful Proposals*. San Francisco: Jossey-Bass, 1995.

Corporate Volunteer Programs: Benefits to Business. New York: The Conference Board, 1993.

Geever, Jane C., and Patricia McNeill. *The Foundation Center's Guide to Proposal Writing*. New York: The Foundation Center, 1993.

Golden, Susan L. "The Grant-Seeking Process." In *The Nonprofit Handbook: Fund Raising*, 3rd ed. Ed. James M. Greenfield. The AFP/Wiley Fund Development Series. New York: John Wiley & Sons, 2001.

————. *Successful Grantsmanship: A Guerrilla Guide to Raising Money*. San Francisco: Jossey-Bass, 1997.

Hall, Mary S. *Getting Funded: A Complete Guide to Proposal Writing*, 3rd ed. Portland, OR: Continuing Education Publications, 1988.

Kiritz, Norton J. *Program Planning & Proposal Writing*, expanded version. Los Angeles: The Grantsmanship Center, 1980.

Lefferts, Robert. *Getting a Grant in the 1990s: How to Write Successful Grant Proposals*. New York: Simon & Schuster, 1990.

Meador, Roy. *Guidelines for Preparing Proposals*, 2nd ed. Chelsea, MI: Lewis Publishers, 1991.

Miner, Lynn E., and Jerry Griffith. *Proposal Planning and Writing*. Phoenix, AZ: Oryx Press, 1993.

New, Cheryl Carter, and James Aaron Quick. *Grantseeker's Toolkit: A Comprehensive Guide to Finding Funding*. New York: John Wiley & Sons, 1998.

Picker, Lester A. "The Corporate Support Marketplace" in *The Nonprofit Handbook: Fund Raising*, 3rd ed. Ed. James M. Greenfield. The AFP/Wiley Fund Development Series. New York: John Wiley & Sons, 2001.

Scanlon, Eugene A. *Corporate and Foundation Fund Raising: A Complete Guide from the Inside*. Aspen's Fund Raising Series for the 21st Century. Gaithersburg, MD: Aspen Publishers, 1997.

Shannon, James P. *The Corporate Contributions Handbook*. San Francisco: Jossey-Bass, 1991.

Weeden, Curt. *Corporate Social Investing: The Breakthrough Strategy for Giving and Getting Corporate Contributions*. San Francisco: Berrett-Koehler Publishers, 1998.

The Internet

Allen, Nick, and Mal Warwick. *Fundraising on the Internet: Recruiting and Renewing Donors Online*. Berkeley, CA: Strathmoor Press, 1996.

Ellsworth, Jill H., and Matthew V. Ellsworth. *The New Internet Business Book*. New York: John Wiley & Sons, 1996.

Glister, Paul. *The Internet*. New York: John Wiley & Sons, 1993.

Graham, Ian S. *The HTML Sourcebook*. New York: John Wiley & Sons, 1995.

Hoffman, Paul E. *Netscape and the WWW for Dummies*. Foster City, CA: IDG Books Worldwide, 1995.

Johnston, Michael. *The Fund Raiser's Guide to the Internet*. The NSFRE/Wiley Fund Development Series. New York: John Wiley & Sons, 1999.

———. "Fund Raising on the Net" in *The Nonprofit Handbook: Fund Raising*, 3rd ed. Ed. James M. Greenfield. The AFP/Wiley Fund Development Series. New York: John Wiley & Sons, 2001.

———. "The Internet and the Regulation of the Not-for-Profit Sector" in *The Nonprofit Handbook: Fund Raising*, 3rd ed. Ed. James M. Greenfield. The AFP/Wiley Fund Development Series. New York: John Wiley & Sons, 2001.

Potts, Jason. "New Media and Direct-Response Fund Raising" in *The Nonprofit Handbook: Fund Raising*, 3rd ed. Ed. James M. Greenfield. The AFP/Wiley Fund Development Series. New York: John Wiley & Sons, 2001.

Swadley, Richard K. *The Internet Unleashed*. 2nd ed. Indianapolis: Sams.Net Publishing, 1995.

Warwick, Mal, Ted Hart, and Nick Allen. *Fundraising on the Internet: The ePhilanthropy-Foundation.Org's Guide to Success Online*. San Francisco: Jossey-Bass, 2001.

Zeff, Robbin. *The Nonprofit Guide to the Internet.* New York: John Wiley & Sons, 1996.

Activities, Benefits, and Special Events

Allan, Sylvia. "Benefit Event Fundamentals" in *The Nonprofit Handbook: Fund Raising,* 3rd ed. Ed. James M. Greenfield. The AFP/Wiley Fund Development Series. New York: John Wiley & Sons, 2001.

Brentlinger, Marilyn E. *The Ultimate Benefit Book: How to Raise $50,000-Plus for Your Organization.* Cleveland: Octavia, 1987.

Brody, Ralph, and Marcie Goodman. *Fund-Raising Events.* New York: Human Sciences Press, 1988.

Freedman, Harry A., and Karen F. Smith. *Black Tie Optional: The Ultimate Guide to Planning and Producing Successful Special Events.* Rockville, MD: Fund Raising Institute (a division of The Taft Group), 1991.

Harris, April L. *Raising Money and Cultivating Donors through Special Events.* Washington, DC: Council for Advancement and Support of Education, 1991.

Ulin, Susan B. "Benefit Event Enhancements." In *The Nonprofit Handbook: Fund Raising,* 3rd ed. Ed. James M. Greenfield. The AFP/Wiley Fund Development Series. New York: John Wiley & Sons, 2001.

Whitcomb, Nicki B. Money-Makers. *A Systematic Approach to Special Events Fund Raising.* Charles E. Alberti, George E. Macko, and Nicki B. Whitcomb, 1983.

Volunteer-Led Personal Solicitation

Brudney, Jeffrey L. *Fostering Volunteer Programs in the Public Sector.* San Francisco: Jossey-Bass, 1990.

Connors, Tracy D. *The Volunteer Management Handbook.* New York: John Wiley & Sons, 1995.

Fisher, James C., and Kathleen M. Cole, *Leadership and Management of Volunteer Programs.* San Francisco: Jossey-Bass, 1993.

Gurin, Maurice G. *What Volunteers Should Know for Successful Fund Raising.* New York: Stein & Day, 1981.

Houle, Cyril O. *Governing Boards.* San Francisco: Jossey-Bass, 1989.

Ilsley, Paul J. *Enhancing the Volunteer Experience.* San Francisco: Jossey-Bass, 1999.

Pidgeon, Walter P. *The University Benefits of Volunteering: A Practical Workbook for Nonprofit Organizations, Volunteers, and Corporations.* The NSFRE/Wiley Fund Development Series. New York: John Wiley & Sons, 1998.

————. *Volunteering: The Leader's Competitive Edge.* Cincinnati, OH: The Union Institute, 1991.

————. "Volunteer-led Solicitations." In *The Nonprofit Handbook: Fund Raising,* 3rd ed. Ed. James M. Greenfield. The AFP/Wiley Fund Development Series. New York: John Wiley & Sons, 2001.

Stratton, Jeff, ed. *Nonprofit Volunteer Management.* Gaithersburg, MD: Aspen Publications, 1994.

Unger, Jane L. "Volunteer Development: Individual and Organizational Considerations." In *The Nonprofit Management Handbook.* New York: John Wiley & Sons, 1993.

Management of Annual Giving Programs

Accounting and Financial Reporting: A Guide for United Ways and Not-for-Profit Human-Service Organizations, rev. 2nd ed. Alexandria, VA: United Way of America, 1989.

Arthur Anderson & Company. *Tax Economics of Charitable Giving*, 13th ed. Chicago: 1999.

Bayley, Ted. "Professionalism, Ethics, and Certification." In *The Nonprofit Handbook: Fund Raising*, 3rd ed. Ed. James M. Greenfield. The AFP/Wiley Fund Development Series. New York: John Wiley & Sons, 2001.

Blazek, Jody. *Tax and Financial Planning for Tax-Exempt Organizations*, 2nd ed. New York: John Wiley & Sons, 1994.

————. *Tax Planning and Compliance for Tax-Exempt Organizations: Forms, Checklists, Procedures*, 2nd ed. New York: John Wiley & Sons, 1993.

Bryson, John M. *Strategic Planning for Public and Nonprofit Organizations*. San Francisco: Jossey-Bass, 1988.

Burnett, Ken. Relationship Fundraising: *A Donor-Based Approach to the Business of Raising Money*. London: White Lion Press, 1992.

Burns, Michael E. *Budgeting Guide for Nonprofit Administrators and Volunteers*. New Haven, CT: Development & Technical Assistance Center, 1995.

Connell, James E. "Budgeting for Fund Raising." In *The Nonprofit Handbook: Fund Raising*, 3rd ed. Ed. James M. Greenfield. The AFP/Wiley Fund Development Series. New York: John Wiley & Sons, 2001.

Connors, Tracy Daniel. *Nonprofit Organization Management: Policies and Procedures*. New York: John Wiley & Sons, 1993.

————, ed. *The Nonprofit Handbook: Management*, 3rd ed. New York: John Wiley & Sons, 2001.

Council for Advancement and Support of Education. *Case Campaign Standards: Management and Reporting Standards for Educational Fund-Raising Campaigns*. Washington, DC: Council for Advancement and Support of Education, 1994.

Day, Duane L. *The Effective Advancement Professional: Management Principles and Practices*. Gaithersburg, MD: Aspen, 1998.

Drucker, Peter F. *Managing the Nonprofit Organization: Practices and Principles*. New York: HarperCollins, 1990.

————. *The Drucker Foundation Self-Assessment Tool for Nonprofit Organizations*. San Francisco: Jossey-Bass, 1993.

Emerson, Jed, and Fay Twersky, eds. *New Social Entrepreneurs: The Success, Challenge and Lessons of Nonprofit Enterprise Creation*. San Francisco: Roberts Foundation, 1996.

Frantzreb, Arthur C. *Not on This Board You Don't: Making Your Trustees More Effective*. Chicago: Bonus Books, 1997.

Fry, Robert P., Jr. *Nonprofit Investment Policies: Strategies to Grow the Funds of Your Organization*. The NSFRE/Wiley Fund Development Series. New York: John Wiley & Sons, 1998.

Gee, Ann D., ed. *Annual Giving Strategies: A Comprehensive Guide to Better Results*. Washington, DC: Council for Advancement and Support of Education, 1990.

Greenfield, James M. *Fund Raising: Evaluation and Managing the Fund Development Process*, 2nd ed. New York: John Wiley & Sons, 1999.

————, ed. *Financial Practices for Effective Fundraising*. New Directions for Philanthropic Fundraising, Number 3. San Francisco: Jossey-Bass, 1994.

————. *Fund-Raising Cost Effectiveness: A Self-Assessment Workbook.* New York: John Wiley & Sons, 1996.

————, ed. *The Nonprofit Handbook: Fund Raising,* 3rd ed. New York: John Wiley & Sons, 2001.

Gross, Malvern J., Richard F. Larkin, and John H. McCarthy. *Financial and Accounting Guide for Not-for-Profit Organizations,* 6th ed. New York: John Wiley & Sons, 2000.

Hasselbein, Frances, Marshall Goldsmith, and Richard Beckhard, ed. *The Leader of the Future.* San Francisco: Jossey-Bass, 1996.

————. Marshall Goldsmith, and Richard Schubert, ed. *The Community of the Future.* San Francisco: Jossey-Bass, 1998.

Hawkins, Kimberly. "Strategic Planning for Fund Raising." In *The Nonprofit Handbook: Fund Raising,* 3rd ed. Ed. James M. Greenfield. The AFP/Wiley Fund Development Series. New York: John Wiley & Sons, 2001.

Herman, Robert D., and Associates. *The Jossey-Bass Handbook of Nonprofit Leadership and Management.* San Francisco: Jossey-Bass, 1994.

Hopkins, Bruce R. *The Law of Charitable Giving.* New York: John Wiley & Sons, 1993.

————. *The Law of Fund Raising,* 2nd ed. New York: John Wiley & Sons, 1996.

————. *The Law of Tax-Exempt Organizations,* 7th ed. New York: John Wiley & Sons, 1997.

————. *A Legal Guide to Starting and Managing a Nonprofit Organization,* 3rd ed. New York: John Wiley & Sons, 2001.

————. "Federal Regulation of Fund Raising." In *The Nonprofit Handbook: Fund Raising,* 3rd ed. Ed. James M. Greenfield. The AFP/Wiley Fund Development Series. New York: John Wiley & Sons, 2001.

Joyaux, Simone P. *Strategic Fund Development: Building Profitable Relationships That Last.* Aspen's Fund Raising Series for the 21st Century. Gaithersburg, MD: Aspen Publishers, 1997.

Kaminski, Andrea. "Women as Philanthropists: A New Approach and A New Voice in Major Gifts." In *The Nonprofit Handbook: Fund Raising,* 3rd ed. Ed. James M. Greenfield. The AFP/Wiley Fund Development Series. New York: John Wiley & Sons, 2001.

Kelly, Kathleen S. *Effective Fund-Raising Management.* Mahwah, NJ: Lawrence Erlbaum, 1997.

————. "Ropes: A Model of the Fund-Raising Process." In *The Nonprofit Handbook: Fund Raising,* 3rd ed. Ed. James M. Greenfield. The AFP/Wiley Fund Development Series. New York: John Wiley & Sons, 2001.

Kennedy, Larry W. *Quality Management in the Nonprofit World: Combining Compassion and Performance to Meet Client Needs and Improve Finances.* San Francisco: Jossey-Bass, 1991.

Klein, Kim. *Fund Raising for Social Change.* Inverness, CA: Chardon Press, 1988.

Kotler, Philip, and Alan R. Andreasen. *Strategic Marketing for Nonprofit Organizations,* 3rd ed. Englewood Cliffs, NJ: Prentice-Hall, 1987.

Larkin, Richard F. "Accounting for Contributions." In *The Nonprofit Handbook: Fund Raising,* 3rd ed. Ed. James M. Greenfield. The AFP/Wiley Fund Development Series. New York: John Wiley & Sons, 2001.

Letts, Christine W., William P. Ryan, and Allen Grossman. *High Performance Nonprofit Organizations: Managing Upstream for Greater Impact.* New York: John Wiley & Sons, 1999.

Levy, Barbara R., and Barbara H. Marion. *Successful Special Events: Planning, Hosting, and*

Evaluating. Aspen's Fund Raising Series for the 21st Century. Gaithersburg, MD: Aspen Publishers, 1997.

Light, Paul C. *Sustaining Innovation: Creating Nonprofit and Government Organizations That Innovate Naturally.* San Francisco: Jossey-Bass, 1998.

Lindahl, Wesley E. *Strategic Planning for Fund Raising.* San Francisco: Jossey-Bass, 1992.

Linzy, Jerry A. "Donor Recognition and Relations." In *The Nonprofit Handbook: Fund Raising*, 3rd. Ed. James M. Greenfield. The AFP/Wiley Fund Development Series. New York: John Wiley & Sons, 2001.

Martin, Lawrence L., and Peter K. Kettner. *Measuring the Performance of Human Service Programs.* Thousand Oaks, CA: Sage Publications, 1996.

McLaughlin, Thomas A. *Streetsmart Financial Basics for Nonprofit Managers.* New York: John Wiley & Sons, 1995.

McLeish, Barry J. *Successful Marketing Strategies for Nonprofit Organizations.* New York: John Wiley & Sons, 1995.

Murray, Dennis J. *The Guaranteed Fund-Raising System: A Systems Approach to Planning and Controlling Fund Raising*, 2nd ed. Poughkeepsie, NY: American Institute of Management, 1994.

Mutz, John, and Katherine Murray. *Fundraising for Dummies.* Foster City, CA: IDG Books Worldwide, 2000.

New, Anne L., and Wilson C. Levis. *Raise More Money for Your Nonprofit Organization: A Guide to Evaluating and Improving Your Fundraising.* New York: Foundation Center, 1991.

Nichols, Judith. *Strengthening Fund Raising through Evaluation.* Chicago: Bonus Books, 1998.

Perlman, Seth, and Betsy Hills Bush. *Fund-Raising Regulation: A State-by-State Handbook of Registration Forms, Requirements, and Procedures.* New York: John Wiley & Sons, 1996.

Perlman, Seth, "State Regulation of Fund Raising." In *The Nonprofit Handbook: Fund Raising*, 3rd ed. Ed. James M. Greenfield. The AFP/Wiley Fund Development Series. New York: John Wiley & Sons, 2001.

Rosso, Henry A. *Rosso on Fund Raising: Lessons from a Master's Lifetime Experience.* San Francisco: Jossey-Bass, 1996.

Schmaedick, Gerald L. *Cost-Effectiveness in the Nonprofit Sector: Methods and Examples of Leading Organizations.* Westport, CT: Quorum Books, 1993.

Spears, Larry C., ed. Reflections on Leadership: *How Robert K. Greenleaf's Theory of Servant-leadership Influenced Today's Top Management Thinkers.* New York: John Wiley & Sons, 1995.

Strand, Bobbi J. "Prospect Development—An Art." In *The Nonprofit Handbook: Fund Raising*, 3rd ed. Ed. James M. Greenfield. The AFP/Wiley Fund Development Series. New York: John Wiley & Sons, 2001.

Warwick, Mal. *The Hands-On Guide to Fundraising Strategy and Evaluation.* Gaithersburg, MD: Aspen Publishers, 1997   .

Watson, Gregory H. *Strategic Benchmarking.* New York: John Wiley & Sons, 1995.

Weinstein, Stanley. *The Complete Guide to Fund-Raising Management.* The NSFRE/Wiley Fund Development Series. New York: John Wiley & Sons, 1999.

Young, Dennis R., and Richard Steinberg. *Economics for Nonprofit Managers.* New York: The Foundation Center, 1995.

Index